THE CAMBRIDGE
ANCIENT HISTORY

VOLUME VII
PART 1

THE CAMBRIDGE
ANCIENT HISTORY

SECOND EDITION

VOLUME VII

PART I

The Hellenistic World

Edited by

F. W. WALBANK F.B.A.

*Emeritus Professor, formerly Professor of Ancient
History and Classical Archaeology, University of Liverpool*

A. E. ASTIN

*Professor of Ancient History,
The Queen's University, Belfast*

M. W. FREDERIKSEN

R. M. OGILVIE

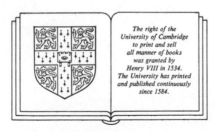

The right of the
University of Cambridge
to print and sell
all manner of books
was granted by
Henry VIII in 1534.
The University has printed
and published continuously
since 1584.

CAMBRIDGE UNIVERSITY PRESS

CAMBRIDGE

LONDON   NEW YORK   NEW ROCHELLE
MELBOURNE   SYDNEY

Published by the Press Syndicate of the University of Cambridge
The Pitt Building, Trumpington Street, Cambridge CB2 1RP
32 East 57th Street, New York, NY 10022, USA
296 Beaconsfield Parade, Middle Park, Melbourne 3206, Australia

© Cambridge University Press 1984

First published 1928
Second edition 1984

Printed in Great Britain at the University Press, Cambridge

Library of Congress catalogue card number: 75-85719

British Library Cataloguing in Publication Data
The Cambridge ancient history
Vol. 7
Pt 1: The Hellenistic world
1. History, ancient
1. Walbank, F. W.
930   D57

ISBN 0 521 23445 X

SE

CONTENTS

BIBLIOGRAPHY

MAPS

TEXT-FIGURES

PREFACE

This volume opens at Babylon in the aftermath of Alexander's death in 323; it closes a little over a hundred years later in 217 with the Peace of Naupactus (between Philip V of Macedonia and his Greek allies and the Aetolian Confederation) and another Peace, in Asia, between Antiochus III and Ptolemy IV, following the latter's victory at the battle of Raphia. Both dates are significant. The first is a more realistic beginning to the new Hellenistic age than the battle of Ipsus in 301 (which was implied by opening Volume VII at that date in the first edition of this work), while the second is famous as the year which Polybius singled out as the beginning of a process of *symploke*, that interweaving of affairs throughout the whole civilized world which was (in his view) to culminate in its domination within a little over fifty years by Rome.

In the first edition, Volume VII covered not only Hellenistic history from 301 to 217 but also that of Rome from the earliest times down to the end of the First Punic War in 241. The vast amount of new material which has become available since 1928, both for Greece and the Hellenistic East (including the Far East) and for Italy, has made it necessary to divide the volume into two parts, with Roman history reserved for the second of these. Nor is that the only difference. The present volume lays less emphasis on military detail and more on social and economic problems than did its predecessor. But general surveys, whether of particular kingdoms or of the whole area of Hellenistic civilization do not provide a substitute for a chronological narrative of events, for without such a framework a general sketch may well fail to convey the sense of historical development. Accordingly, after a preliminary chapter surveying the sources available for the period by Professor F. W. Walbank, the volume opens with an account of the first twenty years from 323 down to 301 by Professor E. Will – a period dominated by the attempt of Antigonus I to uphold the principle of a single empire (under his control) and his failure to accomplish this in the face of rival generals who, even before they combined to destroy him at Ipsus, had themselves assumed the title of king. From this time onwards until the Roman conquest, monarchy was to be the dominant political

institution throughout the eastern Mediterranean (and to some extent in
Sicily) and in Chapter 3 its antecedents, the political machinery which it
devised and the ideology which supported it are discussed by Professor
Walbank. Already before Ipsus, Ptolemy I and Seleucus I had etablished
themselves firmly in Egypt and Asia respectively, where they founded
dynasties which were to last into the first century; but the possession of
Macedonia was still disputed. In Chapter 4 Professor Will carries the
history of the struggle between the Diadochi down to the accession of
Antigonus Gonatas to the throne of Macedonia in 276; in Chapter 7
Professor Walbank takes the history of Macedonia and Greece down to
Gonatas' death, and discusses the growth of the Achaean and Aetolian
Confederations and the character of the Macedonian state in the
Hellenistic period. Two chapters, by Sir Eric Turner and Professor D.
Musti, describe the Ptolemaic and Seleucid kingdoms respectively, and
here no attempt has been made to restrict discussion to the third century:
the development of Ptolemaic Egypt is traced down to the second
century and beyond – though with particular emphasis on the reigns of
Philadelphus and Euergetes I – and the Seleucid kingdom is treated as a
single, evolving, political institution with special attention paid to social
and economic factors, to the relationship between Greeks and non-
Greeks, and to that between central government and the Greek cities. The
problem of the secession of Bactria and Parthia and the chronology of
these events is treated in an appendix. These separate studies of three of
the main political units which went to make up the Hellenistic world are
followed by a central chapter in which Professor J. K. Davies describes
the main cultural, social and economic feature of the Hellenistic age as a
whole, assesses the rôle of the *polis* in this period and examines the
factors which worked for and against its continuing importance in the
Hellenistic scene.

   In a general history such as this it was not feasible to include a full
critical account of the art, literature and philosophical speculations of
the period. That is not because these activities and achievements do not
stand very high indeed in any overall assessment of the Hellenistic age;
indeed, relevant material from all these areas is integrated into the
discussion throughout the volume. But limitations of space ruled out the
kind of detailed treatment which a reader will more naturally seek in
more specialized works.[1] One aspect in which Hellenistic thought
proved especially creative has, however, been given special attention in
Chapter 9: the rôle of science and its application in peace and war. Here
Professor G. E. R. Lloyd discusses the impressive achievements of the
Hellenistic age in physics, geography and astronomy, medicine and the

---

[1] See, for example, the *Cambridge History of Classical Literature* I: *Greece* (forthcoming); M.
Robertson, *A History of Greek Art* (2 vols., Cambridge, 1967); A. A. Long 1974: (H 132).

life sciences, and Professor Y. Garlan's progress in the techniques of war and siegecraft, a field in which the application of scientific discoveries produced noteworthy changes in the way war was waged; given the preponderant rôle of warfare throughout the period, this was something that affected the lives of everybody. In the same chapter, Dr D. J. Thompson describes and assesses the technical level of agriculture in the various parts of the Hellenistic world and the changes introduced in the new environment of the kingdoms; she concludes that they were minimal. Professor F. E. Winter rounds off this chapter with an account of building and townplanning, in which he describes the methods and materials used during the period of three centuries which saw so many cities founded and built, and was outstanding for the originality of its innovations.

After these chapters devoted to particular areas and aspects of the Hellenistic world and life in it, chapters 10 to 12 revert mainly to narrative. In Chapter 10, Professor Meister describes Agathocles' career in Sicily, leaving subsequent events affecting Greeks and Carthaginians in the West (including Pyrrhus' Italian and Sicilian adventures) to the more suitable context of Volume VII.2. In a chapter (11) mainly concerned with the Syrian-Egyptian wars which run like a thread through the fabric of Seleucid and Ptolemaic relations during the whole of the third century, Professor H. Heinen also describes the growth of the smaller kingdoms of Asia Minor, the increasingly important rôle of Pergamum and Rhodes, and the invasions of the Celts, whose inroads and intrusive settlements brought panic to the peoples of Greece and Asia Minor a century after they had first terrified the Romans. The fortunes of the cities of the Black Sea have not been included here, since they receive discussion in an earlier volume (VI) and will be mentioned again in relation to Pompey's campaigns in Volume IX. Finally, in Chapter 12, Professor Walbank carries the history of Macedonia and Greece proper down to 217 with an account of the reigns of Demetrius II, Antigonus Doson and Philip V as far as the conclusion of the so-called Social War.

A word on the bibliography seems in order. This is arranged in sections dealing with specific topics, which sometimes correspond to individual chapters but more often combine the contents of several chapters. References in the footnotes are to these sections (which are distinguished by capital letters) and within these sections each book or article has assigned to it a number which is quoted in the footnotes. In these, so as to provide a quick indication of the nature of the work referred to, the author's name and the date of publication are also included in each reference. Thus 'Tarn 1948, 1.52: (A.58)' signifies 'W. W. Tarn, *Alexander the Great* (Cambridge, 1948), vol 1, p. 52, to be found in section A of the bibliography as item 58'. The number of footnotes and the extent of documentation varies somewhat from chapter to chapter, since it has been left largely to each author to treat his subject as he thought best. The text was complete by the middle of 1982; though a few later publications are mentioned, work which appeared after that date could not normally be taken into account and only exceptionally does it figure in the bibliography.

Planned originally in 1977 in conjunction with Volumes VII.2 and VIII, the work has suffered two blows in the successive deaths of two of the three original editors, M. W. Frederiksen and R. M. Ogilvie; in place of the former the Syndics appointed Professor A. E. Astin. It is also with regret that we record the death of one of the contributors, Sir Eric Turner; the proofs of his chapter have been read by Dr Dorothy J. Thompson. Five chapters and one section of Chapter 9 were written in languages other than English. Chapters 2 and 4 have been translated from French by Francis McDonagh, chapter 6 has been translated from Italian by Dinah Livingstone, Chapter 9b from French by Mrs Janet Lloyd and Chapters 10 and 11 from German by John Powell. The index has been compiled by Jenny Morris.

Two volumes of plates are being published to accompany Volumes VII parts 1 and 2 and VIII, dealing with the Hellenistic World and Early Rome respectively. The first of these contains material relevant to the present volume and references to the plates in it will be found in several chapters.

From the earliest stages in the planning of this volume and throughout its production the editors, past and present, enjoyed the fullest collaboration and encouragement from the staff of the Cambridge University Press, who have been patient in accepting delays and quick to suggest or approve solutions to such problems as have arisen from time to time. We should like to record our gratitude both for this help and for the readiness with which it was always made available.

F.W.W.
A.E.A.

CHAPTER 1

SOURCES FOR THE PERIOD

F. W. WALBANK

From the hundred years following Alexander's death the work of no single contemporary historian has survived other than fragmentarily. Yet the period had been fully covered both in universal histories and in specialized works dealing with particular kings, peoples or regions. In the latter category there are forty-six authors known to have written about the Hellenistic period: all are lost. On the causes of this holocaust one can only speculate. Most works had of course been written in the contemporary Greek idiom (the so-called *koine*), which did not appeal to later scholars (and copyists). Then again, many works may never have existed in sufficient numbers of copies to render them safe against the ravages of time; this was especially likely to be true of local historians. But above all the sheer bulk and length of many works alienated the average reader, and the appearance of résumés, abridgements and even lists of contents created the conditions for a kind of literary Gresham's law to operate, so that the inferior products drove the original out of circulation and hence eventually out of existence.

The disappearance of primary sources is the main problem for the historian of the third century. But there are others. The years from 323 to 217 saw an unparalleled expansion of the Greek world as a result of which Greeks, Macedonians and the peoples of Asia Minor were brought into close contact with the inhabitants of Egypt, Phoenicia, Palestine, Mesopotamia, Iran and central Asia. Everywhere Greeks settled and established a *modus vivendi* of some kind or other with the original populations. But the voice of the non-Greeks is rarely heard. All our sources are in Greek or are derived from Greek. Manetho the Egyptian priest and Berosus the Babylonian were encouraged to write the earlier history of their peoples down to the time of Alexander's death in Greek (for Greeks did not normally learn foreign languages); but we possess no Egyptian or Babylonian account of the period of Alexander's successors (the Diadochi) nor any history of Seleucid Asia written from the point of view of a Persian or a Babylonian, nor of Ptolemaic Egypt from that of a native Egyptian. The Jews, it is true, have left us their own version of the Hasmonean risings of the second century (in the

Maccabees), but only three chapters of Josephus' *Antiquities* (XII.1–3) concern the century from Ptolemy's occupation of Egypt to the loss of Coele-Syria at Panium in 200. Furthermore, within the Graeco-Macedonian milieu itself all our accounts are written from the point of view of the dominant classes in society. The voices of the natives and those of the poor are equally silent; in many places such as Egypt natives and poor tended to be the same people.

The limitations of the source tradition do not end there. For the period after 300 there is no consecutive account of historical events in the eastern Mediterranean basin (other than the brief résumé in Justinus (see p. 7)) until we come to Polybius' description of the rise of the Achaean League and of the Cleomenean War in Book II of his *Histories*. Such important events as the Chremonidean War in Greece and the early wars between Egypt and Syria have to be reconstructed from odd scraps of information eked out with inscriptions and papyri.

Of the lost writers of the period 323 to 217 five stand out as especially important. There is strong evidence that it is these five who have predominantly stamped their character and their version of events on the surviving tradition; and it is possible to gain some impression of the contents and characteristics of their work from later writers who have drawn on them. In this chapter I shall begin by examining these lost writers. I shall then go on to consider those historians whose works survive, either wholly or in part, and how these relate to the primary sources. That done, I propose to discuss briefly some of the other sorts of information available to the historian.

I. LOST WRITERS

By far the most important of the lost historians is Hieronymus of Cardia (died *c.* 250),[1] whose political and military career, first under Alexander (whose archivist he was), then under Eumenes and, after his death, under Antigonus I, Demetrius I and Antigonus Gonatas, gave him a broad military experience and reinforced his judgement as a historian. His *Histories* (their exact title is uncertain) covered the period of Alexander's successors (cf. Diod. XVIII.42) from 323 probably down to Pyrrhus' death in 272, and were the chief source of Diodorus XVIII–XX, which constitutes our only sustained and continuous narrative for the period down to the battle of Ipsus. But Hieronymus is not Diodorus' only source, nor is it certain whether Diodorus used him directly or through an intermediary (though the former is more likely). Hieron-

---

[1] *FGrH* 154; cf. Hornblower 1981: (B 21).

ymus' merits were widely recognized and he was a source[2] for Plutarch's *Lives* of *Eumenes, Demetrius* and *Pyrrhus,* for Nepos' *Life* of *Eumenes,* for Arrian's account of the successors of Alexander, and for Trogus (in Books XIII–XIV of Justinus' summary). As far as the abbreviated version in these later writers allows us to judge, his work was serious and intelligent, and he saw the full significance of what was happening as Alexander's empire fell apart, giving way to the separate kingdoms, the rise of which formed the main theme of his story. Pausanias (1.9.8) accuses him of bias towards Antigonus, whom he served, a charge which can hardly be sustained, though Antigonus does receive considerable attention. Of all the lost primary sources Hieronymus' *Histories* undoubtedly constitute the most serious casualty.

Hieronymus directed his work in part against that of Duris of Samos (*c.* 340–*c.* 260),[3] a pupil of Theophrastus who for many years was tyrant in his native island of Samos. His *Macedonica* covered Macedonian affairs from 370/69 probably down to 281/80, the year in which Seleucus I died (shortly after Lysimachus) and Ptolemy II seized Samos and brought Duris' tyranny to an end. Duris' work, which was used alongside Hieronymus' both by Diodorus and by Plutarch in his *Lives* of *Eumenes, Demetrius* and *Pyrrhus,* was hostile in tone towards the Macedonians, but its main purpose was to entertain the reader and it aimed at creating sensational impressions and specialized in lurid episodes and scenes designed to arouse the reader's emotions. The same characteristics were displayed by Duris' *Life of Agathocles,*[4] which was based on second-hand sources and concentrated on exposing the tyrant's wickedness. Diodorus made some use of this biography for his account of affairs in the West. For Italy, Sicily and the western Mediterranean the most important of the lost sources was, however, Timaeus of Tauromenium (*c.* 350–255),[5] who spent fifty years in exile at Athens, where he wrote his history of the western Greeks down to the death of Pyrrhus. This work was Diodorus' main source for his account of Agathocles. Timaeus was painstaking and accurate and he probably devised the system of chronology based on Olympiad years which Polybius later adopted (Polyb. XII.11.1). He lacked a developed critical sense, but Polybius' virulent polemic against him (especially in Book XII) is exaggerated and unjust.

For the mainland of Greece the most important writer was the

---

[2] Plut. *Eum.* 11, Diod. XVIII.42 and Nepos, *Eum.* 5.4–5 give very similar accounts of conditions in the blockaded town of Nora (which Hieronymus visited as Antigonus' ambassador: Diod. XVIII.50.4). Stratagems of Eumenes and Antigonus recorded in Polyaenus probably also go back to Hieronymus.

[3] *FGrH* 76; cf. Lévêque 1957, 2: (C 46); Kebric 1977, 51–4: (B 23).

[4] See ch. 10, p. 384.

[5] *FGrH* 566; cf. Brown 1958: (B 7); Momigliano 1966, 1.22–53: (B 25).

Athenian (or Naucratite) Phylarchus,[6] who covered the years between
Pyrrhus' death in 272 and that of Cleomenes III of Sparta in 219, and
whose *Histories* in twenty-eight books thus began where Hieronymus
left off. Though he savagely criticizes Phylarchus for emotional writing
(rather like Duris) (Polyb. 11.56–63) and was clearly irritated by his
partisanship for Cleomenes, Polybius nevertheless used him in Book 11
for his own account of Peloponnesian events down to the death of
Antigonus Doson; he was also Plutarch's source in his *Lives of Agis and
Cleomenes* (*Cleom.* 5, 28, 30), and was drawn on by Athenaeus and
followed (probably) by Trogus Pompeius. Polybius' main source for
Greek events before his main narrative opened in 220 was, however, the
thirty books of the *Memoirs* of his fellow-Achaean, Aratus of Sicyon
(271–213),[7] which were designed as an apologia covering his career
down to 220, including the controversial volte-face when he called in the
Macedonians to destroy Cleomenes. Rough in style and marred by
significant omissions, Aratus' *Memoirs* were certainly less reliable than
Polybius asserts (11.40.4). Nevertheless, where their version can be
recovered they provide a salutary corrective to Phylarchus.

There were of course other third-century historians. Demosthenes'
nephew Demochares (*c.* 360–275); composed a work in at least twenty-
one books, mainly on Athens. Diyllus of Athens wrote a history in
twenty-six books ending with the death of Cassander's son Philip;
Proxenus was the author of a flattering biography of Pyrrhus, which
drew on his *Memoirs*; and, for events in the West, there were the
Syracusans Antander, who wrote a monograph on his brother, the
tyrant Agathocles, and Callias, who wrote twenty-two books on the
same subject.[8] Both of these were laudatory in tone and their influence
on existing works has been slight.

II. SURVIVING WRITERS

The earliest historian of the period to have survived in substantial
amounts, and the only one of outstanding merit, is Polybius of
Megalopolis (*c.* 200–*c.* 118).[9] He pursued a public career as a statesman of
the Achaean League down to 168 when, after the defeat of Perseus of
Macedonia, he was compelled along with a thousand other Achaeans to
go to Rome, where he was detained until 150. During these eighteen

---

[6] *FGrH* 81; cf. Gabba 1957: (B 13); Africa 1961: (D 118).

[7] *FGrH* 231; cf. Walbank 1933: (D 73).

[8] *FGrH* 75 (Demochares), 73 (Diyllus), 703 (Proxenus), 565 (Antander), 564 (Callias); on
Antander see Walbank 1968–9, 482–3: (G 10).

[9] Books I–V survive intact, XVII, XIX, XXVI, XXXVII and XL (index volume) were lost by the tenth
century and no genuine fragments survive; the remaining books consist of extracts. See Walbank,
1957, 1967 and 1979 (Commentary): (B 37); 1972: (B 38); 1977: (B 39).

years he became the friend and teacher of P. Scipio Aemilianus (XXXI.23–30) and set about the composition of his *Histories*, originally designed to cover the years 220 to 167 in thirty books, in which he proposed to explain, primarily for Greek readers, 'how and thanks to what kind of constitution' (I.1.5) the Romans had during that period become masters of the whole of the civilized world, the *oecumene*. Later (probably after Scipio's death in 129) he added a further ten books going down to 146 and intended, he says (III.4.6), to enable his readers to judge of the character and acceptability of the Roman empire. An important factor in his decision was, however, his desire to celebrate Scipio's achievements and to recount his own experiences at Carthage, exploring the Atlantic (in a ship provided by Scipio), and as intermediary between the Romans and the defeated Achaeans after the sack of Corinth in 146. For the main part of his *Histories* (as distinct from the introductory Books I and II) Polybius drew on information derived from the careful questioning of eye-witnesses; but for the period down to 217, which included the rise of the Achaean League (in Book II) and, after 220, the Social War in Greece and the Fourth Syrian War between Antiochus III and Ptolemy IV (in Books IV and V), he was obliged to use written sources. Among these, as we have seen, were Aratus and Phylarchus for mainland history. There is in fact some evidence that the account of the rise of Achaea (II.37–70) and the crisis created by the war with Cleomenes was originally a separate work (or the draft for one), which he included in the *Histories* only at a very late date. Polybius' description (in Books IV and V) of the revolts against Antiochus III and the Fourth Syrian War goes back to excellent sources, but these cannot be identified. For later events Polybius was widely used by Livy, Diodorus and Dio Cassius; but for the period down to 217 he is our only continuous source.

After Polybius' death there is a gap of almost a century before we come to another historian directly relevant to the military and political history of this period. We should indeed take some note of Agatharchides of Cnidus,[10] who may have been a former slave who rose to the position of royal tutor at the Ptolemaic court *c.* 116, and composed two histories. One was a work in ten books *On Asia*, dealing with Alexander's successors, the other consisted of forty-nine books *On Europe*, relating events in Greece from Alexander's death perhaps down to the fall of the Macedonian monarchy in 168. Agatharchides also wrote a book *On the Erythraean Sea*, which can be largely reconstructed from extracts in Photius and passages in Diodorus based on it. This monograph contained interesting information about the Ptolemaic

---

[10] *FGrH* 86; cf. Peremans 1967: (B 27); Gozzoli 1978: (B 18).

elephant-hunts, on the gold-mines near the frontier of Egypt and Ethiopia and on similar topics. But neither this work nor the histories, of which little survives, made much impression upon the tradition. Mention should also be made of the *Lives* of *Phocion* and *Eumenes* by Cornelius Nepos, a contemporary of Cicero in the first century B.C.; but they are of small historical value.

The most important source after Polybius is Diodorus of Agyrium[11] in Sicily, who wrote his world history, the *Bibliotheca Historica*, at the time of Caesar and Augustus. Books XVIII–XXI deal with the century down to 217, but the full text goes only to the end of Book XX (the battle of Ipsus), the later books being made up of excerpts from the collection of Constantine Porphyrogenitus (tenth century A.D.), quotations from other authors including Photius, and passages taken from a now lost set of excerpts published in the seventeenth century (the *Eclogae Hoeschelianae*). Apart from occasional remarks, mainly of a moralizing nature, Diodorus is normally content to reproduce his sources, keeping to one author for a long period (with an occasional cross-reference to a divergent view in a second source). Hence the value of any passage in Diodorus is limited to that of its source (if known). As we have seen, for the period here being considered Diodorus reproduced Hieronymus, Duris and Timaeus, and his text provides our main access to those writers. The influence of Hieronymus is evident from the attention which Diodorus gives to Eumenes, Antigonus I and Cassander among the early kings. Whether Diodorus used these sources directly is not certain, though likely. A theory that Agatharchides was an intermediary has gained some popularity, but cannot be proved – though the use of Agatharchides has been demonstrated in some parts of Diodorus. From Book XXI onward the surviving fragments are taken mainly from the parts dealing with Roman history; here Diodorus' main sources were Philinus of Acragas, a pro-Carthaginian historian, for the First Punic War and after that Polybius and Posidonius. Diodorus' chronological scheme marks a retrograde step after Polybius' use of Olympiad years; he employs a framework based on Roman consul years and Athenian archon years (available only as far as Book XX, where the full text stops); but his dates are often inconsistent and must be treated with caution.

Another historian who used Hieronymus (and, for the West, Timaeus) is Trogus Pompeius,[12] a Vocontian Gaul from Vasio, who wrote a universal history in forty-four books entitled *Historiae Philip-*

---

[11] For bibliography see Will 1967, II.472–3: (A 67); cf. Bizière 1974: (B 4). On Diodorus' chronological scheme see L. C. Smith 1961: (C 66): Olympiad years are mentioned occasionally in Books XIX and XX.

[12] See Will 1967, II.493–4: (A 67); for Timagenes as Trogus' main source see Schwab 1834: (B 33); cf. von Gutschmid 1882: (B 19); also Walbank 1981, 351–6: (B 40).

picae (a title perhaps derived from Theopompus' *Philippica*, and certainly indicating a non-Roman slant to the work). Of this there survive only the *prologi* (list of contents) and an epitome made by M. Junianus Justinus, who wrote at some date before or during the lifetime of St Augustine, who mentioned him. The books of Trogus relevant to the period 323–217 are XIII–XVII and XXII–XXIX (Books XVIII–XXI being devoted to the Roman war against Pyrrhus, the early history of Carthage and events in Sicily down to Agathocles' rise to power). Whether Trogus used his sources direct or drew on some sort of compilation has been much debated. His account of the Diadochi clearly goes back directly or indirectly to Hieronymus; but who lies behind his history of the later decades of the century is obscure. One view makes Trogus' main source the *History of Kings* by the Alexandrian Timagenes, who came to Rome in the mid first century, quarrelled with Augustus and became an associate of Asinius Pollio. This hypothesis, which has won some support, encounters serious obstacles, not least Timagenes' attested hostility to Rome, which is not evident in Trogus. But whatever his source or sources and despite the garbled character in which his work has reached us in Justinus' abridgement, Trogus is important as the only authority for many otherwise unknown events.

The importance of Plutarch (*c.* A.D. 50–*c.* 120)[13] as a source is not easily over-valued. This philosopher and polymath, who passed his life moving mainly between his home city of Chaeronea in Boeotia and the sacred shrine of Delphi, where he held a priesthood, was no genius but he was immensely learned, and he had an eye for what was significant. His *Parallel Lives of Greeks and Romans* were intended to exemplify virtue and stigmatize vice in the characters portrayed, and to assist in the promotion of partnership between the two races in the running of a common empire. The *Lives* are not history but they are full of the stuff of history, and where they are available they bring life and personality to all the main actors upon the stage of history. The characters of the Diadochi as we believe we know them – of Antigonus, Ptolemy, Seleucus, Perdiccas, Eumenes and Demetrius Poliorcetes – are largely transmitted, perhaps in part created, by Plutarch. His *Lives* draw on a large number of sources, not always identifiable. Those of *Phocion*, *Eumenes*, *Demetrius* and *Pyrrhus* are relevant to the period of the Diadochi. As we saw, they make great use of Hieronymus and Duris. For the second half of the century those of *Agis* and *Cleomenes* were based mainly on Phylarchus, who was sympathetic to the revolutionary kings, while the *Aratus* draws largely on its hero's own *Memoirs*. The *Philopoemen*, only marginally relevant for this period, was derived mainly from Polybius,

---

13 Cf. Russell 1973: (B 31); on the *Philopoemen* see Walbank 1979, III.780–1 (B 37).

but whether from the *Histories* (additions in that case being due to elaboration by Plutarch himself) or from the historian's independent biography of his predecessor, is uncertain.

Arrian (L. Flavius Arrianus) (c. A.D. 89–after 146),[14] a Bithynian from Nicomedia, was like Plutarch interested in both philosophy and history; but, unlike Plutarch, he followed an active career in the imperial service, holding a consulship, provincial governorship and military commands, thus exemplifying the partnership which Plutarch sought to promote from the seclusion of his study. Eventually he retired to Athens, where he held the eponymous archonship in 145/6. Arrian's most important historical work was his *Anabasis of Alexander*, but the one which concerns the period under consideration, and that only for its first few years, is his *Events after Alexander*. This history, in ten books, has survived only as a summary in Photius, reinforced by two tenth-century palimpsests containing part of Book VII and an Oxyrhynchus papyrus (*PSI* XII.1284) describing part of a battle of 320 between Eumenes and Neoptolemus. A comparison with Diodorus renders it virtually certain that for this work, which covered only the brief years from Alexander's death to Antipater's crossing into Europe in 320 (following the agreement at Triparadisus), Arrian used Hieronymus, though he probably supplemented him from some other unidentified source.

Appian of Alexandria (late first century A.D.–before A.D. 165),[15] roughly Arrian's contemporary, composed a history of the Roman empire on a novel plan, describing in twenty-four books the history of each separate people down to the time it was brought within the controlling power of Rome. His merits, like those of Diodorus, are very much those of his sources; and for the century down to 217 B.C. what survives has little to offer the historian, except that his *Syrian History* (51–70) contains a version of the early years of the Seleucid kingdom from the time of Alexander onwards. Appian's sources are obscure, Hieronymus and perhaps Timagenes' *History of Kings* being among the more important.

Apart from these more substantial sources, information of various kinds (and weight) can be gleaned from a number of other writers. The negotiations at Babylon which followed Alexander's death are most fully described by Q. Curtius Rufus (x.5ff.); his rhetorically elaborated account probably draws on Cleitarchus, but he also uses Hieronymus. For the Lamian War at the very outset of the period there is evidence in

[14] See Stadter, 1980: (B 35). The *Bithyniaca* contains only one anecdote from the pre-Roman period and the *Parthica* a brief account of the Parthian break away from the Seleucids under Antiochus II. For the *Events after Alexander* see *FGrH* 156 F1–11 and the reconstruction in Stadter, *ibid.* 144–52, 235 n.46. Stadter, *ibid.* 148–9, suggests that the source used to supplement Hieronymus was Ptolemy, if his work was published soon after 320 (so Errington 1969, 233–42: (D 54)).

[15] Cf. Will 1967, 11.469–71: (A 67); Gabba 1958, 1–40: (B 14).

the *Funeral Speech* of Hyperides and the *Lives* of *Demosthenes* and *Hyperides* which have come down among Plutarch's works. Pausanias is invaluable for information on sites and localities and has some useful passages dealing with the Diadochi, Ptolemy, Lysimachus and Seleucus, and with Pyrrhus. Pliny's *Natural History* and Athenaeus' *Deipnosophists* contain several valuable accounts, for example Athenaeus' description (v.196a–203b; from Callixeinus) of the great procession held in Alexandria (probably in 271/70) to celebrate the *Ptolemaieia* festival. Photius gives résumés of Books IX to XVI of a local history by Memnon of Heraclea, a work based partly on the third-century history of his compatriot Nymphis (*c.* 310–after 245), which contributes substantially to the history of the area around the Bosphorus and the Black Sea, especially during the years between Corupedium (281/80) and Antiochus I's accession.[16] Memnon's own date is somewhere between Julius Caesar and the emperor Hadrian. The lexicographers Stephanus of Byzantium and the *Suda* also make a contribution of value; the latter, for example, is our sole source for an alliance made between Ptolemy I, Antigonus I and Demetrius Poliorcetes against Cassander, probably in 309/8. For military matters the writers on stratagems are a useful supplementary source. The consular Sex. Julius Frontinus, writing under Domitian, records stratagems of Antigonus I, Antigonus II, Antigonus III, Eumenes of Cardia, Ptolemy I, Ptolemy Ceraunus and Pyrrhus, and the Macedonian rhetorician Polyaenus, in a hasty compilation made for L. Verus, included a number of examples relevant to this period, of which a dozen (probably taken from Duris and Timaeus) concern Agathocles alone. Often, however, it is not possible to be sure which Antiochus or Seleucus Polyaenus is writing about.

Diogenes Laertius' compendium on the lives and doctrines of the philosophers (probably composed in the first half of the third century of our era) is also useful for political history, since many philosophers (e.g. Demetrius of Phalerum, Menedemus of Eretria) followed political careers either within the kingdoms or in their shadow. Finally, for the chronology of the period mention should be made of the verse *Chronica* compiled by Apollodorus of Athens (b. *c.* 180 B.C.) and dedicated to Attalus II of Pergamum and of the *Chronicles* of Porphyry (A.D. 234–early 4th century), who was Plotinus' successor as head of the Neoplatonic school at Athens. This study was utilized by his younger contemporary, Eusebius of Caesarea, in his *Chronica*, a work of which Part I has survived in an Armenian translation and Part II in the Latin version of St Jerome.[17]

These works exemplify the wide variety of sources, not in themselves

16 *FGrH* 434 (Memnon); 432 (Nymphis).   17 On Eusebius see Helm 1956: (B 20).

histories, which can be tapped for historical information. As regards histories proper, some six hundred monographs on cities and peoples are known; not all but many of these contain material relevant to the period 323–217. There are also sources of special relevance to particular fields of study such as the progress of science, and these are listed and discussed in their appropriate place. Naturally, too, contemporary literature contains references to contemporary events. Theocritus' seventeenth idyll is a eulogy of Ptolemy II and his fifteenth gives a vivid picture of life in Alexandria on the occasion of the festival of Adonis.

III. OTHER SOURCES

Only the literary sources can furnish a consecutive narrative. But this is often flat and jejune; nor does a mere sequence of events round off the historian's interests. It is therefore to other fields that he must turn for fresh evidence if he hopes to revise and amplify the literary record and to deepen our ideas about why events happened as they did. Such new evidence is fortunately available and it is constantly increasing in quantity. It falls into one or other of the following categories: inscriptions, papyri and ostraca, coins, excavation records and material remains.[18] They will be discussed here in that order.

(a) *Inscriptions*

From the mid seventh century onwards Greek cities had used durable material, in particular stone and marble, to record information which for whatever reason they needed to publish and keep available. In the Hellenistic period, with the widespread development of new cities, the areas where inscriptions were set up grew in number and came to embrace (as well as continental Greece and the West) north-west Greece and Macedonia, Thrace, Asia Minor, Syria, the Black Sea coast, Mesopotamia, and places further east as far as Bactria and Parapamisadae – though the number of finds remains uneven and depends to a considerable extent on the zeal for their recovery shown in the various modern states in which those areas are now situated.

The use of inscriptions is subject to several limitations. First, one cannot always establish the date and provenance of an inscription. A stone may have been moved, or its contents may give no indication of its

---

[18] Particular mention should be made of the vast amount of archaeological work, including the discovery and publication of important inscriptions, from the Greek cities of the Black Sea in modern Bulgaria, Rumania and the Soviet Union, if only because most of it is still inaccessible to scholars unfamiliar with Bulgarian, Rumanian and Russian. For a survey and references down to 1958 see Danoff 1962: (D 156). See also the Bibliography D (h).

date, while lettering can be an unsure guide within a century or so; moreover, inscriptions were sometimes recopied at a later date. Where known names (e.g. that of a king) are mentioned, it may be uncertain which of two or more homonymous persons is meant; for dynastic names tend to be repeated, and ordinary men often carry their grandfather's name.

While it is rare to find an inscription wholly intact, plausible restoration is possible because inscriptions are usually couched in stereotyped phrases characteristic of a particular chancellery, city or other milieu, and the professional epigraphist can often work wonders in restoring the original text. Restorations by more imaginative and less knowledgeable and disciplined editors can, however, be dangerously misleading, and even the best restoration is not the same thing as having the words on the stone. On the whole there is good reason to regard inscriptions as more reliable than statements in historians. Most inscriptions were contemporary documents, being set up as records of decisions on factual matters; the risk of exposure would be high, were city decrees, royal letters or arbitration decisions to appear in a falsified form. But inscriptions do not always give the full story, and what a city or a king writes on stone as the background to a decision or a decree must be judged like any other public pronouncement, that is as a political statement.

Despite these qualifications, however, inscriptions constitute our main source of fresh information about the Hellenistic world. Their importance is all the greater when they can be studied in groups dealing with the same topic, especially when as far as possible these include all available examples. Evidence of this kind is particularly useful in throwing light on social phenomena such as, for instance, piracy or mercenary service, both of which are prominent in the life of Hellenistic society. There are also many forms of international contact and association which are most effectively illuminated and elucidated from inscriptions. Many, for example, record decrees honouring foreign judges sent in response to a request to judge internal disputes or to arbitrate between cities, usually on questions of boundaries and the possession of territory. Others record grants of *asylia* – immunity from reprisals and so, by extension, virtual immunity from arbitrary or piratical attack – to temples or cities (or both), and yet others the authorization of grants of what is really potential citizenship to the citizens of some other city, in the form of *isopoliteia*.

Many inscriptions are concerned with the international festivals which aroused so much interest and played so important a role in the life of the Hellenistic world. They may show a city acceding to a request for the recognition of some newly instituted festival, the *Asklepieia* at Cos or the festival of Artemis Leucophryene at Magnesia-on-the Maeander, or appointing *theorodokoi* to receive and entertain sacred delegates sent by the city holding the festival to announce its imminence throughout the Greek world. Where festivals included musical and dramatic contests they were attended by actors and other performers, as well as by the athletes who competed in the games. Inscriptions yield information about the rewards granted to the latter by their cities and about the activities of the *technitai* of Dionysus, the professional performers organized in guilds which sometimes seem to operate almost like independent states. Doctors loaned by one city to another in time of war or epidemic also have their services rewarded, along with envoys, travelling poets and musicians, and rich men who earn civic gratitude (and sometimes more tangible advantages) by their large gifts of money either to ransom prisoners, endow a festival or (in some Black Sea cities) pay danegeld to a threatening barbarian neighbour. A whole range of inscriptions throws light on the doings of the ephebes within the cities and on the gymnasium and its officials and teachers. One may also ascertain the status of cities situated within a monarchy or on its fringes by a comparison of their decrees with those of free cities and by studying the magistracies and forms of procedure which the inscriptions reveal. Collections of royal letters or treaties likewise throw light on the relations between kings and other states and on political history generally.[19] A phenomenon such as ruler-cult is also illuminated by the evidence of inscriptions.

A great deal of epigraphical material from the great panhellenic sanctuaries throws light on the social and economic conditions in which the temples were put up and maintained. From Delos, for example, the accounts of the *hieropoioi*, the magistrates responsible for temple administration, provide information on the building and restoration of many shrines and other edifices, such as the sacred houses of Zeus Cynthius and Athena Cynthia built on Mt Cynthus early in the third century; and the inventories of the temples of Artemis and Apollo record the contents of the treasuries, the names of donors and the dates of gifts. From building accounts, such as those from the fourth and third centuries at Epidaurus, the historian can trace the procedures and the economic basis of temple building.[20]

The failure of the literary tradition to provide a firm chronology for the period between 300 and 220 (see above, p. 2) can be in some degree compensated from epigraphical material. One of the two surviving fragments of a chronicle from Paros covers the years 336/5 to 299/8 (originally it went down to 264/3);[21] unfortunately this document is of

---

[19] See *RC* for royal letters; *SVA* II and III.   [20] Cf. Burford 1969: (J 192).
[21] *FGrH* 239.

no real help for the third century. What is more important, Attic inscriptions, which are frequently dated by archon years, have been used to further the reconstruction of the list of archons which breaks off in Diodorus with the end of his complete text in 300 – though it is carried down to 292/1 by Dionysius of Halicarnassus (*Din.* 9).[22] This enterprise has generated formidable controversies and its goal is still very far from being achieved, though as new inscriptions turn up, the options which remain open for archons not yet firmly anchored in position grow progressively fewer. Comparable work has been done on the Delphic archons[23] and on the Boeotian federal archons between 250 and 171 (based on twenty-six military catalogues engraved on a wall at Hyettus).[24] There are two problems here: first, the reconstitution of such a list, and secondly its use for general dating, which depends on the possibility of correlating inscriptions datable in terms of the Athenian or Delphian magistrates with particular events which fit into a general historical context. This is often possible in the case of Athenian material, and the Delphic archon list has a special value inasmuch as it is a means of dating decrees of the Amphictyonic Council. In these the number of Aetolian votes has been shown to increase in proportion to the growth in the number of states in central Greece which the confederacy controlled at any particular time. It thus becomes possible to trace the extension of territory under the confederacy, though this is subject to two qualifications: first, one cannot always equate new votes with the accession of particular areas, and secondly until the list of archons is complete the chronology remains in some degree fluid (see further, ch. 7, pp. 233–4).

   These are a few examples of how particular categories of inscriptions can illuminate areas of history in which the literary record is deficient. But frequently an individual inscription standing alone can be correlated with known events so that it either sets them in a new context or assists in dating them more closely. One or two specific examples will illustrate this point. Our knowledge of the refounding of the Hellenic League by Antigonus I and Demetrius I in 302 would be meagre without the (admittedly fragmentary) text of the actual treaty founding the League, discovered at Epidaurus (*SVA* 446), together with the further information afforded by an Athenian honorary decree for Adeimantus of Lampsacus, who is now known to have served as one of the five original *proedroi* of the organization, and to have sent a letter to Demetrius

---

[22] For recent proposed archon lists see Meritt 1977 (D 95) and Habicht 1979, 113–46: (D 91); but no dates between 261 and 230 are quite certain.

[23] See Daux 1936: (D 77); Flacelière 1937: (D 105); Nachtergael 1977: (E 113); Ehrhardt 1975, 124–38: (D 14).

[24] Étienne and Knoepfler 1976: (D 78).

concerning the ratification of its constitution by the Delphic Amphictyony.[25] Three inscriptions from Athens dating from the archonship of
Nicias of Otryne (266/5) (*SIG* 385–7) throw light on the Athenian
capture of the Museum Hill during Olympichus' liberation of Athens
from Demetrius, probably in 287, an event known otherwise only from
two short passages in Pausanias (1.26.1–3, 29.13). An Athenian decree
honouring Callias of Sphettus which was passed around the turn of the
year 270/69 provides information about the liberation of Athens from
Demetrius and also about a hitherto unrecorded peace made in its train
between Demetrius and Ptolemy.[26] An essential piece of evidence for the
Chremonidean War is the Athenian inscription containing the decree
causing it, which was proposed by Chremonides in the year of
Peithidemus (268/7);[27] this can be supplemented by a further decree
honouring the Athenian general Epichares, which is recorded on an
inscription from Rhamnus (*SEG* XXIV.154). Another inscription from
Rhamnus throws light on the situation in Attica during the Demetrian
War in 236/5 (*ISE* 1.25). Finally, a dossier of documents from Labraunda
in Caria brings information about the dynast Olympichus of Alinda,
which updates his relations with Philip V to the beginning of the latter's
reign and throws light on Antigonus Doson's Carian expedition.[28]

These examples all concern Macedonia and Greece; but the history of
Syria and Egypt has also been illuminated by epigraphical evidence. For
example, the annexation of Cyrene by Ophellas on behalf of Ptolemy I
was probably the occasion for the publication of the so-called 'charter of
Cyrene', in fact a *diagramma* of Ptolemy I.[29] An inscription from
Laodicea-on-the-Lycus[30] provides evidence which may involve redating
the 'elephant battle' of Antiochus I against the Galatians to 270. Events
in Seleucid and Ptolemaic history can also be further elucidated from
inscriptions in languages other than Greek. The First Syrian War
(274–271) between Antiochus I and Ptolemy II would be virtually
unknown but for a cuneiform tablet from Babylon and a hieroglyphic
stele celebrating Ptolemy's victory from Heroopolis (Pithom).[31]
Ptolemy III's return to Alexandria from his invasion of Mesopotamia in
246 is recorded on the 'Canopus decree', a trilingual inscription of
which three copies survive.[32] Pithom yields yet a further document

---

[25] See ch. pp. 58–9.
[26] Shear 1978: (C 62); Habicht 1979: (D 91). Shear dates the liberation of Athens to 286, Habicht
to 287.   [27] *SIG* 434–5 = *SVA* III.476; see ch. 7, p. 236.
[28] Crampa 1969: (B 60); see ch. 12, p. 460 and n. 38.
[29] *SEG* IX.1; see ch. 2, p. 36 with n. 28.
[30] See Wörrle 1975, 59ff.: (B 177); also ch. 11, p. 423 and n. 26.
[31] *BM* 92689; cf. S. Smith, *Babylonian Historical Texts* (London, 1924) 150ff.; for the Pithom stele
see ch. 11, p. 417 with n. 7; Sethe 1904: (F 126), and Bibliography F 116–19.
[32] *OGIS* 56; see ch. 11, 421 with n. 20.

which adds substantially to our knowledge of what happened after the
battle of Raphia (217). This is the stele[33] inscribed in Greek, demotic and
hieroglyphic and recording a decree passed by the synod of priests at
Memphis on 15 November 217, which refers to a punitive expedition
into Coele-Syria lasting twenty-one days, which Ptolemy carried out
after the battle. Finally, we may consider two documents of great
importance inscribed in cuneiform. One is a Babylonian chronicle
published in 1932, the other a king-list contained on a Babylonian
cuneiform tablet which was published in 1974.[34] The former gives a
synopsis of events between 321 and 307 and the latter a list of dates for
the reigns of the kings of Babylon from Alexander down to Antiochus
IV, using the Babylonian calendar; this list, which appears to be reliable
and based on good evidence, allows a much closer dating of events in
Seleucid history.

The study of Greek epigraphical material has been facilitated by the
publication of inscriptions over many years in collections arranged
according to geographical and, as far as is feasible, chronological
criteria. The main works are listed in the bibliography; mention may be
made here of the volumes of *IG* in both the original form and the revised
edition in smaller format (*IG²*). Some volumes originally planned have
for various reasons never appeared and in their place one must consult
other publications. Prominent among these are *Die Inschriften von
Olympia, Inscriptions de Délos, Fouilles de Delphes: Inscriptions, Inscriptiones
antiquae orae septentrionalis Ponti Euxini, Inscriptiones graecae in Bulgaria
repertae*; but there is a fuller list in A. G. Woodhead, *The Study of Greek
Inscriptions*.[35] Later material is published in *Supplementum epigraphicum
graecum* and there are several volumes containing a corpus of inscriptions
from particular sites and areas, e.g. Caria, Sardis, Ilium, Pergamum,
Priene, Miletus, Magnesia-on-the-Maeander, Didyma, Cos, Lindus,
Cyrene, Histria, Scythia, Egypt, Syria. Mention must also be made of the
annual surveys of new material in J. and L. Robert's *Bulletin épigraphique*
published in *Revue des Études Grecques*. L. Robert's *Hellenica* in thirteen
volumes (Paris, 1940–65) and his many other publications together
constitute a contribution without parallel not only to epigraphical
studies but also to numismatics and to Hellenistic history in general.
There are useful selections of historically important inscriptions in
Dittenberger's *Sylloge inscriptionum graecarum³* and his *Orientis graeci
inscriptiones selectae*, in L. Moretti's *Iscrizioni storiche ellenistiche*, and (in
English translation) M. M. Austin's *The Hellenistic World*. New

[33] See ch. 11, pp. 437–9.
[34] Furlani and Momigliano 1932, 462–84: (E 24); *BM* 35603 with Sachs and Wiseman 1954: (E 49).
[35] Woodhead 1981, 103–7: (B 176).

inscriptions are published regularly in excavation reports and in many specialist journals such as *Hesperia*.

(b) *Papyri and ostraca*

A second source of contemporary material which, like inscriptions, is constantly growing in volume, is provided by papyri and (in smaller numbers) by ostraca. Professor Turner has prefaced his chapter on Ptolemaic Egypt with a note (see below, p. 118–19) emphasizing the limitations which hamper the historian who tries to use papyri and correcting the false impression that most existing papyri have by now been published. We can in fact expect the flow of publication to continue for many decades and also hope that as more specialists in demotic are available the present disparity in the number of published Greek and demotic texts will be redressed, to the advantage of all students of Ptolemaic Egypt. The present section is intended to supplement the comments in ch. 5 with some general remarks on the use of papyri by the historian.

The area for which papyri and ostraca are of use is far more limited than that served by inscriptions. For the century following Alexander's death they throw light mainly on the Egyptian countryside and, of course, on the relations between its inhabitants and the representatives of government at various levels. As one descends in the social scale demotic becomes more important as the language of communication, since the lower officials are more likely to be Egyptian. That is one reason why the preponderance of Greek papyri hitherto published creates an unbalanced picture. As regards the contents of papyri, here too there is a contrast with inscriptions. Whereas many of the latter are official records of decrees, grants, letters, treaties and other matters of direct political importance, papyri, though occasionally containing material of that kind, for the most part consist of discarded notes, drafts and documents throwing light on social, fiscal and economic matters, which have survived as mummy wrapping or in rubbish dumps preserved in the dry sand of Upper Egypt. Ostraca were used largely as tax receipts, but might also be a convenient vehicle for memoranda and the like.

Papyri furnish a wealth of information for Egypt such as we possess from no other part of the ancient world. Within the period under consideration the greatest number fall between *c*. 259 and *c*. 215.[36] For this period of rather less than half a century – for which, as it happens, our literary sources are especially unsatisfactory – we are informed (though intermittently) about prices and wages, normal daily food rations, the extreme limits of wealth and poverty, the size of land

[36] See ch. 5, p. 118.

holdings, the composition of families, customs dues, the size and capacity of river craft, the time taken to transport commodities and what it cost, rates of interest, crop yields, the rents of farms and houses, the area of villages, the various categories of land occupation, and above all the thousand and one ways in which government in all its ramifications impinged on the lives of peasants and settlers.[37] Most of this material is undated. There is not a great deal from the towns, at any rate in the early Ptolemaic period, but the powerful and important temples – many of them built or extended by the Ptolemies – have left a wealth of demotic material, some of which is especially interesting for the glimpse it gives of relations between the Greeks and native Egyptians. Alexandria and the Delta have provided virtually nothing since the damp soil there has prevented the survival of papyrus.

Though only exceptionally relevant to political and military history, papyri have made some contributions – and for certain periods contributions of great importance – in that field. Among literary papyri so far discovered a few contain extracts from historical works. There are for instance the fragment of Arrian's *Events after Alexander* found at Oxyrhynchus (see above, p. 8), and a first-century papyrus (*P. Oxy.* 2399) containing a fragment of an unidentified historian writing about Agathocles.[38] Another discovery, which has provoked violent controversy, is of a fragmentary Copenhagen papyrus (*P. Haun.* 6) containing, it would appear (for the document is hard to decipher) six short résumés of incidents of Ptolemaic history during the period of the Third and Fourth Syrian Wars.[39] These include a reference to a certain *Ptolemaios Andromachou* (or *Ptolemaios Andromachos* – both words are in the genitive), to the battle of Andros, to the murder of an unnamed person (Ptolemy 'the son'?) at Ephesus, to an Egyptian advance as far as the Euphrates, and finally to an Aetolian Theodotus (perhaps a man already known from Polybius). This brief document may be a scrap from a set of notes taken by someone reading a historical work. The divergent views about its contents reflect the dearth of reliable information available from this period of Ptolemaic history.

One such almost blank area is that of the Second Syrian War, for which an ostracon and several papyri have produced substantial evidence. The ostracon, from Karnak, appears to refer to Ptolemy II's invasion of Syria in 258/7, a topic which also figures in *P. Haun.* 6;[40] and two papyri, *P. Cairo Zen.* 67 and *P. Mich. Zen.* 100, show that in 258/7

[37] Cf. Préaux 1978, 1.106: (A 48).

[38] See ch. 10, p. 384.

[39] Cf. *P. Haun.* 6; see ch. 11, nn. 19 and 44; new readings in Bülow-Jacobsen 1979: (E 13); and Habicht 1980: (E 28). See Will 1979, I².237–8: (A 67); Bengtson 1971, 11–14: (B 48).

[40] See ch. 11, n. 13, for bibliography; and ch. 5, pp. 135–6, for the problems presented by this document. On *P. Haun.* 6 see the previous note.

Halicarnassus was Ptolemaic and that Ptolemaic naval construction was going on during that year – two facts of considerable interest in the reconstruction of an obscure conflict. The end of the war is also illuminated by several papyri which attest the establishment of cleruchic settlements in the Egyptian countryside in late 253, and by a famous document, *P. Cairo Zen.* 59251, containing a letter from the doctor Artemidorus who escorted the princess Berenice to the borders of Palestine in 252 for her marriage with Antiochus II, as a seal to the peace settlement. For the Third Syrian (Laodicean) War too there is an important papyrus, the so-called *P. Gurob*, which is usually taken to be an official communiqué sent by Ptolemy III to the court at Alexandria, describing the Egyptian advance as far as Antioch at the outset of the war in 246.

These and a few other papyri throw light on specific historical situations. But apart from these there is a vast amount to be learnt from the prosopographical information contained in papyri and this, supplemented by names taken from inscriptions, has been made available in the volumes of the *Prosopographia Ptolemaica*.[41] These provide material illustrating not only political events but also, what is no less important, the administrative structure of the Ptolemaic kingdom and its military organization both in Egypt and abroad.

(c) *Coins*

Coins provide a further useful source of information on the early Hellenistic period. Greek coins of this time fall broadly into three groups: there are royal issues minted by the kings in their own mints, coins produced for the kings in cities under their control, and coins minted by cities on their own behalf. The right to mint was an important aspect of sovereignty. Royal issues usually carry a portrait on the obverse, though not necessarily that of the monarch issuing the coins. Lysimachus and Ptolemy I both struck coins with the head of Alexander; and later many cities around the Hellespont and the Propontis followed this practice. Lysimachus' head was also featured widely after his death. Some coins bearing his head were still being minted under the Roman Empire, reminding us of the protracted life of Maria Theresa dollars. But beginning with Demetrius Poliorcetes it became normal (except at Pergamum) to represent the reigning king (and occasionally his consort) on his own coins. Some of these portraits were assigned the characteristics of gods, for example the horns of Ammon worn by Alexander, or the sun's rays shining from his head on gold coins of Ptolemy III. In

---

[41] Ed. W. Peremens and E. van 't Dack (Louvain, 1950–75) = *Pros. Ptol.*

this way, and also in the subjects represented on the reverse, coins can throw light on royal pretensions and royal cult – though this is commoner under the Roman Empire than in the Hellenistic period.

Coins were an important medium for royal propaganda. A king could celebrate his achievements in words or by easily understood symbols or by a special commemorative issue. Thus a coin of Demetrius Poliorcetes shows a personified Nike (Victory) on a ship's prow to commemorate his naval victory over Ptolemy at Salamis in Cyprus in 306.[42] A study of both separate finds and of the coins contained in hoards can extend knowledge of the economic and monetary policy of cities and monarchs. A good example is that of a hoard, hidden away about 220 at what is now Büyükçekmece and containing silver coins of two sorts, first a number of pseudo-'Lysimachi' (that is, silver tetradrachms of 17 g bearing Lysimachus' head) overstruck with a countermark of Byzantium and Chalcedon, and secondly specimens of two later issues (one from each city) based on a different 'Phoenician' standard with a tetradrachm of 13·93 g.[43] These coins have been convincingly interpreted as evidence for a monetary alliance between the two cities and the imposition of a currency monopoly within their territory at a date shortly before 220, when, as we know from Polybius (IV.38–53), Byzantium was under pressure from the Galatians in the kingdom of Tylis, and in consequence sought to impose customs dues on all goods exported from the Black Sea, until the Rhodians compelled her by war to abandon the practice.

The use of coins as evidence, like that of inscriptions, is not, however, without its difficulties. The historian must start with an open mind about why the coin is there at all. It may have been issued to attract or assist commerce, but equally its existence may merely indicate a need by the responsible authority to make payments, for public works perhaps or more often to meet the costs of war. The function of a coin might vary too according to the metal of which it was made. Judging by their condition when found in hoards and by the figures given by Livy of coined money carried in Roman triumphs of the second century, gold coins were commonly hoarded, not circulated. Silver was the normal medium of international trade, and bronze sufficed for everyday needs and usually had an extremely limited area of circulation. Further, it is not always easy to discover where a coin was struck. As we have seen, some royal heads (e.g. Alexander, Lysimachus) help with neither provenance nor date, since they occur posthumously on a wide range of coins, for many of which the only means of identification may be the monogram of the issuing city, and that cannot always be interpreted. On the other

[42] See Plates vol., pl. 70b.
[43] Thompson 1954: (B 266); cf. L. Robert in N. Firatli, *Stèles funéraires de Byzance* (Paris, 1964) : 86 n. 5; Seyrig 1968: (B 262).

hand, given a large number of Lysimachus coins, it is sometimes possible to use a gradual divergence in features from the original type to establish a chronological sequence. Style, however, is always a risky criterion, especially when used to determine the provenance of a coin, since different cities sometimes employed the same engraver for the dies.

It is not always possible to be sure to what standard a particular coin is minted, since weights were only approximate and could be affected by wear in circulation. In general there were two main systems covering the Greek world at this period. Alexander's adoption of the Attic standard was followed by Lysimachus and later by the Antigonids and Seleucids, with the result that over much of the Hellenistic world, including Athens, Macedonia, Asia Minor and the Seleucid territories as far as Bactria north of the Hindu-Kush, there was a single silver standard with a tetradrachm weighing c. 17 g, and the emissions of the various states were accepted almost interchangeably. In fourth-century pre-Alexander Egypt too the Attic standard obtained, as is shown by the large quantities of imitation Athenian tetradrachms struck by the last Pharaonic and Persian régimes, from c. 375 onwards.[44] After some experimentation Ptolemy I eventually settled on the lighter so-called Phoenician or Cyrenean system with a tetradrachm of 14·25 g, and this standard was also used in Carthage, Cyprus, Syria and Phoenicia and in Syracuse under Hiero II. In continental Greece, however, there were many local currencies with restricted circulation and using different standards.[45]

The dating of issues of coinage is one of the most difficult and most important tasks for the historian using numismatic material. Where coins do not themselves carry a regnal year, the best evidence comes from die-studies and from the collation of hoards. By comparing the amount of wear in the dies and by identifying the use of the same dies for coins with a different obverse (or reverse), it becomes possible to establish sequences of issues. The existence of a relevant hoard furnishes a further criterion for, since an approximate date for the burial of the hoard is usually that of the least worn issues in it, it is possible by comparing the amount of wear of the other issues it contains to establish their relative chronology. The numismatist has other means of dating, such as the quantity of dies known of a particular issue: this may allow conclusions concerning the length of time a particular issue lasted, but clearly there are many variables in such an equation.

In practice the numismatist will as often draw on 'historical' evidence to date the coins as the other way round. But once he has framed a hypothesis that fits the known historical events and the

---

[44] See Buttrey 1982: (F 389).
[45] Cf. Giovannini 1978, 8–14: (B 224); and see below, ch. 8, pp. 276–9.

numismatic evidence, this can be used to fill out the total picture. The revision and refining of hypotheses is part of the normal process of historical research and here the numismatist is only marginally worse off than the historian who uses other material such as inscriptions and papyri.

The study of numismatics is facilitated by the publication of hoards, by detailed surveys of the currencies of particular areas and by the publication of the coins contained in great public and private collections, especially those covered by the *Sylloge Nummorum Graecorum*.[46]

(d) *Archaeology*

Information derived from inscriptions and coins can often be supplemented by the results of excavation; indeed many inscriptions and coins are uncovered in the course of excavation and can only be fully exploited by the historian who studies them in their archaeological context. Knowledge about the cities of mainland Greece and western Asia Minor which play a large role in the history of the Hellenistic period has been greatly expanded as a result of excavation reports. These are available not merely for such centres as Athens (especially the *agora*), Corinth, Argos and Thebes, for the great cities of western Asia Minor such as Pergamum, Sardis, Smyrna, Ephesus, Priene, Miletus and, from the islands, Cos and Rhodes, but also for more remote spots like Pella in Macedonia, Scythopolis in Palestine, the cities of the Black Sea coast, Icarus (Failaka) in the Persian Gulf or the unidentified city at Aï Khanum in Afghanistan.[47] Public buildings, walls, temples, theatres, harbour installations and the street pattern have all been unearthed by the spade, and add to the historian's understanding of the way of life of the city dweller and the dangers he sometimes faced. In addition, by carrying investigations into the surrounding area it is also possible sometimes to throw light on the relations between the *polis* and its *chora*, especially if inscriptions are also available. In Egypt the remains of temples built or enlarged in Ptolemaic times – for instance the vast remains at Tentyra (Denderah), Thebes (Karnak), Esneh, Edfu and Kom Ombo – furnish evidence for the relations between the Macedonian dynasty and the powerful Egyptian priesthood.

A further source of information properly included under archaeology consists of surviving objects – works of art, mosaics or sculpture, or

---

[46] The volumes of the *Sylloge* are gradually appearing. *SNG* Copenhagen (*The Royal Collection of Coins and Medals, Danish National Museum* (42 fasc.; Copenhagen, 1942–69)) offers the most complete coverage to date. See Bibliography B(d) and F(k); for additions to the literature see *A Survey of Numismatic Research*, published periodically by the International Numismatic Commission.

[47] See Plates vol., pls. 17, 26, 27, 30–1 (Aï Khanum), 18 (Failaka), 66 (Pella).

everyday objects of trade and household use. The presence of these in a
particular place cannot always be satisfactorily explained. Objects can
move from where they were made for several reasons – in the course of
commerce, but also as gifts or booty. They may also have been lost or
indeed hidden away in time of danger, like coins and treasure. Their
interpretation therefore presents the historian with problems. But they
can sometimes provide evidence about trade routes to supplement what
is known from finds of coins and from other sources. Unfortunately,
though it is occasionally possible to determine an object's provenance
with certainty – certain types of pottery, for instance, and stamped jars
originally containing oil and wine – this is not always so, and the origin
of many artefacts made of metal, ivory or glass can only be guessed at.
Such articles throw light on economic trends, on the standard of living,
on taste in art and on many cultural assumptions. Finally, it is only by a
combination of methods supplementing the findings of archaeology
with the use of every other sort of evidence that progress can be made
towards the solution of outstanding historical problems; and many must
await the discovery of new source material.

CHAPTER 2

THE SUCCESSION TO ALEXANDER

ÉDOUARD WILL

I. FROM THE DEATH OF ALEXANDER TO TRIPARADISUS (323–321)

At the time of Alexander's death in June 323, the actual military conquest of the East was to all intents and purposes complete. It had come to an end – despite the king's wishes – on that day in 326 when his troops had refused to follow him further across the plains of the Indus. But the organization of this immense empire was still only roughly sketched out and ideally the Conqueror should have lived a good many more years to enable this colossal and disparate body, held together only by the will and genius of the king, to acquire some homogeneity and some hope of permanence. This very year in which Alexander died would in all likelihood have proved decisive from the point of view of his political work. On the one hand, his choice of Babylon as capital (though this choice is not certain) was probably the prelude to a definitive organization of the central administration, a very necessary task, since everything so far had been more or less improvised. On the other hand, certain recent incidents (the *proskynesis* affair, the mutiny at Opis, and so on) must necessarily have led the king to a more precise and at the same time more restricted definition of his powers, of the relations between Macedonians and Persians, and the like. In short, the great epic adventure was over, and the task of reflection was beginning. It demanded prudence and imagination, tact and boldness. No one can say whether Alexander would have been equal to this task (some have doubted it), and his death leaves all the questions open.

The very fact that from the crossing of the Hellespont to the descent into the plains of the Indus everything had depended on the person and the will of the Conqueror meant that on his death the first problem to arise was that of the succession.[1] Alexander had no legitimate son. It is true that the rules of succession in Macedonia had never been very strictly defined: if power in Macedonia had been passed down for many generations within the family of the Argeadae, it had nevertheless

---

[1] Glotz *et al.*: 1945: (A 18) (to which readers are referred for the chapter as a whole); Merkelbach 1954, 123ff., 243ff.: (B 24); Vitucci 1963: (C 72); Schachermeyr 1970: (C 58); Errington 1970: (C 22); Bosworth 1971: (C 6).

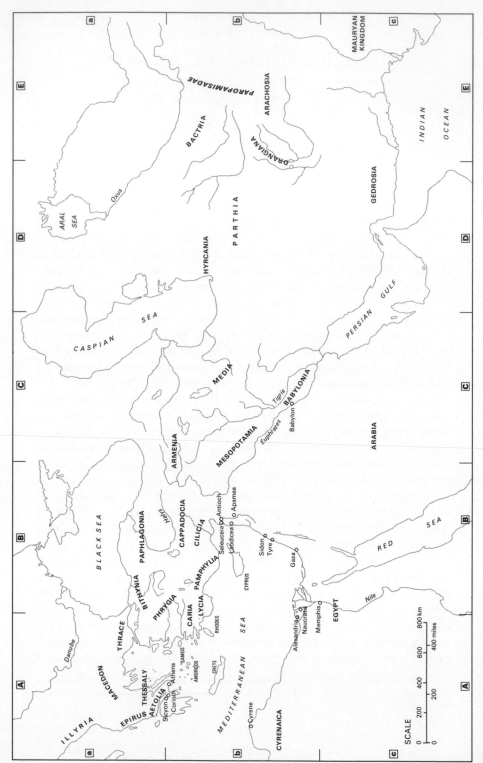

Map 1. The Hellenistic world in the late fourth century.

always been, and still was, necessary to reckon with the assembly of free Macedonians (or, according to a recent hypothesis, of the Macedonian nobility alone), which could impose or ratify successions departing from the normal patrilineal system. The most notable example of these 'irregularities' (which were irregularities only for those who cannot conceive of monarchical succession in any other terms than those of male primogeniture strictly interpreted) was still present in all minds: it was that of Alexander's own father, Philip II, who was certainly not the son of his predecessor but had, without great difficulty, acquired the power which should 'normally' have fallen to one of his nephews. The absence of a legitimate son of Alexander did not, therefore, pose an insurmountable legal problem as long as the royal family was not extinct – and not even then. Alexander had a half-brother, Arrhidaeus, a bastard of Philip II, who could have made an acceptable successor, in law at least, for in fact he was incapable of taking on the tasks left by Alexander, being an epileptic and retarded. Despite the unpromising prospects raised by the possibility of a recognition of Arrhidaeus, the memory of Philip II and of Alexander left so strong an impression on those who survived them (an impression stronger, no doubt, than the simple feeling of loyalty to the dynasty) that no one dared or even thought to raise the dynastic question. Moreover, another circumstance prevented its being raised immediately: Roxane, the widow of Alexander, was pregnant, and so might, within a few months, give her deceased husband a male heir. Between the two possibilities opinions were divided. Perdiccas, who, after Hephaestion's death had held the position of chiliarch to Alexander (the title is a Greek translation of a Persian term meaning 'commander of the thousand' and indicating 'first after the king'), and the members of the royal council indicated their preference for the possible direct heir: a long minority was no doubt not without attractions for the ambitious among them, not least Perdiccas. Roxane, however, was not Macedonian and her son would be half-Iranian, and this prospect was repugnant to the Macedonian peasants who made up the phalanx. These infantrymen, the majority of whom were mainly interested in returning to their homeland and re-establishing contact with the national traditions which Alexander had gradually abandoned, met spontaneously in a tumultuous assembly and, spurred on by Perdiccas' opponents, proclaimed Arrhidaeus king. To avoid a battle between the cavalry, who supported Perdiccas, and the phalangites, a bargain was negotiated: if the child was a boy (as proved to be the case; he was called Alexander [IV]), he would share power with Arrhidaeus,[2] who was given the distinguished (and, for the infantrymen, politically

[2] Granier 1931, 58–65: (D 23); Briant 1973, 240ff., 279ff.: (C 8); Errington 1978: (D 17).

significant) name of Philip (III). This compromise, based on a collegiate kingship shared between an idiot and a minor, was clearly no more than an interim solution. But the interim before what? No one yet knew, or at least no one would yet say.[3]

Even before the child was born, however, the empire he was to inherit had to be governed, and Alexander's companions divided among themselves the duties and the great regional governorships which, in the conquered countries, the Conqueror had allowed to retain their structure and their title of satrapies.

In Europe the aged Antipater, whom Alexander had left behind him on his departure for Asia, retained his previous functions as *strategos*, which made him the all-powerful representative of the monarchy. In practice regent of Macedon, Antipater in addition exercised the Macedonian protectorate over all the regions of Europe which, in one way or another, had been more or less closely tied to the kingdom (Thessaly, Thrace, Epirus, parts of Illyria, etc.) and especially over European Greece, which Philip II had organized within the Corinthian League. Antipater was devoted to the ideas of his contemporary, Philip II; he was the embodiment of loyalty to the dynasty (if not to Alexander himself, of whose development he is known to have disapproved), of prudence, of wisdom, but also of unrelenting energy: without Antipater and the vigilant watch he kept in Europe Alexander's adventure would have been impossible. He was to continue this work until his death, now unfortunately close.

In Asia too provision had to be made for a central authority. Perdiccas seemed marked out for this by his duties as chiliarch. He therefore retained this office (and took the title going with it, which Alexander had not yet conferred upon him) and was thus invested with a power to which all the satraps were theoretically subordinate.

The kings (or at least Philip III, who was as yet sole king) were, however, kings both of Macedon and of Asia, and, since one already was and the other would be for a long time incapable of exercising their kingship in either of these two countries, it was necessary for a person of some standing to undertake, not indeed the exercise of power over the whole empire, but the representation of the sovereigns. This person was Craterus, the most respected member of Alexander's entourage, whose high authority must have been, in the eyes of some, above all a means of curbing the thrusting ambition of Perdiccas. Craterus was named *prostates* of the kings. This office, that of a proxy rather than of a guardian in the strict sense, seems to have been intended to give him supreme control of the army and the finances of the empire, more

[3] Arr. *Diad.* fr. 1.1; Dexipp. fr. 1.1; Diod. XVIII.2; Just. XIII.2–4.4; Plut. *Eum* 3.1; Curt. X.19–31; App. *Syr.* 52.

particularly in Asia. In 323, however, Craterus was not in Babylon; he was en route for Europe (where he was secretly intended to replace Antipater) at the head of the returning veterans, and was later to play a part in events there. But his career was destined to be even briefer than that of Antipater, and in fact he was never able to exercise his powers. Until 321 (the date of the deaths of both Craterus and Perdiccas) the kings were to remain with Perdiccas, who thus assumed in practice the duties which had been conferred, perhaps more in theory than in reality, on Craterus.[4]

Craterus, Antipater and Perdiccas thus formed a sort of triumvirate controlling Alexander's legacy. This triumvirate was totally theoretical, since at the time these decisions were taken Craterus and Antipater could not be consulted, and it was to be shattered by events before long.

There was also a matter of more importance than the division of the supreme powers, and this was the division of the satrapies, for it is this which contains the seed of the dismemberment of the empire. A passage of Pausanias (1.6.2) asserts that the most active initiator of this division was Ptolemy the son of Lagus;[5] if this report is accurate, it probably implies that Ptolemy had an idea at the back of his mind, and we shall probably not be wrong in supposing that it was at his request, or as a result of his intrigues, that Egypt was allocated to him. During his stay in Egypt Alexander had not made the country a satrapy, but tradition asserts that in 323 the title of satrap was used in Egypt by the Greek Cleomenes of Naucratis, one of those appointed by Alexander to manage the finances of Egypt: whether Cleomenes was named satrap by Alexander at an unknown date or whether he had usurped the position, he was now made subordinate to Ptolemy.[6]

In Asia Minor satrapies were given to or confirmed in the possession of two figures destined to become famous later: Antigonus Monophthalmus ('the One-Eyed'), who was installed in western Anatolia (Greater Phrygia, Lycia, Pamphylia),[7] and Eumenes of Cardia,[8] who was sent to Cappadocia and Paphlagonia. The case of this last is somewhat unusual. Eumenes, who was a Greek and Alexander's archivist (and so one of those closest to him and most familiar with his intentions), was unpopular with the senior Macedonian captains, and it may even have seemed desirable to some to remove him from the centre of affairs. From this point of view, Cappadocia represented the gift of a poisoned chalice,

---

[4] Arr. *Diad.* fr. 1.3; Dexipp. fr. 1.3–4; Just. XIII.4.5; Diod. XVIII.2.4 and 3.2 is confused and incorrect.
[5] Seibert 1969, 27ff.: (F 145).
[6] Seibert 1969, 69ff.: (F 145); Vogt 1971: (C 73); Seibert 1972: (F 147).
[7] Wehrli 1969, 32–3: (C 75); Briant 1973, 125ff.: (C 8).
[8] Briant 1972: (C 7).

since this difficult country had not been conquered by Alexander and was administered by a Persian satrap, Ariarathes: in sending this civil servant to take Ariarathes' satrapy from him, there must have been those who expected him to fail. Perhaps, however, this was not the attitude of Perdiccas if there was already an understanding between the chiliarch and the Greek, which is not certain: it might suit Perdiccas to put a reliable man in areas which allowed him to keep an eye on communications between Mesopotamia and Europe.

At the junction of Macedonia and Asia Minor, Thrace was entrusted to Lysimachus.[9] This is also a special case, because Thrace was not a satrapy but a European territory which Philip II had annexed to his realms and which was now detached to form a separate province. It is true that, as a country under threat, Thrace required an energetic soldier to devote himself exclusively to its defence, but to give it to Lysimachus was also to take it away from Antipater.

Ptolemy, Antigonus, Eumenes, Lysimachus: the list (along with the supreme 'triumvirate') embraces the names of those who were to be the protagonists in the confused struggle which was about to be engaged. The other satrapies, in Asia Minor and Syria, in Mesopotamia and in Iran, were entrusted to figures summoned to a less illustrious future: we shall meet some of them in passing; for the moment they may be ignored.[10]

All these men – with the exception of Eumenes and one or two other Greeks – are Macedonians. The death of Alexander meant the removal of almost all Persians, whom the Conqueror had admitted in large numbers to his entourage and placed in administrative posts. In other words, the sort of Macedonian–Iranian condominium over Asia which Alexander had begun to create – not without fierce resistance from the Macedonians – was immediately replaced by the power of the conquerors alone. This, at least, was a tendency which appeared in the summer of 323, and it would be wrong to identify it summarily as the principle which was to govern the whole of the Hellenistic period. Yet nowhere is there any sign, except perhaps in the case of Peucestas in Persis, that the reality of power was ever subsequently shared with Orientals. And the rapid break-up of the Iranian marriages forced by Alexander on his Macedonian companions (only Seleucus kept his Iranian wife) is a further sign that these men did not intend to have descendants of mixed race. The Macedonians, who had criticized Alexander for not keeping all the fruits of their conquests for them, seem henceforth to have been firmly resolved to be the sole masters.

Conflicts were to break out immediately among these new masters of

---

[9] Saitta 1955, 62ff.: (C 57).
[10] Arr. *Diad.* fr. 1.5–8; Dexipp. fr. 1.2–7; Diod. XVIII.3; Just. XIII.4, 9–23; Plut. *Eum.* 3.2.

the empire, the 'Diadochi' ('Heirs'). Nevertheless it is important to note that these conflicts, if they were obviously first conflicts of personal ambition, were also, in this first period, something else and something more: conflicts between the unitary idea, the legacy of Alexander's thinking, and particularist tendencies. Furthermore, these two aspects of the struggles of the Diadochi are inextricably intertwined, inasmuch as the unitary idea simply covers larger ambitions, more on the scale of Alexander's, than do the particularist tendencies. The period we are about to consider is, in short, that which sees the elimination of the unitary in favour of the particularist tendency. Indeed, the latter had already won final victory, despite a last revival of the will to reunite the empire, as early as 301.

To the best of our knowledge, the announcement of Alexander's death aroused no disturbance among the nations of Asia. This inertia is remarkable but, though its interpretation is a delicate matter, it would no doubt be wrong to see it as no more than a general indifference. In the vast stretches of Mesopotamia and Syria the indigenous inhabitants were accustomed to a subjection often stretching back over centuries, and the death of a new conqueror was nothing to cause an upsurge of 'nationalism'. It would no doubt be desirable to draw distinctions – what did Tyre think? what was the atmosphere in Babylon? – but the documents available do not enable us to answer such questions. However, if the inertia of the westernmost regions of the Asian empire was largely the result of apathy, this interpretation would probably be false for Iran. We have of course no more documents in this case than in the other, but if we consider, first, that the Iranians were the former masters of Asia, second, that Alexander had given them a privileged position, and finally, and to anticipate, that Iran was soon to be the main area of anti-Macedonian agitation, we may be inclined to think that the inertia of Iran in 323 was in large measure a waiting game.

While the Asians made no move, the general tranquillity of the empire was on the other hand disturbed, at both extremities, by Greeks.

It was in the far East that the first rising, that of the Greeks of Bactria, took place. This is our first encounter with this country and these people, whose subsequent role is by no means negligible. Who were these Greeks established in eastern Iran, on the northern slopes of the Hindu-Kush? We are told that they were soldiers settled by Alexander in military colonies designed to protect this particularly vulnerable border region of his empire who, weary of their stay in this remote spot, had been demanding repatriation since 325. There must indeed have been such semi-penal colonies, and no doubt their inhabitants chose this moment to revolt or, more accurately, at the news of Alexander's death they renewed a mutiny which had broken out two years before. But certain facts make one hesitate. The satrap of Media, Peitho,[11] who was given the task of suppressing the revolt, would willingly have shown clemency to the rebels (against the orders of Perdiccas) in the hope of making them a base for his personal power, but his Macedonians, contrary to his plans, massacred the Greeks in large numbers. And yet, some eighty years later, a vigorous Greek state was to spring up in this area; heavy Greek immigration in the intervening period is so unlikely that it has been suggested that there may have been a well-established Greek population on these edges of the known world before Alexander's arrival. The only support for the hypothesis is a phrase in Herodotus (vi.9), which indicates that Bactria was a place of deportation in the Achaemenid period. There is a problem here, insoluble in the present state of the sources.[12] But the fact remains that there were large numbers of Greeks in Bactria, that they revolted in 325 and then again in 323, that they survived despite their defeat and the accompanying massacres, and that once calm was restored the satrap appointed to Bactria was a Greek (the Cypriote Stasanor) and not a Macedonian.[13]

At the other end of the empire there occurred an event more serious, more moving and, not least, one better known, the rising of the old states of European Greece.[14] While it is certain that it was the news of Alexander's death which provoked the explosion, it is nonetheless also true that a complex discontent was brewing in Greece. Significantly, that not very intelligent compiler Diodorus Siculus assigns two different causes to the conflict in two different passages of his work.[15] In one place he emphasizes the agitation of the mercenaries in the huge man-market of Cape Taenarum, many of whom were on their way back from Asia and had chosen as leader the general Leosthenes, an Athenian condottiere of whom it is not certain whether he had served Alexander or Darius, but whose hostility to the Macedonians was by this time open. In his other reference Diodorus places the stress on the discontent provoked in Aetolia and Athens by the decree of Alexander ordering the Greeks to recall their exiles, a measure which in particular forced the Athenians to abandon their cleruchy on Samos.[16] Alexander's death brought all these discontents together. The heart of the anti-Macedonian resistance was once more Athens, in Athens the democratic party (the propertied classes would have preferred peace) and within that party Hyperides, the former comrade-in-arms of Demosthenes

[11] Bengtson 1964, I.177ff.: (A 6).
[12] Narain 1957, 1ff.: (E 196); Cozzoli 1958: (C 14).
[13] Diod. xviii.7 presents the rising of 323 as a continuation of that of 325 (xvii.99).
[14] Ferguson 1911, 11–28: (D 89); Lepore 1955: (C 45); Treves 1958: (C 70); Braccesi 1970: (B 6).
[15] Diod. xvii.3.1–3; xviii.8.
[16] Habicht 1957, 154ff.: (B 81); 1970, 253: (I 29); 1972 (nos. 4–5): (B 84); 1975: (C 34); Barron 1962: (C 4).

who, however, had just secured Demosthenes' conviction in the obscure affair of Harpalus.[17] Leosthenes placed at his country's disposal the essentially unpolitical force of his mercenaries, for whom the remains of Harpalus' treasure provided wages. A treaty of alliance was concluded with the rising power of Greece, Aetolia; the Thessalians acceded to it a little later, with some others.

Well led by Leosthenes, the last military celebrity of Athens, and organized in a confederation of autonomous cities and nations which replaced the Macedonians' Corinthian League, the allies won easy successes over Antipater, who lacked troops and was forced to take refuge in Lamia (hence the name of the war). Large numbers of waverers now hastened to support what looked like success. In the Peloponnese, where he had taken refuge after his conviction, Demosthenes, at first hostile to a rising which he judged premature, was soon all action, securing an alliance here and neutrality there. Forgetting the recent past, Athens opened her gates to him and gave him a triumphal welcome – to what was to be his final failure. At the very point when a united Greece seemed to be pulling itself together to break the yoke of masters weakened by the fragmentation of their forces, the tide was already turning. It is true that free Greece had a run of bad luck. Perhaps even before Demosthenes reached Athens, Leosthenes, the only man capable of organizing the common effort, had fallen in battle and his successor had been obliged to raise the siege of Lamia to go and head off the army approaching under the command of Leonnatus, the satrap of Hellespontine Phrygia, who had been summoned by Antipater along with Craterus. Antipater's appeals, while certainly justified by the military situation, were also part of a political strategy. Antipater had offered the hand of one of his daughters to Leonnatus at the same time as he asked for his help; no doubt he wanted to obtain the allegiance of this ambitious young man (with his ties to the royal family), on whom Perdiccas had recently relied. Leonnatus, however, had moved only after receiving another matrimonial proposition, more interesting from his point of view but contrary to Antipater's interests: it had come from the old queen Olympias, who had suggested that he should marry Alexander's own sister Cleopatra (whom Olympias was a little later to offer to Perdiccas himself). It was thus probably with designs on the crown that Leonnatus landed in Thessaly.[18] As for Craterus, he must

[17] Harpalus, who had managed Alexander's finances, had in company with some others turned traitor to the king in 324 and, with the help of his treasure, had tried to carve himself a principality in Cilicia before arriving in Athens with the object of provoking her, and in her wake Greece, to revolt. Divided but cautious, the Athenians had refused to listen to him and Harpalus had gone off again, though not before he had distributed much money among the leading circles in the city – a circumstance which had induced the settlement of several political accounts, and notably the condemnation of Demosthenes for misappropriation of public funds.

[18] Briant 1973, 162ff.: (C 8).

have received Antipater's appeal about the time that the news reached him of his appointment as royal *prostates*. No doubt uncertain of the course to adopt, he waited in Cilicia until the day he learned that Perdiccas was marching on Asia Minor (spring 322). Preferring to place his veterans, who in any case had to return to Macedon, at the service of Antipater rather than to have to face Perdiccas, he now set out for Europe; this choice was to have serious political consequences. In the meantime the situation had developed in Greece. In his encounter with the Greek army, Leonnatus had been defeated and killed, but his army had nevertheless linked up with Antipater. Even now all was not lost for the Greeks. Athens had made a final, considerable, naval effort – but her fleet was defeated off Amorgos.[19] In the forces committed on the two sides, the battle of Amorgos seems comparable only with that of Salamis. Salamis had laid the foundation of Athenian naval power, which now sank for ever in the waters of Amorgos. The classical history of Athens is, as it were, enclosed by these two battles fought for Greek freedom, battles with such different outcomes.

Antipater, meanwhile, had been joined by Craterus: together they marched on Greece and forced the reluctant allies to accept battle at Crannon in Thessaly; the fighting was unspectacular, but emphasized the already advanced decay of the league. Antipater and Craterus, following the practice of Philip after the battle of Chaeronea, skilfully refused to treat with their enemies as a group and so provoked a succession of defections among the last allies of Athens and of the Aetolians. Isolated, Athens had to negotiate in the autumn of 322. Some clauses of the treaty she was forced to sign were no more than the normal price of defeat: payment of a heavy indemnity, the loss of Oropus on the Boeotian frontier, the installation of a Macedonian garrison in the Piraeus. The obligation imposed on the defeated to surrender the leaders of the revolt could also count as a legitimate demand of the victors; Hyperides and Demosthenes, already in flight, were pursued. Hyperides was captured on Aegina and executed. Demosthenes committed suicide at Calauria as he was captured. But the most serious blow for Athens was the measures, disdained sixteen years previously by Philip, against the democracy, which was abolished, perhaps less by a dictatorial decision of Antipater than by the support he gave to the régime's opponents.[20] Once again, but this time more permanently, Athens experienced the oligarchy of defeat, led by the virtuous octogenarian general Phocion and by the corrupt politician who had made his career (out of conviction too, it seems) in the service of the enemy, Demades, an oligarchy protected by the spears of the occupier. Even though a number of

[19] Hauben 1975, 43ff.: (C 37).   [20] Gehrke 1976, 87ff.: (C 29).

upheavals were still to come, for Athens it was the end of her history as an independent city – and it is this that justifies us in having dwelt at some length on these events in Greece in the years 323–322, which are in fact fairly unimportant when viewed in relation to the destiny of the work of Philip and Alexander.[21]

Nevertheless it is important to note that the outcome of the Lamian War meant for European Greece as a whole a worsening of its juridical situation. For the Corinthian League of Philip and Alexander the rebels had substituted their own confederation, and the collapse of this created a void which Antipater and Craterus took good care not to fill: the cities were henceforth subject to Macedon directly and in isolation.[22] If it is true that the Corinthian League had been no more than a fiction designed to mask the Macedonian protectorate in Greece under the cloak of a collective alliance, the new situation had at least the merit of clarity: the Greek cities, without being theoretically deprived of their autonomy, without being legally annexed to Macedon, were tightly bound to her. From this point of view the case of Athens is exemplary.

Greece, then, was pacified by the end of 322 – except for Aetolia. Antipater and Craterus organized a large expedition against this mountainous and difficult region, but it was cut short as the two Macedonians were abruptly summoned east by the news from Asia. The sudden switch was of immense importance, because this unexpected chance offered to the Aetolians is very probably the reason for the important role the Aetolian confederation was soon playing in world affairs. Contrasts have been drawn between the collapse of the 'old' Aegean city, whose revival of patriotism had not restored its ancient military virtues, and the rise of the 'young' mountain people of the west which, in a short time, was to reveal remarkable reserves of political and military energy – but the fact remains nevertheless that the difference in their fates at the end of the struggle they jointly led in 323–322 was in large measure due to the intervention of an unexpected outside factor, the sudden inability of the Macedonians to devote themselves to crushing the Aetolians.

Let us therefore return, with Antipater and Craterus, to Asia, where dangers and complications were already beginning to multiply. While, as we have seen, no 'nationalist' movement threatened Alexander's work in Asia on the morrow of his death, the rivalries of his former colleagues did.

There can be no doubt about Perdiccas' personal ambitions, but it is difficult to define them exactly, particularly as they probably grew

[21] Hyper. *Epitaph.*; Diod. XVIII.9–18, 24–25.5; Arr. *Diad.* fr. 1.9 and 1.12–15; fr. 17; frs. 22–3; Just. XIII.5; Plut. *Phoc.* 23–8; *Dem.* 27ff.; ps.-Plut. *X orat.*; *Dem.* 38ff.; *Hyper.* 11–12.; Paus. 1.25.5.
[22] Bengtson 1964, 1.52–6; 129–32: (A 6).

rapidly in the few remaining months of his life. One fact, however, is clear from his short career: Perdiccas showed a strong desire to complete the work of conquest and to maintain (certainly for his profit) the integrity of the empire against the separatist tendencies of the powerful Macedonian satraps.

Completing the work of conquest was a task which had to be performed, somewhat paradoxically, in the region first reached by Alexander, Anatolia. We have seen that, in the allocation of satrapies, the task of occupying Cappadocia and Paphlagonia had been entrusted, perhaps not without hesitation, to Eumenes of Cardia, who was to be assisted by the satraps of the neighbouring regions, Antigonus Monophthalmus (Greater Phrygia) and Leonnatus (Hellespontine Phrygia). Whether from personal ambition or from reluctance to submit to the authority of a Greek, Antigonus for his part had refrained from action and Leonnatus, who had gone to help Antipater, had been killed. With Eumenes isolated, Perdiccas had gone himself to support him in 322 and had installed him in his Cappadocian province. The success of the enterprise, which served further to round off the empire only a year after Alexander's death, increased the prestige and power of Perdiccas, and his ambition, and still more the impatience felt by some Macedonian satraps at having to accept his authority. This authority had, moreover, recently become more onerous: once Craterus had joined Antipater in Macedonia Perdiccas had not hesitated to claim for himself the title conferred a few weeks earlier on Craterus of *prostates* of the kings.[23] Here was the seed of the first conflict. Perdiccas' main opponent was Antigonus, whom the chiliarch criticized sharply for his hostility to Eumenes. As the official, but hardly legitimate, ruler of Macedonian Asia, Perdiccas thus found himself more or less isolated in the face of suspicious and hostile subordinates. Only Eumenes was genuinely attached to him.

Matrimonial questions also arose to complicate Perdiccas' situation still further. Antipater had three daughters and had opened negotiations about marriage with Perdiccas, Craterus and Ptolemy: in the case of the first two, to make them his sons-in-law was clearly, to Antipater's mind, a way of cementing the 'collegiate leadership' which the events of 323 had placed in control of the empire. Perdiccas had therefore become engaged to Nicaea, Craterus agreed to marry Phila and Ptolemy accepted the hand of Eurydice. Antipater, however, had a redoubtable enemy in the person of the aged Olympias,[24] the mother of Alexander, and Olympias, from her native Epirus, where she lived in exile, devised a plan to play Perdiccas against Antipater: she offered the chiliarch the

---

[23] Bengtson 1964, 1.95ff.: (A 6), but cf. Goukowsky 1978, 197: (A 19).
[24] Hammond 1967, 558ff.: (D 26).

hand of her daughter Cleopatra, the sister of Alexander the Great and widow of Alexander the Molossian. Perdiccas was thus trapped between the promise he had given to Antipater, whose daughter was even then about to arrive at his headquarters, and the tempting visions conjured up by a marriage which would make him the posthumous son-in-law of Philip II, the posthumous brother-in-law of Alexander the Great and the uncle of the young Alexander IV. Had not Philip II come to power as the uncle of the legitimate heir? Perdiccas' attitude seems to have been equivocal. He did not break off the engagement with Nicaea, but neither did he refuse the hand of Cleopatra who, in turn, set out for Asia, which she reached at the same time as Nicaea. Perdiccas, who thought he could still reach agreement with Antipater, married Nicaea. But when, having summoned Antigonus to appear and explain himself, he saw him join Antipater in Europe, Perdiccas realized that all hopes of an accommodation were gone. He repudiated Nicaea and married Cleopatra. This personal affront came as an addition to the reasons Antipater must already have had to mistrust Perdiccas, who could from this point be openly accused of aspiring to the throne – as was probably true.[25]

This is the first time, but not the last, that we find the female factor intervening in Hellenistic affairs. To stress, as some scholars have, that this is something utterly contrary to Greek traditions, according to which women played no part in political life (in the classical period at least), is of little interest: the political and diplomatic traditions of the classical city are no longer relevant here. The new world is one of personal and – already – dynastic politics.

A coalition, the first in a period which was to see so many, now united against Perdiccas all those disturbed by his ambitions:[26] Antipater and Craterus, aroused by Antigonus; Lysimachus who, though immobilized by the long drawn-out war he was forced to wage against the barbarians in his Thracian province, controlled land communications between Macedonia and Asia; and, last, Ptolemy. In other words, Perdiccas, like all those who were to succeed him in the possession of these Asiatic territories, was threatened with a war on two fronts. No doubt judging his moral position rather weak in relation to Antipater and Craterus, more authentic defenders of dynastic legitimacy who also could command the military resources of the motherland, Perdiccas decided to make his first target Ptolemy, an apparently less formidable, though not negligible, opponent and one with whom he had a personal quarrel for his action in diverting Alexander's remains to Egypt when Perdiccas had intended, perhaps against the last wishes of the deceased (the tradition is

[25] Diod. xviii.16.1–3; 22–3; 25.3ff.; Arr. *Diad.* frs. 1.11; 21; 26; Just. xiii.6.1–7; Plut. *Eum.* 3–4; App. *Mith.* 8.
[26] Diod. xviii.25.4; Just. xiii.6.9.

uncertain), to deposit them solemnly in the dynastic vault at Aegae in Macedonia[27] – probably with the intention of seizing power in Europe on the same occasion.

Ptolemy had not as yet played any notable part in these emerging conflicts. Prudent and skilful, he had solidly established his power in Egypt. He had also succeeded in making himself master of Cyrenaica by intervening in the political and social conflicts which divided the Greek cities of the country (322–321). With great skill he had avoided annexing the country to his Egyptian satrapy, but had left the Cyreneans a theoretical independence, granting them a constitution in which he made a place for himself as *strategos* for life, so creating what was in effect a personal union between Egypt and Cyrenaica.[28] Ptolemy had also very early established diplomatic relations with several petty Cypriot kings.[29] The subsequent period was soon to show that, from the beginning of his residence in Egypt, Ptolemy had been laying the foundations of his future policy, one of determined independence. By choosing him as a son-in-law alongside Perdiccas and Craterus, Antipater had no doubt shown that it was from the direction of Egypt that he expected the first attempt at secession. In addition, Ptolemy also enjoyed considerable financial resources, in the shape of the treasure of his predecessor Cleomenes of Naucratis, whose assassination he engineered at the precise moment of his break with Perdiccas. He suspected the Greek of being in secret communication with the chiliarch, and it is likely that, by making himself Perdiccas' agent in Egypt, Cleomenes in fact hoped to be restored one day to his previous position as satrap.

At the beginning of 321, therefore, having failed to get the army to condemn Ptolemy, Perdiccas decided to march first against his southern enemy,[30] leaving the government and defence of Asia Minor to Eumenes. But the expedition ran into both natural and artificial obstacles which denied it access to the valley of the Nile and forced it to mark time in the neighbourhood of Memphis. The result was a conspiracy at Perdiccas' headquarters, and he was assassinated.[31] This murder ended the campaign. On the following day the conspirators invited Ptolemy, who had immediately joined them, to assume the functions of Perdiccas and the guardianship of the kings. Ptolemy

---

[27] The tradition is confused: Arr. *Diad.* frs. 1. 25; 24.1; Paus. 1.6.3; Diod. XVIII.26–8. Cf. Seibert 1969, 110ff.: (F 145); Errington 1976, 141ff.: (A 14).

[28] Diod. XVIII.19–21; Arr. *Diad.* fr. 1.16–19; Just. XIII.6.20; *Marm. Par.* B 11. Epigraphical text of the 'Cyrene charter': *SEG* IX.1 (1938) no. 1; Glotz *et al.* 1945, 281 and n. 88: (A 18); Machu 1951: (C 47); Bengtson 1967, III.158ff.: (A 6); Pagliaro 1956, 101fio (C 55); Fraser 1958, 120ff.: (B 75); Volkmann 1959, 1609ff.: (C 74); Seibert 1969, 91ff.: (F 145); Laronde 1972: (C 43).

[29] Arr. *Diad.* fr. 24. §6 ('the Reitzenstein fragment'); Moser 1914, 12ff.: (F 139); Hill 1940, 156ff.: (D 144); Seibert 1969, 113–14: (F 145).

[30] Diod. XVIII.25.6; 29.1–3; Just. XIII.6.10–17.

[31] Diod. XVIII.33–6; Arr. *Diad.* fr. 1. 28–9; Just. XIII.6.18–19; 8.1–2 and 10; Plut. *Eum.* 5–7.

refused. Wisdom and prudence, certainly, made him wish to keep to the strictly Egyptian policy which he had begun to practise with success, and also a desire to lull suspicions by adopting an attitude of genuine modesty. But perhaps this refusal was prompted by another consideration as well, namely that Ptolemy, determined as he was to assert his independence – though without dramatic gestures – was not anxious to make himself the instrument for maintaining the unity of the empire, which he probably judged impossible and above all did not want.[32]

While Perdiccas thus disappeared from the scene, his adversaries had lately failed in their attempt to subdue Eumenes in Asia Minor.[33] Craterus had even perished there in a major battle the site of which is unknown. These circumstances, which brought about the passing in the space of a few days of the only two surviving colleagues of Alexander with sufficient stature and authority to pull together the whole of his inheritance, allowed Eumenes to take possession of a large part of Anatolia.[34]

A little later, though still in 321, or according to some in 320, the opponents of Perdiccas and Eumenes met at Triparadisus in northern Syria[35] to examine the new situation. The simultaneous disappearance of Perdiccas and Craterus, that is, of two of the members of that fragile triumvirate which had taken over or, more accurately, had been supposed to take over the direction of affairs, but had fallen apart in barely a year, clearly made necessary a reorganization of what was already no more than the shadow of an empire.[36] Since Ptolemy had declined the offer of the regency of the whole, the normal course was for this to be offered to Antipater, who certainly had more than one claim to it and who took on the functions of *epimeletes* of the kings. Nevertheless this concentration of supreme power did little to improve the situation. At the point events had reached, it is doubtful whether anyone could have stopped the rapid process of the disintegration of the empire, but no choice was better suited than that of Antipater to hasten the process still further. This is not to question either the personal capacities of Philip's old collaborator or his devotion to the dynasty; Antipater had given ample proof of both. No, what made this choice ominous for the future was the fact that, while the seat of unrest and intrigue was in the conquered countries of the East, the theoretical centre of power was being once more transferred to Europe, where Antipater intended to take the kings – or the king, if it is true that Philip Arrhidaeus was sole

[32] On Ptolemy's coinage and the chronological difficulties of this period, see Will 1979, I.39–40: (A 67).

[33] Diod. XVIII.29.4–32; Just. XIII.8.3–9; Plut. *Eum.* 5–7; *PSI* XII.1284 (Arrian?).

[34] Errington 1970: (C 22).

[35] Schlumberger 1969: (C 60).

[36] Diod. XVIII.37–9; Arr. *Diad.* fr. 1.30–8; 42–4; App. *Syr.* 53; Just. XIV.1.1.

king after Triparadisus.[37] Having always lived and served in Europe and having followed Eastern affairs merely from a distance and without sympathy, Antipater, who, moreover, was a very old man, would inevitably tend to let events take their course at a moment when there was no longer any sign of unitary feeling on the spot in Asia to resist the pressures of separatism. In Alexander's lifetime Macedon, deprived of the royal presence, had ended by looking in fact like an appendage of the new empire. The return of the kings (under-age kings, too) to Macedon certainly did not reverse this situation, but further accentuated the break between the metropolis and the conquered lands. The unity of the empire was, no doubt, being maintained in theory, but the possible and predictable disappearance of the last of the Argeads would suffice to make this theoretical unity in turn vanish. In essence the appointment of Antipater as regent over the whole empire amounted more or less to returning Macedon to its situation before Alexander, that of a strictly European state. From this moment the profound weakness of Alexander's unfinished work becomes apparent, a weakness which consisted essentially in the fact that old Macedon and the newly conquered countries were bound by nothing more than a personal union. Alexander's empire was not a state,[38] but an artificial aggregate of at least three states, Macedon, Egypt and 'Asia'. Once Alexander had died without leaving an effective successor, the disintegration of this fragile structure was inevitable. We have seen that, even before Triparadisus, Ptolemy had more or less brought about the secession of Egypt. Macedon was currently tending to return to its traditional role as a Balkan kingdom. But, much more important, the arrangements made at Triparadisus contained in germ the dismemberment of the 'kingdom of Asia' itself.

The redistribution of Asian satrapies which was now carried out had the effect (apart from other measures of minor importance) of giving key roles to the two most ambitious and talented figures (apart from Eumenes) surviving from Alexander's staff, Seleucus and Antigonus. Seleucus, one of Perdiccas' murderers, who as yet had had no experience of territorial administration, was given Babylonia – a satrapy which might suggest certain ambitions to a governor with the makings of a politician:[39] had not Alexander, as in Egypt and as the first Achaemenids had done before him in Babylon, assumed the old native kingship? Had he not also intended to give Babylon a place of prominence (like that of Alexandria) within his empire, if not to make it his capital? As for Antigonus Monophthalmus, whose old satrapies were restored, he was

[37] Goukowsky 1978, 198: (A 19).   [38] Errington 1976, 158–9: (A 14).
[39] Funck 1974, 505ff.: (C 27).

charged with waging the war against Eumenes of Cardia, whom the assembly had condemned to death immediately the fate of Craterus was known. For this purpose Antipater, in the name of the kings, had named Antigonus '*strategos* of the royal forces', a title which put at his disposal the military resources of the empire. In addition, Antipater had thought of entrusting Monophthalmus with the guardianship of the kings, but, rapidly made suspicious by the all too evident ambitions of the gentleman, the regent had decided, on the eve of his return to Europe, to take the kings with him, as was mentioned earlier. At this point he had conferred on Antigonus the office of '*strategos* of Asia', which gave the holder of this title more or less unlimited authority over Asian affairs and placed him, in relation to Antipater, in practically the same position as he, as *strategos* of Europe, had occupied in relation to Alexander[40] – but Antigonus did not have the loyalty or the disinterestedness of Antipater.

Antigonus charged in the name of the kings with waging the campaign against Eumenes, the last close partner in Alexander's thought – here was a fine reversal of the situation. The break between Perdiccas and Monophthalmus had been brought about by the obstacles which the latter had placed in the way of the completion of Eumenes' work in Cappadocia, and it was then Antigonus who had put himself at odds with the wishes of the central authority, represented by Perdiccas. Now, with Perdiccas defeated and dead, legitimacy and loyalty changed sides and it was Eumenes, the victim of his loyalty to Perdiccas, who appeared as a separatist and was placed under the imperial ban. In reality, despite the sanction given to this condemnation by Antipater, there was practically no more Argead legitimacy in Asia (further confirmation of the Macedonian withdrawal to Europe): Asia was now no more than the lists where rival ambitions were to clash.

If until the death of Perdiccas there could still be some hesitation about the fate of Alexander's empire, this uncertainty was now removed. Triparadisus, two years after the Conqueror's death, marks the passing of his work and his thought.

II. THE PERIOD OF ANTIGONUS MONOPHTHALMUS (321–301)

The death of Perdiccas enabled a new, strong personality to make an appearance, Antigonus Monophthalmus, who for a period, from pure ambition and without any real concern for the Argead dynasty, was in turn to embody the unitary ideal. One would like to know more about the physiognomy of this great adventurer who almost succeeded where Perdiccas had failed from the start. Despite the lack of detail in the texts

[40] Bengtson 1964, 1.96ff.: (A 6).

relating to him, he is nonetheless one of the Diadochi best understood through his actions, which recall on the one hand the tireless energy of Alexander and on the other the political realism and cunning of Philip II. We shall therefore let his actions speak.

(a) *From Triparadisus to the death of Eumenes (321–316)*

We saw earlier that Antipater and the other Diadochi had given Antigonus the task of continuing the struggle against Eumenes of Cardia,[41] whose victory over Craterus had given him possession of a large part of Asia Minor. Antigonus not only took up the task with vigour; in addition, wishing to round off the territories which constituted his province proper, he did not hesitate to look for any pretext to intervene against his colleagues in the other satrapies of Asia Minor. The result was that very quickly, and in defiance of the arrangements made at Triparadisus, he was in more or less sole control of vast areas of Anatolia.[42] Eumenes had been driven back towards the east and forced to take refuge with a handful of men in the little Cappadocian fortress of Nora, where he was duly besieged.[43] But, at the moment when Antigonus might suppose that he had his opponent by the throat, one of the reversals of fortune in which this period is so abundant forced him to come to terms. The cause of this reversal was the death of Antipater.

The effect of the old regent's death was to introduce a period of acute complications for Alexander's inheritance and to open up new vistas for the ambitions of Monophthalmus. The first question thus raised was who would inherit the position of *epimeletes* of the two kings, Philip III and Alexander IV. Antipater's son Cassander felt that the position was his by right.[44] Antipater, however, had taken a different view and, judging that his son was too young to control the turbulent Macedonian satraps (particularly Antigonus, with whom Cassander had quarrelled as early as 321), he had appointed as his successor one of his companions of the older generation, the man he had left in charge of European affairs on his departure for Asia two years before, Polyperchon.[45] This old officer of Philip was more notable for his military talents than for his political and diplomatic ability. Feeling himself slighted, Cassander quickly broke with Polyperchon and crossed into Asia, where he formed a

[41] On Eumenes: Vezin 1907: (C 71); Westlake 1954: (C 76); Briant 1972–3: (C 7).
[42] Bengtson 1974, 1.106ff.: (A 6).
[43] Diod. XVIII.40–2; 44–7; Arr. *Diad.* fr. 1. 39–41; Just. XIV.1–2.4; Plut. *Eum.* 8.3–11.
[44] Fortina 1965: (C 26); Goukowsky 1978, 94ff.: (A 19).
[45] Diod. XVIII.48.4–49.3; 54; Plut. *Phoc.* 31.1; T. Lenschau, 'Polyperchon (1)', *PW* XXI.2 (1952) cols. 1797–1806.

coalition against the new regent which included Lysimachus and Antigonus, who were shortly afterwards joined by Ptolemy.

It is at this point that one realizes to what extent all accepted ideas are upset from this moment on. Antipater himself, beyond doubt the most loyal representative of the tradition, had acted ambivalently. If the fact of not having passed on his position to his son could be seen as a wise gesture (though in fact Cassander was to show himself infinitely superior to Polyperchon), above all in the sense that it avoided giving any basis for accusations of dynastic ambitions, on the other hand it is certain that, legally, Antipater had no right to appoint his successor and that by making Polyperchon *epimeletes* of the kings and so regent of the empire, he had acted autocratically.[46] The illegality of the procedure was not what shocked the new masters of the empire, however, but the fact that the succession to Antipater aroused secret ambitions in some of them. Lysimachus, Macedon's immediate neighbour, would certainly not have disdained the idea of one day restoring for his advantage the union of Macedon and Thrace, nor Antigonus above all that of ruling on both shores of the Aegean. The Macedonian mirage seems to have exercised such a powerful influence on Monophthalmus that he imprudently released Eumenes, in spite of having him at his mercy, and promised to give him back his satrapy and even more if he supported the venture. Eumenes, whose situation was desperate, hastened to accept; both, of course, were insincere.

As for Ptolemy, his participation in the struggle against Polyperchon had different motives. The death of Antipater gave him the opportunity to throw off the apparent modesty he had displayed so ostentatiously immediately after the death of Perdiccas. As soon as the news of the regent's death reached him, trampling underfoot the promises of Triparadisus as Antigonus had done before him, he invaded the satrapy of Syria-Phoenicia.[47] This action is most important for an understanding of the ideas and policies of Ptolemy and shows (though some modern writers have denied this) the extent to which he had rapidly absorbed the political and strategic traditions of the land of Egypt in which he had established himself as ruler: while no more than a satrap, a high official theoretically subordinate to a central power, admittedly a distant and shadowy one, he fell upon this traditional land of conquest of the great independent Pharaohs. No doubt by acting in this way he was applying what he had learnt from the threat Perdiccas had used against him two years earlier: throughout time Palestine and Coele-Syria had formed Egypt's defensive glacis on her Asian side, and provided her not only with more convenient and closer naval bases than those of Cyprus

[46] Bengtson 1964, I. 60ff.: (A 6).
[47] Diod. XVIII.43; App. *Syr.* 52 (confused and inaccurate).

(which Ptolemy did not yet control) but also with a continental base for eventual operations against northern Syria, Mesopotamia or Asia Minor. But the point to be emphasized above all in this study of the disintegration of Alexander's empire is that by annexing these regions Ptolemy was showing clearly, on the morrow of Perdiccas' failed offensive, that he was determined never again to be dislodged from the valley of the Nile. Nothing shows more clearly that Ptolemy was easily the first of the Diadochi to reveal in his actions a fully worked out policy – one probably worked out even before this year of 319: the fact that this first conquest of Syria-Palestine was, as we shall see, no more than ephemeral makes no difference.[48] So – to return to the coalition against Polyperchon – the Syrian venture was a challenge to the order which Polyperchon symbolized and as it could be foreseen that the new regent would find it difficult to keep his position it was important for Ptolemy to be on the side of his opponents.

Against so many enemies Polyperchon had few resources. But, to counter Cassander, who was already establishing a hold in Greece, he had the idea of playing the Greek card by offering the Greeks the prospect of an improvement in the unenviable lot which had been theirs since the Lamian War. In the name of Philip Arrhidaeus Polyperchon addressed a solemn proclamation to the Greek cities in which, in essence, he drew a veil over the unfortunate events of the Lamian War and announced that royal benevolence was granting a return to the situation existing in the reigns of Philip II and Alexander: this meant mainly the restoration of the constitutions which preceded the oligarchies imposed by Antipater and maintained by his son, and the return of the exiles. Special favours were granted to certain cities, such as a promise to Athens of the return of Samos, though the return of Oropus was refused. It has often been held that this charter granted by Polyperchon was equivalent to a restoration of the Corinthian League;[49] in fact, it has to be recognized that, in the text of the declaration which has come down to us,[50] with the possible exception of a vague reference to the achievements of Philip and Alexander in Greece and a passing mention of the 'peace' on which the League of 338 was based, there is no reference to the legal status or the institutions of the League, which we know, moreover, to have been little more than a shadow at the end of Alexander's reign. Rather than a restoration of the legal position of 338, this was a restoration of the actual position of 323. From a different angle, Polyperchon's proclamation has often been compared with Antigonus' famous appeal to the liberty of the Greeks, which we shall

[48] Moser 1914, 23ff.: (F 139); Volkmann 1959, 1611ff.: (C 74); Seibert 1969, 133ff.: (F 145).
[49] Larsen 1925–6: (A 31).   [50] Diod. XVIII.56.

soon come to, but this comparison is inaccurate, although the aim pursued in turn by Polyperchon and by Antigonus (to win the support of the Greek cities and to detach them from Cassander) was the same. If Polyperchon had proclaimed the liberty of the cities, he would have recognized *de facto* the justice of their revolt in 323; in fact his proclamation was an amnesty, which reminded the Greeks of their fault only to pardon it. Polyperchon's action is thus completely original, without antecedent and without sequel.[51]

And also without much effect. If Polyperchon expected an explosion of enthusiasm and gratitude from the Greeks, he was mistaken. His policy had no more than mixed success. At Athens, in particular, a small expedition was necessary to restore the democracy despite the presence in Piraeus of a garrison of Cassander. Even then, the democracy survived no longer than the time necessary for a bloody settling of accounts (which cost Phocion his life), because the democrats were soon forced by Polyperchon's failures to come to terms with Cassander's troops and with the oligarchs who had taken refuge with them. One of the latter, Demetrius of Phalerum, succeeded in organizing the transition with skill and moderation. At the beginning of 317 Athens concluded a treaty with Cassander the text of which, preserved by Diodorus (XVIII.74.3), is characteristic of the new era: the Athenians are to keep their city, their territory, their revenues, their boats 'and everything else' – but in friendship and alliance with Cassander, who also reserves the right to occupy Munychia 'until the end of the war against the kings'. A property-based franchise, but quite broadly based, was substituted for the democracy: in other words, Cassander imposed on Athens the system of his choice, one which kept power in the hands of that propertied class which already had a long history of sympathy with Macedon. But better – or worse – was to come: 'as *epimeletes* of the city an Athenian citizen of Cassander's choice would be installed', and Diodorus concludes, with what must be involuntary irony, 'Demetrius of Phalerum was elected', the term used implying a formal election by the citizens, presumably by this new restricted citizen body. Athens was to live for a decade under this régime of controlled autonomy. Demetrius of Phalerum, a worthy representative of that Peripatetic intelligentsia which asked nothing better than to turn from the theory of politics to its practice, gave his country, in its mood of self-absorption in a sort of philosophical utopia, a period of excellent internal administration with a touch of 'moral order', in accordance with the more or less genuinely Solonian ideal which has inspired conservative circles since the beginning of the century. It was an ideal which, as we shall see, was

[51] Heuss 1938, 142ff.: (C 41).

never shared by the majority, but as long as Cassander was in charge the majority had no choice but to get used to it.[52]

Seeing Athens escape from his grasp seriously reduced Polyperchon's chances of solidly establishing his influence over Greece. Nor was it long before his power began to collapse even in Macedon. After the destruction of his fleet by that of Antigonus in the Straits and Cassander's rapid recovery in Greece,[53] Polyperchon fell back on the Peloponnese, where his 'liberal' policy had had a slightly better response than in central Greece.[54]

This was the beginning of the bloody drama in which the Argead dynasty, already reduced to a shadowy existence, was finally to disappear. Polyperchon had taken with him the little Alexander IV, but Eurydice, the extremely clear-headed wife of the retarded Philip III, had sided with Cassander and so the two kings were in opposite camps. The ambitious and scheming Eurydice had Cassander proclaimed regent (spring 317),[55] clearly with the intention of seizing the royal power herself, which could only be at the expense of the infant Alexander. Polyperchon, for his part, ever since the death of Antipater and in order to give some prestige to his power, had had the idea of recalling from Epirus the aged Olympias, whom Antipater had spared no effort to keep at a distance from Macedon. Olympias had hesitated long, but at the news of Eurydice's schemes she hastened towards Macedon at the head of an Epirote army and some troops of Polyperchon, and her grandson Alexander IV was brought to her. Olympias succeeded in taking possession of the persons of Eurydice and Philip III Arrhidaeus, whom she immediately had killed (autumn 317), thereby unwisely satisfying old resentments (Philip III was a bastard of Philip II); one of Cassander's brothers met the same fate, together with a hundred or so Macedonian nobles. Cassander himself returned in haste from the Peloponnese, where he had been campaigning against Polyperchon's supporters, and succeeded in having Olympias handed over to him. Her crime had ranged all Macedon against her, the assembly of the army condemned her to death and she was executed in her turn.[56] Thus at the beginning of 316 the infant Alexander IV was left sole king – but he was little more than a hostage in the hands of the new master of Macedon, Cassander, who lost no time in attempting to assert the legitimacy of his own power by organizing a solemn royal funeral for Philip III and Eurydice and

[52] Ferguson 1911, 30ff.: (D 89); Cloché 1923–4: (C 10); Lenschau 1941, 458ff.: (C 44); Bayer 1942: (C 5); Colombini 1965: (C 13); Mossé 1969, 155ff.: (A 43); Gehrke 1976, 105ff.: (C 29).

[53] Engel 1973: (C 21).

[54] Diod. XVIII.55–57.1; 64–75; Polyaenus, *Strat.* IV.6.8. On Demetrius of Phalerum: Diog. Laert. V.75–85; *Suda, s.v.*   [55] Just. XIV.5.1–3.

[56] Granier 1931, 87ff.: (D 23); Errington 1978, 118–19: (D 17).

marrying a half-sister of Alexander the Great, that is, attaching himself personally to the dynasty: this marriage opened up possibilities for him whose realization was highly likely (though not necessarily) to be at the expense of the little king, now his nephew.[57]

While these conflicts were taking place in Europe a more important contest was being fought in Asia. We have seen[58] that Eumenes had accepted Antigonus' self-seeking proposals merely to get himself out of a tight corner; in fact, far from allying himself with Monophthalmus against Polyperchon, he had immediately resumed his own activities, following the ideas of Perdiccas and, probably, of Alexander himself. This made it natural for Polyperchon now to get in touch with Eumenes and, since he still regarded himself as regent, to offer him in the name of the kings the position of *strategos* of Asia which Antipater had formerly conferred on Antigonus. There were thus, for a few months, two rival regents in Europe and two rival *strategoi* in Asia – though, admittedly, Polyperchon and Eumenes were recognized by almost no one but each other. But Eumenes had bad luck with his allies: the failure of Polyperchon and his confinement to the Peloponnese left Eumenes practically isolated, as the death of Perdiccas had isolated him. He nevertheless pursued a quite astonishing military adventure in which he revealed talents rare in men who have made their careers at a desk, an adventure which had already taken him, by 318, from Asia Minor to Phoenicia, where he had seized some of Ptolemy's recent conquests, and was now taking him into Iran. Detail is of little importance here in view of the ultimate failure of these campaigns: hunted by Antigonus, Eumenes was finally surrendered by his troops, tried, condemned and executed (316).[59] These events took place against a background of revolts and rivalries among Iranian satraps – a state of anarchy to which Antigonus, the new sole master of the 'upper satrapies', attempted to put a temporary stop.[60]

Eumenes had doubtless been the last faithful follower of Alexander's ideas, and the cult of Alexander (or at least of Alexander's royal insignia) had helped him to rekindle the failing enthusiasm of his troops. For Eumenes, this fidelity to Alexander's ideas probably did not mean unconditional loyalty to the Argead dynasty. In his attitude to the dynasty he had always manoeuvred, and if in the end he posed as the defender of Alexander's empire and the champion of dynastic legitimacy, he also had no other way of retaining any sort of position for himself: his personal ambitions were perhaps less pure than they seemed

---

[57] Diod. XVIII.49.4; 57.2; 58.2–4; 65.1; XIX.11; 35–6; 49–52.5; Just. XIV.5.8–6.
[58] See above, p. 41.
[59] Diod. XVIII.57.3–63; 73.2ff.; XIX.12–34; 37–44.2.
[60] Diod. XIX.44.4–5; 46–8; Bengtson 1964, I.180ff.: (A 6).

and than modern historians have sometimes thought. With the departure of Eumenes, it was the turn of Antigonus to take up the unitary cause – but on his own account this time and without any real consideration for the last survivor of the Argead line. This was enough for the constellation to shift once more: the Diadochi (with the exception of Polyperchon, as we shall see) were now united against the aged Monophthalmus.

(b) *The first phase of the struggle against Antigonus (316–311)*

Antigonus' victory over Eumenes had given him control of almost all the regions between Asia Minor and Iran inclusive, an outcome which the negotiators of Triparadisus had not foreseen. In these countries Antigonus appointed governors chosen from among his loyal supporters. Then, in a surprise attack on Babylonia,[61] he forced Seleucus to abandon his province (apparently spring 315). Seleucus fled for safety to Ptolemy; his stubborn desire to win back his satrapy made him one of the lynchpins of the coalition against the new conqueror.[62]

As Antigonus advanced deeper into northern Syria he was met by an embassy from Lysimachus, Ptolemy and Cassander carrying an ultimatum in the following terms:[63] Monophthalmus was immediately to return Babylonia to Seleucus, abandon the whole of Syria to Ptolemy, return Hellespontine Phrygia to Lysimachus (who had never possessed it and would thereby have become master of the Straits), and, lastly, cede Cappadocià and Lycia to Cassander (this last point has provoked many discussions,[64] but there is no reason to doubt that Cassander may have had Asian ambitions).[65] In addition he was invited to share Eumenes' treasure with the other Diadochi. The legal justification for these demands was that the war against Eumenes, with which Antigonus had been entrusted at Triparadisus, had been a joint venture and that, consequently, the spoils of the former archivist should be shared among all; further, Antigonus had no right to deprive of their territories satraps who had not supported Eumenes. In reality this ultimatum was a poor disguise for ambitions which clashed with those of the man to whom it was addressed and it is understandable that Antigonus should have rejected it and accepted war. Accordingly, he methodically occupied all the settlements of southern Syria, except Tyre, where the Ptolemaic garrison offered effective resistance; then, with tireless activity, he seized

---

[61] Diod. XIX.55.6; Bengtson 1964, I.111ff.: (A 6).
[62] Hauben 1975, 83ff.: (C 37).
[63] Diod. XIX.57.1; 85.3; Just. XV.1.2; App. *Syr.* 53.
[64] Was it Lycia or Cilicia – or Lydia? To Cassander or Asander? Cf. Tarn 1927, 484, n. 1: (C 68); Aucello 1957: (C 3); Fortina 1965, 54ff.: (C 26); Wehrli 1969, 44ff.: (C 75); Wörrle 1977, 48: (B 178); Will 1979, I.55–6: (A 67).   [65] Braunert 1967, 13ff.: (H 25).

all of Asia Minor he did not already control, from Bithynia to Caria.[66] At the same time he formed an alliance with his former adversary Polyperchon, whom he appointed *strategos* of the Peloponnese, a rapprochement which the breach between Antigonus and Cassander made natural.[67]

In 315,[68] at Tyre, where he had gone to take charge of operations, Antigonus, not content to extend his success in practical terms, also gave his claims a political and legal formulation. A manifesto[69] announced to the world that the assembly of his army had tried and condemned Cassander for various misdeeds, the most important of which were the murder of Olympias (who, as we know, had herself been condemned by Cassander's army for the murder of Philip III) and the detention of Alexander IV and his mother Roxane; further, that the same assembly had proclaimed Antigonus *epimeletes* of the king (a regency which he would thus be able to add to his command of Asia); and finally, that if Cassander refused to submit he would be treated as an enemy. This was the beginning of the battle to the death between Antigonus and Cassander: it was to last thirteen years.

The manifesto which announced Antigonus' new claims and the condemnation of Cassander contained a final article, which boldly proclaimed that the Greek cities were to be free, autonomous and ungarrisoned.[70] This exercise in 'psychological warfare', as it would be called today, was directed mainly against Cassander, who held central Greece, and was intended to detach from him and to draw into Monophthalmus' camp the cities which had fallen into the power of the master of Macedon: the move was clear, and quite fair.

Ptolemy, however, learning of this document, immediately published another in the same terms, 'wishing the Greeks to know that he had no less concern than Antigonus for their autonomy', says Diodorus. Coming from Ptolemy, who also controlled Greek cities, this action might well seem a sham; on the other hand, it also contained an ambiguity, since Ptolemy was an ally of Cassander and the latter, to all appearances, would be the first victim of its proclamations. This total disregard on Ptolemy's part for the interests of his ally can be explained only if we accept that he saw further than the present moment. In the growing conflict between Antigonus and Cassander, the victor, whoever he was, would be master of Macedonia and a candidate for the regency of Alexander's inheritance, and thus for authority over Egypt as

[66] Diod. XIX.58ff.   [67] Diod. XIX.60.1.

[68] Or only in 314: Errington 1977: (C 24).

[69] Diod. XIX.61.1–3; Just. XV.1.3; Manni 1951, 99ff.: (C 48).

[70] Heuss 1938, 146–52: (C 41); Cloché 1948, 108–12: (C 11); Simpson 1959, 389ff.: (C 65); Wehrli 1969, 105ff.: (C 75).

over the other satrapies. The victor, whoever he was, would therefore be
Ptolemy's enemy. And having realized (from Antigonus' actions) that
the freedom of the Greek cities would be the best obstacle to place in the
path of the master of Macedon, Ptolemy was already taking his place
among the 'disinterested' defenders of those liberties.

It goes without saying that in itself the freedom of the Greek cities
was of little interest to either Antigonus or Ptolemy. It was a propaganda
theme which makes its appearance in this period and recurs year in year
out until the intervention of the Romans, who use it in their turn.
Nevertheless it must be stressed here at the outset that the only reason
why this theme could play such a role and be so often repeated was that it
corresponded to an important political problem which was to remain a
live issue throughout the Hellenistic period. That problem was the
position which the Greek cities could and should occupy within the new
territorial and monarchical states which were taking shape in the period
we have now reached. In other words, it was the problem of the
adaptation of the most widespread ancient Greek political formula to a
new political form.

In the circumstances of 315 Ptolemy did nothing to translate his
completely theoretical proclamation into fact. This was not the case with
Antigonus, who made clever play with the freedom of the cities. When
there were signs of unrest in the Aegean islands, and Delos and Imbros
rejected the control of an Athens in thrall to Cassander, Antigonus
encouraged and gave his support to the establishment of a body which
was to have some importance, the *koinon* of the Nesiotes (the
Confederation of the Cycladic Islanders). These circumstances and this
date (315–14) are preferable to the date 308 and Ptolemaic patronage,
which have sometimes been proposed for the foundation of this
confederation.[71] At the same time Antigonus sent agents, money and
troops to Greece in an effort to raise the country against Cassander:[72] his
own nephew Polemaeus was among those in charge of the operation.[73]

Antigonus' establishment of his patronage over the islands and the
occupation of a few places in Greece were not, however, enough to give
Antigonus victory. Fundamentally Monophthalmus was in the same
position as Perdiccas in 321 and facing the same strategic problem, being
forced to fight on two fronts, whereas Cassander had simply replaced his
father on the north-western front. But the situation was made more
complicated than in the time of Perdiccas and Antipater by the presence

---

[71] Durrbach 1907: (C 19); Guggenmos 1929, 12ff.: (C 32); Laidlaw 1933, 95ff.: (D 145); Wehrli
1969, 113ff.: (C 75); Merker 1970, 141 n. 2: (C 50); Hauben 1975, 28ff., 36ff., 101ff.: (C 37).
  [72] Newell 1923: (B 246); Simpson 1955: (C 64); Geagan 1968: (B 80); Bakhuizen 1970, 112ff.:
(B 182); Hauben 1975, 93ff.: (C 37). The chronology of this period is difficult to establish with certainty
and views differ: Hauben 1973: (C 35) (criticizing Bakhuizen 1970, 160ff.: (B 182)); Errington 1977:
(C 24).   [73] Diod. XIX.61.3–4; 62.1–2; 62.9; 68.3–4.

of Polyperchon in the Peloponnese: the rapprochement of Antigonus and Polyperchon was, as we have seen, in the order of things.

No doubt with Perdiccas' unfortunate experience in mind, Antigonus chose to press the main northern offensive himself to give Lysimachus a fright in Thrace and go on to attack Cassander in Macedon itself, while his generals undermined his power in Greece.[74] The attack on Egypt would then be simple, and in the meantime Antigonus' young son Demetrius (the future Poliorcetes) was given the task of looking after Syria-Palestine. The precaution was clearly necessary for it was easy to see that among Antigonus' enemies Ptolemy had a particular aim, namely to recover control of the satrapy of Syria-Phoenicia which he had conquered for the first time in 319 but which Eumenes and then Antigonus had stolen from him.

While Antigonus was making his preparations and trying in vain, by diplomacy and by arms, to force the barrier which Lysimachus' possessions constituted to his plans for an offensive against Macedon, Ptolemy, as was his habit, acted without haste. He strengthened his influence in Cyprus (though Antigonus put up fierce opposition here), on the southern coasts of Asia Minor (Caria), and tried without much success to occupy ports in Ionia.[75] It now seems doubtful whether he formed an alliance with Rhodes as early as 315, as had been thought.[76] However, he hesitated to attack the formidable Monophthalmus directly; and a revolt in Cyrene[77] and another in Cyprus[78] also tied his hands until the end of 313. It was not until 312 that, at the insistence of Seleucus, who was impatient to recover Babylonia, he took the decision to attack Demetrius.[79] Demetrius was overwhelmed at Gaza,[80] and this defeat, which allowed Seleucus to strike into Mesopotamia, forced Antigonus to abandon his northern projects in order to head off Ptolemy – who lost no time in getting back to Egypt.

Seleucus, however, proved so enterprising in Mesopotamia,[81] and showed signs of doing the same in Iran, that Antigonus preferred to seek terms.

As a result peace was agreed in conditions which have been much discussed by modern writers and are still not totally clear.[82] The previous years had already seen attempts at negotiation:[83] rather than a homogeneous coalition, Antigonus faced two groups of opponents

---

[74] On European affairs, the details of which have been ignored here, cf. Diod. xix.63–64.4; 66–68.1; 74; 75.6–8; 77–8; 87–9.

[75] Diod. xix.68–9; 75; 79.6–80.2.   [76] Hauben 1977: (c 39).

[77] Will 1979, 1.60: (a 67).   [78] Diod. xix.79.1–4.

[79] Diod. xix.80–6; 93; Just. xv.1.6–9; Plut. *Dem.* 5–6.

[80] Seibert 1969, 164ff.: (f 145).

[81] Diod. xix.90–2; Plut. *Dem.* 7.2–3. On the problem of the date of the foundation of Seleuceia-on-the-Tigris (311, 306, 300?), bibliography in Will 1979, 1.60–1: (a 67).

[82] Simpson 1954: (c 63); Wehrli 1969, 52ff.: (c 75).   [83] Diod. xix.64.8; 75.6.

(Ptolemy and Seleucus on the one hand and Cassander and Lysimachus on the other), and it was in his interest to separate the two groups by making a separate peace with one or the other. As early as 314 a conference had taken place between Antigonus and Ptolemy, then, at the beginning of 312, another between Antigonus and Cassander. They got nowhere; Antigonus' demands (which can only be guessed at) were probably excessive. After Gaza Antigonus reopened negotiations with Cassander and Lysimachus and, no doubt more modest this time, succeeded in reaching agreement. Ptolemy, finding little pleasure in the prospect of a concentration of Antigonid forces in the south, made haste to join the peace, and a joint treaty was sworn in 311. The articles (if not the actual text) have been preserved:[84] Cassander remained *strategos* of Europe until Alexander IV attained his majority, which amounts to saying that he was to remain *epimeletes* of the young king, the very point on which Antigonus had challenged him in 315. Lysimachus remained master of Thrace and Ptolemy of Egypt; Antigonus received power over 'all Asia'. These clauses, far removed from the claims announced by Antigonus in 315, were essentially, taken literally, a ratification of the status quo. Taken literally, since in fact Antigonus was no longer master of 'all Asia', and this raises the question of the fate of Seleucus. Seleucus does not figure in the treaty (and nor does Polyperchon), which evidently means that the peace of 311 did not include him. Cassander and Lysimachus, the first to negotiate, probably ignored him. In the case of Ptolemy, who had been the host and protector of Seleucus for years, the matter is more surprising at first sight, but comprehensible on reflection: when Ptolemy acceded to the peace Seleucus was already conquering the 'upper satrapies' and no longer needed protection. Ptolemy thus did not betray him by coming to terms with Antigonus. Cassander and Lysimachus may have been showing a certain indifference to Seleucus by abandoning 'all Asia' to Monophthalmus; for Ptolemy this clause can have been no more than form, both because he was following Seleucus' progress with sympathy and because secretly he had not abandoned his ambitions in Syria. Whatever the truth, Antigonus and Seleucus remained at war, and that war was to last until 309/8.

Besides these territorial arrangements, two clauses in the treaty of 311 deserve particular attention. The treaty was still, officially, an arrangement for the management of Alexander's legacy, and not a division of that legacy. The legitimacy of the little Alexander IV was still maintained – but this was certainly no more than a fiction, and a fiction not destined to survive the peace of 311. The clause which assigned the 'generalship of Europe' to Cassander stipulated, as we have seen, that

---

[84] Diod. XIX.105.

this arrangement was to last until the king should come of age. It is likely that none of the parties seriously envisaged this event taking place – but it was a matter of winning time. Nevertheless this clause was the death sentence of Alexander the Great's son since Cassander, having no desire to see the appointed day arrive, lost no time in bringing matters to a head and by 310 had presented his colleagues with a *fait accompli* by arranging the assassination of Alexander IV and his mother, who had been entrusted to his care.[85] We may imagine that this elimination of the direct Argead line by the efforts of the son of the dynasty's most loyal servant was received with a secret satisfaction by the former lieutenants of the victim's father:[86] henceforth no legal obstacle stood in the path of their ambition; henceforth all were equal and no argument could be used to challenge the rights of the strongest. There remained, it is true, a sister and a bastard of Alexander the Great, but it would not be long before they were eliminated in their turn.

Finally, a last clause of the treaty of 311 reaffirmed the right of the Greek cities to autonomy. Under its generously Platonic appearance, this clause was perhaps the most insidious of this whole diplomatic instrument. All the parties had established their control over Greek cities – in Greece (Cassander), in Thrace (Lysimachus),[87] in Asia Minor and the islands (Antigonus), in Cyrenaica[88] and Cyprus (Ptolemy) – and it is clear that none of them intended to let his cities return to independence, which allowed each to find, whenever he might wish, a *casus belli* to use against the others. Antigonus, however, whom it is impossible not to see as the inspiration behind this clause (as his proclamation of 315 suggests), made a great show of translating it into the realm of fact. He sent a letter to the cities under his authority (preserved only in an inscription from Scepsis in the Troad)[89] in which he announced the welcome return of peace and explained the motives for his policy with self-righteous emphasis on his concern for the cities (but omitted his son's defeat at Gaza). Most important, as well as confirming the text of the treaty given by Diodorus, the letter adds a detail of which we would otherwise be ignorant: the cities were invited to join together to defend their freedom and autonomy and to bind themselves to this by an oath as 'those in power' had done. It looks (though it is not certain) as if this is evidence of the establishment of, or of an attempt to establish, a federation of autonomous Greek cities within the emerging 'dynastic' states and guaranteed by them. On the other hand it is odd that this addition to the clause about the freedom of the cities should be preserved

---

[85] On Cassander's motives see Bendinelli 1965: (B 3) and Goukowsky 1978, 109ff.: (A 19).
[86] Though Alexander IV was recognized in Egypt until 305/4 (Atzler 1972: (B 280)).
[87] Will 1979, 1.65: (A 67).   [88] Will 1960, 369ff.: (C 77).
[89] *OGIS* 5 = RC 1. Cf. Heuss 1938, 153ff.: (C 41); Simpson 1959; (C 65).

only in Antigonus' letter, and we may wonder whether this was not a measure taken purely for internal use in Asia Minor and the islands (already organized in a federation, as we have seen) by Antigonus alone in his anxiety to play his role of defender of Greek liberties, if not to the end,[90] at least as far as possible. Be that as it may, it is obvious that Monophthalmus would not have tolerated any attempt by the cities to use their solemnly proclaimed freedom against him, but his skill consisted precisely in showing himself sufficiently liberal for the cities to identify their interests with his. This document is important for an understanding of Antigonus: it shows that this rude warrior of almost uncontrollable ambition was also a subtle politician – one thinks of Philip II.

A final remark on the treaty of 311. It shows clearly that from this point, despite the fiction of Argead kingship, which continued to exist for a further year, there were in fact five states in the place of Alexander's empire. But there was probably still one man, Antigonus, who aspired to merge these five states once more into one. It required the removal of Antigonus to prevent the fragmentation of the empire from ever again being seriously challenged and to allow the real history of the Hellenistic states to begin: this was to take another ten years.

(c) *The second phase of the struggle against Antigonus (311–301)*

The period from the peace of 311 to the fall of Antigonus is complex in the extreme because the advances and retreats of the five fragments of Alexander's empire took place in theatres stretching from the Adriatic to the Indus. Let us try to introduce some order, geographical as well as chronological, into all this. The best course, to get a clear view, is to place ourselves in Antigonus' position, all the more since it is his activities which give everything else what coherence it has. The peace of 311, while at root a defeat for Antigonus, made his territories the key to Alexander's legacy, the centre from which new attempts at expansion came and against which attempts at resistance were directed. Even if some episodes independent of this central seat of the politics of the period prove to have a certain importance, they will here be kept in the background for clarity of exposition.

We have seen that Seleucus did not join in the peace of 311. Having regained control of Babylonia as early as 312 and apparently without too much difficulty, he established himself here in genuine independence (this was to be the starting date for the 'Seleucid era'),[91] even if he did

---

[90] On Antigonus' policy towards the cities see the documents and related bibliography in Will 1979, 1.64–5: (A 67).

[91] Sachs and Wiseman 1954, 205: (E 49); Aymard 1955, 105: (E 2). There is a summary of the problem in Will 1979, 1.67: (A 67).

not at this stage adopt the local royal title (contrary to what has often been thought).[92] From Babylonia he had set out on the conquest of the 'upper satrapies' (the term generally used for the Iranian satrapies) which Antigonus had held since his victory over Eumenes in 316. It seems, moreover, that the memory of Eumenes was not completely dead in these remote regions, and that Seleucus found ways of using it against Antigonus. For Antigonus, consequently, the most urgent task was to take advantage of the precarious calm ensured by peace in the West to try to rid himself of the energetic Seleucus. In this he failed completely. The details are far from being known exactly, but it is certain that after being defeated by Seleucus in an important battle of which neither the location nor the date (though it must have been 309/8) has been preserved, he had to abandon Iran. A treaty was probably concluded between the two opponents because from 308 we find Seleucus involved even further east in a contest with the Mauryan ruler of India, Chandragupta, which implies that by then he was no longer embroiled with Antigonus. And, conversely, from this same date of 308 we find Antigonus involved in Western affairs, which implies that he had ended his struggle with Seleucus.[93]

That the peace of 311 was only a truce hardly needs saying – at least as regards Antigonus and Ptolemy. Certainly, while Cassander and Lysimachus might feel satisfied at having their claims confirmed, in the former case on Macedon and its dependencies, in the latter on Thrace, it is quite clear that Antigonus' ambitions included the conquest of Macedon (which inevitably ranged the others against him) and that Ptolemy had not given up his interest in the satrapy of Syria-Phoenicia, even if there is doubt about whether he aspired to absolute supremacy.[94] For both control of the sea was a condition of success. Both also possessed solid advantages in the eastern Mediterranean. Ptolemy was established in Cyprus,[95] where, in 310, he appointed as *strategos* and governor his own brother Menelaus.[96] Moreover, it was probably at this point that Ptolemy made an alliance with a Greek state which now began to play a major part in Mediterranean affairs, one of the last truly independent and sovereign cities of the old Hellenic world, Rhodes. The date of this alliance is not known. It is not definitely attested until 306,[97] but then in terms which suggest that it had been in existence for some time, though it is impossible that it should go back to the proclamation of Greek liberties in 315.[98] Ptolemy thus held, directly or by alliance, the

---

[92] So Bikerman 1938, 12 n. 5: (E 6); 1944, 74ff.: (E 7); Funck 1974: (C 27).

[93] Diod. XIX.90–2; Plut. *Dem.* 18.2; App. *Syr.* 54 (274–5); 55 (278).

[94] So Seibert 1969, 176ff.: (F 145). *Contra*, O. Müller 1973, 62: (C 51).

[95] Cf. most recently Gesche 1974: (C 30); Bagnall 1976, 39ff.: (F 204). There is a summary of the problem in Will 1979, 1.72: (A 67).

[96] Diod. XX.21.   [97] Diod. XX.46.6.   [98] Hauben 1977: (C 39).

two main island bases bordering on Antigonus' territory. It was also since 315 that Antigonus had been protector of the Confederation of the Nesiotes and as a result was in possession of the 'bridge' which separated his territory from European Greece and Macedon. In addition, he controlled the Phoenician ports, and, despite his solemn guarantee of Greek freedom, the ports of Asia Minor were in practice his. This whole area of the islands and the littoral, divided in this way between Ptolemy and Antigonus, could not but be an area of conflicts. The clause of the treaty of 311 dealing with the freedom of the cities was there to provide pretexts: as early as 310 Ptolemy accused Antigonus (at the time detained in the East by his struggle with Seleucus) of encroaching on that freedom by installing garrisons in certain cities and himself took possession of a number of places,[99] notably the island of Cos, where he placed his headquarters, which proves that his interest at this time was directed towards the Aegean.[100] It is reasonable to suppose that this sudden shift in the situation in the Mediterranean was one factor which made Antigonus decide to draw the conclusion from his Iranian failures and make terms with Seleucus.

Nevertheless the outbreak of the struggle between Ptolemy and Antigonus was to be delayed, as the result of a change in the situation in European Greece. Hitherto Cassander had been seriously embarrassed in Greece by the presence of his old rival Polyperchon in the Peloponnese. In 309 or 308, however, when Polyperchon had managed to send an advance force as far as the borders of Macedon with the intention of there proclaiming king a bastard (real or supposed) of Alexander the Great by the name of Heracles, Cassander judged it more expedient to be reconciled with Polyperchon, to whom he abandoned the Peloponnese and gave the title *strategos*,[101] the young Heracles being sacrificed in the process.[102] Whatever chance the least weak of the Greek cities had had hitherto of playing off Cassander against Polyperchon and vice versa, they now lost; against the newly reconciled pair the Greeks needed outside support. Antigonus, the certified defender of Greek liberties, was indeed maintaining in Greece the troops which had formerly gone there to support Polyperchon, but his representative in Europe, his nephew Polemaeus,[103] had just betrayed him and offered his services to Cassander as a prelude to opening discussions with Ptolemy, who summoned him to Cos. Polemaeus must have given Ptolemy precious details of the situation in Europe. It is difficult to imagine a

---

[99] All the documents are of uncertain date. Miletus: *RC* 14; Seibert 1971, 159ff.: (F 146); H. Müller 1976, 74ff.: (B 112); Wörrle 1977, 55ff.: (B 178); Iasos: Pugliese Carratelli 1967–8, 437ff.: (B 122); J. and L. Robert, *Bull. épig.* 1971, no. 620. Lycia: Wörrle 1977, 43ff.: (B 178).
[100] Diod. xx.19.3ff.: 27; Plut. *Dem.* 7.3.   [101] Bengtson 1964, 1.136ff.: (A 6).
[102] Diod. xx.20; 28; Just. xv.2.3–5.   [103] Bakhuizen 1970, 112ff.: (B 182).

more confused situation – but, to compound the confusion, Ptolemy had Polemaeus murdered and came to an agreement with Demetrius,[104] who was then the representative in Asia Minor of his father Antigonus. The reasons which may have made Antigonus seek a rapprochement with Ptolemy in this way are easy to understand: he could not tolerate a situation in which Ptolemy intervened in Greece on his own but he was powerless to prevent him – so the 'liberation' of Greece would be a joint operation. As for Ptolemy, he no doubt exacted a price for this agreement in the recognition of the places he had just seized on the coasts of Asia Minor.

In fact these considerations are not sufficient to explain this reversal of alliances from Ptolemy's point of view: for him to have been prepared to be reconciled with his most natural and immediate enemies and quarrel with Cassander, other factors must have been involved, and these are perhaps to be found in the fact that it was at this moment that Ptolemy's representative in Cyrenaica, Ophellas, deciding in his turn to play his own game, embarked on a campaign against Carthage in concert with Agathocles of Syracuse and began to recruit troops in Greece and particularly in Athens, in other words, in the area under Cassander's influence. Ptolemy, no doubt informed by Polemaeus, may have feared that Cassander would give indirect support to Ophellas' ambitions in Cyrenaica and the eventual formation of an African state on Egypt's western flank.[105]

A large Egyptian expedition therefore landed in the Peloponnese in 308.[106] Ptolemy seems to have had the intention of forming a federation of Greek cities (a revival of Philip II's League of Corinth?), but his appeal, accompanied by appeals for money and provisions, met little success. He did not insist, made his peace with Cassander (who no doubt supplied all the balm his feelings required) and withdrew his army, though not without leaving garrisons in a number of places (Corinth, Sicyon, Megara and others), a tactless act on the part of a 'liberator' of Greece.[107]

Antigonus sent his son Demetrius to Athens.[108] The moment was opportune since Cassander was occupied with a campaign towards Epirus. Demetrius was welcomed as a divine liberator by the enthusiastic Athenians (307),[109] and Demetrius of Phalerum, Cassander's

[104] Suda, s.v. Demetrios (cf. SVA. III.433).
[105] Will 1964: (C 78) (but contra, Bakhuizen 1970, 126; (B 182); Laronde 1971: (C 42)).
[106] Diod. xx.37.1–2; Suda, loc. cit.
[107] Moser 1914, 37ff.: (F 139); Kolbe 1916, 530ff.: (F 134); Fritze 1917, 20ff.: (F 131); Bengtson 1964, 1.142ff.: (A 6).
[108] Diod. xx.45–46.5; Plut. Dem. 8–14; Suda, loc. cit.; Ferguson 1911, 95ff.: (D 89).
[109] Taeger 1957, 1.264ff.: (I 78); Cerfaux and Tondriau 1957, 173ff.: (I 18); Habicht 1970, 44ff., 255: (I 29).

protégé, went into exile.[110] The oligarchy supported by Cassander gave way to a restored democracy[111] – but one under Antigonid patronage. The blow was all the harder for Cassander in that his expedition to Epirus, the occasion for Demetrius' venture, ended in failure.

The friendship between Antigonus and Ptolemy was no longer-lived. As early as 306 conflict broke out between them in the area of their most vital interests. Antigonus plucked his son from the delights of Athenian life and put him in charge of a large offensive against Cyprus.[112] Plutarch, in his *Life of Demetrius* (15), notes that the prize of victory was to be, not Cyprus nor even Syria, but general supremacy: at least that was Monophthalmus' intention. Ptolemy suffered the most shattering defeat of his career:[113] Cyprus passed into the hands of the Antigonids and stayed there for more than ten years. Antigonus, anxious to exploit his success, immediately organized a double expedition, by land and sea, against Egypt. Success, which he anticipated, was meant to cover his rear during his subsequent operations against Cassander.[114] The operation was a total failure. Ptolemy was saved.[115]

Accordingly Antigonus turned back towards the Aegean. Between his now long-established protectorate over the Confederation of the Nesiotes and newly conquered Cyprus there was now only one obstacle left which prevented his complete control of the sea – Rhodes.[116] The Rhodians, who had had to give in to some of Monophthalmus' demands between 315 and 311, had nevertheless refused to take part in either the Cyprus or the subsequent Egyptian campaign: their interests placed them clearly in the Ptolemaic camp, even without a formal alliance. Now, showing that the freedom of the Greeks was of concern to him only insofar as it did not conflict with his ambitions, Antigonus ordered his son to take Rhodes. It was a famous siege,[117] in which the poliorcetic resources employed by Demetrius won him the name with which he has gone into history, Poliorcetes, 'taker of cities'. Yet he failed to take Rhodes, which Ptolemy kept supplied with food. After a year's siege (305–304), he had to seek terms. The Antigonids recognized the liberty of the Rhodians (a proof that the root of the problem of the freedom of the cities in this period is not so much a legal doctrine as a balance of forces), and they in turn agreed to form an alliance on the express condition that it would never be invoked against Ptolemy. The Rhodian episode is important. The preservation of the island's freedom is the source of the prosperity it enjoyed for more than a century and of the

110 Bayer 1942, 93ff.: (C 5).   111 L. C. Smith 1962: (C 67).
112 Diod. xx.47–52; Just. xv.2.6–9; Plut. *Dem.* 15–16; App. *Syr.* 54.
113 Seibert 1969, 190ff.: (F 145); Hauben 1975, 107ff.: (C 37); 1975–6: (C 38).
114 Hauben 1975/6: (C 38).   115 Diod. xx.73–6; Plut. *Dem.* 19.1–2.
116 Hauben 1977, 330ff.: (C 39).
117 Diod. xx.81–8; 91–100.4; Plut. *Dem.* 21–2.

important role it played during this period. Nor were the Rhodians in any doubt about the scope of their success: it was to commemorate the raising of the siege that they erected at the entrance to their harbour, in honour of Helios, the high god of the island, the famous Colossus which the ancients counted among the seven wonders of the world. As for Ptolemy, the success of the Rhodians compensated him somewhat for the loss of Cyprus.

Since the murder of Alexander's son in 310 and the extinction of the Argead dynasty none of the Diadochi had dared to usurp the Macedonian royal title. Antigonus was the first to take this step and to have himself granted by acclamation the title of *basileus*, which he shared with his son. The occasion was Demetrius' triumph in Cyprus in 306. Antigonus' act has a very clear significance: by proclaiming himself *basileus* he was claiming to be the successor of the last real king, the Conqueror; by associating his son with himself he was indicating his intention of founding a dynasty; and by the very act of assuming Alexander's title and diadem, he was laying claim to Alexander's legacy. In other words, he was declaring ambitions hitherto left implicit.[118]

But the two kings' lack of military success in their expedition against Egypt induced Ptolemy in his turn to assume the royal title (305/4).[119] It is important to make it very clear that in Ptolemy's case this act has nothing like the same significance as in the case of Antigonus. As *basileus*, we have just said, Antigonus claimed to inherit the whole of Alexander's legacy – Egypt naturally included. Ptolemy, on the other hand, had no such claims: in also taking the royal title, his main intention was probably to challenge Antigonus' status in the area he, Ptolemy, had reserved for himself – he was proclaiming his sovereignty over Egypt. The proclamation was addressed to the Macedonians; for the native Egyptians the title *basileus* had no significance. In Egyptian eyes, the only dignity Ptolemy could assume was the traditional Pharaonic kingship, which Alexander had certainly assumed. That Ptolemy had behaved as a Pharaoh from the beginning (just as, we are told, Seleucus behaved as a king with the barbarians) is a plain fact, even though it has recently come to light that he maintained the fiction of Alexander IV's reign as Pharaoh after the young king's murder. Whether, at some moment or other of his career, he had himself crowned Pharaoh at Memphis is, on the other hand, doubtful – but it matters little for our purposes. The assumption of the royal title of Macedon in 305 was not an act of domestic policy; it was an act of foreign policy: against Antigonid pretentions to universal kingship Ptolemy was asserting his particular, limited sovereignty – though a sovereignty which he too claimed to derive from Alexander's.

---

[118] Ritter 1965, 84ff.: (I 62); O. Müller 1973: (C 51).
[119] Volkmann 1959, 1621–2: (C 74); Samuel 1962, 4ff.: (F 399); O. Müller 1973, 93ff.: (C 51).

In the months that followed Cassander, Lysimachus and Seleucus in turn proclaimed themselves *basileis*. It is possible that Cassander, as the author of the extinction of the legitimate line, made himself king in the same spirit as Antigonus (though the evidence is that he, and he alone, used the title *basileus Makedonon*),[120] but Lysimachus and Seleucus[121] were clearly imitating Ptolemy; in other words, they were challenging Antigonus' claims to sovereignty over what we may from now on call their states – but in no sense themselves, individually, claiming sovereignty over the whole.[122]

The moment is important; this is the birth of the Hellenistic monarchies, if not in fact (since something similar had existed in practice since Triparadisus), at least in law. Just as first Perdiccas' unitary ambitions, and now those of Antigonus, had contributed heavily to accelerating the territorial fragmentation of Alexander's empire, so Antigonus' claims to Alexander's royal power provoked, in reaction, the fragmentation of that power – even though Antigonus in all probability had no such intention, since he never seems to have admitted the kingship of his rivals.[123]

It was now to be left to force to settle the question of the new order: would legitimacy in future derive from the pleasure of Antigonus or from that of his opponents?

Despite the two successive failures suffered by the Antigonids at the gates of Egypt and at Rhodes, it looked for many years as though the rival monarchies – certainly those of Cassander and Lysimachus – would be no more than ephemeral, because the prospects at this point for Monophthalmus and his son in Greece and the Aegean looked at first very favourable.

As early as 307 Cassander had set out once more on an assault on Greece, and quite quickly succeeded in confining Ptolemy's garrisons to Corinth and Sicyon. This offensive had the further effect of inducing the Antigonids to raise the siege of Rhodes in 304. As early as 303, however, Demetrius Poliorcetes had begun to eliminate completely the influence of both Cassander and Ptolemy from the region of the isthmus.[124]

It was at this point, in the spring of 302, that there occurred one of the most interesting episodes in the Greek policy of the Antigonids, the setting up of a federation solidly grouped around Antigonus and his son. This venture, despite its lack of any real future, seems to have been more serious than those of Polyperchon and Ptolemy, and above all we know

---

[120] *SIG* 332; Goukowsky 1978, 201: (A 19).
[121] See above, p. 52 n. 91.
[122] So Cohen 1974: (C 12).
[123] Diod. xx.53.2–4; Just. xv.2.10ff.; Plut. *Dem.* 17–18; App. *Syr.* 54.
[124] Diod. xx.100.5–7; 102–3; Plut. *Dem.* 23–7; Moser 1914, 58ff.: (F 139). For Demetrius' coinage, bibliography in Will 1979, I.78: (A 67).

more about it, thanks mainly to epigraphic evidence:[125] inscriptions give us glimpses of the federal institutions and even enable us to build up a picture of Demetrius Poliorcetes' principal agent in the carrying out of this task, Adeimantus of Lampsacus.[126] This league, which, like that of 338/7, seems to have been based at Corinth, is generally interpreted by modern writers[127] (after Plutarch) as a restoration of the league of Philip II, though some have denied this. What we know of the federal institutions does seem to justify the comparison, but the difference in circumstances explains why doubts could be expressed. In 338 the foundation of the League of Corinth had been the conclusion of Philip's Greek policy, the end of a long enterprise which had started from Macedon; its essential purpose had been to organize a 'common peace' in Greece, and the alliance for other purposes was merely secondary. In 302, however, the situation was practically the reverse. While it is certain that, in Poliorcetes' mind, the new League of Corinth was, like the old, to be a means for controlling Greece (an Antigonid garrison was installed in Corinth, and was to remain there for sixty years), nevertheless it was also, and above all, to be one starting point among others for the seizure of Macedon from Cassander. The league of 302 was, therefore, for a time a weapon of war against the ruler of Macedon and from this point of view the 'symmachy' became the primary objective, with the 'common peace' as no more than a distant goal. If the Antigonid offensive against Cassander had been crowned with success, then, but only then, the league of Corinth of 302 might have acquired a similarity with that founded by Philip, that is, it would have become exclusively an instrument for Macedonian domination of Greece, in the framework and under the cover of a firmly re-established 'common peace'. If, of course, the league had lasted . . .

While Demetrius was organizing Greece in this way, his father was pressing ahead with his preparations in Asia: Macedon was to be caught in a vice. Cassander, feeling that the days of his power were numbered, attempted to negotiate, but the aged Antigonus, seeing success at last within his grasp and with old age leaving him little time to lose, refused: his ultimatum gave new cohesion to the union of his opponents.[128] Cassander first obtained the support of Lysimachus, who faced as great a threat as himself. Ptolemy's was automatic, and finally Seleucus, who had been occupied for several years by affairs in India, now realized that an Antigonid victory in the West would once more compromise his situation and, at an uncertain date (between 305 and 303?)[129] made peace

[125] *IG* iv².1.68 (cf. *SEG* 1.75; ii.56; iii.319; xi.399). *ISE* 1.44: sv A iii.446.
[126] Robert 1946, 15ff.: (c 56); Daux 1955: (c 15); *ISE* 1.9; ii.72.
[127] Bengtson 1964, i.154ff.: (A 6); Hampl 1938, 58ff., 113ff.: (A 20); Ferguson 1948: (c 25); Wehrli 1969, 122ff.: (c 75).   [128] Diod. xx.106–13.   [129] Hauben 1974: (c 36).

with the Mauryan Chandragupta, surrendering to him territories in the Paropamisadae and in Arachosia and Gedrosia the extent of which has often been discussed, as have other enigmatic clauses of this treaty.[130] The allies decided, in a risky gamble which, however, proved correct, to sacrifice the defence of Macedon to an offensive in Asia Minor, which forced Antigonus to recall his son from Europe. The combined operations of Cassander, Lysimachus and Seleucus (with Ptolemy on his own playing his very personal game by invading Coele-Syria) resulted in a complete reversal of the situation: in the summer of 301, at Ipsus in Phrygia, Lysimachus and Seleucus completely crushed the Antigonids, thanks particularly to the elephants supplied by Chandragupta.[131] The aged Monophthalmus himself was left on the battlefield.

After Ipsus, a division of the spoils of the Antigonids was necessary.[132] Lysimachus took Asia Minor as far as the Taurus, with the exception of a few places in Lycia, Pamphylia or Pisidia, which seem to have come into the hands of Ptolemy[133] (where they were not already in his possession), with the exception also of Cilicia, which was given to one of Cassander's brothers, Pleistarchus,[134] though this little state was to be short-lived. Cassander made no demands, but he evidently expected to have a free hand in Greece from now on, even though Demetrius Poliorcetes, who had escaped by a hair's breadth from the disaster of Ipsus, retained strong positions. Seleucus laid claim to Syria, but he was unable to annex it completely because Ptolemy, who had refrained from appearing at Ipsus as arranged, had immediately set about methodically occupying the southern half, as far as the river Eleutherus.[135] The conquerors of Antigonus, suspicious, ordered Ptolemy to surrender this territory to Seleucus, but he refused. Seleucus, invoking the old friendship between himself and Ptolemy, agreed provisionally to let the territory go, but not without making it clear that he was not renouncing his rights over Coele-Syria:[136] this was the origin of what are called the Syrian wars, which were to involve the two kingdoms in lengthy hostilities. Reduced to the northern half of the country, which was to take the name of Seleucis, Seleucus, following the policy of colonization begun by Antigonus, founded especially the four towns of the 'Syrian tetrapolis' (Antioch-on-the-Orontes, Seleuceia-in-Pieria, Laodicea-on-Sea and Apamea) which were henceforth to be the heart of his kingdom.[137]

[130] Summary of the discussions and bibliography in Will 1979, 1.265–6: (A 67).
[131] Elephants on Seleucus' coins: Newell 1938, 38ff., 115ff., 121ff., 229ff.: (B 249).
[132] Diod. XXI.1.5; Just. XV.4.21–2; Plut. Dem. 28–30.1; 31.4.
[133] Bibliography in J. Seibert Historia 19 (1970) 347ff.
[134] Robert 1945, 55ff.: (B 142); Schaefer 1951, 197ff.: (C 59).
[135] Otto 1928, 37ff.: (E 46); Seyrig 1951, 208ff.: (E 173); Volkmann 1959, 1624: (C 74).
[136] Bikerman 1947: (E 154).
[137] Seyrig 1968: (E 174) and 1970: (E 53); Marinoni 1972: (E 39).

In one sense, the disappearance of Antigonus Monophthalmus marks the end of an era. After him, even if the unitary idea still haunted the thoughts of his son (which remains uncertain), even if it passed through the mind of Seleucus as a fleeting desire on the eve of his death, from this point onwards there was to be no policy devoted seriously, stubbornly, like that of Antigonus, to reviving Alexander's empire. Besides, that union of Asia and Europe had been made possible for a moment by exceptional circumstances (the euphoria caused by Philip's successes, the Achaemenid collapse, Alexander's personal prestige) and too many centrifugal forces stood in the way of its being reconstructed. Antigonus himself had learnt this since, for all his desire to bring territories in Asia and in Europe under his authority, as early as 307 the facts themselves had given the lie to this claim; from the day when the Antigonids' activity had crossed the Aegean from Asia to Europe, father and son had been obliged to divide responsibilities, Antigonus keeping Asia for himself and delegating Demetrius to Europe, to recall him only in the hour of danger. Thus for the Antigonids Asia (an Asia already severely reduced by the fact of Seleucus) and Europe had in reality been no more than two territories artificially linked by a dynastic bond. In contrast, what Lysimachus was to achieve for a moment was to be different in scope and character from Antigonus' dream. Antigonus' death on the battlefield of Ipsus marks the final passing of the idea of an empire reviving that of Alexander, if not inherited from him. That is by no means to say that Alexander's work was totally and finally ruined. Beneath the collapsing territorial unity another unity, deeper and more important for the future of the world, was coming into being, taking root and growing, and spreading too, if at the cost of its purity; this was the unity of civilization of the Hellenistic world. In this chapter (as in chapter 4) it is primarily the political aspects of that unity with which we shall be concerned, but these are not the least interesting aspects since, from many points of view, what was taking place in these years was the birth, even now obscure, of the 'modern' conception of territorial states with no claims to universality which seek to co-exist, as far as their interests allow, in a system of unstable equilibrium. This may be not at all what Alexander would have wished to leave to posterity but it is nonetheless his legacy, since without his work the experiment could never have started. And even then Antigonus Monophthalmus had to disappear from the scene in the debacle of Ipsus before the fragmentation of the world newly opened to Graeco-Macedonian civilization could be assured beyond all challenge.

CHAPTER 3

MONARCHIES AND MONARCHIC IDEAS

F. W. WALBANK

I. THE NEW POLITICAL PATTERN

Within twenty years of Alexander's death his empire had split into separate states, whose rulers had taken the title of king. In future most Greeks were to live under the shadow of monarchic régimes. Some lived in cities situated within the kingdoms, and even the inhabitants of mainland Greece and such islands as stayed independent were subjected to their pressure, while many from time to time were forced to endure their garrisons. The immediate presence of monarchy affected all aspects of life, including political theory and philosophical speculation. It was the exceptional city that could escape making some sort of accommodation with one or other of the new monarchies and political theory now had to start from the premise that kingship was the best form of state. This was an assumption not too difficult to accept in as much as it was far from novel. Throughout the fourth century a strong current of anti-democratic thought had advocated monarchy as the most stable régime and the one best able to defend the power and prosperity of the rich. According to Aristotle (*Pol.* VII (v).10.3, 1310b9ff.), kingship is the resource of the better classes against the people, whereas a tyrant is chosen from the people to be their protector against the notables. Such notions fell in with the new political developments which followed after Alexander; but they were not their cause, for the monarchic régimes had sprung naturally out of the break-up of Alexander's empire, left without an effective heir.

To fifth-century Greeks monarchy was something remote. Except in the hated and supposedly corrupt form of tyranny it either belonged to the heroic age (and was therefore familiar in an idealised form from Homer and tragic performances) or it survived in backward and peripheral areas like Thrace, Macedonia, Epirus, Cyprus and Cyrene. At Sparta, and less obviously in some other cities, kingship had been incorporated as a sort of magistracy or even reduced to a ritual office within the structure of the city. In its absolute form monarchy seemed a form of government suited only to barbarians, slavish by nature, and the King *par excellence* was of course the King of Persia. In the fourth century the older cities, which hitherto had dominated Greece but were

62

now weakened by protracted warfare and could not afford the more sophisticated fighting techniques and the high cost of hiring mercenaries, gradually yielded place to new centres of power and, after Chaeronea, to Macedonia under Philip and Alexander. Alexander's eastern expedition encouraged the military and autocratic aspects of his rule, and in this respect his successors, the Diadochi, followed in his footsteps. It is symptomatic of the military character of the new states that of the fourteen Seleucid kings from Seleucus I to Antiochus VII only two, Antiochus II and Seleucus IV, died at home.[1]

The new kings were forceful and ambitious men who relied on their armies and mostly ruled in lands where monarchy was traditional. There was really no feasible alternative. The nature of their rule, and one at least of its problems, are sketched in a passage quoted in the *Suda*:

It is neither descent nor legitimacy which gives monarchies to men but the ability to command an army and govern a state wisely, as was the case with Philip and Alexander's Successors. For Alexander's natural son got no help from his kinship with him owing to his weak character, whereas those who were in no way related became kings over virtually the whole inhabited world.[2]

The first Successors to take the royal title were Antigonus and Demetrius, after the latter defeated Ptolemy at Salamis in Cyprus in 306;[3] they were followed by Ptolemy himself and Seleucus in 305/4 and, soon afterwards, by Cassander and Lysimachus.[4] Others – including Anatolian rulers not of Graeco-Macedonian origin – followed suit over the next decades, beginning with Zipoetes of Bithynia in 297 and Mithridates of Pontus in 296 (or 281).[5] What these claims to royalty really signified can only be surmised; but it seems more than likely that while Antigonus and Demetrius were staking a claim to the whole empire, their rivals were merely asserting their right to kingship within the areas they governed.[6]

Though they were in fact jointly successors to Alexander's empire and their kingship in a sense followed on from his (and that of his ill-starred heirs), the Diadochi based their claims to kingship not on succession, but on their personal achievements. Each government had to work out its own particular relationship, on the one hand to the indigenous peoples who lived within its frontiers and were accustomed to monarchy, and on the other to the Greek cities which were not. But

[1] Bikerman 1938, 13: (E 6); Seleucus IV was assassinated.
[2] *Suda s.v. βασιλεία*=Austin 37; cf. Adcock 1953, 170: (I 5); Bikerman 1938, 12: (E 6).
[3] See above, ch. 2, pp. 57–8; cf. Préaux 1978, I.184: (A 48).
[4] Plut. *Dem.* 18.1–3; Just. *Epit.* xv.3.10–12.
[5] Memnon, *FGrH* 434 F 12, 4–5; Diod. xx.111. For the dates when the other monarchies were established in Asia see Préaux 1978, I.184 n. 2: (A 48).
[6] Cf. Aymard 1967, 94: (I 9).

despite these variations there emerged a new political form, Hellenistic monarchy, characterized by enough common traits to justify treating it as one institution. Graeco-Macedonian in origin and scarcely influenced from the East, it is to be found not only in the successor states, but also in regions which had never formed part of Alexander's empire at all, such as Epirus and the Syracuse of Hiero II; and, as we have just seen, its forms and structure were adopted by non-Greek and semi-Greek states in Asia Minor.

The new monarchies presented Greeks with an ideological problem. Wherever they lived, they had to adjust to a dominant royal power and to find an acceptable place for monarchy within their political philosophy without losing their self-respect and (as far as possible) without discarding their traditional commitment to freedom. Earlier on some cities had had to live under the Great King; but the new relationship was more intimate and more ambiguous. It called for and very soon elicited a new political theory, capable of reconciling Greeks to their situation under an autocratic government and at the same time holding up an ideal image of the king against which his actual treatment of the cities could be measured. Between theory and political reality there were obvious divergences, but also considerable interplay, as each to some extent modified the other. But since monarchy and monarchical theory do not altogether coincide in their origins, we shall look at the former first.

II. THE CHARACTER OF HELLENISTIC MONARCHY

First it is necessary to get one source of confusion out of the way. It has been widely argued that the Antigonid monarchy in Macedonia differed in important respects from monarchy in the other kingdoms. As a national institution rooted in the Macedonian people, it was subject (it is alleged) to constitutional limitations which did not apply to the other kings. The king of Macedon was *primus inter pares*, whereas the others enjoyed personal and absolute rule. This view rests on slender foundations, namely the residual powers of the assembled Macedonians to appoint a new king by acclamation and to act as judges in cases of high treason. The arguments in favour of the Macedonians' having possessed such powers are examined elsewhere in this volume[7] and need not be repeated here. They furnish no support for thinking that during the period after Alexander Macedonia differed constitutionally from the other monarchies. There was certainly a closer relationship between the king of Macedon and his people than existed elsewhere; to

---

[7] See below, ch. 7, pp. 225–7.

that extent it was a national monarchy. Moreover, there are five known inscriptions dating from Amyntas, the son of Perdiccas III in the fourth century, down to Philip V, in which the king describes himself as 'king of the Macedonians'. That is a formula not available for use in any other kingdom. But there is nothing 'official' about the phrase, which implies neither that the Macedonians possessed constitutional rights nor yet that the king was exercising greater autocracy over them (both views have been propounded). The formula 'king of the Macedonians' is comparatively rare and is probably used when the king (or in Amyntas' case someone else) wanted to make a special point.[8] It is noteworthy, too, that more treatises *On Kingship* seem to have been written for the early Antigonids than, for example, for the Ptolemies. So perhaps they were more interested in the philosophic justification of kingship. But this conclusion is not certain and in any case would have no bearing on Macedonian rights.

We may then assume that like their fellow-kings the Antigonids represented the state.[9] Their position inside the kingdom differed from that of others only in nuances – there was for example no official dynastic cult in Macedonia. Nor is this similarity surprising. Directly or indirectly all the dynasties went back to Alexander; and two Antigonid kings – Demetrius I and Antigonus II – had, earlier in their careers, exercised what it is customary to call a personal monarchy. In addition, there was a gradual process of assimilation which in time led the various monarchies to resemble each other more and more and to adopt similar institutions and conventions affecting their interstate relations. Macedonia was in no way exempt from this development. Nor does any ancient source imply that the Macedonian monarchy differed in any substantial regard from the others. It is therefore legitimate to examine the general character of Hellenistic kingship without drawing fine distinctions, except in minor respects, between 'national' and 'personal' monarchies.

One such minor difference we have just examined: the use of the title 'king of the Macedonians'. Elsewhere (with one exception)[10] Hellenistic kings were not described as rulers of a particular people or country, but

[8] For this formula see *IG* VII.3055 (Lebadeia: Amyntas); *SIG* 332 (Cassandreia: Cassander); *SIG* 573 and 574 (Delos: Philip V); *Lindos* II inscr. 1 no. 2 (Lindus: Philip V). Against Aymard 1967, 100–22: (I 9), see Errington 1974, 23–9: (D 16).

[9] Aristotle, *Pol.* v.8.5.1310b, links the Macedonian monarchy with those of Sparta and Epirus, not as traditional monarchies rooted in the state (so Aymard 1967, 149 n. 5: (I 9)), but as monarchies that have won merit by settling or gaining territory; and when, in *Pol.* v.11.2.1313a, he refers to monarchies with limited powers he mentions Sparta and the Molossians, but not Macedonia.

[10] In a letter to Cos (*RC* 25 = *SIG* 456) Ziaelas calls himself 'king of the Bithynians' and this has been taken as evidence of 'national feeling' in Bithynia. But it was epistolary convention everywhere (including Macedonia) for a king to style himself simply (e.g.) 'King Antigonus', and the solecism here seems simply to be the product of an incompetent chancellery.

simply, *tout court*, as kings. That is, of course, within the Greek context. To their indigenous subjects they had other titles. Cuneiform documents describe Antiochus I as 'the powerful king, the king of the world, the king of Babylon, king of the lands';[11] and the Ptolemies, as Pharaohs, were kings of 'Upper and Lower Egypt'.[12] But these native titles were irrelevant to the Graeco-Macedonian population, in whose eyes the claim to kingship was not dependent on the possession of a particular piece of territory. Once he had been so recognized, a king might (like Demetrius Poliorcetes) lose all his territory and still retain his title. On the other hand it was important to his status and his renown that he should control territory, in which he could exercise his kingship (and from which he could draw revenues and recruit troops); and claims to territory were never lightly relinquished. Conquest was the strongest title to land, as Polybius (XXVIII.1.6) records of Antiochus IV who, at the outset of the Sixth Syrian War, was determined to maintain his hold on Coele-Syria and Phoenicia, since he 'regarded possession through warfare as the surest claim and the best'. Earlier Antiochus III had drifted into war with Rome through his determination to recover the Chersonese and the cities in Thrace which his ancestor Seleucus I had won by his victory over Lysimachus (Polyb. XVIII.51.3–6).

'Spear-won territory' was important partly because it was concrete evidence of victory:[13] and victory was one of the main attributes of royalty, for it was a demonstrable proof of merit and an uncontrovertible claim on the loyalty of troops and subjects. Commenting on the triumphant eastern expedition of Antiochus III, Polybius remarks (XI.34.15–16) that

in a word he put his kingdom in a position of safety, overawing all his subjects by his courage and his efforts. It was in fact this expedition which made him appear worthy of the throne, not only to the inhabitants of Asia, but to those of Europe likewise.

It was after this expedition that Antiochus assumed the epithet 'the Great'. Merit thus recognized was a personal quality. Yet, somewhat illogically, it tended also to become attached to the king's family and so served as a justification for dynastic succession. To ensure that one's kingdom passed peacefully to one's heir was, naturally, a prime objective of most kings. It was to facilitate an easy transition from one reign to the next that it became customary for a king to raise his eldest son to co-regency during his own lifetime. Early examples are the co-

---

[11] Bikerman 1938, 6 n. 1: (E 6).

[12] *OGIS* 90 (= Austin 227), l.46, τήν τε ἄνω χώραν καὶ τὴν κάτω; for the Egyptian versions see E. A. Wallis Budge, *The Rosetta Stone in the British Museum* (London, 1929); Plates vol., pl. 3.

[13] Diod. XVIII.43 of Ptolemy who τὴν . . . Αἴγυπτον ὡσανεί τινα < βασιλείαν > δορύκτητον εἶχεν.

rule of Antiochus I alongside Seleucus I and Demetrius I alongside Antigonus I; but it was practised in most monarchies, and when this occurred the younger king was frequently trained for the succession by being given an independent command. Concern for the consolidation of the dynasty may also have been behind the adoption of brother–sister marriage at Alexandria – a custom which the Greeks found odd, though they soon learnt to tolerate it and to make flattering references to Zeus and Hera. The first such union was that of Ptolemy II with Arsinoe. In their case the marriage was probably engineered by Arsinoe's strong-minded and ambitious character, but it will have continued as a regular custom of the Ptolemaic dynasty, perhaps partly because it had parallels in earlier native Egyptian practice,[14] but also because of the merits of such a marriage in consolidating the royal family and avoiding the complications that could arise from inter-dynastic unions.[15] An extreme example of such a marriage is the polygamous union of Ptolemy VIII Euergetes II with his sister Cleopatra II and her daughter (and his niece) Cleopatra III. Hellenistic kings were normally monogamous, though this often went with a succession of wives. Brother–sister marriages are primarily to be found in Alexandria, but there is one probable example in the Seleucid family, if indeed the wife of Antiochus, Antiochus III's eldest son, was the latter's daughter Laodice.[16]

Part of the necessary glamour of kingship was secured by the wearing of special clothing and symbols of royalty – though compared with eastern monarchies this remained on a fairly modest level. Kings adopted the Macedonian military uniform with boots, a flowing cloak and a broad-brimmed hat (or in war-time a helmet).[17] In addition they wore a diadem[18] on the head (or over the helmet), consisting of a white or purple and white headband with two loose ends behind. Other outward signs of kingship were crowns, presented as an expression of gratitude by Greek cities (later these were commuted into sums of money), purple robes (though others besides the king could wear these), a sceptre and a ring with a seal-stone. The Seleucid seal bore an anchor, the sign of Apollo. The king's appearance, often idealised, was rendered familiar to his subjects through sculptures and representations on the coinage.

[14] See Hopkins 1980, 303–54: (F 266); for another view see below, ch. 5, pp. 136–8.

[15] Cf. Aymard 1953, 400–1: (I 8).

[16] Mørkholm 1966, 49: (E 43). It has been suggested that this Laodice subsequently married her two other brothers, Seleucus IV and Antiochus IV; cf. Bikerman 1938, 25 n. 1: (E 6). See against this somewhat unlikely succession of marriages, Aymard 1967, 243 n. 1: (I 9).

[17] Cf. Aymard 1953, 401: (I 8); Bikerman 1938, 32: (E 6); Préaux 1978, I.210: (A 48).

[18] Cf. Ritter, 1965: (I 62). On the diadem as a symbol of kingship cf. Polyb. xxx.2.4. For examples, see Plates vol., pls. 4a, 4c, 4d; 11; 14; 22b; 56b; 65b, 65c, 65d.

III. THE MACHINERY OF MONARCHICAL GOVERNMENT

Though the first generation of kings was much occupied with warfare, they already had considerable experience in governing the provinces of Alexander's empire and from the outset they had to apply themselves to civil administration in their own kingdoms. The survival of evidence on this subject is uneven, and though written sources preserve some details, most of our information depends on the chance survival of papyri and inscriptions. Consequently far more is known of Egypt than of anywhere else, because of the papyri found there. The general picture is of a bureaucracy which begins by being fairly rudimentary, but fills out and solidifies as time goes on. In the early days of the kingdoms competent and reliable men were put to tasks which needed doing without too much regard for the title of the post they nominally held,[19] but after a time a number of what might be termed ministerial posts became established, and these often bore the same or similar titles in the various kingdoms: for example, the secretary-of-state, head of the chancellery and responsible for official correspondence,[20] the grand vizier or prime minister,[21] and the chamberlain in charge of the court and bodyguards.[22]

The court is a typical feature of the new kingdoms, and gradually it takes on an elaboration which recalls the monarchies of Persia and Pharaonic Egypt rather than anything Greek. Set up in the capital, around the royal palace, it contained slaves, eunuchs and a variety of servants with specialized functions ensuring its smooth running. There were bodyguards to watch over the king's safety, and there were doctors to minister to his health. But, most important of all, the king was surrounded by his Friends (philoi), whom he appointed to a position close to his own person, where they enjoyed an intimate relationship profitable to both parties, and he often rewarded them with gifts of land which established them among the propertied class, whose support was vital to the security of his rule. These Friends were of the king's own personal choosing and might come from anywhere in the Greek world. A king's Friends would not necessarily be taken over by his successor. Since with the exception of Macedonia the new monarchies were the

[19] See below, ch. 6, pp. 185–6.
[20] Polyb. IV.87.8. ἐπὶ τοῦ γραμματείου (Antigonid); XV.27.7, ὁ πρὸς τοῖς γράμμασι τεταγμένος (Ptolemaic); XXX.25.16, ἐπιστολαγράφος (Seleucid); cf. Bikerman 1938, 197: (E 6); Walbank 1979, III.453: (B 37), for inscriptional evidence.
[21] Polyb. V.41.1, προεστὼς τῶν ὅλων πραγμάτων; cf. II Macc. XI.12, ἐπὶ τῶν πραγμάτων; cf. Bikerman 1938, 197 (E 6).
[22] Polyb.IV.87.5, ὁ ἐπὶ τῆς θεραπείας τεταγμένος; cf. Bikerman 1938, 36: (E 6); Corradi 1929, 297–8: (A 11).

personal creation of their founders and had no roots in the native population – for Alexander's policy of racial fusion and collaboration with the Persians had soon been rejected by the Seleucids and had never been even contemplated in Egypt[23] – there was no indigenous nobility on whose help the king could draw. He had to build up his own governing class and he generally chose his helpers on the basis, not of birth or wealth, but solely of ability: to get on with him and to carry out whatever duties he assigned.[24]

The earliest contemporary reference to Friends occurs in a letter from Lysimachus to the city of Priene dating to around 285,[25] in which the king, the Friends and the army are said to have received greetings of goodwill from Prienean envoys. But Friends are to be found in all Hellenistic courts, where they form a council of state in daily session, advising the king on matters of policy – though it remains his prerogative to take the decision. Meetings of the royal council are often mentioned in literary sources, for example that of Ptolemy IV discussing what to do about Cleomenes of Sparta (Polyb. v.35.7–13), or that of Antiochus III, meeting on several occasions over the revolt of Molon (Polyb. v.41.6, 49.1, 51.3); and an interesting dossier of inscriptions dating to the years 163–156 from Pessinus in Galatia reveals the active role of one of the Friends of Attalus II in securing the reversal of a decision to go to war, after a discussion lasting several days.[26]

The Friends were almost invariably Greeks or Macedonians; Egyptians, Syrians, Jews and Iranians were alike excluded.[27] Many, but not all, were exiles from their own cities. They flocked to Alexandria, Antioch and later Pergamum from all parts of the Greek world, seeking wealth, status and an opportunity to exercise skill and power. Nor did they simply form the council round the king. They were also a reservoir of talent from which the king chose his military officers, his governors of provinces, his ministers of state, his high priests and his ambassadors. There was little or no specialization. Artists, writers, philosophers, doctors, scholars – all were possible recruits, but once they became the king's Friends they might be drafted to any task. The Stoic philosopher Persaeus ended his life – Stoically – by suicide, when he failed to save the Acrocorinth, where Antigonus Gonatas had made him commandant;

---

[23] Whereas Seleucus I had a Bactrian wife, the mother of Antiochus I, there were no later dynastic marriages with Iranians. Against the view that Ptolemy I first contemplated an Egyptianizing policy see below, ch. 5, pp. 126–7.

[24] On the Friends see Habicht 1958, 1–16: (H 85); on the changing attitudes of Greeks in the independent cities towards them see Herman 1981: (I 32).

[25] *RC* 6; king, Friends and army are often mentioned together as three focal points of importance in a Hellenistic kingdom; cf. *I. Magnesia* 86, ll.15ff.; *OGIS* 219 (=Austin 139), ll.12ff.; Polyb. v.50.4–9; Habicht 1958, 4: (H 85). For a later reference to Lysimachus' Friends in 292 see below, p. 70.   [26] *RC* 61; cf. Virgilio 1981: (E 98).

[27] Hannibal at Antiochus III's court is a noteworthy exception.

the doctor Apollophanes carried his point of view in Antiochus III's war-council in 219; and the poet and scholar Hegesianax (who had, appropriately, written a Trojan history) served as Antiochus' ambassador to Rome.

The king and his Friends looked to each other for assistance. Their relationship was that of a partnership based ultimately on self-interest. Hellenistic kings, in the early days at any rate, could not normally draw upon the hereditary loyalty which an established monarchy can command; but nevertheless the institution of the Friends fostered a sense of mutual obligation and goodwill, so strong at times that when in 292 Lysimachus was threatened by a Thracian army and 'his Friends kept urging him to save himself as best he could . . . he replied to them that it was not honourable to look after himself by abandoning his army and his Friends' (Diod. XXI.12). King, army and Friends must stand together; and on this occasion Lysimachus was taken prisoner (though he was later released).

The exclusion of non-Greeks from this circle probably reflected the prejudices of the Greeks and Macedonians rather than any incapacity or reluctance to serve on the part of the native population. Racial prejudice was characteristic of the Graeco-Macedonian caste within the kingdoms at least throughout the late fourth and the third centuries. That it extended well down in the social scale can be seen from the fact that in the Seleucid kingdom it was only after two or three generations that men with native names appear as holders of administrative posts at any level, and even then they are few in number – never more than 2.5% from a sample of several hundred names – and these few are employed chiefly as commanders of local units.[28]

During the fourth and third centuries the king's Friends are distinguished by social and geographical mobility and personal initiative; but in the second century there was a gradual hardening into a bureaucracy. With dynastic succession firmly established in all kingdoms, their rulers could now claim a new authority based on the concept of legitimacy; and the Friends, from being a group of individuals closely linked to the king by bonds of mutual interest, swelled in number to become a large, stratified and hierarchical administrative class, in which status was defined by the conferment of honorific titles, inflated in both number and verbiage. In the Seleucid kingdom a series of ranks can be traced, beginning with Friends (*philoi*) and ascending through First Friends (*protoi philoi*), Honoured Friends (*timomenoi philoi*), First and Most Honoured Friends (*protoi kai protimomenoi philoi*), organized in various 'orders'. Ranking above them are numerous individual 'kinsmen' (*syngeneis*) – their relationship to the king was fictitious – a category which perhaps embraced his so-called 'foster-fathers' (or 'tutors') (*trophes*) and his 'fellow-pupils' (*syntrophoi*).[29] The nomenclature in the Ptolemaic kingdom is even more variegated. Most of the recorded categories appear to be purely honorific and constitute a hierarchic structure which has little to do with any actual duties performed. This is probably equally true of Pergamum and the Seleucid kingdom as well as of Egypt, where the rich papyrus finds have enabled the system to be most clearly delineated.[30]

The court and the Friends were essential to the successful functioning of government; but although they shared in the work, power rested constitutionally in the hands of the king and the state was embodied in his person. In consequence he was also the source of law; and his relationship to the law – whether as well as creating it he was also in some sense bound by it – was a much debated issue which will be discussed below (pp. 80–1). In everyday administration the king's decisions (they were not called laws, *nomoi*) had to be published throughout the kingdom and in the cities under the king's control. The royal will was indicated in documents promulgated through administrative channels or in letters despatched to the cities. The latter were written in the first person (usually the royal plural) and sent directly to whoever was concerned, whereas the former – they were usually called *diagrammata*, though other terms were used – were couched in the third person (with the verbs in the imperative) and issued by the king or his central office and were equivalent to a general proclamation with the force of law.[31] When addressing cities the king seems to have tried, when possible, to have his decisions incorporated in their laws, perhaps in the interest of good relations, but also because city laws could be expected to command greater permanence than a royal enactment. An example of this procedure is to be found in a letter from Attalus III to the council and people of Pergamum, sent shortly before his death in 133, in which he expresses his wish that provisions for establishing a cult of Zeus Sabazius in the temple of Athena Nicephorus shall be incorporated in the 'sacred laws' of the city.[32]

A request of this kind raises a problem which none of the kings wholly solved. How best was the king to establish satisfactory relations with the Greek cities? The usual method was a combination of force and

[29] Cf. Bikerman 1938, 41–2: (E 6); and see below, ch. 6, pp. 179–80. For examples in other kingdoms see Holleaux, *Études*, III.230–5.

[30] For other details see Mooren 1975; (F 286) and 1977: (F 287); and below, ch. 5, p. 165.

[31] For other types of document used see Préaux 1978, II.199–200: (A 48), and De Francisci 1948, II.490–5: (D 8).

[32] RC 67. The laws are called ἱεροί because they concern city cults, and they are perhaps to be distinguished from secular laws, πολιτικοὶ νόμοι.

cajolery in a proportion which varied according to the location and strength of the city and the political constellation of the moment. Whatever the juridical position – whether the city concerned was an ally in reality or merely in name[33] – a king exerted as much pressure as he felt he could; and in the new cities in the Seleucid East independence can never have been more than a façade since they were normally under a royal governor (*epistates*) in command of a garrison. For all that, official communications were couched in courteous terms and usually elicited decrees praising the kings as bringers of peace, protectors and liberators. The other side of the coin can be seen in the generous gifts which the kings bestowed – corn in time of food shortage, the building of theatres, gymnasia, porticoes and walls (and the repairing of these when they began to crumble), the furnishing of ships' timber, the reduction of taxes, the financing of artistic competitions and the endowment of festivals and cults. The native temples too, being centres of power which had to be conciliated, received gifts and patronage. The attitude of the recipients towards these gifts was mixed. Usually greed or sheer necessity prevailed and a fulsome resolution was passed, praising the donor and saluting his generosity. But to a free city or a federal body outside a king's direct control such gifts could spell danger and even present a threat to political independence. When in 185 Eumenes II offered the Achaean League 120 talents, the interest on which was to be used to fund the paying of council members, the offer was harshly rejected as compromising the League's freedom – for, added one member, 'the interests of democracies and kings are naturally opposed, and most debates, and those the most important ones, deal with our differences with the kings' (Polyb. XXII.7.3; 7.8–8.8). The motives behind such offers were mixed. Certainly some were intended to win goodwill or an alliance; but there was often an element of genuine philanthropy alongside the desire to figure as a philhellene.[34] For cities inside a kingdom motives were somewhat different. There benefactions could only provide a partial compensation for the presence of a governor and garrison and the payment of tribute. A city might be 'liberated'; but often this meant simply that it had passed from the power of one king to another. For such cities acts of generosity might be no more than signs of temporary embarrassment or uncertainty on the king's part. 'Perhaps', writes Polybius (XV.24.4),

it may be said of all kings that at the beginning of their reign they talk of freedom as of a gift they offer to all and style all those who are their loyal adherents friends and allies, but as soon as they have established their authority, they at once begin to treat those who trusted them not as allies but as slaves.

---

[33] For the position under the Seleucids see below, ch. 6, pp. 204–9.
[34] Cf. Préaux 1978, 1.205–7: (A 48).

Singled out among the cities of a kingdom was its capital, where the king himself resided and maintained his court – Pella, Pergamum, Antioch, Alexandria. Here there could be no real independence (though, as we have just seen, the Attalids maintained the pretence of addressing letters to the governing body of Pergamum as though to an independent city). Invariably the capital was privileged, since to have it adorned with splendid amenities redounded to the glory of the dynasty. Alexandria stood in a class by itself, with fine buildings and research facilities of every kind. The two Libraries and the Museum, and the distinguished work carried out there by mathematicians, doctors and geographers as well as literary critics, are described later in this volume.[35] Alexandria also possessed an observatory, a zoo and an anatomical institute; but the royal botanical gardens, used for the acclimatization of fruit trees, were at Memphis.[36] There were also libraries in other capital cities – a public library at Antioch (where the poet Euphorion was librarian under Antiochus III), while the one at Pella was the private possession of the kings. The Pergamene library was second only to the great library in Alexandria, which it sought unsuccessfully to rival.[37]

These magnificent foundations helped to foster the image of the king as a patron of culture. The context was of course entirely Greek, for nothing of this had relevance to the indigenous populations which made up the greater part of the Ptolemaic and Seleucid kingdoms. The relationship between the king, committed to Graeco-Macedonian culture and a familiar style of life, and his native subjects with their own languages and religions posed the perpetual problem of establishing a tolerable compromise. In a fictional account of a banquet at the court of Ptolemy II, described by a Jewish writer, 'Aristeas', in his *Letter to Philocrates* (267), the king puts the question: 'How is one to accommodate oneself to all the different races in the kingdom?'; to which one of the Jewish sages who are being entertained replies: 'By adopting the appropriate attitude to each, making justice one's guide'. It is an answer that offers little detailed guidance in a complicated situation. Egypt, with its more or less homogeneous native population (if one forgets temporarily the Jewish diaspora in Alexandria) was a different and simpler problem than the mélange of races and cultures in the Seleucid dominions. But both houses were alike in stepping into the shoes of an earlier dynasty. Seleucus I could draw on the traditions of the Achaemenids (though he wisely opted to be called King of Babylonia in Mesopotamia) while in Egypt the Ptolemies were Pharaohs. In theory, as we have seen, all authority was centred in the king. But neither Ptolemy nor Seleucid could afford to neglect the native power structures

[35] See below, ch. 5, pp. 170–2.
[36] *P. Cairo Zen.* 59156; cf. Préaux 1978, 1.233: (A 48); and below, ch. 9c, Agriculture, p. 366.
[37] Préaux 1978, 1.235: (A 48).

inside their kingdoms. In Asia Minor and the far eastern provinces the Seleucids had to take account of minor rulers, chieftains and dynasts who acknowledged the king's over-riding sovereignty. But it was in particular the great temple complexes which played a special role in both kingdoms. It is now being recognized that, contrary to some earlier opinion, the Seleucids found it expedient to encourage and conserve the ancient temple states which were so central to the religion and economic life of Anatolia.[38] In Egypt the kings exerted some pressure on the priesthood in the early third century: its wealth was curtailed and restricted to what was required for the maintenance of the temples. But from the time of Ptolemy III there was a burst of temple-building which brought new strength and prestige to the priesthood. In the second century, under Ptolemy V, the Rosetta decree shows king and priests closely allied at a time of revolt, social misery and dynastic weakness.[39]

Temples and local dynasts, then, both give the lie to the official pretence that all power resided with the king. But above all it was by his control of the army that he reigned, and through its loyalty that he could maintain his rule. That loyalty he secured in various ways, as paymaster, as the original source of land on which many of the troops, both in Egypt and in the Seleucid realm, were settled, but not least through the *charisma* surrounding his person, which rendered him a formidable opponent to any rebel.

'When the armies advanced against each other', relates Polybius (v.54.1), describing the final engagement between the young Antiochus III and the rebel Molon, 'Molon's right wing remained faithful and vigorously engaged Zeuxis' force, but the left wing, as soon as they closed and came in sight of the king, went over to the enemy, upon which Molon's whole force lost heart' – and Molon quietly committed suicide. A factor in the creation of this belief in a divinely favoured personality with an overwhelming claim to men's loyalty may well have been the impression produced by the frequent repetition of such cult titles as 'Saviour' and 'Benefactor' which marked the king out from ordinary men (see below, pp. 93–4). In naval engagements too the king's person could be decisive. 'How many ships is my presence worth?', enquired Antigonus Gonatas, when told that the Ptolemaic fleet outnumbered his own.[40] Loyalty is a vital matter and depends very much on how the monarchy and the king himself are generally regarded. This then is perhaps a suitable point at which to turn our attention to the ideal concept of kingship prevalent during the Hellenistic age; for it is images of this kind that help to mould and sustain an institution.

---

[38] See below, ch. 6. pp. 196–8, for a list and discussion of these.
[39] See below, ch. 5, pp. 166–7.
[40] [Plut.] *Apophtheg.* 183 C; see below, ch. 7, p. 239 n. 40. The occasion is probably the battle of Cos.

IV. SOURCES FOR THE CONCEPT OF THE IDEAL KING

Though the Hellenistic monarchies emerged from the fragments of Alexander's kingdom, the ground had already been prepared ideologically by political and philosophical speculation on kingship during the earlier decades of the fourth century. Consequently, when the Greek world found itself facing a crop of kings, there was already a body of doctrine in existence ready to interpret, account for, justify and, it might be hoped, contain this disconcerting phenomenon. Discussion on monarchy and the qualities that make a king occur in many fourth-century writings. The publicist Isocrates wrote a laudatory biography of the late king Euagoras of Cyprus, and this served as a model for Xenophon's encomium on the Spartan king Agesilaus. The second half of that work listed the profusion of Agesilaus' virtues: he was god-fearing, just, generous, incorruptible, self-controlled in food, drink and sexual pleasures, courageous, patriotic and the enemy of barbarians. Both authors wrote other works portraying the qualities of the ideal king. Xenophon (*Oec.* 21.12) asserted that it was a divine accomplishment (*theion*) to rule over willing subjects. He wrote his *Cyropaedeia* nominally as a fictional biography, but in fact to survey the qualities that go to make up a good king and general, illustrated from the education of Cyrus the Great; and his *Hieron* discussed the difference between the tyrant and the true king in the form of a dialogue between Simonides and Hiero of Syracuse. In the long run, however, neither of these was perhaps so influential as two other works by Isocrates, the *Ad Nicoclem*, published shortly before Nicocles' accession in Cyprus in 374/3 and before the appearance of the encomiastic biography of his father, Euagoras, and the *Nicocles*, an exhortation to his leading citizens, placed in the mouth of Nicocles himself, in which he stresses his own qualities of justice, moderation and self-control – none of which in fact was possessed by the historical Nicocles! – and urges the superiority of kingship over both aristocracy and democracy, because of its permanence and stability. The many quotations from this work in later writers and in papyri are proof of its popularity in the Hellenistic age and later in Byzantine times and in the early Renaissance. Works such as these were designed partly to flatter the king, but also to influence him. An anecdote recorded in ps.-Plutarch (*Apophthegm.* 189D) relates how Demetrius of Phalerum urged Ptolemy to read books on kingship and the general's art, since he would there learn what his Friends did not dare to tell him.

In his *Nicocles* Isocrates touched on the problem of the ideal constitution, a constant preoccupation of philosophers, including both Plato and Aristotle. For Plato the best constitution was that giving power to philosopher-kings (*Rep.* 499B–C), but in the *Politicus* (294A) he

swung over to the view that a wisely conducted monarchy was superior
to a constitution based on the rule of law; and in the *Laws*
(IV.711E–712A) he argued that if you could find a man with a truly royal
character and a 'divine passion for self-control and justice', then the best
thing to do was to hand over the city to him.[41] It is only in the absence of
such a man that the city has to fall back on the rule of law. As for
Aristotle, despite the long discussion of monarchy in Book III of the
Politics (III.14.1, 1284b35ff.), it is not easy to discover how he finally
related monarchy to the best constitution. In a famous phrase (*Pol.*
III.13.13, 1284a9–10)[42] he declared that a man whose virtue and political
capacity put him beyond comparison with any of his fellows might truly
be called 'a god among men' and be a law to himself; but in the real
world of Greek cities he can find no place for such a man and concedes
that when one such arises 'the argument in favour of ostracism is based
upon a certain justice' (*Pol.* III.13.22, 1284b15). Throughout the fourth
century there was much speculation on this subject and Plato had even
undertaken an ill-starred expedition to the court of Dionysius, the tyrant
of Syracuse, in an attempt to put his theories into practice. In particular,
the relationship between the king and the laws was debated inconclus-
ively and at length. Clearly, then, monarchy had a strong appeal to
philosophers and thinkers at this time. There is however no evidence
that monarchic theory had as yet made much headway outside certain
intellectual circles. To the ordinary man monarchy was not an
institution suited to Greeks. 'The Greeks', Isocrates affirmed (*Philip*
107), 'are not accustomed to tolerate monarchies, whereas other peoples
cannot live their lives without a rule of that sort.' Moreover, as we have
seen, the political speculations of philosophers and publicists played no
part directly in the rise of the Hellenistic monarchies. What they did was
to furnish these monarchies with the trappings of a respectable ideology,
once they were established.

By then, however, the question was no longer one of deciding what
was the ideal form of state but rather of providing a philosophical
justification for what was there and had to be lived with. Treatises *On
Kingship* soon appeared in considerable numbers, many at the solicitation
of kings – especially, it appears, those of Macedonia[43] – but others no
doubt intended by a combination of exhortation and flattery to persuade
their recipients to allow their governments to develop along the right

---

[41] Such a man would be free to break the laws and to send men off, for instance, to found new
colonies, whether they wanted to go or not, and to enrol new citizens at will (*Polit.* 293C–E); cf.
Mossé 1962, 383–8: (I 46).
[42] Similar phrases are found earlier and appear to be used conventionally; cf. Ehrenberg 1938,
73–4: (I 23).
[43] Fraser 1972, 1.485: (A 15); see above, p. 65.

lines (as upper-class Greeks conceived them). Undoubtedly a vast Hellenistic literature on kingship once existed, though one may doubt whether many of the kings were seriously interested in framing a consistent and comprehensive philosophy of the king's role and function;[44] nor, apart from its known vogue in Macedonia, can we say with certainty whether any other courts encouraged this sort of speculation. Aelian (*VH* II.20) indeed records a story that Antigonus Gonatas, who encouraged the Stoics at his court in Pella, once told his son that their rule was 'a sort of glorious servitude'; but, even if it is true, as it could be, not too much importance should be attached to this remark, for it is hard to detect any practical application of Stoic precepts in the realities of Antigonus' government.

Among the earliest works *On Kingship* was one by Aristotle – in addition to his treatment of the subject in the *Politics*; and Theophrastus too wrote a treatise under that title, dedicating it to Cassander. Others are attributed to Demetrius of Phalerum and, among the Stoics with whom the subject was particularly popular, to Zeno, Cleanthes, Sphaerus and Persaeus; Persaeus (like Euphantus of Olynthus, a philosopher of the Megarian school) dedicated his work to Antigonus. There were also countless others, including one by Epicurus. What detailed arguments they put forward is unknown. A few fragments of Theophrastus' treatise have survived,[45] but the rest are merely titles.

Fortunately there are other works, written by or going back to Hellenistic authors, which have either survived complete or in part or can be reconstructed, from which it is possible to form some notion of the general philosophic framework within which Hellenistic kingship was presented. If, and it seems fairly certain, much of the first book of Diodorus' *History* derives from the historian and Sceptic philosopher Hecataeus of Abdera's *On the Egyptians* (*Aegyptiaca*),[46] it tells us something about a strange work written at the court of Ptolemy I, probably before the end of the fourth century, which drew on many sources, including Herodotus and the Egyptian priests. The last section (Diod. 1.69–95), which describes the customs of the Egyptians, contains an idealised picture of Ptolemy whom it shows as a king who, far from exercising unlimited rule, has his everyday routine prescribed down to the minutest detail by sacred law and custom. In this way he is obliged to act so as to confer benefits on his people and so win their gratitude, thus

---

[44] Adcock 1953, 177: (I 5).

[45] Cf. Theophr. fr. 125–7; Diog. Laert. v.42.49; Athen. IV.144e; *P. Oxy.* 1611.

[46] *FGrH* 264; cf. Murray 1970, 141–71: (I 49); Sinclair 1951, 284: (I 69); Fraser 1972, I.496–505: (A 15). The theory of Spoerri 1959; (I 72), followed by Burton 1972: (B 8), that Diodorus has drawn on a large variety of authors in Book I, which in consequence contains little from Hecataeus, is to be rejected.

conforming to a concept of kingship shared by both Greeks and
Egyptians. Basically, however, Hecataeus' picture is Greek and whatever in it began as Egyptian has been translated into Greek terms so as to
make it acceptable and comprehensible to his Greek public. Ptolemy as
the slave of Egyptian temple laws and taboos has little resemblance to
the realities of his kingship, and one can only speculate on how he
received this eccentric account of his functions.

The next relevant source is the *Letter to Philocrates*[47] by a writer who
calls himself Aristeas and purports to give a contemporaneous account
of the visit of seventy-two Jewish sages from Palestine, six from each
tribe, to the court of Ptolemy II in order to provide him with a Greek
translation of the Septuagint for the great Library. 'Aristeas' was a
hellenized Jew writing in Alexandria, but his date is uncertain. He lived
at least a century and a half after Philadelphus, but for a closer date the
evidence is indecisive; dates proposed vary between 160 and 100 B.C.,
with support also for various dates in between; a date around 160 is
perhaps the most likely.[48] The account of the translation of the scriptures
occupies only a small part of the work. A large section (180–294) is taken
up with a banquet given by Ptolemy upon Aristeas' arrival with the
scriptures from Jerusalem, at which the sages are subjected in turn to a
series of questions and reply with answers ending in each case with a
particularly Jewish nuance and a reference to God. Many of these
questions concern the nature and problems of kingship, and despite the
strong Jewish flavour throw a good deal of light on Hellenistic views on
kingship. Though it is going too far to say that the *Letter* incorporates a
work *On Kingship* as one of its sources,[49] nevertheless it is perhaps the
best surviving source on this topic.

Something can also be derived from the fragments, preserved in
Stobaeus, of three pseudo-Pythagorean treatises, written in Doric, on
kingship: their authors – whose names may be pseudonyms – are
Ecphantus, Diotogenes and Sthenidas, and their dates, like that of
Aristeas, are controversial. It is likely, however, that they wrote in the
second century A.D., though Ecphantus may well be as late as the third.[50]
The difficulty in using them for Hellenistic ideas is the great variety of
sources, many of them late, on which they draw. Diotogenes stresses the

[47] See Fraser 1972, I.696–703: (A 15) and for texts and editions *ibid.* II.972 n. 122; cf. Pelletier
1962: (I 58); Meecham 1935: (I 42).

[48] See, on the date, Fraser 1972, II.970–2 (160 B.C.): (A 15); Momigliano 1969, IV.213–24: (A 38),
and Murray 1967, 337–71: (I 48) (*c.* 100 B.C.).

[49] Murray 1967, 351–2: (I 48), criticizing Zuntz 1959, 21–36: (I 98).

[50] Stobaeus, *Ecl.* IV.6.22, 7.64 (Ecphantus); 7.61–2 (Diotogenes); 7.63 (Sthenidas). Goodenough
1928: (I 28), followed by Thesleff 1965; (I 81), dated them to the early Hellenistic period; but Delatte
1942: (I 20) has made a strong case for putting them in the second century A.D. (cf. Fraser 1972,
II.701–2 n. 55: (A 15)), and Ecphantus may belong to the third (Aalders 1975, 28 n.96: (I 3)).

resemblance of the king in his kingdom to god in the universe; he is god's representative on earth and the embodiment of the law. His triple function as supreme commander, dispenser of justice and overseer of divine cults corresponds to the Homeric division of powers as set out in Aristotle; [51] but in his enumeration of the duties of the king Diotogenes seems to be drawing on Stoic sources. The very short extract from Sthenidas follows a similar line, though his 'king who is a sage' seems to be a reversal of the Platonic or Stoic 'wise man who rules'. The paternal aspect of his king recalls Aristotle (*Eth. Nic.* VIII.12, 1160 b 26) but is also characteristic of Stoic thought. Ecphantus presents a special problem. He has an altogether more mystical concept of the universe and of the relationship of the king to god within it; the king mediates between god and man in a universe bound together in cosmic harmony.[52] Little of this is likely to be Hellenistic. The difficulty with all these three writers is to isolate ideas which are patently drawn from a wide range of sources spread out over several centuries. Nevertheless, where themes in their work can be traced back to Plato, Aristotle or other pre-Hellenistic sources, it is possible to make a cautious use of their texts.

All these three sources – Hecataeus, Aristeas and the pseudo-Pythagorean treatises – are alike in presenting a mixed picture. All contain some Hellenistic elements; but these are contaminated, in the first two by material derived from Egyptian or Jewish priestly sources and in the third by doctrines belonging to a later period. Fortunately, however, there is a further source which is not exposed to the same handicap and can be used as a control on the literary sources, and that is the evidence of contemporary inscriptions and papyri.[53] These documents fairly reflect the official view of royalty put out through the royal chancelleries or echoed in texts issued through the regular organs of the cities in circumstances which lead them to express the sort of sentiments the kings would want to hear. They can also be supplemented from symbols appearing on the coinage, for example the cornucopia placed on some Ptolemaic coins to indicate the care of the royal house for the prosperity of Egypt.[54] The composite picture which emerges is of course an idealised one, like that in the treatises. Both are in marked contrast to the historians, who not only give a down-to-earth account of the kings' political and military activities, but sometimes, as if in resentment at their power and domination over the cities, take their revenge by retailing anecdotes trivializing and denigrating their conduct.[55] Such

[51] Stob. *Ecl.* IV.7.61; cf. Arist. *Pol.* III.14.7. 1385 b 9.
[52] See Delatte 1942, 288–90: (I 20).
[53] Schubart 1937 (1), 1–26: (I 65); 1937 (2), 272–88: (I 66).
[54] See Plates vol., pls. 4b and 11.
[55] Jane Hornblower 1981, 235: (B 21).

stories, we must remember, also furnish valid evidence for current views about monarchy. A good example is the kind of anecdote which describes an encounter (usually fictitious) between a philosopher and a king – Cineas and Pyrrhus (Plut. *Pyrrh.* 14), Bion and Antigonus Gonatas (Diog. Laert. IV.44–7), Sphaerus and Ptolemy IV (Diog. Laert. VII.177)[56] – in which the philosopher scores over the ruler and in his implied criticism of absolute power acts as the spokesman of the city Greeks. Anecdotes have always been a safety-valve in times of political oppression.

From sources such as these,[57] despite their shortcomings, it is possible to assemble a picture of Hellenistic monarchy as the kings wished it to be envisaged and as, to some extent, it was envisaged. Though an ideal, up to a point it was able to influence reality and prevent some of the worst excesses characteristic of absolute power. It is the king's personal qualities which form the justification of his rule; and the absolutism of his rule itself provides the field within which those qualities find their fulfilment.[58]

The relation of the king to the law constitutes a special problem. If his power is unlimited, he creates the law: so is he also bound by it? In practice the king was expected to behave in a moderate and responsible manner. It is very rare for the theory that law was embodied in the king to be alleged in mitigation of outrageous conduct. We are told, it is true, that Anaxarchus brought up this argument to console Alexander after he had killed Black Cleitus; and the parallel with Zeus which Arrian puts into Anaxarchus' mouth was also used in implied justification of what Greeks believed to be the incestuous marriage of Ptolemy II to his sister Arsinoe.[59] It is Diotogenes who provides the clearest statement that the king is living law (*nomos empsychos*), though he does so with a qualification: the king, he says, is either the embodiment of law or one who governs in accordance with law.[60] This is reminiscent of a passage in Ps.-Archytas' treatise *On Law and Justice* (Stob. IV.1.135), where a distinction is made between animate law embodied in the king and

---

[56] Further examples in Préaux 1978, 1.226–7: (A 48).

[57] Others include Plutarch's *In principem indoctum*, which draws on standard earlier material; ps.-Plutarch, *Regum et imperatorum apophthegmata*; and from the east the *Milindapañha* (*Questions of Milinda*) – Milinda is the king Menander: on the last see Tarn 1951, 414–36: (I 79). At a more practical level the emergence of 'kingly' qualities (later to be institutionalized) can be traced in the narrative account of the relations built up between the successors of Alexander and their armies in the course of their campaigns; cf. Hornblower 1981, 210–11: (B 21).

[58] Cf. De Francisci 1948, II.493–4: (D 8).

[59] Arr. *Anab.* IV.9.7; Theoc. *Id.* XVII.132; Aalders 1969, 323 n. 28: (I 2).

[60] Diotogenes in Stob. *Ecl.* IV.7.61, ὁ δὲ βασιλεὺς ἤτοι νόμος ἔμψυχός ἐντι ἢ νόμιμος ἄρχων· διὰ ταῦτ' οὖν δικαιότατος καὶ νομιμώτατος. In this sense the phrase βασιλεὺς νόμος ἔμψυχος is first found in Philo, *de vita Mosis*, II.4. On the history of the phrase, from Eur. *Suppl.* 430f. onwards, see Delatte 1942, 245–9: (I 20); Aalders 1969: (I 2).

inanimate law embodied in the written code; but there the king does not enjoy absolute monarchy, since it is only through his observation of the law that his position as king is legitimated. Being the living mouthpiece of the law does not free him from the obligation to observe the law. Similarly in the *Cyropaedeia* (VIII.1.22) Xenophon describes the leader whose keen eye watches for transgressions of the law and punishes them as 'the seeing law' (*blepon nomos*) without any suggestion that he is thereby freed from observing the law himself. There is reason to think that the same limitation is implied in Diotogenes.[61] Whether that is so or not, and if it is so, whether the formulation goes back to the Hellenistic period, must remain uncertain. In any case, it does not, of course, make any difference to the fact that in reality the Hellenistic kings were free to legislate as they wished.

V. THE HELLENISTIC PICTURE OF THE KING

Having briefly examined the nature of the available sources, we are now in a position to consider the idealized picture of the Hellenistic monarch which emerges, with some consistency, from these. First and above all, as we have already seen, the king is portrayed as victorious. It was usually following on a victory that Alexander's successors had assumed their royal titles. Curiously this emphasis on victory does not lead kings to exult in the destruction of their opponents. It would be misleading to attribute to the Hellenistic courts a political concept of a 'balance of power' as it is understood in modern times. But such a balance certainly existed in practice. Wars were fought to achieve limited ends like the acquisition of territory, not to wipe out the enemy; for that the Hellenistic world had to await the arrival of Rome. It is also anomalous, given this emphasis on victory as the hall-mark of kingship and the trumpeting of it as a virtue in such titles as Nicator, Ceraunus, Nicephorus and the like, that the available sources have so little to say about the duties and qualities which are specifically related to a king's performance in waging war. This is certainly a strange omission, in as much as the king's position depended on his having won it in conflict or being prepared to defend it in conflict. But it is perhaps part of the same attitude of mind that Hellenistic kings do not boast of the number of the enemy they have slaughtered in the way familiar from Egyptian and Assyrian temple reliefs, Sassanian rock-carvings and the records of Roman triumphs. This is, of course, true only in the Graeco-Macedonian context. As Pharaohs, the Ptolemies were represented on the Egyptian temple walls in the traditional role and poses of their predecessors.

[61] So Delatte 1942, 248: (1 20).

Because he is victorious the king can protect his people and be their saviour and benefactor amid the dangers that threaten them. 'Saviour' (*soter*) and 'Benefactor' (*euergetes*) are well-known cult titles, mainly of the Ptolemies, but both are found used of Antiochus the Great,[62] though he never adopted them officially; and one of the Jewish wise men in the *Letter to Philocrates* (240) defines the king's duty as 'preserving the lives of men'. It is in this context and employing a metaphor obvious in Mediterranean lands and familiar since early times in Greece – it need not, therefore, be borrowed from ancient Egypt, Sumeria or Mesopotamia – that the king is called the shepherd of his people.[63] For this role the king must be brave. His courage (*andragathia*) is mentioned in several decrees, where it is combined with other royal virtues.[64] The king often fought in person; and if hunting was a popular sport among Hellenistic kings, that was at least in part because it was a sound training for battle.[65] When the Friends of Ptolemy V praised his prowess on the hunting field (Polyb. XXII.3.5–9), they were singling out his achievements in a pursuit traditionally esteemed both in Pharaonic Egypt and in the Hellenistic world.

Not unnaturally, it was towards supposedly defensive ends that the king's bravery was directed. He was the champion of civilization against barbarism, a theme illustrated notably on the Pergamene Altar of Zeus, with its reliefs depicting the battles of the gods against the giants and symbolizing the wars fought by the Attalids against the Galatians (Plates vol., pl. 61). The role of the Antigonids as protectors of the northern frontiers of Greece was also frequently underlined by their propagandists, and it was alluded to on a significant occasion by the Roman general Flamininus.[66] Similarly, but with a slight whiff of blackmail, Euthydemus emphasized his services in repelling the nomads of the steppes in order to extract an agreement with Antiochus III (Polyb. XI.34.5). Kings were also applauded as the guardians or restorers of peace. This aspect of kingship is frequently mentioned in Egypt, where Ptolemy III is praised, in the Canopus decree of 238 (*OGIS* 56 (=Austin 222), ll.12–13), for having 'maintained the country at peace by fighting in its defence against many nations and their rulers', and in the decree passed at Memphis in 196 Ptolemy V is similarly praised for his defeat of the rebels at Lycopolis (*OGIS* 96, ll.19–28). These examples are taken from decrees of the synod of the Egyptian priests and show that we are here dealing with a motif that goes back to Pharaonic Egypt. But the last question put by Ptolemy II to the Jewish sages in the *Letter* of Aristeas

---

[62] *OGIS* 239: cf. also *P. Ent.* 78.   [63] Cf. Aalders 1975, 24–5: (I 3).

[64] E.g. *OGIS* 219 (=Austin 139), l.34 (Antiochus I); 332, ll.22–3 (Attalus III), ἀρετῆ[s] ἕνεκεν καὶ ἀνδραγαθίας τῆς κατὰ πόλεμον, κρατήσαντα τῶν ὑπεναντίων.

[65] Cf. Polyb. XXXI.29.3–5 with Walbank 1979, III.512–13: (B 37).

[66] Cf. Polyb. IX.35.2; XVIII.37.9; Livy XXXIII.12.10.

(291–2) was: 'What is the greatest thing in royalty?' and the reply: 'It is that the subjects may always enjoy peace and obtain justice promptly in the courts.' Here peace is linked with justice to provide the two greatest boons the king can confer upon his subjects. Justice is of course the classic virtue. It was in the search for justice that Plato built his ideal republic and it is justice that Theophrastus has in mind when, in his work *On Kingship*, he affirms that the true king rules with the aid of the sceptre, not of the sword (*P. Oxy.* 1611, ll.42–6). Justice depends on the kings' obedience to the laws, 'so that by practising justice they may improve the lives of their peoples'; so Aristeas (279), and the same emphasis on the administration of justice is to be found in Diotogenes (Stob. IV.7.61). That it was widely felt to be an essential quality of the king can be seen from the many appeals made by the Egyptian peasants to the king for help against the excesses of his own bureaucracy.

Justice and wise administration demanded different qualities from those needed to defend the land from its enemies, to keep the peace and to create harmony (*homonoia*). In his dealings with his people the king must be generous (*philanthropos*) and magnanimous (*megalopsyches*). Generosity (or humanity) – that is the meaning of *philanthropia* – was not a quality expected of a ruler in classical times; but it is one of the commonest words in the vocabulary of the Hellenistic inscriptions, applicable to the king's subjects as well as to himself. Aristeas (265) reckons the *philanthropia* and the *agapesis* (affection) of his subjects as the supreme acquisition that a king can possess.[67] The word *philanthropia* was indeed so commonly used at this time that in Egypt it came to have the specific meaning of an amnesty. Magnanimity (*megalopsychia*) is also an essential royal quality. Seleucus II, for instance, shows magnanimity and gratitude towards his benefactors (*OGIS* 229, ll.6–7). But there are other virtues that a king must display. He must be pious (*eusebes*) towards the gods and affectionate (*philostorgos*) towards his subjects.[68] He must be wise (*sophos*), possess intelligence (*phronesis*) and show self-control (*enkrateia*) – 'the greatest empire of all', says Aristeas, and in a king that means, paradoxically, not to go out for new territories and glory (221–2).[69] He must be reasonable (*epieikes*), which implies a certain gentleness even in reproving those who are at fault (Aristeas, *Letter* 207); and he must avoid all excess, sloth and hedonistic behaviour, be a lover of truth and accessible to his subjects. He must throw his weight on the side of what is good, in short he must be a man of the highest moral stature.[70]

[67] See also Aristeas, *Letter* 208, on how a king can render himself humane by cultivating a sense of pity.
[68] E.g. *RC* 35, l.12.
[69] *OGIS* 332: Attalus III's virtue (*arete*), understanding (*phronesis*) and munificence (*megalomereia*) are to be recorded beneath his statue.   [70] Murray 1967, 357–8: (I 48).

Naturally kings were wealthy. And in the ideal picture it was their duty to possess wealth – provided they avoided greed. 'The king should possess riches', says Diotogenes (Stob. *Ecl.* IV.7.62), 'but only to the extent that they are essential to benefit his friends, relieve the needy and defend himself justly against his enemies.' The proper use of wealth is important: Polybius (V.88–90) has some harsh words for contemporary kings who are miserly with their wealth, and Aristeas (205) makes a Jewish sage urge on Ptolemy II the need not to waste wealth on futile display, but to use it generously to win the affection of his subjects – thus following the example of God himself. But in fact, no matter what Aristeas might advise, lavish consumption for display was charac- teristic of the great monarchies, and our sources dwell on the grand procession through the streets of Alexandria organized in honour of his parents by Ptolemy II and Antiochus IV's triumphal celebrations at Daphne near Antioch.[71] Like the rich palaces in which they lived and held their courts,[72] these served the purpose of advertising their wealth, which was a symbol of greatness and a means of exercising power and influence. Wealth and display both thus contributed to the royal image, and this in turn helped to sustain the monarchic governments throughout the Hellenistic world.

VI. MONARCHY AND RELIGION

Hellenistic monarchy was closely associated with religion and the gods. This is hardly surprising, for the primitive kingship of the Homeric stamp, which lay not too far behind Macedonian monarchy, possessed priestly duties, and in addition the kings who had until recently reigned in the lands which now constituted the territory of Hellenistic kingdoms had been closely involved in their own national religions. During the period we are considering religion and monarchy interact in several ways to add solemnity and authority to the king's office. Broadly speaking, we can identify four main channels along which religion affects the role of the king. First, the royal dynasty and its members frequently stand under the protection of particular gods or goddesses, whom they identify as the protectors of their house; secondly, kings are sometimes assimilated to certain gods or even in some cases identified with them; thirdly, special cults for kings (and queens) are set up by cities within or without the kingdom – a complex institution with many aspects; lastly, there is dynastic cult in the full sense, that is officially established worship of the dead and sometimes of the living members of

---

[71] Athen. v203c; Polyb. xxx.25.1–26.9.
[72] Cf. Bikerman 1938, 33: (E 6) on Seleucid palaces. For the development of the palaces and other buildings on the acropolis at Pergamum see Hansen 1971, 234–84: (E 122).

the royal house. These are four separate cult practices, but they cannot be treated wholly in isolation from each other. In particular, it is difficult to draw a clear line between the worship of patron gods, who are often ancestors of the dynasty, and that of gods of the ordinary pantheon who appear to be identified with members of the ruling house; or between the special cults of the ruler set up by individual cities and the official dynastic cult, for often an epithet used in the one turns up as a cult-title in the other. One might be tempted to try to distinguish cults which arose spontaneously from cults imposed as an act of official policy. But this would be of doubtful value, for it is rarely possible to ascertain whether a cult really arose spontaneously or not. And it is even more difficult to find out what ruler-cult truly signified, in religious as well as political terms, to those practising it.

With those cautionary remarks we may now turn our attention to the role of patron deities in relation to the dynasties over which they were placed. Since in one sense all the new monarchies began as usurpations, it was natural for them to try to legitimate their pretentions by adopting some special divine protector chosen from among the still venerated Olympian gods and goddesses; and it strengthened the king's position further if it could be conveniently and authoritatively revealed that he was in fact directly descended, like a Homeric hero, from some deity or other. In support of the legitimacy of their rule the Antigonids stressed their (probably fanciful) relationship with the Argeads (Polyb. v.10.10). They thereby acquired Heracles as an ancestor, and Heracles' club appears as an emblem on their coinage. Antigonus Gonatas issued a series of tetradrachms showing the head of Pan, perhaps in recognition of Pan's help at the decisive battle of Lysimacheia.[73] The Seleucids took for their special patron Apollo of Miletus, for he had prophesied Seleucus' royal destiny.[74] Apollo was also given out to be the ancestor of the dynasty (*OGIS* 219 (= Austin 139), ll.27–8), and manifest proof of this was the fact that his symbol, an anchor, was to be found as a birthmark on Seleucus' thigh (Justin. xv.4.2). The Attalids similarly claimed the protection of Dionysus Cathegemon.[75] These special relationships did not, of course, deter the various royal houses from the worship of other gods and goddesses as well and from founding cults and temples to them.

Divine patronage and divine ancestry were closely connected with the custom of assimilating kings to particular gods. This practice, like ruler-

[73] Plates vol., pl. 70e. One specimen shows Pan with the features of Antigonus Gonatas; see the frontispiece to Tarn 1913: (D 38). Against the view that there was an epiphany of Pan at the battle of Lysimacheia, see however Pritchett 1979, III.32–4: (J 151).

[74] Diod. XIX.90.4; cf. *RC* 22, ll. 4–5.

[75] Hansen 1971, 451–3: (E 122).

cult, is ignored in the treatises on monarchy.[76] It appears to have been especially prevalent in Egypt, where J. Tondriau has listed some twenty assured and fifteen possible examples, identifying various Ptolemies with Dionysus, Apollo-Helios, Eros, Heracles, Hermes, Poseidon and Zeus.[77] Of these the most important is Dionysus, who was closely associated with the dynasty, perhaps even from the time of Ptolemy I. An inscription copied at Adulis in the sixth century A.D. describes Ptolemy III as sprung from Heracles on his father's side and Dionysus on his mother's side (OGIS 54 = Austin 221); and two later members of the dynasty, Ptolemy IV Philopator and Ptolemy XII Auletes, were equated with Dionysus; so too was the Roman M. Antonius at the very end of the Ptolemaic period.[78] Of these Ptolemy XII incorporated the title 'the god New Dionysus' (theos Neos Dionysos) to form part of an elaborate official nomenclature (OGIS 186, 191) – and he stands alone in doing so, for no other Hellenistic king is known to have included a title identifying him with a god in his official style. The real significance of such a title is not easy to discover. Nock has suggested[79] that Ptolemy XII may have been influenced by the Pharaonic concept of his reincarnation of Osiris; but Antony's assimilation to Dionysus-Osiris, like that of Cleopatra to Isis-Aphrodite (already anticipated on her coinage at the time of Caesarion's birth) is more likely to have been a political gesture – though in her case the religious feeling behind it was probably genuine. There were precedents in the assimilation of both Arsinoe II and Berenice to Aphrodite.[80]

Identification with a god takes place, though less frequently, in other dynasties. From the Seleucid kingdom, for example, we hear of priests of Antiochus (I) Apollo Soter and of Seleucus (I) Zeus Nicator at Seleuceia-in-Pieria (OGIS 245 = Austin 177). And one should probably interpret in the same way coin types which point to the identification of a ruler with some god, for instance Zeus's head with the features of Alexander Balas on a contemporary Seleucid coin,[81] or the Macedonian tetradrachm in which Pan's head has the features of Antigonus Gonatas.[82]

---

[76] Cf. Aalders 1975, 26: (I 3).

[77] Tondriau 1948(2), 127–46: (I 84); 1950(I), 404–5: (I 86); 1953, 441–56: (I 88).

[78] Tondriau 1946, 149–67: (I 82); 1950(2), 293–312: (I 87). Cerfaux and Tondriau 1957, 207: (I 18).

[79] Nock 1972, I.147: (I 54).

[80] Nock 1972, I.217–18: (I 55). Whether a phrase such as 'Aphrodite Berenice' implies identification or merely a sharing of the temple between two 'deities' remains uncertain. See below, p. 87, on temple-sharing.   [81] Cf. Bikerman 1938, 217: (E 6).

[82] See above, n. 73. This coin forms one of a series in which Pan usually has his normal features. There is a parallel in Coan coins representing Heracles with the features of Mausolus, which form part of a series in which the god usually has his own features. (B. V. Head, Catalogue of the Greek Coins [in the British Museum] of Caria, Cos, Rhodes, etc. (London, 1897) Pl. xxx.6–8). Nock 1972, I.146: (I 54), quotes other examples of this phenomenon and suggests that it should be regarded as a kind of visual comparison rather than an identification. The same will hold good for Pan as Gonatas.

VII. RULER-CULT

More varied in both its form and its implications is the religious practice commonly known as ruler-cult. Ruler-cult is a form of worship offered to a king, though this is a simplified description of a complex institution, which shares some affinity with the practice of assimilating a king to a particular god, which we have just been considering. The impetus to ruler-cult comes primarily from the worshippers, not from the ruler himself. It is characteristic of the Hellenistic age, when cities stand in constant need of protection and are, perhaps, less confident than they had been that the traditional gods can provide this: but it has a background in the fourth century. To anyone brought up in the tradition of Christianity there appears to be an insuperable distinction between honouring a king as a superior person and worshipping a god. To the Greek, however, these two extremes are bridged by a number of fine gradations of attitude and behaviour; and our sources either through uncertainty or in some cases with deliberate ambiguity do not always make these differences clear.

An example of one such overlap arises in connexion with the custom, common in Egypt but also found elsewhere, of introducing a king or queen into a temple of one or other of the traditional deities, so that he or she may receive worship as a 'temple-sharing god' (*synnaos theos*).[83] This practice was anticipated in a literal sense by Demetrius Poliorcetes' actual residence in the Parthenon at Athens, and apparently in the temple of Apollo at Delos,[84] but the first clear example of sharing temple-honours is that of Arsinoe II, who was included posthumously in the cult of the Egyptian god in each locality. From then on temple-sharing is a regular practice in Ptolemaic Egypt, where it had Pharaonic precedents;[85] and there is an example from Pergamum, where a cult of Attalus III was established in the temple of Asclepius at Elaea during his lifetime and sacrifices instituted on the altars of Zeus Soter, Zeus Boulaios and Hestia Boulaia (*OGIS* 332).[86] Here a typical ambiguity arises, since the relevant text does not make clear (and was perhaps not intended to make clear) whether the sacrifice was 'to' or 'for' the king. Furthermore, it makes an important difference in temple-sharing whether the ruler is granted a cult-statue (*agalma*) for worship, or simply an image (*eikon*) not intended for cult. Attalus III specifically receives an

[83] Cf. Nock 1972, 1.202–51: (I 55). This practice has obvious affinities with the assimilation of kings and queens to gods and goddesses discussed above, pp. 85–6.

[84] Cf. Nock 1972, 1.204: (I 55); Plut. *Dem.* 10.12; *IG* XI.2.146, l.76, ὅτε ὁ βασιλεὺς ἐξέπλευσεν, τὸν κόπρον ἐξενέγκασιν ἐκ τοῦ ἱεροῦ μισθωτοῖς ΔΔΗΗ.

[85] For a list of recorded examples from the Ptolemaic period, see Nock *ibid.* 235.

[86] Cf. Nock 1972, 1.219: (I 55); Robert 1937, 17: (B 139).

agalma, but he was also given an equestrian statue in gold (*eikon chryse ephippos*) on a column in the most prominent spot in the market-place alongside the altar of Zeus Soter. The same two honours – an *agalma* and an *eikon* – are voted by the actors' guild for Ariarathes V of Cappadocia (*OGIS* 352). Later, however, the distinction between the two words, *agalma* and *eikon*, is not always maintained. Thus an image of Ptolemy V designed to receive cult is referred to in the Rosetta inscription (*OGIS* 90 (=Austin 227), l.38) as an *eikon*, nor is this an isolated example.[87] Once established in the temple of the god (or goddess) it was only a short step for a king or queen to be identified with the main incumbent. One cannot always tell whether or no that step has been taken.

Though it impinges on the institution of 'temple-sharing', ruler-cult has a different origin. It appears to arise more or less spontaneously. In the earlier period it is merely a recognition that such and such a king is in fact a god, and should in consequence receive worship;[88] the setting up of a cult does not *create* a god any more than canonization within the Roman Catholic Church creates a saint. Ruler-cult also has part of its background in hero-cult, for heroes, like kings, were often men of divine descent who had bestowed benefits on mankind. Founders of cities were also regularly worshipped as heroes and virtually all Hellenistic kings could claim to have done this. Heroization no longer had the rather local associations of earlier hero-cults. At Athens, for instance, altars and heroic shrines (*heroa*), attended by libations and hymns, were voted for Adeimantus, Oxythemis and Burichus, three of Demetrius Poliorcetes' followers, in 302/1; they are now known to have been men of considerable importance, not, as Demochares represented them, mere toadies and parasites.[89] Their heroization was a counterpart to the deification voted a little earlier for Demetrius, and underlines the similarity between the two grades of honour. Nevertheless ruler-cult is not derived from hero-cult.

Another point relevant to the development of ruler-cult has already been touched on. As we have seen (p. 76), there were several commonly used expressions which undoubtedly illustrate the fragility of the boundaries which Greeks of the classical period set up between men and gods. It was not unusual to say of some outstanding person that he was, or soon would be, or ought to be, regarded as a god among men. Isocrates (IX.72) regards the phrase as a poetic exaggeration, like calling a man a 'mortal divinity' (*daimon thnetos*). But it was clearly something a little more serious than that to some people. Aristotle, for instance, said that if you could find such a man you ought to offer him complete

---

[87] Cf. Nock 1972, 1.346 n. 8: (1 55).
[88] Later this distinction was obscured: cf. Badian 1981, 29–30: (1 10).
[89] *FGrH* 75 F 1; see Robert, *Hellenica* II (1946) 65ff.; Habicht 1970, 55–8: (1 29).

obedience. Plato (*Rep.* VI.500C–D) had asserted that the philosopher-king 'by conversing with what is beautiful and divine himself becomes beautiful and divine', though he qualifies the statement with the words 'as far as is possible for a mortal'. Neither Plato nor Aristotle is seriously suggesting by this kind of language that the philosopher-king or the outstanding person is in any real sense a god. Nor, when Isocrates wrote to Philip II of Macedon to say that, if he followed up the victory of Chaeronea by subjugating the barbarians and the Great King, 'nothing will be left for you but to become a god' (*Epist.* 3.5), is this to be read as a literal statement of fact. These are metaphors, but their common use contributes to the breaking down of what we should regard as clearly defined categories. It was by a similar half-metaphorical use of language that a Greek (and later a Roman) might remark that someone of outstanding quality was divine (*theos*), a god or 'a god to me'; one might even say which god he was.[90] But this too is not to be regarded as literally identifying the person thus singled out with a god, though it may have implied that for the moment the speaker *thought of him* as a god.

There was, it is fair to note, another strand of Greek thought which firmly rejected any idea of such an overlap between gods and men – as, for example, when Pindar (*Nem.* 6.1ff.) says that 'one is the race of men, one the race of gods . . . yet a power that is wholly sundered parts us, in that the one is nothing while for the other brazen heaven endures as an abode unshaken for evermore'. It was this point of view that was expressed in Callisthenes' speech opposing the proposal to accord Alexander obeisance (Arr. *Anab.* IV.11.2–9).

It has been argued that this traditional attitude which firmly divided men from gods was already weakening in the early decades of the fourth century, with the granting of divine honours to various generals and kings even before the reign of Alexander. The first and perhaps the most convincing instance of this is that of Lysander, the Spartan commander who, Duris of Samos reports (*FGrH* 76 F 26 and 71), was the first Greek to whom the cities erected altars as to a god. This was done by the Athenian oligarchs in Samos; and though the fragments of Duris do not say that it took place in Lysander's lifetime, Plutarch, who had read Duris' full text, clearly believed that it had. Furthermore, Plutarch's statement that the Samians renamed the festival of the *Heraea*, calling it the *Lysandreia*, seems to be confirmed epigraphically.[91] The evidence for this incident seems therefore to be quite strong; but there is a long time to wait before it has a sequel. The libations and prayers offered in 357 to

[90] Cf. Nock 1972, I.145: (I 54), quoting [Eur.] *Rhesus* 355: οὔ μοι Ζεὺς ὁ φαναῖος; Delatte 1942, 130 n. 2: (I 20), for bibliography.

[91] *Arch. Anz.* 1965, 440; Habicht 1970, 243: (I 29); Badian 1981, 37–8: (I 10), queries the date of the institution of the *Lysandreia*.

Dion in Syracuse 'as to a god' (Plut. *Dem.* 29.1) were far from being the equivalent of formal deification; Diodorus (XVI.20.6) is evidence only for the award of heroic honours.[92] The only other examples of deifying men around this time come from Macedonia, where some rather late evidence attests a cult of Amyntas III at Pydna during his lifetime and one of Philip II, also during his lifetime, at Amphipolis; in addition an inscription from Eresus (*OGIS* 8a) mentions altars of Zeus Philippius, but this may be merely a cult to Zeus the protector of Philip. There is also evidence for a cult to Philip at Philippi,[93] though this would probably be as founder. Finally, on the day of his death at Aegae Philip arranged for his statue to be carried along with those of the Twelve Gods (Diod. XVI.95.1) – a striking spectacle, but one inviting homage rather than worship.[94] All in all, this evidence does not add up to a great trend towards the deification of human beings during the period before Alexander. It cannot all be dismissed, but clearly we are concerned with something on a small scale, of only occasional occurrence – and that mostly in Macedonia rather than Greece. The change came with Alexander.

During Alexander's lifetime many cults in his honour were es-tablished in the Greek cities of Asia Minor.[95] Their date is uncertain. It has been generally assumed that they were set up following liberation from the Persian yoke in 334/3, but a later date is possible. Callisthenes' speech against the proposal to accord obeisance to Alexander in Bactria in 327 (Arr. *Anab.* IV.11.2–9) contains no indication that he was already being widely worshipped in the Greek world; so perhaps the cults belong to Alexander's last years, in which case they may link with his request for divine honours from the Greeks of Europe in 324/3.[96] On the reception of that request we are not well informed; but it was apparently acceded to at Athens, where at the same time heroic cult was set up for his dead friend Hephaestion. Later the statesman Demades was to be fined ten talents for his part in the matter.[97] At Sparta an anecdote (Plut. *Mor.* 219E) reports that Damis proposed that 'if Alexander wishes to be a god, let him be a god'. Other cities evidently followed suit, for the envoys sent from the Greek cities to Alexander at Babylon in spring 323

[92] Habicht 1970, 10: (I 29); cf. Badian 1981, 42: (I 10). On heroization, see Hornblower, 1982, 254ff.: (E 73).

[93] I am grateful to Dr Pierre Ducrey and Dr M. B. Hatzopoulos for the text of an unpublished inscription from Philippi, presented to the Eighth International Epigraphical Congress (Athens, 1982), which attests the existence of two sacred precincts to Philip in that city; see also Habicht 1970, 26: (I 29).

[94] Cf. Griffith in Hammond and Griffith 1979, II.682–3, 692–5: (D 29).

[95] For a list of the cults see Habicht 1970, 17–28, 245–6, 251–2: (I 29); they come from the Ionian League, Priene, Ephesus, Erythrae, Bargylia, Magnesia-on-the-Maeander and Ilium, and from the islands of Rhodes and Thasos. Badian 1981, 60–3: (I 10), dates them after 327.

[96] Habicht 1970, 28–36, 246–52: (I 29); Préaux 1978, I.241: (A 48); Badian 1981, 54: (I 10).

[97] Aelian, *VH* II.19; Hypereides, *Epit.* 6.21; Athen. VI.251b.

came 'wreathed in the manner of sacred envoys to honour some god' (Arr. *Anab.* VII.23.2).[98]

The Alexander-cults in Greece proper will scarcely have outlasted his death.[99] But the precedent had been established and within the next few decades cults were being set up all over the Greek world in honour of the new rulers. These were primarily an expression of gratitude by those setting them up, resembling in this the cults to Alexander in Asia Minor. The first we know of comes before the spate of royal titles, for it was in 311 that Scepsis voted a cult image (*agalma*) and divine honours to Antigonus Monophthalmus. But the inscription recording this (*OGIS* 6 = Austin 32) reveals the existence of an earlier festival for Antigonus, which probably also involved divine honours. Those of 311 were decreed in gratitude for the recent peace made with Cassander, Lysimachus and Ptolemy and the guarantee of freedom for the Greek cities which Antigonus had extracted from them. It seems certain that Scepsis will not have been alone in paying these honours, and that many cities passed similar decrees for Antigonus at this time. A little later, in 307, we find Antigonus and his son Demetrius being worshipped as Saviours (*Soteres*) at Athens, following Demetrius' liberation of the city; new tribes were named after the two generals and the cult of the *Soteres* must link with their role as tribal eponyms.[100] In 304 Demetrius received another cult as 'the god who steps down' (*theos Kataibates*), an epithet commemorating the occasion and place where he descended from his horse or carriage when he returned to liberate Athens from Cassander.[101] Ten years later, after an interval under the tyrant Lachares, Athens once again came into Demetrius' hands and once more the liberation and restoration of democracy – and an unexpected gift of wheat – were celebrated with cult. It was a little later, in 290, that the famous hymn was sung, which inspired Athenaeus' comments on the servility of the former victors of Marathon: the text was recorded by Duris of Samos (*FGrH* 78 F 13 = Athen. VI.253e = Austin 35) and an extract reads:

O son of the most mighty god Poseidon and of Aphrodite, hail! For other gods are either far away or have not ears, or do not exist, or heed us not at all; but thee we can see in very presence, not in word and not in stone, but in truth. And so we pray to thee.

---

[98] The Greek is ὡς θεωροὶ δῆθεν and Fredericksmeyer 1979 [1980], 3–5: (1 25), has shown that this phrase indicates 'what was then considered as real or true, but was subsequently shown to be *not* real or true'. Badian 1981, 56–8: (1 10), argues less cogently that it means 'what might then have been considered as real or true but was in fact not true'. If they were really nothing but ambassadors, it is not clear why they came garlanded at all.

[99] For a short-lived attempt by Eumenes of Cardia to institute a posthumous cult of Alexander in the army see Diod. XVIII.60.4–61.1; Launey 1949–50, II.945–6: (J 143).

[100] Habicht 1970, 44–8: (1 29); cf. Woodhead 1981, 357–67: (1 96).

[101] Habicht 1970, 48–50: (1 29).

This hymn constitutes one of the most striking testimonies to the attitudes which led to ruler-worship in a time of need and uncertainty. It also confirms that such cult was not, at any rate in the third century, part of the mere routine of royal flattery. The absence of such cults can also have its significance. The fact that so far there is no firm evidence of any cult for Antigonus Gonatas in Greece must surely link with his reputation there, not as a liberator, but as the sponsor of tyrants.[102]

The granting of such honours to the early Antigonids before Gonatas can be paralleled in other dynasties. In 304, after Demetrius' failure in the famous siege of Rhodes, that city established a cult for its patron Ptolemy I under the title of Saviour; and this was later supplemented by the worship of Ptolemy and Berenice.[103] The Island League also celebrated Demetrius' expulsion from the Aegean with a cult for Ptolemy I set up on Delos in 287/6 (*SIG* 390 = Austin 218); a decade earlier, in 306, the same League had chosen the same island to establish a festival for Demetrius himself (*IG* XI.1036). The islanders also set up a cult for Ptolemy II during his lifetime, but the context is not known.[104]

The only cult known for Cassander was as the founder of Cassandreia (*SIG* 332), but there were cults of Lysimachus at Priene, Samothrace and Cassandreia, all set up in the 280s.[105] Ilium honoured Seleucus I in his lifetime, probably in gratitude for its liberation from Lysimachus,[106] and Seleucus was also worshipped in Erythrae, Colophon and Magnesia-on-the-Maeander.[107] The Attalids were receiving divine honours even before Attalus took the title of king after his Galatian victory in 241; there is some evidence of cult honours being paid to both the founder of the state, Philetaerus, and his successor Eumenes.[108]

These are only a selection of the ruler-cults established during the generation following Alexander. The practice grew in subsequent decades and centuries, and continued under the Roman Empire. Ruler-cult is to be found in all parts of the Greek world and it included a variety of forms, largely derived from the cult practices accorded to the gods. At the heart of the cult was a sacrifice, normally of an animal but sometimes including incense and libations, and performed on a definite day, either four-yearly, annually or monthly. The cult might be associated with a

---

[102] It is unlikely that *IG* XII Suppl. 168 is to be attributed to Gonatas.

[103] Diod. xx.100.7–8; Paus. 1.8.6; M. Segre, *BSAAlex.* 34 (1941) 29ff. = *Bull. épig.* 1949, 120; Habicht 1970, 26 and 109–10: (I 29). The royal pair are probably Ptolemy III and Berenice II.

[104] Durrbach, *Choix*, no. 21.

[105] Priene: *OGIS* 11; cf. Robert 1937, 183–4: (B 139) (probably 286/5). Samothrace: *SIG* 372 (between 288 and 281). Cassandreia: *SIG* 380 (between 287 and 281). Cf. Habicht 1970, 38–9: (I 29); Préaux 1978, 1.249: (A 48).

[106] *OGIS* 212; cf. Robert 1937, 172ff.: (B 139).

[107] Habicht 1970, 85–8, 91: (I 29). For a list of cults to Seleucid monarchs see Bikerman 1938, 243–6: (E 6).

[108] For the cults of Pergamum see Hansen 1971, 453–70: (E 122).

temple, a precinct or an altar; its ceremonial was performed either by a specially appointed priest or by the priests of some other divinity. Usually it was linked to a festival, named after the recipient, such as the *Ptolemaieia* at Alexandria, or the *Antigoneia* and *Demetrieia* of the Island League on Delos. It might be connected with the festival of some god, frequently Dionysus – in this way combining the maximum of publicity with some degree of economy – or it could take place independently on the monarch's birthday or on the anniversary of its inception. The festival usually included contests, which could be musical, literary or gymnastic (with athletic competitions) or a combination of these; and there was also likely to be a procession, accompanied by the singing of a paean. Sometimes too the voting of a cult was celebrated with the institution of a new dating era or by the naming of a month after the honorand; we hear of months called *Seleuceius* at Ilium, *Antiocheon* at Laodicea-on-the-Lycus, *Demetrion* at Histiaea and Athens and *Anti-ocheon*, *Laodikeon* and *Stratonikeon* at Smyrna. Similarly tribes were named after kings who received cult, for instance *Antigonis* and *Demetrias* (and later *Ptolemais* and *Attalis*) at Athens, or *Seleucis* in Colophon, Magnesia-on-the-Maeander and Nysa. The kings or queens who received the cult often had special epithets connected with the particular circumstances which gave rise to its institution. We have already noted that of Demetrius *Kataibates*. The other epithets commonly used were God (*theos*), Saviour (*soter*) and Benefactor (*euergetes*), but these are not to be regarded as permanent cult titles, but rather as applying to the honorand in the context of a specific cult. Consequently the same king may be saluted by different titles in different cities. As it happens, these titles – not unnaturally – coincide with those frequently found in official dynastic cult; but their use in the city cults is quite different. One may suspect, however, that a title conferred by a city in the course of a special cult, for example *Soter* used of Ptolemy at Rhodes, was often a forerunner of an official dynastic title.[109]

What did such cult really mean to those instituting it and to the kings who received it? In many respects it seems to resemble the worship accorded to gods. But that is perhaps because it originates as an act of gratitude for a specific benefit, usually of the kind for which it was hitherto normal to offer thanks to the gods, for example preservation from the enemy, the restoration of freedom or succour in time of famine and distress. Early examples of ruler-cult are all very specifically linked to an occasion of this kind and invariably describe the nature of the king's services rather than his innate qualities; it is his benefactions, not his virtues, that are being acknowledged. Only towards the middle of

[109] On these connected aspects of cult see Habicht 1970, 134–59: (I 29).

the third century does the practice become more or less institutionalized. The reason for the decree is now described in stereotyped phrases: for example, the town of Itanus in Crete alleges as the reason for voting honours to Ptolemy III and Berenice (*IC* III Itanos 4 = *SIG* 463 = Austin 267) Ptolemy's continuing to maintain the city's freedom, i.e. doing nothing; and no attempt is made to justify the honours voted to Berenice.

But that comes later. In the early decades the honours go to the king because he does what the god is expected to do – and often does it more effectively, as the Athenian hymn to Demetrius Poliorcetes makes quite explicit. The implied criticism of the gods in that hymn is unparalleled in its outspokenness. Usually respect for the gods, which remained strong, would lead such feelings to be concealed. A much more typical response is to be found in an item of the *Temple Chronicle* at Lindus (*FGrH* 532 F 1, D3, ll.95ff.) recording that at the time of Demetrius' attack the goddess had saved the island – by calling in Ptolemy! By doing the god's work a king qualified to receive the homage due to the god, and this was all the easier because many honours traditionally paid to the gods were also legitimately paid to men. According to Aristotle (*Rhet.* 1.5, 1361a28ff.),

honour is a recognition of a good reputation for benefactions, and it is with justice that honour is accorded especially to those who have conferred benefits, though he is also honoured who is a potential benefactor . . . (34ff.) Honours consist of sacrifices, metrical and non-metrical commemoration, privileges, sacred enclosures, the right to front seats, tombs, images (*eikones*), meals at public expense, barbarian honours like obeisance and keeping at a distance, and, what is common to all, gifts.

These are all honours properly accorded to men: Aristotle is not speaking here of cult. Yet clearly many of those mentioned – sacrifices, sacred enclosures, statues – are also closely associated with ruler-cult; and the reasons for conferring them are the same, benefits received or the hopes of benefits to come. Here there is plenty of opportunity for ambiguity and this can be compounded by the uncertainty which sometimes occurs as to whether a sacrifice is being carried out 'to the king' or 'for the king'.[110] In addition it is not clear, and was probably not clear to contemporaries, whether the according of 'honours equivalent to those for a god' (*isotheoi timai*), such as were voted to Philopoemen after his death at Megalopolis in 183 (*SIG* 624), implied that the person honoured was regarded as a god or not. It might rather seem that in such cases – and perhaps too in ruler-cult – the recipient was

[110] See above, p. 87; for similar ambiguity under the Roman empire, when sacrifices were said to be 'of' the emperor, thus leaving undefined whether they were 'to him' or 'for him', see Price 1980, 33: (1 60). In an anecdote related by Philo, *Leg. ad Gaium* 356–7, the emperor Gaius challenges the Jews on that very point.

being treated as a god while it was recognized that he was in fact a man. But the same ritual and even the same phraseology may have conveyed different meanings to different people or indeed at different periods. An analysis of the dedications associated with ruler-cult reveals a trend away from sacrifices to the king in the direction of sacrifices made on his behalf, while the number of festivals and sacrifices grows. This may imply a decline in the *religious* importance of these cults; and it has been plausibly suggested[111] that by the second century the cities had come to accept the fact of monarchy, and no longer needed to express their relation to the kings in terms of deification. This may well be true. It would correspond to the institutionalizing of the cults, which can be seen in the increasingly perfunctory nature of the explanations offered when the city conferring cult attempts to justify it (see a above, p. 94).

We have been considering ruler-cult as a spontaneous expression of gratitude by the cities, but it also appears in private dedications. Indeed, in Egypt, where, apart from Alexandria, city life hardly existed at all, the main dedications are those of individuals, not cities; and in that kingdom, without the framework of independent city life, the domi-nation exercised by the central government and the native temples is very strong. Elsewhere too the spontaneity of ruler-cult as an expression of gratitude should not be exaggerated, for it is an institution which exists in a political context and the form it takes is a response to a complicated and usually unwelcome set of circumstances. The kings and generals themselves create the climate of pressure and danger, from which they receive gratitude for succouring its victims. Often, too, hints must have been given – and taken. The very first example considered above – the granting of cult to Antigonus and Demetrius by the city of Scepsis – comes in response to a letter from Antigonus which underlines his concern for the freedom of the Greeks. One certainly cannot exclude the possibility that the Scepsians (and others) were left in little doubt what was expected of them.

Ruler-cult evidently filled a need. It was only in the fourth century during and after the reign of Alexander that it was resisted. Callisthenes, notably, in his opposition to the proposal to offer obeisance (*proskynesis*) to the king, asserted the old distinction between men and gods, and at Athens Hypereides (*Epit.* 6.21) complained that his fellow-citizens had been forced

to see sacrifices accorded to men, the statues, altars and temples of the gods disregarded, while those of men were sedulously cared for and the servants of these men honoured as heroes.

But Hypereides' sense of outrage is largely provoked by his political

[111] Price 1980, 28–43: (1 60).

hostility to the pro-Macedonian party at Athens; the charge of impiety is being exploited to make a political point.[112] It is significant that all later criticism of ruler-cult takes the form of attacking those who propose to confer cult on a particular king on the grounds that the recipient is unworthy and his supporters scoundrels: their proposal is not so much impious as merely shameful.[113] There is no sign of opposition based on the assumption that ruler-cult is in itself outrageous and sacrilegious.[114] There could be no clearer indication that in ruler-cult the Hellenistic age had devised a political and religious institution which fulfilled a real need in organizing and lubricating relations between the free cities and their new rulers. At the same time ruler-cult, for the ordinary man in the Greek cities and in the directly governed parts of the kingdom alike, provided an incentive – how powerful one can only guess – to direct his loyalty towards the king, and the very cult-titles themselves will by constant repetition have helped to reinforce the picture of the king as saviour and protector.

VIII. DYNASTIC CULT

Ruler-cult arose spontaneously in the cities – though, as we have seen, the concept of spontaneity requires careful definition in this context. It has to be clearly distinguished (as it has not always been) from dynastic cult instituted by the various ruling dynasties themselves and organized within the central administration of the kingdoms. The dynastic cults have thus a quite different origin from the city cults, though, as we saw earlier (p. 85), they shared some features with these. Compared with the city cults they were slow to appear, perhaps because they could not find a place so long as Alexander's successors were merely generals and not yet independent kings. Why they arose has been much discussed and variously explained. A popular view is that they were intended to reinforce the power of the ruling house. There is, however, no evidence that power could be derived from a religious cult, though clearly cult and the festivals connected with it could give added lustre to a dynasty and so add to its popularity. Perhaps a more convincing explanation of dynastic cult is that it was intended to provide a specific form of religious worship and ritual for the royal house itself and the vast number of bureaucrats and army personnel directly connected with it.[115] The members of the royal family no longer belonged to a Greek city with its gods and cults; and most of their Friends, soldiers and officials were likewise displaced persons. Dynastic cult provided them with the framework of religious observance necessary to a rounded life at that

[112] Habicht 1970, 217: (I 29).   [113] Cf. Charlesworth 1935, 17: (I 19).
[114] For discussion see Habicht 1970, 213–21: (I 29).
[115] Bikerman 1938, 249–56: (E 6).

time, and one moreover that consolidated loyalty around the king. As we have already noted, the royal houses encouraged certain city cults. Seleucus paid special honour to Apollo of Miletus, claiming Apollo as his ancestor (p. 85). But he was also responsible for organizing the great religious precinct of Apollo and Artemis at Daphne near Antioch.[116] Similarly the Attalids, not the city, were responsible for setting up the cult of Dionysus Cathegemon at Pergamum.[117] It was to reinforce these and similar cults set up by the kings that dynastic worship was introduced.

It begins in Egypt with the cult of Alexander, which perhaps already existed by 290. It was a national cult with an eponymous priest whose name was used to date both Greek and demotic contracts,[118] and quite distinct from the cult which had been set up to Alexander shortly after his death as the founder of Alexandria.[119] Following Ptolemy I's death in 283, his successor Ptolemy II in 280 proclaimed him a god with a special cult as the Saviour (*Soter*) and instituted elaborate games, the *Ptolemaieia*, to celebrate this. Ptolemy I's wife Berenice, who died in 279, was also included in the cult and the two together are referred to as the Saviour Gods (*theoi soteres*).[120] The next development came when Ptolemy II added the cult of himself and his queen (and sister) Arsinoe to that of Alexander under the name of the Brother-Sister Gods (*theoi adelphoi*) (*P. Hibeh* 199); this probably took place in 272/1 before Arsinoe's death, thus introducing the cult of the living monarch. Subsequently new pairs of rulers (and their queens) were added to the royal cult. But for some unexplained reason the Saviour Gods were not included in the dynastic cult until the reign of Ptolemy IV.[121]

This cult of the dead and living Ptolemies, going back to Alexander, was for the benefit of the Greeks in Egypt. But their names were also incorporated into the worship of the Egyptian temples. The Canopus decree of 238 (*OGIS* 56 = Austin 222) records the institution of a cult of the Benefactor Gods (*theoi euergetai*), that is Ptolemy III and Berenice II, quite distinct from the Graeco-Macedonian state cult. This is specifically declared to be in recognition of Euergetes' gifts to the temple. Similarly the Rosetta stone of 196 (*OGIS* 90 = Austin 227) shows that a synod of priests meeting at Memphis in November 197, on the anniversary of Ptolemy V's accession, passed a decree containing elaborate arrangements for the placing of his image in the temple and other details of cult in recognition of his benefactions to Egypt and to the priests, and of his defeat of the rebels at Lycopolis. These two inscriptions show clearly

[116] RC 44, l.21; cf. Bikerman 1938, 252: (E 6).   [117] RC 65-7.
[118] Cf. Préaux 1978, 1.256: (A 48).   [119] Habicht 1970, 36: (I 29).
[120] Fraser 1972, II.367-8 n. 229; 373 n. 283: (A 15).
[121] Fraser 1972, II.369 n. 237: (A 15).

that the cult of the Ptolemies, bearing their Greek cult-titles, also found a place in the native temples. This cannot have had the significance to the king that the dynastic cult possessed, but it was clearly important as helping to cement the relations between the ruling house and the powerful Egyptian priesthood.

The dynastic cult in the Seleucid kingdom took a rather different shape and was slower to develop. Antiochus I proclaimed his dead father Seleucus a god with the cult-title Seleucus Nicator and a temple and sacred enclosure at Seleuceia-in-Pieria; it was called the *Nicatorium* (App. *Syr.* 63). But this was merely a private cult. The first Seleucid king under whom there is evidence for a state cult was Antiochus III, who probably instituted it to include the worship of himself and his ancestors; later, in 193/2, he added a cult of his queen Laodice. But whereas in Egypt there was a single dynastic cult in Alexandria, in the Seleucid kingdom there was a different high-priest (and for the cult of Laodice a different high-priestess) in each satrapy.[122] These priests had authority over the lower priests of the dynastic cult, but there is no evidence that they controlled the priests of the city cults in any way.[123] The dead rulers are given cult-titles, but this is not so for the living rulers who, until after the reign of Antiochus IV, were included in the cult, but without a cult-title. In Egypt it is also in the second century, under Ptolemy VIII Euergetes II, that the living king uses such a title in official documents.[124] But the frequent use by others of cult epithets, and frequently of the same ones for the same king, must indicate that at least unofficially they were acceptable and accepted.

In Pergamum there is some evidence for local cults of Philetaerus, the founder, and for the kings;[125] and Attalus III shared the temple of Asclepius at Elaea (above, p. 87). But there was no dynastic cult in the real sense. Macedonia too shows only city cults and no dynastic cult organized by the state.[126] There remain only the small half-Greek kingdoms, but from one of these, Commagene, there is evidence of how dynastic cult could develop in a land with a strong Iranian influence. A large monument erected on Nimrud Dagh contains a long inscription (*OGIS* 383) of Antiochus the Great, god just and manifest, philoroman and philhellene, setting up a state cult with a priest and prescribing

---

[122] *RC* 36; Robert, *Hellenica* VII (1949), 17–18; *CR Acad. Inscr.* 1967, 281–96; cf. *OGIS* 245 = Austin 177 (a list of priests of earlier members of the dynasty included in cult at Seleuceia-in-Pieria).

[123] Bikerman 1938, 247–8: (E 6); the 'general and high-priest of Coele-Syria and Phoenice' mentioned in *OGIS* 230 has probably nothing to do with the dynastic cult: cf. *RC* p. 159 n. 7; Cerfaux and Tondriau 1957, 236 n. 6: (I 18).

[124] Bikerman 1938, 250: (E 6); *OGIS* 141–2.

[125] *OGIS* 764, l.47, for a sacrifice in a gymnasium to Philetaerus Euergetes; see further above, n. 108.

[126] For Amyntas III and Philip II, see above, p. 90.

various rituals and procedures, including the erection of statues, both *eikones* and *agalmata*, to his deceased ancestors and to the living monarch. The general pattern of cult is Seleucid, but a reference to 'the Fortune of the king' has been thought to translate the *hvarenó* of the Persian royal house.

IX. CONCLUSION

The religious aspects of Hellenistic monarchy have been examined at length; but their part in the total picture should not be exaggerated. Ruler-cult, in Adcock's words,[127] was not the root of Hellenistic monarchy: it was rather the leaves on the branch – though it did perhaps have an important role in helping to reconcile the Greeks of the cities to a new political constellation which may have brought distinct economic advantages to some citizens, while clashing with their aspirations towards freedom and, in many cases, with their past experience. But it was not the cities that were to put the monarchies to the test. Well before the end of the third century the Hellenistic world was under pressure from the East and by the year 200 pressure was growing quickly from the West as well. It was to be from Rome that destruction came.

The Romans had as deep a distrust of monarchy as any citizen of a free *polis*. The crimes of Tarquin were learnt by every Roman at his father's knee and the history of the early Republic was studded with incidents in which dangerous and untrustworthy men had tried unsuccessfully to overthrow the republic and set up a monarchy in its place. In their earliest contacts with the Hellenistic powers the senators found kings curious and strange, to be treated with a mixture of suspicion and alarm. Cato, typically, defined a king as 'a carnivorous animal' (Plut. *Cato mai.* 8.8). But after their experiences with Pyrrhus and Hiero of Syracuse and even more after Cynoscephalae and Magnesia, the Senate no longer doubted that the Roman consul or proconsul was more than a match for any king. The famous meeting between C. Popillius Laenas and Antiochus IV at Eleusis near Alexandria, at which the latter was ostentatiously humbled in front of his Friends, was intended as a demonstration of the power which the republic now exercised over the kings of the East (Polyb. xxix.27.1–7). Before long Eumenes was being expelled from Italy through a message conveyed to him at Brundisium by a lowly quaestor and Prusias II of Bithynia encouraged to debase himself by slavish prostration on the floor of the Senate House (Polyb. xxx.18.3–7; 19.6–8). By the first century kings were pawns in Roman politics; the remnants of the Seleucid legacy were swept up by Pompey and the question of who should put Ptolemy Auletes

[127] Adcock 1953, 175: (1 5).

back on his throne and for how much was tossed about between the triumvirs. By this time such kings as survived did so as clients of Roman nobles. But there was an irony in the fact that the very process of annihilating the Hellenistic kingdoms had accentuated the conditions which made the survival of the republic impossible. It was no coincidence that the year which saw the destruction of the last – and in many ways the most remarkable – of the Hellenistic monarchies at Actium also saw the beginning of a monarchy, under another name,[128] which was to survive at Rome for five hundred years. As a result the legacy of Hellenistic kingship lived on in the Roman Empire, its ideology and its institutions, secular and religious alike, now adapted to the requirements of a universal monarchy.

[128] Cf. Appian, *Praef.* 6.

CHAPTER 4

THE FORMATION OF THE HELLENISTIC
KINGDOMS

ÉDOUARD WILL

I. THE ADVENTURES OF DEMETRIUS POLIORCETES (301–286)

Having narrowly escaped from the massacre of Ipsus,[1] Demetrius
Poliorcetes had hurled himself at Ephesus: Asia might be lost, but he had
to keep control of the sea. At sea, the position of Antigonus' son
remained solid. The confederation of the Nesiotes remained, for the
moment, loyal to him and Cyprus was still firmly in his grasp, as were a
number of coastal towns in Asia, from Asia Minor (though here
Lysimachus rapidly established his power, which made the inhabitants
long for the days of Antigonus) to Phoenicia (Tyre, Sidon). In European
Greece, where Pyrrhus of Epirus, from exile, was for a time Demetrius'
representative,[2] the recently restored League of Corinth soon fell apart
and Demetrius found himself restricted to a certain number of seaboard
towns, chief of which was Corinth. To his great disappointment, Athens
gave him notice: the servility of the Athenians had enabled them to
tolerate many extravagances on Demetrius' part and even many
sacrileges (such as the installation of his harem in the Parthenon and his
scandalously irregular initiation at Eleusis), but the bill was heavy.
Freed from the costly encumbrance of Demetrius' protection, the
Athenians, under the semi-tyrannical government of Lachares, lost no
time in renewing their ties with Cassander, whose eviction had been the
occasion for wild rejoicing in 307.[3] Happily for Demetrius, he still had
his fleet (the Athenians even returned to him the squadron posted in
their waters) and was indisputably master of the sea.

There can be no doubt that the loss of his father was the heaviest blow
Poliorcetes could have suffered. In the collegiate kingship of the
Antigonids, Antigonus had been the head, the mind, the will, Demetrius
the arm acting in the West. Duly directed, Demetrius, with his gifts of
generalship and tactical skill, had rendered great services to the common
cause, even though his rashness and thoughtlessness had sometimes

[1] Elkeles 1941, 31ff.: (C 20); Manni 1951, 41ff.: (C 48); Wehrli 1969, 151ff.: (C 75).
[2] Bengtson 1964, 1.164ff.: (A 6); Lévêque 1957, 106–7: (C 46).
[3] Ferguson 1911, 126ff.: (D 89); De Sanctis 1928: (C 17) and 1936: (C 18); Fortina 1965, 111ff.: (C 26); Bingen 1973, 16ff.: (B 185).

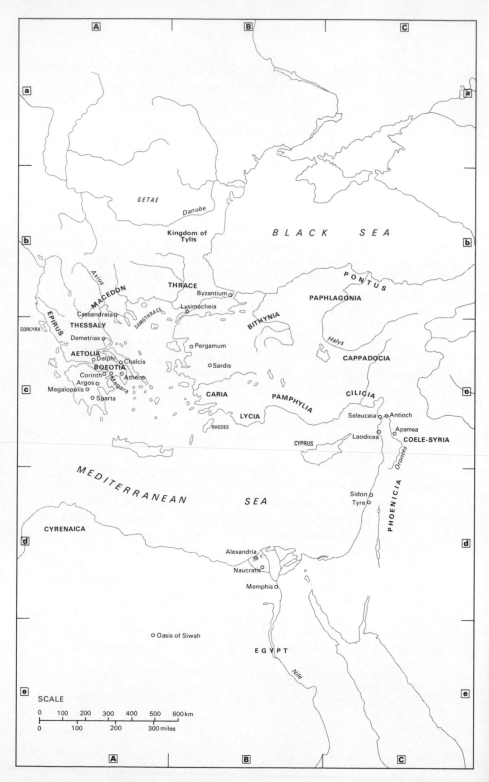

Map 2. The eastern Mediterranean *c.* 275 B.C.

Within the map:

GETAE

Danube

Kingdom of
Tylis

BLACK   SEA

PONTUS

THRACE

Byzantium

PAPHLAGONIA

Axius

MACEDON

Lysimacheia

Cassandreia

SAMOTHRACE

BITHYNIA

EPIRUS

THESSALY

Halys

CORCYRA

Demetrias

Pergamum

CAPPADOCIA

AETOLIA

Delphi

Chalcis

Sardis

BOEOTIA

Corinth

Athens

Argos

Megara

CARIA

CILICIA

Megalopolis

Sparta

PAMPHYLIA

Seleuceia

Antioch

LYCIA

Apamea

RHODES

CYPRUS

Laodicea

COELE-SYRIA

Orontes

MEDITERRANEAN

SEA

Sidon

Tyre

PHOENICIA

CYRENAICA

Alexandria

Naucratis

Memphis

Oasis of Siwah

EGYPT

Nile

SCALE

0   100   200   300   400   500   600 km

0   100   200   300 miles

proved disastrous, most recently at the battle of Ipsus. Left to himself, he naturally retained his military qualities but was to give free rein to his instability and his lack of judgement and political sense. As a result, the whole of this second part of his career has a dizzying quality, though it is impossible, and would be futile, to go into detail here about his numerous about-turns.[4]

Was Demetrius Poliorcetes, at this point in his career, pursuing the dream of unity which had inspired his father? It is possible – but, both because of his volatile temperament and the circumstances which made his situation unstable (and which he did not always use to best advantage), we do not find in his actions the same stubborn continuity which marked those of Antigonus. Rather than the man of the distant prospect doggedly pursued, Demetrius was a man of the present moment ready to drop the substance for the shadow. If indeed he retained the hope of recovering what Ipsus had deprived him of, and winning yet more, this hope was not to have much influence on the course of events; until Ipsus Antigonus had been the formidable champion who had to be contained and then crushed; afterwards his son was no more than a foreign body to be eliminated. His activities, which kept the world in suspense for fifteen years, seem in retrospect to have been accidental rather than essential to the history of the period. The essential, after a short pause, was to be the rise of Lysimachus' power and the reaction which finally broke it.

Among the four continental territorial kingdoms, it was thus Poliorcetes' empire over islands and sea which kept him in the game, and, very soon, a new reversal of alliances which enabled him to fight back.[5] This reversal came about over the question of Coele-Syria. Seleucus, as we have seen, had declared that he was maintaining his claims on this country despite Ptolemy's seizure of it, and Ptolemy on his side was determined not to surrender an inch of it. A conflict was thus predictable quite soon and, against Seleucus, what more advantageous alliance could Ptolemy have found than one with the new master of Asia Minor, Lysimachus? So it came to pass, and the agreement was strengthened by marriages. Ptolemy gave Lysimachus and his heir presumptive, Agathocles, two of his daughters, the half-sisters Arsinoe (the daughter of his mistress, soon to be his wife, Berenice) and Lysandra (daughter of his wife Eurydice, herself the daughter of Antipater). The marriages were to be the cause of tragic shifts of fortune.[6]

Caught between Lysimachus and Ptolemy, Seleucus too needed an alliance. Cassander was far away and had no interest in a quarrel with his

[4] Diod. XXI.1.4; Plut. Dem. 30–31.2; Pyrrh. 4.3; Paus. 1.25.6–7; 26.1–3.
[5] Just. XV.4.23–4; Plut. Dem. 31.2; 32.1–2; Memnon, FGrH 434 F 4.9; Paus. 1.9.6; 10.3; OGIS 10.
[6] Saitta 1955, 120ff.: (C 57); Seibert 1967: (A 57).

neighbour Lysimachus or with Ptolemy, who could cause him problems in Greece. On the other hand, Demetrius Poliorcetes was a natural enemy both of Ptolemy, because of his presence in Cyprus, and of Lysimachus, because of his designs on Asia Minor. Seleucus therefore made overtures to the son of Antigonus and an alliance was concluded at Rhossus in Syria, once again cemented by a marriage: the aged Seleucus married Demetrius' young daughter Stratonice (she was shortly afterwards to become the wife of Antiochus, the son of Seleucus,[7] when his father made him joint ruler and heir,[8] and placed him in charge of the 'upper satrapies').[9] Demetrius' gain from the rapprochement was the little Cilician state ruled by Pleistarchus, which Seleucus sacrificed to him.[10]

However, the friendship did not last and these two allies soon quarrelled again, though in circumstances which are obscure. Demetrius on the one hand attempted a rapprochement with Ptolemy, though without success. Meanwhile it was a constant source of irritation to Seleucus that Demetrius possessed naval bases bordering on his territories, and he demanded that Demetrius surrender Cilicia, Tyre and Sidon to him. Having nothing but the sea for an empire, Demetrius could not agree to the loss of these few important bases, which helped to ensure his possession of Cyprus. The rapprochement between Seleucus and Demetrius was thus shortlived.[11]

New possibilities were opened up for Demetrius in 298 or 297 by the death of his old enemy Cassander. Antipater's son had, all in all, firmly disproved the anxieties his father had shown about him in keeping him out of power in favour of Polyperchon. Though he remains one of the least well-known figures of his period, Cassander's activity in Macedon had shown him to be an energetic politician, prudent and far-sighted, though often brutal and totally lacking in scruples. In his last years Cassander had been relatively inactive on the international scene: ill-health must have been a factor, but probably there was also a desire to give his kingdom a breathing-space after the turbulent years it had experienced since the death of Alexander. But Cassander died too soon to prevent his work from being immediately compromised, because his three sons were still young, and the eldest, Philip IV, barely survived him. Accordingly a period of minority now began in Macedon under the regency of the queen mother.[12]

---

[7] Plut. *Dem.* 32–3; App. *Syr.* 59–62.

[8] *OGIS* 214=*Didyma* II.424; Newell 1938, 231ff.: (B 249).

[9] Bengtson 1964–7, II.80ff.: (A 6).

[10] The only basis for a reconstruction of the very confused situation on the coasts of Asia Minor at this time is inscriptional material, and even then the picture is very uncertain: cf. Will 1979, I.88–9: (A 67).   [11] Plut. *Dem.* 32.3; 33.1.

[12] Just. XVI.1; Plut. *Dem.* 36–7; *Pyrrh.* 6.2–7.1; Diod. XXI.7; Paus. IX.7.3; Euseb. *Chron.* (Schöne) 231–2.

The circumstances were too tempting for a man as impulsive as Demetrius Poliorcetes to resist the desire to exploit them without delay. Accordingly, forsaking the borders of Asia for Europe, Demetrius descended on Greece in 296, tried to blockade Athens, failed, rushed to the Peloponnese, returned to Attica and, in 295, laid siege to the city, where Lachares was in command. A squadron of Ptolemy's ships failed to lift the blockade and Athens fell at the beginning of 294,[13] as the first deaths from hunger occurred. Demetrius immediately left for the Peloponnese, where he had to secure his rear before advancing northwards, but, as he was about to attack Sparta, he received bad news. During all this time Ptolemy had been robbing him of Cyprus, Seleucus of Cilicia and Lysimachus of the Ionian towns he still held.[14] Minor matters for the moment to Demetrius who, as in 302, saw Macedon within his grasp. In Macedon at this time bloody struggles were dividing Cassander's heirs: the two young kings, one of whom had murdered his mother, were engaged in a bitter struggle for power. In the autumn of 294 Demetrius, leaving Greece in the care of his son Antigonus Gonatas,[15] invaded the kingdom, seized the younger of Cassander's sons and put him to death, forced the other, Antipater, to take refuge with Lysimachus and had himself proclaimed king of Macedon by his army. The usurpation was only too obvious, and yet Demetrius could claim some right by virtue of his marriage to Phila, Cassander's sister. With all Cassander's descendants out of the way, Demetrius, through his wife, was left the sole heir of those to whose ruin he and his father had devoted all their energy, and Phila seems to have shared her husband's ambitions. The conquest of continental Macedon does not seem to have made Demetrius abandon his interest in Aegean affairs: it is striking to note that he gave his kingdom a new capital on the coast, Demetrias, on the gulf of Volo in Thessaly. Even though Demetrius' reign over Macedon was not to last long, it was to have its importance for the future, since it laid the foundation for the future legitimacy of his son and of the dynasty which was subsequently to rule the country until the Roman conquest.

The very next year, taking advantage of Lysimachus' difficulties in the area of the Danube (where he was for a time a prisoner of the Getae),[16] and despite the fact that Lysimachus had recognized him, Demetrius yielded to this new temptation to set out again for Asia and invaded his neighbour's territories. However, the news of a united rising of the Boeotians and Aetolians brought him quickly back (292/1).[17] This rising was backed by a figure we have as yet scarcely met, the famous Pyrrhus.

---

[13] *IG* II². 1.646; Habicht 1979, 2–8:(D 91).

[14] *SIG* 368; Plut. *Dem.* 35.2.

[15] Tarn 1913, 36ff.: (D 38).

[16] Paus. I.9.8; Diod. XIX.73; XXI.12; Just. XVI.1.19; Saitta 1955, 85ff., 116ff., 124ff.: (C 57).

[17] Flacelière 1937, 57ff.: (D 105); Wehrli 1969, 173ff.: (C 75). The Aetolian–Boeotian treaty: *SVA* III.463.

While the young Pyrrhus' career had already been very eventful, it is at this point that he makes his real debut in major politics, and if he is all along indisputably pursuing his own ends, at this point he is still also pursuing (perhaps without altogether realizing it) those of Ptolemy. It is worth our while to dwell for a moment on this aspect of the history of the period.[18]

We saw previously how, as early as 315, Ptolemy had taken a lofty stance in support of Greek liberties. In 308 his intervention in Greece, somewhat contradicting these liberal principles, had been unsuccessful; it had been a lesson for Ptolemy, who henceforth attempted to make his actions accord with the principles he professed to hold. The events which followed Ipsus were to give Ptolemy the opportunity to practise with skill and success a policy which would today be called one of 'containment' with regard to Macedon, a policy which was in part expansionist (at sea and in the islands) and partly propagandist and a search for influence (on the Greek mainland) – principles which were the foundation of the Greek policy of the Ptolemies in the third century. It was easy to foresee that the succession to Cassander would unleash, as we have just seen that it did, Poliorcetes' ambitions and the first proof that Ptolemy did foresee this revival of the Macedonian question was a clearly anti-Macedonian gesture on his part, the restoration of Pyrrhus to his hereditary territories.

Dynastic conflicts the details of which do not concern us here had twice forced Pyrrhus to leave Epirus for exile: once in 317 (when he was two) and again in 302. On the latter occasion Epirus came under the influence of Cassander, the protector of King Neoptolemus. Even before this, in order to arm himself against Macedonian influence, Pyrrhus had sought closer relations with the Antigonids, and in 303 Demetrius had married a sister of Pyrrhus, Deidameia – not the only case of princely polygamy in the period. It was therefore natural for Pyrrhus to seek refuge with his allies in 302, and he fought at their side at Ipsus. Shortly afterwards in 299, as part of his attempt to achieve a rapprochement with Ptolemy, Demetrius had sent him his brother-in-law Pyrrhus as a hostage and pledge of his goodwill. The rapprochement with Egypt, as we saw, came to nothing, but Pyrrhus, no doubt resentful at having been used as a hostage, and since his sister Deidameia had meanwhile died, stayed in Alexandria, where he became a friend of Ptolemy, who gave him as wife Antigone, a daughter of his mistress Berenice by a first marriage. Immediately the news of Cassander's death was known, Ptolemy helped Pyrrhus to re-establish himself in Epirus, probably in 298–7: he had presumably realized that the young prince did not have the spirit of a vassal and that, whoever was to be master of

18. Plut. *Pyrrh.* 1–5.1; Just. XVII.3.16–21; Paus. I.11.

Macedon in the years to come, its western frontiers would be well guarded by the hot-headed 'descendant of Achilles' and relative of Alexander the Great. The system was further reinforced by a triangular alliance with Agathocles of Syracuse: Agathocles, who had also recently made an Egyptian marriage (perhaps even marrying the sister of the princess Pyrrhus had married) gave one of his daughters, Lanassa, to Pyrrhus, whose wife Antigone had meanwhile died; the bride brought her husband the island of Corcyra as a dowry. In this way there was a solid guarantee against any Macedonian push towards the Adriatic with an additional threat from the West hanging over the kingdom.[19]

Events were to confirm the correctness of Ptolemy's views: even before Demetrius had established himself in Macedon, Pyrrhus had intervened in the quarrels of Cassander's sons and occupied the western borders of the kingdom. The conditions for a bitter rivalry were created.[20] It is important to note that there is no proof that in 292–1 (any more than in 293, the date of an earlier Boeotian rising against Demetrius) the Boeotians acted, or that Pyrrhus and the Aetolians tried to support them, at the express instigation of Ptolemy. However, the two events correspond nicely to two aspects of Ptolemy's policy, his propaganda in favour of Greek freedom and his support for an anti-Macedonian Epirus. While there may have been no immediate stimulus from Ptolemy, these were nevertheless fruits of Alexandrian policy.

Despite this Pyrrhus and his Aetolian allies arrived too late to be successful.[21] Demetrius Poliorcetes put down the Boeotian rising and, to avenge himself on Pyrrhus (and also to acquire a naval base in the West to curb Aetolian piracy), in 291–90 he proceeded to seize Corcyra[22] Lanassa's dowry – and Lanassa herself, who had already separated from Pyrrhus. The following years were taken up with confused and largely fruitless fighting between the two adversaries, in the course of which the Aetolians acted in conjunction with Pyrrhus. A peace was, however, agreed in 289, though we do not know its terms.

These sterile battles gradually took their toll of Demetrius, and of his popularity,[23] particularly in Greece, where the precariousness of his situation had forced him to follow a brutal policy very different from the one which had earned him so much sympathy during the lifetime of his father. From now on we find no more talk of the freedom of the cities or of the League of Corinth; indeed those machines of war but lately directed from outside against Cassander had no purpose now that Demetrius had taken Cassander's place. But, more seriously, his popularity began to

---

[19] Nenci 1953: (C 53); Lévêque 1957, 83ff.: (C 46); Hammond 1967, 567ff.: (D 26).
[20] Lévêque 1957, 125ff.: (C 46).
[21] Plut. *Dem.* 39–41.2; 43.1; *Pyrrh.* 7.2ff.; 10.2ff.
[22] Elkeles 1941, 56–7: (C 20).   [23] Plut. *Dem.* 42.

wane even in the kingdom of Macedon, which was being exhausted by these futile wars.

Demetrius, however, seems not to have understood, in 295 and succeeding years, that Ptolemy, after robbing him of Cyprus, would not stop there. In fact, between 291 and 287 (the dating, based mainly on epigraphic material, is uncertain), Ptolemy succeeded in taking over the island territories of the Antigonids, and the Confederation of the Nesiotes came under Egyptian protection.[24] Ptolemy did not have great difficulty in winning the good opinion of the islanders; Demetrius' rule and his fiscal demands, here also, had become intolerable, and inscriptions show that the change was welcomed. Relief from taxation, respect for civic institutions and the showing of a measure of respect for the Federal Council were enough to gain acceptance for the presence of a 'nesiarch' (governor of the islands) in the service of Ptolemy, a man who had the skill to make himself popular, as the decrees in his honour show.[25]

While he was thus losing his island bases, Demetrius (according to Plutarch) was constructing vast projects for the reconquest of Asia,[26] and assembling a naval force so large that a coalition began to form against him. In 288/7 Ptolemy was depriving him of Sidon[27] and Tyre while his continental neighbours Lysimachus and Pyrrhus, who had most interest in his downfall, were attacking Macedon.[28] Abandoned by his army, Demetrius was reduced to his fleet and his kingdom was divided among the conquerors.[29] At length, in spring 287, Athens revolted, and when Poliorcetes a little later made a final attempt to regain it he was frustrated by the arrival of Pyrrhus.[30]

Demetrius fell back once more towards Asia,[31] leaving his remaining European possessions in the care of his son Antigonus Gonatas.[32] He tried to seize coastal regions belonging to Lysimachus, failed, fell back on territories belonging to Seleucus, saw his army melt away day by day and was finally captured in 286 after being hunted down in the Taurus mountains. Seleucus offered him a gilded cage on the banks of the Orontes, and the Taker of Cities died in 283, only a little over fifty but worn out by a life divided between incessant warfare and no less

[24] Moser 1914, 83ff.: (F 139); Fritze 1917, 31ff.: (F 131); Guggenmos 1929, 88ff.: (C 32); Laidlaw 1933, 103ff.: (D 145); Bagnall 1976, 136ff.: (F 204).
[25] Merker 1970, 150ff.: (C 50).
[26] Plut. *Dem.* 43; *Pyrrh.* 10.5–6. Questioned by Fellmann 1930, 17ff.: (D 18).
[27] Where King Philocles became one of Ptolemy's principal admirals: Merker 1970, 143–4: (C 50); Seibert 1970, 337ff.: (C 61).
[28] Geyer 1928, 17ff.: (C 31); Lévêque 1957, 151ff.: (C 46); Saitta 1955, 129ff.: (C 57).
[29] Plut. *Dem.* 44–6; *Pyrrh.* 11–12.6; Paus 1.10.2.
[30] Shear 1978: (C 62); Habicht 1979, 45ff.: (D 91).
[31] Geyer 1928, 19–20: (C 31); Elkeles 1941, 64ff.: (C 20); Will 1979, 1.97: (A 67).
[32] Tarn 1913, 89ff.: (D 38).

incessant debauchery. Plutarch did not miss the opportunity to philosophize about this sad end.[33]

Nevertheless it would be quite misleading to exaggerate the importance of the death of Demetrius Poliorcetes: for the future of the Hellenistic world the event counted less than had the death of his father and even than that of Lysimachus was to do. Since Ipsus Demetrius had been superfluous in the concert of new states gradually achieving stability: hurled by the debacle of 301 into a fluid situation, caught between Cassander, Lysimachus, Seleucus and Ptolemy, Demetrius had only one chance of surviving, to take the place of one of the other four. The death of Cassander had offered him the opportunity, and he seized it energetically – but he had been unable to hold on to it because he totally failed to realize that it was no longer an age for vast dreams, but for limited ambitions. After 294/3, the time of his establishment in Macedon, Demetrius was less a victim of the world situation than of his excessive temperament, his *pleonexia*, which prevented him from being content with a kingdom in which there seems to have been every chance of remaining secure, provided only that he showed a little wisdom. What Macedon and its European appendages needed now was a new Philip II, but Demetrius had not inherited from his father what made Antigonus resemble Alexander's father – nor was he Alexander. There was no longer any room for this unstable personality in a world looking for its equilibrium, and it was through him that the stabilization of Macedon was delayed for another fifteen years.

Nevertheless the career of Demetrius Poliorcetes is of historical interest. It can perhaps be seen as the symbol, as it were, both of the dimensions and of the internal limits of the new world: its dimensions, which were those of an adventurous generation which Demetrius, who roamed from Iran to the Adriatic and from Pontus to Arabia, had the misfortune to survive, and its internal limits, which were those of a new political philosophy which might be called pragmatism. This vast world had now become the crucible in which a new civilization was beginning to form, the scene of profound exchanges of ideas, of fertile religious syncretisms, of the silent but effective comings and goings of merchant fleets and caravans, but it was no longer the unbounded space into which an Alexander had been able to lead his army. Demetrius Poliorcetes' mistake had been his complete failure to realize that his father's defeat had meant the end (for the moment) of universal ambitions and that the age of political frontiers had arrived, frontiers within which there were new tasks to be performed by spirits more settled than his own.

[33] Plut. *Dem.* 46ff.

II. FROM THE APOGEE OF LYSIMACHUS TO THE RE-
ESTABLISHMENT OF ANTIGONUS GONATAS (286–276)

The removal of Antigonus Monophthalmus had already meant a remarkable increase of power for Lysimachus. Hitherto the master of Thrace had filled the obscure but useful role of defender of the northern borders of the Graeco-Macedonian world. Ipsus had enabled him to seize Asia Minor and raise his modest kingdom to the status of a first-rank power. With one foot in Europe and the other in Asia, Lysimachus' kingdom had features which foreshadowed later political structures and its capital, Lysimacheia, founded in 309/8 on the site of Cardia, had obviously been planned as a capital for the Straits, though also as a capital for a period in which the Aegean, Macedonia and Greece were still more of a focus of interest than Pontus or the Danubian regions. The occupation of the northern half of Macedonia in 288/7 at the expense of Demetrius, which could not fail to stimulate claims to the southern half, had further increased the importance of Lysimachus' state, and its ruler might well have seemed to have a chance of achieving what the Antigonids had attempted in vain, if not the re-establishment of Alexander's empire (there is no sign that Lysimachus had any thought of this), at least a kingdom centred on the Aegean sea with all the coasts held by the same sovereign. Lysimachus' new position could not fail to arouse the anxious attention of his colleagues, Seleucus, his closest Asiatic neighbour, and the Ptolemies (Ptolemy I had handed over to Ptolemy II in 285 and died in 283), whose new Aegean territories were now confronted, on all sides except the south, by the new 'Thracian' empire. An old man when he finally reached the front of the stage, Lysimachus showed himself determined not to waste time but to be quick in realizing the potential of his new situation.[34]

It was implicit in the logic of this situation that Lysimachus should first try to rid himself of Pyrrhus in Macedonia and Thessaly. Their alliance had been formed against Demetrius, and with him gone and his son Gonatas reduced to a precarious position,[35] Lysimachus had no more reason to show consideration to Pyrrhus, all the more since it was clear that the king of Epirus could expect no help from anyone. Pyrrhus had previously enjoyed the support of the Aetolians and of Ptolemy, but they had been alienated by his Macedonian ambitions. The only power of any weight in Greece at this time, the Aetolian League,[36] had reached an understanding with Pyrrhus against Demetrius Poliorcetes when he

[34] The literary sources for the years 287–281 are disastrously meagre.
[35] Tarn 1913, 111ff.: (D 38).
[36] Tarn 1913, *loc. cit.*; Flacelière 1937, 8off.: (D 105); Lévêque 1957, 164ff.: (C 46).

had seized Macedon but, once Pyrrhus was master of Thessaly and of the southern half of Macedonia (a position which, as with that of Lysimachus, led him to entertain pretentions to the rest of the country), he encountered nothing but suspicion and hostility from the Aetolians. Of course, in attempting a rapprochement with Lysimachus, the Aetolians ran the risk of exchanging Charybdis for Scylla, and there is no better illustration of the impossibility of any genuinely independent Greek policy in the conditions of the new era: between acceptance of domination interrupted by largely unco-ordinated movements of revolt for the weakest and a short-sighted policy of rapid seesawing for the less weak there was little room for a genuinely Greek policy. Allies of Pyrrhus against Demetrius, friends of Lysimachus against Pyrrhus, ready for reconciliation with Pyrrhus once he was pushed back to Epirus – what else could the Aetolians do? They survived by skilful manoeuvring. Better times would come for them. As for the Ptolemies, their position was more delicate. Ptolemy I Soter had certainly played off Pyrrhus against Demetrius a few years earlier and it might even now have been in Alexandria's interest to support him against Lysimachus, whose expansion in Asia and Europe was a potential threat to Egypt's Aegean interests. Ptolemy, however, also had reasons for preserving his good relations with Lysimachus in case Seleucus should assert his claims to Coele-Syria. With the pressures of these contradictory interests, it was a difficult game to play. Ptolemy seems to have abandoned it, and did not intervene on either side. A degree of senile inhibition, and perhaps also a degree of fluctuation in Egyptian policy during the transfer of power to Ptolemy II, which occurred at this very moment, may be part of the explanation for Alexandria's abstention in the game which was now beginning in Europe. It should be added that the matrimonial ties which had been formed between Alexandria and Lysimacheia had proved productive of frightening complications (to be discussed later) which were not calculated to facilitate a very flexible exercise of Ptolemaic diplomacy.

This left the way clear for Lysimachus: for although Pyrrhus made an alliance with Gonatas, it was to little purpose since the latter was in no position to offer much help. From the summer of 285 southern Macedonia and Thessaly began to fall, almost without a struggle, into the hands of Lysimachus,[37] and Pyrrhus turned back to place his ardour and his talents at the service of his ancestral domains,[38] pending the time when events in the West should present him with his great temptation.

At this time Lysimachus' kingdom included Thrace as far as the Danube[39] (with the exception of Byzantium, a free city), Macedon and

---

[37] Plut. *Pyrrh.* 12.7–9; Just. XVI.3.1–2; Paus. I.10.2.
[38] Lévêque 1957, *loc. cit.*: (C 46).   [39] Mihailov 1961: (D 158).

Thessaly (with the exception of the recently founded capital, Demetrias, which Gonatas had succeeded in holding), plus Asia Minor
(with the exception of the two kingdoms of Pontus and Bithynia, the
royal eras of which go back to 297/6, and the Paphlagonian principalities). The European Greek cities, too, were broadly sympathetic to
Lysimachus from hatred of the Antigonids, since Gonatas still held
Corinth, Piraeus (though it is not certain that he succeeded in keeping
it), Chalcis and some other towns, mainly in the Peloponnese. However,
Lysimachus does not seem to have envisaged any active policy in
Greece.

   But this new power was soon to collapse. Within his own territories
Lysimachus earned hatred, both from Greeks and Thracians, by his
fiscal severity and his harshness. Heavy demands seem to have been
made in particular on the Greek cities of Asia Minor; admittedly the
sympathy which many of them had shown for the Antigonid cause and
the resistance they had sometimes offered to the establishment of the
new authority deprived Lysimachus of any pretext for playing in his turn
the role of champion of liberties.[40] Beyond his boundaries his advances
and his ambition inevitably aroused anxiety. One incident would be
enough for risings to break out and outside interventions to be justified.
That incident was the murder of his son Agathocles.

   Hellenistic history was rarely to witness a more entangled 'vipers'
knot' than that which the Egyptian marriages had formed at the court of
the aged Lysimachus after Ipsus. It will be remembered that Arsinoe, the
daughter of Ptolemy and his mistress Berenice, had married Lysimachus, while Lysandra, the daughter of Ptolemy and Queen Eurydice, had
married the heir-apparent Agathocles. Arsinoe, both queen and mother-
in-law of her half-sister, having had several sons by Lysimachus, had
vowed to ensure the succession of the eldest of these at the expense of
Agathocles, her stepson, who was, nevertheless in his prime and a
valued assistant of his father's. We do not know exactly how she
achieved her ends but the fact remains that Lysimachus let himself be
manoeuvred by his wife and in 284/3 or 283/2 Agathocles was put to
death by order of his father.[41]

   This dynastic crime seems to have removed the last underpinnings of
Lysimachus' support. It is likely that it alienated from the king
collaborators without whom his power could not survive. Feeling the
hatreds and resentments rising towards him, Lysimachus struck and
roused new hatreds. Abroad Seleucus was being urged to act by

[40] Andreades 1930, 6ff.: (C 2); Bengtson 1964, 1.209ff.: (A 6); Saitta 1955, 97ff.: (C 57); M.
Thompson 1968, 163ff.: (B 270). Additional sources and bibliography in Will 1979, I.101–2: (A 67).
[41] Just. XVII.1.3–6; Memnon, *FGrH* 434 F 5.6; Paus. 1.10.3–4 (an analysis of the sources in
Longega 1968, 44ff.: (F 136)). Cf. most recently Heinen 1972, 7ff.: (A 21) (listing earlier work).

Lysandra, Agathocles' widow, who had sought refuge at his court, and no doubt also by Ptolemy Ceraunus. Ceraunus, the son of Ptolemy I and Eurydice (and so Lysandra's brother), had been excluded from the Lagid succession in favour his half-brother Ptolemy (II), the son of Berenice, on the day Ptolemy I had repudiated Eurydice to marry his mistress. He had then followed Lysandra to the court of Lysimachus, where his presence must have further aggravated the hostility between Lysandra and Arsinoe. After the murder of Agathocles Ceraunus had accompanied Lysandra to the court of Seleucus, and incited him to make war on Lysimachus. His own aims are obscure; perhaps he was already thinking of Macedon, which we soon find him invading. Seleucus was also receiving other appeals, coming from Asia Minor: among others Philataerus, the governor of the citadel at Pergamum, offered Seleucus his troops, his treasury and his influence.[42]

Seleucus yielded to persuasion. In 282, or perhaps in the middle of the winter of 282/1, he invaded Asia Minor, encountering no difficulty at all, for the promised support was effective. The encounter took place at Corupedium, near Sardis, at the beginning of 281.[43] Here Lysimachus met the same fate as his comrade Antigonus twenty years before at Ipsus, and Seleucus immediately took possession of his adversary's Asian territories.

The collapse of Lysimachus seemed to open to Seleucus the way to his native land, to that Macedon which all the Diadochi except Ptolemy had, at one moment of their career, dreamed of possessing, as though they expected it to lend legitimacy to their power. But, at the end of summer 281, when Seleucus, having crossed the Straits, seemed to be showing an intention of collecting the Macedonian inheritance for himself (though we have little precise information about his later plans), he found Ptolemy Ceraunus in his path. The dispossessed son of Ptolemy I, seeing the evaporation of the share he probably hoped for in the spoils of Lysimachus, assassinated his benefactor Seleucus with his own hand and fled to Lysimacheia,[44] where, posing as the avenger of the leader defeated at Corupedium, he managed to have himself acclaimed king of Macedon by the army.[45]

Thus disappeared the last survivor of the great generation of the Diadochi. Fortunately for his territories, Seleucus had carefully secured the succession during his lifetime by making his son Antiochus I joint ruler. Antiochus, however, who was governor of all the upper satrapies,

[42] Just. XVII.1.7–12; App. *Syr.* 62; Memnon, *loc. cit.;* Paus. 1.10.5; Euseb. *Chron.* (Schöne) 233–4.
[43] Place: Glotz *et al.* 1945, 372 and n. 86: (A 18). Date: Sachs and Wiseman 1954, 202ff.: (E 49). Aymard 1955, 106: (E 2); Heinen 1972, 20ff.: (A 21).
[44] Sachs and Wiseman 1954, *loc. cit.*
[45] Granier 1931, 119ff.: (D 23); Ritter 1965, 108ff.: (I 62); Heinen 1972, 63ff.: (A 21); Errington 1978, 130–1: (D 17).

was at this moment far from where crisis was once again brewing, and prevented by numerous obstacles from intervening rapidly. Only Antigonus Gonatas, still master of his fleet and of a few Greek bases, could with an effort try to overtake Ceraunus by landing in Macedonia before this unexpected pretender reached there from Thrace. Ceraunus outstripped him, however, and, with Lysimachus' fleet at his command, inflicted a defeat on Gonatas which shattered his hopes: there was now no obstacle to Ptolemy's taking possession of Macedon. There he found his half-sister Arsinoe who, after the death of her husband Lysimachus, had succeeded in escaping to Cassandreia after Corupedium, and – despite all the hatreds which had existed between them – he married her: their interests seemed momentarily to coincide. But, when Ceraunus had had two of her three sons by Lysimachus murdered, Arsinoe fled to Samothrace, then to Egypt (where she later married her brother Ptolemy II).[46]

Was Macedon at last to find peace in unity under the rule of a Ptolemy? The moment was still far away. After the rivalries of pretenders and dynastic struggles, it still had to face a barbarian invasion and anarchy.

Lysimachus' kingdom, like its predecessor the Macedonian province created by Philip II, had, as we have said, played the obscure but essential role of rampart for the Greek world against the barbarians beyond. In this respect, the collapse of Lysimachus was disastrous: it left that northern frontier exposed at a moment when the pressure was particularly intense. The barbarians who were the traditional threat to the northern part of the Greek world, the Thracians and Scythians (who had no doubt already become mixed with the Getic tribes against whom Lysimachus had fought), had around this time been reinforced by Celts.[47] At this date Celtic expansion was no longer in its infancy: Italy and Rome had experienced it more than a century before. At the end of the fourth century, however, a new unrest appeared in the Celtic world and peoples long established in western and central Europe were forced to set out on their travels once more as a result of pressure on them from new arrivals belonging to the great Belgic group. For our present purposes the important detail is that the thrust at this time was towards the east and south east, into the Danube basin and the Balkans. Bands of Celts had begun to make their appearance in these areas from the beginning of the fourth century, and both Cassander and Lysimachus

---

[46] Just. XVII.2; Memnon, *FGrH* 434 F 8.1–7; Euseb. *Chron.* (Schöne) 235–6; App. *Syr.* 62; Paus. 1.16.2; Volkmann 1959, 1597–9: (C 74); Longega 1968, 57ff.: (F 136); Heinen 1972, 63ff.: (A 21).

[47] Just. XXIV.4–8; XXV.1–2; Diod. XXII.3–4, 9; Paus. 1.4, 16.2; x.19.5–23; Memnon *FGrH* 434 F 8.8, 11; Euseb. *Chron.* (Schöne) 235–6; Polyb. IV.46. Exhaustive bibliography in Nachtergael 1977: (E 113).

had had to defend the borders of their territories against them, or against peoples displaced by them.

It must be realized that the defence of the Thraco-Macedonian border areas depended not only on military forces, but also on a system of diplomacy to secure, when needed, the collaboration of the mountain peoples. Lysimachus had had forty years' experience of the business, while Ceraunus was completely ignorant of the frontier problems of the kingdom he had so daringly usurped. By his failure to reach an understanding with his neighbours the Dardanians, he unwittingly forced them to make common cause with the invaders, who were able to pour into Thrace and Macedonia, particularly along the usual penetration route of the valley of the Axius (Vardar). This left the young king no alternative but to confront the Gauls in open country: his army was crushed and he himself killed (at the beginning of 279 or perhaps even the end of 280). His two successors (his brother Meleager and a nephew of Cassander's, Antipater) proved incapable of restoring the situation and made no more than brief appearances on the throne; only the *strategos* Sosthenes (who refused the crown)[48] prevented the country from sinking into complete disintegration.

The defeat of Ceraunus left the road to Greece open to the Celtic bands. One of these, under a certain Brennus, penetrated as far as Delphi, where the sanctuary was saved by a snowstorm miraculously sent by Apollo. The tradition relating to the sack of Delphi is late and false; in fact, the peoples of central Greece, the Boeotians, Phocians and especially the Aetolians, had hastily organized resistance, and the Celts, severely tried by guerrillas in the mountains, made a brisk retreat northwards,[49] through Thessaly and Macedonia, in the direction of the Thracian Chersonese, where a large body was destroyed by Gonatas – whose activities at this period we shall examine shortly.

The invasion of Macedonia and Greece, however, was no more than part of the Celtic tide and, while the 'miracle' of Delphi, commemorated by the festival of the *Soteria* (in honour of Zeus *Soter*), made the episode particularly celebrated,[50] it was mainly outside Greece that the Gaulish thrust left lasting traces. Thrace, for example, was invaded by other bands and a Celtic kingdom known as the kingdom of Tylis was to survive there until the end of the century, occupying much of Lysimachus' former territory. In particular, western Asia Minor was invaded by yet other groups, though this was later and in special circumstances (see below, pp. 422–3).

[48] Bengtson 1964–7, II.383ff.: (A 6); Briant 1973, 324ff.: (C 8).
[49] Flacelière 1937, 93ff.: (D 105).
[50] Though not all the documents which commemorate it are contemporary as is the decree from Cos (*SIG* 398). Those from Athens and Chios (*SIG* 402 and 408) are later: cf. Klaffenbach 1952, 1623ff.: (D 92); Pélékidis 1961, 53ff.: (D 96); Nachtergael 1977, 211ff.: (E 113).

The Gaulish invasion, which had put Macedonia to fire and the sword and deprived the country of its king, had also given the son of Demetrius Poliorcetes his chance.[51] The defeat Gonatas had suffered on the occasion of his first attempt on Macedonia, immediately after the assassination of Seleucus, had had very serious consequences for him since many Greeks had seen these events as a new opportunity to shake off the Macedonian yoke. The leadership of the movement this time was taken by Sparta, whose king, Areus, something of a megalomaniac, dreamed of no less than the restoration of the old Peloponnesian confederacy. A certain number of cities (the most important of which, Argos and Megalopolis, did not, moreover, join with Sparta) had driven out their Antigonid garrisons. Corinth, however, was in the hands of Gonatas and barred the way to the north, where Demetrius' son still retained Piraeus, Chalcis and Demetrias – those 'fetters' of Greece which were to play such an important part in the history of the dynasty. Avoiding a direct confrontation with Gonatas, Areus had embarked on a marginal war against the Phocians, a war which was fatal to him and forced him to abandon his plan.[52] However, anti-Macedonian movements in Athens, Megara and Boeotia had made Gonatas' position so precarious that, content to keep a firm hold on his remaining possessions, he had for the moment abandoned the attempt to regain a foothold in Macedonia and had resumed on his own account his father's last and unsuccessful venture, an attempt to win a place in Asian affairs. Circumstances might have seemed more favourable to this than in 287/6. The defeat of Lysimachus and the subsequent murder of Seleucus had stimulated an independence movement in northern Asia Minor and the region of the Straits which presented a serious challenge to the far-stretched sovereignty of Antiochus.[53] Gonatas might reasonably wonder whether this was not an opportunity to fish in troubled waters[54] – all the more since Antiochus was detained by disorders in Syria. After all, the past of the Antigonids had been more glorious in Asia than in Europe: might not the same be true of their future? It is unfortunately impossible to know exactly what happened in these areas at the moment of the Celtic inrush and the Macedonian disaster.[55]

But this disaster rearranged yet again the elements of the problem for Gonatas. The new interest the European scene held for him may have made him look less favourably on Asian ventures which, after all, involved a certain risk – and Antiochus can only have encouraged him to turn towards Europe. It was no doubt in this spirit that their reconciliation took place, probably in 278.[56]

[51] Tarn 1913: (D 38).   [52] Just. XXIV.1; Flacelière 1937, 8off.: (D 105).
[53] Memnon, FGrH 434F9–10.   [54] Ferguson 1911, 155: (D 89).
[55] Will 1979, I.109: (A 67).
[56] Just. XXV.1.1. Cf. Bengtson 1964–7, II.336 n. 1: (A 6).

At the beginning of 277, as he was trying to gain a foothold in Thrace, Gonatas encountered, in the area of Lysimacheia, a large band of Gauls whom he succeeded in luring into an ambush and wiping out.[57] This feat of arms (the only heavy defeat inflicted on the Celts in these years) had the double effect of putting a stop to the Gaulish invasion in Europe and opening the way to Macedonia to the victor. Gonatas could now present himself in Macedonia not merely as a dubious pretender, the son of an unpopular and dethroned king, but as a true *Soter*. We do not, indeed, know anything of the manner of his return, but nevertheless in 276 he was master of the country and of its Thessalian appendage.[58]

So the pattern of the great Hellenistic kingdoms was finally fixed, under the three dynasties – the Ptolemaic, the Seleucid and the Antigonid – which were to preside over their destinies until their respective ends. The great game of diplomacy and war, and also of economics, which was for so long to provide the life-force of this new world, had already begun in Asia.[59]

[57] Just. XXV.1.2–10; 2.1–7. For a discussion of the date: Nachtergael 1977, 167 and n. 191: (E 113).

[58] The date of Gonatas' seizure of power in Macedon, the end of 277 (Nachtergael 1977, 168, n. 192: (E 113)) does not coincide with his first regnal year, which is 283 (Chambers 1954, 385ff.: (D 6)).

[59] See below, ch. 11.

CHAPTER 5

PTOLEMAIC EGYPT

E. G. TURNER

PRELIMINARY NOTE ON THE PAPYRUS SOURCES

This note is intended to issue two warnings. The first is that the historian of Ptolemaic Egypt cannot call at will on written sources contemporary with the period he is describing. From the time of Ptolemy I Soter at the moment of writing this note (January 1980) I know of only two certainly dated Greek papyri, and some six scraps, to which should be added some thirty private documents in demotic Egyptian. The first ten years of Ptolemy II are also blank. A trickle of texts commences in the late 270s B.C.; from about 259 B.C. it becomes a flood which lasts down to about 215 B.C. Thereafter there is comparative poverty till the middle of the second century. The end of this century is well documented for the Fayyûm villages, and there exist a few papyri of the first century B.C. Chronological continuity is assured by the Greek and Demotic ostraca (normally stereotyped tax receipts), not by papyri. Yet only part of the stage which is Egypt is thus flood-lit: above all the Fayyûm, the area most recently won from the desert, the first to revert to desert and in consequence to conserve its archives over twenty-three centuries. But no documents survive from the Delta, the richest and most populous area of Egypt; from Alexandria only such texts as were fortuitously carried up-country. In Middle Egypt Memphis (through its necropolis at Saqqara), el-Hiba, Heracleopolis, Hermopolis, Oxyrhynchus, Lyco-polis intermittently offer finds containing thinly spread and discontinu-ous information. The Thebaid moves in and out of the gloom, for the most part shrouded in darkness, except for its tax receipts on potsherd. Papyrologists and historians of the last two generations have been dazzled by the bright lighting and too ready to extrapolate and generalize from their new information. It is only one of many great services to scholarship of Claire Préaux that she first called attention to this discontinuity in time and place of the evidence, and warned against the supposition that any pattern that may be identifiable under full flood-lighting continues into the unilluminated areas.[1] On herself and her

---

[1] Two examples in minor matters: a cavalry-man's holding in the Memphite nome is 120 arouras, in the Arsinoite 100 arouras. In the Arsinoite nome fishermen receive a state wage; in the Thebaid they have no wage but hand over a quarter of their catch. A major example (to be discussed on pp. 143–4) is provided by the competence of the *dioiketes* Apollonius.

pupils she imposed the discipline of noting date and provenance of texts offered in evidence, and her judgement has repeatedly been proved sage.

The second warning is against the supposition that the bulk of the papyrus evidence is now published and generally available to scholars. It has several times been asserted recently (i.e. in 1978 and 1979) that the major finds of Greek papyri of the Ptolemaic period are published. But the reader should bear in mind the body of petitions acquired by the Sorbonne in 1978 (*enteuxeis* which link with the texts from Ghoran and Magdola already known), the mass of cartonage in Lille or the imposing array of undismounted mummy masks in Oxford, the possible return from which is unknown. Moreover work on demotic texts is only just beginning to get into its stride. One reason why this chapter differs radically from the one it replaces (written fifty years ago by a scholar of wide sympathies and voracious reading) is the progress made by demotic studies during the interval. There are now vigorous centres of demotic in England, Belgium, the Netherlands, Germany, France, Italy and the United States of America (a list which is not exhaustive). Two major finds of demotic material made by W. B. Emery, H. S. Smith and G. T. Martin at Saqqara in 1966–7 and 1971–2, mainly of the fourth and third centuries B.C., promise invaluable Memphite background material for the subject of this chapter;[2] a deposit found by the French School at Luxor in 1970 and 1971 promises equally well for Thebes in the third century B.C. The dream oracles from Saqqara contribute to knowledge of the opening years of Ptolemy VI. The demotic book of law practice from Hermopolis is now at last in scholars' hands. A regular rhythm of future publication is to be looked for.

The statement of a distinguished Egyptologist is especially appropriate to this study: 'nothing can be gained by relying on unwarranted assertions in the books of our predecessors; only patient collecting of facts may in future replace mere guesses by more exact knowledge'.[3] Since 1927 great progress has been made in the collection of 'facts' from Greek papyri about the Ptolemies (in the *Prosopographia Ptolemaica*, for instance, or F. Uebel's monumental lists of cleruchs). But the analysis of these 'facts' is still only in the preliminary stage.

I. PTOLEMY I

On the death of Alexander the Great on 13 June 323 B.C. Ptolemy, son of Lagus and Arsinoe, obtained from Perdiccas, the holder of Alexander's seal, the right to administer Egypt. He lost no time in taking possession

---

[2] Exciting preview in Smith 1974: (F 148).
[3] Černý 1954, 29: (F 230), on the subject of consanguineous marriage (below p. 137 n. 40).

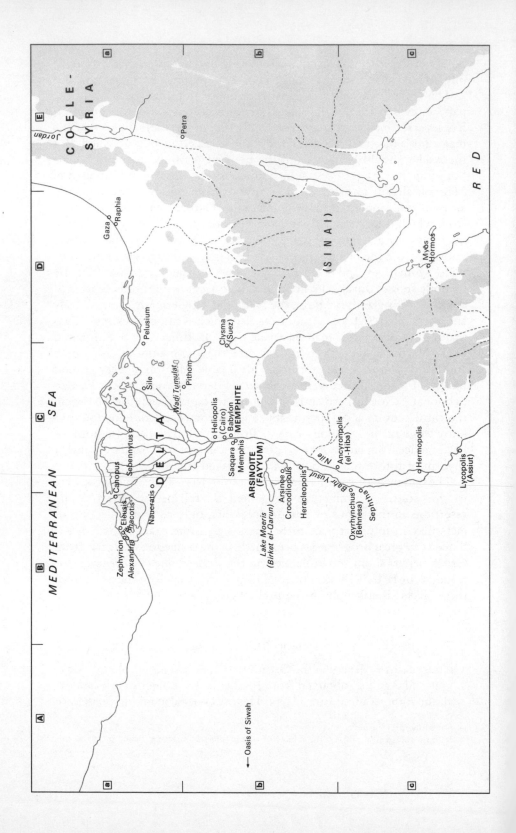

MEDITERRANEAN SEA

COELE-SYRIA

Jordan

RED

(SINAI)

Petra

Gaza
Raphia

Pelusium

Sile
Wadi Tumulat
Pithom

Clysma
(Suez)

Myos
Hormos

Heliopolis
(Cairo)
Babylon
MEMPHITE

DELTA

Zephyrion
Alexandria Rhacotis
Eleusis
Canopus
Sebennytus
Naucratis

Saqqara
Memphis

ARSINOITE
(FAYYUM)

Lake Moeris
(Birket el-Qarun)

Arsinoe
Crocodilopolis

Heracleopolis

Bahr Yusuf

Ancyronpolis
(el-Hiba)

Nile

Oxyrhynchus
(Behnesa)

Sephthis

Hermopolis

Lycopolis
(Assiut)

⟶ Oasis of Siwah

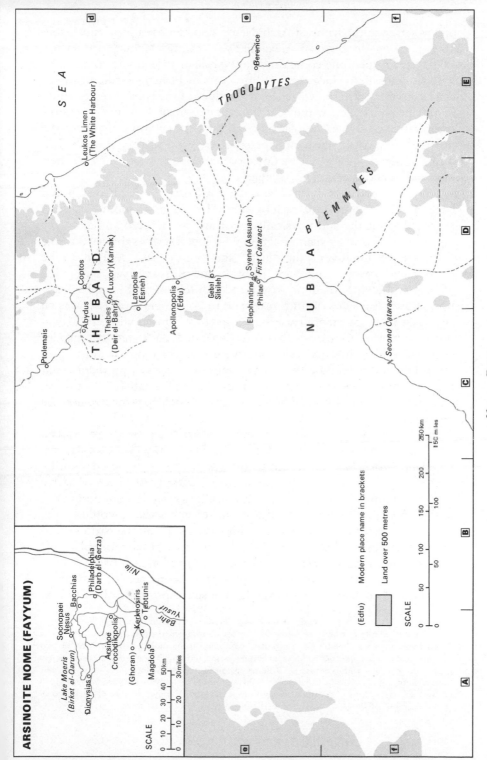

Map 3. Egypt.

ARSINOITE NOME (FAYYUM)

Lake Moeris
(Birket el-Qarun)

Socnopaei
Nesus
Bacchias

Philadelphia
(Darb el-Gerza)

Dionysias

Arsinoe
Crocodilopolis

(Ghoran) o

Kerkeosiris

Tebtunis

Magdola

Nile

Bahr Yusuf

SCALE
0 10 20 30 40 50km
0 10 20 30 miles

SEA

Leukos Limen
(The White Harbour)

TROGODYTES

BLEMMYES

Ptolemais

Abydus
Coptos

THEBAID

Thebes (Luxor) (Karnak)
(Deir el-Bahri)

Latopolis
(Esneh)

Apollonopolis
(Edfu)

Gebel
Silsileh

Elephantine Syene (Assuan)
Philae First Cataract

NUBIA

Second Cataract

Berenice

(Edfu)   Modern place name in brackets

Land over 500 metres

SCALE
0   50   100 150 200 250km
0   50   100   150 miles

of it as satrap in the name of Arrhidaeus, who had been proclaimed sole king, pending the birth of Alexander's posthumous child (pp. 25–6).

It is worth spending some time on the rule of Ptolemy I (Soter, as he will here be called) since the first fifty years of Ptolemaic rule in Egypt can be characterized only through the actions of the ruler. For the study of this period which witnessed the foundation of Ptolemaic government, retrospective extrapolation from the better known Egypt of the 250s B.C. will falsify historical perspective. And history described in terms of personality is not inappropriate to an age when men by their personal qualities effectively shaped events.

Soter had marched with Alexander the Great to Afghanistan and back, and had commanded a Division. He was now about forty-five years old. Mentally and physically vigorous (he fathered an heir at the age of sixty), he was a man of action who successfully submitted to the discipline of intelligent diplomacy and policy, and refused to be discouraged by apparent failure. As brave and skilful captain, sage judge of men and affairs, memoir-writer and hail-fellow-well-met, he knew how to attract friends of both sexes and to hold their loyalty. It was an age when a man could not carve out a career for himself without carving out careers for his friends. Success depended on attracting men of adequate calibre for the tasks that were also their opportunities, on rewarding and defending them, and continually consulting them about innovations of policy. The need for a springboard to satisfy his personal ambition was what attracted Soter to Egypt. No deeper motive need be looked for.

In a conference of the Successors at Triparadisus (see p. 37) Soter's envoy maintained that Egypt was his by right of conquest, it was 'spear-won land' (*doriktetos ge*).[4] From whom had it been conquered? Not by Soter from the Egyptians, for there is no mention anywhere of native resistance to him. Just possibly there is an allusion to the conquest in 332 B.C. by Alexander the Great.[5] But to make such a claim would hardly distinguish Soter's case from that of his rivals, since all the parties owed their territories to Alexander's original conquests. Much more plausible is a reference to Soter's repulse of Perdiccas in 321 B.C.; possibly also to Soter's forceful take-over of Egypt from Cleomenes of Naucratis. Cleomenes had held from Alexander himself a position of authority.

[4] Diod. xviii.39.5 and 43.1 (in the latter passage Perdiccas is specially mentioned).

[5] Cf. Diod. xix.85.3, where *doriktetos chora* seems to apply to the whole territorial area of Alexander's conquests. Possibly Diodorus gives two different meanings to the term. In the two passages cited in n. 4 a reference to Alexander cannot be the meaning. The word *doriktetos* is used in the context of a claim to Egypt asserted by Soter against his fellow Diadochi. It is the reason why Soter and not, e.g., Antigonus or Seleucus should hold Egypt. In any case the term has nothing to do with an assertion to legal title of ownership of the land of Egypt, a sort of manifesto of 'nationalization' of the land, as claimed by Rostovtzeff 1953, 1.267: (A 52).

Since Egypt was a province of the Persian empire, his post is correctly described as a satrapship by the ancient historians when they forsake generalities; it is an unnecessary guess of some modern historians that he was 'administrator' (*dioiketes*). He used his office to extract double dues from the Egyptian priesthood, and to hold Aegean and mainland Greece to economic ransom during a famine by means of a ruthless monopolistic exploitation of exports of Egyptian corn. One of Soter's first acts was to entrap him and put him to death.

'Soter', wrote Diodorus, probably drawing on the histories of Hieronymus of Cardia, who himself played a part as diplomatist in these troubled times, 'succeeded to (*parelabe*) Egypt without putting himself at risk; towards the natives he behaved generously (*philanthropos*), but he succeeded to (*parelabe*) 8,000 talents, and began to recruit mercenaries and collect military forces.'[6] A modern German historian[7] aptly quotes this passage in support of his characterization of the antithesis between generosity towards the natives and reliance on non-Egyptian soldiers as the fundamental and permanent basis of Ptolemaic rule. The claim is too sweeping, but it is appropriate to Soter's action in 323/2 B.C. The term translated 'generously' (*philanthropos*) represents not merely the abstract quality of generosity (*philanthropia*) which theory demanded in a king; it refers to his *philanthropa*, the acts of clemency traditionally incorporated in a proclamation to his subjects in Egypt by a king on his accession. [8] Soter is informing his new subjects that one satrap has succeeded another, and that the new one will not repeat the abuses of his predecessor.

Diodorus' specific statement on Soter's recruiting accords with the expectations of common sense. Alexander's successors acted according to the law of the jungle, and Soter's first need was to secure himself militarily against treachery or invasion. On marching away to the East in 331 B.C. Alexander the Great had left an occupation force in Egypt of 20,000 men, presumably Macedonians and Greeks, under the command of the Macedonians Balacrus and Peucestas. The latter was presumably commander at Memphis, since an 'out-of-bounds' notice to his Greek troops has been found at Saqqara.[9] As capital of Egypt and key to the Delta and the Nile valley Memphis must have been garrisoned. Balacrus may have commanded at Pelusium, the frontier town on the land route

---

[6] Diod. XVIII.14.1.

[7] Bengtson 1967, III.15: (A 6).

[8] From the Egyptian New Kingdom a classic example is the decree of Horemheb, the general who became Pharaoh after Tutankhamun, Breasted 1905, III.22–33: (F 154) (revised version and translation in Pfluger 1946, 260–76: (F 163); Smith 1969, 209: (F 166). Examples from the Ptolemaic period are also discussed by Wilcken, *UPZ* I. p. 497; Koenen 1957: (F 273); they do not include the present passage. The best known is *P. Tebt.* 1.5 (see below, p. 162). See also above, p. 83.

[9] Turner 1974, 239: (F 336).

from Syria. A fleet of thirty warships was commanded by Polemon son of Theramenes. It is highly probable that Soter continued these arrangements. Pelusium was shortly to hold up a succession of would-be invaders; Memphis was the goal which Perdiccas failed to reach in 321 B.C. A garrison may have continued to man the southern frontier at Elephantine. The Persians had maintained a detachment of Jews on guard duty there (some of their Aramaic documents may date as late as the time of Soter[10]). A Greek marriage-contract drawn up in 311 B.C. (probably in Egypt because of its dating formula) and found there shows a Greek presence at Elephantine early in Soter's reign. But their task may have been civil, not military. A Greek papyrus letter of about 250 B.C. mentions Greek soldiers billeted near Edfu. Soter's only Greek city foundation, named Ptolemais after him and sited in Upper Egypt near the modern Assiut, must have contributed to the stability of that region.

A skeleton order of battle of the Ptolemaic forces at Gaza in 312 B.C. can be extracted from Diodorus.[11] Soter marched to Pelusium with 18,000 foot soldiers and 4,000 cavalry composed of Macedonians, of mercenaries and of a mass (*plethos*) of Egyptians; of the latter 'some had missile weapons or other [special] equipment, some were fully armed [that is, for the hoplite phalanx] and were serviceable for battle'. In 307 B.C. Demetrius was surprised that those of Soter's troops he had taken prisoner at Cyprian Salamis refused to change sides. 'They had left their gear (*aposkeuai*) behind in Egypt with Soter.'[12] Mercenaries at this date normally changed sides without fuss. It looks as though Demetrius' prisoners in 307 B.C. were cleruchs (*klerouchoi*), later called *katoikoi*, professional soldiers attracted by Soter to serve as a reserve army by settling them in Egypt on holdings of land. Perhaps the policy decision to settle cleruchs in Egypt was taken early in Soter's rule. By inducing experienced foreign soldiers to settle in Egypt Soter could expect their loyalty: they had a stake in their adopted country as well as the means of a permanent livelihood. The concept of small-holder soldiers sprang from three sources: it was in conformity with Macedonian custom; it had precedents in Pharaonic Egypt, and under the Saites the *machimoi* (native soldiers) had enjoyed personal small-holdings of ten arouras and come to the notice of Herodotus; a third source was the Athenian cleruchic system, an origin which must be taken seriously.[13] Expropriation of land above all had caused bitter enmity towards the Athenian cleruchs; no

---

[10] Harmatta 1961, 149: (F 256), dating these documents to about 310 B.C.
[11] Diod. XIX.80.4.   [12] Diod. XX.47.4.
[13] The argument can only be sketched here. The Athenian institution had a long and complex history. One must take into consideration not only the Athenian decree of the late sixth century B.C. about the Salaminian settlers (ML no. 14), but Thucydides' statement at III.50 (with the comments of A. W. Gomme, *A Historical Commentary on Thucydides* (Oxford, 1945–81) II.327–32) of the terms on which cleruchs were sent to Lesbos in 427 B.C. It should be noted that in 322 B.C. Athenian cleruchs

evidence has survived to show whether similar displacements made
Soter a target of resentment (traces of such feelings are found in the
rather different conditions of the Fayyûm in the 250s B.C.). It is quite
possible that there was exploitable, but never irrigated, good land
available without the need to displace sitting tenants. A decision to
attract foreigners to settle in Egypt to serve as a professional soldiery
could be presented to Egyptians without the implication of Egyptian
military inferiority. The new method had an advantage over that used
against the Persians between 404 and 342 B.C., when Egypt had
depended on the assistance of Greek professional fighters. On completion of their contract these fighters had returned to their homes in
Greece carrying their golden handshake in the form of specially minted
coin. By settling them on the soil of Egypt the satrap retained the
coinage in Egypt, perhaps brought additional land under cultivation
and offered his troops a permanent retainer. Such might have been the
presentation of a policy destined to have far-reaching consequences. *De
facto* the new military settlers were in a privileged social and economic
class; *de facto* their dispersal through the length and breadth of Egypt
drew attention to the Greek way of life; moreover it provided an
unobtrusive military solution for an occupying power. Garrison towns
could be few in number, and Soter could adhere to the principle of
Alexander the Great (it was probably much older) that civil and military
authorities were to be kept separate.

If it was true that only Macedonians or troops of equivalent
equipment, training and resoluteness could meet Macedonians in the
phalanx it was also true that in a barter economy only Greeks knew how
to put coined money profitably to work. Moreover only a Macedonian
princess could provide Soter with an heir acceptable to Macedonians.
Charmers though the Egyptian girls were, only one of Soter's many
mistresses was Egyptian. Of the six persons described before 300 B.C. as
particular friends of the king – Andronicus, Argaeus, Callicrates,
Manetho, Nicanor, Seleucus, the nucleus of the later court hierarchy –
only one, Manetho, was Egyptian.[14] Without any overt declaration of
policy or rejection of partnership, a pattern was being set. It was to
Macedonians and Greeks that the Macedonian ruler gave positions of
command in the army or the élite troops, of executive decision-making
in the administration, and of trend-setting in court manners and
etiquette. Greek became the language of polite society, of administ-

---

who had been settled in Samos for forty years were evicted on the return to their homes of the native
Samians. The recruiting agents of Soter must have notified him of their availability, for it is the year
after his need for soldiers had begun to make itself felt. In the third century B.C. it is possible to list
by name from papyrus documents some twelve cleruchs in Egypt of Athenian origin.

[14] Mooren 1978, 54: (F 288).

ration and of command. In their own country Egyptians required the help of an established corps of interpreters (met later in the Zenon papyri) to approach authority.

The view just outlined has not been universally accepted by modern historians. Some have argued that Soter's satrapship was consciously Egyptianizing at its beginning, and that only later did the pendulum swing in favour of a pro-Greek policy. They point to the high military office held by Nectanebo (Nekhtnebef), described in his hieroglyphic memorial (of Ptolemaic date) as 'nomarch of Sile and at Sebennytus [i.e. of Nomes XIV and XII], commander of foreigners in Nome XIV and commander-in-chief of his majesty's armies'. The titles (and precision in translation does not come easily) may be inflated. The third may mean commander of (Jewish?) mercenaries, the last 'Commander-in-chief of Egyptian troops'. This Nectanebo was grandson of an Egyptian military commander, and his maternal grandmother was sister to Nectanebo I (380–363), among the last of Egypt's native kings.[15] They point also to Petosiris, priest and magnate, whose influential family, owning great estates at Hermopolis, can be traced for two generations before and after him. Inscriptions in his exquisite private tomb pour scorn and detestation on unnamed intruding sovereigns (they must be the Persians),[16] and by inference he built his tomb and composed its inscription under the Ptolemies. Attention is also drawn to the sympathetic account of ancient Egypt (largely utilized by Diodorus) written in Greek by Hecataeus of Abdera before 315 B.C., when Theophrastus quotes it;[17] and to Soter's friendly relations with the Egyptian priesthood revealed in the hieroglyphic satrap stele[18] and in the encomia bestowed therein on the Pharaoh Qabbash (as yet unplaced in time). It is further urged in favour of this view that Soter did not at once make Alexandria his capital but kept his headquarters at Memphis, where the satrap maintained a palace in royal state and furnished the first resting-place for the body of Alexander the Great, hijacked by a resolute stroke of propaganda as the *cortège* was on its way to the Oasis of Siwah.

But these examples will not sustain the thesis. Nekhtnebef's is the last known case of what might be expected if Egyptian troops were employed; Petosiris is the last known Egyptian landowner to have built a family tomb designed and painted in the old tradition of the nobles; even if Soter commissioned Hecataeus to write a work as briefing for his administrators, no commitment to continue Pharaonic policy is in-

---

[15] Confusion has been caused by the conventional rendering 'prince'.

[16] See considerations adduced by Lefebvre 1923–4: (F 378) and further particularized by Roeder 1939, 731ff.: (F 381).

[17] Eicholz 1965, 8–12: (J 5), quoted by Murray 1970, 143: (I 49); see further Stern and Murray 1973, 159ff.: (F 369).

[18] English translation in Bevan 1927, 28–32: (F 127).

volved; in the satrap stele, itself of uncertain date, the endorsement of Soter as recoverer of sacred images stolen from Egyptian temples by the sacrilegious Persians is shown by its later frequent recurrence (for instance in the Karnak ostracon of 258 B.C. (pp. 135–6) or the Canopic decree of Euergetes[19] of 239 B.C.) to be an agreed formula of accommodation between church and state. Soter's remaining at Memphis is easily explained on military grounds: until he could feel confident that his military establishment could contain an invasion from Syria, Soter will have found Memphis strategically preferable to Alexandria. The later of the dates indicated by the satrap stele for the removal to Alexandria is preferable, that is about 313 B.C.

Nor is there any evidence for a swing of the pendulum. Both the Egyptological history, written in Greek, by the learned Manetho of Sebennytus and the organization of the worship of Sarapis under royal sponsorship with the help of Timotheus the Eumolpid belong late in Soter's rule. Their 'Egyptianizing' is almost contemporary with the welcome given in 297 B.C. to Demetrius of Phalerum, spiritual godparent of the Greek Museum and Library in Alexandria and mentor to Soter on the privileges, prerogatives and duties of kingship, and also a friend of Sarapis, reputed healer of his blindness. Well before that date Soter had founded his city of Ptolemais and called on the services of Greeks at Assuan (close to 311 B.C. as *P. Eleph.* 1 shows).

In a country in which the natives outnumbered the newcomers by a factor of between a thousand and a hundred to one, Soter had to find his administrators where he could and seek for co-operation of the governed. Perhaps this is the period in which a formula much used in petitions of about 240–220 B.C. was invented.[20] The official action recommended is sketched out in a phrase beginning: 'Best of all, effect a reconciliation between the parties. Failing that . . .' It is a time when another quality later prized in officials would have been needed: that is, the quality of *proedria*, literally 'the right to be consulted first'. In difficult circumstances the moral effect of taking and retaining the initiative in discussion would have saved many an awkward situation: such for instance as that of the Greek shepherd Hermias who reports to Zenon in 249/8 B.C. that 'we would have kept *proedria* if your messenger had not turned up empty-handed'.[21]

After so much subjective argumentation[22] it is pleasant to conclude by

[19] Translated by Bevan 1927, 208–14: (F 127).   [20] *P. Ent. passim.*
[21] Cf. Crawford 1978, 199: (F 240). She does not quote the example referred to (*PSI* 380).
[22] Professor H. S. Smith has drawn attention to a serious omission from the account given above. I quote his own words:
'The system inherited from the Persians and the Nectanebos is still imperfectly understood. But about the latter one thing is clear – and it goes back to the Saites, and well beyond. That is, the temples were the principal land-owning and income-centralizing branch of the state. Royal

advancing two converging lines of objective evidence. The first is
Soter's coinage. In his early minting he shows himself a loyal satrap to
Philip Arrhidaeus, and to Alexander's posthumous son. Ambition
reveals itself in the coins of about 312–311 B.C. On the obverse is
Alexander the Great's head covered with the elephant scalp; on the
reverse, Zeus enthroned with the legend *Alexandrou* gives place on
silver tetradrachms to the image of Athena Alcidemus with the legend
Alexandreion Ptolemaiou (='Alexandrian, of Ptolemy').[23] At some time
between 312 and 305 B.C. minting on the Attic standard is abandoned in
favour of the standard of Rhodes or Chios. This, it may be guessed, will
have been the period in which the official acrophonic numeral notation
in Greek documents, pre-eminently if not solely in use in Attica,
revealed in use in Egypt by papyri recently discovered at Saqqara,[24] was
dropped in favour of the Milesian 'alphabetic' notation. From 305/4 B.C.
Soter's gold staters, silver tetradrachms, bronze obols, carry his own
portrait. The coin series reveal his progress from governor to monarch,
resident king of Egypt.

The second line of evidence (already drawn on by anticipation) is
furnished by the dating system of Soter as satrap and as king. Soter does
not use his own regnal years for dating till some moment during the year
7 Nov. 305–6 Nov. 304 B.C. The Greek documents adopt a different
system from the demotic. They continue Soter's years as satrap, that is
they trace back year 1 of his reign retrospectively to 324/3 B.C. (very
probably to 3 June 323 B.C., the date of Alexander the Great's death) and
their year 40 is 285/4 B.C. The demotic documents take as year 1 the
moment when Soter's assumption of the position of Pharaoh was
accepted by the Egyptian priesthood, some time in the Egyptian year
305–4 B.C., so that 285 B.C. is year 18. It has indeed been argued[25] that
this assumption of the powers of Pharaoh was proclaimed on the
Egyptian New Year's Day, 1 Thoth=7 November 305 B.C. Be that as it
may, the important point to take is that Soter made no attempt to
harmonize the two systems. He was content to leave the choice between
them to his Egyptian and to his Greek subjects.

At this point it may be helpful to review the continuities of life in
Egypt, starting with ineluctable natural constraints. The geographical
factor of fundamental importance is a great river.[26] Egypt *is* the Nile.

donations to temples allowed these institutions to develop better cultivation, higher income, to
employ more workers, to endow more priesthoods, thus creating a larger administrative force,
and to provide more income and services to the state. And the priesthood was no body of
secluded hierophants (as sometimes depicted), but a corps of practical business and public men
who provided the main administrative muscle of the state.'

[23] Discussion in Fraser 1972, II.10–11: (A 15); cf. E. S. G. Robinson in Rostovtzeff 1953,
III.1635–9: (A 52).

[24] Only one has so far been published: Turner 1975, 573: (F 337).

[25] Samuel 1962, ch. 1: (F 399).   [26] Butzer 1970, 62: (F 129).

From the sea to Assuan is a little less than 1,100 km. Going inland from the Mediterranean the traveller first traverses the 'gift of the river', the prolific Delta. The area (and consequently the name) has the shape of the fourth letter of the Greek alphabet written as a capital. It is upside down, an inverted equilateral triangle, its base depending on the sea; its apex is the point, close to modern Cairo, Roman Babylon, Egyptian Memphis, from which the river branches into a fan of streams. Southwards from this spot to Assuan, about 880 km, Egypt consists of the narrow Nile valley. It is a corridor of green between vari-coloured desert and hills, nowhere more than 30 km wide, averaging about 11 km, and sometimes, as at Gebel Silsileh, narrowing to a mere pass between cliffs. At Luxor and Assuan the valley wears an aspect and climate to delight the senses, even in the heat of summer. Very different is the asperity of Nubia further south, inhospitable, infertile, sometimes cold in winter, always scorching hot in summer. Through its length the river is a first-class waterway. Above Assuan it is a usable route (see below, p. 139) by which to penetrate to the heart of the African continent (an additional 4,300 km to Lake Victoria Nyanza, but hard going from the second cataract, or the swamps south of modern Khartoum). Use of this waterway turned the ordinary Egyptian into an excellent sailor, albeit a sailor in inland waters. In their sacred barques the gods visited each other at festival time; when the whole valley was inundated every Egyptian 'messed about in boats' in order to move from his village to his neighbours'. An annotated sketch-plan from Zenon's papers outlines the earth-work needed to protect the temples of a new settlement against flood and river creatures.[27] In 321 B.C. patriotic crocodiles devoured at least a thousand of Soter's enemies during Perdiccas' mismanaged invasion, and they even come to the notice of Theocritus.[28]

To its valley floor and its Delta the Nile gave life in abundance. Greeks commented on the profusion of flowers all the year round, not merely in spring. Crops of cereals, pulses, vegetables, oil-seeds, dates, orchard fruit, grapes for the table and the wine-press were of great richness and variety. Pasturage maintained herds of cattle, sheep and goats, the desert offered game, the marshes wild-fowl, duck and delicious fish such as the salmon-like *thrissa* that is invoiced for Alexandrian kitchens in the Zenon papyri. Every year between late June and November (a miracle to non-Egyptians who expected a river to run low at that season) the Nile rises in flood and covers the whole valley floor; fish can be caught far from the main channel. For Egyptians this was the natural time of holiday and festival, for no work could be done on the land. After the flood passed its peak, the water could be directed

[27] *P. Mich. Zen.* 1.84 (257–255 B.C.).
[28] Diod. XVIII.35.6; Theocr. XVII.98, πολυκήτεα Νείλου.

through dykes and basins to achieve maximum effect, and to reach areas that might otherwise be unirrigated. When the water receded, it left behind a deposit of life-giving mud. Egypt is the 'black land', *melangaion*, Kemit in Coptic. The alluvium provided a perfect bed for seeding and planting. After the flood there followed a survey, the literal meaning of 'geometry', to satisfy both cadastral and fiscal purposes.

The mountains and deserts flanking the valley formed a natural barrier to an invader. From time to time a foray might descend from the interior, or a hostile force penetrate the Delta from the sea or from Syria. But at north and south nature offered strong points to guard against such incursions, and the flanks could not be turned. Being by nature a stay-at-home to whom the idea of burial in foreign soil was unbearable, the Egyptian also became a man of peace, not war. His natural defensive system tended to insulate him from the surrounding world. Nature provided a setting likely to engender a closed society and a self-contained economic system inside a unified political frame. As a Belgian scholar[29] has put it, the Egyptian cultivator was still living in the Bronze Age when Alexander the Great arrived.

To add a historical dimension to the objectivities of nature is bound to introduce subjective interpretation, over-simplified when it essays to generalize developments spread over three millenia. But society and politics do show certain constants. So long a valley could not become a political unit without a strong central authority. The reconciliation of fiercely hostile neighbouring districts, the so-called 'nomes', the union of 'the two lands' of Lower and Upper Egypt and military defence of the whole called for a king. Measurement of the effects and effectiveness of the annual flood demanded surveyors and recorders, in short a bureaucracy. Both the king and his officials had to be sustained by the primary producer, the cultivator; and the latter's fears and terrors, his need for rites to ensure fertility, to guarantee the flood and maintain the continued existence of the created world evoked a hard-working priesthood (p. 127–8 n. 22) to mediate between cultivator and the supernatural.

The cultivator worked all day and every day for more than two-thirds of the year. But sometimes the Nile (its height measured on the Nilometer at Assuan – and indeed in every nome) did not reach a sufficient height at flood time to prevent distress. Had the cultivator practised self-control (birth-control there was none) and the population of the valley been kept to a figure which a 'low' Nile would sustain, the cultivator might have been the happiest and most prosperous of men. The optimism of mankind and the greed of rulers seeking to bring

---

[29] Bingen 1970, 39: (F 210).

additional soil under cultivation may intermittently have allowed the
population to rise to a figure which only a 'high' Nile could maintain –
this generalization is a guess that it would be hard to substantiate
precisely. The Egyptian cultivator, for all his physical labour and
exposure to endemic riverine and insect-borne disease (especially
ailments of the eyes), was still an object of envy to his counterpart in
neighbouring countries. In the deserts of Sinai the Israelites who
escaped from thraldom remembered the fleshpots of Egypt. In Ptolemaic Egypt the cultivator probably rarely tasted Zenon's wild-boar
haggis; but it may be guessed that a savoury roast pigeon or duck was
eaten at a festival, washed down by beer (the native 'barley Dionysus'),
and accompanied by spontaneous music and dancing, the rattle of the
castanet and the magic of the story teller. In law the cultivator was a
freeman, not a slave or helot, and had as much right to the king's justice
as any of 'the great ones'.

The king's officers, by contrast, congratulated themselves on the
perquisites of their profession. A whole genre of propaganda literature
dwells on the delights of being a scribe in contrast to the pains endured
by the poor flogged cultivator or weaver, realistically displayed on the
painted walls of the tombs of Old Kingdom nobles, for instance the
mastabas of Ti or Mereruka at Saqqara. At the annual sowing the scribes
who follow the surveyors issue seed corn and note the proportion of the
crop to be repaid at harvest (it is an unanswerable and almost
meaningless question whether this proportion should be called rent or
tax). Harvesting, storage, transport overland and down-river no doubt
differed not at all from the picture of them in the Greek papyri
(pp. 149–50). In Ptolemaic Egypt all these services must either be paid
for by a supplementary levy on the harvest or else performed personally
by the cultivator. It is unlikely that this practice is a Ptolemaic innovation, even though specific and unequivocal Pharaonic evidence cannot
be cited. In both Pharaonic and Ptolemaic Egypt the cultivator can be
called on for personal service in corvée, to maintain the canals and
drainage dykes, to tow a stranded obelisk off a sandbank, to keep guard
over the king's barges. In both, the bureaucracy is self-perpetuating and
self-multiplying; whether or not it is corrupt depends on the vigour of
central control. Administrative papyri have revealed shocking scandals
under the Ramessides in the twelfth century B.C.;[30] corruption in
Ptolemaic Egypt will be reported later.

It was accepted that when they travelled the king and the king's men
could call for horses, mules and donkeys. 'The lord hath need of him'
was an accepted explanation for the requisitioning of a colt. Entertain-

[30] Černý in *CAH*³, II.2, ch. 25, sect. iv.

ment and quarters must be provided. The court could exact the refinements of life, objects of daily use of a craftsmanship that delighted the eye, commodious palaces and villas, graceful and gracious women, flowers and poetry. Similar demands on behalf of the gods were unquestioningly accepted. In imposing buildings was celebrated the daily liturgy that renewed creation; the Wilbour papyrus[31] shows that in about 1150 B.C. 14% of the cultivable land between the Fayyûm and Assiut was assigned to the temples. Ritual offered a prominent place for the monarch himself; Pharaoh was the true intermediary between gods and men. As such he was the 'son' of the gods when he sat on 'the throne of Horus the living', and he exclusively was represented carrying out the services of the gods. A bad king is an enemy of the gods, *theoisin echthros* in Ptolemaic documents, the bringer-back of chaos.[32] At the moment of coronation in the religious ceremony the king is acceptable as Horus himself (the King's ambivalent nature is set out more precisely on p. 168). This formula could be regarded as a form of accommodation between theocracy and autocracy, which had often in the past been in unstable equilibrium and were to be so again under the Ptolemies. This undoubtedly oversimplified account will help the reader to stand outside a history written from the European viewpoint. Usually attention is focussed on what the Greeks had to give and the Egyptian contribution is under-rated. Undeniably the Greeks brought with them initiative, energy, intelligence, new technology, an outsider's experience and institutions; but they deployed these gifts in a land of high culture with a respect for craftsmanship and philosophical thinking (imaginative rather than logical), and a tradition of social and political stability. For almost every aspect of Hellenistic government in Egypt there is a Pharaonic precedent as well as a Greek one. A historian must trace the tension between them and analyse the counterpoint of the *interpretatio Graeca* and the *interpretatio Aegyptiaca*.

At the same time this account will show the delicacy of the task. Egyptology has become an autonomous discipline and the historian of Greece and Rome cannot but admire its achievement. He becomes aware of his own enormous advantage in starting from a historiography based on human activities and capacities, from eye-witness accounts which comprehend all aspects of man's functions, not a certain selected number, and the availability of adequate documentary material for their verification and the disclosure of their unexpressed assumptions and prejudices. The Egyptologist does not have these resources. He has to

---

[31] Černý, *ibid.* 611, 1004–5.

[32] Koenen 1959, 103: (F 274). Professor H. S. Smith has suggested to me that the Greek phrase is equivalent to demotic Egyptian *bwt ntr(w)* 'the abomination of the gods'. The Greek phrase is applied (flippantly?) by an individual to a tax-collector in *P. Tebt.* III.768.2 (116 B.C.).

work with an imperfectly understood linguistic system in an un-vocalized notation. The continuous narratives available to him were written by non-Egyptians up to two or more millennia after the events they purport to describe. Writings in Egyptian characters may be categorized briefly as follows.[33] In hieroglyphic writing the monumental inscriptions in temples are mainly ritual in nature, those in tombs are mainly funerary formulae, traditional autobiography, official and priestly titles. The cursive hands, hieratic and its successor demotic, were used for imaginative literature; and for a fair bulk of documents, administrative, legal, epistolary, business and personal. Among them great documents of state, like the survey register of the Wilbour Papyrus or the inventory of royal donations to temples in the great Harris Papyrus, were rare. These documents are so widely spread over Egyptian history, so localized, and often so confined in their reference that they yield only a fragmented picture of Egyptian society at any one time. Because of this limited reference over a limited time-scale it is not possible to start from an accepted description of an institution of pre-Ptolemaic Egypt and observe the innovations introduced by the Ptolemies; indeed the opposite is more likely to happen, that Ptolemaic practices are projected backwards. The historian may often suspect Pharaonic antecedents but fail to document them: and his instinct may be justified by some future discovery. For instance, the absence of 'protection rackets' from the records of Pharaonic Egypt does not warrant the inference that they did not then exist. It is not possible to state with certainty that the leading official of Saite and Persian Egypt was a financial administrator rather than a political officer.[34] And there is no evidence available to support the assumption of some historians, an assumption reasonable in itself, that Egypt was in administrative chaos after the Persian Occupation of 342–332 B.C.

II. ADMINISTRATION, ECONOMY AND SOCIETY UNDER PHILADELPHUS AND EUERGETES

Section One, it might be thought, should have included a note on the geographical facts governing the possibility of military action by Pharaoh outside Egypt. Ptolemaic military doctrine held that to keep open the land route for his armies to operate abroad (whether by

---

[33] For the substance and the formulation of the four following sentences I am heavily indebted to Professor H. S. Smith.

[34] Dr W. J. Tait in *P. Tebt. Tait* pp. 30ff. has shown that the demotic title applied in the Ptolemaic texts to Apollonius *dioiketes* is found twice in pre-Ptolemaic texts applied to a high-ranking officer; once in the Persian period, once at a date under dynasties XXVII–XXX. Dr Tait allows me to say that further investigations not yet published confirm his conclusion that this pre-Ptolemaic official was a finance officer.

Pelusium–Gaza or Wadi Tumulat and Sinai), the king must control, that is garrison, not only the southern Syrian coast and the Jordan valley, but Lebanon and Antilebanon and the territory lying east and south of these mountains ('hollow Syria'). Was this doctrine or dogma? Merely to pose the question shows that the answer will be found in military appreciations rather than geographical imperatives. Others discuss the question in this book. Here it will be enough to observe that the Ptolemies were unwilling to abandon the land routes, even though conditions had changed radically. In the mid fourth century the strategic importance of Cyprus for the defence of Egypt was demonstrated by Euagoras' tenacious defence of the island against the Persians. During Alexander's march through Syria a fleet based on Cyprus had covered his western flank and facilitated his march to Pelusium. Alexander had read the military lessons right when he founded Alexandria. From Egypt itself his new foundation removed the dangerous hiding places of beaten guerillas pausing to recoup (Inaros and Psammetichus in the 450s, and the so-called Libyans of the late fifth century); above all, it gave Egypt a door to the west for a two-way traffic of goods and ideas, as well as providing a secure base for a navy. But the Ptolemies were unwilling to rely on their navy alone for the power of entering or leaving Egypt with armed forces. Nevertheless they built up that navy as the means of distant military action: its maintenance was a major item in their military budget, its successes and failures a barometer of their fortunes. Usually it fought far from its home base: in the decisive battle of history, the battle of Actium, more than 1,100 km away. Other foreigners before the Ptolemies had sat in Egypt on the throne of the Pharaohs, but no Egyptian king had undertaken strategic campaigns reaching into the Aegean.

Military and naval campaigns and the underlying principles of Ptolemaic foreign policy are analysed elsewhere in this book (see pp. 442–5). There will be no discussion here whether they should be read as aimed at an aggressive, defensive, religious, mercantile or economic imperialism. No more is needed than to note the points of interaction between foreign and domestic policy. First is an enormous military and naval expenditure on warships, mercenaries and elephants. A second factor was the need to import materials that could not be home-produced: timber and pitch for ship-building, for instance. Import requirements were more than balanced by export possibilities; the Ptolemies could offer articles of fine Egyptian craftsmanship, for which there was much demand, guaranteed by a rigorous control of quality: linen, papyrus, faience and, later on, glass; for diplomatic ends or straightforward sale they could release a sizeable proportion of the known world's grain crop. A third factor was the desire to attract into

Egypt men of talent or possessed of special skills, and to reward them appropriately. Such men were ready to seek service more demanding and remunerating than could be offered by the bourgeois opportunities of the declining Greek city-state; and in a world competing for their skills and laying stress on prestige it was important for kings to be seen to be successful.

The relative weight to be attached to these factors, the motives underlying particular actions to realize them, and their influence on Egyptian domestic issues are topics that have been and may long be expected to remain a preoccupation of scholars. The reader should be warned that the view of Philadelphus' rule propounded in this chapter is not the accepted one. Its administration is usually held up to unbounded admiration: it is supposed to exemplify Greek resourcefulness and intelligence, the splendid financial returns obtainable from energy and enterprise, and a strong overall control which established equilibrium between immigrant and native. It promised in the 270s to be all these things. In spite of a series of expensive military and naval failures, it achieved much. But its show of brilliance was attained by disastrous fiscal and social policies. Philadelphus was committed to an inexorable demand for progressively growing revenue. By the 250s total mobilization of the resources of Egypt was the driving principle of its economic, social and fiscal organization.

This view is no more than a hypothesis and it must be tested in the pages which follow. The first step is to consider a recent discovery. This is a large piece of terracotta bowl found at Karnak in 1969/70 and inscribed in ink with a long text in demotic.[35] A paraphrase of this text might run:

Register of patrimony: orders have been given to make a complete registration in writing, capable of verification, and to put it in the hands of Phoenix (*Pȝmjk*) the chief treasurer (*mr–ḥtm*)[36] in the year 28, month Thoth, of the king who triumphed over the pro-Persian king at the time of the Syrian journey, put in his hands by his scribes and district agents from Elephantine to the Mediterranean, specifying nome by nome, that is 36 [corrected to 39] districts . . .

The enumeration includes the growth of the sown crops, state of irrigation, type of land concerned, areas unwatered and unsown, extent of small-holdings, orchards and vineyards, leases, the position of the

[35] Found by the French school, and hereafter referred to as 'the Karnak ostracon'. Thanks are due to Bresciani 1978, 31: (F 222), for a prompt preliminary publication (photograph and translation into Italian, no transcription) and the promise of a definitive edition. In a text of such central importance and difficulty the last word will not be said for some time. I am indebted to Dr W. J. Tait for answering my queries about it. See also ch. 11, p. 419 n. 16.

[36] No historical argument should at present be based on the supposed Greek form of the name or title.

priests. It finishes: 'Sum total of expenditure for the welfare of Egypt and its sublime independence, and that of its cities and its temples.'

Many features in this text require elucidation: the linguistic connotations of the conceptual terms employed need to be unravelled (does 'patrimony', for instance, mean 'the property of an individual or institution' or 'the resources available in Egypt'?); another question is whether the motivation is merely traditional, the propaganda theme of triumph over a king heir to the Persians having already been shown to be a formula for agreement between king and priests (see p. 127 above). Supposing it to be no more than propaganda, it is still striking that the theme should be invoked at this time and for this purpose. Thoth year 28 is the beginning of the Egyptian regnal year following[37] the year in which the 'Revenue Laws' were issued and the so-called Second Syrian war began, and so falls in 258 B.C. This war is only hinted at in the ostracon, but the implication of its final phrase is that the thoroughgoing fiscal system described and codified is intended to support it.

In order to judge the validity of this implication the reader must first consider some salient features of Philadelphus' rule: his marriage, his conspicuous expenditure on pageantry, his personality. In this survey a short characterization of the principal Greek papyri will also be given.

The name *Philadelphos* ('loving his sister') by which posterity knows Ptolemy II was not applied to him in the singular number during his lifetime. It was reserved for his full sister and second wife, Arsinoe *Philadelphos* ('loving her brother'), an intelligent and tempestuous Macedonian princess outstanding even from a line of passionate and intelligent Macedonian women. Her irresistible personality led to her official deification during her lifetime, the first 'western' queen to enjoy such honours (below p. 168). She had already been married to her half-brother, Ptolemy Ceraunus. Now she engineered the marriage to her full brother, forcing him to divorce and banish his first wife in order to comply. The fact that Philadelphus agreed indicates a characteristic ambivalence in his personality and in his rule. The marriage gave occasion for scurrilous jests and scandal in Alexandria and throughout the Greek world. Recently modern historians have grown reluctant to believe that those ancient writers who comment on this particular marriage[38] (as distinct from commentators on brother and sister marriage in general) are to be accepted as evidence that Philadelphus and Arsinoe were adopting a practice in common use in Egyptian society in the third century before Christ. Egyptologists admit that in Pharaonic

[37] Assuming both ostracon and the Revenue Laws use the Egyptian regnal year.

[38] Examples of the former Paus. 1.7.1 (but he wrote four centuries later), Memnon *FGrH* 434 F 8.7 (garbled in extract since the censure is applied to Ptolemy Ceraunus), of the latter Diod. 1.27.1–2 (connected with Isis' marriage to Osiris, a passage usually treated as Diodorus' own comment).

times some Pharaohs married their full sisters: an instance quoted in an earlier volume of this history is that of 'Queen Neferu (III), the sister and apparently one of the wives of Mentuhotpe II', the great Mentuhotep of the Middle Kingdom who reigned before 2000 B.C.[39] But that the practice was ever widespread has been challenged. One obstacle to a generalized affirmation is semantic. The same word in Middle and New Kingdom Egyptian (typically in New Kingdom love poetry in the hieratic script) was used for sister and for the loved one, and consequently could be extended to mean wife, as often in New Kingdom tomb reliefs and stelae. Whether a marriage, royal or private, was fully consanguineous can often not be determined. However even the most strict of Egyptologists is ready to admit the existence of some fully consanguineous marriages in the royal house, and from the Eighteenth Dynasty onwards among private persons. The latest Pharaonic documentary example I can adduce belongs to the tenth century B.C., that of the Libyan commander Pediese and his wife who was also his sister Taere (persons close to the royal house in Dynasty XXII).[40] Was there continuity? Are there documentary records of the practice in Persian Egypt? Neither Herodotus nor Hecataeus of Abdera notice it. It should also be remarked that in demotic Egyptian contracts, it would be surprising to find the word for brother/sister extended to mean marriage partner.

Yet that extension was suffered after 280 B.C. in Egypt and nowhere else in the Greek world by the Greek words for brother/sister. It is hard not to see this semantic change developing out of social usage. The marriage of Arsinoe and Philadelphus undoubtedly kept power inside the family. The pair might have reasoned that compensation for possible alienation of Greek support could be obtained from an appeal to the imagination and affections of Egyptian subjects by representing the necessities of ambition and naked power as recourse to or revival of Egyptian tradition. It is for Egyptologists to report whether in 280 B.C. the synod of Egyptian priests would or could have given a different account of the supposed tradition from that set out here, and to make

---

[39] See W. C. Hayes, *CAH*[3] I.2, pp. 478, 481.

[40] The most strict of Egyptologists is J. Cerný (n. 3 above). Pediese, 'the great chief of Me', Breasted 1905, IV, no. 774a: (F 154); Cerný 1954, 23: (F 230). For guidance on Egyptian linguistic usage I am deeply indebted to Professor H. S. Smith. [Normally work unavailable till after April 1980 is not taken into account. But Hopkins 1980: (F 266) (which I had not seen) is too important not to be inserted. He gives a notable analysis of the incest taboo, and a strict documentation of the numerous examples of brother–sister marriage in Roman Egypt, the implication being that so widespread an institution must have developed its roots over a long period of time. An explanation is needed also for the equality with men enjoyed by Egyptian women in marriage and divorce contracts. I have sympathy for his contention that it is inappropriate and may be misleading to impose legal rules of evidence on literary and liturgical texts. For the Ptolemaic period Egyptologists must take up his challenges.]

precise the limits within which their account was framed. Philadelphus and Arsinoe could have reasoned that Greek protests (unlikely to be pushed home by the beneficiaries of royal patronage) could be countered by mustering Greek precedents. For Theocritus and Callimachus to cite the sacred marriage of Zeus and Hera, full brother and sister, is not so lame a defence as has often been supposed. Besides, Athenian law accepted marriage between a half-brother and half-sister if the shared parent were the father, Spartan law if it were the mother. Such precedents, however, are not adequate support for those who argue that full consanguineous marriage was a Greek custom introduced to Egypt by Greeks. After the 270s private individuals no doubt followed the example of their sovereigns, but not in large numbers: the examples of such marriages verifiably attested in Greek and demotic documents before the Roman period can be counted on the fingers of one hand.

Philadelphus must have welcomed the advertisement of dynastic solidarity offered by his marriage to Arsinoe. He had succeeded to the throne although he had an elder half-brother, the child of Soter's first wife Eurydice. With or against Soter's wish, the ancient Egyptian device of a co-regency[41] had indicated where the succession would lie. The moments of transfer of power are flash points in the history of personal rule; they offer dangerous moments of weakness, to be seized by revolutionaries at home or enemies abroad; round the apparent candidates for the succession parties form, motivated by self-interest and conflicting policies. In 283 B.C. there are only traces of a struggle: Demetrius of Phalerum backed the wrong candidate and withdrew from Egypt. It is not known whether Philadelphus was adept enough to keep his hands clean.

This marriage must have taken place before 274 B.C., and it could have been as early as 279 B.C.[42] In 279/8 B.C., probably on the fourth anniversary of Soter's death, the magnificent festival of the *Ptolemaieia* was first celebrated.[43] In glorifying the founder of the dynasty by implication it glorified his heir. It was thereafter to be held every four years, the *pentheteris* par excellence of the Zenon Papyri. Such festivals, attended by invited delegates especially from Greece and the Eastern Mediterranean,[44] built up Philadelphus' international prestige and

[41] Kienitz 1953, 95: (F 159). The co-regency began in Dystros (March/April) 285 B.C. This was eventually, but not immediately, accepted as the first year of Philadelphus' rule. The retrospective dating caused havoc in the dating systems of Philadelphus (below, pp. 146–7). I accept the arguments of Koenen 1977, 43–5: (F 275). Year 14 in *P. Hib.* II.199 is retrospectively dated, i.e. it is Julian 272/1 B.C. Year 4 in the inscription published by Wörrle 1978: (B 179) can also be retrospective.

[42] Fraser 1972, II.367–8 n. 229: (A 15).

[43] See most recently Shear 1978, 33ff.: (C 62), and this volume p. 417.

[44] H. Braunert 1951/2, 262: (F 220), points out that no persons from Arabia, India, Carthage or Massilia appear among the dedicators of the Hadra vases. They may have been invited for all that.

displayed his determination to assert the status of a first-class power for Egypt. That of the *Ptolemaieia* claimed and was accorded parity with the Olympic games, and its competitions included Greek athletic, musical and equestrian events; yet its celebration possibly incorporated some Egyptian elements from a *heb-sed* or anniversary festival, the dead king being associated with a festival for a living ruler. The reigning king was present in person, and spectators and competitors had a chance to crave a boon. The Egyptian relish of festivals matched that of the Greeks, and Philadelphus exploited this prop of power with consummate mastery. Inspiration from Egyptian models is likely for some of his other festivals. Theocritus in *Idyll* xv, his most felicitous dramatic poem, takes as centrepiece the prima donna's cantata evoking the tableau of the death of Adonis; the crowded streets and galloping war horses are part of the accompanying pageantry. The most famous *pompe* of all, the pomp and circumstance described by Callixeinus (Athenaeus 196a), with its parade of lions and elephants and spectacular floats, could be illustrated only by combining elements out of the Parthenon frieze with frescoes in the tombs of the Nobles of the New Kingdom, or the reliefs in the temple of Hatshepsut at Deir-el-Bahri.

Mention of Hatshepsut prompts a momentary digression on the imports from India and Africa. The traffic, with the one large exception of the elephant, is of the same character as that of the New Kingdom: Callixeinus' account of the procession speaks of Ethiopian tribute bearers, ebony, leopards, panthers; and papyri reveal perfumes and ostrich eggs. Nor is there much change in the routes these goods followed – from Somaliland or Aden to a Red Sea port, then by caravan to Coptos, from there up or down the Nile. The Nile itself was exploited a little. Soter's expedition to Ethiopia reported the exact latitude of Meroe, and Theocritus knows of the rock of the Blemmyes. But from the second cataract southwards its passage was too difficult and territory too inhospitable for it to serve as a corridor of regular traffic. Philadelphus re-opened the canal from Heliopolis to Suez by the Wadi Tumulat and Pithom.[45] But a waterless, harbourless coast and head winds made for slow northward voyages to reach Suez. The preferred Red Sea harbours were further south – Myos Hormos, the White Harbour, Berenice, Ptolemais of the Elephants. No doubt these are among the 'designated' harbours (a standard Ptolemaic administrative term) mentioned in the *Periplus Maris Erythraei*. From the northern Berenice in the late second century[46] five merchants risked their privately borrowed capital in a venture to the spice-bearing land. East of Bab el Mandeb they will have been seeking cargoes of spices, gem-

[45] Oertel 1964, 32: (F 291).   [46] Wilcken 1925, 86: (F 346).

stones, sacred cows and hunting dogs. The secret of the periodicity of the monsoons may have been penetrated as early as the late second century B.C.; the evidence seems clear that regular direct sailings to India did not begin till the first century after Christ.[47] Aden (Arabia Eudaemon) remained the important centre for exchange. From it to Europe there were two routes in addition to that by the Egyptian coast: the sea route up the west coast of Arabia and the parallel caravan route on shore terminating at Petra. South of Gardafui, Philadelphus', Euergetes' and Philopator's elephant hunters pursued their dangerous mission, to catch what the Adulis inscription terms 'Trogodytic and Ethiopian' elephants. A specially-built elephant transporter (*elephantegos*), vulnerable to storms, carried provisions on the southward trip, and brought back the elephants which fought at Raphia.

What kind of man was the king who set these expeditions in motion? In the Greek world Theocritus projected the image of Philadelphus the philhellene: 'kindly, cultured, gallant, as pleasant as may be; knows his friend, and knows his enemy even better. As a king should be, he's generous to many, and doesn't refuse when asked; but you mustn't always be asking, Aeschinas.'[48]

The Greek documents show Philadelphus living up to this image: experimenting, asking questions, an intellectual as well as a voluptuary, organizer of a zoo as well as a Museum (unkind critics compared his professors to his singing birds). The fact remains that he knew how to talk to the talented group of men whom he attracted, and moved without formality, if not always at his ease, among them. Perhaps he depended on them individually more than a king should. 'Where is Apollonius?' reads a papyrus, 'the king needs to consult him.'[49] The impression is given that issues were handled as they arose, and that the king had a temperament that reacted to crises. The king's scorn sometimes blazed out in public humiliation.[50] After Arsinoe's death Philadelphus possibly felt deeply the absence of a guiding personality. He could give continuing support to a man he trusted: Apollonius *dioiketes* enjoyed such support for fifteen years. The rewards of royal patronage were high; a small-holding and a good standard of living for a soldier; for men of organizing ability a salary, a palazzo in Alexandria, sinecure priesthoods, perhaps a gift estate (for instance, a city in Asia Minor,[51] or in Egypt 'Ten Thousand Arouras'= 2,500 hectares, a territory greater than that of two populous villages). Such largesse

[47] Fraser 1972, I.181–4: (A 15), supersedes all previous analysis.
[48] *Idyll* XIV.62, translated by A. S. F. Gow.
[49] *P. Cairo Zen.* 1.59066.
[50] *P. Petrie* III.42 H 8.6 = Witkowski 1911, no. 6: (F 152). Metrodora writes to her husband, Cleon, Senior Engineer for Irrigation Works, that she will stand by him in his disgrace.
[51] Wörrle 1978, 201–46: (B 179).

carried the opportunity of private enrichment as added bonus. Of course there were risks to be taken by an ambitious man. The gift of an estate could be revoked. The court had its own internal tribunal of enquiry.[52] Some of Apollonius' predecessors, Telestes and Satyrus perhaps, seem to have fallen out of favour.[53] From such successes and failures among its members the court gradually built up a body of precedent and protocol. Under Euergetes, when Zenon's friend Hermocrates incurred the king's displeasure, the decision of the internal court of enquiry was conveyed in writing to the king by the Chancellor (*hypomnematographos*), Dositheus, not by Hermocrates' departmental superior 'because it is the custom for things to be done this way'.[54]

The minute of this formal decision has unfortunately not survived. Hermocrates' case is known from the 'Zenon archive' already mentioned, which it will be helpful to characterize briefly. It is self-evidently a collection of papers personal, official, miscellaneous, tidily docketed and preserved by Zenon, a jackdaw of a man, in his house at ancient Philadelphia, modern Darb-el-Gerza. The desert sands encroached on it and saved the papers till they were unearthed fortuitously by fellahin about 1914–15.[55] In spite of efforts to assemble all the papyri at Cairo important parts of the find have been dispersed throughout the world.[56] The archive contains only a few letters written by Zenon himself, for he did not as a rule keep copies of outgoing letters. But there are incoming official and private letters addressed to him, correspondence exchanged between other parties, affidavits, receipts, loans and leases, some of which have no immediate connexion with Zenon. In total there are perhaps two thousand items (an item may be a chit of three or four words or a register several feet long). As publication progresses, the total may be increased or reduced – reduced as fragments in various collections are identified as portions of a known item.

Zenon himself was a Carian, son of Agreophon of Caunus. Carians had a long tradition of service in Egypt as mercenaries and as managers. In Memphis in Saite times they formed a separate ethnic group, Caromemphites alongside Hellenomemphites. Some of the funerary stelae pillaged from their cemetery were found at Saqqara in 1968–70.[57] No family ties of Zenon to Egypt are known. He presumably offered his

[52] The text cited in n. 54 refers to an *anakrisis*, a term that occurs elsewhere in the Zenon archive. It is tempting to see in this particular course of enquiry the origin of the second-century *to en tei aulei kriterion* of P. Lond. VII.2188, 89:   [53] Skeat 1948, 80: (F 324).

[54] P. Mich. Zen. 55.26: (F 62); CPJ 1.127(a): (F 9). If the Dositheus of this text really is to be identified with Dositheus, son of Drimylus, his period of office exceeded eighteen years.

[55] A very few appeared on the market as early as 1911. See T. C. Skeat on P. Lond. VII.1974: (F 59).

[56] See the bibliography in Préaux 1947, 87: (F 141); Turner 1980, 202: (F 149); Pestman and others 1981: (F 18).   [57] Masson 1978: (F 281).

services in about 261 B.C. to Ptolemy, who gave him the usual arrival present, and assigned him to his *dioiketes* Apollonius (himself guessed on very slight grounds[58] to have been a Carian). Zenon's ability was quickly recognized, and he was appointed to various offices of trust: in Palestine about 259/8 B.C., then at Apollonius' side in Alexandria or on tour in Egypt. In 256 B.C., after an illness, he was put in charge of the 'Ten Thousand Arouras' in the Fayyûm, one only of the gift estates (*doreai*) granted to Apollonius, and served him till about 246 B.C. Apollonius dismissed him, then himself disappears from view; whether through death, disgrace or the advent of a new king is not known.[59] Zenon remained at Philadelphia apparently without benefit of higher protection till at least 234 B.C.[60]

It is important that his papers should be seen in perspective. Superficially they tell a success story; looked at more closely they show signs of strain in the economic and social system of Egypt, and an analysis attempted later (pp. 149–53) may reveal whether these strains are inherent, predictable and cumulative or merely temporary. At the moment it should be noted that the problems facing Zenon on Apollonius' estate are not typical of traditional Egyptian farming and rural administration, though experience of such farming would have been useful to a man who had to invent his own solutions. Zenon himself may be regarded as the ideal civilian immigrant: resourceful, energetic, able to initiate and organize and to express himself in terse Greek phrases, normally lucid but ambiguous when evasiveness is desirable, touched occasionally with literary reminiscence. Success brought him a good livelihood, a country villa, challenging daily work; he remained a man of frugal habits, interested in more than material rewards. He sponsored young athletes and musicians, equipped a palaestra, had books sent down from Alexandria, for himself or his brother Epharmostus; to commemorate his favourite hound Tauron who saved his life from a wild boar he commissioned two epigrams, one in elegiac, one in iambic verse. Zenon represents middle-management. Apollonius, his personal rather than official superior, is an altogether exceptional character. More than fifty letters from him survive, curt, to the point; he spares neither himself nor his staff. One long account of the issue of lamp oil to his travelling retinue shows that work went on after dark in the bakery, the stables, the secretariate and the butler's pantry, where Bannaeus cleans the silver by lamplight. Apollonius was intolerant of the slipshod, especially carelessness in money matters – his

[58] Principally the dedications to Zeus Labraundus (*P. Mich. Zen.* 31.6) and Apollo Hylates, *OGIS* 1.53.1.
[59] No certainties are supplied by the much corrected draft petition *P. Cairo Zen.* v.59832. Cf. n. 122 below.   [60] *P. Lond.* VII.2019.

household noted with surprise his severe reaction to the discovery that seven talents had been disbursed from his travelling safe without reference to him. His great abilities, his very success in pleasing Philadelphus, may have distorted appreciation of the general administrative situation. Should not a distinction be made between the man and his office? Some historians have written of Apollonius as the king's 'all-powerful' finance minister, almost as his prime minister. This may be his personal achievement. It has no foundation in the archive. Financial transactions have to be recorded, and will occupy a disproportionate place in the papers of a financial administrator. That under the Saites, Persians and Nectanebos a high financial official enjoyed the same title in demotic Egyptian (p. 133 n. 34) must have been valuable to Apollonius in his dealings with the population of Egypt. But there was no automatic continuity between Pharaonic and Ptolemaic Egypt. Apollonius has the ear of the king; so do a number of other important men whose files have not survived. It is doubtful whether Apollonius helped in policy decisions. When, in the second century (p. 165) protocol has fossilized honorific titles into a hierarchy, a *dioiketes* occupies a relatively lowly position. It is perhaps rash to put in order of precedence the competing band of men who can be labelled as ministers of so moody a king as Philadelphus. But it may be guessed that Apollonius' official place was at best sixth, and may have been as low as tenth. Above him must be ranked the royal *epistolagraphos*,[61] Ptolemy's secretary or *ab epistulis*, who has to advise on diplomacy and draft letters to brother monarchs and sovereign states; the *hypomnematographos*, the king's Chancellor or *a commentariis*; perhaps the officer who drafted royal edicts, *ho epi ton prostagmaton*, Ptolemy's *a libellis*; one or more field marshals and admirals, the Governor of Cyprus, possibly the President of the Museum and the Governor of Alexandria. Another common assumption, that Apollonius was the sole finance minister, is also open to question. A recent study[62] has made a strong case for several *dioiketai* being simultaneously in office later in the third century. In the schedule of nomes issued under the authority of Apollonius in the Revenue Laws, only twenty-four are specified by name.[63] The list finished with 'The Thebaid' – which, as is known from other papyrus sources, was itself divided into nomes.[64] Was 'The Thebaid' under the charge of another than Apollonius? The question is not to be answered by noting the

[61] For the spelling see *P. Lond.* VII.1930.160 and T. C. Skeat's note.

[62] Thomas 1978, 189: (F 331). the use or absence of the definite article with *dioiketes* is not significant. Petitions are addressed indifferently to 'Apollonius *dioiketes*' and 'Apollonius the *dioiketes*'. The latter would in any case mean simply 'the *dioiketes* of this province'.

[63] *P. Rev.* cols. 31 and 60–72 (the names differ in the two lists). The Karnak ostracon (above, n. 35) offers a total of 36 (39) nomes.

[64] *P. Eleph.* VII.12 (225/4 B.C.).

absence of records that Apollonius' personal tours of duty took him to the south of Egypt. Alexander the Great had supported the principle of collegiality for his first civil officials, the nomarchs Doloaspis and Petesis. In the Karnak ostracon (pp. 135–6) above) no argument can be based on the demotic title or form of the name given to the principal officer; but Apollonius is not mentioned.

These considerations have importance for another reason. It is hard to believe on *a priori* grounds[65] that the organizational ideas seen in the papyri of the 250s are a sudden upsurge that had to wait for that decade for their conception and elaboration. It was in the 270s that Theocritus was beating the drum for Philadelphus and the king was organizing his most outrageously extravagant procession. But it is in the early 260s (about 268/7 B.C.) that new ideas of fiscal exploitation (Model II, below pp. 151–4) were in process of conception and application.[66] It is an accident of discovery that has concentrated scholarly attention on the next decade.[67]

A different type of administration was applied to the land (*chora*) of Egypt from that used for the Greek cities. The latter, Naucratis, Ptolemais and then supremely Alexandria, enjoyed their own laws and a theoretical self-government, more a source of pride than of power. The laws of Naucratis, the oldest Greek foundation in Egypt, are cited as paradigms when Antinoopolis was being founded by Hadrian; about A.D. 270 victory for an athlete, musician or poet in the games at Naucratis still carried valuable tax immunities.[68] As already seen, Alexandria did not become the most famous of Alexander's foundations by accident: Alexander had sensed the opportunities awaiting a city that gave Egypt a door to the west. Its streets were laid out on a Hippodameian grid, with adequate space inside the walls for five districts (*grammata*) labelled One to Five (*alpha, beta, gamma, delta, epsilon*, the first five letters of the Greek alphabet in their numeral signification).

---

[65] And there are suggestions in the papyri themselves. The Revenue Laws mention the name of Satyrus in connexion with the collection of the *apomoira*. Simaristus' *dioikesis* is still unexplained.

[66] This is not the place to work it out in detail, but a possible hypothesis is that agreement over the collection of the *apomoira* marked the first stage of the new fiscal system in about 268/7 B.C. The *apomoira* was collected from year 18 onwards (*P. Rev.* col. 37) by Greeks, but in kind not in cash. It has been argued by P. W. Pestman (1967, 6: (F 398)) that the institution of the 'Revenue year' (the year beginning Mecheir 1, late March in 267–265) belongs to this period. *P. Hib.* 1.43 shows that the manufacturing system envisaged in *P. Rev.* for sesame oil was operating in 261 B.C.

[67] The reclamation of the Fayyûm was proceeding apace in 259 B.C. The consulting engineer Cleon was still at work. In some documents the nome is called the 'nome of the Lake' (Limnites, Limne); its capital was then called after Arsinoe as it was itself renamed Arsinoites, and many of its villages were christened after members of the ruling house or favourite divinities. The German archaeologists who dug the site of Philadelphia (Viereck 1928: (F 341)) found no remains below the new settlement. Nevertheless one day archaeological exploration may supply evidence of earlier Ptolemaic occupation at some sites, both in the Fayyûm and elsewhere.

[68] *P. Oxy.* XXII.2338; Coles 1975, 199ff.: (F 238).

Philadelphus found architects to erect buildings that were to make the city a wonder of the world: a lighthouse to guide mariners into the newly constructed harbours that gave safety to shipping on a coast dangerous in summer because of northerly winds. The square fenestrated tower of the Pharos, surmounted by a fire-basket and by the statue of Zeus the Saviour, is commemorated in Poseidippus' epigram and in glass beakers manufactured for the tourist trade.[69] The founder was himself enshrined (in the manner of Napoleon or Lenin) in a magnificent mausoleum, some say of glass, some of gold. This building may have been commissioned by Euergetes who certainly added the great Serapeum. The amenities and situation of this new city attracted an assorted population, foreigners, Egyptians, Jews (originally, it is said, a large body of prisoners of war, who elected to remain and formed the most important single minority group). The right to full citizenship was restricted to Macedonians and Greeks, and some of the privileges of their citizen law (*politikos nomos*) are set out in the so-called 'Dikaiomata' roll,[70] material excerpted by an advocate to use for procedural proof. Politically they were registered in demes (the names of some forty are known), the organizational nucleus of a Greek city's traditional governing Council and Assembly. Did the institutions of Council and Assembly ever exist and function? The most recent historian of Alexandria argues that they did[71] but were abolished in successive stages at dates unknown. Certainly neither was in existence when Augustus took over Egypt. City business at that time was conducted by a series of city officers – the *exegetes*, city *hypomnematographos*, *archidikastes* and the Night General. In the third century B.C. a city officer was Superintendent of the City; he was either replaced or supplemented by a royal General of the City.

Throughout its history, Alexandria remained set apart from Egypt: it was 'Alexandria by Egypt'. As a Greek city it had its own dependent territory (*chora*), but that territory was not the whole *chora* of Egypt. The land of Egypt was administered in the manner traditional to the Pharaohs: the old-style royal offices of nomarch,[72] royal scribe, village scribe or village officer (*komogrammateus* or komarch) continued in being; except for the first on the list, they were predominantly exercised by Egyptians. The nomarch may be presumed to have controlled a

[69] Plates vol., pl. 6. Hackin 1954, 101–3 and figs. 359–63: (F 377).

[70] *P. Hal.* Add *BGU* xiv.2367.

[71] Fraser 1972, 1.94ff.: (A 15). Only one example survives on stone of the prescript normally found in a decree of Council and Assembly; a decree of the 260s B.C. is quoted word for word in a papyrus of Satyrus *On the Demes of Alexandria*, *P. Oxy.* xxvii.2465. It implies the existence of both and assigns important duties to the *prytaneis*, who are normally presidents of the Council. Cf. Robert 1966, especially 192ff.: (1 63).

[72] Or the 'officer in charge of the nome' (*proestekos*), *P. Rev.* 43.

whole nome,[73] a district or circumscription, often of great antiquity, clustered round an important religious or commercial centre. Later that centre is to become the metropolis of the nome, lacking the political institutions of a Greek city but filling many of its functions. In the third century B.C. an additional subdivision, that of the area authority (*toparchy*), was inserted into the system, to give in ascending order village, toparchy, nome; the Fayyûm had an idiosyncratic organization by divisions (*merides*). On to this administrative hierarchy was imposed a new parallel financial one: the *dioiketes* had his own local officer in each nome, his *oikonomos*; confronting the *oikonomos* and his subordinates was a hierarchical series of collectors and auditors (*logeutai, logistai, eklogistai*) and of checking clerks (*antigrapheis*). All of these are civil officers, for civil and military control were separated, as far as present knowledge goes: the proviso is necessary, for there are several puzzles. The 'Revenue Laws', for instance, are addressed to military authorities, *strategoi*, hipparchs, *hegemones*, as well as to civilian officials and police officers. This same document envisages the possibility of alternates for several officials: the phrase 'to the nomarch or the toparch or in his absence, the *oikonomos*' clearly does not mean that the offices are hierarchically equivalent, but that for the immediate purpose any one of them will do.[74] When manpower is short rigid demarcation is a luxury.

Specialist officers (surveyors, law-officers, etc.) have been omitted from this outline by territorial competence and departmental function of the upper echelons of the Ptolemaic bureaucracy in the 250s. It is a bureaucracy that has earned a varied assessment. Hear one authority: 'one of the most rigidly centralized bureaucracies that the world has ever seen'; another writes, 'This Hellenistic state reached a height of administrative and economic control that posterity can only regard with astonished admiration.'[75] Both judgements require qualification. The centralization is not complete: in Philadelphus' bureaux four different systems of dating were in use concurrently, and both the addressee in a document or letter and a modern historian have to guess which. Documents may be dated (i) by the Macedonian calendar and regnal year, beginning on the day of the king's accession (a lunar year bedevilled by the intercalation of an extra month every other year); (ii) by the Egyptian civil calendar (a year of 365 days) beginning on 1 Thoth, the regnal years dating from his accession (the usage of demotic Egyptian

[73] In the present state of the evidence it is impossible to give a generally accepted account of nomarchies named after individuals and nomarchs co-extensive with nomes. See *Pros. Ptol.*, *Studia Hellenistica* 9(1953)73. Arrian's application of the term to *Doloaspis* and *Petesis* is probably a misuse; and the correctness of the emendation of 'nauarchies' to 'nomarchies' in Diod. XIX.85.4 is by no means self-evident.
[74] Samuel 1966, 213ff.: (F 317).
[75] Jones 1971, 297: (A 26); Bengtson 1967, III.1: (A 6).

scribes); (iii) by the Egyptian civil calendar, the regnal years dating retrospectively from the beginning of his co-regency with Ptolemy Soter (the usage of the Greek scribes); (iv) by the so-called 'financial year' which used the Egyptian civil calendar, but began on 1 Mecheir instead of 1 Thoth.

The favourable judgement takes the documents of this bureaucracy at their face value: instructions are treated as having the same evidential value as reports of orders executed. What has been termed the jewel of Greek administrative papyri, *P. Tebt.* III.703, is a long series of detailed instructions about his duties probably issued early in the rule of Euergetes by a *dioiketes* to an *oikonomos*. The oikonomos is to make frequent tours of inspection to ensure that standards are being maintained and to pounce on evasion. It has been pointed out[76] that the document falls into a long tradition of instructions to scribes, and that its closing moral exhortations are a literary genre.

The reality, both in Pharaonic and in Ptolemaic Egypt, may be different, and the whip too may play its part[77] in the relationship between officials and the governed. But the bureaucracy does have certain ideals, and a minimum basic training. Scribes, like priests, worked so that their sons might succeed to their office. An administrative college at Memphis is revealed by Wilcken's analysis of a famous Paris papyrus.[78] The aspirant to public service was set down to copy a file of official correspondence (incidentally, precious to the historian) written in 164 B.C. by the *dioiketes* Herodes. He then went on to essay the composition of letters. *P. Tebt.* III.703 somewhat evasively hints at the prospects of promotion: 'if you emerge without blame from these duties you will be thought capable of higher ones'. But no regular system of promotion, no *cursus honorum* or specially quick promotion to reward initiative has been traced. Remuneration is normally by monthly salary and corn-ration.[79] A clever official will find ways to add to his income by doing business on his own account. In Apollonius' enterprises it is often difficult to distinguish between those undertaken on behalf of the king and those intended for his own profit; Zenon did much contracting on his own account; highly placed Alexandrian officials invest in transport or vineyard operations. A civil servant could expect gifts (*xenia*, *stephanoi*) from petitioners and callers: and to get something done it is advisable to call in person. Zenon himself, once permanently based at Philadelphia, found that Alexandrian colleagues, formerly his close friends, no longer took any notice of his letters.[80] The crown tried to

[76] Crawford 1978, 195ff.: (F 240).   [77] Turner 1966, 79: (F 335).
[78] *UPZ* I.110. The candidate's own exercises in letter writing are *UPZ* I.144, 145.
[79] Known for the royal scribe in 241/40 B.C. from *P. Lille* I.3. 40ff.
[80] *P. Cairo Zen.* II.59150 and Edgar's note.

prevent outright corruption by insisting on the presence, when private financial transactions are involved, of a checking clerk – a rule like that by which two signatures are often needed on a modern bank cheque. But there are many letters in the Zenon archive from officials who gang up to defeat the regulations or to do down an Egyptian colleague. Apollonius and Zenon themselves are honourable exceptions. Corruption and collusion apart, the system discouraged initiative in taking decisions. Better to avoid responsibility and stick to the rule book, the *diagramma*. From this sprang slackness, *rhathymia*, long delays in reaching decisions or paying out salaries, and downright callousness in ignoring positive distress. The modern reader wryly notes that phrases such as 'laying everything else aside', 'instantly', are favoured epistolary tags.

These remarks do not penetrate the outer skin of appearances. Where eventually did responsibility lie in the civil service? What was the nature of that responsibility? A profounder understanding requires the unravelling of the complex nexus of economic, social and legal obligations binding individuals and institutions. The keenest cutting edge of analysis has been that of the Brussels school led by Claire Préaux[81] and independently continued by Jean Bingen. Because of their work in particular this chapter reads quite differently from that written by M. I. Rostovtzeff in 1926. Rostovtzeff's varied descriptive phrases – nationalization of the land, treatment of Egypt by Ptolemy as his private estate,[82] centralized directed economy, *étatisme*, paramountcy of the crown – can be seen to be no more than half-truths. Consider, for instance, the phrase 'ownership of the land': the supposed prop offered by the phrase 'spear-won land' (*doriktetos ge*) has already been knocked away (p. 122). It can and will be shown that private ownership in land existed throughout the Ptolemaic period. However, the ideal principle was not surrendered that, except for land relinquished by the king, all land belonged to the king, and it was given classic expression in a document of the late second century[83] at a time when theory and practice stood poles apart. The phrase 'centralized directed economy' goes back to the first editor's interpretation of the 'Revenue Laws' papyrus.[84] The

---

[81] Préaux 1939: (F 306); *ead.* 1961, 200–32: (F 309); *ead.* 1978, 1.358ff.: (A 48), and the personal confession (376 n. 7) on the view of Rostovtzeff, 'que j'ai moi-même trop accentuée, à mon gré d'aujourd'hui, dans mon *Économie royale*'. For the papers of J. Bingen see the Bibliography, F(h).

[82] It is premature to throw into the scales the phrase 'patrimony of Egypt' from the Karnak ostracon (p. 135).

[83] *P. Tebt.* 1.5 (118 B.C.) *ge en aphesei*, 'land in relinquishment'. In my opinion all attempts to give this phrase a fiscal or administrative sense fail on philological grounds (Herrmann 1955, 93: (F 264); Seidl 1962, III: (F 367); Seidl's kite, 1973, II: (F 368) will not fly). The attempt by Modrzejewski 1979, 164: (F 360), to construe *alle* as 'also other lands which are *en aphesei*' is implausible when it is observed how frequently in other clauses of this text the draughtsman or excerptor has employed the word *allos* as a safety net to catch items not specifically mentioned.

[84] Nothing said here is to be construed as denigration of B. P. Grenfell's great achievement in the publication and pioneer explanation in 1896 of two long and difficult papyrus rolls, without benefit of parallels.

term 'Laws' is, however, misleading: it confers the authority of systematic comprehensive legislation on what are in fact ad hoc regulations to maximize the revenue returns in unrelated and limited fields of economic activity.[85] In particular the supposed 'crop-sowing schedule' (diagraphe tou sporou) has been demonstrably misinterpreted.[86] The schedule was not a directive imposed on the nomes after elaboration in Alexandria on the basis of a system of budgetary priorities and intensive paper calculations; it was an estimate made by district officials (without consulting the primary producers) as a working list of attainable crop proportions, to be put into practice as far as possible and transmitted to higher authority for information and tax calculation. The paramountcy of the crown (to basilikon) in no way excludes the participation of private capital in development schemes, indeed the participation of such capital is encouraged. The paramountcy is enunciated as an ideal and the need to assert it in itself suggests that the involvement of privately owned capital may have been felt to be on such a scale as to constitute an encroachment.

In forbidding advocates to represent parties involved in legal action against the treasury[87] Philadelphus is showing royal high-handedness. One wonders what he would have thought of the appeal to his ruling made more than a century later.

Two models of the nexus of obligations can be constructed. The first takes as base the handling of Egypt's fundamental source of wealth, the corn crop. It was grown mainly on royal land (ge basilike) by royal cultivators (basilikoi georgoi). The firm Ptolemaic evidence comes from the archive of the village scribe of Kerkeosiris, dated to the second half of the second century B.C. But there is no reason for thinking the pattern of the third century to have been any different. The traditional pattern involved a partnership between the king and his cultivators. The king issued the seed corn and supplied necessary agricultural implements, the cultivator grew the corn. At the moment of receiving the seed the latter accepted the obligation[88] to pay a proportion of the produce, the exact figure of artabas being governed by the quality of the land and the extent of the inundation. There was no written lease between the partners.[89]

[85] This is the view set out in Bingen 1978(2): (F 214).
[86] The old interpretation was first shown to be untenable by P. Yale 36. See Vidal-Naquet 1967: (J 167). There is still much that is obscure.
[87] P. Amh. II.33=C. Ord. Ptol. 23 (259 B.C.., cited in 157 B.C.).
[88] When this obligation is expressed by an oath, imposed cultivation or forced lease is involved.
[89] Historians and lawyers, with honourable exceptions, have failed to notice that the survey fills the functions of a lease. For a hundred years they have been looking for something that is not there. The absent phantasm they term a general diamisthosis, at which rents on royal land would be adjusted and changes of tenancy agreed. But the noun does not appear in the indexes to P. Tebt. III and IV; in BGU VI.1216.49 and P. Tebt. 1.72.450, its only occurrences in an enormous published literature of landed tenancies, it applies to uncultivable land. The verb form (also occurring once only, P. Tebt. III.826.17) is restricted to one special and mysterious class of land. Shelton 1975, 268: (F 322),

After the harvest the corn was thrashed on the public threshing floor under the eye of both cultivators and royal officers; the king claimed his due proportion, the cultivator retained the rest. It was the principal sustenance of himself and his family till the same moment next year. He was free to sell it if he wished and could spare it; but he may already have accepted a lien on a part of it, had he gone hungry before the harvest and taken out a loan to be repaid then. The cultivator's problem was to stay alive from one harvest to the next; the king's to dispose of his corn to the best advantage. It was stored temporarily in royal barns supervised by *sitologoi*, then transported on donkey and mule back to the nearest river harbour by a guild of transporters. At the harbour it was loaded into a river boat. Often this was chartered by a private contractor from a company which invested in such boats. If the charterer is not himself captain, the ship will sail under an Egyptian skipper: to Rhacotis if it goes down river, but it may go up river to the garrison at Syene, or indeed the corn may be distributed en route.[90] At each transfer, receipts were exchanged, so as to clarify responsibility if the quantity were short when the corn reached its destination. The precaution was necessary. Pilfering of goods in transport was common. Invoices of produce sent to Alexandria by Zenon show that game, fruit, fish and wine rarely arrived intact.

The obligations, therefore, in Model I are in part legal, in part social and traditional. Among the former is the chain of receipts stretching from the village *sitologoi* to the receiving officer at Alexandria. Second-century evidence shows that the traditional and social ones were to some extent safeguarded by the public conscience of village society and very probably by family ties. The king's officers, his royal and village scribes responsible for the survey, the village elders who proferred advice are under continual scrutiny. 'Forcible suasion' (*peithananke*), the euphemism of the second century, is not thereby made impossible, but it cannot escape publicity.

The handling of the corn crop admitted private capital only in one restricted field, transport by river.[91] Royal resources were supplemented by privately owned vessels. Investors in such boats often turn out to be

demolishes these examples as bad readings or restorations. See in general Crawford 1971, ch. 2: (J 158); and J. C. Shelton at *P. Tebt.* IV.p. 7: 'Registration in tax rolls . . . with information recorded in registers . . . is perhaps all that was officially needed to assure a tenant rights and responsibilities over a given piece of land'. Michurski 1956: (F 282) anticipated some of these points.

[90] Rhacotis: *P. Ryl.* IV.576.5; Syene: Reekmans and van't Dack 1952, 149–95: (F 316). On the corn transport a vast bibliography exists. On the river boats clarity is brought in the recent summary by Scherer 1978, 95ff.: (F 319); and the list of boats and personnel compiled by Hauben 1971, 259ff.: (F 258); 1978, 99ff.: (F 260). See also Meyer-Termeer 1978: (F 354).

[91] Did Pharaoh manage on a smaller transport fleet by leaving his grain in village warehouses for longer periods?

highly placed officials; Euergetes' queen Berenice is also named.[92] In the case of her ownership it is tempting to see an underlying statecraft: the queen's fleet of corn ships, perhaps a dowry or gift, displayed in action the purveyor of plenty symbolized in the cornucopia which she is represented as holding on the faience oenochoe used in state ritual.[93]

Private capital was, however, utilized on a larger scale in developing and exploiting a wide range of primary produce other than corn and the manufactures based on it. In this field a more complicated model is needed. Model II can, by greatly simplifying, be reduced to the following essentials. On manufactured goods and on agricultural raw materials other than corn the tax was demanded in money (in all, that is, except the *apomoira*, the tax of one sixth for the upkeep of the cult of Arsinoe imposed on vineyards). To pay the tax the primary producer had first to sell his crop. The state bought it off him at prices fixed by itself. Additionally the state retained the right to process the crop so acquired (whether as tax revenue or by state purchase) into manufactured goods (oil from oil-seeds or olives, beer from barley, linen from flax, etc.). The manufactures were processed in state-owned and state-supervised factories. Finally, the state licensed firms of capitalists to sell the goods either wholesale or retail at prices fixed by itself.

This is the system which seems to result from the application in practice of the so-called Revenue Laws of Ptolemy Philadelphus. It excited the admiration of three generations of economic historians who saw in it either an economic system designed to maximize production or else the rigorously planned and directed economy associated with state socialism. This seemed especially to be true when to the sketch in the previous paragraph was added an interpretation of the sowing schedule, *diagraphe tou sporou* (the words occur in the Revenue Laws), that made it an organ of quantitative planning.

Jean Bingen has recently demonstrated[94] that the reality is something other than the construction placed on it. In the two rolls themselves the five surviving sections (on the treatment of money taxes, on the *apomoira*, on the oil tax and the oil monopoly, on control of the banking system), the first and last are so damaged that they are not independent witnesses. What remains is a miscellany of instructions, in which at times earlier regulations show through. The instructions frequently use the word 'law'; nevertheless, these texts do not lay down a régime

[92] *P. Ryl.* IV.576 has both. See Hauben's lists cited in n. 90. Against the identification of this Berenice as Euergetes' consort, see Hauben 1979, 68: (F 261).

[93] Plates vol., pl. 12; Thomson 1973: (F 382). One is tempted to add that such propaganda is specially appropriate to the famine years 245 and 240 B.C. But the motive was traditional on the faience. For a slightly different suggestion, Bonneau 1971, 127: (F 218).

[94] Bingen 1978(2): (F 214).

constructed by a rigorous intellectual exercise in fiscal philosophy. They display a pragmatic adaptation to Egyptian conditions (extensive thickly-populated territories, shortage of official manpower) of the tax-farming system evolved in classical Greece to make good the absence of trained officials of integrity required to collect those taxes on which the return was unpredictable. New evidence will be required to answer the question how far the instructions were actually put into operation, or whether the quantities and kinds specified in the sowing schedules were in fact collected.

A prime need in the system was cash to lubricate it, and expertise in accounting. It was advantageous to the state to call on private capitalists for the former, and to arrange a division of the latter between capitalists and officials so as to obviate corrupt book-keeping and yet leave incentives to secure a good return on the investment. The actual collection was kept in the hands of state officials, the *logeutai*; but the amounts collected were entered in the ledgers of banks run by private capitalists licensed by the king. Budgeting was the task of the capitalists, who were given access (often not without the intervention of a high official) to state statistics. Having made a budget for their firm, the capitalists would make a bid, and post a bond as guarantee. In theory the state would have a choice of bids – it is assumed that the highest bid would secure the contract. After acceptance of a bid and the start of the tax year, royal officials (the *oikonomos* and his checking clerk), the capitalists bidding for the tax and the bankers had a monthly meeting to examine and distribute the receipts. If there was an excess over their bid, the tax firms retained it (their *epigenema*), if there was a deficit they were required to make it good. At the monthly meeting the primary producer, the craftsman in the manufactory, the licensed retailer were not represented. The aim of the system was not to encourage production, not to control the economy, but to secure the highest possible return for the king from taxation and from sales in the home market: that is, it was fiscal, not economic or socialistic. Whether or not it was also mercantilist requires a leap in the chain of evidence – the undisputed elements are the facility of mercantile control offered by a country with so few points of exit, the undoubted presence all over the Mediterranean world, the Black Sea, and the Near East of Egyptian manufactured articles of high quality and the great demand for them. But that the king encouraged manufacture so that he alone might sell is not established.

Both the models described require their own bureaucracies, the first an agricultural one, the second a split hierarchy of accountants. In Model I the main elements were inherited from Pharaonic Egypt, in Model II they are mainly Greek innovations, and money guarantees replace social obligations. A number of Pharaonic elements were incorporated in

Model II at the craftsmanship stage – weavers, brewers, etc. The craftsmen took an oath to remain at their task. In the oil-factories a limitation of movement was placed on the oil-processors (*elaiourgoi*). They are described as 'stationed in each nome' and their persons were subject to seizure if they attempted to leave it. Similarly, five Egyptian brickmakers imported from other nomes by Zenon to Philadelphia in 256 B.C.[95] took an oath to remain till their construction task was finished. There is room for Egyptian participation at the bid stage (the advertisement was posted in demotic Egyptian as well as Greek), and at the moment of licensing retail sales, such as 'the monopoly of lentil broth' contracted for the Oxyrhynchite village of Sephtha in 247 B.C. by Chaiemnegois.[96]

In addition to the subjects specifically covered in the Revenue Laws (wine, grapes, currants, etc.; orchard fruits; oil; flax; banking) it was according to Model II that a whole range of other products and taxes were treated, and this model was also applied to taxes in Ptolemaic foreign possessions.[97] Often the details can only be glimpsed. Items included are the production and taxing of salt (monopoly production, but the tax basis is so much per head), of spices, soda (*nitron*), papyrus, the stamp-duty on conveyancing (*enkyklion*, that is circulation tax); quarries, mining and hunting. All of these are accompanied by a bewildering variety of minor dues, some reckoned as proportions, some as fixed amounts per head, the diversity and ingenuity of which can be seen in the indexes to the great collections of Greek ostraca.[98] To these economic returns should be added the taxes in corn and in money paid by cleruchs on their holdings, and contributions in cash or kind received from the temples, the complex evidence for which cannot be examined here. And there are the enormous customs dues paid for import and export from Egypt, as well as the internal tolls collected at several stations inside Egypt from traffic passing up and down the Nile.

The total revenues of Egypt under Philadelphus at an unknown moment of his rule are stated by St Jerome to have amounted to 14,800 talents and one and a half million artabas of corn. The reliability of the figures is doubtful; for their appreciation too many assumptions have to be made for discussion here to be worth while. It would be interesting also to know what sums were in the treasury at Philadelphus' accession. The monetary figure, it is noted by Claire Préaux,[99] would in terms of wages (a third-century mean of two obols a day, perhaps a high estimate) put at the king's disposal 750,000 working years of ordinary labouring

[95] *P. Rev.* col. 44; *P. Cairo Zen.* 1.59133.   [96] Uebel 1964, 165: (F 339).
[97] *P. Tebt.* 1.8 = Wilcken, *Chr.* 2: (F 91).
[98] Wilcken 1899, II: (F 105); J. G. Tait *et al.*, *O. Tait*: (F 101).
[99] Préaux 1978, 1.364 n. 1: (A 48).

men. It is clear that the ancients were enormously impressed by these figures.

If the general outline of Model II is accepted, then the system implies the presence in Egypt of a Greek social group possessing monetary resources and the permission to invest them.[100] Because of their participation in estimating, checking, accounting, as well as the provision of capital by way of advance payments, they may be regarded as in a sense the king's partners, beneficiaries alongside the king in what have usually been represented as enterprises jealously reserved for the crown. In the preceding paragraphs they have been termed 'capitalists', 'investors'; but there is no need to imagine them as individually commanding large sums. In the Revenue Laws there is a great variety of terms to describe them: 'the holder/administrator/purchaser/manager of the contract'. Most interesting are 'the shareholder' or 'the chief buyer and his partners'. The shareholders may have been persons like Zenon himself, penniless immigrants, but hard workers who understood what methods and associates were needed to help them make their fortunes. The high rate of interest legally exactable, 24%, twice that obtainable at Delos, suggests that the authorities were ready to encourage the flow of capital into Egypt. Such is the figure that appears in the earliest surviving loan, which dates to 273 B.C. That few such contracts have survived may be fortuitous, though not necessarily if even higher returns could be earned by other types of investment.

Belgian scholars have collected evidence to show so many loans of cash in the last years of Euergetes and the early years of Philopator as to display recognition of a way of earning interest from capital.[101] By this time, also, it is possible to point to a number of small consortia, often a Greek and an Egyptian in partnership, thriving on cleruchic distress by leasing small-holdings (property to which the lessor may often have no title to ownership, it being theoretically owned by the crown to which it should have reverted).[102]

It is likely that in this class of tenure as elsewhere in Egypt possession created a presumption of ownership, and the exact legal title of a piece of land had in practice become irrelevant. Cleruchs on mobilization seek the aid of their friends, who without power of attorney find tenants on their behalf. These factors render modern juridical classification particularly difficult. The Demotic Law handbook from Hermopolis[103] mentions the 'lord of the land' (who is not the king); the section of which a Greek translation has been discovered alludes in both demotic

---

[100] Acknowledgement must again be made to J. Bingen (n. 94 above).
[101] Reekmans 1949, 324–42: (F 314).
[102] Bingen 1978(3), 74: (F 215).
[103] Mattha 1975, col. VI.3–4: (F 353). P. Oxy. XLVI.3285, fr. I, ll. 1–3. It is the allusion to purchase 'by the father' that arouses suspicion about title.

and Greek to 'land purchased by the disputant's father in accordance with a contract'. House property was accepted as security from tax-farmers of the *apomoira*, and sold off by the revenue officials when the farmer was in default.[104]

Mention of the Demotic Law book calls attention to a conspicuous absence from this chapter: an exposition of the systems of law in force in Egypt, their application to individuals or to groups, and the courts which enforced their provisions. It was once thought possible to distinguish between Greek citizen laws (for instance, the law of Alexandria), Greek law in a sort of generalized form (governing Greeks living in the *chora*) and the laws of the land (*tes choras* – or *enchorioi* – *nomoi*) to which Egyptians were subject. On this view a system of itinerant courts, *chrematistai* for Greeks, *laokritai* for Egyptians, administered the appropriate laws. But this schematic distinction runs up against a number of difficulties. What kind of generalized Greek law could exist to apply to a Greek owning no allegiance to any city or corporate institution? How could it have come into existence? Does the status of the litigants or the language of the contracts (Greek, demotic Egyptian) govern the choice of court, procedure and precedent? There is evidence which tends to both conclusions, and it is not a simple matter of a temporal difference (one procedure in the third century, one in 118 B.C.). How is status established? Greek and demotic papyrologists do not agree whether a status designation which from the Greek is translated 'Persian, of the epigone' and from demotic 'Ionian (i.e. Greek) born in Egypt' is one and the same, why these pseudo-ethnics should have been chosen, under what conditions it was obligatory to declare them, and what was the legal effect of such a declaration. And a further complication is added by the undoubted erosion of legal rights, and interference in judicial process by the administration.

As between Greeks and Egyptians, it is an inescapable conclusion that under Philadelphus the balance held fairly by Soter became tilted in favour of the immigrants. The court itself looks westwards: it sends competing athletes to the games of homeland Greece, rewards the victors, has its connoisseurs of silver plate and poetry, entertains ambassadors from the whole known world. No Egyptians at all are found among the holders of high office, or on the bridge of the king's men-of-war. In commerce and the civil service it remained helpful to have Egyptians in the team. Nevertheless moral recriminations began to be bandied about.[105] 'Nowadays no ruffian slips up to you in the street Egyptian-fashion and does you a mischief – the tricks those packets of

---

[104] Wilcken, *Chr.* 110.12: (F 91) (200 B.C.).
[105] Rostovtzeff 1953, III.1644: (A 52), for references up to 1941, and the case for Egyptian resentment.

rascality used to play', gossips Theocritus' Praxinoa. The papyri confirm that much pilfering went on. The moral worlds of Greeks and Egyptians were very different: an Egyptian would think shame to go back on an oath, a minor matter for a Greek. Much of the evidence in this field is equivocal. Zenon's correspondent who says he is despised because he cannot speak Greek[106] would carry more weight if his name were known and it were certain that he was an Egyptian. The eight petitioners in the *Enteuxeis* would also carry more weight when they ascribe their ill-treatment to their being 'foreigners' (*xenoi*), if it were not that two such pleaders are Egyptians from other nomes; 'outsiders' is the proper rendering of the Greek. Two special areas of friction can be observed – the institution of billeting and the obligation to use money to transact business or pay taxes. Billeting, tolerable over a short period, over an extended one could not fail to create conflicts. Billetees peremptorily sold and assigned their lodgings or used them to raise a mortgage; questions arose of the number of rooms in a house a billetee could claim. As early as the 270s B.C. the king laid down by royal decree that half the house went to the billetor, half to the billetee; this and other enactments were repeated in the 240s B.C.[107] Owners of lodgings found tricks to frustrate the billeting officer. One method was to block up the doors of a house and build altars in front of them. The full subtlety of this manoeuvre lay in the fact that the altars would be dedicated to the reigning sovereign, and the proprietors were testing the loyalty of would-be billetees.[108] As was no doubt intended, the billeting officer referred a decision to higher authority.

A second cause of friction was the substitution of cash payments for barter or trading in kind. The first two Ptolemies minted in gold, silver and copper. From some time about 270–260 Philadelphus issued copper coins in large denominations, but the standard for official transactions was the silver coinage. Model II (p. 151) required a succession of such transactions. To each bargain would have to be added banker's commission and also premium or agio, the payment for conversion of copper coins into silver.

Even these gains at the expense of the primary producer did not satisfy the financial wizards of Alexandria. A dossier of 256 B.C. has been convincingly interpreted by Jean Bingen[109] as an attempt to apply the norms of Model II to Model I. Apollonius, through Panacestor, Zenon's predecessor, had agreed with a group of Egyptian cultivators to grow a corn crop for him. The original agreement

---

[106] This translation of ἑλληνίζειν is inescapable.

[107] *C. Ord. Ptol.* 1–4, 5–10.

[108] *P. Petrie* II.12(1), in part in Wilcken, *Chr.* 449 (242 B.C.). The subtlety was pointed out by L. Robert in *Welles Essays*, especially pp. 187–8: (I 63).   [109] Bingen 1970, 35: (F 210).

envisaged shares $-\frac{1}{3}$ to Apollonius, $\frac{2}{3}$ retained by the cultivators. Shortly before harvest Apollonius arbitrarily altered the agreement. His new offer, euphemistically called concessions, *philanthropa*, was that the cultivators settle on the basis of an estimate calculated from a survey of the green standing corn (*syntimesis*). The cultivators asked for time to think; four days later they took sanctuary in a temple. Bingen argues plausibly that the phrase *syntimesis* committed the cultivators to a cash payment as well as changing the framework of the whole transaction. Under Model I the cultivator knew his obligations, but he knew his rights also: share-out on the threshing floor. In this example the corn was apparently not harvested at all, and the result was damaging to both parties.

Any outline of Egyptian society in the third century B.C. should pay special attention to the matched coherence of two social groups, the cleruchic settlers and the priests. The social rôle of the cleruchic settlers has already been remarked (pp. 124–5): their dispersal throughout the land of Egypt (which meant penetration of villages as well as nome capitals), their introduction and advocacy of Greek ideas and techniques to the cultivators among whom they moved. When there is military mobilization, they may become absentees. It is unlikely that individuals – and the same is true of priests – farmed the land themselves. The priests, because of the shift system of taking duty, were also dispersed throughout the land and villages of Egypt, also were neighbours to the cultivators, also formed a homogeneous group. To be a priest was almost the only career open to an Egyptian of talents. The priests in each temple were not on continuous duty. Except for its superintendents, each temple's priests were organized into shifts (*phylai* is the Greek term), four up to the time of the Canopus decree of 239 B.C., thereafter five.[110] The four-shift system, like the four-month periods of Egyptian barter accounting, was based on the ancient division of the year into three seasons of inundation, sowing, harvest. Under it a priest performed a month's continuous duty celebrating the daily liturgy. Then a new shift took over and he went about his own business, usually that of superintending the farming of his own leased plot of temple land; and he did not return to temple duties for three months. There was little that marked priests off from ordinary men. Their heads were shaved (the origin of the tonsure), they did not go bare-foot, they wore linen, and when on duty observed certain prescriptions of ritual purity. No doubt they had also a certain gravity of demeanour. But they were allowed to marry and to raise a family, bringing up a son in the hope of succession. They moved as ordinary men among ordinary men in the ordinary tasks of life. This explains their effectiveness as guardians of tradition and

[110] See Sauneron 1957: (F 188).

disseminators of news, even rumour. By such media a ready circulation was available for stories about Alexander the Great and Nectanebo, the last native Pharaoh, and wishful thinking about disasters to fall on Alexandria such as is embodied in the Potter's Oracle.[111] Cleruchic settlers and working priests, both distanced slightly from their immediate neighbours, formed two complementary groups which it was essential to maintain in counterpoise.

This equilibrium was seriously endangered in the early years of Euergetes' rule. Rostovtzeff has already called attention[112] to what he terms 'the native revolt in Egypt in the time of Euergetes' and later suggests 'the possibility that some of the oppressive measures of Euergetes' time were temporary, caused by the great strain of the Syrian war, which lasted to 240 B.C.' Since 1941 there have been considerable additions to the evidence on which Rostovtzeff relied. His inferences are supported strongly by the re-interpretation of a 'literary' papyrus in Copenhagen (see p. 420 n. 19): and by the secure dating of *P. Tebt.* III.703 to the early years of Euergetes because of its parallels with the new *P. Hib.* II.198, which is definitely fixed to shortly after 243/2 B.C.[113] In both appears a preoccupation with runaway sailors: 'Royal sailors' (*basilikoi nautai*) they are termed in the latter text, 'persons who have been branded with the (royal) mark'[114] and they are to be treated with the same ruthlessness as 'brigands'. Furthermore the cleruchic administration was in very great disorder between 246 and about 240 B.C.; and in addition the Nile inundation was seriously inadequate in 245 B.C. and disastrously so in 240 B.C.[115] Earlier in this chapter it was hinted that strains such as might lead to a breakdown are to be observed in the 250s B.C., and the economic system of this decade was labelled a 'total mobilization'. In January 250 B.C. Apollonius ordered a certain Demetrius to contact the royal scribes, the chiefs of police and the *phores* in order to make a survey and with a gang of labourers to 'fell native timber, acacia, tamarisk and willow to provide the breast-work for the

---

[111] C. H. Roberts, *P. Oxy.* XXII.2332, for the theory of political intention, and a dating in the time of Euergetes; a new text and discussion in Koenen 1968, 178–209: (F 176), and 1974, 313–19: (F 177). Préaux 1978, I.395: (A 48), sees this whole literature as eschatological, not political. Cf. Fraser 1972, I.681, II.950: (A 15); Peremans 1978, 40 n. 14: (F 298).

[112] Rostovtzeff 1953, III.1420 n. 212: (A 52). He uses in particular the evidence of *P. Tebt.* III.703 (Fayyûm) and *UPZ* II.157 (Thebaid).

[113] Bagnall 1969, 73: (F 201).

[114] No certainties about the functions of these 'royal sailors' have emerged from the considerable discussion about them. M.-Th. Lenger and I, who edited the original text, have been under fire for suggesting that the Ptolemaic fleet was powered by galley slaves. We made no such suggestion. But the differing provenances of the three texts (Fayyûm, Heracleopolis, Thebes) prompt another unanswerable question: was a squadron of the Ptolemaic seagoing navy diverted up the Nile to deal with native rebels?

[115] Evidence discussed by Bonneau 1971, 123ff. and synoptic tables, 222ff.: (F 218).

men-of-war'.[116] Between 250 and 248 B.C. Zenon suffered crippling financial embarrassments.[117] Between these dates also analysis of his accounts has revealed that salaries and corn rations were cut by a sixth.[118] The indications from the Zenon archive can be discounted as due to Zenon's poor health, unwise speculation or to local difficulties. But it is also possible to interpret the evidence cumulatively, as part of a series of events. If one looks forward, one must add the impressive evidence for troubles in the early years of Euergetes, as well as the revocation of Apollonius' gift-estate. A backward look suggests that poor harvests resulting from inundations is an unsatisfactory explanation. The scene of the sullen peasants described earlier (on p. 157) was a legacy to Zenon in 256 B.C. from his predecessor Panacestor. In 258 B.C. merchants in Alexandria, who included would-be exporters, were required to surrender their gold coinage for reminting in the royal mint, the unspoken suggestion being that it is for the profit of the king.[119] This, it will be remembered, is the year to which the Karnak ostracon is dated. It is the time at which the Revenue Laws were being elaborated. My reading of the evidence is this: the 250s B.C., so far from being a decade of creative financial ideas, are a decade of anxiety in which the screw is tightened progressively and the pressures of an already oppressive exploitation directly cause the explosion of the 240s B.C. Without his competitive dynastic wars the story could have been different. It was Philadelphus, not Philopator, who bankrupted Egypt.

III.   FROM EUERGETES I TO EUERGETES II

The title of this section is a concession to the limitations of the evidence available. Towards the close of his life, after over fifty years of nominal rule, in about 121–118 B.C., Euergetes II came to terms with his sister Cleopatra II and his wife Cleopatra III. The reconciliation was marked by a long act of amnesty, most of which has survived in copies on

---

[116] Fraser and Roberts 1949, 289–94: (F 196) = *SB* VI.9215: (F 88). In l. 15 restore the definite article in the plural. The word translated 'trackers' (*phores*) might also mean 'thieves', 'convicts', and is found again in *P. Hib.* II.198. The poor timber concerned was used on Nile boats, but surely only in an emergency on warships.

[117] *P. Cairo Zen.* 59327 shows him pawning silver plate. *P. Lond.* VII.2006–8 detail a whole series of shortages, see T. C. Skeat's note. Cf. *PSI* 378.

[118] Reekmans 1966: (F 315). *P. Lond.* VII.2004 shows this cut in effect by February 248 B.C.

[119] *P. Cairo Zen.* I 59021. The vulgate interpretation (little more than a guess) is that Philadelphus wished to apply his own Ptolemaic standard throughout the Ptolemaic dominions. Bagnall 1976, 176: (F 204), concludes from an examination of coin provenances that it is broadly true that only Ptolemaic issues circulated in Syria, Cyrene and Cyprus; this is entirely untrue of other Ptolemaic possessions overseas. It is to be noted that Soter himself in 304 B.C. set an example of reminting at lower weight. The collector of the hoard found at Phacous systematically rejected reduced-weight tetradrachms, Jenkins 1960, 34ff.: (F 390); Nash 1974, 29: (F 393).

papyrus (hereafter referred to as *P. Tebt.* 1.5).[120] It is almost the last major Greek papyrus document of the Ptolemaic age. Its provisions reveal a world utterly different from that of Euergetes I. The seed sown by the disastrous policies of Philadelphus had borne fruit.

At the end of the previous section signs of the failure of that policy were enumerated. As a result of failure the succession of Euergetes I to Philadelphus turned out to be a moment of greater peril than the succession of Philadelphus to Soter had been. Euergetes was hurriedly recalled from a victorious campaign in Syria to confront simultaneous palace revolution and Egyptian domestic revolt.[121] He was able to master the situation. The policies of Philadelphus could not be entirely reversed, but they might be mitigated by a simultaneous effort of strength and a display of conciliation.[122] The spirit of conciliation is evident in the treatment of petitioners to the king. In Ptolemaic Egypt if a subject thought himself wronged, one means of redress was to seek audience of the king, armed with a statement of the grievance. The technical term 'enteuxis' implies a meeting face to face. That it is Greek suggests derivation from Macedonian prerogative; but Egyptians sought redress with equal readiness and confidence of success,[123] as if the practice was also established in their own tradition. The written petitions of this period found at Ghoran and Magdola are now routed automatically through a high-ranking army officer, the *strategos*. Moreover, he noted meticulously what the next stage in redress should be.

The handling of petitions to the king is the clearest evidence at present available of the new functions of the *strategos*. What military duties he retained – what military operations he commanded during the

[120] Edited by Grenfell and Hunt in 1906. Revised text taking into account the other copies, *C. Ord. Ptol.* 53ff. *P. Tor.* 1 = *UPZ* II.162 is the latest long papyrus.

[121] I accept the restoration in *P. Haun.* 6 fr. 1.15–16 of εἰ μὴ τότε Αἰγυπτίων ἀπ[όστασις ἐγένετο (or the like), because the compiler of this cento can be shown to have drawn on accurate and unexpected information in other sections (e.g. the archon's name in l. 22) and the restoration is supported by Justin 27.1.8 and Porphyry *FGrH* 260F243. See below, ch. 11, p. 420 n.19.

[122] It is possible that the withdrawal of Apollonius' gift-estate in the Fayyûm was part of a deliberate policy. I can find no incontrovertible mention of a gift-estate at work under Euergetes, a period well represented in the papyri. The search is complicated by the use in Greek of the word *dorea* for a grant of benefits in money (see the list assembled by W. Westermann, introd. to *P. Col. Zen.* II.120). Early in the reign of Philopator gift-estates are again in evidence. A Chrysermus, member of a prominent Alexandrian family (on them L. Koenen 1977, 19: (F 275)), had one in 219/18 B.C., *P. Ent.* 60, 2. The date of grant is uncertain, nor is it clear whether it was suspended under Euergetes. The same uncertainty applies to the gift-estate of Sosibius mentioned casually in 138 B.C. in *P. Tebt.*, III.2, 860, 17, 67, etc., where in l.2 the name Agathocles occurs also in an ambiguous context. This Sosibius is presumably the athlete of Call. fr. 384 Pf., priest of Alexander 234/3 (Ijsewijn 1961, 76: (F 269)) and regent of Philopator, Fraser 1972, II.1004: (A 15). Mooren 1975, 63 and 75: (F 286), maintains the older view of two distinct persons.

[123] *P. Ryl.* IV.563.

opening years of Euergetes – are unknown.[124] But as early as about 240
B.C. he is found acting alongside the nomarch; in 236 B.C. he joins the
nomarch and the latter's checking clerk to investigate locust damage to
vineyards.[125] He is becoming immersed in the administration of the
nome, of which he is shortly (if not at once) to become head. Historians
have concentrated on the development of his powers as civilian official.
It is at least as important to notice that the separation of civil and military
powers had been officially abandoned. In a crisis, the brigadiers had been
called in to put the country to rights. To have a high military officer
responsibly assessing the pros and cons of calling in troops was an
improvement on a situation in which the civil power summoned aid
from the military,[126] but neither side took any responsibility. Moreover,
the *strategos* had been given strict instructions to conceal the iron hand in
the velvet glove.

The policy worked. So did resolute action to mitigate famine and
minimize disorder caused by poor inundations (p. 158) above). Individuals were required to register 'for present needs' the amount of
corn in their possession.[127] 'Grain was purchased at high prices in Syria,
Phoenicia, Cyprus and elsewhere; special shipping was chartered to
transport it.' The quotation is from a decree passed in honour of
Euergetes and his consort by a synod of priests meeting at Canopus in
239/8 B.C.[128] The record was cut on stone in Greek, in hieroglyphic and
demotic Egyptian, and five copies have been found (at several places in
Egypt). Law and order (the Greek term is *eunomia*; 'respect for the law'
or 'a state enjoying good laws') was furnished to subjects of the crown.
Peace had also been made with the gods: the temples gave thanks for
benefits received, the gods for worship, the cult of Apis and the sacred
animals was maintained, the sacred images carried away by the Persians
were restored. In sober terms characteristic of a Greek honorary decree,
Euergetes received the same sort of praise as had been offered to Soter in
the Satrap stele. The Ptolemies again became large-scale benefactors of
the temples – indeed temple builders. Philadelphus had given gifts to the
sacred animals, especially on the occasions of embalmments, but had
undertaken no major work of this kind. In this very same year Euergetes
made a progress to Edfu to lay the foundation deposit for the great

---

[124] The papyri are singularly unhelpful on Ptolemaic military institutions. The situation could be
transformed by the discovery of a body of papers corresponding to those of the Roman third-
century H.Q. at Dura-Europus.

[125] *P. Hib.* II.198; *P. Tebt.* III.772. *P. Col. Zen.* II.120, on which Bengtson (1964–7, III.32: (A 6))
relies, is a broken reed, since the inference depends on a supplement which is not self-evident.

[126] Such was apparently the situation in *P. Hib.* I.40.17 (260 B.C.): cf. *P. Hib.* I.44 = *P. Yale* I.33,
and discussion.

[127] Wilcken, *Chr.* 198 (2 Dec. 241 B.C.). The date and phrase *eis ta deonta* suggest an emergency,
not a routine declaration.

[128] *OGIS* 56; Sauneron 1957, 67: (F 188).

temple of Horus, construction of which was to be continued for more
than a century by his successors. He also built the temple of Osiris at
Canopus (where the synod met), the naos of the temple of Isis at Philae,
and commenced work at Assuan and Esneh. In the framework of this
building policy, the foundation of Euergetes of the great Serapeum of
Alexandria (above, p. 145) finds a natural place.

A century after the death of Euergetes I, the second Euergetes issued
his amnesty decree. Though not intact, it contains sixteen clauses
rehearsing releases from sundry obligations granted by the reconciled
sovereigns (such as from the penalties for alleged involvement in
brigandage, payment of accumulated arrears in corn and money taxes)
and at least twenty-eight general enactments (*prostagmata*). Release the
crown can grant directly to its own cultivators, officials, soldiers;
enactments are aimed at third parties intervening between the crown and
a beneficiary. The latter ban such illegalities as unauthorized re-
quisitions, wrongful seizures by customs officers, possession of land
without title, interference with priests and with temple revenues
(especially under the guise of protection rackets), short-circuiting of
prescribed court procedures or the established rules about the language
in which a hearing is to be conducted. The whole is called 'the decree of
generous concessions (*philanthropa*)'.[129] The term is traditional (p. 123
above); it is also a euphemism of officialdom. In fact, the king is prisoner
of events, not their master. This set of *philanthropa* is only one of a series
stretching over the second century.[130]

It may be helpful to supplement this catalogue by a composite picture
of conditions in second-century Egypt. The reader must bear in mind
that the outline given offers to a state of intermittent anarchy a spurious
impression of continuity and uniformity; moreover the phenomena
must not be considered as described in a causal relationship. None the
less some of the elements of disintegration that confronted Euergetes I
between 246 and 240 B.C. will be recognized. Prominent among them is
the collapse of law and order in civil life. Official documents prescribed
measures against brigands, gangs, deserters, runaway sailors, drop-out
civilians.[131] No doubt the effect on civil life can be exaggerated. People
learned to live with it, as the twentieth century has adjusted to mugging,
violence, terrorism.

But there were occasions of downright revolution or civil war, and
periods during which the king's writ did not run in parts of Egypt. This

---

[129] *P. Tebt.* 1.74.3.

[130] *P. Kroll=C. Ord. Ptol.* 34, 186 or 163 B.C.; *UPZ* 111, 164 B.C (cf. *UPZ* 110); *UPZ* 161, 162,
c. 145 B.C. See *C. Ord. Ptol.* 'Allusions', 247ff.

[131] Drop-outs are explicitly connected with brigands in *P. Tebt.* 1.5.6–7. A sweep by a *strategos*
against brigands attacking visitors to the great Serapeum at Saqqara in *UPZ* 1.122.9 (157 B.C.). Cf.
UPZ 1.71.7

was the case between 206 and 186 B.C. in the Thebaid. In autumn 206 B.C. an Egyptian whose name is usually transliterated Harmachis seized the temple at Edfu, and then marched north, drove the Greeks out of Thebes and occupied it. There he was crowned 'Harmachis who lives for ever, beloved of Isis, beloved of Amonrasonter the great god' and reigned for six years. Greek armies were back in Thebes in 199/8 B.C., but failed to hold it, and a second king Anchmachis was installed and maintained his rule till August 186 B.C., when Epiphanes' general Comanus won a definitive victory.[132] Perhaps connected with this revolt is a graffito on the walls of the chapel of Osiris at Abydus: an Egyptian has scratched in Greek characters a few lines in the Egyptian language, 'Year 5 of Pharaoh Hurgonaphor, beloved of Esi and Osiris . . .' The rank of Comanus is described cautiously by the latest student of the question as 'that of an official of extraordinary powers appointed in an emergency situation, which certainly in some ways approximates to the post of an *epistrategos*'.[133] To judge by the etymology of his name, this official should be a 'super-brigadier'. An earlier generation of scholars saw in him a generalissimo of Upper Egypt.[134] The moderns argue whether that is a fair description of his functions and territorial competence, whether the office was only filled in an emergency, whether two *epistrategoi* may have held the position simultaneously. After Comanus fourteen possible appointees can be listed. Clarity will not be reached till it can be established what military functions were still performed by a titular *strategos*.

Other Egyptians enjoyed short-lived military successes; Dionysius Petosarapis in 164 B.C., Harsiesis about 130 B.C.[135] Hints appear in the papyri of troop movements in Middle and Upper Egypt:[136] the mercenary troopers at the headquarters at Ptolemais; the fortification of Hermopolis and Syene. No continuous account is possible.

Such difficult conditions officials[137] described as 'non-intercourse'

---

[132] de Cenival 1977, 10: (F 229), and Zauzich 1978, 157: (F 349), have put forward a case for transliterating as Horonnophris and Anchonnophris, W. Clarysse 1978, 243: (F 231), as Hurgona-phor and Chaonnophris. Clarysse's interpretation explains the graffito Hurgonaphor (*SB* 7658 = Pestman *et al.* 1977, I no. 11: (F 109)) and utilizes a new papyrus (Clarysse 1979, 103: (F 232)) referring to destruction and violent death as far north as Lycopolis in middle Egypt 'in the *tarache* at the time of Chaonnophris'. Moreover the Onnophris element in the name characterizes 'a resurrected king restored to power and prosperity by the piety of his son Horus' (Gardiner 1950, 44: (F 173)), and reveals a nationalist programme put forward by this native dynasty. So does the name Harsiesis taken by the short-lived native king of 132 B.C.

[133] Thomas 1975, 112: (F 330).

[134] Martin 1911: (F 280). Against Thomas' agnostic approach see E. van 't Dack's review in *Chron. d'Égypte* 51 (1976) 202–6.

[135] Koenen 1959, 103: (F 274).

[136] E.g. *P. Grenf.* 1.42; Wilcken, *Chr.* 447; *P. Berl. Zilliacus* 7.

[137] I pass over changes in the structure of the bureaucracy, such as the disappearance of the nomarch, the emergence of the *epimeletes*, and the institution of the *idios logos* (officer in charge of

(*amixia*) or 'disturbance' (*tarache*). To carry out their tasks they bullied and threatened. Their impotence matched their prolixity, and their peculations were motivated by the need to recoup the cost of buying their way into office – a practice clearly attested in the second century.[138] At village level or above, officials organized protection rackets.[139] Inadequately irrigated land, or soil not cleared of wind-blown sand, went out of cultivation. Confiscated land and land 'under deduction' (ἐν ὑπολόγῳ) was sold at auction, leased at lower rates or assigned on a forced lease. Cultivators who could not meet the claims made on them abandoned their lands (*anachoresis*) and took refuge in a temple, whose right to protect them was acknowledged in repeated enactments. Shortfalls in the currency were made good by manipulation of the copper currency, which was not accepted for tax purposes, and its relationship to silver, the recognized standard. For the eleven years from 221 to 210 B.C. the government pretended there was no inflation,[140] and wages were paid at the old rates but taxes collected at the depreciated level dictated by freely rising prices, estimated at 400% in this decade. In 210 B.C. copper became the official inland currency, and was cut loose from silver, no longer in adequate supply. When it was needed (e.g. to pay for imports) the price of a silver drachm was 240 copper drachms, 480 by 183/2 B.C. No wonder the victors returned from Raphia were disillusioned and disenchanted. Apart from the direct effect on living standards, loss of confidence in the currency inhibited long-term credit. A family that had to borrow in order to stave off hunger found money-lenders ready to offer short-term loans. Such loans were superficially attractive, for no interest was charged; but they included savage penal clauses. The money-lenders (who constituted a profession by the later third century) gambled on the expectation of insolvency. The bankrupt debtor, whether cultivator or artisan, dropped out and left his village: one more sanctuary seeker, active revolutionary or member of the anonymous Alexandrian mob.

Such a situation offered few temptations to immigrants. Furthermore they were offered a lower scale of rations and of pay than hitherto. The nominal area of small-holdings on offer was reduced, their allocated area in real terms smaller still.[141] In any case, there were fewer Greeks to emigrate from the homeland, itself depopulated.

The phenomena of weakness and misery that the documents present

non-predictable revenues). *P. Haun.* 11, important for the history of the office of the *idios logos*, should be dated to 182 B.C., not 158 B.C. The inference was drawn by the Louvain school in *Pros. Ptol.* VIII (e.g. 56 no. 445) from two demotic texts in Zauzich 1968, 37 and 85: (F 153).
[138] For a *strategos*, *P. Tebt.* 1.5.19 (118 B.C.); for a village scribe Menches, *P. Tebt.* 1.10 (119 B.C.).
[139] *P. Tebt.* 1.40; 1.5.60 (118 B.C.).
[140] Reekmans 1949, 324–42: (F 314).
[141] See the table compiled by J. C. Shelton, *P. Tebt.* IV, p. 39.

must be reinforced by general considerations about the personal weakness of the kings from Philopator onwards. For three accessions in a row (Philopator, Epiphanes, Philometor) the new king was a minor, and regents were unscrupulous men. The weak personality of the sovereign encouraged the growth of parties headed by ambitious individuals. They might be in support of one or other prince, king or queen; or of a policy – choice for instance of foreign alliances (Macedon or Rome) or domestic patronage (Egyptians or Greeks). Both motives of policy might be united in destructive force. Between Perdiccas in 321 B.C. and Antiochus Epiphanes in 170–168, no foreign army penetrated Egyptian territory. Antiochus invaded easily and subsequently issued edicts as Pharaoh. His short-lived occupation was quickly ended by Roman intervention. But Egypt had to live for the next century with the consequences: demonstrated subservience to Rome; a dynasty craftily divided against itself; revival of nationalistic feeling.

So gentle a king as Philometor was forced to take up arms against a gross and unscrupulous brother; the feud was bequeathed to Philometor's sister-wife Cleopatra II and his daughter Cleopatra III. It is commonly supposed that the institution of a system of court ranks and titles, by playing on the vanity of courtiers, was intended as a bond between monarch and ministers. The nomenclature makes its appearance with four titles in the first decade of Epiphanes' reign: two others were probably part of the original series (*syngenes, ton somatophylakon*, nos. 1 and 6 in the list); three additional titles were later added (nos. 1(a) and 2(a) in the list). The complete list runs in descending order:

1.   'kinsman' (*syngenes*)
1(a). 'of rank equivalent, *homotimos*, to kinsman'
2.   'of the order of first friends' (*ton proton philon*)
2(a). 'equivalent to the first friends'
3.   'leader of the bodyguard' (*archisomatophylax*; later 'of the class of leaders of the bodyguard')
4.   'of the class of friends' (*ton philon*)
5.   'of the class of successors' (*ton diadochon*)
6.   'of the class of bodyguards' (*ton somatophylakon*).

There is not yet agreement about whether the titles are honorary *ad hominem* or whether a particular office carries a particular ranking. L. Mooren, the latest student of the phenomenon in depth,[142] argues strongly in favour of a separation between court rank and office. For historians and prosopographers the matter is not an idle quarrel. It is a question of how far inferences about the importance of officers and offices may be drawn from the presence of absence of such titles.

[142] Mooren 1975: (F 286), 1977: (F 287).

The monarchy was under pressure from a different section of society, namely the priests. The black basalt slab found at Rosetta in 1799 which provided the key to decipherment of the hieroglyphs through its matched inscriptions in Greek, hieroglyphic and demotic Egyptian, records a decree of a priestly synod at Memphis in 196 B.C.[143] The Greek text gives the formulae of Egyptian piety, and is in strong contrast to the severity of the Canopic decree in honour of Euergetes. Monarch and priests needed each other. The king, in particular, could no longer afford to turn his back on so useful a group of allies, who, when they met in synod, always claimed to speak on behalf of Egypt. In this period the High Priests of Memphis return to prominence, and make a parade of their unbroken pedigree.[144] In the second half of the century a highly placed priestly office, that of the *phritob*,[145] who seems to have had judicial powers, is held concurrently with a court title by a Greek called Ptolemy. Further evidence is needed before it can be positively asserted that he was titular head of the priesthood; but it is not unlikely.

A cycle of misery has been described in this outline. Where did it begin? Did it have any single over-riding cause? Polybius made some obiter dicta on the Egyptian situation which have attracted great attention. 'Picking up heart after the rout at Raphia, the Egyptians were no longer able to tolerate an imposed system (*to prostattomenon*), but sought a leader and a personality (*prosopon*)[146] in the conviction that they were strong enough to assist each other.' Claire Préaux has illuminated Polybius' observations by showing that his account of Philopator as a moral debauchee belongs to a tradition of character-painting, and is very probably drawn from a different source than his factual observations on Egyptian nationalism.[147] The latter carry no moral judgements. Indeed Polybius' picture of an apathetic prince with apathetic ministers contradicts his own account of their actions. Polybius belonged to the generation after Philopator, he personally visited Alexandria; his judgements are entitled to respect. His phrase 'the Egyptians no longer were able to tolerate an imposed system' is true, even though not the whole truth. What is striking to the modern observer is the speed with which the domestic Egyptian scene changed. Within a few years it could appear to break down completely; or go from apparent breakdown to recovery inside a similar interval. During the breakdown it is hard to discriminate between cause and symptom. Physical explanations, such as poor inundations, are inadequate explanations: poor harvests could be

---

[143] The occasion of the decree has been much discussed: anakleteria, *sed*-festival, defeat of a revolt in the Delta? For the last-named, Pestman 1965, 157: (F 299).

[144] Reymond and Barns 1977, 1–33: (F 185); Crawford 1980, 1: (F 169).

[145] *P. Lond.* VII.2188.61; *UPZ* 1.51.18.

[146] Polyb. v.107. *Prosopon* should perhaps be rendered 'persona'.

[147] Préaux 1965, 364–75: (F 310).

met by resolute action, as Euergetes I proved. Morale was more difficult to restore. Loss of it showed on three planes: on the religious level there was a widespread feeling that chaos had triumphed again over the established order, an enemy of the gods occupied the throne, Seth was victorious over Horus; on the moral level, the governed refused their consent to their governors; on the administrative and political level, it was believed that coercion could be beaten by non-co-operation.

Some historians have written of the equilibrium established by the early Ptolemies. The phrase will serve if analysed as follows: Egypt was a country of, say, seven million Egyptians and 100,000 immigrants. The latter class could not expect to maintain a claim to an equal, much less to a larger, share of the products unless they contributed (or were considered to contribute) a qualitatively much more important share. To create the illusion was the task of statesmanship. Soter, and more surprisingly Euergetes, succeeded in the task. Philadelphus had every advantage in his favour, but pressed his success too hard and frittered away his assets. After Raphia followed sterile stalemate.

IV. RELIGION, LITERATURE, ART

In the first section of this chapter the task of the historian of society and administration in Ptolemaic Egypt was described in a musical metaphor: to trace the counterpoint in the *interpretatio Graeca* and the *interpretatio Aegyptiaca* of the contributions of Greeks and Egyptians respectively. In the study of religious practice and belief, of systems of ideas and artistic and moral values the same metaphor may be used. It is valid if it implies that the constituent themes retain a recognizable identity, but in contrast and combination form a larger whole. But it is dangerous if it tempts the investigator to seek deliberate design in that larger whole, to be realized by conscious policy through centuries of the historical process. Moreover, this is a field where sharply edged definitions are likely to be falsified. The themes themselves are transformed. Boundaries become blurred, and it is not unknown for there to coexist in the minds of men ideas which, if logically worked out, would prove mutually exclusive.

In her mature work on the Hellenistic world,[148] Claire Préaux has set out her conclusion, that 'the expansion of the Greeks into what had been Alexander's empire did not create a new mixed civilisation'. The tendency of this chapter and section is to reinforce her conclusion. Fusion or integration was neither a conscious element of policy nor a result of the presence of the Ptolemies in Egypt. But willy nilly there was inter-penetration. In some areas of human experience the mere fact that men were put on their guard sharpened their awareness of it.

[148] Préaux 1978, especially II.680ff., 'Le bilan de l'âge hellénistique': (A 48).

In public acknowledgement of Ptolemy as god there was almost no contact between the Egyptian and Greek worlds of ideas. For the Egyptian, Pharaoh was divine on three planes. When a god recognized him as son and put the kingdom into his hands, this action expressed the recognition of him by his subjects as legitimate king; when he sat on the throne of Horus he was himself very god; when Pharaoh entered the inmost sanctuary of a temple, it was to take part as priest in the supreme rites of the liturgy. All could not be well with the world unless all three conditions were fulfilled: the king's divinity was a public matter. For the Greek, worship of his king as canonized hero, then as god, sprang from individual personal influences. The first Ptolemy received his salutation as Soter from Rhodians, not the Greeks of Egypt, because he had been their physical 'saviour' in time of siege. A founder of a city also often received cult worship as a 'hero'. Alexandria had its cult of Alexander as founder, and Soter came to share in it. At some date after 311 B.C. the worship of Alexander was extended from the city to the whole of Egypt. It remains a puzzle for historians why Soter also was not worshipped throughout Egypt, and later associated with the worship of Alexander: only in the cities (Alexandria, Ptolemais certainly) did Soter receive cult offerings. A great leap in the development took place in Philadelphus' 14th year: Alexander's priest was also entrusted with the cult of 'the divine brother and sister' (*theoi adelphoi*). If, as I hold, that is the 14th year on chronological system (ii) (see p. 146), Arsinoe was still living. The innovation lay in the full divinization during their lifetime of queen and king, not the lesser novelty of apotheosis of a dead queen, with whom her surviving consort was associated. The leap is explicable in terms of the deep impression left by Arsinoe's masterful personality. Alive, she was the subject of private dedications found not only in Egypt but in many ports of the Mediterranean; dead, she was not only one of the 'brother and sister gods', she also had her own priestess, who had the same title *kanephoros* as the basket-bearer of Demeter. There was also a city cult and spontaneous worship of her in private sacrifice as the Marine Aphrodite[149] by Alexandrian citizens. This worship called for minute regulation in a sacred law decreed by the prytanes. After this great step, every Ptolemy and his consort joined their predecessors and received cult in their lifetime: the 'benefactor gods' (*euergetai*) etc. appear in the dating clauses of documents till scribes tired of writing out the full list.

In addition to Aphrodite, in a short survey there is occasion to single

---

[149] *P. Oxy.* XXVII.2465, with the explanations of L. Robert in *Welles Essays*, 192ff., and especially 199: (163). He emphasizes the use of sand as bed for the sacrifice and the fire of split logs used to burn up the green pulses.

out only Demeter and Dionysus from the Greek pantheon as gods who still retained a hold in Egypt. Demeter, Greek goddess of the springtime, was worshipped at Eleusis near Alexandria (and in the city) in Mysteries modelled on the Attic Rite. Dionysus was god of wine, joy, life. Like Alexander, he had conquered the East; he was also an ancestor of the Ptolemies, a point stressed in the deme names of Alexandria as well as villages in the Fayyûm such as Bacchias, Dionysias. His cult received a central position in the great procession described by Callixeinus. And Philopator in his megalomania fancied he had a special relationship with him.[150]

It is hard to gauge the sincerity of feeling evoked by Greek private worship. In the ordinary Egyptian there was no doubt of his depth of feeling towards the divine. The great temple buildings included many lesser shrines as well as their central holy of holies. In these, ordinary men and women could express a personal involvement with the numinous. Both in their shrines, and in their progresses across the waters, the gods of Egypt gave answers to simple enquiries about every day courses of action: 'if it is profitable for me to plough the bank of the lake this year, year thirty-three, and not to sow, extract this enquiry', so runs a request written in demotic Egyptian submitted in the second century to Sobekh (Souchos), the crocodile god of Socnopaei Nesus;[151] submitted alongside it was its pair, the same question formulated as a negative, 'if it is profitable for me not to plough, etc.'. The matched slips of papyrus for this oracle were inserted into an urn, and one was drawn out as if it were a lottery ticket (the bean oracle at Delphi worked on a similar system). Such questions were asked about an intended journey, a purchase or lease, the expectation of return of an absent member of the family.

Another illustration might be furnished from dedications and prayers to Isis and Osiris and deities associated with them (in particular, the sacred animals in which they were incarnate, the Apis bull, for instance, who will have been visited by every traveller to Memphis). Isis suckling the infant Horus is one of the most popular types of Egyptian bronze dedications of the late period. Son and husband had been torn from her by the powers of evil, but Isis recovered them by her steadfastness. She prefigured the Madonna in having endured the tribulations of all women. Osiris eventually found his home among the blessed, but to attain it he had triumphed over wickedness. In Memphis, Osiris and Apis together, the resurrected god and the living god, received worship

---

[150] It seems very likely that 215/14 B.C. is the *terminus ante quem* not *post quem* of the royal decree (*BGU* VI.1211: (F 7)) ordering the registration of the worshippers of Dionysus.

[151] Bresciani 1975, nos. 1–2 (F 107). Cf. P. W. Pestman, *P. Mil. Vogliano* III, p. 195; Smith 1974, 18: (F 148) (Osiris-Apis); Youtie 1975, 253ff.: (F 194) (a pair addressed to the Pantocrator and St Philoxenus).

and answered enquiries and prayers.[152] Sarapis was the Greek interpretation of Osiris-Apis, Oserapis, Osor-Hapi.[153] Sarapis was given a royal installation at Alexandria by Soter, so that his Greek subjects might also have the comfort of the god's miracle-working powers. Soter was not creating a cult intended to unify Greeks and Egyptians. They did not share hymn-books in the Serapeum; Sarapis was not worshipped under that name by Egyptians in Egyptian temples (Ptolemy son of Glaucias 'detainee', *katochos*, of Sarapis at Memphis, was a Greek). But Osiris-Apis continued to answer prayers at Memphis; in Alexandria the Greek visitor made his pilgrimage and bowed the knee before the image of Sarapis in his great temple erected by Euergetes. The god had other centres in Alexandria – that of Parmeniscus or Parmenio;[154] many a shrine for immigrant Greeks up-country; and shortly a trail of temples stretching across the Mediterranean to Delos, Athens, Rome.

If, in the religious life, Egyptian themes prevailed, literature and science (except medicine) were dominated by the Greeks. Their studies might be termed a secular religion. The Museum was christened after and dedicated to the Muses, the inspirers of song, music and dance. But they were now worshipped with the head rather than the heart. They lost spontaneity on leaving their native mountains, Olympus, Parnassus, Helicon. They travelled to low-lying Alexandria with (or perhaps better, in) their books, their new sanctuary was a Library. Museum, Library and Secondary Library were associated though separate foundations. Scholarship joined poetry in their foundation. The most distinguished scholars were perhaps mathematicians, doctors, geographers (see pp. 351–2). Their students, too, sprang from poetry. Aristotle and his followers had taken all knowledge as their province; they had accumulated a working library in the Peripatos in Athens; they conducted historical research by quoting and analysing the verses of Solon; probably they were the pioneers of the line-by-line commentary on a poetic text. This genre, that of the *hypomnema*, was for long considered an Alexandrian invention; but it is found fully developed in a papyrus roll recovered at Derveni near Thessaloniki that cannot have been copied later than about 300 B.C.[155] The roll contains just such an

[152] Examples in Smith 1974, 18, 74: (F 148). E.g. 'a man asks Osiris-Apis to bring shame on a woman'. In *UPZ* I.1 a woman asks Oserapi in Greek to bring shame on a man (both probably fourth century B.C.).

[153] Established by Wilcken in *UPZ* I.1927. Among forms in conventional use for the name are Oserapis (Wilcken); Osiris-Apis, Smith 1974: (F 148). In the foundation plaques of the great Serapeum of Alexandria, the demotic writing of the name is commonly vocalized as Osor-Hapi, Fraser 1972, I.250: (A 15). Bivar (1979, 741: (F 168)) sees in the Aramaic Ḥstrapati of the recently deciphered trilingual inscription from Xanthus in Lycia the Old Persian *xšaθrapati* 'an old Iranian epithet of Mithra' and makes an identification with 'supposedly Egyptian Sarapis', whose origin he now traces back to Iran.

[154] R. Pfeiffer on Call. fr. 191, Diegetes 4.

[155] Bibliography in Turner 1980, 183 n. 4, 200 n. 4: (F 149).

exegesis of an Orphic verse cosmogony. Scholars not only studied poetry, they wrote it. The Muses of learning and of wit were invoked in order to rescue the old genres of literature in a world that no longer needed them. A catalogue of names is of little value in the short space here available. But mention should be made of Philitas of Cos, tutor to Philadelphus, Callimachus of Cyrene, Asclepiades of Samos, Zenodotus of Ephesus, Lycophron of Chalcis; of Theocritus and Apollonius surnamed the Rhodian. Eratosthenes and Aristophanes of Byzantium were in the line of Zenodotus as scholar-librarians, followed by Aristarchus. Callimachus is generally believed never to have held the post of titular librarian,[156] but he left his mark on the library as cataloguer. If ever a librarian deserved the title of creative genius simply from cataloguing it was he. His *Pinakes* set a standard for the ancient world, and a modern bibliographer could take pride in scholarship of so high an order.

The scholarly achievement of Alexandria was the crowning glory of Ptolemaic Egypt. Its legacy, still fruitful in the modern world, was twofold: on one side, definitive advances in science and learning (see pp. 321–52), on the other the establishment of methodical scientific discipline. The Jews were introduced to the principles of scholarship in Alexandria, as well as taught that literature may be an art-form in addition to a divine revelation. The inspired Seventy of the Septuagint turned into Greek the Hebrew sacred scriptures, no longer understood by the numerous and progressive Jewry of Alexandria. Their members are frequently mentioned as energetic ministers and subjects of the Ptolemies. The Alexandrian Jew, Ezechiel, took the story of Moses and Exodus for a Greek tragedy (*Exagoge*).

The tasks to which this scholarship addressed itself – translation of the Septuagint, the geographical systems of Eratosthenes or the geometrical of Euclid, even Callimachus' own inventory of all Greek literature – were conceived on a grand scale. They match the spirit which erected the Pharos, or Bryaxis' over-life size statue of Sarapis. Because of Callimachus' victorious theories about poetry, Alexandrianism has come to stand for preoccupation with the minute and the miniature, or else with escapism from reality: in literature the Epyllion, the Idyll, the pastoral, the epigram; in craftsmanship the cameo (exquisitely cut onyx as in the Tazza Farnese), porcelain, the painted glass beaker, exquisite embroidery. But there had been other schools of thought; Apollonius of Rhodes wrote a long epic poem well enough to survive, his predecessors in the Alexandrian epic did not. They were a testy crowd, the members

---

[156] Largely on the strength of *P. Oxy.* x.1241. But this anonymous, mutilated and erratic list cannot be cited against a librarianship of Callimachus before that of Apollonius son of Silleus (e.g. in the 260s B.C.) without a generous injection of hypothesis.

of the king's Senior Common Room. But if malice is the spice of wit, intellectual life cannot have been dull in the time of Philadelphus.

Callimachus' preoccupation with the traditions of Greece had also led to over-emphasis on his and his circle's apparent refusal to draw on the teeming life of Egypt for subjects. In Alexandrian poetry shepherds are from Cos, Sicily or possibly Arcadia, certainly not the Fayyûm; the fishermen who illustrate the resourcefulness of poverty are Greek islanders, not Libyan or Nilotic.[157] It is almost as though the Greek artist deliberately turned his back on the genre scenes of his adopted country. But this is not true of the choroplast, the worker in terracotta or faience, who portrayed the fellah with sagging paunch, basket slung over his shoulder on his way to market.[158] And it is not entirely true even of Callimachus himself. In his evocation of the awakening of a city from sleep,[159] is it certain that the screech of the axle in the busy main road, the water-drawer's shanty,[160] the hammering of the bronzesmiths contains nothing of Alexandria? Again few subjects could appear more remote from everyday than Callimachus' witty and delightful *Lock of Berenice*.[161] Euergetes' consort, queen Berenice, promised to dedicate a lock of hair to Aphrodite at Zephyrium on her husband's return from the third Syrian war.[162] The dedication was made, but one day the curl could not be found. Conon the astronomer then discovered it among the constellations. In Plutarch's narrative, Isis searching for Osiris snipped off a curl and dedicated it at Coptos as a token of mourning. A Greek writer of the Roman empire and a Greek proverb speak of Isis' hair being shown at Memphis. Did Berenice or Callimachus know of this incident in the mythology of Isis? Indeed, did it figure in the story in the third century B.C.? There is a delicious irony in its rejection from the Isis story by an Egyptologist as a borrowing from the Greek.[163] Whichever answer is correct, it is of interest to the theme of this chapter. In the monumental field a counterpart to this phenomenon has been identified by P. M. Fraser.[164] He points out that in marble dedicatory plaques there is a change in the second century B.C. 'The simple unadorned rec-

---

[157] Theoc. *Id.* XXI.18 προσέναχε θάλασσα.

[158] Thompson 1979, 175ff.: (F 384). She lists similar works; as in *Ptolemaic Oinechoai* (F 382) she stresses that faience is an Egyptian not a Greek material.

[159] Fr. 260 Pf. 54ff. from *Hecala*, which creates the expectation that Athens is the place.

[160] *Hydrophoros* is a description of an artisan class in *P. Petrie* III.137.7; *P. Ent.* 78.1.

[161] Fr. 110 Pf. The suggestion here reported is made by Thompson 1979, 175ff.: (F 384).

[162] Callimachus' own words are too fragmentary to show the precise point in time and location of the dedication. The *diegetes*, Hyginus and others say 'Berenice promised she would dedicate the lock' if her husband was returned.

[163] J. Gwynn Griffiths, edition of Plutarch, *de Iside et Osiride* (Cardiff, 1970) n. 14; Lucian, *adv. indoct.* 12, *Paroemiogr. gr.* II, p. 170. Note that a Greek inscription and a papyrus, both of Roman date, contain dedications to 'Isis of the Lock', Griffiths *loc. cit.,* with the correction of H. C. Youtie, *ZPE* 13 (1974) 239.

[164] Fraser 1972, I.191, II.323 n. 6: (A 15).

tangular plaque is usually replaced by a larger stele with curved upper section, containing a representation of a sacred figure or scene such as had been traditional in Pharaonic Egypt.'

The *Lock of Berenice* is a learned esoteric poem – an 'in' poem for an 'in' group. When literature becomes élitist, only an élite can understand it: an essential background is all Greek literature for the Alexandrians, as is a great deal of English, indeed of world literature for *The Waste Land*. Nevertheless papyrus finds show that Callimachus as well as Menander was read in the third century B.C. in up-country Egypt; so were Homer, Stesichorus, Euripides, Plato, the Peripatetics, the doctors. It is unprofitable to speculate on whether these books were the property of private persons, such as Greek officers, or privates, or even the courtiers from Alexandria who possessed second homes in the Fayyûm. They may also have been part of the stock of a gymnasium library. The gymnasium was a club which offered intellectual as well as physical amenities. Restricted to Greeks it helped them to preserve a national identity as well as a national heritage. And the cleruchs did their best to find Greek women to marry or live with, as is shown in the names of their wives and mistresses. When Egyptians were admitted to hold *kleroi*, Greek small-holders tended to reserve for themselves the title *katoikoi*, after the top class of cleruchs, the catoecic cavalrymen (*katoikoi hippeis*) who appear as early as 257 B.C.[165] At lower social levels, in families of Greeks who took Egyptian wives, both a Greek and an Egyptian name was often used for all members of the family.

In Nectanebo's temple at Saqqara a Hor might wonder whether King Philometor would gain greater benefit from receiving dream warnings in demotic, the first language of the dreamer, than in inadequate Greek versions. Hor, like many of his class, had a limited facility in Greek. But he is among the élite who can write and read in the Egyptian tongue. For there is also an Egyptian élitism; Egyptian-speakers were, in the main, illiterate. There could be no counterpart to the Greek's Homer in the houses of Egyptian cultivators. But the Egyptian was by no means unappreciative of imaginative literature, and he had an ear for a rhetorical device or a pithy phrase. For all his millenia of past history, the present came to him as the supreme experience, and myth retained an actuality that it had lost for the literate Greek.

Three abiding effects of the interwoven counterpoint of cultures may be cited in conclusion to this chapter. The term 'Hellene' came to stand indifferently for Macedonian, Athenian, Alexandrian, Cretan, even Thracian. For everyday dating the simple and practical Egyptian calendar system ousted the elaborate Greek cycles that called for

---

[165] *P. Mich. Zen.* 9.6–7.

disturbing insertions of extra months. The Egyptians took over and adapted the Greek alphabet as a notation for their own language. A hesitant attempt at it in the early second century B.C. has been noticed (p. 163); the idea fermented and emerged as Coptic, fully formed not later than the second century of the Christian era.

CHAPTER 6

SYRIA AND THE EAST

D. MUSTI

I. ORGANIZATION, THE MONARCHY, THE COURT

Of the various Hellenistic kingdoms which arose out of the dissolution of Alexander the Great's dominions, that which most resembled the empire conquered and for a time ruled over by the Macedonian king was the Seleucid kingdom. It was similar in size and structure, in racial and social composition, in its economic functioning and in its political ideology. This kingdom sprang from the struggles of the Diadochi and was consolidated in the battles fought by Seleucus I against Antigonus Monophthalmus, Demetrius Poliorcetes an Lysimachus. It was to last, formally, until its final subjection to Rome and the reduction of the small parts of it that still remained to the condition of a province, in the course of Pompey's reorganization of the East in 63 B.C. The conflict with Rome makes it convenient to divide the history of the kingdom (which began in 312 B.C. with the official initiation of the Seleucid era and thus lasted a little less than 250 years)[1] into two clearly distinct periods. Following its defeat by Rome in 189 B.C. and the subsequent peace of Apamea in 188, the Seleucid kingdom finally lost its control of western Asia Minor (the part which lies to the west of the Taurus Mountains). It had ruled this region for nearly a century, with some interruptions and upheavals caused by the rebellion of Pergamum, the Galatian invasion, the civil wars and revolts led by Antiochus Hierax and Achaeus, and conflicts with other kings who tried to dispute its possession. The change in the size of the kingdom between the first and the second periods of Seleucid history also brought with it a change in its general political orientation. Before the peace of Apamea, it was mainly concerned with the regions bordering the eastern Mediterranean and more specifically the Aegean Sea; afterwards, it was influenced more by the process of disintegration, by dynastic struggles and by the ferment of the various nationalities. In this context, the outstanding historical figure was Antiochus III (the Great), who restored the kingdom, both eastwards and westwards, almost to the boundaries which it possessed at the death of its

---

[1] The beginning of the Seleucid era in Babylon is dated to 1 Nisan (= 3 April) 311 B.C. For the Macedonians, after the adoption of the title 'basileus', it is conventionally placed in the autumn of 312. Cf. Bikerman 1944, 73–6: (E 7); Samuel 1972, 245–6: (A 53).

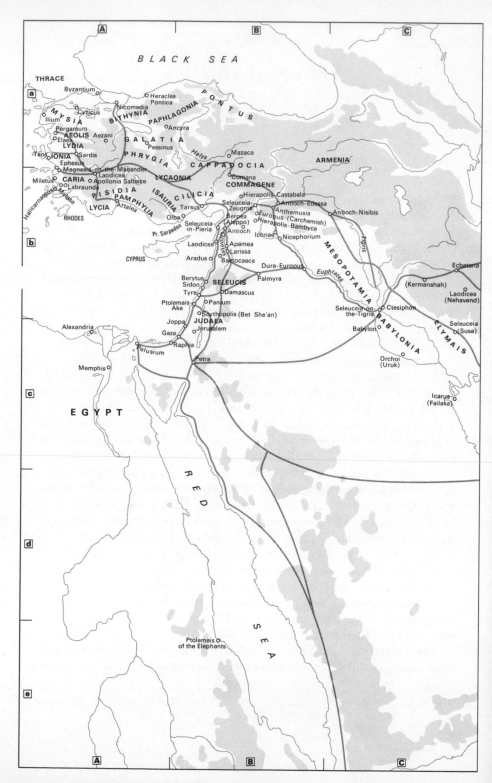

BLACK SEA

THRACE
Byzantium

MYSIA
Ilium
Cyzicus
Nicomedia
Heraclea
Pontica
BITHYNIA
PAPHLAGONIA
PONTUS

Pergamum
AEOLIS
Elaea
Aezani
Ancyra
GALATIA
Pessinus

LYDIA
Teos
IONIA
Sardis
PHRYGIA
Halys
Mazaca
CAPPADOCIA
ARMENIA

Ephesus
Magnesia-on-the-Maeander
Laodicea
Miletus
CARIA
Apollonia Salbace
LYCAONIA
Comana

Labraunda
COMMAGENE

Halicarnassus
Mylasa
PISIDIA
ISAURIA
CILICIA
Hierapolis-Castabala
Antioch-Edessa
Antioch-Nisibis

RHODES
LYCIA
PAMPHYLIA
Attalea
Tarsus
Seleuceia-
Zeugma
Anthemusia
Europus (Carchemish)
MESOPOTAMIA

Olba
Beroea
(Aleppo)
Hierapolis-Bambyce

Pr. Sarpedon
Seleuceia-
in-Pieria
Antioch
Ichnae
Nicephorium
Tigris

CYPRUS
Laodicea
Apamea
Larissa

Aradus
Bartocaece
Dura-Europus
Euphrates

Berytus
Sidon
Palmyra
Ecbatana
(Kermanshah)

Tyre
SELEUCIS
Damascus
Laodicea
(Nehavend)

Ptolemais-
Ake
Panium
Seleuceia-on-
the-Tigris
Ctesiphon
BABYLONIA
ELYMAIS
Seleuceia
(Susa)

Alexandria
Joppa
JUDAEA
Scythopolis (Bet She'an)
Babylon

Gaza
Jerusalem
Orchoi
(Uruk)

Pelusium
Raphia
Petra
Icarus
(Failaka)

Memphis

EGYPT

RED

SEA

Ptolemais
of the Elephants

Map 4. Hellenistic Asia

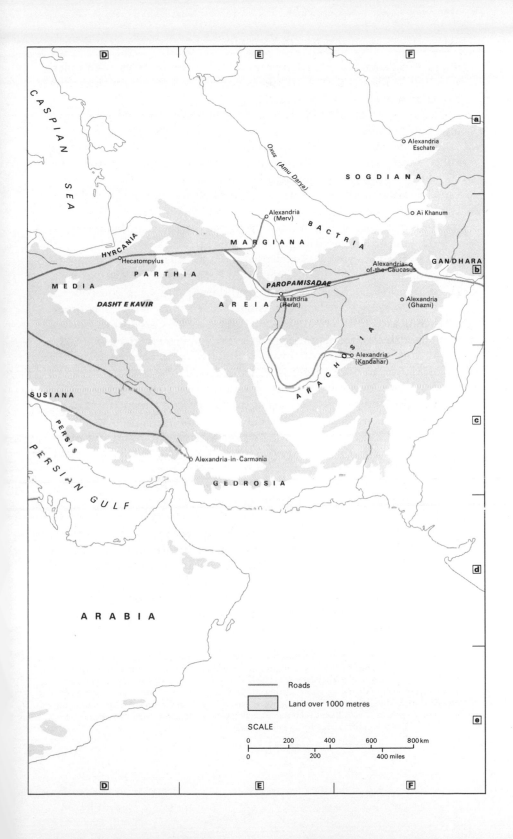

CASPIAN SEA

Oxus
(Amu Darya)

SOGDIANA

o Alexandria
Eschate

o Ai Khanum

BACTRIA

Alexandria
(Merv)

MARGIANA

HYRCANIA
o Hecatompylus

Alexandria o
of-the-Caucasus

GANDHARA

PARTHIA

MEDIA

PAROPAMISADAE

DASHT E KAVIR

AREIA

Alexandria
(Herat)

o Alexandria
(Ghazni)

Alexandria
(Kandahar)

A R A C H O S I A

SUSIANA

PERSIS

o Alexandria-in-Carmania

GEDROSIA

PERSIAN GULF

ARABIA

a

b

c

d

e

——— Roads

Land over 1000 metres

SCALE

0   200   400   600   800 km

0   200   400 miles

founder, Seleucus I, and so appears to some extent as its re-founder, although he lived (till 187) to experience the first heavy blow dealt it by Rome in the war of 192–189 B.C.

The second period (187–63 B.C.) can, however, also be subdivided into two periods:

(a) That during which the state was still a solid political and economic entity, with a sense of its fundamental unity and legitimate power. This lasted from the reigns of Seleucus IV and Antiochus IV Epiphanes (the sons of Antiochus the Great) to those of Demetrius I, Antiochus V Eupator, Alexander Balas and Antiochus VI, and largely corresponds to the period during which Roman policy in the eastern Mediterranean appears simply as one of hegemony (196–146 B.C.).

(b) A second period in which the seeds of discord, sown by the accession to the throne of the two sons of Antiochus the Great (Seleucus IV and Antiochus IV) successively, and the appearance in consequence of two dynastic branches increasingly in conflict with each other, resulted in violent and bloody conflicts, usurpations, secessions (such as that of the Jews), reductions in the territory subject to the king (at the hands of the Parthians), the loss or eclipse of legitimacy and even the appropriation by foreign dynasties from Armenia and Commagene of dynastic traditions and legitimate rights over the kingdom.

After this short historical sketch, it will be convenient to examine various aspects of the Seleucid kingdom in its classic form, that is to say at the time of its greatest extent. However we shall also note some of the divergences caused by the complex incidents and disturbances which have been briefly described.

The kingdom founded by Seleucus was a personal, rather than a national, monarchy.[2] It consisted in the rule of a king (*basileus*) belonging to the dynasty founded by Seleucus. The territory over which the authority of the king extended was inhabited by various peoples, without ethnic unity. Unlike the documents mentioning the king of Macedonia, in which in addition to the *basileus*, and subordinated to him, we have the *Macedones*, the official Seleucid documents mention the king but no people (*ethnos*). Had a people been mentioned, given the dynastic origin of the Seleucid dynasty and the ethnic composition of the army, at least in the early decades, it could only have been the *Macedones*

---

[2] For this difference, sometimes denied without reason, see Aymard 1967, 100–22: (I 9); Musti 1966, 111–38: (E 44); and other works indicated in the Bibliography. For a different viewpoint see Errington 1978: (D 17). The character of personal monarchy is perhaps also inherent in the term Σελευκίς, especially if this means (at least in the early period of Seleucid history) 'land or dominion of Seleucus'. (Cf. Musti 1966, 61–81: (E 44)). For a broader notion of Σελευκίς (in the third century B.C.) with respects to Συρία Σελευκίς (as also including Cilicia) see also Ihnken 1978, 41 n. 2: (B 93). On Συρία Σελευκίς in Strabo see below, p. 189 n. 21.

again, here too in Syria. The absence of any indication of a people beside the title (and name) of the king is a matter of greater positive than negative significance. This positive significance was as an expression of the dynasty's resolve not to represent the *basileia* simply as the rule of Macedonian (or Graeco-Macedonian) conquerors over the various subject peoples, who were, in order of their conquest, the populations of Mesopotamia and Syria, Iran, Asia Minor and Palestine – in short, Semitic peoples together with Iranian and Anatolian elements. After an early period during which the capital was in Mesopotamia (Seleuceia-on-the-Tigris: *c.* 311–301), it was transferred, perhaps for a short time, to the new foundation of Seleuceia-in-Pieria and then, finally, to Antioch-on-the-Orontes. At this point the geographical, political and (partly, at least) the economic centre of gravity moved to Syria. The burden, but also the advantage of a more direct rule, now fell most heavily on the Semitic populations of Syria (and as before, of Babylonia). But this did not mean that the Seleucid kings became formally 'kings of the Syrians'.[3]

The inscriptions found in the Seleucid kingdom use terms which taken together provide some indication of its personal structure. Besides the king appear the friends (*philoi*) and the military forces of land and sea (*dynameis*).[4] The former term (*philoi*) stresses the personal structure of the kingdom: it indicates a characteristic aspect of the monarchical institution as such. But it is also of interest to seek its antecedents; the institution appears in an eastern context (in the Achaemenid kingdom and its Mesopotamian predecessors) as well as in that of Macedonia. The 'king's friends' form his council. Participation in this body does not depend on the local origin of its members. Precisely because the council is formed with absolute autonomy by a king endowed with absolute power, persons who are strictly speaking foreigners, since they come from outside the kingdom, can become members of it. The court was thus a prop for the king and at the same time a vehicle of international relations, open to politicians, soldiers and scholars, drawn (usually) from the Graeco-Macedonian elements. Among the 'Friends' there were various categories, arranged according to a more or less rigid hierarchy: *timomenoi, protoi kai protimomenoi*, 'honoured men', 'first and especially honoured men'.

The Seleucid monarchy (like the Ptolemaic and other Hellenistic monarchies) was also acquainted with the category of 'relations' of the

[3] On the argument for the Macedonian presence cf. Edson 1958: (E 19), and also some remarks in Musti 1966, 111–38: (E 44). On the different capitals of the kingdom in the different periods, cf. Downey 1961: (E 157); Will 1979, 1.60: (A 67); Marinoni 1972: (E 39).

[4] Cf. e.g. *OGIS* 219, 20–9; Habicht 1958, 3–4: (H 85); Orth 1977, 44, 55–8, 67, 170–1, *passim*: (A 46).

king (*syngeneis*). Often (and especially in the early days of the kingdom) these people were in fact blood relations of the sovereign; but later on the title became purely honorific.[5]

The true basis of the Seleucid monarchy was, however, the armed forces (*dynameis*). Its power was based on these and this fact determines the whole structure and history of the kingdom. The Seleucid monarchy had the typical characteristics of a military monarchy: this basic fact explains the colonization, the type of relations with the natives, the limited success of attempts at hellenization, and the sense of precariousness pervading the whole history of the kingdom – to mention an external factor which of course does not embrace the whole reality of Seleucid history, but is nonetheless an aspect that cannot be ignored. Balancing, and sometimes contrasted with, all these features stands the policy of the sovereign, resting specifically on the ideology of a personal and multiracial monarchy, a privileged relationship for the cities (*poleis*), a much-trumpeted respect for their freedom and democracy (*eleutheria kai demokratia*), and, all in all, a claim to principles inspired by the policies of Alexander the Great and Antigonus Monophthalmus, who served as models for the Seleucid kings.

Power, then, was exercised by the king, his 'Friends' and the armed forces, and the object of their rule was the territory (*chora*) and the subject population. More specifically cultivators of the royal lands (*basilike chora*) were called royal peasants (*basilikoi laoi*): they were not slaves but their status was akin to that of rural serfs. However their position cannot be described precisely without reference to the villages in which they lived.[6]

The distinction between cities, peoples and dynasts (*poleis, ethne, dynastai*) is sometimes considered peculiar to the Seleucid kingdom. But in fact, although these terms are sometimes to be found in Seleucid inscriptions, they also occur, all or some, and in various combinations, in other texts, literary and epigraphical. These are not, in the writer's view, distinctions valid only within the kingdom. They are rather complex designations of the complex reality of the Hellenistic world considered as a whole – which is how it is considered in the texts of the chancelleries of Hellenistic sovereigns. For throughout the Hellenistic world there were *basileis*, that is true and proper kings, *dynastai*, princelings or local lords, *ethne*, populations with little or no civic

---

[5] Cf. Momigliano 1933: (E 42); Mooren 1968: (F 285). For the Ptolemaic ambience there are surer indications of the meaning, function and hierarchy of titles such as ὁ συγγενής, τῶν πρώτων φίλων, ἀρχισωματοφύλαξ, τῶν φίλων, τῶν σωματοφυλάκων, τῶν διαδόχων. Cf. Trindl 1942: (F 333) and especially Mooren 1977: (F 287). Mooren does not think that the council of 'Friends' had lost its political role by the beginning of the second century B.C., particularly in Egypt (as against Habicht 1958: (H 85)).

[6] On the condition of the *laoi* see below, p. 203 n. 45.

structure and often dominated by the *dynastai* or even the *basileis*, and *poleis*, the cities which enjoyed at least a certain level of autonomy.[7]

II. GEOGRAPHICAL DESCRIPTION OF THE SELEUCID KINGDOM

The nucleus of the state was in the arc spanning the area from the Persian Gulf, across the Plain of Babylonia and Giazirah (literally 'the island') to the broad valley of Aleppo, the coast of Hatay (Myriandrus) with its many ports, Seleuceia-in-Pieria, the plains of Apamea and Laodicea, and on to the plain of Cilicia. This was the compact economic, strategic and political nucleus: Mesopotamia, Syria and Cilicia.

Immediately behind this nucleus lie other areas:

(1) First there is the high desert plain of modern southern Syria (probably ancient Coele-Syria), crossed by a few hills and valleys. On the edges of this region there were cities, most of which developed late, especially in the Roman period but also in late Hellenistic times: Palmyra and Damascus, both important stops on caravan routes and both destined to play a special role in the following period, when their economic function became more important during the political and economic crisis of the Seleucid state.

(2) Iran: this is a region mainly composed of mountains and desert, but also including fertile zones such as Gilan, Mazandaran with Gurgan, immediately to the south of the Caspian Sea. The general function of Iran in the structure of the Seleucid kingdom and its relations with the sovereign will be discussed in the next paragraph. Here we simply note the interest, from the military point of view, of the road that connected the nucleus of the Seleucid kingdom (with Mesopotamia as the principal departure point, and in particular the ancient capital of Seleuceia-on-the-Tigris with its royal residence) with northern Iran, that is the region of Media. This road was wedged between the Caspian Mountains (south of the Caspian Sea) and the Salt Desert (Dasht-e Kavir).

It is no accident that one piece of evidence for the cult of the Seleucid rulers, Antiochus III and his 'sister-wife' (*adelphe*)[8] Laodice, comes from Nehavend, the Seleucid Laodicea, and another from Kermanshah, both probably stops on a main mountain-road from Mesopotamia to Media. Similarly, the parallel evidence from Durdurkar in Phrygia was also found along another 'umbilical cord', this time connecting the heart of the kingdom with one of its various offshoots, western Asia Minor.[9]

[7] It is in this fuller sense that the formula is employed, for example, in Diod. XIX.57.3. Cf. also *OGIS* 228, l. 11; and Herzog-Klaffenbach 1952, no. 2, ll. 8ff.: (B 89).

[8] The title is formal: Laodice was not in fact Antiochus' sister.

[9] Cf. Robert, *Hellenica* VII (1949) 5–29; VIII (1950) 33–75; *CR Acad. Inscr.* 1967, 281–97: (B 146) (for the copies of the letter of Antiochus III on the institution of the cult of Laodice side by side with his own).

(3) Outside the borders of Iran itself, but still within the Iranian (or Iranian-Scythian) orbit, there were outposts set up by Alexander, some of which were preserved, at least for a time, by Seleucus I and Antiochus I. To the north-east of modern Mashhad, on the plain of what is today Turkmenistan, exposed to the attacks of tribes (whom we now know to have been much more sedentary than was previously imagined and to be distinguished from the surrounding nomads) there was Antioch-in-Margiana (Mary, till 1937 called Merv). A little further to the east, in the region of Ferghana (beyond Maracanda-Samarkand), there was Alexandria Eschate ('the last'). The domain of Seleucus I also extended behind the mountains of Band-i-Baba, Hararajat and the Chain of Paropamisadae (Hindu-Kush) into modern Afghanistan, to where the high plain allows the possibility of settlement and cultivation and where there arose some of the many Alexandrias founded by the great Macedonian: Alexandria-Herat, Alexandria-Kandahar, Alexandria-Ghazni (below Kabul), Alexandria-of-the-Caucasus and Alexandria-on-the-Oxus, probably to be identified with Aï Khanum, at the confluence of the Amu Darya and the Kowkcheh.[10] Here in ancient Bactria, Seleucid rule survived for a few decades, continuing that of Alexander the Great. However, while Seleucus I was still on the throne, control was relinquished over the level region of the Indus (now Pakistan) and the Punjab (North-West India).

A notable feature of the two regions described above was the presence of transit routes furthering communication and trade. Besides the great road joining Mesopotamia via the passes of the Zagrus into northern Iran (which, besides its fundamental military role and its function as a link with the outposts of Graeco-Macedonian rule, may have also been used as a trade route with the regions of Central Asia), there were the roads which followed the course of the Tigris or the Euphrates to the Persian Gulf. The Seleucid presence is also documented by inscriptions from the third century B.C. in an island opposite the mouth of the Tigris in the northernmost corner of the Persian Gulf; this is Failaka, the ancient Icarus. The roads following the course of the two great rivers crossed the Syrian heartland and went towards the ports either of northern Syria or (after the acquisition of Phoenicia, Palestine and southern Syria) of Phoenicia.

The history of roads in the Seleucid kingdom, and in particular those connecting the regions east of the Tigris and the Euphrates with the

---

[10] On the seventy Alexandrias attributed by tradition (Plut. *de Alex. fort.* 1.5) to the great Macedonian, and on the difficulty of giving them a precise location, cf. Tcherikower 1927, 145–6: (A 60); Tarn 1948, II.171–80, 232–59: (A 58). Specifically on Alexander's foundations in Bactria and Sogdiana: Diod. XVII.24; Strabo XI.11.4.C. 517; on the cities founded in Margiana: Curt. VI.10.15–16. On the cities in the Indus delta: *ibid.* IX.10.2. For Aï Khanum, cf. n. 67.

shores of the Mediterranean, can be divided, according to Rostovtzeff, into two distinct periods. The first was before the Seleucid victory of Panium (200), which gave the kingdom of Syria control over Phoenicia and Palestine, and the second after this victory and especially after the peace of Apamea between Syria and Rome (188 B.C.). In the third century B.C. and in the second till the peace of Apamea, the roads most frequently used for trade were the northernmost ones (Rostovtzeff singles out two between Antioch and Mesopotamia: one ran from Antioch-on-the-Orontes in the direction of the Euphrates, which it crossed at Zeugma, and then continued through Edessa and Antioch-Nisibis to join the Persian road leading to the upper satrapies; the second followed the same route to Zeugma but then, having crossed the Euphrates, descended to the Plain of Mesopotamia and followed the Anthemusia–Ichnae–Nicephorium route to join the road dating from the Persian period which led to Babylon and Seleuceia-on-the-Tigris). In the second century B.C. another trade route became important, the desert road, connecting Seleuceia-on-the-Tigris by a more southerly route, which ran either through Damascus, or even further to the south through Petra, with the ports of Phoenicia and Palestine respectively.[11]
(4) Asia Minor was a land of great variety, which expressed itself in its landscape, its geographical and economic characteristics, and in its political history. Consequently Seleucid rule, which in Cilicia was solid and produced typical and long-lasting results, proved to be less stable elsewhere.[12] In particular Asia Minor possessed certain characteristic empty spaces, which to some extent reflected the dimensions and directions of the conquests and rule of Alexander the Great. The Seleucids seem, for example, not to have gained a firm foothold in the mountainous regions of Armenia and in their outliers in Asia Minor. The sources speak of a 'Seleucid Cappadocia' (and also of military operations by Seleucus I near a River Lycus in Armenia), but in these regions Seleucid rule was strictly limited.[13] The chain of mountains in Pontus, which follows, at some distance, the coast line of eastern Anatolia and enters the Asiatic hinterland, put Pontic Cappadocia beyond Seleucid control. But neither did internal Cappadocia – the region whose centre was the royal temple-city of Comana – become truly subject to Seleucid rule; and this was also, and even more decidedly, the

---

[11] See especially chs. 4–6 in Rostovtzeff 1953: (A 52).

[12] On forms of 'democratic' life in Seleucid Cilicia, in particular at Tarsus and Magarsus (Antioch-on-the-Cydnus and Antioch-on-the-Pyramus respectively), cf. Musti 1966, 187–90: (E 44) (differing from Welles 1962: (E 101)), on the basis of the inscription from Karatas (*SEG* XII.511; Robert, *CR Acad. Inscr.* 1951, 256–9).

[13] On *Καππαδοκία Σελευκίς*: Appian, *Syr.* 55.281; on Seleucus' operations on the Lycus: Plut. *Demetr.* 46.7–47.3; Musti 1966, 71–3: (E 44).

case with Bithynia.[14] In short, vast inland regions of eastern Asia Minor, behind the mountains of Armenia, the Antitaurus and the Taurus, escaped conquest and rule at the hands of both Alexander and the Seleucids, and on the whole the Graeco-Macedonian presence was also episodic during the period of the Diadochi.

The Graeco-Macedonians thus did not control the whole length of the ancient royal Persian road, which ran from Ephesus to Sardis, entered Phrygia, and after leaving that region passed over to the east of the River Halys (Kizil Irmak) into those parts of eastern Anatolia which, as we have seen, were outside Seleucid rule. Persian rule seems to have penetrated more deeply into these regions inhabited by peoples of Anatolian and Iranian origin. The expansion organized by the Seleucids into Asia Minor did not therefore follow the route of the ancient Persian royal road but rather the one followed by the Ten Thousand in Xenophon's *Anabasis* or by the army of Alexander the Great: from the Troad to the high plains of Phrygia in western Asia Minor – these were not without their fertile areas – and then, turning sharply towards the coast, across the Taurus (and the pass of the Cilician Gates) into Cilicia and the modest coastal plains of the Gulf of Alexandretta. This route was followed in reverse (in an effort to retain connexions with western Asia Minor and the Aegean) in the course of Seleucid expansion under Seleucus I, then under Antiochus I and especially under Antiochus III.

Cyprus remained outside Seleucid control. Its possession would indeed have required (and also stimulated) a proper naval policy. But that was something which remained embryonic in Seleucid history; the Seleucid navy was only consistently developed in the last decade, more or less, of Antiochus III, that is during the brief period from the victory of Panium to the peace of Apamea (200–188 B.C.) during which the Seleucids controlled the ports of Phoenicia (and also, it should be noted, the forests of Lebanon, which were an excellent source of timber for ship-building).

III. ADMINISTRATIVE DIVISIONS AND PERSONNEL

Because of the large expanse of territory ruled over by the Seleucid kings, not only was it divided from the outset into districts, which we shall examine later, but above that there was a division into large territorial areas, which meant, alongside the central nucleus of the kingdom under the direct administration of the king and his generals, the creation of true viceroyalties. This need for some breaking up and territorial distribution of power arose primarily from the size of the

[14] On the sanctuary of Ma at Comana in Cappadocia, Strabo XII.2.3. c. 535–6; on the sanctuary duplicating it at Pontic Comana see also Strabo XII.3.32. c. 557.

kingdom and, in consequence of this, the existence of vast peripheral areas subject to less rigorous control, in which the work of unification and transformation went on less intensively. These areas were strategically more exposed and they already possessed less responsive political and economic systems. Relations between them and the central power were more difficult, and it was therefore necessary for these to be more indirect than those existing between the central power and the nucleus of the kingdom. However, the creation of these 'viceroyalties' or 'special commands', as they were called, solved a problem arising from the fact that the monarchy was hereditary, in short a dynasty. Especially during the early decades of Seleucid history, these 'special commands' were usually reserved for members of the royal dynasty; in particular, the heir to the throne was given command over the 'upper satrapies' (*ano satrapeiai*), comprising the Iranian regions (sometimes the term also included Mesopotamia).[15] The other special command was the governorship of Sardis, that is, the territories of western Asia Minor lying west of the line running from the River Halys to the Taurus mountains. The existence of a governorship of Sardis is clearly attested as early as the Persian period, during which we find the title and function of the *karanos*, the viceroy of the Achaemenid king, who resided at Sardis and exercised jurisdiction over the lands of western Asia Minor. Many modern scholars (beginning with H. Bengtson, who is best acquainted with the post of general (*strategos*) in the Hellenistic period) hold that this governorship was re-established in the Seleucid kingdom immediately after the conquest of western Asia Minor, that is after Seleucus I's victory over Lysimachus at Corupedium in 281 B.C. Although this possibility is not to be excluded, it should be pointed out that there is no positive evidence for the unification of these regions under a single command before the middle of the third century B.C. (The first certain governor is Antiochus Hierax, the brother and later the opponent of King Seleucus II. His successors, Achaeus, who also belonged to the dynasty and rebelled against Antiochus III, and Zeuxis, are also well known.)[16] Moreover, it does not seem necessary nor even likely that the conditions of considerable confusion which characterized Seleucid rule in Asia Minor would have recommended the too rapid creation in these

[15] For the problems of the special commands of the East and the West, cf. Bengtson 1964–7, II.1ff.: (A 6); Orth 1977, 124–6: (A 46); different views in Musti 1957, 275–8: (B 113); 1965, 153–60: (E 87); 1966, 107–11: (E 44).

[16] On the position of Zeuxis see Musti 1966, 109–11: (E 44); Olshausen 1972: (E 89); Walbank 1979, III.109 (*ad* Polyb. XII.16.4) and 785: (B 37). Zeuxis is the most interesting and (with some gaps) the best documented example of the career of a Seleucid official (222–190 B.C.). The brothers Molon and Alexander were invested at the accession of Antiochus III (so I interpret Polyb. v.40.7) with the command of the ἄνω σατραπεῖαι (one Media, the other Persia). However, on these two see (for a partly different interpretation) Schmitt 1964, 116–50: (E 51).

regions of an extraordinary power, whose holder could at once have strengthened himself by alliance with individual cities, thus constituting a serious threat to the central authority. In the writer's opinion the unification of power in these territories was caused by dynastic pressures: but these then had the foreseeable consequences of encouraging rivalry within the family and secession from the central and legitimate power of the king of Antioch.

It has been said that in the Seleucid state there was no proper council of ministers, no 'cabinet'. At any rate the functions of 'prime minister' were apparently performed by persons with the title 'charged with affairs' (*epi ton pragmaton*);[17] and both at central and regional level we can distinguish the functions of the *dioiketes* who, in accordance with the principal meaning of the word *dioikesis*, appears to have been responsible for financial administration. At local level there is the *oikonomos*, who was probably the administrator of the district governed by a general (*strategos*) or more specifically of the royal property (beneath him was the *hyparchos* with executive functions); but the *oikonomos* can also mean the administrator of individual properties (e.g. that of the queen Laodice II). It is also difficult to define the exact position of the official known as 'in charge of revenues' (*epi ton prosodon*) in the Seleucid kingdom. Once this position was thought to be a very high one, comparable in some degree to the *dioiketes*; but now it is held to be more equivalent in rank to the *oikonomos*. The relevant sources would suggest that there was a development in the function of the *epi ton prosodon* in the later stages of Seleucid history to the detriment of the *oikonomos*, whom he replaced. It is, however, very difficult to assign a single rigid value to designations which are of their nature generic, or to establish a rigorous hierarchy between the various functions, outside particular contexts in which the different functions are defined and co-ordinated in relation to each other. Also to be noted are the offices of the *eklogistes* (accountant), the *epistolographos* (secretary) and the *chreophylax* (the keeper of the register of debts) (the latter at Uruk).[18]

If we are certain of the existence of a special command of the 'upper satrapies' from the time of the reign of the founder of the Seleucid empire, and of a special command of western Asia Minor from the middle of the third century B.C., we can then go on to enquire how the

[17] On the ἐπὶ τῶν πραγμάτων (which was the position of Hermias and Zeuxis under Antiochus III) cf. Walbank 1957, 1.571 (*ad* Polyb. v.41.1), *idem* 1967, 11.452 (*ad* Polyb. xv.31.6): (B 37); Schmitt 1964, 150–8: (E 51).
[18] On the ὕπαρχος cf. RC 18–20 and p. 371. We should also mention the γαζοφυλάκιον (treasury): RC 18, ll. 20–1. On the relations between βασιλεύς, στρατηγός, ὕπαρχος, βυβλιοφύλαξ, *ibid.*; Musti 1957, 267–75: (B 113); 1965: (E 87). On the ἐπιστολογράφος (Dionysius at the time of Antiochus IV) and on the χρεωφύλαξ (keeper of the register of debts, attested at Uruk), cf. Rostovtzeff 1928, 165, 167, 181: (E 48). On the διοικητής, J. and L. Roberts, *Bull. épig.* in *Rev. Ét. Gr.* 83 (1970) 469–71; 84 (1971) 502–9. On the ἐπὶ τῶν προσόδων and the ἐγλογιστής, *ibid.* 1954, 292–5.

kingdom was organized administratively. Here it is advisable to avoid *a priori* generalizations and assumptions, such as, for example, taking it for granted that they did not adopt the Persian model at all. According to Herodotus (III.89) the Persian empire at the time of Darius was divided into twenty satrapies. These had their own governments (*archai*) and were obliged to pay a certain fixed tribute (*phoros*). One is dealing here with an administrative and financial form of division which is reflected in the terminology used to describe the functioning of the Seleucid kingdom: in the sphere of military administration *strategos* for the governor, *satrapeia* for the area he controlled, and in that of finance and taxation the *dioiketai* and *oikonomoi*. Herodotus listed twenty satrapies during the reign of Darius (III.90–4):

1. Ionians, Magnesians, Aeolians, Carians, Lycians, Milyans, Pamphylians
2. Mysians, Lydians and others
3. Phrygians, Thracians (in Asia), Paphlagonians, Mariandyni, etc.
4. Cilicians
5. Phoenicia, Syria-Palaestina, Cyprus
6. Egypt, Libya and Cyrene
7. Sattagydae, Gandarians, etc.
8. Susiana
9. Babylonia-Assyria
10. Media
11. Caspian regions
12. Bactria
13. Armenia and surrounding regions
14. Inhabitants of the Persian Gulf
15. Sacae and Caspians
16. Parthians, Chorasmians, Sogdians, Areioi
17. Paricanians and other peoples of Asia
18. Matienians, etc.
19. Moschians, Tibarenians, Macrones and Mossinoecians, etc.
20. Indians

Some of these certainly did not form part of the Seleucid kingdom. But for those that did, can these divisions have remained the same in the Seleucid kingdom in all its parts? We find the 'upper satrapies' clearly attested. This means that there is no doubt that the Iranian and Mesopotamian regions, which (at least in some periods) belonged to them, were divided into satrapies, that is according to the model of the Achaemenid administration.

The organization of the official cult of the sovereign can also be useful for tracing the Seleucid administrative divisions. In Coele-Syria and Phoenicia at the time of Antiochus III (end of the third century B.C.) we

find a *strategos kai archiereus* ('general and high priest'), Ptolemy, son of
Thraseas. He is known to us through a dossier referring to him found at
Bet She'an, on the site of the ancient Scythopolis in Palestine.[19] The
association of these duties appears to be characteristic of the Ptolemaic
organization for it is also found in Cyprus. So when we find, in parallel
epigraphical texts deriving from two centres in Iran and one in Phrygia,
indications pointing to a territorial competence possessed by the high
priests of the cult of the sovereign (of the king and queen respectively), it
is probable that these also represent administrative divisions (perhaps
satrapies or subdivisions of satrapies). If there was a 'general and high
priest' for Coele-Syria and Phoenicia, it is probable that there existed an
administrative subdivision corresponding to the territorial competence
of the high priests in other regions too. Moreover, Appian (*Syr.* 62.328)
attests the existence of at least seventy-two satrapies in the Seleucid
kingdom: perhaps the number is exaggerated and includes 'subdivisions' of satrapies in the true and full sense. W. W. Tarn regarded
Appian's seventy-two satrapies as eparchies, meaning stable (and rigid)
subdivisions of true satrapies (and at the same time as larger units than
the hyparchies). Bengtson was more flexible on the whole question. He
considered Appian's seventy-two satrapies as the historical result of the
splitting up of a lesser number of larger units. This splitting up was
caused on the one hand by spontaneous thrusts in the direction of
autonomy and on the other by pressure from the central authority
(especially under Antiochus III) in an attempt to reduce the power of the
governors of over-large satrapies by dividing them up into smaller units.
In any case it is not possible to attribute a rigid terminological and
technical value to such a broad term as *eparchia* (which generally
corresponds, as Bengtson rightly observes, to the Latin *provincia*).

Thus there must have been divisions analogous to those existing
under the Achaemenids in the Seleucid period. (This is shown by the
mention of the *strategoi* who were in charge of the satrapies themselves.)
For the first half of the third century B.C. we find attested the satrapies of
the Hellespont, Lydia and Greater Phrygia (not counting Cilicia and
Cappadocia) in Asia Minor; the satrapies of Arachosia and Gedrosia,
Bactria, Parthia and Hyrcania, Media, Persis and Susiana, in the East;
and the satrapies of Syria Seleucis (about whose history during the third
and second centuries B.C. there is still much uncertainty), Mesopotamia
and Babylonia in the central part of the kingdom. Thus, according to
Bengtson, there were at least fourteen satrapies during the third century
B.C. Later, as we saw above, their number could have increased. At any
rate we find others attested, as for example, in 188 B.C., when the list of

---

[19] For the dossier of Scythopolis (Bet She'an) cf. Landau 1966: (B 101); and the remarks of J. and
L. Robert *Bull. épig.* in *Rev. Ét. Gr.* 83 (1970) 469–73.

satrapies in western Asia Minor contained the addition of at least Caria, Lycia and Pamphylia.[20] And Syria Seleucis, at least at the end of the second century B.C., was divided into more satrapies, but these were considerably smaller administrative divisions (consisting of a city and its territory).[21] This leads us to think that (at least at a certain stage of their history) the Seleucids tried to set up a more complex organization than the Persian, corresponding to the greater urban, political and administrative development in their state compared with that of the Achaemenids.

IV. MILITARY AND NAVAL ASPECTS

We have quite a large amount of information on the history and composition of the Seleucid army. However this does not tell us anything about the lower ranks, unlike in Ptolemaic Egypt, for which a vast papyrological documentation has survived. Our knowledge of the Seleucid armed forces mainly derives from literary texts. These consist of Diodorus' account of the career of the first of the Seleucids; Appian's *Syrian History*; Polybius' description especially of certain moments in the history of Antiochus III, like the battle of Raphia, fought (and lost) in 217 B.C. against Ptolemy IV Philopator, or the treaty (of Apamea) with Rome in 188, and in the history of Antiochus IV such as the great parade at Daphne in 166 B.C.; Livy's account of the battle of Magnesia-by-Sipylus (190 B.C.), etc.[22]

The presence of genuine Macedonians in Seleucus I's army is explicitly attested, and is also verifiable from the tradition of colonization and the many military foundations (*katoikiai*), some of which (only in the course of time however) were to become true cities (*poleis*). These *katoikiai* are particularly attested in western Asia Minor; but they also

[20] Cf. Bengtson 1964 7, II particularly 12–18: (A 6). For my part I do not entirely exclude the existence of a district of Ionia under a particular delegate of the king: Musti 1965: (E 87), in particular.

[21] On the concept of Συρία Σελευκίς, attested particularly in Strabo XVI.2.1–21. C. 749–56, see Musti 1966, 61–81: (E 44).

[22] The principal texts for the composition of the Seleucid army are: Diod. XIX.113; XX.113.4; XXXIII.4a, but especially those relative to the battles of Raphia (217 B.C.: Polyb. V.79–85) and of Magnesia-by-Sipylus (190 B.C.: Liv. XXXVII.37–44; Appian *Syr.* 30–6) and the Daphne parade (166 B.C.: Polyb. XXX.25). Cf. Bikerman 1938, 51–97: (E 6); Walbank 1957, I.607–10: (B 37); *idem* 1979 III.448–53; Bar-Kochva 1976: (J 136); Galili 1976/7: (E 160). For the location of Daphne: it should be kept near Antioch-on-the-Orontes and can probably be identified with Bêt el Mâ; Horain's proposal (1963: (E 33)) to locate it near Gerasa is not acceptable. Compared with the army marshalled at Raphia, Antiochus III's army at Magnesia contained a more conspicuous presence of Anatolian contingents. The Iranian element decreased from Raphia to Magnesia and then again to Daphne. At Daphne, the presence of contingents (mercenaries or regular soldiers) from Asia Minor could have been a symbol of provocation or revenge against Rome by Antiochus IV, more than twenty years after the mutilations inflicted on the Seleucid empire by the treaty of Apamea.

appear elsewhere. They find an echo in place names (cf. p. 179 n. 3), which are recorded in literary texts, and in the Macedonian personal names of men or divinities (as the epigraphic finds increasingly show). *Katoikiai* often arose on the site of native villages (or groups of villages).[23]

From the beginning the Seleucid kingdom must have disposed of mixed forces, that is to say of armies in the composition of which a large part was played by local elements, drawn especially from regions whose social structures involved and encouraged strong warlike traditions, regions in short inhabited, or at least dominated, by warrior tribes. Thus in 217 B.C., besides a phalanx of 20,000 men (mainly Graeco-Macedonians), Antiochus III's army comprised a nucleus of 5,000 Iranians and Cilicians armed like *euzones* (select troops), about 10,000 natives armed in the Macedonian manner, 2,000 Persian and Agrianian archers and slingers, 1,000 Thracians, about 5,000 Medes (and Iranians in general), distinct from the first group of Iranians in not being select troops, about 10,000 Arabs, 5,000 Greek mercenaries, 2,500 Cretans and Neo-Cretans, 500 Lydian lancers and 1,000 Cardacians. This was the infantry, divided, of course, into the heavy infantry (the first half) and the light. After that there was a strong cavalry force, comprising 6,000 horsemen and 102 'beasts' (elephants); the custom of using these had been introduced by Seleucus I who had taken it over from the Indians. (The Indian king Chandragupta had given him a large number of elephants and these contributed largely to his victory over Antigonus Monophthalmus at Ipsus in Phrygia in 301 B.C.) According to these figures the army amounted to about 70,000 men. Looking at the numbers and kinds of forces in this valuable account provided by Polybius for one of the first years of the reign of Antiochus III, we see that the Iranian element was strongly represented, and partly entrusted to the command of a native of Media and partly placed under that of a Macedonian. We also note the Arab contingent, commanded by a local ruler. A third element in this army was the Anatolian (Cilicians, Cardacians). And of course the contribution of the Greek mercenaries is also significant. Three local components (Iranians, Arabs, Anatolians) are important enough to be explicitly mentioned by Polybius – they are largely homogeneous contingents with some autonomy – and by comparison the other components (especially those from the regions of Syria in the broad sense and from Mesopotamia) are relatively insignificant and are almost lost in the mass of 10,000 men picked from the 'whole' kingdom. Perhaps this means that in regions like Syria and

---

[23] The Seleucid *katoikiai* are epigraphically attested in Asia Minor. Literary texts also speak of them for the regions east of the Taurus, but rarely: Bar-Kochva 1976, 22–9: (J 136). It is difficult to say how significant or decisive this is.

Mesopotamia, which were the nucleus of the Seleucid kingdom, there was a greater density of Graeco-Macedonian soldiers, as was natural in the nerve centre of the state. And this was probably the reason for the particular social structure of these regions (Syria and Mesopotamia), in which the mass of soldiers of largely Graeco-Macedonian origin and the people, who were often *laoi*, villagers, formed two distinct entities. The army could, however, be a means of collaboration and fusion between country and city people, if recruitment was drawn not only from the *katoikiai*, as is universally admitted, but also from the cities as well.[24] Whereas the differences between the *ethne* made for separateness in the country, conditions in the cities and in centres comparable with them served to encourage mixing and even a degree of fusion – especially by way of mixed marriages. Syria's central position in the Seleucid kingdom and the closeness of the capital, Antioch-on-the-Orontes, explain the particular importance, from the military point of view, of Apamea, which was the seat of the main barracks of the Seleucid kingdom and was the southernmost and furthest inland of the four cities of Syria, being sited to the south-east of Antioch (and of Laodicea) and east of the Orontes.

We know little about the structure and organization of the Seleucid fleet. The title of 'navarch' attested for a fleet operating in the Caspian Sea and the Persian Gulf must also have been held by the commanders of larger fleets; but this does not prove the existence of an admiral in chief. We have a series of accounts about naval operations of a military character. Except for some belonging to the reign of Antiochus I and recorded by Memnon, these, however, refer to the time of Antiochus III rather than the earlier period. For the period of Antiochus I we are told about an Athenaeus, known from an Ilian inscription, who was *epi tou naustathmou*, that is, in charge of the military port and also perhaps the arsenal at the time of the Galatian War, and, perhaps in this period too, a Seleucid navarch, Alcippus, in an inscription from Erythrae. There were naval fleets in operation, accompanying the military operations under Seleucus II and Antiochus III, during their campaigns in Asia Minor. The Seleucid fleet was drastically hit by some clauses in the treaty of Apamea, which restricted its movement (it might not sail west of the Calycadnus and Cape Sarpedon) and limited its number of ships.[25]

---

[24] The fact that the cities could also provide troops for the Seleucid army is positively attested in Polyb. xxx.25.6 (πολιτικοὶ δὲ τρισχίλιοι, in this case cavalry). On the problem in general cf., however, Bikerman 1938, 74–7, 87: (E 6); on the difficulty, already raised by Bikerman, in establishing a clear connexion between the concession of a *kleros* and the imposition of military obligations, cf. Cohen 1978, 51ff.: (E 16).

[25] On the Seleucid navarchs, cf. Plin. *NH* vi.21.158 (Patrocles, *praefectus classis* at the time of Seleucus and Antiochus I); Polyb. v.43.1 (Diognetus in the period of Antiochus III); a decree honouring a navarch (Alcippus) and trierarchs, who appear to be in the service of the Seleucid king

One clause of the treaty, as preserved by Polybius (XXI.43.13), both illuminates the past history of the Seleucid navy and informs us in particular about the limitations imposed on it by this treaty for at least fifteen years. This clause states that Antiochus must hand over the long ships and their gear and tackle and not have more than ten *kataphraktoi*, that is, ships with a deck (or, according to another interpretation, not more than ten *aphraktoi*, that is ships without a deck). Neither can Antiochus have any vessel with (more than?) thirty oars, and not even that for war purposes.[26] If the reading *aphraktoi* is correct, the decision taken by the Romans at Apamea was certainly more harsh than the one concerning Philip V of Macedon, who was allowed at least five covered ships. Later, however, the Seleucid fleet was restored by Antiochus IV, largely with the invasion of Egypt in mind; and the last mention of a fleet occurs under Antiochus VII.[27]

The two principal bases were certainly Seleuceia-in-Pieria and Ephesus. But if the number of records preserved really indicates the particular importance of the Seleucid fleet in the first years of the second century B.C., that is, in the period of greatest activity towards the Aegean under Antiochus III, this was certainly due to the conquest of Phoenicia and the use of Phoenician ships and crews. As noted above, the cities of Phoenicia provided timber useful for ship-building. And we may suspect that the scarcity of records of naval operations of a warlike character from the period before Antiochus III (except for the fleet which supported the operations of Seleucus II against the cities of Ionia, cf. Justin. XXVII.2.2) is to be explained in the light of the situation before the Fifth Syrian War, in which the Seleucids were victorious, and thereby gained control of the cities and regions which traditionally provided ships and crews. Livy (XXXIII.19.9–11) relates the rebuilding of the navy by Antiochus III; and later we have specific references to crews of Sidonians, Tyrians and Aradians for Phoenicia and Sidetans for Pamphylia. Thus it is no accident that during the third century B.C. the Seleucid kingdom is not distinguished by particular naval exploits of a warlike character. The new importance the fleet acquired under Antiochus III is shown by the fact that in 197 B.C. the sovereign himself took command of it.[28]

should, it appears, be dated during the reign of Antiochus I (Engelmann-Merkelbach 1972, 106–16, no. 28: (B 68)). The inscription which mentions Athenaeus is *RC* 12, ll. 4f. Plin. *NH loc. cit.* and 11.67.167 mentions the exploration of the Hyrcanian and Caspian Seas (and the Indian and Caspian) by a Seleucid fleet under the first two kings respectively. For the testimony of Memnon, cf. *FGrH* 434 F 10 and 15.

[26] On this problem, cf. McDonald-Walbank 1969: (E 84).
[27] Cf. Bikerman 1938 (on I *Macc.* 15.3 and 14): (E 6).
[28] Livy XXXIII.19.9–11.

V. TAX SYSTEM AND ECONOMIC LIFE

Seleucid authority over the cities of the kingdom was exercised by laws, the presence of garrisons and the imposition of taxes; this is expressly attested by Polybius (XXI.41.2). This tribute (*phoros*) was usually raised through the various communities. 'The Seleucids', writes Bikerman, 'demanded *phoros* from the Greek cities of Asia Minor, from the rulers of Upper Asia, such as Xerxes of Armosata, and from the peoples and cities of Palestine, including Jews and Samaritans and hellenised communities such as Gazara, Joppa and the Greek city founded by Antiochus IV in Jerusalem.'[29]

Literary texts and inscriptions attest the existence of a personal tax (poll tax, called *epikephalaion* and perhaps also *syntaxis*), a tax on sales (*eponion*), a tax on slaves (*andrapodikon*), a tax on salt (*peri ton halon*), a 'crown tax' (*stephanitikos*), that is a tribute raised by the state as a 'crown', i.e. as an offering to the sovereign, an extraordinary tax (*eisphora*) and taxes on the use of harbours and on imports and exports.[30] In this respect, a fragment of Flavius Josephus (*Ant. Jud.* XII.138–44) is of particular importance. It is the text of a letter from Antiochus III to the Jews (now regarded as authentic at least in substance) which allows exemption from the more humiliating taxes to the priests of the Temple in Jerusalem. It has been rightly observed that this exemption operated a social class distinction within the Jewish people and introduced a state of privilege for one section of it.[31]

These are the known taxes but it is improbable that they represent the real hub of Seleucid finance. The basis of this must have been the tribute from the royal lands, that is, from the lands cultivated by the 'king's peasants' (*basilikoi laoi*): but records about this are scarce. The cases noted above (peoples from the peripheral regions and the Greek cities) represent particular and specific situations and, what is more, situations which attract our notice at what may be called a 'negative' moment, that is, when they obtained the concession of *immunity* (an occasion which in these regions and cities, which were to some extent dependent but being

[29] Bikerman 1938, 106–7: (E 6).

[30] On the basis of an inscription of Labraunda (Crampa 1972, no. 42: (B 60): a decree of Eupolemus, governor in the name of Cassander) a distinction has been made between taxes imposed by the king on cities and collected by them (ἐπιγραφή or ἐπιταγὴ βασιλική) and taxes imposed directly by the king on subjects (βασιλικὰ τέλη); cf. Moretti 1977, 331ff.: (H 148); Hahn 1978, 12–16: (E 30). For the above-mentioned taxes see also Jos. *Ant. Jud.* (quoted in the text). On the δεκάτη in the area of the 'satrapic' economy, ps.-Arist. *Oecon.* II.1345 b 30ff.; in particular, Hahn 1978, 15–16: (E 30).

[31] See Vidal-Naquet 1980, 63: (E 176).

peripheral tended therefore to be centrifugal, must have been quite frequent for political reasons). One of the most noteworthy and best known dossiers of inscriptions concerns the concession of immunity from the payment of tribute; in it the league (*koinon*) of the cities of Ionia is exempted from payment of contributions to *ta Galatika*, that is, the war tax paid to the Seleucid sovereign to finance operations against the Galatians, at the time of King Antiochus I or, less probably, during the reign of Antiochus II.[32]

We could also refer to various other records about the transferring of the royal lands to the jurisdiction of a city, which must have entailed payment of tribute to the city itself and consequently the lessening of the rights of the central authority to exact tribute. For example there is the case of the attribution (*prosorismos*) to a city of the Troad of land assigned to Aristodicides of Assus in the time of Antiochus I, or the case of the possible attribution to the territory of a city of Asia Minor of a property sold for the sum of 30 talents by Antiochus II to his ex-wife Laodice.[33]

Some indication of the mechanism for the raising of taxes by the Seleucid sovereign can be gained from the famous inscription of Laodice (see above; and cf. in particular *RC* 18), with its reference to a village (*kome*), a '*baris*' (see below, p. 196), a piece of land belonging to the village (*chora*), its inhabitants (*laoi*), and also the annual income from it (*prosodoi*); and likewise from the so-called Mnesimachus inscription, which comes from Sardis and contains various indications of how the property of a great landowner is made up, the rights he exercises, his labour force, and the payments and tributes in kind and in cash which the peasants have to pay (there is mention of jars of wine, taxes rendered in money and in labour, and other revenues accruing from the villages, col. 1.12–13). If, for comparison, we were to replace Mnesimachus' name with that of a Seleucid functionary, who might, for example, have the title of *oikonomos*, we should probably have some notion of how in practice the Seleucid sovereign's property rights operated financially over the villages and the lands which formed the royal estates (*chora basilike*).

The Mnesimachus inscription comes from the temple of Artemis at Sardis. It should probably be dated *c*. 200 B.C. and is normally taken as evidence of the property relationships in force within the Seleucid kingdom, although, in fact, in col. 1 l. 2 there is mention of a certain Antigonus as author of the attribution of the property (*ousia*) to the

---

[32] On the concept of tribute εἰς τὰ *Γαλατικά* cf. *OGIS* 222–3; *RC* 15; Orth 1977, 89–92, 98: (A 46) (tribute 'for the financing of the war against the Galatians', not a contribution for the payment of a tribute to the Galatians). On the distinction between φόρος, εἰσφορά, σύνταξις see Moretti 1977, *loc. cit*. (n. 30).

[33] On the donations to Aristodicides and to Laodice II, cf. *RC* 10–13 and 18–20; Musti 1957, 267–78: (B 113); 1965, 153: (E 87); Atkinson 1968: (E 58); Orth 1977, 150 n. 5: (A 46); Funck 1978: (H 70) and other works on the *basilike chora* cited in the Bibliography.

person who speaks in the first person in the inscription. It was thought this might be Antigonus Monophthalmus, but of course this would not suit a date of *c.* 200 B.C. Other data seem more certain, although not all the relationships are clear. It is evidently an inventory of the possessions of a debtor to the temple of Artemis. These possessions include villages and land-lots (*komai* and *kleroi*), with their respective taxes, and dwelling-plots (*oikopeda*) and persons (*laoi*). The whole appears to constitute an *aule*, outside which there are houses belonging to *laoi* and (this time) slaves (*oiketai*), orchards (*paradeisoi*) and arable lands. What is particularly unclear is the process by which the relationship between the land-lots and the property of Mnesimachus has arisen. By what right can Mnesimachus count on them and their taxes? What is his relation to them and their holders? Did the *kleroi* become his property in all senses; that is, do we find here proof of the rapid appearance of a process of alienation of the lands once given to the cleruchs, in spite of the declared rule of inalienability? However, we note that the tribute paid from the *kleroi* is notably lower than that paid from the villages. And the term *aule* must be considered as a technical term indicating a large property, with a very complex origin and constitution.[34]

We find an analogous complexity of formation in a large property mentioned in an inscription from Denizli, dated to the month of Peritios of the 45th year of the Seleucid era (= January 267 B.C.), that is, from the reign of Antiochus I.[35] In it we read of the (rather informal) decision of an 'assembly' (*ekklesia*) of the inhabitants of Neonteichos and Kiddioukome, to honour Achaeus, a high Seleucid functionary, who is called 'lord of the place', and on whose property there are at least three villages. Honours are also paid to an *oikonomos* with the Semitic name of Banabelus and an *eklogistes*, that is, an accountant, whose name is Lachares. To complicate relations between the 'lord of the place', Achaeus, and the three villages, these same villages have a sort of political life: a form which is perhaps still somewhat shadowy. Although there is an assembly, there appear to be no magistrates of the community and not even a council (*boule*). This means that in this case *ekklesia* may signify a meeting or assembly of a fairly informal kind; and though the privilege of sitting in the front seats at public festivals (*proedria*) granted to Banabelus and Lachares resembles a privilege granted also in true and proper cities, it is not in fact clearly defined as to the place and occasions on which it might be exercised. The Denizli inscription does indeed throw an interesting light on the relationship between landowner and villages. Given the presence of quasi-political forms of life, this relationship seems to be equivalent to a particular right of the landowner

[34] For the inscription of Mnesimachus, Buckler-Robinson 1912: (B 55); 1932, no. 1: (B 56).
[35] On the inscription of Denizli, Wörrle 1975: (B 177).

to some form of tribute. Thus it is possible that ancient local structures survived under the Seleucids (and perhaps even developed towards political forms of autonomy) but that, in property relationships and on the economic level in general, landowners were imposed or super-imposed upon these communities from above (through the institution of the royal gift estate (*dorea*)) and that they were thereby entitled to exact a tax on what the communities produced.

It is immediately apparent that agriculture is the basic form of production in the Seleucid kingdom and that the royal estates constitute a particularly large and certainly the most important form of property. From the flat river valleys of Syria to the plain of Mesopotamia, the scattered peripheral plains and high plateaux of Iran, where cultivation of the soil or pasturage was practicable, the fertile lands of Cilicia, it is possible to indicate the geographical contexts we must presuppose for the royal estates and for the *laoi*, that is the peasant population, which lived on the land and worked it. But we have only partial knowledge of the organization of such estates: the specific terminology, an important clue to organization, appears mainly in inscriptions; but inscriptions containing important indications concerning both terminology and organization come mainly, as we have seen, from western Asia Minor. In these texts we find the terms describing types of habitat: the *kome*, that is, the village; the *baris*, that is, probably, the farm (possibly with some fortification – in a sense a villa); the *epaulis* (perhaps meaning something similar); rather more general, but still describing a rural place, the *chorion* or *topos*. Then we find terms indicating the inhabitants or, more specifically, their social condition: the *laoi*, the *oiketai*; terms relative to types of cultivation: *paradeisoi* (orchards), etc. This is the fundamental form of property which fits into an historical tradition of social and economic relations belonging specifically to Asia, characterized by the presence of an absolute master (in this case the king (*basileus*)) and a dependent population (*laoi*), among whom there can occasionally exist conditions of actual slavery, though this does not seem to be the norm.

But besides this type of agrarian property, there are certainly others, such as the great private estate, which was perhaps thought of merely as a concession from the king who 'suspended' his rights in favour of his protégés (important people in the kingdom, people the king wished to reward or favourites, or perhaps ancient landowners) to whom he ceded his right of possession or title to the property. There were also (in Syria, Babylonia, Iran, Cilicia and the inner regions of western Asia Minor) all the temple possessions, which made up a conspicuous part of the Seleucid territory: lands with their villages annexed to sanctuaries, and with a population which would provide the indispensable personnel to serve the sanctuaries (*hierodouloi*). These estates were organized structures, in habitat, in the ceremonies and festivals they celebrated, in the services they offered, in the supplies at their disposal. This meant that a part of the population who worked on the 'sacred lands' were also required to engage themselves in functions strictly concerned with the temples as such.[36]

Quite contrary to opinions current a few decades ago, we are now accumulating an increasing weight of evidence in support of the view that even though the Seleucids pursued for at least a century and a half a policy of urbanization of the territories subjected to them, they did not engage in a systematic programme of secularization of temple lands in favour of the state, private landlords or individual cities. In fact they increasingly appear as the great conservers of the ancient temple structures (and perhaps also of the tribal structures), granting space for more or less developed forms of city life (and, consequently, for urban forms of property), only where that was possible, that is to say on the site of ancient cities or on the site of villages included within the *chora*.

The most recent interpretations of the temple policies of the Seleucids (those of Broughton and L. Robert)[37] question the idea of ruthless secularization proposed by Ramsay. But earlier M. Rostovtzeff had already maintained that the Seleucids pursued a policy of intervention in temple finances and an anti-temple policy in general, *only* with regard to some eastern sanctuaries and *only* from the reign of Antiochus III onwards.

Among the temple cities (or states) attested in Seleucid territories only in the post-Seleucid era, but for that reason probably existing in the same form under the Seleucid dynasty, we have at least the following: (a) In the Syrian–Phoenician–Cilician nucleus of the kingdom, the sanctuary of Zeus at Baetocaece facing Aradus; the sanctuary of the Syrian Goddess at Hierapolis (Bambyce); the temple of Bel Marduk in Babylonia; the sanctuary of Zeus at Olba and that of Artemis Perasia at Castabala in Cilicia. (b) For Iran we have the sanctuary of Anahita at Ecbatana and the temple of Bel in Elam (Elymais), whose riches were pillaged by Antiochus III in 209 and again in 187 B.C. after the peace of Apamea with Rome, which imposed such heavy burdens on the finances of the kingdom of Syria; the sanctuary of the island of Icarus in the Persian Gulf (Failaka) dedicated to Artemis and provided with *oiketai* (Plates vol., pl. 18). Antiochus IV tried to attack the wealth of the sanctuary of Artemis (who is probably to be identified with Nanaia) in Elam, but he died shortly after his attempt to despoil the temple.

---

[36] On *hierodouloi*: Debord 1972: (H 44); Waldmann 1973: (E 100); Archi 1975: (E 57); Kreissig 1977: (E 35); Musti 1982: (I 51); Welwei 1979: (E 55).

[37] On the temple policy of the Seleucids: Broughton 1951: (E 63); J. and L. Robert 1954, 295–6: (E 94); Musti 1977, 241–6: (H 150).

However he had succeeded in laying his hands on the treasures of the temple in Jerusalem. On this subject Flavius Josephus, the hellenized Jew, had an interesting argument with the Greek historian Polybius, whom he greatly admired (expressly declaring him to be a 'good man' (*agathos aner*) and often imitating his way of writing history): for the Greek Polybius, Antiochus IV's sudden death was caused by the fact that he had 'wanted' to rob the treasures of the temple of Nanaia; Josephus on the other hand held that divine vengeance had struck him down, not because he had wanted to despoil a temple, and failed, but because he had in fact succeeded in ransacking the temple of the Jews.[38] (c) Beyond the Taurus Mountains, in Asia Minor, in regions which were at least temporarily under Seleucid rule, the sanctuary of Ma at Comana in Cappadocia, and the temple state associated with it, which were still flourishing in the time of Strabo the geographer (1st century B.C.–1st century A.D.); inside Phrygia, which was later occupied by the Galatians, the sanctuary of Cybele (and the associated temple state) at Pessinus and the temple of Zeus at Aezani (for the history of which in the Hellenistic age we have re-engraved Hellenistic texts dating from the Hadrianic period); the sanctuary at Apollonia Salbace in Caria (for which we have also epigraphic confirmation of the existence of sacred villages (*hierai komai*), and a population, the *Saleioi*, attached to this sanctuary); also in Caria there was the sanctuary of Zeus at Labraunda, from which we have a rich dossier of epigraphical texts, throwing light on various aspects of the relations in the second half of the third century B.C. between Seleucid sovereigns (Seleucus, probably II), Macedonian sovereigns (Antigonus Doson and Philip V), the city of Mylasa (subject to the dynast Olympichus) and, of course, the sanctuary of Zeus itself, with its priestly dynasty.[39] Obviously the various cities to be found in Seleucid territory which have the name Hierapolis also largely belong in the same category.

Besides these three fundamental types of landed property, there were the lands transferred by the process of *prosorismos* (analogous to the Roman *adtributio* and already mentioned above) to the territory of cities, and the vast areas reserved for the planting of colonies (*katoikiai*), which

[38] For testimonies on the Seleucid kings as despoilers of Iranian temples: Polyb. x.27 (Antiochus III at Ecbatana in 209); Diod. xxvIII.3, xxIX.15; Strabo xvI.1.18.C. 744; Justin. xxxII.2.1–2 (the same king in Elam). Cf. also Musti 1968, 420: (E 45). For Antiochus IV: cf. Polyb. xxxI.9.1–4 and the respectful polemic of Flavius Josephus, *Ant. Jud.* xII.358–9; *contra Apion.* II.84.

[39] On the sanctuary of Zeus at Baetocaece: Seyrig 1951: (E 173); Rey-Coquais 1970: (B 125). On the sanctuary of Zeus at Labraunda (Caria) and Olympichus of Mylasa: Crampa 1969–72: (B 60). On the sanctuary of Icarus: Jeppesen 1960: (E 193); Altheim-Stiehl 1965: (B 42); Musti 1966, 180–1: (E 44); Cohen 1978, 42–4: (E 16). On the sanctuary of Pessinus in the Attalid and Roman periods: *RC* 55–61; Virgilio 1981: (E 98). On the sanctuary of Artemis Perasia at Castabala (Cilicia): Dupont-Sommer-Robert 1964: (E 66). On the sanctuary of Aezani: Laffi 1971: (E 75). On Apollonia Salbace: J. and L. Robert 1954, 285–312: (E 94).

at least in the beginning were military colonies, often of Macedonian, Graeco-Macedonian or mixed origin, but which over the course of time gave way, at least in part, to colonies of inhabitants of the Seleucid empire itself, transferred more or less forcibly from one region to another (for example from Judaea to western Asia Minor, or from localities – some of them Greek – in Asia Minor to Iran), sometimes with the clear military object of acting as garrisons, sometimes with different aims varying according to place and circumstances.[40]

This is one of the aspects of the intensive process of colonization, which the Seleucids carried on throughout the kingdom from the reigns of the first two sovereigns (Seleucus I and Antiochus I) and then throughout the whole of the third century and also during part of the second century B.C. The process often brought about a significant urbanization of the territory and sometimes at least caused the rise of *katoikiai* which frequently extended themselves in groups over whole areas. Many cities were founded with names like Seleuceia, Antioch, Laodicea, Apamea, and particularly in Syria Seleucis, and more specifically in so-called 'Pieria', there was a concentration of cities with Macedonian or Greek names, such as Europus, Cyrrhus, Edessa, Beroea, Larissa, etc.[41] Around these there were colonies of Macedonians, groups of rural settlements which either received a general ethnic name containing an allusion to their (at least partly) Macedonian origin, or simply adapted pre-existing names (whether indigenous place names or place names connected to a precise historical origin). It is not always easy to distinguish rigorously between cities (*poleis*) (of Seleucid foundation) and colonies (*katoikiai*), because the former too could be subject, like the latter, to forms of administration, or at least control, exercised by the central power, and on the other hand the latter, given that they were, one and all, communities, might develop forms of self-government and self-administration which made them institutionally similar in some respects (and perhaps in some cases more and more so over the course of time) to the *poleis* (through the presence of magistrates, councils and perhaps forms of assembly). The difference between them was more marked on the social and economic level, because when proper cities were created, this was probably accompanied by the rapid development of forms of private property. On the other hand, the territory of the *katoikiai*, at least according to the intentions of the central power and during one or two generations of colonists, was

---

[40] On the transference of colonists from one region of the kingdom to another: Jews in Lydia and Phrygia, Jos. *Ant. Jud.* XII.147; Schalit 1960: (E 50); Cohen 1978, 5–9: (E 16); Magnesians from Magnesia-on-the-Maeander to Antioch (in Persis) *OGIS* 233; Orth 1977, 114–16: (A 46). In general see also Bar-Kochva 1976, 20ff.: (J 136).

[41] The *locus classicus* on Seleucid colonization is Appian, *Syr.* 57.295–8.

collective property. However, individual ownership will in many cases have ended up creating forms of private property (or at least its immediate pre-conditions).

Seleucid colonization cannot easily be reduced to a single pattern. This is not so much (or not only) because of the scantiness of the evidence we have about it, but also, and probably to a greater extent, because of the remarkable elasticity of the colonial policy of the Seleucids, which adapted itself to the different conditions prevailing in the various parts of their composite kingdom. This emerges from the most recent research on Seleucid colonization, which also confirms some of its predominant characteristics, which distinguish it from that of the Ptolemies. Seleucid colonization consisted essentially in the settlement of groups of colonists, with a certain tendency (probable but not completely demonstrated) to preserve in the countryside a firm distinction and separation between the colonists and the earlier, but still surviving, indigenous population. In Egypt, on the other hand, the Graeco-Macedonian colonists appeared to have been scattered throughout the countryside and to have been absorbed as individuals into the pre-existing economic (and also socio-economic and cultural) structures.[42] Perhaps this was also reflected in the matter of property rights: in Seleucid regions we find evidence of forms of ownership which were to some extent collective or at least associative; one may compare the *hekades*, groups of land-lots (*kleroi*), attested in Dura-Europus. Another general aspect, also confirmed by the most recent research on Seleucid colonization, is the difference between the colonization undertaken by Antiochus IV in the mid second century B.C. and the attempts at colonization and urbanization made by the first Seleucids, and in particular by the first three sovereigns of the dynasty, from Seleucus I to Antiochus II: in the second century it was a question at most of the re-foundation of ancient Seleucid colonies, re-foundations which sometimes involved new names (e.g. Antiochia) and probably also the arrival of new colonists, who did not however come from outside the kingdom of Syria but from within it. The colonies of the period of Antiochus IV were therefore not so much a continuation of the immigration from outside the confines of the kingdom but rather a revitalization of ancient centres, probably by the movement of population groups within the kingdom of Syria, a process which had had

---

[42] On the problems concerning colonization, besides the classic work, Tcherikower 1927: (A 60), see also Cohen 1978: (E 16) (a balanced synthesis) and Briant 1978, 57–92: (E 12), on the limited extent to which the policy of colonization functioned in promoting integration and other social ends, with doubts concerning the very concept of 'hellenization'; a distinction is made between a zone 'outside' the Seleucid foundations, where relations of production remained constant, and one 'inside', where there was a development of private property. However, it is difficult to distinguish with precision between outside and inside zones.

precedents in the history of Seleucid colonial policy, for example under Antiochus III.

The inhabitants of the *katoikiai*, whom we find particularly in Asia Minor, but who must also have existed in the central regions of the kingdom (Syria and its surrounding areas and Mesopotamia) and in Iran, provided a pool of human labour – even if not the only one – for the recruitment of soldiers for the Seleucid phalanx. However there is no proof that inhabitants of the true *poleis* founded by the Seleucid kings did not also help to fill the ranks of the Seleucid regular army.

It appears, however, that we should accept the general position of Bikerman,[43] according to whom the great labour pool for recruitment to the infantry of the Seleucid army consisted of 'Macedonians' from the Seleucid colonies. Only exceptionally was the population of the cities drawn upon. The indigenous population was able to supply manpower for the light infantry and the cavalry, but in fact for the heavy infantry 'the inexhaustible reserves of manpower available to the Seleucids, successors of the Achaemenids, remained unexploited and unexploitable'.

Now that we have considered the forms of agrarian property, we are in a position to analyse the Seleucid economy in its agricultural aspect. The products will have been: corn and grapes in Syria, corn and fruit from various trees in Mesopotamia, vegetables and fruit from trees in Lebanon and Phoenicia, and elsewhere in western Asia Minor. In individual cases, it is not clear by what method the sovereign exacted his share of the products of the soil, how he accumulated this and how he converted it into money. In Asia Minor the system must have been essentially that of a fixed amount, if the introduction of a quota, the tithe, by the Romans after the creation of the province of Asia was regarded as a novelty. However, the tithe system (*dekate*) was known in the so-called satrapic economy mentioned by ps.-Aristotle. For Judaea we have evidence for the rendering to the Seleucid authority of one third of grain products and one half of 'wood' products (i.e. timber).[44] But these quantities are especially large and were probably a substitute for a form of personal tax, calculated on a smaller scale. This was perhaps the high price paid in exchange for a guarantee that the principle of the pre-eminent ownership by the sovereign would not be introduced into the region. However, the principle of the predominance of royal land (*basilike chora*) was introduced, with all its unpleasant consequences, direct or indirect, involving the creation of gift-estates (*doreai*) and of city lands (*politikai chorai*), which impinged to some extent on ancient

[43] Bikerman 1938, 67–78, in particular 69: (E 6).

[44] Cf. for the tribute of ⅓ of the corn and ½ of the 'wood' produce, I *Macc.* 10.29–30; Kreissig 1978, 72: (E 36).

rights and traditional forms of property, viz. small and medium-sized private property.

Besides agriculture, especially in the cities (although not exclusively there), crafts and the trade associated with them both flourished. There was public and private building connected with the process of urbanization. Large cities were built and were divided into different quarters, in which different specialized occupations were pursued. Some were devoted to the requirements of government, administration and cult activities, security and defence, supplies and the creation of reserves of all kinds, as well as to the prestige of the new state and ways of expressing this, and to the requirements of urban life. In addition to building activity, there was metal work, which covered everything from work in bronze for the manufacture of arms, to the activities of the gold and silver smiths (the capital, Antioch-on-the-Orontes, was a centre for the latter; we have a record of this for the period of Antiochus IV in Polyb. xxvi.1.2). Glass objects were produced, especially in Phoenicia, on the coast between Ake and Tyre. Phoenicia was also famous for the production of purple (at Tyre), obviously in connexion with the general development of the textile industry (for which Sidon had always been famous). It was also famous for naval production (Strabo xvi.2.23–5, c. 757–8). Because of the large natural demand, ceramic workshops were widespread from Asia Minor to Mesopotamia; the latter produced glazed terracotta pots, especially at Ctesiphon, and faience at Seleuceia-on-the-Tigris. The textile industry, already mentioned, was also widespread and flourished in inland Syria as well as on the coast.

It was natural that in the cities, especially those on the coast but also the inland ones, which had a strong commercial character (and often well developed crafts), the organization of work and the relationships of production were different from those that appear to have been prevalent in the vast rural areas of Seleucid territory, which were subjected more directly to the royal administration. On the royal estates they were relationships of dependence, rather than slavery, and filtered through the pattern of habitation and the social structure of the village. But in the highly developed urban centres with large and complex craft enterprises and, in consequence of this, a concentrated workforce, we may speculate whether there were not present all the conditions necessary to encourage the development of forms of direct and total personal 'dependence', in short a form of 'chattel' slavery. This must have been encouraged in some way by the presence of 'rural serfdom' (on the royal estates and also on temple properties) and by the persistence of traditions of nomadism and piracy which included kidnapping (often tolerated by the central and local authorities) and thus considerably increased the slave trade, both outside the kingdom (in the second century B.C. particularly through Delos) and inside it.[45] There are indications – direct or indirect – particularly in inscriptions from areas under Seleucid control, of the existence of true slaves[46] and these are undoubtedly to be found (alongside numerous 'serfs' or persons in conditions of relative dependence) on the lands belonging to the great private properties. It is, however, disputed whether in the highly populated cities, with strongly developed crafts and maritime trade, the bulk of the workforce employed in non-agricultural work were actually slaves or merely people in a dependant position. It has been denied that the predominant mode of production, even in the cities with highly developed crafts, trade or shipping, was through the use of slaves.[47] What, for example, was the condition of the ancestors of those who in the Roman period were the famous linen workers in the Cilician city of Tarsus? Slaves or 'half free'? Certainly the Tarsus linen workers (*linourgoi*) referred to in Dio Chrysostom (xxx.21–3), under the Roman Empire, were free and the orator strongly defends their participation in the citizenship (*politeia*) of Tarsus; a *politeia* in which the dyers (*bapheis*), tanners (*skytotomoi*) and carpenters (*tektones*) already took part. This shows Tarsus to have been a city in which most of the artisans were citizens (even if they had to pay tax for the privilege); but difficulties were raised concerning the linen workers. This passage is sometimes taken as proof that the linen workers of Tarsus were 'free' workers in the Roman era and had been so in the preceding Seleucid era. The problem is in fact considerably more complicated. Dio's first reference to the linen workers occurs in a perplexing phrase: 'some people are accustomed to call these men linen workers'.[48] Is he here referring to the high grade workers, and possibly even to the *owners* of the workshops, or to the whole of the workforce? Among the artisans admitted to the citizenship of Tarsus were, for example, the tanners. That was also the case in fifth-century Athens, where one thinks of the famous Cleon; but it is not of course to be supposed that all Athenian activity connected with the working of leather was carried out by free workers. Would Cleon not perhaps have had slaves under him? In Tarsus these *linourgoi* of the Roman period, these 'linen workers', whose name seems so strange to Dio, could have been the master linen workers or the heads of workshops or even the

---

[45] On the problem of the *laoi*, cf. especially, besides the classic work of Rostovtzeff 1953: (A 52), Briant 1972: (E 60); Levi 1976, esp. 53–86: (H 130); Debord 1976/7: (H 45); Welwei 1979: (E 55). On the problem of the trade in Syrian slaves to the West, treated in detail by Rostovtzeff, see Crawford 1977: H 38); Hopkins 1978: (A 24); Musti 1980: (H 151).

[46] The terms ἀνδράποδα or δοῦλοι have this meaning more definitely than the word οἰκέται or the more ambiguous παῖδες or highly ambivalent σώματα.

[47] On aspects of the craftwork and trade in the regions of the Seleucid kingdom, see the long discussion by Kreissig 1978, particularly 74–88: (E 36).

[48] §21, τούτους δὲ εἰώθασιν ἔνιοι λινουργοὺς καλεῖν.

owners (assuming that there were enough of them to form a 'mob' (*ochlos*), as Dio says). Perhaps they had fallen into poverty. Certainly in the Roman period they were able to point to parents and even ancestors of Tarsian origin (§21) but their social condition may have been less favourable earlier. Above all it is difficult to define the condition (slave or free?) of the 'genuine' linen workers (whose existence should be admitted *e contrario*), since those referred to by Dio are only 'linen workers' in an equivocal sense. They could for instance have been slaves belonging to the so-called 'linen workers' referred to here. As we can see, the evidence could be disputed indefinitely but it does not afford a firm basis for saying that the workforce in the linen industry at Tarsus was *totally* or *fundamentally* composed of free workers.[49] The situation of the workers who produced and dyed cloth at the end of the fourth century B.C. at Teos, at a time when the city was not yet under Seleucid sovereignty, was probably different. They were most likely *andrapoda* (cf. *SEG* 11.579, ll. 11ff., a text which is not completely clear), that is to say, slaves (perhaps not working in factories but in houses). This particular condition of a part of the working population seems, however, to be explained mainly by the traditional economic structure of an ancient Greek settlement, whereas, if we look at the structure of production in Seleucid agriculture (which was the fundamental form of production in the state), there are good reasons to deny the widespread existence of slavery. As for the condition of the artisan and mercantile workforce, it does not yet seem possible to say with certainty that slavery played a limited part in it: the fundamental social and economic structure of the kingdom was probably also reflected to some extent in the society and economy of the cities. But the problem is to know *to what extent*; and one is bound to ask whether it can really be said that in cities, and especially in those cities of the Seleucid kingdom which had highly developed trade and crafts, there did not exist the slavery which is generally to be found in the Greek world wherever artisanship and trade flourished and there was a dense urban population.

VI. RELATIONS WITH THE GREEK CITIES

In considering the relations between the Seleucid kingdom and the Greek cities one must distinguish between the new Seleucid foundations and the 'old cities' which existed before the Seleucid period and even before that of Alexander and the Diadochi. The former were mainly

[49] On the λινουργοί of Tarsus, besides Kreissig 1978, 177: (E 36), cf. Cracco Ruggini 1980, 60–4: (E 17), who stresses the poverty of the 'linen workers'; however the sum of 500 drachmas which they could not pay (Dio. *loc. cit.* 21) is said by her (72 n. 42) to be 'considerable'. Moreover, she puts forward the hypothesis (not completely unlike the one here presented in the text) that the λινουργοί were 'originally' *laoi* or *hierodouloi* who had migrated to Tarsus.

situated in the central regions of the kingdom (Syria and neighbouring areas, Cilicia, Mesopotamia, Iran), although there were some also in other parts of the kingdom, especially in western Asia Minor. However, Seleucid foundations should properly also include those pre-Seleucid cities which date back to the period of Alexander, or to the age of Antigonus, Lysimachus or others of the Diadochi, if they were re-founded, and perhaps also re-named, by Seleucid sovereigns. It would be difficult to deny that, in the cities which they founded, the Seleucid kings exercised direct control through their functionaries, even when these cities possessed magistrates, councils and perhaps also their own forms of assembly, that is to say all the organs characteristic of civic autonomy. In cities of Syria or Mesopotamia, for example, we find mentioned the figure of the royal *epistates*, the superintendent (or prefect) placed by the central power over the organs of autonomous administration. It is in cities of this kind (at Laodicea-on-Sea and, it appears, also at Seleuceia-on-the-Tigris) that we also find attested the existence of a body whose members bear the Macedonian name of *peliganes*, probably a council with a significantly dominant role in the political life of the cities in which it is found.[50]

The relation between the central government and the 'old' Greek cities was certainly more distant and more indirect. It was also very complicated. We see this relationship in action principally in the cities of western Asia Minor. This was territory peripheral to the heart of the kingdom, not always easily controllable and yet extremely important. Its importance sprang from strategic and general political reasons, for it guaranteed contact with the Aegean Sea and so with the traditional Greek world, and it was the cause of confrontation and frequent rivalry with other Hellenistic powers such as Macedonia, Egypt and Pergamum. Whereas the regions of the Seleucid 'nucleus' had a fundamental unity and compactness, reflecting the economic and political autonomy which they enjoyed, political crises were most likely to occur in Seleucid relations with the territories and the cities of western Asia Minor. It was here that the Seleucid king had contact with the ancient Greek cities of Asia, and indirectly with the Greek peninsula in general. It was here too that he was confronted by traditions (and aspirations) of freedom, autonomy and democracy; and it was here that he paid homage, essential for propaganda and political reasons, to the great Greek sanctuaries.

For some decades there has been heated discussion on the form and

---

[50] On the ἐπιστάτης and the πελιγᾶνες at Seleuceia-on-the-Tigris: Polyb. v.48.12 and 54.10 (here, however, the manuscript tradition gives ἀδειγᾶνες); at Laodicea-on-Sea: Roussel 1942–3: (B 154); Musti 1966, 123–4: (E 44). A position analogous to that of an ἐπιστάτης could have been held by the Sophron placed in charge of Ephesus, ἐπὶ τῆς Ἐφέσου (Athen. XIII.593 b–d) by Seleucus II: on him see Orth 1977, 151–2: (A 46).

substance of the relationships between the Greek cities (in particular, for the reasons mentioned above, those in Asia Minor) and the Hellenistic kings in general, especially the Seleucids who concern us here. On the formal level scholars are agreed: a city normally figures in a relation of 'alliance' (*symmachia*) with the sovereign. It appears in fact that we cannot and should not distinguish between cities 'within the territory' (*chora*) and those 'in alliance' (*symmachia*). However, the substance of the relationship is notoriously more controversial. In 1937 a book by Alfred Heuss stressed, in relation to the *Idealtypus* of king and Greek city (an explicit reference to the theory and terminology of Max Weber), the fundamental independence of the Greek cities, whose political and constitutional structure had remained the same during the classical and Hellenistic periods and also as they passed from the control of one sovereign to that of another. Examples of interference by Hellenistic monarchs were mere *factual* occurrences which left no constitutional traces. To this 'idealizing' theory E. Bikerman replied by stressing the empirical and more genuinely historical aspects of the situation. Bikerman, at about the same time as the publication of Heuss's book, published a fundamental volume on the *Institutions des Séleucides*, which gave a realistic picture of the administrative apparatus and political methods of the Syrian dynasty. In its reference to a series of particular situations this book was so precise and well argued that it became the necessary point of departure for any study of the relations between the central power and the Greek cities, allied to the sovereigns, but often, in fact, situated in a position of heavy dependence on them. On the other hand it remained and still remains necessary to show the various gradations in the position of these cities. There is still no reason to question the absence of regular royal functionaries (like the *epistatai*), operating *within and above* the political structures of the city, in western Asia Minor. One must also distinguish between the purely propagandist and the more genuine aspects of the proclamations made by the sovereigns about the preservation (or restoration) of freedom (*eleutheria*), autonomy (*autonomia*) and sometimes democracy (*demokratia*) (though the royal chancelleries usually preferred to pass over the latter). Some other scholars have insisted on the incompatability of liberty and civic autonomy with monarchical power. Although this is true in principle, it would be a mistake to take account only of the formal aspects of freedom (*eleutheria*), which were infringed every time there was an intervention by the sovereign.[51] It would also be unrealistic to

[51] On this theme, cf. Heuss 1937: (A 22), Bikerman 1938: (E 6) and 1939: (H 12). On the incompatibility between the freedom and autonomy of the cities and the power of the king see Orth 1977: (A 46), D. Musti, 'Formulazioni ideali e prassi politica nell' affermazione della supremazia romana in Grecia', in *Tra Grecia e Roma*, by various authors (Rome, 1980) 55–66.

refuse to consider the actual room for external and internal political action, which the cities, with some difficulty, tried to win or preserve. It is this which makes sense of the episodes involving the 'restoration' of freedom, autonomy (and even democracy) celebrated by the cities or recognized and perhaps even publicized by the sovereigns. Finally one would be showing little regard for the far from irrelevant (although not abundant) documentation, if one were simply to equate the political pattern of relations between the Seleucid kings and the Greek cities with the experience and political conduct of all their predecessors or of the other Hellenistic monarchies. Our first task then is to make some distinctions.

There were cities which in general preserved their independence and, even though they were linked with different sovereigns at different periods, made it clear that they did not have to submit to the opinion or interests of a single one of them. One thinks first of Miletus, which succeeded in maintaining relations of dignified alliance, not without some form of subjection, with the Seleucids: this is shown in a decree in honour of Apame, the wife of Seleucus I, and one in honour of Antiochus, son of Seleucus, before he ascended the throne as Antiochus I. The city suffered, successively, the overlordship of Lysimachus, Demetrius Poliorcetes and the Ptolemies: but apparently not uninterruptedly. In their relations with the Seleucids (who re-established themselves under Antiochus II Theos after the tyranny of a certain Timarchus)[52] a particular role was played by the specific connexion of the Seleucids with the sanctuary of Apollo at Didyma, a divinity whom the Seleucids considered to be the founder of their family (*archegos*).[53]

Among the ancient Ionian cities, an important role was also played by Ephesus, which was refounded on a different site from that of the ancient city of Lysimachus and which, in the middle of the third century, was one of the royal residences under Antiochus II. The relation between Samos and the Seleucids was more like that of Miletus. The Seleucids did interfere, however (although under pressure from interested citizens and to put right abuses committed by their own administration), in matters regarding the landed property of the citizens of Samos in the plain of Anaea on the mainland. Here, moreover, their position as islanders helped to determine their particular relationship.

The city of Ilium appears to have been more closely dependent on the Seleucids. We have from there a law against tyrants which suggests an intervention by the Seleucids to restore normal conditions after a period

---

52 On the tyrant Timarchus: Musti 1966, 153–4: (E 44); Will 1979, 1.235–6: (A 67).

53 On the Milesian decrees: Wiegand-Rehm 1958, nos. 479–80: (B 172); in general, Müller 1976: (B 112). On Apollo ἀρχηγός: *OGIS* 212, 13–14; 219, 25ff.; Musti 1966, 95–8, 106–7, 140, 149: (E 44); Günther 1971: (E 27); Orth 1977, 45, 73, 75: (A 46).

of political and social disturbances marked by the appearance or threat of a tyrannical régime.[54] Reference has already been made to the special position of Sardis as the residence of the governor of the Seleucid rulers 'on this side of the Taurus': however this position is also firmly attested with Antiochus Hierax (the brother of Seleucus II who rebelled against the legitimate king) (242–228), with Achaeus, the cousin of Antiochus III, who as usurper for some years maintained the secession of Asia Minor from the government at Antioch,[55] and then, still under Antiochus III, with the legitimate governor Zeuxis.

It is natural that the position and story of Pergamum should have a place apart in the history of Seleucid Asia Minor. It was the seat of the royal treasure under Lysimachus. It was transferred by the treasurer Philetaerus to the alliance of Seleucus after Corupedium (281 B.C.). Thereafter it progressively asserted its independence. The first limited manifestations of this appeared under Eumenes, and ended in the definitive proclamation of himself as king by Attalus I. Attalus had consolidated his power and prestige with a famous victory over the Galatians and cleverly exploited the opportunity provided by the disturbances in western Asia Minor which were caused by the Celtic invasion from the third decade of the century onwards.

The history of the relations of the Seleucids with western Asia Minor, from the time of Seleucus I to the battle of Magnesia and the peace of Apamea, can be divided into the following periods:
(1) One of relations based rather on diplomacy than on hegemony, which lasted until Corupedium (312–281 B.C.).
(2) The most critical period as regards actual crises (and scarcity of documentation), which stretches from the beginning of the reign of Antiochus I until the early years of the reign of Antiochus II (c. 280–258).
(3) Consolidation during the latter years of Antiochus II's reign (until his death in 246 B.C.). This can be traced for example at Miletus and in other cities of Ionia, but its existence is also proved by gestures of liberality like that of the sovereign to Priene.
(4) The new critical period of the Laodicean War (246–241), with the connected crisis in the central power and the appearance as governor of Sardis of Antiochus Hierax, at war against his brother Seleucus II.
(5) The period of the secessions of Hierax and Achaeus.
(6) The glorious but short-lived restoration due to Antiochus III.

In the better periods (the reign of Seleucus I, the later years of Antiochus II and the period of Antiochus III) but also to some extent in

---

[54] On the Seleucids and Samos, cf. *SEG* 1.366; the law of Ilium against tyrants: *OGIS* 218 (= Frisch 1975, 62–80, no. 25: (B 78)). Important for all the cities is Magie's classic work (1950: (E 81)).

[55] On Achaeus and his revolt, see especially Schmitt 1964, 158–88: (E 51); Walbank 1967, II.63–6, 93–8: (B 37).

the rest there is a particular characteristic of the relations between the central Seleucid power and the ancient Greek cities of Asia Minor. This is the special attention and respect shown by the Seleucid sovereigns towards the political forms of democracy and the principle, proclaimed at least verbally, of freedom (*eleutheria*).[56]

In general the Seleucid monarchy exhibited a certain respect for what has been called the proud susceptibility of the 'bourgeoisie' of the Greek cities and for the forms and political ideologies to which this had given rise; but at certain moments, for instance under Antiochus III in the first years of the second century B.C., on the eve of the encounter with Rome and in conscious expectation of this, there was an appeal to *demokratia* in the fullest sense as a régime with a 'popular basis'. In about 190 B.C., during his last years, Antiochus III in fact played the popular card, in order to win the sympathies of the masses.[57]

As regards both these aspects of Seleucid policy there is a great deal to be learnt from the study of the rich epigraphic material from Teos, published magisterially by P. Herrmann.[58] We find documented here a special relationship between the king and the city, with its democratic traditions and popular organs of government. Teos in turn had a cult of the Seleucid sovereign, the forms of which recall those documented in other Greek cities of Asia Minor, such as Ilium and others.

If, however, the relationship between the central power and the different cities of Asia Minor was varied, so too was that between the central power and the native populations. An important part of the region will have consisted of royal estates (*basilike chora*) occupied and worked by the royal peasants (*basilikoi laoi*). But it should not be forgotten that it was in this region of the Seleucid kingdom, in Anatolia, that there existed a particularly marked distinction between peoples (*ethne*) and rulers (*dynastai*) (see above p. 178). The former were autonomous populations living in tribal conditions and jealously guarding fairly strong forms of independence; they lived in Lycia, Pisidia, Pamphylia, Isauria and Lycaonia. The latter were small local lords in a relationship of fairly tenuous dependence on the central power, such as Olympichus of Mylasa or the dynasty of the Teucridae at Olba in Cilicia.

[56] On *demokratia* in Seleucid inscriptions, Musti 1966, 138–45: (E 44); 1977, 280–2: (H 150). On the political life of a Seleucid foundation in Roman imperial times, Robert in Gagniers *et al.* 1969, 279–335: (B 195).
[57] Besides the 'popular' traits evident in the policy of Antiochus III before and during the conflict with Rome, which I have discussed elsewhere (1966, 160ff.: (E 44)), note also the marked benevolence towards the poor (the ἀσθενοῦντες), displayed by Queen Laodice (II or III), whose letter precedes that of Antiochus III, but was inscribed under him, in an inscription of Iasus (Pugliese Carratelli 1967–8, 445–6, ll. 13–14, 23: (B 122); J. and L. Robert, *Bull. épig.* 1971, 502–9).
[58] Cf. Herrmann 1965: (B 85). On the *asylia* of Teos on the eve of the Roman-Syrian war cf. Errington 1980: (E 67).

VII.   RELATIONS WITH IRAN. RETREAT FROM FURTHER
ASIA. GROWTH OF THE PARTHIANS. GREEKS IN BACTRIA
AND INDIA

The repeated attempts of the Seleucids to keep Asia Minor and many
ancient Greek cities of the Aegean under their control reflected
understandable political aims and were in line with an historical
tradition of successive empires in those parts. The precise role of the
Iranian regions and the policies pursued there by the Seleucid sovereigns
are less clear, bearing in mind that, in comparison with the Persian
empire, the axis of the Seleucid kingdom was markedly further to the
west. All in all, in the second half of the reign of Seleucus I the axis of the
Seleucid empire is still perhaps more correctly defined as Syro-
Mesopotamian (with the possible addition of Cilicia) than as Syro-
Anatolian. In any case the formation of a unity, an economic and
political nucleus between the Tigris and the Mediterranean, through the
rise of the Seleucid state, is an undeniable fact, which distinguishes it
significantly from the more eastern location (geographical, economic and
political) of the Persian empire.[59]

A first aspect of the problem is to define the Iranian policy of the first
Seleucids, to ascertain the extent and meaning of their undeniable
engagement and progressive disengagement. It is a problem (or group
of problems) which must be seen first and foremost in geographical and
chronological terms.[60]

Between 305 and 303 Seleucus I made war on the Indian king
Chandragupta (Sandrakottos or Sandrokottos in Greek), who ruled
over the valley of the Indus, modern Pakistan. But the peace with which
he ended that war was a compromise and in effect an act of renunciation.
Thus at the outset one must determine the western limits of the Mauryan
kingdom of Sandrokottos – who was the grandfather of Aśoka, the
author of several edicts, engraved on cliffs, among them a famous

[59] Seyrig 1970: (E 53) stresses the innovative aspects connected with the foundation of Seleuceia-
in-Pieria and Antioch-on-the-Orontes, with respect to previous traditions of settlement and trade,
and the pointedly philo-Macedonian character of the colonizing work of Seleucus I. The
importance of the area around Aleppo, on the other hand, particularly in regard to communications
and exchanges with the regions of the interior, may go back to very ancient times, as is shown by the
extraordinary discoveries of Ebla (Tell Mardikh), the city of northern Syria about 80 km south of
Aleppo, on the road to Hama and Damascus, where recent archaeological excavations have enabled
us to locate the centre of a flourishing state, with considerable commercial interests, dating back to
the third millenium B.C., and have brought to light the remains of a royal palace and an extremely
rich archive of clay tablets.

[60] On Seleucid policy towards Iran, the pages of Will 1979, I.262–314: (A 67), are illuminating (cf.
also *idem.* 1982, II.51–69, 344–55, 400–10, 413–16: (A 67)).

bilingual Greek and Aramaic edict from Alexandria-Kandahar.[61] The question is to ascertain how much of the conquests of Alexander the Great were kept by Seleucus I. After establishing himself in Babylonia in 312, Seleucus had pushed on into Bactria and from there to India (which included at least the valley of the Indus) but he later surrendered to Chandragupta at any rate the eastern part of Gedrosia and Arachosia and the territory of the Paropamisadae (that is the eastern part of modern Afghanistan, the south-west part of Pakistan and Beluchistan). But did the region of Alexandria-Kandahar fall under Mauryan rule at the time of Sandrokottos, or later under his son Bindusara, or only during the reign of his grandson Aśoka? Under Seleucus I (or Antiochus I) or under Antiochus II? And how far east did Seleucus advance?[62]

These questions must remain without a precise answer, although we can reasonably say that Seleucid rule in Gedrosia and Arachosia must have shown its weakness from the time of Seleucus I. The expansion of the Seleucid empire to the central and north-eastern regions of Iran carried with it the serious problem of whether it was really possible to administer and control these vast regions, interrupted by mountain chains and deserts and inhabited by diverse tribes. But it is no accident that they maintained a tenuous but longer lasting relationship (first a link that was also political, then at least a cultural and perhaps always a commercial link) with the central regions of the new Graeco-Macedonian empire. These countries appear to be fairly distant from the Greek world on the map, but looked at more carefully, it is clear that they occupy a position with which it was very easy to maintain communications owing to the existence of ancient roads, which had been retravelled, re-explored and militarily consolidated first by Alexander, then by Antigonus, and after him by Seleucus. This explains why Bactria maintained cultural relations with the Seleucid world for a longer time than Gedrosia or Arachosia and why for at least two centuries it remained an outpost of hellenism. Likewise the middle and higher reaches of the Indus remained notably exposed to Greek cultural influences.

Seleucid interest in ruling over at least part of the Iranian heritage left by Alexander the Great to the Graeco-Macedonians undoubtedly persisted under Antiochus I. Evidence for this lies first in Antiochus I's own experience of governing the 'upper satrapies', that is the Iranian regions (apart from Mesopotamia), while his father was still alive (viz.

[61] Cf. Tucci *et al.* 1958: (E 208); Schlumberger *et al.* 1958: (E 200); Thapar 1961: (E 207); Pugliese Carratelli-Garbini 1964: (E 197).

[62] The references to Antiochus (II) in the second and especially the thirteenth of the great rupestrian edicts of Aśoka seem to make a clear distinction between the Seleucid state and that of Aśoka himself.

before 280 B.C.). Then there is Antiochus' own Iranian origin: he was the son of Seleucus and Apame, a daughter of the Bactrian Spitamenes (according to Arrian, *Anab*. VII.4.6). Finally there is the presence of cities named Antioch as far afield as Margiana (if the name really dates back to the first Antiochus). However it is certain that in the first decade of his reign (280–270) Antiochus I had to face difficulties and conflicts in Asia Minor and Seleucis (meaning Syria Seleucis or perhaps, more generally, the Seleucid dominions east of the Taurus). It is difficult to say how many years of his reign he devoted to political (and even military) intervention in the Iranian regions, extending to the farthest north-eastern areas. Positive evidence is lacking. But everything leads us to suspect that the reign of Antiochus II (261–246 B.C.) represented the first serious crisis for the Iranian possessions of the Seleucids and for their whole Iranian policy.

As to the purpose of this policy, there is no doubt that its military aspects of defence and consolidation were of particular importance. By accepting and maintaining the general character of Alexander the Great's advance and conquest and by assuming the control of Bactria, they guaranteed the coherent defence of the 'umbilical cord' that connected this region with the central parts of the kingdom. Both areas were alike protected by the whole outpost of Iran, which acted as a first line of defence. It is true that Seleucid policy also had its more aggressive aspects designed to penetrate more deeply into the Iranian regions and link them more closely with the central nucleus of the Seleucid state and empire. There will have been economic interests concerned with the exploitation of local resources, the appropriation, at least in part, of lands belonging to the local aristocracy, and the guarding of trade routes. Seleucid colonization also left its marks here, and this is a fact of general importance, even though the main over-riding purpose of the colonies in these regions appears to have been military. However the general impression remains – and although this is a summary judge-ment, it is valid and apposite and also one expressed in the ancient sources – that Iran, both in Media and Persis, which made up its central part and richest regions, and in its almost legendary offshoots in Bactria and Sogdiana, was for the Seleucid kingdom a sort of grandiose outpost, an extraordinary bulwark,[63] but, ultimately, something marginal to the economic and political unity which was growing up in the Syro-Mesopotamian heart of the state. This seems to be reflected in the difference in social structure between the Iranian regions and those of Mesopotamia. In Iran during the Achaemenid period and probably, at least partly, during the Hellenistic age, there existed an aristocracy of

[63] On the idea of a bulwark against the barbarians, cf. for example Polyb. XI.34.5.

landlords, a warrior nobility who owned vast tracts of land. In the Mesopotamian regions the fundamental structure (one may term it 'Asiatic') was based on the village and on the royal power and so on a more direct relationship of despot and subjects. There was in short little or no mediation, so to say, through a nobility of local lords enjoying some independence of the sovereign power – or displaying in relation to the central authority marks of dependency basically connected with well-defined forms of property-owning and personal rule. In Iran there was a strong intermediate power (both economic and military, and so in a sense political) and it was this which, far more than in Syria or Mesopotamia, prevented the Greeks becoming firmly established ethnically, politically, culturally and economically – except when the Greek element itself took on a separatist role, providing pretexts and support for the autonomist tendencies of the population and primarily of the local aristocracy.

After Antiochus I, the first Seleucid king to set foot in Iran was Seleucus II, between 230 and 227. His campaign did not have results in any way comparable to the successes achieved by Antiochus III, whether in the war against the usurpers Molon and Alexander for the reconquest of the central and western parts of Iran (227–220 B.C.) or in the glorious 'anabasis' which followed (212–205/4 B.C.). Although these wars enabled Antiochus III to consolidate his authority in large areas of Iran and to assume or be granted the title of Great King (*megas basileus*), they did not result in a reconquest of Parthia and Armenia – though indeed he did win some remarkable victories against their kings, which at least succeeded in restraining for a time the Parthian advance towards the west. As for the more eastern regions such as Bactria or Gandhara, Antiochus the Great had to be content with small acts of formal recognition which brought him certain immediate practical advantages.[64]

There is a problem about the chronology of the withdrawal of the Seleucid kingdom from Bactria and the more westerly Parthia. There is a 'high' chronology, which places at least the initial stage of the process of separation in the reign of Antiochus II, and a 'low' chronology, which transfers the whole of these events to the reign of Seleucus II and in particular to the period of the so-called 'War of the Brothers' (between Seleucus II and Antiochus Hierax, *c.* 240/39–237 B.C.). The 'high' chronology has been supported chiefly by Bikerman and the 'low' in

[64] Walbank 1967, II.231–42 and 312–16: (B 37) (on the expedition against Arsaces of Parthia and Xerxes of Armenia and on the relations with Euthydemus of Bactria and Sophagasenus the Indian who ruled in Gandhara). Antiochus recognized Euthydemus' title of *basileus* and obtained elephants from him; he promised one of his daughters as a wife to his son Demetrius. With Sophagasenus his relation was clearly more distant: it was a renewal of φιλία and a concession of elephants and financial payments by the Indian king (for whose identification see Walbank, *locc. citt.*).

various studies by J. Wolski.[65] It is of course not merely a chronological problem, since it is one thing to say that Bactria and Parthia broke away from the Seleucid kingdom by taking advantage of internal discords occurring there, and another to say that under Antiochus II the shift of the axis of the kingdom towards the west was accelerated and that this in itself in some degree prepared the ground for, and encouraged, the great secessions of the regions of northern and north-eastern Iran.

The chronological uncertainty derives of course from the different (and contradictory) sources regarding the facts just mentioned – and that problem is discussed below in an appendix.[66] There it is argued that the following stages can be traced in the defection of the eastern provinces:

(1) Rebellion of the Greek (or Graeco-Macedonian) satraps of the two peripheral regions, viz. Diodotus of Bactria and Andragoras, satrap of Parthyene.

(2) During the last years of the reign of Antiochus II, nomadic tribes, Scythians or Parnians, under the command of one Arsaces (or of Arsaces and Tiridates) began their movement from the Scythian steppes towards Parthyene. They murdered the governor, who was already in rebellion against the central power, and set up an independent state, which they then consolidated during the reign of Seleucus II.

The formation of the Parthian state was thus primarily the victory of a nomadic over a settled element. However these nomads were in turn linked with settled populations in the Scythian area and these gave them vital support.

Bactria had enjoyed a significant urban development with the coming of Graeco-Macedonian rule and considerable hellenization of former centres, such as Aï Khanum at the confluence of the Oxus (Amu Darya) and the Kowkcheh. The city has been uncovered in the course of the excellent French excavations. A palace, a theatre, a gymnasium and other buildings were found, but the hellenization of the city can also be deduced from the discovery of Greek inscriptions and the traces left by papyri (which have been associated with the work of Clearchus of Soli).[67] Evidence for the economic development of Bactria has been provided particularly by coins of the Greek kings of the second century

[65] Cf. Bikerman 1944: (E 7); Wolski 1947: (E 210) and 1956–8: (E 211) (followed in substance by Schmitt 1964, 64–6 and 70–6: (E 51)); Will 1979, 1.301–8: (A 67).

[66] See pp. 219–20. Doubts about the historicity of Arsaces and/or Tiridates in Wolski 1959, 1962 and 1976: (E 212, 214–15).

[67] On the excavations at Aï Khanum, cf. Schlumberger-Bernard 1965: (E 201); Bernard 1967: (E 182) and CR Acad. Inscr. 1966–72, 1974–6, 1978 (accounts of the palace, theatre, gymnasium, other buildings): (E 181). See Plates vol., pls. 17, 26. On the canalization of the surrounding territory, going back to the time of the Achaemenid sovereigns and, even before, to the Bronze Age, and lasting till the Middle Ages, which was in use during the Hellenistic period (and in a different social and economic context) by the new Greek landowners, cf. Gentelle 1978: (E 190); Briant 1978, 77–8: (E 12).

(Plates vol., pls. 35–6). Thus Bactria continued to have an autonomous existence. Its population did not change (or become radically integrated with native elements) after its separation from the Seleucid kingdom, as was the case with Parthyene.

In Parthyene there was a change, or at least a modification, in the population caused by the displacement of the original settled element by the nomads. The history of Bactria reflects the loosening of the Seleucid hold on the Iranian regions and the withdrawal by the Greeks of that area from its relationship and links with the central power (in Syria and Mesopotamia). There were also thrusts towards autonomy by the Iranian population: but in Bactria the latter remained undisturbed, either in subordination to, or side by side with, the Graeco-Macedonian element (and in itself the diversity in their modes of settlement and social organization, with the one group living in towns and the other in tribes and in some cases as nomads, may even have contributed to their establishing some kind of compromise, precarious though it was). Central and northern Iran, on the other hand, was overrun by a wave of nomads of Scythian origin, called Parnians, and this resulted in a new dynasty.

Movements towards independence can be traced in Persis (Phars). There coins of the *fratadara* (or *frataraka*?) of Persepolis-Istachr point to something of the sort but are difficult to date; suggestions vary between the reign of Seleucus I and that of Seleucus IV. The identification of the Seleucus mentioned in a passage of Polyaenus (VII.39–40) in the context of fighting between Macedonians and Persians is no less uncertain.[68]

The anabasis of Antiochus III (212–205/4) which took him into Media, Hyrcania, Parthia and Bactria, did not result in a renewed subjugation of these last two regions. King Euthydemus of Bactria obtained recognition of his formal sovereignty from Antiochus III. The Parthian kingdom too began to expand gradually to cover the whole of Iran (under Antiochus IV) and Mesopotamia (in the course of the conflicts between the two branches of the Seleucid family descended, as we have already seen, from Antiochus III). During the long reign of Mithridates I of Parthia (175–138 B.C.), Parthian control expanded over large areas of Seleucid territory. The second century B.C. also marked the end of the brief flowering of the Indo-Greek kingdoms, which had expanded considerably towards the valley of the Indus under Demetrius I and later, under Demetrius II and Menander.[69]

[68] On the rebellion of Oborzus (Vahuberz), Will 1979, I. 280: (A 67); 1982, II.350: (A 67).

[69] For a dating in the epoch of Demetrius I, son of Euthydemus, of the Greek advance into Gandhara and the plain of the Indus, see Tarn 1951: (E 206); against Narain 1957: (E 196); Simonetta 1958: (E 204); Woodcock 1966: (E 217) (for a lower dating, referring to Demetrius II, son of Antimachus Theos, and especially Menander and Apollodotus, of the expansion into the plain of the Indus and of the succeeding expansion towards the Ganges and the south). The role of

In the second century B.C., after the efforts at expansion towards Egypt and Palestine and the attempts to extend his power towards Iran by Antiochus IV, one can detect a gradual flaking away of the Seleucid kingdom. All the peripheral regions were lost, Judaea (through the revolt of the Maccabees), the cities of Phoenicia and southern Syria, parts of Iran and then Mesopotamia (through the expansion of the Parthians as mentioned above); and there is evidence for the development of neighbouring states, independent or hostile, such as Commagene and Armenia. Before it finally became a Roman province, the Seleucid kingdom even lost its dynastic identity and, for several years between 83 and 69 B.C., was under the rule of an Armenian king, Tigranes.

VIII. CONCLUSION

Rostovtzeff's general conclusion in the previous edition of the *Cambridge Ancient History* concerning the historical outcome of the creation of the Seleucid kingdom tends to be pessimistic. Two desirable consequences singled out by Rostovtzeff, the foundation of cities and hellenization, were, according to him, only scantily achieved. Confirmation of this can be derived from what happened in the sphere of religion and of culture generally. The local religions showed an impressive staying power. As for Greek culture, only a few names stand out: a couple of philosophers, a poet (Meleager of Gadara), an historian (Posidonius), who seems to Rostovtzeff to be much less Syrian than the fact that he was born at Apamea might suggest. In Rostovtzeff's opinion the achievement of Seleucid Syria is to be assessed historically as a posthumous contribution. In the general history of culture, the Seleucid empire functioned merely as a vehicle of transmission. Sassanid Persia, Christian Armenia and Syria, pre-Islamic Arabia, the culture of Gandhara and Taxila are unthinkable without the role of intermediary played by the Seleucid kingdom.

This pessimistic picture cannot be fundamentally disputed. It can only be filled out with greater detail and illuminated by introducing new perspectives. Meanwhile there is need, in the historical field generally, of a deeper analysis of the very concept of hellenization and politicization; and that means, first and foremost, defining the social context in which the process of hellenization and politicization took place. The policy of hellenization is usually seen as the expression of a programme of the Seleucid dynasty carried out in collaboration with the aristocratic strata of the population. Of course in some regions, and especially in areas and

Eucratides is also disputed. He appears to have fought Demetrius II *c.* 171 B.C. and taken power in Bactria (cf. especially Masson 1961: (E 195)). On these problems see Will 1982, II.343–52, 400–4: (A 67), and Habicht in vol. VIII of the present work.

communities not previously hellenized, Seleucid policy was directed primarily towards the aristocracies; and it was at this level that more or less fragile agreements could be concluded. The classic case of a hellenizing movement, which did not penetrate the more dense strata of the population and, although it made headway among some of the aristocracy, ran up against national and religious resistance with strong popular support, was the hellenizing policy pursued by Antiochus IV in Judaea. Elsewhere, however, for example in the previously hellenized area of western Asia Minor, which had its own distinct and characteristic political traditions, Seleucid policy was not exclusively directed at an understanding with the aristocracy and higher classes. There on the contrary Seleucid policy could present itself in a variety of hues and offered the possibility of broader political alliances which sometimes (as in the Romano-Syrian war) reached down to, and involved, even the lowest classes of the population. Thus hellenization and politicization did not always and everywhere mean a break with the popular base. They varied according to regions and also according to periods and situations. Where the dynasty succeeded in its intention of creating large urban centres, the conditions could arise for a certain cultural fusion between Greeks and natives. This follows from the considerations put forward above on the basis of recent studies concerning the forms and effects of Seleucid colonization. Furthermore, we have slightly better documentation (and information) than was available in Rostovtzeff's time on at least two aspects of the policy of the Seleucids: first, their policy towards the temples, cities and temple properties can be shown to be more respectful than was previously thought and, secondly, the spread of Greek culture and aspects of Macedonian culture (as seen from the cults and place names) was larger and more potent than was previously thought. The Graeco-Macedonian colonists and their de- scendants show a capacity to express their culture which is seen to be proportionately greater, the more archaeological and epigraphical documentation we have available. Of course this does not prove that there was a strong and deep hellenization of the natives, although the evidence for this too is constantly increasing (for example in the most recent studies and publications on the cultural situation in Hellenistic and Roman Cappadocia). However the cultural vitality of the Graeco-Macedonian colonies and settlements was a remarkably widespread phenomenon.

On the other hand, hellenization does not seem to be an adequate criterion for judging the historical success of the creation of the Seleucid kingdom. Altogether, the Seleucid state, if one looks both at the top and at the base, appears to be a society of the asiatic or 'ancient oriental' type, of which the fundamental characteristics are a monarch who is 'lord of the land', on the one hand, and an immense peasant population, which inhabits it in a condition of dependence but *not of slavery*, on the other. In this society the causes of crisis are introduced and develop alongside the introduction of new economic forms at variance with the 'ancient oriental' aspects, which however remain the basic ones. The new forms consist in the development of urbanization and trade together with a limited development of slavery. Seleucid society does not seem however to have been able to develop these new forms to the point of a fully established system of slavery, which would have been to its own profit. Syria was to become rather the great reservoir of slaves for the western Mediterranean, where slavery flourished from the second century B.C. at least to the end of the first century A.D.

As for the causes of the decline and fall of the Seleucid empire, for which Rostovtzeff stresses (not without some uncertainty and contradiction) both the external (aggression by Rome and the Parthians) and the internal factors (poor cohesion, dynastic conflicts, internal anarchy), it now seems that they are to be looked for chiefly in the internal structure of the Seleucid world, and in the strong attraction which this structure exercised on a state like Rome which was orientated towards rule over other areas of the Mediterranean world, and on the needs and the social forces operative within the Roman state.

In this context Rostovtzeff's definition of Posidonius as a phenomenon completely extraneous to the history of Syria becomes a little less probable. True, Posidonius grew up and expressed himself in antithesis to the society of Seleucid Syria. But for that very reason his experience as a historian was in vital relation (though of a dialectical character) to Syria's historical experience. In the light of what has been said above, it will for example become clear how the interest in social history – and in the history of slavery in particular – which characterizes Posidonius' work, arose, what it reflects and what, in a complicated fashion, it is reacting against. To complete his literary, historiographical and general cultural education, Posidonius certainly had to leave Syria and move to the old Greek cities, such as Athens and Rhodes. But as regards his special place as a historian, he can be understood and he receives the full recognition that is his due only when he is seen against the background of the political, social and economic history of Syria. It is therefore no accident that the most important evidence which we possess on these historical aspects, comes to us from the geographical work of Strabo, who derived it largely from Posidonius of Apamea.

THE DATE OF THE SECESSION OF BACTRIA AND PARTHIA FROM THE SELEUCID KINGDOM
(see pp. 213–16)

The chronology of the secession of Bactria and Parthia from the Seleucid realm is obscure owing to the inconsistent information afforded by the sources, and opinion has swung between a 'high' dating, which places the initial events in the reign of Antiochus II, and a 'low' dating which brings them down to that of Seleucus II. There is a reference to the 'War of the Brothers', 'duorum fratrum regum, Seleuci et Antiochi, discordia', in Justin (XLI.4.3 ff.). There is also a curious reference to an Antiochus called Callinicus (who was apparently *also* called Seleucus) in the Byzantine historian Syncellus (p. 284 Bonn). The 'high' dating is decidedly the more probable; considerations in favour of the 'low' dating are sometimes based on forced interpretations of the fundamental texts. Without going into all the particulars, I limit myself here to making some observations about some aspects of the exegesis of our texts, which do not seem to me to have been sufficiently exploited.

(i) There is a clear reference to the period of Antiochus II regarding the *Parthian secession* in a fundamental text of Arrian (*Parthica* fr. 1). The name of the Seleucid governor in this text is Pherecles, whereas in Syncellus it is Agathocles, and elsewhere it is Andragoras, but this is a difficulty, or rather a variant, which remains on any chronology. But Justin (XLI.4.3) also refers to the consulate of Manlius Vulso and Atilius Regulus as the date of the beginning of the invasion of Parthyene. It is true that he also speaks here of Seleucus II, but the consular date (256 or 250) represents a chronological element independent of Seleucid chronology. Wolski interprets that as an element of weakness, but in fact, because it is a 'foreign body', it could constitute an element of strength. It is certain that we cannot claim Justin's reference to the *fratrum discordia* as proof of a late date (Seleucus II) for the *beginning* of the invasion of the Parni into Parthia, because Justin (with noteworthy coherence here) himself distinguishes two phases: (1) a first phase linked to the consulate of Vulso and Regulus (though indeed dated anachronistically under Seleucus II), which is the date of the *beginning* of the Parnian invasion and the secession of Parthia; (2) a second phase, in which the *discordia fratrum* '*dedit impunitatem*': that is, in which the secession was consolidated, but *in the course of time*.

(ii) It is not certain nor is it indeed probable that the fragment of Strabo XI.9.2, c. 515 contains any mention of the War of the Brothers of *c.* 240/39–237.[70] The

[70] Strabo XI.9.2.C. 515: νεωτερισθέντων δὲ τῶν ἔξω τοῦ Ταύρου διὰ τὸ πρὸς ἄλλοις εἶναι τοὺς τῆς Συρίας καὶ τῆς Μηδίας βασιλέας τοὺς ἔχοντας καὶ ταυτα, πρῶτον μὲν τὴν Βακτριανὴν ἀπέστησαν οἱ πεπιστευμένοι καὶ τὴν ἐγγὺς αὐτῆς πᾶσαν οἱ περὶ Εὐθύδημον, ἔπειτ᾽ Ἀρσάκης, ἀνὴρ Σκύθης κτλ. On the fragment cf. also the analysis of Will 1979, 1.305–6: (A 67) (who suggests a different chronological view); and the edition of F. Lasserre, *Strabon, Géographie* (Livre XI) (Paris, 1975) 91 and 140.

correction πρὸς ἀλλήλους instead of πρὸς ἀλλήλοις of the manuscript tradition, represents a modification of the traditional text which is almost as slight as the other proposed correction (πρὸς ἄλλοις), but it presupposes a distinction between the king of Media on the one hand, and the king of Syria on the other, which does not correspond to that between Seleucus II (who was king of Syria and Media, etc.) and Antiochus Hierax (the sovereign of western Asia Minor). However, the presence of the words καὶ ταῦτα ('these regions as well') renders the correction πρὸς ἄλλοις (the kings of Syria and Media were busy with 'other regions' or 'other affairs') somewhat attractive. On the other hand, from the chronological point of view, the whole passage of Strabo labours under the difficulty created by the reference to Euthydemus of Bactria and consequently by the chronology (which is far too late) that Strabo appears to attribute to these events. In addition the meaning of ἔξω τοῦ Ταύρου is open to limitless argument, but in principle one must surely admit a reference to those oriental regions, Bactria and Parthia, about which Strabo goes on in the same passage to mention particular, individual events.

(iii) We therefore have no clear and decisive evidence in favour of putting the defection of Parthia 'under Seleucus II'. For Justin's first piece of evidence is linked with the chronology of the consuls of 256 (or 250) B.C. and thus one solution is *at least* as good as the other. His second testimony, moreover, that relative to the *discordia fratrum*, clearly refers to the conclusive stage of the Parthian rebellion. And finally Syncellus' evidence is not in the form given by Wolski ('a Seleucus whose second name was Antiochus'), but, if we follow the text, exactly the reverse ('an Antiochus whose second name was Seleucus'). Certainly there is the attribute Callinicus which we know was given to Seleucus II. But how far is an epithet in honour of a victory decisive for singling out a particular sovereign? On the other hand there is at least one strong piece of evidence in favour of Antiochus II, that of Arrian; and there is also the consular date given by Justin. Furthermore the official beginning of the Parthian era was 1 Nisan 247 B.C., a year which falls firmly within the reign of Antiochus II.

However, even if it began under Antiochus II (and that would be almost in the logic of things, given the reduced commitment to an Iranian policy under this sovereign), the secession of Bactria and Parthyene took place over a period of years, and that was apparently the period stretching from the last years of Antiochus II to the period of the war between Seleucus II and Antiochus Hierax.

CHAPTER 7

MACEDONIA AND GREECE

F. W. WALBANK

I. ANTIGONUS GONATAS AND PYRRHUS

His victory over the Gauls at Lysimacheia left Antigonus Gonatas
master of Macedonia; but for several years his hold on the country
remained precarious, and was threatened by rivals whose elimination
was his first concern. Of these the most dangerous were Cassander's
nephew Antipater and Ptolemy, the surviving son of Lysimachus and
Arsinoe; there was also a certain Arrhidaeus. Furthermore the port of
Cassandreia was held by a Greek demagogue, Apollodorus. Using
Gaulish mercenaries Antigonus had dealt with all the pretenders within
a year. To expel Apollodorus he employed an arch-pirate, Ameinias,
who later entered his regular service. Apollodorus was executed and
Ptolemy, the son of Arsinoe, took refuge with Ptolemy II; he and his
descendants are later found ruling the town of Telmessus in Lycia,
which was assigned to him by Ptolemy II. Hardly were these rivals
disposed of, however, when Antigonus had to face a more serious
challenge. In the later months of 275 Pyrrhus, the king of Epirus,
returned home from the fiasco of his wars in Italy and Sicily (see vol.
VII.2), and soon afterwards, perhaps in spring 274, he invaded
Macedonia. Having defeated Antigonus at a spot Plutarch calls 'the
Narrows' – it may be the Aous gorge south of Tepeleni in southern
Illyria – he pursued him into Macedonia, whereupon the Macedonian
army defected to the invader. Antigonus had to flee to Thessalonica, and
very soon Pyrrhus was in control of both Macedonia and Thessaly.

The view has been advanced[1] that in invading Macedonia Pyrrhus
was acting as agent for Ptolemy II who, it is assumed, being now
married to his half-sister Arsinoe, Lysimachus' widow, will have sought
to secure the Cyclades against Macedonian attack by setting Arsinoe's
son Ptolemy on the Macedonian throne. It seems, however, far more
likely that Pyrrhus was acting on his own behalf. He was a man given to
impulsive acts, and a raid undertaken in the first instance for plunder –
since he needed pay for his soldiers – may well have developed into
something more when he encountered weak resistance. But Pyrrhus
failed to consolidate his gains, and the violation of the royal tombs at

---

[1] By Tarn 1913, 259ff., 445: (D 38); against this see Lévèque 1957, 560–1: (C 46).

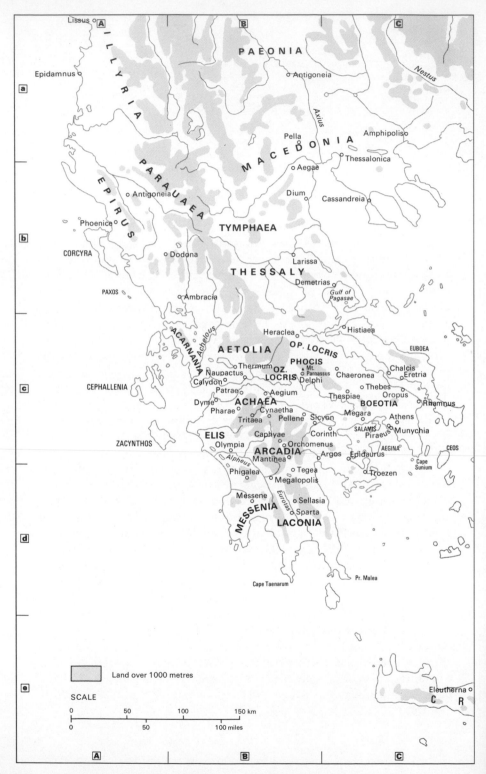

Map 5. The Greek mainland and the Aegean.

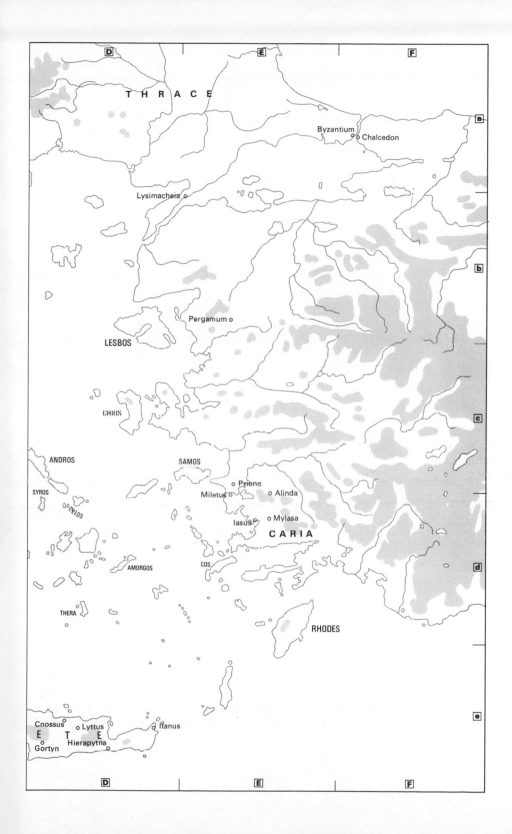

THRACE

Byzantium
○○ Chalcedon

Lysimacheia ○

Pergamum ○

LESBOS

CHIOS

ANDROS

SAMOS

SYROS

Priene ○
Miletus ○ ○ Alinda

Iasus ○ ○ Mylasa

CARIA

AMORGOS

COS

THERA

RHODES

Cnossus ○ ○ Lyttus ○ Itanus
E T E
Gortyn ○ ○ Hierapytna

Aegae by the Gaulish garrison which he installed in the town turned feeling against him. Very soon he withdrew to Epirus where, on the invitation of Cleonymus, the son of Cleomenes II and a pretender to the Spartan throne, he set about preparing to invade the Peloponnese. Macedonia he left in the hands of his son Ptolemy, who there inflicted a further defeat on Antigonus. A passage in Teles' diatribe *On Poverty*[2] records some impartially cynical, if somewhat unjust, comments of Bion of Borysthenes on Pyrrhus' role as a tomb-robber and on the cowardly flight of Antigonus.

In 272 Aetolian neutrality, coupled with positive help from Achaea and the goodwill of Megalopolis and Elis, enabled Pyrrhus to cross into the Peloponnese, where most of Antigonus' Peloponnesian allies quickly fell away. Pyrrhus then advanced on Sparta by way of Megalopolis. But meanwhile, having regained control of Macedonia, Antigonus quickly conveyed an army south by sea to Corinth, determined even to assist Sparta, if that was the best way to make an end of Pyrrhus' ambitions. Sparta offered a successful resistance to Pyrrhus and in the autumn he was diverted to Argos, where the anti-Macedonian faction offered to deliver up the town to him. On the way his son Ptolemy, who had rejoined him from Macedonia, perished in an ambush laid by Areus, the king of Sparta; and at Argos Pyrrhus found Antigonus camped on a nearby hill and the Argives anxious to assert their neutrality. The town was essential to him as a base, however, and with the help of partisans he forced an entry by night. Antigonus thereupon sent in his son Halcyoneus with Macedonian forces, Pyrrhus was trapped and soon after dawn was killed by a tile flung by a woman from a roof-top. So perished a man notable for his instability of purpose and failure to follow up any policy to its conclusion, yet for all that outstanding among the figures of his generation. Antigonus sent Pyrrhus' son Helenus back to Epirus, where his elder brother Alexander succeeded to the throne. Pyrrhus' mercenaries were incorporated in Antigonus' army.

II. ANTIGONUS AND MACEDONIA

Only now, with Pyrrhus dead, could Antigonus turn his attention to the rehabilitation of his kingdom. Since Cassander's death twenty-five years earlier Macedonia had been devastated by Gaulish invasion and torn apart by the successive attempts of Demetrius, Pyrrhus, Lysimachus, Seleucus and Ptolemy Ceraunus to seize and hold it. Now at last it possessed a firm and capable ruler; and though his task was no easy one he enjoyed some advantages not shared by his fellow-kings in Antioch and Alexandria. By this time the Macedonian people over whom he

---

[2] *Teletis reliquiae*[2] (ed. Hense), 43.

ruled had long since coalesced into a homogeneous population and he was himself one of them. The separate elements of Thracian, Anatolian or Illyrian origin had now been absorbed; the outlying principalities were subordinated to the central government at Pella, and the upper class at any rate was strongly hellenized.

Alexander's expedition and the subsequent wars had imposed a heavy burden on Macedonian resources and manpower. At a single stroke half the men of military age had been swept from their native land; casualties had been heavy and of the survivors many never returned. A few, it is true, came back rich, but they were a minority, and such wealth as they brought with them could hardly compensate for the losses which Macedonia continued to sustain from the emigration of younger men to the new kingdoms in Asia and Egypt during the fifty years following Alexander's death. Antigonus' cautious policy in Greece (see below, pp. 229–32) was probably designed to allow Macedonia to recover from her exhaustion. In such fighting as was necessary he quite deliberately spared his national troops by leaving them to farm the land and calling them up rarely; instead he relied chiefly on mercenaries – Greeks, Illyrians and Gauls from the Balkans – to do his fighting and garrisoning. Unfortunately there are no firm figures for Macedonian manpower under the Antigonids before the reign of Antigonus III and Philip V over half a century later. Some scholars have argued that the minting of an adequate and reliable silver coinage by Antigonus II shows his reign to have been a time of Macedonian prosperity;[3] but the argument is of limited validity, for Antigonus is unlikely to have minted with commercial ends in view, but rather to meet military demands, and in any case the volume of Antigonus' coinage has been exaggerated.[4] Certainly Macedonia never attained anything like the level of wealth found in Egypt and some other Hellenistic states; a hundred years later, in 168, the land tax brought in only a little over 200 talents a year.[5] There were of course other sources of national wealth besides agriculture and pasturage. The still extensive forests (furnishing timber and pitch, both essential for ship-building), the silver mines of Mt Pangaeum and a little gold were all capable of contributing to the wealth of the kingdom once conditions were stable. Whether mines and forests were a royal monopoly is not clear. There was certainly 'king's land' out of which domains were granted; but on the conditions of land tenure in Macedonia the sources tell us virtually nothing.

Within Macedonia, in contrast to the other Hellenistic states, the king's autocratic power was subject to the restriction of certain vestigial

[3] For example, Rostovtzeff 1953, 1.253: (A 52); on Gonatas' coinage see Merker 1960, 39–52: (B 240), with the criticism of Ehrhardt 1975, 75–8: (D 14).
[4] Cf. Ehrhardt 1975, 75–109: (D 14).   [5] Plut. *Aem.* 28.4.

popular rights. It was a traditional prerogative of the Macedonian people, operating very often through the army-assembly, to appoint a new king by acclamation and to act as judges in cases of high treason.[6] But how far these rights were exercised under Antigonus and his successors is another matter. Of the circumstances attending Antigonus' accession no record remains; but fifty years later Antigonus III is said by Plutarch (*Aem.* 8.2) to have been raised to the throne by 'the leading Macedonians', and in practice it was probably some such group rather than any popular assembly which in time of crisis took the decision. Their advice, it is true, may have been validated by the people or the army; but nothing of the sort is recorded, nor has any decree by any Macedonian assembly been found. Once he was appointed, the army took an oath to the king, but its wording has not survived; nor is it known whether the king swore a reciprocal oath, as the king of the Molossians did.

There is evidence that constitutionally 'the Macedonians' were an element in the Macedonian state, however slight and however ineffective their powers. A fragmentary treaty between Antigonus III and Eleutherna (*SVA* 501) was made with 'Antigonus and the Macedonians'; a dedication set up on Delos to celebrate Antigonus III's victory over Sparta in 222 (*SIG* 518) reads: 'King Antigonus, son of King Demetrius and . . . and the allies from (the spoils of) the battle of Sellasia to Apollo' – where the missing words can only be 'the Macedonians', as in the treaty of 215 between Philip V and Hannibal (Polyb. VII.9.1); Philip V is honoured on a Delian inscription by the 'corporate body (*koinon*) of the Macedonians' (*SIG* 575); and a dedication to the Great Gods on Samothrace is made on his behalf by the Macedonians (*Hesperia* 48 (1979) 16). Furthermore, the Macedonians were included among the members of the Hellenic Symmachy set up by Antigonus III in 224/3 alongside the Greek federal states (Polyb. IV.9.4); and towards the end of Philip V's reign coins were issued in the name of 'the Macedonians' as well as by various regional groups and cities inside Macedonia.[7] But in reality the powers of the Macedonians amounted to very little. Treaties were normally made in the king's name alone. The exceptional mention of the Macedonians in those with Eleutherna and Hannibal may connect with the reference to the Greek allies which occurs in both documents. There is moreover no hint anywhere in Polybius that the Antigonids had to take account of any popular rights; and though, following a long-standing custom, the Macedonians in contact with the king displayed an outspokenness in addressing him

---

[6] For a sceptical view of these rights see Errington 1978, 77–133: (D 17).

[7] See Walbank 1940, 265: (D 43).

which is quite unlike anything found in the other Hellenistic monarchies, frankness and power are by no means synonymous. The simple fact is that for all practical purposes the Antigonids were the state.

In its organization, too, Macedonia came increasingly to resemble the other Hellenistic monarchies. The king's Companions, prominent during the reigns of Philip II and Alexander, are not found after the latter's death, but the Friends (*philoi*), who constituted a Council of State in most kingdoms including Macedonia, are their Hellenistic counterpart. Like Philip II's Companions they were chosen from outside as well as inside the kingdom and they were in essence the king's men, personal to him; his successor need not retain them, and when the young Philip V wanted to assert his independence one of his earliest actions was to rid himself ruthlessly of the Friends whom he had inherited, some as guardians, from Antigonus III. The Friends constituted an important element in the royal court. As under Alexander, this court also continued to include Bodyguards (*somatophylakes*), a group of high-ranking officers who stayed close to the king night and day, except when assigned confidential duties, Royal Pages (*basilikoi paides*), the sons of nobles and others of high family, themselves future Friends and officers, and 'foster-brothers' (*syntrophoi*), boys from the same social group chosen to be brought up with the royal princes. We hear, too, of several posts paralleled in the bureaucratic and military structure of other kingdoms: the Secretary of State, the Treasurer, the Captain of the Bodyguard and the Captain of the Peltasts (a body of infantry resembling Alexander's hypaspists). Most of the evidence comes from the reign of Philip V, but in essentials the organization will no doubt already have existed under Antigonus II.

Economically Antigonid Macedonia benefited from a substantial growth in urbanization. Under Philip II and Alexander the highland areas – Elimiotis, Orestis, Lyncestis, Eordaea and Pelagonia – were still divided into cantons with virtually no cities, and though lower Macedonia was organized with communities consisting each of a city with its territory, only a few of these cities other than the Greek colonies along the coast were more than market towns; an exception to this, as excavations have shown, was the capital at Pella. Under Alexander's successors, however, cities multiplied. Cassander had initiated two important foundations, both probably in 316 – Thessalonica, a synoecism of several small towns at the head of the Thermaic Gulf, and Cassandreia, incorporating the cities of Pallene. Both had large Greek populations, but a growing national consciousness of being Macedonian is reflected in the fact that during the Antigonid period citizens of all Macedonian cities, whatever their origin, now style themselves Macedonians.[8] Outwardly the cities reveal the structure and institutions of Greek democratic states. Inscriptions containing decrees granting *asylia* (literally, freedom from reprisals (see below, p. 235)) to the temple of Asclepius at Cos in 242[9] provide evidence that Cassandreia had a council and Thessalonica a council and assembly, and since an assembly is also mentioned at Philippi and Amphipolis, it seems probable that all, including purely Macedonian cities like Pella and Aegae, possessed both institutions. Like cities elsewhere they were divided into tribes and demes, and inscriptions also mention generals, law-guardians (*nomophylakes*), treasurers, archons and priests. They carried on an active exchange of embassies with cities elsewhere and made honorific grants of *proxenia*[10] to citizens of those cities, just as if they were independent city-states. But this impression is quite misleading, for in fact they were wholly subservient to the king, who installed in them royal governors (*epistatai*), royal judges (*dikastai*) and other officials, whose control was exercised both indirectly and, when necessary, directly. Thus a letter written by Philip V to his representative in Thessalonica, Andronicus (*IG* x.2.1, no. 3) forbids the municipal authorities to interfere with the revenues of the temple of Sarapis without permission from the royal governor and judges; and under Antigonus II the decrees granting *asylia* to the Coan Asclepieum indicate that the decisions conveyed have the king's approval. Within these limits however the cities of Macedonia enjoyed local autonomy, administered their own funds and could even confer a local citizenship.

The full integration of the coastal cities as part of Macedonia both strengthened the kingdom economically and contributed to the growing hellenization which characterized Antigonus' reign. Under the regency Macedonia had lacked the lustre of a royal court; but both Antipater and Cassander maintained links with the Peripatetic school at Athens, and Cassander patronized the visual arts. The confusion of the two decades following his death ended all this, but under Antigonus II Pella once more became a minor centre of patronage and culture – though indeed Macedonia never possessed the wealth to compete with cities such as Antioch or Alexandria. Nevertheless, Pella extended its hospitality to many writers of distinction, in particular Aratus of Soli, who like Antigonus himself had been a pupil of the Stoic Menedemus. Aratus was the author of a famous and popular work, the *Phaenomena*, a

---

[8] The one apparent exception is Cassandreia; but the Cassandreians must also have considered themselves Macedonians, for a city decree of 242 conferring *asylia* on the Coan Asclepieum mentions the good will of Cos towards 'King Antigonus, the city of Cassandreia and all the rest of the Macedonians' (*SEG* XII.373).

[9] Herzog and Klaffenbach 1952, 1: (B 89).

[10] A *proxenos* was originally the representative of a foreign state in another city; but *proxenia* had by this time become a mainly titular honour.

Stoic poem on the physical universe, the rising and setting of the stars and the lore of weather-signs. Zeno, the founder of the Stoic school, had also taught Antigonus, but declined an invitation to come to Pella. Persaeus of Citium came in his place and stayed on as tutor to the king's son Halcyoneus. As a courtier and as a politician and general he found a career outside philosophy, ultimately committing suicide when as commander of the Acrocorinth in 243 he failed to prevent its seizure by Aratus (see below, p. 251). Persaeus' treatise *On Kingship* shows the current philosophical interest in the new monarchies. Other visitors to Pella were Timon of Phlius, who wrote lampoons, satyr-plays and various philosophical works, and Bion of Borysthenes, the wandering Cynic teacher and writer.

Even more important were the historians, who included Marsyas of Pella, author of a history of Macedonia and perhaps the first native writer of importance, and Antigonus' own half-brother Craterus, who published a collection of Athenian decrees with a commentary. But the main figure was Hieronymus of Cardia, the most outstanding and – as far as one can judge from fragments – the most reliable writer on the events from Alexander down to Pyrrhus' death in 272. Originally in the service of Eumenes of Cardia, he transferred his allegiance to Antigonus I after Eumenes' death and remained loyal to his house until his own death around 250. Other branches of literature also flourished at Pella; they included the works of the tragedian Alexander of Aetolia and Antagoras of Rhodes, author of a Theban epic. But the influence of Greek culture was not restricted to literature and philosophy: the discovery of several outstanding pebble mosaics at Pella, an impressive tomb with highly competent tomb paintings at Lefkadhia and the great Hellenistic palace at Vergina (Aegae) near the site of the tombs of the Macedonian kings are sufficient indication that at the higher levels at least Macedonia was now in no sense a cultural backwater; and continuing excavations at Pella are revealing an impressive Hellenistic town.[11]

III. MACEDONIA AND GREECE IN 272

The consolidation of Macedonia was impossible without security both against barbarian attacks from the north and against interference by Hellenistic rivals. In setting up his capital at Pella rather than in any of the coastal cities Antigonus asserted his return to a traditional policy

[11] On the Pella mosaics see Robertson 1965, 72–89: (B 312); 1967, 133–6 (B 313); Petsas 1965, 41–56: (B 311) Plates vol., pl. 139. Robertson dates them with some hesitation to the late fourth century under Cassander. On the Lefkadhia tomb see Petsas 1966: (J 239); Plates vol., pl. 671. On the palace at Vergina see Andronikos and Makaronas 1961: (J 172); Andronikos 1964: (J 171); Plates vol., pl. 69.

and also perhaps demonstrated his concern for the interior of his realm. Strong defences in the north, east and west were essential not only for Macedonia but (as the Gaulish invasion had showed) for Greece as well. On Antigonus' policy in Thrace no evidence survives; but it seems unlikely that he ceded the area east of the Nestus to Antiochus[12] in the settlement of 278 (see above, ch. 4, p. 116). The coins of Lysimacheia continued to feature Lysimachus, and that suggests that this area maintained an uneasy independence of both Macedonia and the Seleucids until the reign of Antiochus II. To the north the upper Axius valley was occupied by the kingdom of Paeonia; like the Molossians (and the Macedonians themselves) the Paeonians formed a commonalty (*koinon*) with a king. Paeonia had briefly recovered its independence at the time of the Gaulish invasion; at Olympia the *koinon* honours King Dropion as its 'founder' (*SIG* 394). Antigonus probably took no immediate steps to recover Paeonia, but that he did so later is shown by his foundation of a new city called Antigoneia, probably near Banja in the Axius valley. On the western frontier likewise the provinces of Tymphaea and Parauaea were left in Epirote hands. In all these three areas the indications are that Antigonus sought a quick settlement which would leave him free to concentrate on home affairs. Thessaly was more essential and its recovery was not long delayed. Delphic records show the Thessalians represented at Amphictyonic meetings even after the organization fell under Aetolian control in 277; but since throughout the third and early second centuries states directly under Macedonia normally withdrew their representatives from the Amphictyonic Council while it was dominated by the Aetolians, the absence of Thessalians from the Council from 276 onwards indicates that Macedonian control of Thessaly had been reimposed from that time onwards.

It was a basic principle of Macedonian policy to deny southern Greece to Ptolemy or any other rival power and for this purpose the minimal requirement was control of the sea-route by way of Demetrias, Chalcis and, if possible Piraeus, to Corinth. Philip V was later to dub Demetrias, Chalcis and Corinth the 'fetters of Greece'; they constituted the foundation of Macedonian power in the south of the peninsula. Antigonus had managed to hold on to these coastal strongholds even when he still did not yet control Macedonia and (probably since 280/79, when he was attacking Antiochus I) he had entrusted Corinth to his half-brother Craterus, whose command also took in Chalcis, the Piraeus (which defected during the war with Pyrrhus, but was recovered in 271/70) and several other states. Within this area Craterus governed almost as an independent viceroy.

The Macedonian system based on this command in Corinth derived

----

[12] So Tarn 1913, 168: (D 38); Beloch 1927, IV.2.355ff.: (A 5).

strength from the pro-Macedonian or Macedonian-controlled states of the Isthmus and the Peloponnese, where they served to counter the ambitions of Sparta. The long Spartan tradition of hostility to Macedonia was interrupted briefly following Antigonus' help to Areus during Pyrrhus' invasion; but Areus soon reverted to his earlier enmity and, subsidized by Egypt, showed himself in addition anxious to play the part of a Hellenistic king in a manner well outside the traditions of Sparta. Sparta's enemies were ranged in varying degrees of support on the side of Macedonia. Both Elis and Megalopolis had pro-Macedonian tyrants. In Elis, it is true, Aristotimus survived only six months before falling to the blows of tyrannicides; but at Megalopolis Aristodamus established himself more firmly and held power for around two decades. The chronology of his rule cannot be firmly ascertained; but one famous incident, the defeat and death of Areus' son Acrotatus while attacking Megalopolis, will belong to the later part of his reign (c. 255). The position in Argos is less clear. Aristippus, who had supported Antigonus at the time of Pyrrhus' attack, bears a name which suggests that he was a forebear of the later dynasty of Argive tyrants (see below, pp. 247–8), but that he himself exercised tyrannical power is not attested. Nor was Macedonian control continuous there, since in the 250s Argos was a centre for anti-Macedonian conspirators (see below, p. 243). Sicyon at this time fell under a series of tyrants, whose relation to Antigonus is not entirely clear. Cleinias, for instance, the father of the future Achaean leader Aratus, who exercised a beneficent autocracy during the early 260s, had close family links with both Ptolemy and Antigonus.

    Elsewhere Macedonian control was maintained with garrisons, as at Troezen, whence the Spartans were expelled c. 272, and at Megara. Corinth, it may be noted, though the centre of the Macedonian command, was itself a privileged city; on one occasion it can be seen exercising a vote on the Amphictyonic Council, and it retained coining rights.[13] The position at Athens is rather different. Athens' representation on the Amphictyonic Council between 277 and 265 need not in itself attest her independence, since she could be enjoying a specially privileged position like Corinth. But her independence is confirmed for 271/70 by the passing of a decree honouring the democrat Demochares in that year,[14] and for 270/69 when, in the archonship of Sosistratus, special honours were voted for Callias of Sphettus who, as a Ptolemaic mercenary captain, had brought help in liberating Athens at the time of the democratic rising against Demetrius Poliorcetes in 287 (see above, ch. 4, p. 108);[15] Athenian sympathies are also indicated by the treaty

13   Flacelière 1937, 200: (D 105).
14   Plut. X Orat. vit. 851 D (Attic archonship of Pytharatus).
15   On the date see, against Shear 1978: (C 62), Habicht 1979, 45–67: (D 91).

sworn with Aetolia in 272 (*SVA* 470).[16] The Piraeus, however, remained in Macedonian hands without a break.[17] The deprivation of their main harbour continued to be a constant irritation to the Athenians, which was ultimately to lead to war. Thus by 270 Craterus was in the firm possession of a considerable territory which included the Isthmus and Euboea, together with several key cities and fortresses, while further south, in the Peloponnese, a zone of Macedonian influence varying in intensity from city to city derived strong support from the tyranny in Megalopolis. Further north, on his western frontier, Antigonus left the Epirote monarchy undisturbed, probably seeing in it a counterweight against the Illyrians. A factor of more concern, since the defeat and death of Pyrrhus, was the growing strength and influence of the Aetolian League.

IV. THE RISE OF AETOLIA

The Aetolians occupied a rough and mountainous territory on the north shore of the Corinthian Gulf; their land was not rich and the inhabitants supplemented a scanty living derived from agriculture with piracy, brigandage and mercenary service. At the time of the Peloponnesian War they were loosely but effectively organized in three main tribes together with some sub-tribes; but either towards the end of the fifth century or early in the fourth, and certainly before 367, Aetolia had developed into a federal state possessing a central government and made up of units consisting of cities with their territories. In the third and second centuries, when evidence is fuller, there existed (though not perhaps in all parts of the federation) districts known as *tele*, intermediate between the central government and the individual cities. Examples are known of *tele* centring on Stratus and West Locris; the second of these possessed a local official called a boularch, so presumably it had its own local council.[18] There is no reason to suppose that this political reorganization brought any great change to Aetolian life in general; and for many purposes tribal affiliations clearly continued to be important.

The Aetolian League possessed a primary assembly consisting, it would seem, of all adult male citizens and meeting twice a year, once in spring at the so-called *Panaetolica*, which was held at various towns in turn, and again in autumn at Thermum, when the elections took place; in addition extraordinary meetings were called when required. The

---

[16] This belongs to a time when Athens was sending *hieromnemones* to the Amphictyonic Council. See Flacelière 1937, 190: (D 105).

[17] Pausanias' reference (1.26.31) to Olympiodorus Πειραιᾶ καὶ Μουννχίαν ἀνασῳσάμενος, is probably to be interpreted as a successful defence against Cassander's troops around 305, rather than as a recovery in 272; see Habicht 1979, 102–7: (D 91).

[18] Larsen 1968, 197: (A 33).

assembly had wide and democratic powers; it was responsible for striking alliances, admitting new members, conferring citizenship, despatching and receiving embassies and sacred delegates (*theoroi*), electing magistrates, passing laws – though a board of *nomographoi* was responsible for their periodic review and revision – and making war and peace. There was also a council (*boule, synedrion*) consisting of representatives whose number was proportionate to the military strength of the contingents furnished by the various cities, and this body stayed in permanent session. It provided continuity in the administration between meetings of the assembly and it served as a federal court; but its effectiveness was hampered by its size, since it contained over 1,000 councillors. Consequently there was also a smaller, elected body, the *apokletoi*, who acted as a permanent committee of the council under the presidency of the chief magistrate, the general. Magistrates were elected annually in autumn by the assembly meeting at Thermum. They consisted of the single general (*strategos*) who could be re-elected, but only after an interval, a secretary (and from a date not later than 207 a second secretary assigned to the council), a cavalry officer (hipparch), an *agonothetes* (to preside at the *Soteria* festival at Delphi) and a steward (*tamias*) or stewards. The large numbers taking part in both the assembly and the *synedrion* reflected democratic principles, but made them ineffective instruments for quick action and led to more and more decisions, including those affecting foreign policy, being taken by the *apokletoi*. In the course of the third century the administration of Aetolia thus became increasingly oligarchic.

Socially and economically Aetolia remained backward. Although the constituent units of the league were cities, these were mainly small. Aetolia proper was not highly urbanized and the more prominent Aetolian cities, such as Naupactus or Heraclea, were situated in areas which had been annexed to the league. Insofar as there was a capital it was at Thermum, which was little more than a temple and the site of an annual fair and festival. There and at Delphi the more important inscriptions were set up; but whether the Aetolian archives and treasury were also kept at Thermum is not recorded.

The Aetolians had won themselves great prestige by their courage in defending Delphi at the time of the Gaulish invasion (see above, ch. 4, p. 115), and this they exploited to gain possession of Delphi itself and increasingly to dominate the Amphictyonic Council which administered the shrine. During the sixty years following the Gaulish inroad the confederacy steadily expanded its territory, and this growth can be traced in broad outline through the increase in the number of votes on the Amphictyonic Council which were controlled by the Aetolians. This was brought about by their appropriating places on the Council which belonged by tradition to states now incorporated in the Aetolian League. Unfortunately our knowledge of the details of the process is hampered in various ways. In the first place the dating of many of the relevant documents is still controversial; indeed until the table of Delphic archons is firmly established many dates must remain subject to query. Secondly, although it is clear that any increase in the number of Aetolian delegates must imply the acquisition of, or at least a claim to, new territories, which these were on any particular occasion is often a matter for speculation, since the Aetolian delegates might come from any part of the confederation, regardless of which vote they were exercising; nor can one be sure that when the Aetolians lost their control of some territory entitled to send a *hieromnemon* to the Amphictyonic Council, they invariably abandoned their claim to its delegate. One must therefore envisage the possibility that the Aetolians maintained their claim to delegates representing lost territories, or in the case of an ally still sending *hieromnemones* in its own name that exiles were used as representatives.

For the period with which we are immediately concerned the picture is, however, fairly clear.[19] In 277, the year of Antigonus' victory at Lysimacheia, the first Amphictyonic list since the Aetolians took over Delphi shows them controlling two votes, and these are probably those of the Ozolian Locrians and Heraclea-on-Oeta.[20] The fact that the Thessalians still hold the presidency shows that they had not yet been reconquered by Antigonus (see above, p. 230), whereas their absence from the Council the next year must indicate that they had now once more come under Macedonia. In that year (276) the Aetolians control a third vote, which may be that of the Dolopians. By 272 they exercise five votes, probably after incorporating the Aenianes, and documents of 268 furnish the first evidence for their possessing six votes; the new acquisition is likely to have been Doris. Thus in under ten years the Aetolian Confederacy had extended its territory eastward as far as the Malian Gulf.

The Aetolians had a bad reputation in Greece and this largely outweighed such gratitude as was felt for their good services in preserving Delphi from the Gauls. This reputation has been relayed to posterity by the Achaean historian Polybius, who is directly or indirectly responsible for most of our information about a people which throughout most of the third and second centuries was the enemy of his native Achaea. There is however no reason to question his account

[19] The Amphictyonic lists from 277 to 193/2 are conveniently assembled in Flacelière 1937, 386–417: (D 105).

[20] Cf. Will 1979, 1.212: (A 67). The first list (archon Hieron) should be assigned to 277: cf. Klaffenbach 1939, 194: (D 107); and lists 2, 3 and 4 (Flacelière 1937, 386–7: (D 105), archons Aristagoras and Charixenus), consequently belong to 276 and 275.

(XVIII.4.8–5.2) of their regular addiction to privateering and their custom of allowing their nationals to participate in any war against any state, even where Aetolia was itself neutral and the belligerents their allies. Aetolian access to the Malian Gulf meant that the Aegean now became exposed to piratical attacks. In these circumstances other states frequently found it advantageous to secure from the Aetolians (as also from the other people much given to piracy, the Cretans) grants of immunity from legalized reprisals (*asylia*), which often meant in effect immunity from piratical outrage; and when in spite of such immunity piracy occurred (as it often did), it was helpful if in addition the injured party had previously received a grant of *isopoliteia* from Aetolia. *Isopoliteia* represented potential Aetolian citizenship which could be made actual if the individual to whom it was granted came to live on Aetolian territory, but it also served to give an injured party access to the courts of his assailants for the purpose of securing legal redress. Grants of *asylia* and *isopoliteia* were made to both individuals and communities; and complaints against their violation were sometimes heard by the Aetolian assembly acting as a federal court. Such grants were conferred by other states too, but they were especially valuable when made by peoples such as the Aetolians and Cretans for whom, often in consequence of their poverty or national traditions, piracy was a way of life. Willingness to make such grants may be regarded as evidence of a growing humanity during the Hellenistic period, and this is also exemplified by an increasing readiness to settle disputes by arbitration rather than in the old way by fighting (see further below, ch. 8, p. 313). But grants of *asylia* and *isopoliteia* were not without advantage to the Aetolians themselves, who could subsequently use the privileged cities as bases for depredations elsewhere.

The Aetolians also used grants of *isopoliteia* as a political means of extending their power. In addition to the direct annexation of contiguous areas revealed by the Amphictyonic documents and the bringing of neighbouring states under Aetolian influence without annexation – an example of this is the control exercised over Boeotia after 245 (see below, p. 249–50) – the Aetolians also attached many states to them by grants of *isopoliteia*, especially where they were separated geographically from the federation. Such grants were made at various times to Ceos, Cephallenia, Chios, Oaxus on Crete, and Lysimacheia, Cius and Chalcedon;[21] and *isopoliteia* was also employed in the Peloponnese, where Phigalea and Messene were linked to Aetolia in this way.[22] Much of the evidence for the use of *isopoliteia* by the Aetolians

---

[21] Cf. *SIG* 522=*SVA* 568; *SEG* 11.258+*SEG* XVIII.245 (Chios); *IC* II Vaxos, nos. 18 and 19 (Oaxus); Polyb. XVIII.3.11 (Lysimacheia, Cius, Chalcedon); for Cephallenia see Flacelière 1937, 284 n. 3: (D 105).   [22] *SIG* 572=*SVA* 485.

comes from a period later than that now under consideration. But already the Aetolians had exploited the years of Macedonian anarchy and Antigonus' preoccupation with the consolidation of his position at home and in Greece to extend their territorial base. The events of the next decade were to afford them new opportunities for expansion.

V. THE CHREMONIDEAN WAR

In the autumn of 268 Macedonian progress in southern Greece was interrupted by the outbreak of a war directed against the Macedonian positions there and led by Athens and Sparta. The main evidence for its outbreak is an inscription containing an Athenian decree moved by Chremonides who, along with his brother Glaucon, was one of a group of anti-Macedonian statesmen active in Athens at this time.[23] The decree (*SVA* 476), which is dated by the Athenian archonship of Peithidemus (268/7) and is accompanied by the text of the alliance now made between Athens and Sparta, accuses Antigonus of treaty-violation (though of which treaty or treaties is uncertain) and enumerates the allies lined up behind the two powers, namely Elis (now rid of its tyrant Aristotimus), the Achaean League (which had recently been refounded: see below, p. 244), Tegea, Mantinea, Orchomenus, Phigalea, Caphyae and some Cretan cities;[24] it also indicates that the movement was supported by Ptolemy II with whom Athens was already allied. The wording of the decree is redolent of panhellenic sentiment and recalls the glories of past struggles against those who have tried to enslave the cities, and another inscription from Plataea, containing a decree of the '*koinon* of the Greeks' honouring Glaucon, Chremonides' brother, for his solicitude towards the shrine of Zeus Eleutherios, provides further evidence of the extent to which the movement sought to recall the former great occasion when Athens and Sparta had fought together in unity to save Greece.[25] Thus the Chremonidean War (as it has been called from the name of the proposer of the decree) looked back to the struggle against the Persians as well as to Demosthenes and the Lamian War for inspiration in this new chapter in the fight against Macedonia for Greek freedom.

Why Ptolemy, who after his father's share in the Athenian revolt against Demetrius Poliorcetes (see above, ch. 4, p. 108) had remained inactive throughout the struggle between Pyrrhus and Antigonus, chose the early sixties to stir up a war against Macedonia is not recorded in our sources and has been a cause of much speculation. He may indeed,

---

[23] See Pouilloux, *Mélanges Préaux* 1975, 376ff.: (D 98); Étienne and Piérart 1975, 51ff.: (B 70); Habicht 1976, 7ff.: (D 60).

[24] Possibly Gortyn, Itanus, Olus, Aptera, Rhithymna, Polyrrhenia and Phalasarna; see, however, van Effenterre 1948, 203–4: (D 143); Heinen 1972, 143ff.: (A 21). For an alliance between Polyrrhenia and Phalasarna, instigated by Sparta, sometime before 275, see *SVA* 471.

[25] Étienne and Piérart 1975, 51ff.: (B 70).

as some have supposed, have been incited by Arsinoe II, who had retired to Egypt after her short-lived marriage to Ptolemy Ceraunus, and had there married Philadelphus, also her half-brother. But the reference in the decree of Chremonides to Ptolemy's acting 'in accordance with the policy of his ancestors and his sister' (lines 16–17) is perhaps to be interpreted mainly as a gesture of respect. Arsinoe had died two years earlier (in 270) and the hypothesis[26] that even after her death Ptolemy II continued to share her ambition to provide a kingdom for her son by Lysimachus seems less probable now that it is known that the Ptolemy who figures on various papyri and ostraca as co-regent with Philadelphus between 267 and 259, and who perished at the hands of Thracian soldiers in Ephesus after a revolt against the king, was not the son of Lysimachus.[27] If Arsinoe had a role in the Chremonidean War, it has certainly been much exaggerated, especially by those writing before the date of her death was known.

Others have argued that Ptolemy was induced to stir up a revolt against Macedonia from economic considerations and that he feared to see the Peloponnese dominated by Antigonus lest this should lead to the drying up of an important market for Egyptian corn, or indeed that he suspected Antigonus of seeking to build up the Piraeus into a trade rival of Rhodes and Delos.[28] Neither view is convincing. Indeed a far more likely explanation of the war is that Philadelphus was alarmed at the prospect of Antigonus' restoring Macedonian naval power, for this would constitute a manifest danger to the ring of outposts and the Aegean protectorate with which the Ptolemies sought to secure the approaches to Egypt.[29] A naval revival must have seemed all the more dangerous to Ptolemy in the light of the friendship now existing between Macedonia and the Seleucids. However, Ptolemy's motives are not easily discernible since after the initial impulse the assistance which he rendered to the allies was half-hearted and inadequate.[30] At the outset, however, the stimulus from Egypt struck an echoing note both at Athens, where the group around Chremonides cherished nostalgic hopes of achieving complete independence with the recovery of Piraeus, and also at Sparta, where Areus I clearly hoped himself to establish a domination over the Peloponnese.[31] The war was fought with vigour,

[26] Tarn 1913, 290ff.: (D 38); Sartori 1963, 117ff.: (D 101).

[27] On 'Ptolemy the Son' see RC, p. 75 (no. 14, l. 9); H. Volkmann, PW, 'Ptolemaios (20)', cols, 1666–7. His identity remains uncertain.

[28] See Tarn 1913, 241ff.: (D 38); Rostovtzeff 1953, I.215ff.: (A 52); and against this view Will 1979, I.180ff.: (A 67), analysing Ptolemaic foreign policy.

[29] Will 1979, I.220–1: (A 67).

[30] Hence Habicht 1979, 111–12: (D 91) argues that the main impetus for the war came, not from Ptolemy at all, but from Athens itself, bent on the recovery of the Piraeus.

[31] For dedications to Areus I see SIG 433 (by Ptolemy II); ISE I.54 (Orchomenus). But SIG 430 (Delphi) is a dedication to Areus II, the infant son of Acrotatus; see De Sanctis 1911–12, 267–77 (D 125); Flacelière 1937, 457: (D 105); contra Will 1979, I.223 (A 67); Oliva 1971, 215–16: (D 132).

except by Ptolemy; but it ended disastrously for the allies with the capitulation of Athens in the archonship of Antipater (perhaps 262/1).[32] Its significance lies in the fact that it was the last co-ordinated attempt of the two traditional leaders of Greece, Athens and Sparta, to raise a comprehensive movement of revolt against the common enemy.

No coherent account of the war survives and its course has to be reconstructed from isolated events recorded in often indifferent authorities. Antigonus' possession of Corinth and the Isthmus route prevented the Spartans and Athenians from linking up by land. The Spartans made several attempts to force their way through; the account in Pausanias (III.6.4–6) has been plausibly interpreted to imply three campaigns, in 267, 266 and 265, in the last of which Areus met his death.[33] The Macedonians in Corinth reinforced the Isthmus lines with a garrison on Mt Oneium[34] and directed attacks by land and sea against Athens. These attacks are illustrated by an inscription discovered in the temple of Nemesis at Rhamnus (which was in Athenian hands for at least the early part of the war). This document (*SEG* XXIV.154), which records honours voted at Athens to the general Epichares for his efforts directed towards getting in the grain and other services, furnishes evidence that Antigonus employed pirates against Attica, as he had done earlier against Cassandreia (see above, p. 221).[35]

The help accorded by Ptolemy was unimpressive. Probably in 268/7 he despatched his admiral Patroclus to Greece, where he may indeed have landed some troops in Attica in order to garrison one or other of the strongpoints, which have been identified as operative at this date, at Koroni, Heliupolis, Patroklou Charax on the island of Ghaidhouronisi and elsewhere;[36] but this is not certain for the only place on the mainland for which the actual presence of Ptolemaic troops is attested is Rhamnus. Patroclus certainly brought no expeditionary force to Attica nor did he furnish Areus with the help he had promised; inscriptions (*IC* III.iv.3; *OGIS* 44) show him operating from a base at Arsinoe (Coresia) on Ceos and active at Itanus in Crete and also in Thera, but on the mainland his collaboration was half-hearted and unsuccessful. Either Ptolemy lacked a firm commitment to the war he had provoked or he was diverted by unrecorded Macedonian naval activity in areas such as the Asia Minor

[32] Cf. Bousquet 1958, 77–82: (B 51); Heinen 1972, 180ff.: (A 21); Étienne and Piérart 1975, 59–62: (B 70), who show that since an Athenian *hieromnemon* last appears on the Amphictyonic Council in the year of the Delphic archon Pleiston and that this is in 262/1, Athens cannot have capitulated before that year.

[33] Cf. Diod. xx.29; Plut. *Agis* 3.4; Heinen 1972, 199–202: (A 21). A revolt by Galatian mercenaries in Antigonus' employ is mentioned in Just. *Epit.* xxvi.2 (cf. Trogus, *Prol.* 26).

[34] Cf. Stroud 1971, 143ff.: (B 207).

[35] For concern for the crops see also *IG* II².668, ll. 8–10 (265, archonship of Nicias of Otryne).

[36] Cf. McCredie 1966, 113–15: (D 93); Heinen 1972, 162–3 (with map on 164): (A 21).

coast which were more vital to his interests. Athens held out courageously for several years, but eventually was forced to capitulate, probably in 262/1. A Macedonian garrison was installed on the Museum hill, no doubt, as Pausanias says (III.6.6), as a condition of peace.[37] Whether the Piraeus had remained Macedonian throughout the war is not certain; but if not it certainly became Macedonian now.

While the war was going on in southern Greece, Alexander of Epirus, encouraged by his recent success in warding off an attack by the Illyrian king Mytilus, took advantage of Antigonus' preoccupation with Athens and Sparta to invade Macedonia; whether Ptolemy was behind this move is unknown. Antigonus withdrew briefly from Corinth to Macedonia and very soon Alexander was not merely expelled from that country but also from his own – though from his refuge in Acarnania he soon regained his throne (c. 260).[38] These events are perhaps to be connected with a treaty made about this time between Acarnania and Aetolia (SVA 480), regulating frontiers and establishing a mutual exchange of *isopoliteia* and rights of intermarriage and of the acquisition of land between citizens of the two states. A plausible hypothesis[39] attributes this temporary rapprochement of the two usually hostile states to the mediation of Alexander of Epirus, who may have played upon their shared fear of Macedonia to bring them together and engineer his own restoration.

The Chremonidean War probably had a sequel in a naval victory for the Macedonian fleet over that of Ptolemy. In two places Plutarch attributes a story about 'Antigonus the second' to the occasion of a sea-battle off Cos (though in a third passage, where he speaks of 'Antigonus the old man', he links it with a battle of Andros).[40] The battle of Cos was an important victory commemorated by Antigonus with the dedication of his flag-ship to Apollo. About its date there have been many hypotheses,[41] but if (as seems likely) it fell at the end of the Chremonidean War, it was probably fought in the spring of 261, since on the one hand it must come after the capitulation of Athens (since Antigonus received petitions in that city after his victory)[42] and on the other a Delian inscription dated to the archonship of Tharsynon (261) (IG XI.2.114) speaks of the existence of peace in the Aegean at the

[37] Cf. Apollodorus, FGrH 244 F 44 (archonship of Antipater).

[38] Just. Epit. XXVI.2.9–12, where Antigonus' defeat by Alexander is to be rejected as a doublet of his defeat by Pyrrhus' son Ptolemy during the war with Pyrrhus; nor will Antigonus' twelve-year-old son Demetrius have commanded the Macedonian army which invaded Epirus.

[39] Klaffenbach 1955/6, 46–51: (D 108).

[40] Plut. de seipsum landando 545B; apoph. regum 183 C; cf. Ath. V.209e; attributed to Andros in Plut. Pel. 2.4.

[41] Cf. Momigliano and Fraser 1950, 113–14: (D 34).

[42] Diog. Laert. IV.6.39 (life of Arcesilaus).

time. If Cos was fought in the spring of that year,[43] it may have been followed by a Macedonian attack on Miletus mentioned on another inscription (*Milet* 1.3, no. 139). The Ptolemaic admiral will have been Patroclus who, according to an anecdote in Phylarchus,[44] challenged Antigonus to meet him at sea. The date of Cos cannot however be regarded as firmly fixed; but if it does indeed belong to 261 it must be seen as setting the seal on Antigonus' victory in the Chremonidean War by delivering a severe blow to the naval power of Egypt. Ptolemy's poor showing in the war may indicate that Cos was not the only advantage that Antigonus' new fleet had brought him.

VI. THE RESULTS OF THE CHREMONIDEAN WAR

The Chremonidean War ended with a resounding victory for Macedonia, but the advantages which it undoubtedly brought to Antigonus were greater in some areas than others. The failure of Athens and Sparta to co-ordinate their attack left Corinth firmly in his hands, or rather in those of his half-brother Craterus. In addition Athens and Attica were now also under Macedonian control. Chremonides and Glaucon both escaped to Egypt, where they later pursued distinguished careers under Ptolemy II, and their place at Athens was taken by politicians loyal to Macedonia.[45] More immediately Macedonian officers, including an *epistates*, directly responsible to Craterus˙were installed in Attica with garrisons at several points – Munychia and the Piraeus, Sunium, Salamis and the frontier posts of Panactum and Phyle; and inscriptions show Antigonus appointing Macedonian officers to Athenian posts of hipparch or *strategos*, the appointment being subsequently ratified by the people.[46] For Athens it was indeed a time of humiliation. The activity of the assembly was curtailed and for several years few resolutions were passed which did not echo the wishes of Macedonia. The minting of coins was temporarily suspended,[47] and this together with the Macedonian control of the harbours and ships contributed to a progressive economic decline. The military defeat also coincided with the end of a cultural era. Zeno of Citium died around the end of the war and the comic poet Philemon about the same time. Philochorus stayed on in

[43] Antigonus' flagship which sprouted parsley and was therefore called the *Isthmia* (Plut. *Quaest. conv.* 676D) *may* be that dedicated after Cos; but, if we ignore the 'miracle', its name need not imply that the battle was fought in a year with an 'even' number in the Julian calendar (so Will 1979, I.225: (A 67); Tarn, *CAH* VII (1928), 862). The ship can equally well have been built at Corinth and so named as a compliment to the city (so Tarn 1913, 345: (D 38)).

[44] *FGrH* 81F1 = Ath. VIII.334a.

[45] See the later decrees of Salaminian cleruchs for Heraclitus (*SIG* 454), the Eleusinian decrees for Aristophanes (*SIG* 485) and the Athenian inscription honouring Phaedrus of Sphettus (*IG* II².682).   [46] *SEG* III.122–3.

[47] Cf. Hackens 1969, 706 and n. 2: (B 228).

Athens, but was executed for treasonable communications with Alexandria, and with his death the pursuit of Attic local history, with all its pride in past achievements, came to an end.[48] In 256/5 Athenian freedom was nominally restored;[49] but what this really meant is unclear. Perhaps the garrison was removed from the Museum hill;[50] but there was no relaxation of Macedonian control. Sparta suffered no comparable loss of freedom thanks to her geographical situation, but the failure of Areus' attempt to impose her hegemony on southern Greece was compounded by the death of Acrotatus while attacking Aristodamus of Megalopolis (see above, p. 231). Spartan weakness was deep-seated and is best considered in relation to the revolutionary movement which first made itself felt under Agis IV twenty years later (see below, pp. 252–5).

Antigonus' victory consolidated his hold on southern Greece and the Isthmus, but the situation further north was less satisfactory for Macedonia. During the Chremonidean War the Aetolians, nominally neutral, had in fact favoured the allies. An inscription shows them approaching Ptolemy and Antigonus impartially with a request for the granting of security to those attending the Pythian and Pylaic festivals;[51] but the recognition of the Alexandrian *Ptolemaieia*, which proclaimed Soter's divinity, by the Amphictyonic Council in 262/1, almost twenty years after the setting up of this festival, but coinciding with the capitulation of Athens,[52] can only indicate that the Aetolians were at the least unimpressed by the Macedonian victory in Attica and that they were leaning more decidedly to the side of Ptolemy. Meanwhile the League had been making further acquisitions. In the Delphic archonship of Damaeus (265/4) the Locrians continued to exercise one vote on the Amphictyonic Council, but from the next year (that of Damosthenes) this disappears and instead, under Damosthenes and Pleiston (262/1), the Phocian vote rises from two to three, an increase which evidently reflects the annexation of Epicnemidian Locris by Phocis.[53] From the archonship of Peithagoras (probably 260/59) onwards, however, Phocis is once more reduced to two votes, the lost vote having gone to Aetolia, which now has seven; the conclusion will be that Epicnemidian Locris has now joined the Aetolian Confederation, thus extending still further the Aetolian seaboard on the Straits of Euboea.[54] Shortly afterwards the Aetolian votes rise to nine, the additional votes probably representing the annexation by the League of the part of Phocis to the south around Mt Parnassus, and perhaps the western part of Phthiotic Achaea. The

---

48 Cf. Jacoby 1949, 107ff.: (B 22).   49 Euseb. *Chron.* II, p. 120.
50 Briscoe in Garnsey and Whittaker 1978, 149: (H 73).
51 *FD* III.1.479; cf. Heinen 1972, 139ff.: (A 21).
52 *ISE* II.75; Étienne and Piérart 1975, 59ff.: (B 70).
53 Cf. Klaffenbach 1926, 68–81: (D 81).
54 Cf. Flacelière 1937, 198: (D 105).

fact that the units making up the confederation were cities with their territory facilitated its acquisition of part of a state like Phocis or Phthiotic Achaea. The effect of these territorial acquisitions was to bring the Aetolians gradually nearer to the Pagasean Gulf. Also by extending the area controlled by Aetolia around the Malian Gulf they made it easier to threaten Macedonian communications with southern Greece. In these circumstances the continued control of Corinth became even more important. So long as this fortress was in the loyal hands of Craterus all was well; but, as events were to show, so great a concentration of power under one man might prove dangerous, should Craterus' eventual successor waver in his fidelity to the king of Macedonia.

The war in the Aegean appears to have been less decisive than that on land – though indeed there is little reliable evidence concerning the balance of naval power in the years following the end of the Chremonidean War. It has been widely assumed that the battle of Cos, whether it was fought in 261 or a few years later, dealt a decisive blow to the Ptolemaic control of the Aegean.[55] Delos, it is pointed out, now becomes the scene of Antigonid dedications;[56] no Ptolemaic nesiarch is attested after about 260:[57] and a number of inscriptions which mention a King Antigonus – from Syros, Ios, Amorgos, Cimolos and Cos (together with one similar inscription from Ceos mentioning no royal name)[58] – suggest that Macedonia was now the dominant power in the Aegean. This evidence is inconclusive, however. It is now agreed that no political conclusions are to be drawn from dedications on Delos, which was open to all parties for such a purpose, regardless of political affiliations.[59] The Nesiote League moreover continued to exist at least until the Second Syrian War between Antiochus II and Ptolemy II (see below, ch. 11, pp. 418–19), and this is hard to reconcile with the assumption that Ptolemy lost control of the seas at Cos; and indeed the royal register recorded a substantial war fleet in commission at the time of Ptolemy II's death, though this may have been built in 250.[60] There is furthermore no evidence that Antigonus himself intervened in the Second Syrian War nor that the mysterious naval battle of Andros (see below, pp. 248–9) was an event in that war. Finally it remains uncertain whether the inscriptions from the islands bearing the name of Antigonus belong to Antigonus II or Antigonus III, and until this can be determined

[55] Cf. Cary 1951, 137: (A 10); Huss 1976, 215–16: (F 133).
[56] For the foundation of the *Antigoneia* and the *Stratonikeia* (the latter named after Stratonice, the bride of his son Demetrius) by Antigonus in 253 see *IG* XI.2.287B, ll. 124ff.
[57] Cf. Merker 1970, 159ff.: (C 50).
[58] *IG* XI.4.1052 (Syros); XII.5.570 (Ceos); 1008 (Ios); XII.7.221–3 (Amorgos); Jacobsen and Smith 1968, 184ff.: (B 95) (Cimolos); *GDI* 3611 (Cos); cf. Will 1979, I.232, 238–9: (A 67).
[59] See Fraser 1960, 4ff.: (B 76); Bruneau 1970, 579ff.: (H 30); Will 1979, I.232–3: (A 67).
[60] Appian, *praef.* 10; *SB* VI.9215.

they cannot be safely used as evidence for a Macedonian thalassocracy in this decade. As far as one can tell Ptolemy suffered a substantial defeat at Cos, but it has yet to be shown that he had been ousted from his general control of the Aegean.

VII. ARATUS OF SICYON AND THE ACHAEAN LEAGUE

The dearth of evidence which renders the Macedonian role in the Aegean obscure during the years following the Chremonidean War is paralleled in southern Greece. There, as has been indicated, the peace left Antigonus firmly in control of the Isthmus, while a pro-Macedonian tyrant, Aristodamus, held Megalopolis as a bulwark against any initiative from Sparta. All seems to have remained quiet for about ten years. Then, in 251, in the Dorian town of Sicyon, which had recently been subject to several violent political changes, a significant event took place. Several years earlier, in 264, its ruler Cleinias, who was a guest-friend of both Antigonus and Ptolemy, had been murdered by one Abantidas, who set himself up as tyrant; Cleinias' seven-year-old son Aratus was rescued and lodged at Argos, where he grew up in safety. Twelve years later in 252 Abantidas was himself murdered by tyrannicides and when his father Paseas attempted to rule in his place he too fell at the hands of a certain Nicocles, who seized the tyranny for himself. There is no evidence that in themselves these changes had made much impression on Antigonus; certainly Nicocles, though not directly his man, was not hostile to Macedonia, for under his tyranny the royal stud continued to be maintained on Sicyonian territory.

Aratus was twenty in 251 and already busy plotting against the tyranny in Sicyon. He and a group around him, which included Ecdemus and Demophanes,[61] later famous as tyrannicides in their native city of Megalopolis and for the constitution which they set up in Cyrene,[62] seem to have gone about their plotting at Argos in complete freedom, which probably indicates that the city was not yet under its later pro-Macedonian tyrants. Relying on the guest-friendship of his family Aratus first appealed to Antigonus for assistance in liberating Sicyon; but he, while not rebuffing him, did nothing positive.[63] Evidently Aratus assumed that Antigonus had no special commitment

---

[61] Their names are variously recorded: Ecdemus and Demophanes (Polybius), Ecdemus (or Ecdelus) and Megalophanes (Plutarch), Ecdelus and Megalophanes (Pausanias).

[62] On the activity of Ecdemus and Demophanes at Cyrene see Polyb. x.22.2 and Plut. *Philop.* 1. On Magas' death (see Ch. 11, p. 419) his widow Apame called in Demetrius the Fair, a son of Demetrius Poliorcetes, but he was murdered at the instigation of her daughter Berenice, subsequently wife of Ptolemy III Euergetes. Whether the Megalopolitans were invited to collaborate with Demetrius (like them a pupil of Arcesilaus of Athens) or after his overthrow is uncertain. See Will 1979, 1.245–6: (A 67).   [63] Plut. *Arat.* 4.3.

to Nicocles and might therefore be willing to give support to the son of Cleinias. But when this was not forthcoming, he decided to act alone, and in May 251 by a daring coup carried out with the help of a private band of troops, he seized Sicyon; the tyrant fled and the liberators confiscated his property. The liberation of Sicyon was a signal for nearly 600 exiles, victims of Nicocles or of earlier tyrants, to return home, and faced with serious social and economic problems arising out of this Aratus took the bold and, as it proved, far-reaching step of uniting Dorian Sicyon to the Achaean League. His aim was to acquire for Sicyon the strength and stability that would come from belonging to a larger body; but the accession of Sicyon to the Achaean League was to prove the first move towards the transformation of an ethnic confederacy into a large body which was ultimately to embrace virtually the whole of the Peloponnese. How far it was the return of the exiles which led Aratus to take this step is not recorded; but insofar as they were all presumably enemies of tyranny, their restoration cannot have pleased Antigonus, who is indeed reported as eyeing Aratus with dislike because of the liberation of Sicyon.

The Achaean League had only recently been reconstituted. After being active as a federal body in the fifth century it had fallen into some obscurity from around the middle of the fourth century and little is recorded of its activities at that time. In 280, however, the cities of Dyme, Patrae, Pharae and Tritaea came together, and in 275/4 Aegium, which controlled the federal shrine of Zeus Homarios, rejoined the confederacy, followed shortly afterwards by Bura, Ceryneia (both of which had been under tyrants), and, it would appear, Leontium, Aegeira and Pellene; an inscription (*SEG* 1.74) also shows Olenus joining as an eleventh member after 272, but by the time Polybius was writing that city no longer existed. Originally the revived league elected two generals annually, but in 255/4 the constitution had been changed to provide for the appointment of a single annual general, who entered office in May and who might not be elected in two consecutive years; this move, for which the Aetolian League was perhaps the model, made for greater efficiency while maintaining safeguards against a concentration of too much power in one man's hands. The first holder of the single office was Margus of Ceryneia, a man clearly most influential in the early years, but who then lapses into obscurity until Polybius reports his death in action in 229.

Originally meetings of the League had taken place at the shrine of Zeus Homarios outside Aegium; but from 255 onwards the assembly met in the city of Aegium. According to Polybius (II.37.9–11) the Achaeans had 'the same laws, weights, measures and coinage as well as the same magistrates, council-members and judges'; but there is some exaggeration in this statement, for the cities kept their own laws in addition to those of the federation, and though their weights and coins followed the Aeginetan standard, throughout the third century all minting was done by the separate cities, federal currency appearing only from about 190 onwards. There were federal magistrates including (besides the general) ten *damiurgoi*, a secretary and a hipparch, as well as an under-general (*hypostrategos*) and an admiral, the former apparently responsible for commanding the forces of a district (*telos*), such as those existing in Aetolia.

There was also a primary assembly, which held four meetings a year (*synodoi*), open to all men of military age,[64] at which the federal council (*boule*), open to men aged 30 and over, and magistrates were also present. The magistrates are referred to collectively as the *synarchiai* and include the *damiurgoi* who formed a board along with the general. Elections were held annually, in the spring during most of the third century; but at some date after 217 (or in that year) the time of the elections was changed to autumn so that, as in Aetolia, generals entered office at the end of the campaigning season and could, if necessary, devote the following winter to military preparations. It was perhaps at the same time as this change was made that a new kind of meeting was introduced. Henceforth, in addition to the regular *synodoi* special meetings might be summoned, in certain clearly defined circumstances, and these 'summoned meetings' were called *synkletoi*. The only occasion when a *synkletos* might (and indeed must) be summoned was to decide on war or alliance or to receive a communication from the king of Macedonia (at the time when Achaea was a member of the Hellenic Symmachy presided over by him: see below, ch. 12, pp. 467–8) or, in the second century, after Achaea had switched its allegiance to Rome, to receive a written communication from the Roman Senate. Such special meetings normally consisted (like *synodoi*) of all men of military age, but meetings of a more limited composition (e.g. men of thirty or over) could be summoned in certain circumstances. Since the League was often involved in war the army could act, and on several occasions is known to have acted, as an assembly of the people. The changes mentioned above reflected the more delicate diplomacy necessitated by the domination of powerful states such as Macedonia or Rome; and the clear definition of the circumstances in which a *synkletos* was to be called protected the Achaeans against dislocation of ordinary life by the mischievous convocation of special meetings, but also against the rushing through of ill-considered and dangerous measures at ordinary assemblies. These

---

[64] The composition of the Achaean assembly has been much debated. For the evidence and arguments in support of the interpretation given here see Walbank 1979, III.406–14: (B 37).

met normally at Aegium, but in the second century they began to be held in other cities as well.

Polybius praises the Achaean League as a political system distinguished by equality, freedom of speech and genuine democracy, and its institutions give some grounds for the claim.[65] Nevertheless officeholders appear to be drawn from a fairly narrow group of families, probably belonging to the landowning class; nor is it likely that poorer citizens could habitually make the journey to the assembly at Aegium (or elsewhere) four times a year. It is noteworthy that a second-century inscription from Olympia recording a boundary decision between Sparta and Megalopolis refers to the democratic constitution of Achaea but links it with the word *eunomia* ('orderly government'), which is elsewhere characteristic of oligarchic governments. Socially the Achaean League favoured stability and the *status quo* against calls for land-distribution or debt-cancellation. It was to this confederation that Aratus now united Sicyon and in which he was subsequently to play a major role.

VIII. ANTIGONUS, CORINTH AND ARATUS

Shortly after uniting Sicyon with Achaea Aratus received a gift of twenty-five talents from 'the king', but Plutarch who reports this (*Arat.* 11.2) leaves it uncertain which king is meant – Antigonus or Ptolemy. Either is possible. Ptolemy later became Aratus' paymaster; but Antigonus, though irritated that a young man had acted against Nicocles on his own initiative, may have hoped to buy his support. Whichever the donor was, Aratus used this money to ransom Sicyonian prisoners of war. It thus did nothing towards solving the problems created by the quarrels between the returned exiles and the present occupiers of their land, and consequently soon afterwards and probably in 251/50 Aratus undertook a voyage to Egypt to solicit support from Alexandria. He arrived there after an adventurous voyage, in the course of which bad weather forced his ship to put in at a port on the Macedonian-held island of Andros, and Aratus himself narrowly escaped capture by fleeing to the larger neighbouring island of Euboea. From Ptolemy Philadelphus Aratus obtained a gift of forty talents immediately and the promise of 110 talents in instalments, a method of payment no doubt designed to give the donor a chance to observe whether he was going to receive his money's worth. Antigonus is said to have tried to counter this diplomatic setback by some remarks delivered at a dinner in Corinth, in which he cast doubts on Aratus' attachment to Ptolemy and alleged that 'now that he has been behind the scenes and

[65] Polyb. II.38.6; 44.6; IV.6.5; XXII.8.6; XXIII.12.8; cf. *SIG* 665.

observed that everything in Egypt is play-acting and painted scenery, he has come over entirely to us'.[66] The anecdote is dubious; but if there was some such attempt to discredit Aratus with Ptolemy, it had little success. Meanwhile, either before or after the liberation of Sicyon, Antigonus suffered a much more serious setback when Ecdemus and Demophanes assassinated Aristodamus and liberated Megalopolis, the important outpost of Macedonian power in the Peloponnese.[67] It was perhaps in response to this that Antigonus helped Aristomachus to set up a tyranny at Argos, which was to prove for many years a strong support for Macedonia, and a bulwark against the extension of Achaean power in the Peloponnese.[68]

The fall of Aristodamus was a serious matter: but worse was to come. At some date around 250 Antigonus' brother Craterus, the governor of Corinth, died and Antigonus assigned his command to Craterus' son Alexander, thus creating the impression of a dynastic succession; and shortly afterwards, perhaps in 249, Alexander revolted and declared himself independent of Macedonia.[69] An inscription from Eretria (*IG* XII.9.212), honouring a Macedonian Arrhidaeus, one of his supporters, gives Alexander the title of king. This revolt was a disaster of the first magnitude for Antigonus, for it deprived him of his two chief garrison towns, Chalcis and Corinth – though not indeed of Piraeus which appears soon afterwards under a Macedonian general loyal to Antigonus and independent of the Corinthian command. To win support in Euboea Alexander withdrew the Macedonian garrisons from the cities, as a convincing restoration of the same Eretrian decree records; it was a gesture recalling that of his grandfather Demetrius I in 304.[70] The Euboean League was also revived. Although it cannot be proved, it is likely that Ptolemy was behind these events. Plutarch (*Arat.* 18.2) refers to attacks made by Aratus against Alexander, which evidently date to the time before the viceroy revolted from Antigonus, and may indeed represent a *quid pro quo* for the Ptolemaic subsidy to Achaea and were

[66] Plut. *Arat.* 15.3.

[67] On the subsequent activity of these two men at Cyrene, where they established a new constitution, see above n. 62.

[68] Paus. VIII.10.5 records a battle of Mantinea which, if it ever took place, belongs about this time. According to his account the Spartans under Agis besieged Megalopolis but were defeated near Mantinea (with the loss of Agis) by a combined army of Mantineans, Megalopolitans under Lydiades (the later tyrant) and Leocydes, and Achaeans and Sicyonians under Aratus. This story presents so many difficulties (e.g. Agis did not die at Mantinea, Aratus would hardly command the Achaean army when so young, the alignment of Achaea and Sicyon with Megalopolis against Sparta is highly improbable) that it is best dismissed as unhistorical. See Urban, 1979, 38–45: (D 117) against Beloch 1927, IV.2.253–7: (A 5).

[69] Many scholars date Alexander's revolt to 252 (cf. Will 1979, I.316–18: (A 67)); but the order of events in Trogus, *Prol.* 26, on which this view rests, is not chronological. For the arguments in favour of dating the revolt *c.* 249 see Urban 1979, 14ff.: (D 117).

[70] Cf. Picard 1979, 272–3: (B 252).

possibly one of the factors which persuaded Alexander to rebel. When, shortly afterwards, the Achaeans made an alliance with Alexander, now an independent ruler, these attacks naturally ceased.[71]

Antigonus did not let his nephew's defection go unchallenged. An Athenian inscription (*ISE* 1.23) honouring Aristomachus of Argos shows that for some time Macedonian attacks were levelled against Corinth from Argos and Athens; but evidently the balance of the fighting favoured Alexander, for the conflict ended in a peace secured by payments to Alexander by Aristomachus.[72] A Salaminian decree honouring Antigonus' general in the Piraeus (*SIG* 454) shows Alexander using pirates to put pressure on the Athenians during this struggle.[73] Whether the Megalopolitans shared in the attacks on Corinth is not recorded; the absence of any reference to Megalopolis in the Athenian decree for Aristomachus is not evidence that they did not, for there was no reason for the Athenians to mention Megalopolis in that context.

Antigonus' failure to shake Alexander's power by these attacks from Athens and Argos was in contrast to the growing strength and prestige of the Aetolians who about this time made a public gesture designed to assert their position of eminence in central Greece, their influence at Delphi and their past services to Greece generally. In the year of Polyeuctus' archonship at Athens (either 247/6 or, more probably, 246/5)[74] the Aetolians reorganized the annual Delphic *Soteria*, commemorating the delivery of the shrines from the Gauls in 279, as a panhellenic festival, to be celebrated every fourth year; its general acceptance would be tantamount to an admission by the Greek cities of the Aetolian right to control Delphi and the Amphictyonic Council, which had the responsibility for administering the festival both before and after its transformation.[75] In its expanded form the *Soteria* was first held in 245/4; and it was also in 245 that Antigonus established two new festivals concerned with the dedication of vases at Delos, the *Paneia* and the *Soteria*. Unfortunately the occasion which prompted this celebration is not known. If the naval battle of Andros in which 'the old man' Antigonus defeated Sophron (who was perhaps the man mentioned on an inscription from Labraunda and so possibly a Ptolemaic governor of Caria) was fought about 246, the new festivals may commemorate that

[71] Plut. *Arat.* 18.1.

[72] Aristomachus remained a supporter of Antigonus, but he preferred to keep the war away from his own frontiers.

[73] Brulé 1978, 3–6: (H 29) argues that they were Cretans.

[74] Cf. Pélékidis 1961, 53ff.: (D 96) (247/6); Nachtergael 1977, 211ff.: (E 113) (246/5).

[75] For the terms of the invitation and its acceptance see *SIG* 408 (Athens); *SIG* 402 – better Wilhelm 1922, 7: (B 174); cf. Robert 1933, 535–7: (B 136) – (Chios); *FD* III.1.481 (one of the Cyclades), 482 (Tenos), 483 (Smyrna); cf. Flacelière 1937, 133ff.: (D 105).

victory;[76] but that would depend on assuming that Macedonia was involved in the Laodicean War, and for this there is no evidence. The date of the battle of Andros must still be regarded as uncertain; indeed, despite Plutarch's reference to Antigonus as 'the old man' the possibility cannot be entirely excluded that the battle was fought and won by Antigonus III. Alternatively, then, the vase festivals were instituted to celebrate some unrecorded victory on the northern frontiers of Macedonia. Trouble there in the immediately preceding years would also serve to explain Antigonus' strangely indirect and ineffective reaction to the revolt of Alexander the son of Craterus. A suggestion that the Delian foundations were intended as a response to the Aetolian reorganization of the *Soteria* at Delphi[77] seems on the whole less likely, for a vase-festival at Delos would hardly compete in Greek estimation with a penteteric festival at Delphi; and in any case even on this explanation the vase festivals would require some nominal success to celebrate.

In 245 Aratus, now twenty-six years of age, was elected general of the Achaean League for the first time. His generalship saw the initiation of an aggressive policy towards the Aetolians, who had attempted a coup at Sicyon shortly before its liberation from Nicocles in 251. Aratus took a raiding party across the Corinthian Gulf into Locris and Calydon, and at the same time persuaded the Boeotians who, ever since the annexation of southern Phocis (above, p. 241) had made the Aetolians into neighbours, had regarded them with suspicion, to ally themselves with Achaea and to attack Aetolia. This proved disastrous. The Aetolians quickly retaliated by invading Boeotia, and though the Boeotian general Abaeocritus appealed to Aratus for help and Aratus marshalled an army reputedly of 10,000 men (an impossibly large figure), before he could bring it over the Isthmus of Corinth to Abaeocritus' support, the Boeotian general and 1,000 of his men had been defeated and had perished at Chaeronea. Boeotia, shattered by this blow, at once capitulated and allied itself to Aetolia. The military weakness of Boeotia at this time is confirmed by a federal law on military preparedness mentioned in a decree from Thespiae, which required the cities to provide military instruction for the boys;[78] clearly such measures had come too late. It was probably now that Boeotia was obliged to surrender Opuntian Locris, which she had annexed in 272, though she

---

[76] For the battle of Andros see Trogus, *Prol.* 27; Plut. *Pel.* 2; T. Larsen on *P. Haun.* 6; Momigliano and Fraser 1950, 107–18: (D 34). On Sophron ('Sophrona' was Müller's correction of the MS of Trogus 'Oprona') see Crampa 1969, no. 3, and Habicht's review, 169: (B 60). For a date *c.* 246 see Tarn 1913, 378ff.: (D 38); *contra*, Bikerman 1938, 368–83: (D 3). For the view that Andros was a victory by Doson see Merker 1960, 39–52: (B 240).

[77] So Will 1979, 1.323: (A 67). [78] Cf. Roesch 1972, 66–7: (D 84).

was allowed to keep her representation on the Amphictyonic Council.[79] Thus the effect of Chaeronea was to strengthen the power of Aetolia; and while it cost Achaea an ally, it can hardly have given any satisfaction to Antigonus.

In the same year (245), however, Antigonus had an unexpected stroke of good fortune. Alexander of Corinth died, and his widow Nicaea yielded to Antigonus' proposal that she should marry his son Demetrius, who was presumably to discard his existing wife Stratonice, the sister of Antiochus II. According to the rather sensational account in Plutarch, on the day of the wedding Antigonus left the procession, made his way up the Acrocorinth and by sheer bluff had himself admitted to the citadel. Once master of this he installed the philosopher Persaeus as governor, with Archelaus as garrison-commander under him.[80] The wedding was abandoned, Nicaea was jettisoned and Stratonice reinstated for at any rate another five years (see below, ch. 12, p. 446). With his seizure of Acrocorinth Antigonus also recovered the rest of Alexander's splinter-kingdom including Euboea and the fortress of Chalcis. The Euboean League was suppressed and Macedonian garrisons were once again introduced into the cities of the island.[81] This coup by Antigonus supervening on the defection of Boeotia from their alliance was a serious setback to Aratus and the Achaeans, who had also to take account of a continuing Aetolian interest in the western Peloponnese, which constituted a potential threat to the League.

In the first place a Messenian decree (*SVA* 472) records the establishment, in the years immediately before 240 and perhaps in 244, of *isopoliteia* and a treaty of mutual assistance between Messenia and Phigalea, states which had hitherto been at loggerheads despite the fact that both were friends of Aetolia. The agreement, reached at the instigation of the Aetolians and the Phigaleans, served to consolidate the Aetolian position in the south-western part of the Peloponnese. About the same time Lydiades of Megalopolis made himself tyrant of that city, probably with Macedonian help, since he is later a supporter of Antigonus and Demetrius II. At some time during his tyranny he ceded Alipheira to Elis, for reasons which Polybius does not specify;[82] it could have been for help given at the time he became tyrant or for some other reason later, such as the ransoming of prisoners.[83] Elis must also have gained possession of Triphylia at this time, since that area was subsequently returned to the Achaean League, of which Megalopolis was by then a member. Whether this more or less peaceful penetration was accompanied by Aetolian raids depends on the dates attached to

[79] Cf. Klaffenbach 1939, 199 n. 2: (D 107); Beloch 1927, IV.2.432: (A 5).
[80] Bengtson 1964–7, II.354–5: (A 6).   [81] Picard 1979, 274–8: (B 252).
[82] Polyb. IV.77.9–10.   [83] Urban 1979, 87 n.412: (D 117).

various incursions into the Peloponnese mentioned by our sources out of context. It is on the whole more likely that these attacks occurred a year or two later (see below, pp. 254–5).

Hemmed in by Elis to the west, by the new tyranny at Megalopolis to the south and by Macedonian Corinth to the east, the Achaeans depended for any further expansion on some new initiative; and from the time Antigonus recovered Acrocorinth Aratus set about working on a bold plan to take it from him. This project came to fruition at midsummer 243 when, with the help of traitors within the garrison and leading a small force of 400 men, he penetrated the city by night and by the use of speed and great audacity took the citadel after only a little fighting. Persaeus, the Macedonian governor, overwhelmed with guilt at its loss, committed suicide.

At one blow Aratus had thus wholly reversed the balance of power in southern Greece. Corinth, with its two ports of Cenchreae and Lechaeum, giving access to the two seas, now joined the Achaean League, followed quickly by other states. A fragmentary inscription from the Asclepieum at Epidaurus (*SVA* 489) contains part of the agreement by which Epidaurus now became a member of the Achaean League; enough of it survives to show that freedom from garrisons, the maintaining of the constitution, the laws and the lawcourts, and the settlement of disputes were among the matters dealt with. Besides Epidaurus, Megara and Troezen both joined Achaea, thus establishing federal authority firmly on the Saronic Gulf and thrusting a wedge of hostile territory between Antigonus' nearest outposts in Attica and the tyrants in Argos and Megalopolis. It has been estimated[84] that the territory now controlled by the League amounted to 5,500 km², and this sudden accession of strength to Achaea was as unwelcome to the Aetolians as it was to Antigonus. According to Polybius,[85] Antigonus thereupon entered into a compact with the Aetolians to partition Achaea; but neither party took any immediate action. It is at least possible that a parallel agreement between Aetolia and Alexander II of Epirus to divide up Acarnania,[86] which Polybius twice mentions along with the proposed partition of Achaea, belongs to the same date and was countenanced by Antigonus against his immediate interest in the hope of obtaining Aetolian help against the Achaeans.[87]

Meanwhile the Achaeans, having thus given proof of their ability to deal Macedonia a substantial blow, cemented their relations with Alexandria by electing Ptolemy III as leader (*hegemon*) of the League,[88]

---

[84] Beloch 1925, IV.1.621 n. 3: (A 5).   [85] Polyb. II.43.10; 45.1; IX.34.7; 38.9.
[86] Polyb. II.45.1; IX.34.7; cf. Just. *Epit.* XXVIII.1.1.
[87] Alternatively, it may be slightly earlier at the time of the revolt of Alexander of Corinth.
[88] Plut. *Arat.* 24.4.

probably an honorary post – despite the reference to leadership by land and sea – and one designed mainly to indicate gratitude for past, and the expectation of future, subsidies; and it was perhaps with Ptolemaic encouragement that, in the spring of 242, Aratus launched an attack over the Isthmus against Attica, in the course of which he raided the island of Salamis. It was no doubt as an act of policy that, whereas he had enslaved the Macedonian prisoners captured at Corinth, he now chose to release without ransom the free citizens whom he took in Attica. About this time the Achaeans made an alliance with Sparta, the old enemy of Macedonia.

IX. AGIS IV OF SPARTA

The death of Areus near Corinth in the Chremonidean War had deprived Sparta of an ambitious and aggressive leader, and that of his son Acrotatus in an attack on Megalopolis was a further blow. But quite apart from the loss of individual leaders Sparta in the mid third century faced serious economic difficulties, which would in any case have made it difficult for her to fulfil the kind of role which Areus had envisaged. Already at the time when Aristotle was writing his *Politics*, internal developments at Sparta had led to a great concentration of wealth, especially in the hands of heiresses, and a consequent decline in the number of citizens to around 1,000;[89] and since then this trend had become more pronounced. Its causes cannot be confidently identified, but it is not unlikely that one factor was the wealth brought back by mercenaries returning from abroad. This had been used to buy up land, thus reducing still further the number of those with sufficient property to qualify for citizenship. When in 244 or 243 Agis IV ascended the Eurypontid throne, the number of full Spartiates had fallen to 700, and of these perhaps about a hundred were extremely rich. If we can believe Phylarchus,[90] half the land now belonged to women.

Agis' primary aim was probably to win power for Sparta and glory for himself; but he saw that any revival of Spartan military strength depended on carrying through a radical programme including economic and social changes capable of restoring the citizen body to an effective size. His proposals were related to that end. For the year 243/2 one of his followers, Lycurgus, was elected to the ephorate and he put forward measures to implement Agis' radical plans, representing them however as the reintroduction of the ancient Spartan way of life, known and venerated as the system of Lycurgus, the traditional and somewhat shadowy Spartan lawgiver. His programme provided for the division of

[89] Arist. *Pol.* II.9.1270a15ff.   [90] Plut. *Agis* 7.5.

the central part of Laconia, the 'city land' (*politike chora*) lying between Pellana, Sellasia, Taygetus and Malea, into 4,500 lots, which were to be assigned to dispossessed Spartiates and, since there were not enough of these, to other selected 'inferiors' (*hypomeiones*),[91] *perioikoi* and even foreign residents, to make up the number. Similarly 15,000 lots were to be created in perioecic territory and assigned to landless *perioikoi* capable of bearing arms. The ancient messes, the *syssitia*, which had fallen into desuetude, were to be revived to the number of fifteen in all and with a membership of 200 or 400, and the traditional Spartan *agoge* with its organization of the boys into age-groups was to be restored. After being passed in the assembly, the *apella*, these proposals were rejected by a small majority in the council, the *gerousia* – according to Plutarch (*Agis* 11.1) by one vote (though in a council of thirty that is not possible unless someone was absent). Since the Agiad king Leonidas, the successor of Acrotatus' son Areus II, who died as a child, was behind the opposition, Lycurgus had him indicted for having married a foreign wife and deposed, his place being taken by Cleombrotus, Leonidas' son-in-law.

When the new board of ephors for 242/1 proved sympathetic to the rich and reinstated Leonidas (who had taken sanctuary in the temple of Athena of the Brazen House), Agis and Lycurgus had them expelled from office and Leonidas fled to Tegea. The new board of ephors which replaced those deposed contained Agis' uncle Agesilaus and he, Plutarch records, then carried through the legislation necessary to cancel debts, but not the land-distribution essential for the creation of new citizens and the strengthening of the numbers of *perioikoi*. The young men supported Agis; but the poorer citizens generally, once their condition was ameliorated by the cancellation of the debts which burdened their property and threatened their status as citizens, were reluctant to share with others the privileges which citizenship conferred, and the rich naturally resisted any reduction in the size of their estates. Consequently the creation of the new lots and the proposed increase in the size of the citizen body, which was essential to the fulfilment of Agis' ambitions, were postponed; and at this moment the internal course of the revolution was interrupted by events outside.

In response to the compact between Antigonus and the Aetolians and perhaps too as a means of countering the seizure of the tyranny at Megalopolis by Lydiades (see above, p. 250), an event which threatened both Sparta and the Achaean League, Aratus had contrived an alliance between these two states; the exact date is uncertain and it may have been before Agis' accession. The first appeal to the terms of this alliance came, however, in 241 when the Aetolians, either urged on by Antigonus or

[91] The *hypomeiones* probably included men of non-citizen origin as well as dispossessed citizens: cf. Oliva 1971, 177–8: (D 132).

perhaps alarmed at an unsuccessful attempt by Aratus to take the town of Cynaetha,[92] which will at this time have been under the control of their allies in Elis, invaded the Peloponnese by way of Boeotia and the Megarid. Learning in advance of their proposed invasion Aratus appealed to Sparta, and Agis was sent north with a Spartan army. Evidently he had already made some progress in drilling and organizing this force, for its well turned out appearance inspired popular admiration and some alarm in Aratus and the richer element in the cities of Achaea. The meeting of the two armies at Corinth was followed by a council of war, at which Aratus imposed his view that a pitched battle should be avoided; and soon afterwards he dismissed both his own forces and those of Agis. Social revolution was not without its advocates in many cities, and unwillingness to let Agis' army advertise the Spartan movement too widely may help to account for Aratus' dismissal of Agis and his army. Plutarch (*Agis* 14) emphasizes the suspicion evinced by the rich in Achaea for his innovating ways. The expedition heralded Agis' downfall, however, for he arrived back in Sparta to find Agesilaus moving towards a tyranny. Shortly afterwards his political enemies seized power, recalled Leonidas, expelled Agesilaus and drove Agis to take sanctuary in the temple of Athena of the Brazen House. Cleombrotus was spared and went with his wife into exile, but Agis was tricked into leaving sanctuary and, along with his mother and grandmother, who had supported his plans, was executed. In consequence the completion of the Spartan revolution was postponed for nearly a decade and a half.

Shortly after Agis' dismissal by Aratus, the Aetolians marched over the Isthmus into the Peloponnese unresisted. But when they attacked Pellene in eastern Achaea, Aratus fell upon them as they plundered the town, inflicting a defeat and heavy losses. This invasion, which thus ended in disaster for the Aetolians, was probably not their only incursion into the Peloponnese about this time. Polybius mentions, unfortunately out of context, several Aetolian raids associated with outrages against temples, which should no doubt be dated to this period and perhaps to the year 241.[93] They include an invasion of Laconia by Charixenus and Timaeus and the plundering by Timaeus of the temple of Poseidon at Taenarum and the temple of Artemis at Lusi – which perhaps indicates an approach by way of Elis and Messenia. A passage in Plutarch (*Cleom.* 18.3) speaks of the Aetolians carrying off 50,000 slaves from Laconia, perhaps on this occasion. The figure is improbably high, but the success of these raids may reflect the military weakness of Sparta following the abrogation of Agis' reforms. There were also Aetolian

    [92] Polyb. IX.17; cf. Walbank 1936, 64–71: (D 74).   [93] Polyb. IV.34.9; IX.34.9.

attacks on the temple of Poseidon at Mantinea led by Polycritus and on the Argive Heraeum led by Pharycus. In 241 the tyrant of Argos was a Macedonian client, but this need not have weighed greatly with an Aetolian raiding party against the attractions of easy plunder.

X. ANTIGONUS' LAST YEARS

Except in encouraging the Aetolians to attack Achaea and Sparta, Antigonus was strangely inactive in southern Greece during the years following Aratus' seizure of the Acrocorinth in 243. He may have been distracted by trouble on the northern frontiers which has not been recorded in the sources; but he was by now an old man and perhaps no longer able to react energetically to provocation. However this may be, it was probably in 241/40 that peace was made between Antigonus and Achaea and also between Achaea and Aetolia, perhaps all as part of a single settlement.[94] This did not, however, deter Aratus from continuing his drive against Argos and Athens. For a peace-time attack against Aristippus, Aristomachus' successor as tyrant in Argos, the Achaeans were arraigned, by some procedure which is not explained, before a Mantinean court (Mantinea being at this time an independent city) and were required to pay as damages the perhaps nominal sum of 30 minae.[95] This attack probably took place in 240 and in the same year Aratus raided Athens and the Piraeus, the latter several times, though always unsuccessfully. Already, perhaps, before peace was made with Aetolia he had gained possession of Cynaetha.[96]

In the winter of 240/39 Antigonus died. His long reign had given Macedonia time to recover from the weakness and devastation of the years between Cassander's death and 276, and he had encouraged this recovery by carefully husbanding Macedonian resources and manpower and by making use of mercenaries wherever possible. His foreign policy had been cautious and defensive. Towards the expanding Aetolian League he had been patient and unprovocative,[97] taking no retaliatory measures when various states lying between Thessaly and Attica were incorporated into the league and apparently content to resort to a sea-crossing and the route through Euboea to maintain his communications between Demetrias and the Macedonian garrisons at Chalcis, Piraeus and Corinth. His policy was one of wary neutrality, broken only in his last years when after Aratus' capture of Corinth he entered into a positive, and as it turned out short-lived, alliance with Aetolia against

---

[94] Plut. *Arat.* 33.1–2.   [95] Plut. *Arat.* 25.5.   [96] Cf. Walbank 1936, 64–71: (D 74).
[97] See, however, Roesch 1982, 351: (D 85), for an unpublished inscription recording an attack by Antigonus on Cytinium in Aetolian Doris a little before 243.

the Achaean League. The control of southern Greece, secured by garrisons and, especially in his later years, by the support of friendly tyrants in Argos, Megalopolis and other smaller cities, was itself defensive in conception, designed to debar any political enemy access to Greece; and since the agreement made with Antiochus in 278, that meant primarily Ptolemy.

The challenge from Ptolemy came in the Chremonidean War, but proved wholly inadequate to support Athens and Sparta; and though the details are obscure (see above, pp. 239–40, 242–3), Antigonus seems to have won a naval victory over the Ptolemaic fleet off Cos, which shook but did not shatter Ptolemaic naval power. Unfortunately, as we saw, the evidence is insufficient to allow a satisfactory assessment of Macedonian power in the Aegean. On land the failure of Athens and Sparta left the Macedonian system unimpaired and it was only with the revolt of Alexander and, more important, the growth in the power of the Achaean League and the capture of Corinth by Aratus in 243 that this system was seriously shaken. Subsequently either the inertia of old age or unrecorded fighting on the northern frontier prevented any serious attempt by Antigonus to repair the damage.

Antigonus was a pupil of Zeno and himself a Stoic. An anecdote illustrates his generosity of spirit (*philanthropia*), telling how when his son ill-treated some of his subjects he reproved him with the words that 'our kingship is a kind of glorious servitude (*endoxos douleia*)'.[98] But too much should not be made of this, for there is no evidence that Stoic theories of kingship exercised the least influence on his policy or his statesmanship. Though he was joined at court by Persaeus, it was as a politician and an officer that the Stoic served him. As a man Antigonus is attractive and leaves a favourable impression. He was humane and modest, rejecting flattery and enjoying good relations with his family and especially with his sons. But his death left his successor Demetrius face to face with serious problems.

[98] Ael. *VH* II.20.

CHAPTER 8

CULTURAL, SOCIAL AND ECONOMIC
FEATURES OF THE HELLENISTIC WORLD*

J. K. DAVIES

I. SOURCES AND APPROACHES

Four documents may serve as a framework for this chapter. The first is a much-discussed papyrus of the mid third century B.C., *P. Lille* 29, now generally agreed to be part of the municipal lawcode of Naucratis or Ptolemais.[1] In the surviving fragment, §1 concerns the procedure to be followed if a slave is prosecuted 'as if a free man'. If convicted his master may appeal, and if he loses the appeal, 'execution of penalty is to be carried out according to the laws about slaves except insofar as the royal ordinance forbids'. §3 specifies that 'slaves too may give evidence', and that they may be tortured 'unless (the judges) can judge from the pleadings deposited'. §4 lays down procedures when a master is or is not found responsible for a delict committed by his slave. In one eventuality the slave is to be whipped at least one hundred strokes, to be branded on the forehead 'as the royal ordinances enjoin', and to be sold abroad: though §2, in apparent contradiction, forbids the export, whipping, and branding of slaves (but a qualification may be lost in a lacuna). These laws, like those of Alexandria (*P. Hal.* 1), do not merely reveal once again how 'there was no action or belief or institution in Graeco-Roman antiquity that was not one way or other affected by the possibility that someone involved *might be* a slave'.[2] They also illustrate the complex relationship, attested in all the monarchies, between royal and civic law; the extent to which Greek-style slavery was taking root in Egypt, at least in the three *poleis* (less so, it appears, in the countryside (*chora*)[3]); the debt which they owe, in dialect and content, to Athenian style; and the ambivalence, even clearer here than in classical Athenian

---

* Adequately to survey so broad a field within the confines of one chapter is beyond the capacity of its author. I have tried instead to do two things: (a) to broach the theoretical problems of methods, approaches, and boundaries, and (b) to sketch the main topics, with their source materials and references to pertinent scholarly work. For the subject matter of the chapter as a whole Rostovtzeff 1953: (A 52) is still fundamental, with valuable supplements and *aggiornamenti* in Will *et al.* 1975: (A 68), Bianchi Bandinelli 1977: (H 11) and Préaux 1978: (A 48).

[1] Republished as Mitteis, *Chr.* 369: (F 92) = Meyer 1920, 243 no. 71: (H 142). Discussion and bibliography in Bieżuńska-Małowist 1974, 122ff.: (F 209).

[2] Finley 1980, 65: (H 64).

[3] Bieżuńska-Małowist 1974, 111 nn. 13–14: (F 209).

law, between slave as object of rights and slave as intermittent subject of rights.

The second document is a statue base from Sidon recording, in a dedication and a twelve-line Greek elegiac poem, the victory of Diotimus son of Dionysius in the chariot race at Nemea. His victory, c. 200, was claimed to be the first by a Sidonian.[4] His name and patronymic are Greek, as are the title of his civic office, *dikastes* ('judge'), and the phrase Σιδωνίων ἡ πόλις ('city of the Sidonians'), while the poem invokes the old legend that Sidon was the mother city of Thebes. Yet he was presumably not ethnically Greek, and his title is a calque of Aramaic *sufet*. Since other third-century documents reveal an extreme sensitivity to the Greek/non-Greek boundary, Diotīmus' invocation of Cadmus may have been no mere poetic decoration but an essential cultural passport.[5] Yet Romans with no better mythic claim to be Greeks were admitted to the Isthmia of 228, and were even diplomatically allowed to win;[6] youths from Byblus and Sidon won contests at the *Apollonia* on Delos as early as c. 270;[7] and by the 180s Tyrian and Sidonian corn-merchants with Greek names were getting proxeny-status from Oropus (*ISE* 64). Diotimus' victory, and the way it was recorded, was part of a complex network of cultural transformation which saw all the hitherto distinct civilizations of the Mediterranean littoral reach out to master and absorb at least some aspect of Greek culture or to present themselves in Greek dress to an increasingly hellenophone international audience – a movement which Greeks themselves welcomed complacently and enveloped within the matrix of a living and still fertile mythology.

The third document, brief enough to be quoted in full, is a letter sent c. 185–175 B.C. by a Cretan town to the Aetolian government.[8]

The marshals and the city of the Axians send greetings to the [*synedroi*] and the general and the cavalry-general of the Aetolians. You know Eraton our fellow-citizen, who sailed off on a military service to Cyprus, took a wife and had two sons, Epicles and Euagoras. It chanced that, Eraton having died in Cyprus, Epicles and their mother were taken prisoner and Epicles was sold at Amphissa. Epicles paid off the ransom money and lives among you in Amphissa. He is a fellow-citizen of ours, as are his children Erasiphon and Timonax and his daughter Melita. You will therefore act honourably by considering how, if anyone injures them, he may be prevented by you (from

---

[4] Moretti 1953, no. 41: (B 110)=Austin 121, with Bikerman 1939: (B 50).
[5] See n. 329. The *logos* of Hdt. VIII.137–9 on the Argead kings of Macedon had an identical function (cf. Hdt. V.22).
[6] Polyb. II.12.8; Zonaras VIII.19. For the *logoi* legitimating Roman kinship with Greeks see Momigliano 1975, 13ff.: (A 40), and for other Hellenizing mythic pedigrees see Bikerman 1939, 95: (B 50).
[7] *IG* XI.2, 203A68.   [8] *SIG* 622B=*IC* II.v.19*.

doing so) both publicly and privately: and how the record of common citizenship may endure for ever.

Inscribed at Delphi together with a formal acknowledgement by the Aetolians,[9] the letter throws a harsh light on contemporary social conditions – on the need for Cretans to seek employment as mercenaries elsewhere; on the dangers of piracy and the slave trade (though ironically enough a Cretan is the victim here rather than, as more usually, a perpetrator); on the erosion of citizenship boundaries and the new kind of interstate relationship commonly denoted by the word *isopoliteia*; and on the need for protection and the forms it took.

The fourth document is from Phrygia, a decree of Apamea-on-the-Maeander[10] which may date from the Galatian War of 160–166.[11] It honours a citizen, Cephisodorus son of Ariston, who, already complimented in previous decrees, had recently, as gymnasiarch, been honoured by the young men and had erected statues of King Eumenes II and of his brother, later King Attalus II. More recently still, if the restorations are correct, he had dedicated 3,000 drachmas on behalf of the king on an occasion when corn supply to soldiers was in question, and was now giving a further sum of money the income of which was to provide for an annual assembly of the ephebes and boys during the festivals of Hermes and Heracles. The document reflects much which is specifically Hellenistic: the dominant role of the wealthy citizen in running and financing his city's activities; the pivotal position of the prominent citizen who is also a courtier; the inter-penetration between city finance and royal finance; the practice, by now widespread, of creating foundations to yield a steady income for cult or charitable purposes; and the importance which the gymnasium had come to have as the 'identifying institution of Greek culture' especially in colonial areas such as inland Asia Minor.

Polybius and the poets apart, and especially for the social and economic historian, the Hellenistic world is a world of documents such as these. To decrees of individual cities, diplomatic correspondence, lawcodes and regulations, and dedications we may add statue bases, decrees of religious, local, or semi-autonomous bodies, lists of office-holders or of victors in athletic and musical festivals, accounts of administrative boards, and manumission-records as well as the ubiquitous inscribed gravestones. The Greek and demotic material from Egypt adds petitions, private letters, contracts, bureaucratic records and memoranda, certificates and land surveys as well as the evidence for the

---

[9] *SIG* 622A = *IG* IX².1.178.
[10] Buckler 1935, 71 no. 1: (B 57) = *Monumenta Asiae Minoris Antiqua* VI.173, with *Bull. épig.* 1939, 400, and *Bull. épig.* 1961, 685.
[11] Robert, *Hellenica* XI–XII (1960), 124 n. 6.

literature in vogue, old or new. In this and other respects Hellenistic documentation contrasts with that of the classical period. That most of the documentation of the classical period emanates from Athens is not an accident of survival but an index of Athens' untypical obsession with making the records of government accessible. In contrast, the documents of the third and second centuries are spread geographically much more widely and evenly. The bulk of it comes from Egypt, the Aegean, Delphi, Asia Minor, and Crete, but the rest of mainland Greece, the Black Sea and the Levant are well represented, with a scatter of evidence from further east, though Sicily and Greek Italy remained epigraphic deserts. As we have it, this material largely correlates with the spread and distribution of Greek *poleis*, but that is not true for Egypt, and the kinds of ephemeral public and private documentation preserved there will certainly not have been unique to Egypt. Elsewhere, of course, it was only documents inscribed on stone which survived, created in emulation of the Athenian mania for publicity and reflecting the general though unsystematic establishment of civic and local archives.[12]

Such material presents acute difficulties of concept and method. First and least, most documents are trivial as individual items of information. They begin to yield their full potential as evidence only when comparable documents are placed in sequence or viewed in the aggregate. True, much work of this kind has been done. One may cite, for example, studies of charitable foundations, of the rise and fall of commodity prices, of royal letters, of Athenian prytany decrees, of laws on land-distribution and debt, of decrees of *isopoliteia* and many others,[13] but large and crippling gaps still remain, e.g. in the study of liturgies and voluntary gifts (*epidoseis*), of amphora-handles as evidence of the flow of goods, or of emigration from Greece as a whole to the new territories.[14]

Yet, and secondly, such studies carry the danger of interpreting society through the particular category of document under discussion. Even in the aggregate, they can feed the dangerous assumption that existing evidence can be used inductively and positivistically as the building-blocks of an interpretation of a whole area and epoch. The fact is that there need be no correlation whatever between what is recorded and what is structurally important – a proposition illustrated for this period by the absence of population figures, or by the debate between Wilhelm, Klaffenbach, and others over the actual importance and utility to the recipients of the endless recorded grants of proxeny.[15] Those

12 Klaffenbach 1960: (B 98).
13 For foundations see n. 387; for prices Glotz 1916: (H 80) (Delos) and Heichelheim 1930: (H 91), with Heichelheim 1935, 856ff.: (H 92) (corn-prices). Other topics: Welles 1934 (*RC*); Dow 1937 (2): (H 49); Asheri 1966 and 1969: (H 4–5; Gawantka 1975: (H 76).
14 Cf. the comments of Rostovtzeff 1953, III.1463 n. 22: (A 52), and Schneider 1967, I.130 n. 2: (A 56).   15 See n. 324, below.

whose concern (as in this chapter) is with an overall large-scale description of society have to seek a framework for themselves and to justify it.

Here a third difficulty arises, stemming from the fact that cultural historians such as Kaerst and Schneider[16] tend to see things differently from social and economic historians. This is not just because their primary source material is literary and physical – the poets and geographers, Athenaeus, and the direct and doxographical tradition of post-Aristotelian philosophy, or the surviving luxury or everyday items of household or personal adornment, mosaics, statuary, coinage as an art form, and the remains of houses, sanctuaries, and city walls. It derives rather from the twin desires to see literary evidence as the mirror of reality and to see the influence of literature and the history of ideas as actively moulding the development of society. Yet such desires are perilous. Granted, social historians would be much the poorer without access to Theocritus xv (the *Adoniazousai*) or the more lurid pieces of Herondas, but questions of author's purpose (and obsessions), of literary convention, and of the requirements of patronage must play at least as much part in evaluating Hellenistic poetry for a historian's purposes as they do in evaluating the artistic creations of any age.[17] Specific to our period, furthermore, is a preoccupation with social extremes. The escapist fantasy involved can be obvious: few will suppose that Theocritus iv–vi accurately reflect the living conditions or cultural level of the goatherds of Magna Graecia. Elsewhere the fantasy can be a subtle trap, illustrated all too well at the other end of the social scale by the catastrophically misguided way in which Rostovtzeff used the evidence of the size of dowries in Menander without qualms in his sketch of the early third-century Athenian bourgeoisie. It has needed the evidence for the median size of dotal *apotimemata* (property mortgaged as security) attested on the *horoi* (markers) to bring reality back into the description.[18]

The assumption that literature and the history of ideas are active forces exemplifies a fourth difficulty. A sketch such as this chapter has to choose and to reflect in its structure certain assumptions about the lines of force in society, but cannot discuss them *au fond*, while the general interpretative formulae currently available both cover an unconvincingly wide spectrum and are individually vulnerable. One may instance the classic Marxist view of the Hellenistic period as a specific phase in the

[16] Kaerst 1926–7: (A 28); Schneider 1967–9: (A 56).

[17] Cf. for example the analysis (essential for its understanding) of Theocritus xvii as encomium by Meincke 1965, 85–164: (H 139), and Cairns 1972, 100ff.: (H 32), against Gow *ad loc.* or the verdicts quoted by Meincke 1965, 144 n. 3: (H 139).

[18] Rostovtzeff 1953, 1.163ff.: (A 52); Finley 1952, 79–81: (H 59).

linear development of a slave-exploiting society, hindered from progres-
sing further by its inherent contradictions;[19] or Tcherikover's view of it
as a period of revolution 'which all over the world broke up the fixed
framework of tribe, *polis*, and family, and put in their place the will of the
strong individual';[20] or, implicit or explicit in Rostovtzeff's great
treatise, notions of competition between slave and free,[21] of two-way
interactions between Greek ambitions and 'the solid mass of Orientalism' (p. 133), of a Mediterranean-wide market, of price/demand
fluctuations, of mercantilist governments (e.g. p. 455), and of 'the unity
and homogeneity of the Hellenistic world from the point of view of
civilization and mode of life' (p. 1040). Even with respect to specific
institutions the interpretative gulf can be unmanageably wide. One may
cite the widespread system of *paramone*, whereby a formally freed slave
was contractually bound to remain in the service of his/her ex-owner
until a fixed period had elapsed, until the ex-owner(s) had died, or until
other specified conditions were fulfilled. The system is well attested in
over 1,000 manumission documents at Delphi from 201 B.C. onwards,[22] as
well as in others from elsewhere in central Greece, the Aegean, and
further afield. It is disputed whether the (common but not universal)
participation of a god in the manumission-transaction was a recently
developed additional sanction[23] or reflects older practices of *hierodouleia*
(temple-slavery) and *asylia* (asylum);[24] whether the participation of the
state in the transaction, as in Thessaly and at Oeniadae (*IG* IX^2.1.2.419,
ll. 1ff.), stems purely from reasons of publicity and fiscal interest, or has
deeper roots;[25] whether the *paramone*-system was purely Greek in form[26]
and represented a formalization of older Greek customs,[27] or whether it
was adopted and adapted from Near Eastern practice;[28] whether the
publication of the *paramone*-document was intended to attest and protect
the ex-slave's 'free' status or to ensure his performance of the duties
specified; and whether the system reflected the period's greater
humanity and leniency in the treatment of slaves[29] or rather the desire of
owners to recapitalize the values of older slaves so as to replace them by
younger ones.[30] In the face of such deep diversities of view about these

[19] Ranowitsch 1958: (H 180).
[20] Tcherikover 1959, 159: (A 61).
[21] Rostovtzeff 1953: (A 52); but see now Finley 1980, ch. 2: (H 64).
[22] In general Rädle 1969, 140ff.: (H 178), and Roscoe and Hopkins in Hopkins 1978, 133–71: (A
24), who cite the extensive previous bibliography. List of documents in Bömer 1960, 29 n. 7: (H 21).
[23] Bömer 1960, 11: (H 21).
[24] Cameron 1939: (B 58); Sokolowski 1955: (H 216).
[25] Thessaly: Babakos 1966, 19ff.: (H 7).   [26] Robert 1936: (B 138).
[27] Rädle 1969, 56ff.: (H 178).
[28] Koschaker 1931: (H 115); Schönbauer 1937: (H 204); Mendelsohn 1949: (H 140); Samuel 1965:
(H 196).   [29] Westermann 1955, 40: (H 240).
[30] Roscoe and Hopkins in Hopkins 1978 (A 24).

and other phenomena, prudence requires that they should not be used as the basis of any interpretative superstructure. Yet that is to preclude any kind of creative understanding.

There remains a fifth difficulty, at once the most basic and most intractable, that of defining the field of enquiry. The Hellenistic World is normally taken to denote areas where the language of government and literature is Greek, where the personnel of government, the leisure class, and the clerisy is largely Greek or assimilated Greek, where there is interchange of Greek-style goods and perhaps their production as well, and where forms of buildings (towns, houses, temples, palaces) and artistic production (sculpture, reliefs, jewellery, plate, etc.) are clearly linked with Greek models and styles and belong to the international to-and-fro of ideas and representations. That is too one-sided. What we are following is a process of colonial expansion and settlement, wherein Greek culture and institutions spread outwards – or are encouraged or imposed by Greek-orientated governments – in patterns which change through time, yield markedly different consequences from one region to another, or in town as against country, or within the leisure class as against the peasantry, and tend to impinge first at the top of society. One has only to think of the very limited hellenization of the kingdom of Meroe,[31] initiated by the third-century King Ergamenes, or, clearest of all, the complex reaction to aristocratic hellenizers in Palestine after 180 B.C. Most historiography, ancient and modern, has accordingly concentrated on the Greek component in the interaction of cultural influences in the period and area. That attitude is made all the easier since non-Greek literary productions – demotic Egyptian texts and inscriptions, Phoenician inscriptions, neo-Babylonian cuneiform texts, Hebrew and Aramaic texts outside the Bible such as the Talmud and the Mishnah – are much less accessible than the Greek. When no such texts are available it can even be hard to acknowledge that a culture exists at all in any but the anthropological sense. Yet it hardly needs pointing out that such an intellectual framework is basically colonialist. It undervalues the non-Greek cultures and cultural components, often enough by lumping them together in an undefined category of 'Orientalism'. (It is probably no accident that the notion 'Hellenistic' is not conveyed by any word in contemporary Greek and is a specifically nineteenth-century invention).[32] By concentrating on the common element, it also prejudges questions of the unity of Hellenistic society, to which, as we shall see, much more complex and nuanced answers need to be offered.

[31] For which see Shinnie 1967: (H 213); Schneider 1967, 1.587 n. 1 (references): (A 56); Fraser 1972, II.295 n. 333: (A 15), and Hintze 1978: (H 101).
[32] Momigliano 1935: (H 145); Préaux 1965: (H 175); Bravo 1968: (H 26); Momigliano 1970: (H 146).

The essential will therefore be to beg as few questions as possible. What follows is organized under three broad headings: (1) economic activities and interactions (§§II–V), (2) the role of the kings in creating the parameters of society (§VI), and (3) the transformation of the *polis* as a focus of social life (§VII–VIII). Throughout, the emphasis will be not so much on the delineation of broad patterns as on the co-existence and interaction – close or loose, spasmodic or continuous – of a large number of layers or *loci* of action. That this will yield a picture of incoherence and contradiction will simply be a fact about a plural society, wherein the members of a single political entity show fundamental differences and discontinuities in institutions, culture, and social structure, lack a common social will, and owe their political juxtaposition to the influence of external factors, *imprimis* to power wielded from the outside.[33]

II. DEMOGRAPHIC PROBLEMS

The most basic demographic facts are unknown, for no reliable picture can be drawn of population figures in most areas, or of changes in them. The only exception is Egypt, for which Diodorus (1.31.7) reports a population of about 7 million 'in antiquity' (τὸ πάλαιον, by which he probably means the early Ptolemaic period). His figure for the population in his own day is 'not less than 300 myriads [i.e. 3 million]', but since he also reports the 'free' population of Alexandria-by-Egypt in his own day as 'over 300,000' (XVII.52.6), and since Josephus gives a figure of 7,500,000 for Egypt excluding Alexandria (*BJ* II.385), it is usually assumed that Diodorus' anomalous figure of 3 million is mistaken or corrupt,[34] and that the *laos* (the tied peasantry) continued to comprise at least 7 million. Diodorus' figures stem from the 'sacred registers' and therefore have some authority. Figures for the slave population of Egypt (*P. Harris* 61) and of Ptolemaic Palestine (*C. Ord. Ptol.* 21–2) were similarly known to the government, but are not known to us, so that estimates both for Alexandria and the *chora* vary widely. Since even in the Roman period slaves appear to have comprised no more than 13% of the total population[35] and at least in the *chora* may well have been less during the Ptolemaic period,[36] estimates of 400,000 slaves for Ptolemaic Alexandria are probably too high.[37]

---

[33] Thus M. G. Smith, *The Plural Society in the British West Indies* (Berkeley-London, 1965) and L. Kuper and M. G. Smith, *Pluralism in Africa* (Berkeley-London, 1971), developing the ideas of J. S. Furnivall, *Colonial Policy and Practice* (London, 1948) 302–12.

[34] Cf. Rostovtzeff 1953, 1136–7 and 1605 n. 73–4: (A 52); Fraser 1972, II.171 n. 358: (A 15).

[35] *WO* 703: (F 105); Westermann 1955, 88: (H 240). Even lower figures are reckoned in Karanis (Westermann 1955, 120–2; Geremek 1969, 40: (H 77)).

[36] Bieżuńska-Małowist 1974, 134ff., esp. 140: (F 209).

[37] *Ead.* 141, against Fraser 1972, II.171 n. 358: (A 15).

Elsewhere such figures barely existed, for the census known to have been taken by Demetrius of Phalerum for Attica in or soon after 317 is unparalleled,[38] and of its figures of 21,000 (adult male) citizens, 10,000 metics, and 400,000 slaves the last is generally disbelieved.[39] At most, kings and cities and governments knew the size of their available military manpower, and occasionally made lists of those available.[40] Otherwise demographic interest arose only for fiscal or moralizing motives. In consequence, estimates of population have to be made on the basis of indirect indices such as the size of military forces,[41] the size of excavated towns such as Dura or Priene,[42] or the level of corn donations.[43] The frailty of them all is patent.

Drifts of population are a little clearer. Basic to our period is the fact that the movement of ethnic Greeks and Macedonians into the new kingdoms was substantial enough to form a cultural determinant for centuries. All the same, its scale should not be exaggerated. By the time of Raphia (217) military colonization in the Seleucid empire seems to have allowed a recruitment potential of 42,000 heavy-armed infantry, mostly of Macedonian origin,[44] 3,000 light-armed infantry of Thracian origin, and 8,000–8,500 cavalry of more varied origin. The corresponding figure for Egypt at the same battle was rather lower, probably of the order of 30,000+ Greeks and 4,000 Gauls and Thracians.[45] Though in assessing that figure it must be remembered that Egypt had hitherto been able to recruit mercenaries without difficulty, and that the boundary between mercenary and military settler was highly permeable, yet for this battle above all others the Egyptian régime will have recruited every available Greek before adopting the dangerous expedient of recruiting 20,000 Egyptians to the phalanx (Polyb. v.65.9).[46]

It is true of course that military manpower is only part of the picture. To these figures we must add those too old to fight ($\dot{\alpha}\pi\dot{o}\mu\alpha\chi o\iota$), a trickle of immigrants in the intelligentsia and the administration, and a

---

[38] Ctesicles, FGrH 245 F 1 ap. Athen vi.272c.

[39] Ferguson 1911, 54 n. 3: (D 89); Gomme 1933, 18ff.: (H 82); Westermann 1941: (H 236).

[40] E.g. IG xii.9.241 (Eretria, early third century). Such lists are to be distinguished from those of particular forces or garrisons, mostly recruited from among professionals. For a survey of known lists see Launey 1949–50, 1.66ff.: (J 143).

[41] Thus Beloch 1886, 13ff.: (H 10).

[42] Rostovtzeff 1953, 11.1141: (A 52).

[43] E.g. those to Miletus by Eumenes II, as by Hiller von Gaertringen 1932, 1610: (H 100).

[44] This figure excludes the 2,000 Jewish families sent as military colonists by Antiochus III from Mesopotamia and Babylonia to Lydia and Phrygia (Jos. Ant. Jud. xii.147–52, with Bar-Kochva 1976, 213 n. 8: (J 136), and Cohen 1978, 5ff.: (E 16).

[45] Seleucid forces: see Bar-Kochva 1976, 39ff.: (J 136), against the much lower estimates of Jones 1940, 23: (A 25) (15,000 plus: Ehrenberg 1969, 149–51: (A 13), implies a low estimate but gives no figures) or the much higher estimates of A. Segré 1934, 267: (F 320), and Edson 1958: (E 19). Ptolemaic forces: see Walbank 1979, 111.773: (B 37), with references.

[46] For a contrary view see Ch. 11, pp. 438–9.

fluctuating number of mercenaries on short- or long-term contracts (of whom some might well become military colonists), as well as an unquantifiable influx of traders, opportunists and general hangers-on. Some of these latter are the immigrant Greeks and Carians of the Zenon papyri,[47] who will no doubt have had their unrecorded counterparts in Syria. Others will have come to strengthen the original foundations, such as the men from Magnesia-on-the-Maeander sent on the urging of Antiochus I to 'help in increasing the people of Antioch'.[48] Others were to form a continually growing class of unprivileged 'Greeks' without citizenship at Alexandria, and their presence elsewhere will help to account for the huge populations of formerly Seleucid cities recorded for the Augustan period.[49] Yet mercenaries served only when they could be paid, served where they were sent, might move from one employer to another, might move west rather than east and south,[50] and might hope to be more fortunate than Eraton of Axus (p. 258 above) and to return home *en grand seigneur* like Stratophanes in Menander's *Sicyonius*. Again, it is likely that many of the 'Greeks' in Alexandria or Antioch were either freedmen, whose relocation therefore reflects the activity of the slave trade rather than voluntary movement from Greece, or acculturated non-Greeks such as Diotimus of Sidon (p. 258 above) may have been. All in all, the drift of Greeks south and east to the new colonial areas cannot have represented a mass exodus.

Nor were counter-drifts lacking. The Jewish diaspora into Asia Minor, Greece, Egypt and Cyrene, Syria and Mesopotamia was an important demographic fact, though it cannot yet be quantified.[51] Equally unquantifiable (though not necessarily insignificant) are anecdotal references such as Plutarch's to the four Syrian brothers who were resident in Corinth in 243 (*Arat.* 18.3), or the evidence from Diogenes Laertius and elsewhere for the *patris* of the post-Aristotelian philosophers who lived and worked in Athens. After 300 few of those he names were Athenians (Polemon and Crates being exceptions) or mainlanders, fewer still from the West till the later second century B.C.: most are from the Aegean, Propontis, or Cyrene, with more and more (especially among the Stoics) coming from Levantine and even Mesopotamian cities as the

[47] Rostovtzeff 1953, II.1073–7: (A 52), Fraser 1972, I.67ff.: (A 15); Pestman *et al.*, 1981: (F 140).

[48] *OGIS* 233 = Austin 190, ll. 14ff.

[49] For Alexandria cf. Fraser 1972, I.51: (A 15). Antioch: Strabo XVI.2.5. C 750 says it had a slightly smaller population than that of Alexandria or Seleuceia-on-the-Tigris, which allegedly had a population of 600,000 in Pliny's time (*NH* VI.122). Apamea is said to have had 117,000 citizens at the census of Sulpicius Quirinius in A.D. 6 (*ILS* 2683). For other figures and discussion see Cumont 1934: (E 155), Rostovtzeff 1953, I.498–9 with III.1439 n. 276: (A 52), and R. P. Duncan-Jones, *The Economy of the Roman Empire: Quantitative Studies* (Cambridge, 1974) 260, n. 4.

[50] E.g. the Attalid garrison of Lilaea in Phocis, recruited largely from Asia Minor (*FD* III.4.132–5, with analysis by Launey 1949–50, I.71ff.: (J 143)).

[51] Tcherikover 1959, 287ff.: (A 61).

Hellenistic period wears on. However, such evidence may tell us only about themselves: philosophers are demographically insignificant. Much better evidence comes from the gravestones of foreigners, for they provide at least a trace element and reveal proportions (though they are probably biassed in favour of the literate and the prosperous). For instance, there certainly came to be a substantial colony of Syrians at Delos,[52] and of Syrians and Egyptians at Demetrias in Thessaly,[53] and Rhodes shows tombstones of Alexandrians, Antiochenes, and Laodiceans in considerable numbers.[54] Again, the 60 or so Hellenistic gravestones of foreigners buried at the unexceptional town of Eretria show a fairly even pattern of movement: of those recorded 15 are islanders (all but one from outside Euboea), 11 are from central Greece, 9 from Asia Minor, 8 from the Peloponnese, 7 from the south and east Mediterranean, and another 7 from Thessaly, Macedon, and Thrace.[55] Clearer still is the pattern from Hellenistic Athens, where, though naturally many ethnics are well attested, three stand out above all: Antiochenes (108), Milesians (114), and Heracleots (196).[56] Both they and the next best attested nationalities – 35 from Ancyra (bewilderingly), 27 from Sinope, 26 from Alexandria, 22 from Thrace, and 15 each from Amisus, Apamea, and Corinth – show a strong and unmistakable westward drift. Equally, the massive importation of Italian slaves sold in Greece during the Second Punic War must have had some demographic effect.[57]

Such evidence of migration suggests that many cities were hosts to a large and perhaps growing number of non-citizen immigrants and their descendants, whose presence posed problems of status-assimilation. Some cities eventually resolved them by large-scale enfranchisements (thus Miletus in the third century) or by allowing the purchase of citizenship:[58] others dodged them by resorting to grants of *isopoliteia* (see below). Either way, the basis and definition of community were perforce changing, with further consequences which will be traced below. However, this evidence also suggests that the drain of mercenaries, colonists, and other opportunists from old Greece to the new colonial

---

[52] Roussel 1916(I), 84–95: (H 189); Masson 1969, 682ff.: (H 137).

[53] Arvanitopoulos 1952–3: (B 279); Masson 1969, 682ff.: (H 137), with *Bull. épig.* 1970, 207. Sidon (8) and Ascalon (6) are the best represented, followed by Macedon (6), Crete (8) and Aradus (4), then by many towns with two or three representatives, including Tyre (2). For Phoenicians at Rhodes see Fraser 1970: (B 77).

[54] See Fraser 1960, 29 nn. 5–7: (F 171), and Fraser 1972, II.289 n. 290: (A 15).

[55] *IG* XII.9.786–843, and *IG* XII Suppl. 629–37. These figures exclude gravestones dated by the editors in the imperial period, but include three of the fourth century.

[56] *IG* II².7882–10530. Again, these figures are only of gravestones dated by Kirchner in the 3rd–1st centuries B.C.

[57] Hatzfeld 1913: (H 89), Hackens 1968 (2): (B 227).

[58] See n. 323, below. For Miletus see Hiller von Gaertringen 1932, 1602–3: (H 100).

territories during the third century was being compensated by other movements of individuals, often from those same colonial territories, so that regional population densities need not have changed appreciably. Yet Polybius says explicitly that

in our times the whole of Greece has suffered a shortage of children and hence a gradual decrease of the population, and in consequence some cities have become deserted and agricultural production has declined, although neither wars nor epidemics were taking place continuously . . . This evil grew upon us rapidly and overtook us before we were aware of it, the simple reason being that men had fallen a prey to inflated ambitions, love of money, and indolence, with the result that they were either unwilling to marry, or if they did marry to bring up the children that were born to them; or else they would only rear one or two out of a large number so as to leave these well-off and able in their turn to squander their inheritance (XXXVI.17.5–7).

His remarks have prompted much discussion[59] and have tended to be accepted at their face value, even though most of the evidence adduced in his support either proves nothing[60] or is not specific enough in area and period to be invoked.[61] Yet it may be doubted whether his evidence proves what it is claimed to do, for those able to aspire to 'inflated ambitions, love of money and indolence' or to squander their inheritance can only have been the tiny minority of wealthy families: the pattern of behaviour he describes is a class phenomenon, not a demographic phenomenon. It may be seen in action in two other contexts, which further reveal that its roots lie deeper in the past than Polybius implies. The first is Larissa in 217, as reflected in Philip V's two well-known letters of September 217 and August 215,[62] in which he instructed the city to enfranchise its *katoikoi* 'so that the land will be more fully cultivated' (first letter, l. 9) or 'so that. . . . the land will not lie shamefully fallow as now' (second letter, l. 30). What is crucial is that between 217 and 215 opposition in Larissa to the measure had been strong enough to have it annulled till Philip's fierce second letter had it reinstated. The problem is to understand exactly what was being opposed. It will not have been the mere presence of the *katoikoi* (for they

---

59 Walbank 1979, III.680: (B 37).

60 Thus for example explanations in terms of the exposure of children, which is well attested from Hesiod onwards: for recent references and discussions see Vatin 1970, 228–40: (H 230); Pomeroy 1976, 68ff.: (H 170); Engels 1980: (H 56); Golden 1981: (H 81). That the poets of New Comedy make such use of the motif is a fact about the artistic influence of Euripides and the appeal of the motif to audiences, not a fact about social behaviour.

61 As for example with most of the epigraphic evidence for small families adduced by Tarn and Griffith 1952, 100: (A 59), and accepted by Rostovtzeff 1953, II.623ff.: (A 52). Similarly, the evidence for large families in later Hellenistic Athens adduced by Ferguson 1911, 374: (D 89), concerns the office-holding class on Delos and cannot be used as demographic evidence against Polybius.

62 *SIG* 543 = *ILS* 8763 = *IG* IX.2.5.517 = Austin 60 with Habicht 1970, 273ff.: (B 83). and Salviat and Vatin 1974: (B 156).

were there already), perhaps not even their enfranchisement, so much as the economic consequences. Since their enfranchisement was envisaged as allowing a fuller cultivation of land we must assume that in some way not specified they were to receive vacant land, and that opposition came from those who preferred the existing pattern of landownership, even if it meant a small citizen body and fallow fields, to a redistribution, even if it meant cultivated fields and a 'strong city' (l. 30).

Much the same can be said, though more confidently, of the opposition to Agis and Cleomenes in Sparta a generation earlier (see pp. 252–5, 457–8). Here too resistance to the redistribution of land and to the enlargement of the citizen body came from the wealthy luxury-loving land-monopolising few; here too, though the Phylarchan tradition in Plutarch takes up Aristotle's theme of 'lack of men' (*oliganthropia*) caused by faulty inheritance laws[63] and speaks of a shrunken citizen body a mere 700 strong,[64] Sparta's subsequent military achievements, and Cleomenes' force of no fewer than 6,000 'Lacedaemonians' at Sellasia in 222 (Plut. *Cleom.* 28.8) show clearly that there was no intrinsic lack of men to occupy the *kleroi* which the revolution had made available. In this way the motifs of Sparta's revolution foreshadow events at Larissa, or Polybius' analysis as more narrowly interpreted, or other attempts to redistribute land[65] closely enough to require an explanation common to them all. Yet it is inadequate to point to the drives of greed and luxury, as Polybius or Phylarchus in Plutarch do, for they were scarcely peculiar to the Hellenistic period, while Phylarchus' additional explanation in terms of changes in the inheritance law (the *rhetra* of Epitadeus) is indeed relevant but fails to identify which changes of attitude and priority in Spartan society allowed those changes to take place. We shall do better to consider the military imperatives to maximize the number of citizen hoplite soldiers which in the archaic period had called into existence laws such as those of 'Lycurgus' or Solon which aimed to keep constant the number of *kleroi* and of the proprietors of those *kleroi*. Once adequate military manpower was available from other sources such as subordinate allies (as with Sparta in her great days) or mercenaries, the prime argument for maintaining citizen numbers or for controlling the allocation of land lost its force, and the natural tendency of wealthy oligarchies to maximize property holdings could be given fuller rein. It is no accident that Philip's motive in trying to resist this shift at Larissa was not merely agronomic: as his reference to 'a strong city' and his invocation of the growth of Rome show, it was also (and maybe fundamentally) military.

[63] Plut. *Agis* 5 (Fuks 1962 (3), 250: (D 128), notes that 'the word is not expressly used', but that it reflects the underlying theme nonetheless); Arist. *Pol.* 1270a34, 1306b36–7, 1307a35–6.

[64] Plut. *Agis* 5.6, with Fuks 1962 (3), 245–9: (D 128), and Oliva 1971, 211–12: (D 132).

[65] See the list in Asheri 1966: (H 4).

III. THE DEGREE OF ECONOMIC INTERPLAY: ARTEFACTS AND INSTITUTIONS

In this way demographic problems interlock with those of landowner-ship and land use, and thereby with those of the economy in the widest sense. Of all aspects of Hellenistic society this latter is still the least well charted or accessible, and is in consequence the most complex and controversial. Indeed, for reasons which will appear, it is far from certain that a 'Hellenistic economy' as such existed, in the sense of a continuous market-defined exchange of the whole range of goods and services throughout the eastern Mediterranean, for an economy as thus defined is not to be confused with an economy in the sense of a number of segmental sets of activities conducted under more or less closely comparable social, fiscal, technological, and climatic conditions with a certain degree of interplay between them: that an older generation of scholarship[66] interpreted such interplay as revealing a unified 'Hellenis-tic economy' defines the problem, but does not solve it. Signs of interplay are of course undeniable, ranging from the rise and fall of commodity prices on Delos,[67] the great increase in known shipwrecks – and therefore probably in maritime trade – after 200 B.C.,[68] the circulation-patterns of such coinages as were not purely local,[69] the complementarity of Rhodes and Alexandria,[70] or the growth of Mediterranean-wide institutions and practices,[71] to the distribution of artefacts as various as Alexandrian glass or faience or containers for wine and olive oil.[72] The challenge is rather to develop satisfactory criteria by which to decide whether the evidence (including that of such interplay) suggests a picture of many local and largely autarkic economies, or one of micro- or macro-regional economies stimulated by local economies, or one of a zonal economy of the whole eastern Mediterranean; while, even if such criteria can be suggested,[73] there remains the challenge of finding the evidence to which to apply them. What follows will therefore be primarily an exercise in description.

The three most basic propositions are also the least well documented. First, most gainful activity, especially the production of the basic 'Mediterranean triad' of corn, wine, and olive, will have gone on just as

---

[66] Cf. particularly Heichelheim 1930: (H 91) and Rostovtzeff 1936: (H 188); major counter-considerations in Préaux 1969: (H 176).

[67] Glotz 1913 and 1916: (H 79–80).   [68] Hopkins 1980, 105–6: (H 108).

[69] See pp. 277–82, below.   [70] Fraser 1972, 1.164: (A 15).   [71] Bogaert 1968: (H 17).

[72] Brashinsky 1973: (B 53); Sherwin-White 1978, 236ff.: (D 146).

[73] E.g. the proportion of goods by value finding a final market more than x km away from their place of origin or manufacture; the proportion of the adult working population engaged in producing such long-distance commodities.

it had done for centuries. Second, such primary agricultural production will have continued to occupy the vast majority of the labour force, whether slave, serf, or free. Third, most of their produce will have been consumed within a comparatively short radius (of the order of 30 km) of the locus of production. It is in the nature both of the activities themselves and of the evidence for them that these propositions are hard to prove. The second and third need little comment. For the second, though no figures of direct relevance are attested anywhere for the Hellenistic period, it is to be assumed that as for any pre-industrial society, in conditions which rarely allowed a ten-fold yield (often much lower), food production will have required the labour of at least 80% of the adult population as a whole, men or women, slave or free.[74] For the third, the costs of land transport will have rendered economically prohibitive any mechanisms for ironing out peaks and troughs of production in areas not accessible by ship. We must therefore envisage an underlying pattern, distinguished by local famines and local gluts, of production for local consumption without recourse to trading or to a 'market'. That will apply throughout the eastern Mediterranean and will apply not merely to the 'triad' but even more to vegetables and fruit.[75]

The first proposition deserves longer consideration. It is largely an inference, whether from survivals of the use of comparable techniques and tools from antiquity till recent times, or e silentio from the lack of notable advance in technology or in agricultural productivity. Each element in the argument needs some qualification, the first because continuity of practice can never be formally proved, the second because some innovation and some systemization of knowledge are attested in our period. Evidence of innovation comes mainly from Egypt, above all from the Zenon papyri, and is at first sight extensive. We hear of new techniques of drainage and irrigation, double-cropping, the use of iron plough-shares, the import and acclimatization of new types of wheat and fruit trees, the creation of vineyards, the extension of olive-growing, and the import of Arabian and Milesian sheep.[76] Other instances of large-scale drainage/irrigation systems are attested in Babylonia, Thessaly,

[74] For the hypothesis of this figure for Republican Italy see Hopkins 1978, 19ff.: (A 24); for crop-yields see Mayerson in Colt 1962, 211ff. at 227ff.: (B 189); Duncan-Jones (op. cit. n. 49) 49 n. 4 and 51 n. 1, and Rickman, 1980 (2), 261: (H 182).

[75] Burford 1960–1: (H 31); Duncan-Jones (op. cit. n. 49) 366–9; Rickman 1980 (1), 13ff.: (H 181). Much of the portrait painted for the agricultural pattern of the later Roman Empire by C. E. Stevens ('Agriculture and rural life in the later Roman Empire', in Cambridge Economic History of Europe I² (Cambridge, 1971) 92–124) can be applied with little change.

[76] Rostovtzeff 1922: (J 164); Johannesen 1923: (F 270); Schnebel 1925, passim: (J 165); H. A. Thompson 1930: (J 166); Préaux 1939, 120: (F 306); corn, double-cropping: Rostovtzeff 1953, I.56–7, 391–9 and 363–4 with III.1403ff. nn. 150–61: (A 52); irrigation: Préaux 1969, 56–7: (H 176), Préaux 1978, II.476–8: (A 48).

Euboea, Boeotia, the Crimea and Bactria:[77] of acclimatization of plants in Syria and Babylonia:[78] of selective breeding in Epirus and probably at Pergamum.[79] So too handbooks on agriculture in general or on particular aspects of it proliferated, kings themselves such as Hiero II of Syracuse and Attalus III of Pergamum being among the fifty and more Greek authors quoted by Athenaeus or cited as authorities by Varro (RR 1.8–9), Pliny (NH XVIII.22) and Columella (1.1.8). All the same there is room for doubt about how far-reaching the effects of this activity were. Some at least of the literary work seems to have had interests not so much agronomic as taxonomic (e.g. Theophrastus), dietetic (e.g. Diphilus of Siphnos, Phylotimus), or lexical (Tryphon). Again, much of the work of transplantation and acclimatization may have remained experimental and marginal, for luxury and ostentation, and most of it (not only in Egypt) is likely to have been the product of the convergent fiscal pressures, felt and transmitted by the kings, to reduce imports by developing home-grown alternatives and to improve revenues by improving yields.[80] It is therefore dangerous to use the example of Apollonius and Zenon, in close touch with court policy and disposing of considerable risk capital, as typical even of wider circles among the colonialist Greeks in the new kingdoms, let alone of the indigenous populations. Furthermore, such accounting systems as we can see in use, even on large estates such as Apollonius', derived from those used by city administrations, and like them were designed to prevent embezzlement rather than to quantify each input into each activity and thereby to reveal net profit or loss. A truly 'rational' or 'scientific' agriculture was therefore impossible.[81] Lastly, though some irrigation techniques may have represented genuine innovations, other 'innovations' were rather on the Achaemenid model (cf. ML 12), viz. the transfer to a new area of plants or techniques already in use elsewhere. That is not to deny, but rather to locate more precisely, the scope of such enterprise and impulse to improvement as can be seen.

Nonetheless such transfers are part of the evidence that by c. 300 B.C. the eastern Mediterranean had long since ceased to comprise purely a set of local subsistence economies, at least in the sense that on to the underlying pattern had come to be superimposed widespread production for a market, involving transport and exchange over long distances. It begs fewest questions if the remaining evidence for such interplay is

[77] See references in Rostovtzeff 1953, II.1160–2, 1198, and III.1608–9 nn. 95–6: (A 52); Préaux 1969, 62 n. 2: (H 176). For Bactria (Aï Khanum) see references in Briant 1979, 1398f. and 1414: (H 28).
[78] References in Rostovtzeff 1953, II.1162–8 with III.1609–12 nn. 97–109: (A 52).
[79] For Epirus ibid. II.1163 with III.1609 n. 99; for Pergamum ibid. I.563 with III.1451 n. 330, but OGIS 748 and RC 62 prove only the ownership of large tracts of pasture land by the dynasty, not necessarily any particular policies about their exploitation.
[80] Thus Rostovtzeff 1953, passim: (A 52), surely rightly.
[81] Grier 1934: (F 254), Mickwitz 1937: (H 144), Ste Croix 1956, 37–8: (H 192).

set out by genre. First come general statements in literary sources such as Diodorus' remark in the context of Demetrius' siege of Rhodes in 305, that though the Rhodians tried to stay on good terms with everyone, 'their inclination was towards Ptolemy, for most of their revenues came from merchants sailing to Egypt: in general the city was sustained from that kingdom' (Diod. xx.81.4). So too the outbreak of war between Rhodes and Byzantium in 220, triggered by Byzantium's imposition of tolls on maritime trade through the Bosphorus (Polyb. iv.47.1), is placed by Polybius in a context in which 'the islands which surround the Pontus provide both cattle and slaves in the greatest quantity and of the highest quality; and as for luxuries, the same regions not only supply us with honey, wax, and preserved fish in great abundance, but they also absorb the surplus produce of our own countries, namely olive oil and every kind of wines. In the case of corn there is a two-way traffic, whereby they sometimes supply it when we need it, and sometimes import it from us.'[82] Though, as Polybius goes on to relate, other resentments against Byzantium were also involved, it is significant both that the effect of the Byzantines' action on the terms of trade was enough to make non-Rhodian sea-traders apply pressure on Rhodes and that Rhodes did respond to that pressure on the politico-military level (Polyb. iv.47.1–3).[83]

A second type of evidence comes from the distribution of surviving artefacts. Many categories of them are involved, and the purview of what follows is limited. Highly desirable though it would be to bring up to date the surveys which Rostovtzeff provided of the artefact production of the various regions of the Hellenistic world, neither space nor the competence of a single scholar would allow such an enterprise here. Furthermore, as will appear, the firm evidence of interplay and of exchange of goods yet available from artefact distributors is still embarrassingly limited.

Virtually the only artefacts the distribution of which has been studied systematically are the large containers (*amphorae*) which survive in huge numbers and whose handles tended to be stamped with a state's symbol and/or magistrate's name(s).[84] The most convenient (but intentionally

---

[82] Polyb. iv.38.4–5. The evidence for corn-imports *into* the Black Sea area, now considerable, is set out in Pippidi 1953: (B 117), Rostovtzeff 1953, iii.1462 n. 20: (A 52), Pippidi 1971, 99ff.: (D 166), Stefan 1974: (H 220), *ISE* ii.128 and 132, with Moretti *ad loc.*

[83] For this war cf. Seyrig 1968, 191–2: (B 262), and Habicht 1959, 1088: (E 69). One may legitimately compare events ten years earlier, when sea-traders harrassed by semi-official Illyrian piracy in the Adriatic complained effectively enough to the Roman Senate to trigger off the First Illyrian War in 229 (Polyb. ii.8.1–3). On both occasions collective action by the sea-traders (πλωιζόμενοι in both contexts of Polybius) has to be assumed.

[84] There is still no detailed overall study. See Fraser 1972, i.161ff. with ii.277ff. nn. 227–32: (A 15), Brashinsky 1973: (B 53), and Sherwin-White 1978, 237ff.: (D 146), for references, above all to the work of V. R. Grace: (B 292–4); add now Säflund 1980: (B 314) for the material from Labraunda.

far from complete) summary of distribution figures does show some of
the main traffics.[85] Of 113,469 handles reported by Sherwin-White, no
fewer than 98,047 (86·4%) are Rhodian, and of them about 80,000 were
found in Alexandria. No other state begins to approach such figures,
though Cos, with 1,925 handles reported, shows a similar proportion
from Alexandria (1,480, or 75·9%). In contrast, stamps of the second-
biggest supplier, Cnidus – 6,222 in all reported – gravitated towards
Delos (4,525, or 72·7%, found there). Given the preponderance of
amphorae in known shipwrecks of the Hellenistic period,[86] it is fair to
see in these and other figures[87] a reflection of one of the main
components by bulk (perhaps the principal one) of eastern Mediterranean trade in the Hellenistic period. All the same, though the potential
of this material is immense, its present evidential value is limited.
(i) Only a handful of states, mainly Aegean islands or in the Black Sea
(but none from the Greek mainland), adopted the practice of stamping
amphorae, but it cannot be assumed that they alone were major
producers. (ii) The reasons why handles were stamped are not clear –
whether for fiscal reasons, as a guarantee of origin or of capacity, or as a
date.[88] (iii) The commodities carried in them are still a matter of
guesswork.[89] (iv) The relative and absolute chronology of most series is
still too loose for the ebbs and flows of production to be traceable with
the chronological precision (e.g. by decade) which would alone provide
the really valuable economic evidence. All that emerges clearly at
present is that the predominance of Rhodes seems to have reached its
peak, predictably enough, in the years before and after 200 B.C., but did
continue (at least in Egypt) even after the political and economic
convulsions of the 160s.

   The distribution of other pottery artefacts is even harder to evaluate,
for several reasons. The comparative neglect of Hellenistic pottery is
only now being made good, and the place or area of manufacture of

[85] Sherwin-White 1978, 238–9: (D 146). Omitted are sites where Coan handles have not been
found, as well as, e.g., the stamps of Thasos and elsewhere found on Thasos (Bon and Bon, 1957: (B
282)), stamps from sites in Italy and the West such as Marseilles (Benoit 1961: (B 183)), Fraser 1972,
II.274 n. 214: (A 15)), etc. For Rhodian stamps cf. still Nilsson 1909: (B 307), with Grace 1934, 214ff.:
(B 292); Grace 1953, 116ff.: (B 294); Grace in Talcott et al. 1956, 138ff.: (B 321).
[86] Benoit 1961: (B 183).
[87] E.g. those which show how stamps of Black Sea cities are found largely within the Black Sea
area, or the concentration of amphorae from Italy at Delos and Alexandria above all (see the table in
Sherwin-White 1978, 238–9: (D 146)). Further finds and identifications will sharpen the picture but
are unlikely to alter its main outlines much.
[88] See Grace 1949, 176–8: (B 293), and Bon and Bon 1957, 35ff.: (B 282) (but also Finley 1965, 28ff.:
(H 63)).
[89] If indeed the amphorae were not themselves sometimes the commodity, as Fraser argued was
the case for some of the Rhodian imports to Alexandria (Fraser 1972, I.168 with II.289–90 nn. 282
and 284: (A 15)). Others, he argued, went empty from Rhodes to Laodicea, and took wine thence to
Egypt (ibid. I.167, in the light of Strabo XVI.2.9, C. 752).

several major fabrics either remains unknown[90] or has only recently been ascertained,[91] while other local fabrics remain unstudied.[92] However, one development is clear and paramount, the gradual decentralization of production. In proportion as the Athenian red-figure tradition fell ever further behind contemporary advances in panel painting as the fourth century progressed, so correspondingly, at least for fine pottery, customers' tastes in Greek areas seem to have turned increasingly towards pottery which either eschewed decoration (e.g. Athenian black glaze) or carried simpler and much less ambitious decoration (e.g. West-slope ware) or recalled the forms and decorative motifs of metalwork (notably the so-called Megarian bowls). True, there were exceptions,[93] but their distribution and appeal remained local or specialized, while those of wider appeal could be and were much more easily imitated by local workshops without loss of quality[94] than could be classic black- or red-figure. A crucial component of this process was the move towards mould-made wares, which could be given elaborate decorative ornament with less labour and without becoming slapdash (Plates vol., pls. 165, 170). Hellenistic pottery therefore shows a paradox: while there developed an artistic *koine* (comparable to the linguistic *koine*) which produced a very similar range of fabrics and allowed a very rapid circulation of ideas,[95] that *koine* came to be served by many local schools and workshops whose products therefore seem on the whole to have travelled much less far than the classic wares had done. In consequence, though some individual movements can be detected, no general pattern of shipping movements can yet be assembled from the distribution of Hellenistic pottery fabrics.

Much the same picture holds true of other artefacts. For instance the

[90] E.g. the Lagynos group of jugs (Leroux 1913: (B 304); R. M. Cook 1960, 207: (B 286); Plates vol., pl. 166), or Hellenistic 'Pergamene' (Waagé in Rostovtzeff 1953, III.1639ff.: (A 52); Waggé in Waagé 1948, 18ff.: (B 333)).

[91] E.g. the clay-ground 'Hadra' vases (Fraser 1972, 1.33 with II.104 nn. 248–9, 1.139 with II.245 nn. 50–1: (A 15); Plates vol., pl. 83)) found especially in Egypt but now thought to have been made in Crete (Callaghan 1978, 15: (B 188)), or the variety of 'Megarian' bowls which show Homeric scenes on their relief decoration, now localized in Macedon and the Gulf of Pagasae (see Sinn 1979, 27ff.: (B 318)). [92] E.g. that of Cos (Sherwin-White 1978, 233: (D 146)).

[93] E.g. the black-figure amphorae which continued to be made to serve as prizes at the Athenian *Panathenaea* (Dow 1936: (B 288); Peters 1942: (B 310); J. Boardman *Athenian Black-figure Vases* (London, 1974) 167ff. and 237), the *oinochoai* and other vases made for the purpose of Ptolemaic ruler-cult (D. B. Thompson 1973: (F 382)), or the wares produced by the third-century schools at Canosa in Apulia or Centuripa in Sicily (references in R. M. Cook 1960, 353: (B 286); add Trendall 1955: (B 332)), which preserved some remnants of the major S. Italian school of the fourth century.

[94] E.g. (a) *West-slope ware* (Plates vol., pl. 167), made first in Athens from the late fourth century onwards (H. A. Thompson 1934, 445–6: (B 331) but subsequently made elsewhere; (b) *White-ground Hadra vases*, nearly all made in Egypt but imitated at Rhodes (B. F. Cook 1966, 7 n. 3: (B 285)); and (c) *Megarian bowls* (Plates vol., pl. 168), which seem to have been made in almost every major centre.

[95] Cf. Callaghan 1978: (B 283) on the rapid dissemination of a particular motif from Corinth between *c.* 150 and 146 B.C.

terracotta figurines which regained popularity and became a widespread
minor art form from the late fourth century onwards may have first
taken their new direction in Athens but were soon being made in
numerous centres in a remarkably uniform ('Tanagra') style.[96] So too
precious metalwork and jewellery, surviving in much greater quantity
from the period between the late fourth century and c. 250 B.C. than
either earlier or later, shows a 'basically homogeneous' style practised
by smiths not only in Athens or S. Russia, as for silver-ware in the
classical period,[97] but also in an increasing number of other centres
attested either by literary evidence (e.g. Antioch or Alexandria),[98] by
concentration of finds (e.g. Tarentum),[99] or by rational inference. In any
case the contribution by weight and bulk of such goods to the carrying
trade will have been minimal, as will that of bronze-wares for domestic
use or decoration;[100] that of weaponry might well have been more
substantial, but such material as there is has still not been studied
intensively.[101]

There remains coinage, the one body of artefact material which should at
first sight provide the best evidence for the intensity and directions of
interplay and exchange, if only because the quantity of material can
easily be assessed and because the originating state or area and the
approximate date of emission can usually be determined.[102] The
evidence is in fact much less straightforward to interpret than it appears,
but it is certainly available in adequate quantity. By the late fourth
century coinage was being issued by nearly all major and most minor
states on the Mediterranean littoral.[103] True, Rome and Sparta held out,
Rome till the end of the fourth century, Sparta till 280,[104] and the coin
issues of many smaller states were spasmodic or were confined to small
silver and bronze,[105] but such reluctances or inabilities were more than

[96] See Plates vol., pls. 171–2. For a bibliography see Rostovtzeff 1953, III.1461 n. 17: (A 52), and
Higgins 1967, 154ff.: (H 99).   [97] Strong 1966, 91: (B 320).

[98] Polyb. XXVI.1.2 ap. Athen. v.193d (Antioch in 160s B.C.) (Downey 1961, 98: (E 157)); Athen.
v.197c–203c, with Rostovtzeff 1953, 1.374–6: (A 52), and Fraser 1972, 1.136–7 with II.239–40
nn. 25–32: (A 15).

[99] Wuilleumier 1930: (B 275). Cf., however, the increasing evidence for the specific traits of
Graeco-Bactrian art (Saranidi 1980: (H 197); Litvinskiy and Pichikayan 1981: (B 203)).

[100] See Rostovtzeff 1953, 1.122–3, 374ff. and II.1212–13: (A 52).

[101] See Rostovtzeff 1953, II.1212–22 at p. 1221: (A 52). The topic is not touched on in Launey
1949–50: (J 143) or Bar-Kochva 1976: (J 136).

[102] General sketch in Préaux 1978, 1.106–10 and 280–94: (A 48).

[103] Carthaginian coinage appears to have begun in the late fourth century, though the precise
date is not clear: G. K. Jenkins and R. B. Lewis, Carthaginian Gold and Electrum Coins (London,
1963); Warmington 1964, 153: (H 232); Will 1979, 1.176 n. 1: (A 67).

[104] This is not the place to rehearse the question of early Roman coinage: see M. H. Crawford,
Roman Republican Coinage (Cambridge, 1974) 1.35ff.; Burnett 1977: (G 12), and vol. VII.2. For
Sparta see Walbank 1957, 1.731: (B 37), and Hackens 1968 (1): (B 226).

[105] E.g. Chalcis: Picard 1979, 346–7: (B 252).

outweighed by the huge issues of Philip II and by the output of the new mints established throughout the erstwhile Persian empire by Alexander and the Successors. Through them must have passed some part at least of the captured Achaemenid treasure of 170,000–£190,000 talents,[106] not to mention the revenues which each successor was clearly at pains to maximize and to monetize. In consequence the early Hellenistic period saw a major qualitative shift towards the use of coined metal as a medium for exchange or transfer of resources: that no fewer than 1,900, or 79·6% of the 2,387 Greek coin hoards known in 1973 were buried in the three centuries from 330 to 31 B.C. is a rough but fair reflection of the change in this respect from the classical period. Of course the transformation was not total, for the Persian empire had long used Greek coin and had long minted its own,[107] while effective and sophisticated systems of exchange without the use of coin had long functioned in Babylonia[108] and elsewhere (e.g. Carthage), and will have continued to do so. Nonetheless the shift was real, and was both reflected and reinforced by the spread of more or less barbarous imitations of Greek coinage made by communities on the Greek fringe in the Balkans and elsewhere.[109] The challenge is therefore to insert the numismatic phenomena of increased and widespread minting and circulation within a plausible politico-economic model. Since awareness that this is not a simple matter has grown apace in recent years, it may be as well to set out systematically some of the factors involved before attempting any generalized description.

First, because easily measurable, is the range of different weight standards. Once Alexander had abandoned, for reasons which need not here concern us,[110] Philip II's use of the Chalcidian standard in favour of the Attic standard (1 dr. $= 4 \cdot 3$ g, tetradrachm of c. 17·2 g), the spread of his, his Successors', and continuing Athenian tetradrachm coinage went far to create a monetary *koine* for the eastern Mediterranean. Numerous surviving hoards, especially from Asia Minor in the Seleucid period and from the Levant and Near East, reflect it,[111] and its prevalence was reinforced in the third and second centuries by the minting in many cities of coins modelled on the issues of King Lysimachus of Thrace[112] and by

[106] Diod. XVII.66.1–2 and 71.1 (169,000 tal.); Diod. XVII.80.3 (180,000 tal.); Justin XII.1.1 (190,000 tal.). We need not concern ourselves here with the discrepancies in these and other figures (see Bellinger 1963, 68ff.: (B 216), with Strabo XV.2.9. C. 731, with determining how much was already in coin, or with identifying the coinage immediately created (Bellinger 1963, 72).

[107] Schlumberger 1953: (H 202).

[108] Dandamayev 1969: (E 18); Bogaert 1966: (H 16).

[109] Cf. May 1939, 164ff.: (B 239) (Damastion); Robert 1967, 37ff.: (B 255); Youroukova 1976: (B 276); Youroukova 1980: (B 277); Scheers 1980: (B 257).

[110] Schlumberger 1953, 27: (H 202); Bellinger 1963, 29–30: (B 216).

[111] E.g. *IGCH* 1398–1406, 1410–14, 1423–6, 1446–51, 1515–16, 1523–44.

[112] Seyrig 1963, 22ff.: (B 261).

the resumption by Athens of large-scale coining in the so-called New Style after *c.* 164.[113] However, some states such as Corinth, Rhodes, or the Achaean League after its recreation in 281/80 saw no reason to alter their own existing standards, and these were not marginal coinages. Between 340 and *c.* 308 Corinth and her associated states in the West produced coins of traditional type and standard (1 dr. = 2·9 g, stater of 8·6 g) in such quantity as to predominate in hoards buried in Sicily between 340 and 290, and to give way only gradually to the lighter coins which Agathocles minted from *c.* 295 onwards.[114] Rhodes, again, produced a small coinage on the Chian-Rhodian standard (1 dr. = 3·9 g, tetradrachm of 15·6 g) till late in the third century, but more prominently in the years before and after 200, to judge from surviving hoard material.[115] As for Achaea, though her coins may not have had the homogeneity Polybius claimed for them till after *c.* 196,[116] they did thereafter, and were minted on a large enough scale to provide the largest single component in twelve of the twenty-five hoards in which Achaean League coins are found.[117] Furthermore, there were secessions from the Attic-Alexandrian standard. One is known to have been transitory, namely the issues made by Byzantium and Chalcedon of coins on the 'Phoenician' standard from the 230s till the war of 220, for reasons evidently to do with the Danegeld which Byzantium was then paying to the Gauls.[118] Two others were long lasting and of major importance. The first occurred *c.* 310, when Ptolemy I initiated the first of three successive weight-reductions of his silver currency. By *c.* 290 these had yielded a tetradrachm of *c.* 14·25 g, again more or less corresponding to the 'Phoenician' standard,[119] which continued thereafter and was (remarkably) perpetuated by some of the Seleucid kings for the dominions in Coele-Syria conquered in the Fifth Syrian War.[120] The second secession was the creation of the so-called 'cistophoric' coinage, which was minted on the Rhodian standard (tetradrachm of *c.* 12·60 g) by numerous cities within the Attalid sphere of influence from the 180s or even later till well into the first century B.C.[121] The varying

[113] For this date see Lewis 1962: (B 238), Hackens 1965: (B 225), and Boehringer 1972: (B 217) against the higher date of 196 adopted by M. Thompson 1961: (B 267) and defended by her in M. Thompson 1962: (B 268).   [114] Talbert 1974, 161ff.: (G 18).

[115] This is an impression only, drawn from survey of the 80 hoards listed in *IGCH* as containing Rhodian material.

[116] Polybius II.37.11, with Chantraine 1972: (B 219) against M. Thompson 1939: (B 265) and M. Thompson 1968: (B 271); Walbank 1979, III.761: (B 37).

[117] *IGCH* 242–3, 257–8, 260–2, 270–1, 301, 330, 2053.   [118] Seyrig 1968, 191–2: (B 262).

[119] Fraser 1972, II.239 n. 24: (A 15); Mørkholm 1980: (F 392).

[120] Seyrig 1973, 121: (B 263), correcting Bikerman 1938, 216: (E 6).

[121] The introduction of the cistophoric coinage has been progressively down-dated in recent years, and has now been placed, not as by Seyrig 1963, 22ff.: (B 261), in 188 or soon after, but after 167: see Kleiner and Noe 1977, 10–18: (B 231), with further contributions to the debate by Mørkholm 1979: (B 244), Kleiner 1980: (B 232), Mørkholm 1980: (B 245), Bauslaugh 1981: (E 118). I am grateful to Mr P. J. Callaghan for those last references.

reasons for such choices and changes of standard will be in part explored below, but some notion of their effect needs to be formulated at once. It is often said that the effect of the adoption or retention of particular standards was to create economic isolation or a 'closed economy'.[122] Such statements are at best fierce oversimplifications. By that token Rhodes, with a standard shared by few mints save Chios and Cos in the third century, should have suffered thereby, which hardly appears to have been the case: understandably, for nothing intrinsically precluded the free convertibility of different currencies when weighed as the bullion which (as reasonably pure silver) they all basically comprised.[123] That is not to deny the existence of 'closed economies', at least in the sense that (e.g.) Ptolemaic coins barely appear in Seleucid areas or indeed outside the Ptolemaic monetary zone of Cyrene, Cyprus and Syria, while Seleucid and other foreign coins do not appear in Egyptian hoards.[124] However, the creation and continuance of such exclusions is not a matter of standard but of the degree of informal willingness to accept foreign coin, of the reliability and frequency (or otherwise) of facilities for exchange, and above all of the presence or absence of legal prohibitions created by fiscal policy.

A second factor is the need to identify the routes and mechanisms which yielded the distribution of coins attested by hoard and other evidence and now increasingly becoming the object of detailed study.[125] At least five major mechanisms can be isolated: (i) the payment of military forces, especially but by no means only of mercenaries;[126] (ii) moneys paid by the kings as subsidies to cities in difficulty,[127] as bribes to

[122] E.g. Will 1979, I.78: (A 67), and Préaux 1978, I.248. (A 48), for the Ptolemies; Seyrig 1963, 22ff.: (B 261), and 1968, 190–1: (B 262), for cistophori.

[123] It is pertinent that many hoards contain silver as money and silver as plate buried together, the ensemble being evaluable only by weight.

[124] Fraser 1972, I.136 with II.238–9: (A 15); Bagnall 1976, ch. 8: (F 204).

[125] Any bibliography of this work can only be partial and exempli gratia. Some major recent studies of Hellenistic hoards are Wallace 1956: (B 274), M. Thompson 1968: (B 271), and Seyrig 1973: (B 263). The circulation of coins of certain mints or regions has been studied, by inter alios, de Laix 1973: (B 235) (Aetolia); Hackens 1969: (B 228) (Boeotia); Shelov 1978: (B 264) (Bosphorus); Seyrig 1963: (B 261) and Schönert-Geiss 1970: (B 260) (Byzantium); Picard 1979, 307ff.: (B 252) (Chalcis); Le Rider 1966: (B 237) (Crete); Hackens in Bruneau and others 1970, 387ff.: (J 190) (Delos, in part); Robert 1951, 179–216: (B 253), L. Robert, Hellenica XI–XII (1960) 63–9, and Robert 1967, 37: (B 255) (Histiaea); Hackens 1968(1): (B 226) (Peloponnese); Le Rider 1965, 435–51: (B 236) (Susa); Dunant and Pouilloux 1958, 214ff.: (H 53) (Thasos); Robert 1951, 69–100 and 243–5: (B 253), Bellinger 1961: (B 215), and Robert 1966, 94–114: (B 254) (cities of Troad). Not all of these studies pay equal attention to the two sorts of distribution map or survey required, (a) that of the find-spots of the coins of a given mint or city, and (b) that of the mints or cities of origin of the coins found in one area (for the distinction L. and J. Robert 1954, 332–3: (E 94)). Exemplary are Dunant and Pouilloux 1958: (H 53) and Picard 1979: (B 252).

[126] Griffith 1935, 264–316: (J 141), and Launey 1949–50, II.725–80: (J 143), both making much use of OGIS 266; Ducrey 1970, 653ff.: (E 121).

[127] E.g. by Philetaerus to Cyzicus in and after 280 (OGIS 748 = Austin 194, with Atkinson 1968, 44ff.: (E 58)), by Euergetes to Rhodes after the earthquake (Polyb. v.89 and Diod. XXVI.8), by Attalus I to Sicyon early in 197 (Polyb. XVIII.16.3–4, Livy XXXII.40.8), by Epiphanes to the Achaean League

politicians,[128] or as gifts for the creation of monuments or works of art;[129] (iii) simple seizure, whether through reprisal, through banditry or piracy, or through the capture of booty in more or less regular war;[130] (iv) taxation:[131] and (v) trade. To assess the relative importance of each of these mechanisms is an enterprise barely begun[132] and not yet capable of being satisfactorily expressed in general principles.[133] All that can safely be said is negative: the assumption, still widespread, that coin circulation reflects trade relations above all is not safe enough to allow it to dominate whatever model of circulation we hope to construct.

A third factor is the effect of governmental intervention for fiscal and other reasons. Such intervention took various forms. First, since minting was profitable,[134] all kings followed the Athenian fifth-century example and attempted to control coining within their own territories, to the point where the issue of tetradrachms was a symbol of sovereignty maintained (as by Rhodes or Byzantium) or of autonomy conceded, as possibly by Alexander,[135] more certainly by the Seleucids, rarely in the third century but much more frequently from 126 onwards,[136] and certainly by Eumenes II, in whose extended kingdom after 188 cities given autonomy struck cistophori while those not given autonomy did not.[137] Athens' resumption of tetradrachm coining after c. 164 is to be

in 171 (Polyb. XXIII.9.3), or the offer by Eumenes to the Achaean League in 185 (Polyb. XXII.7.3). For parallel examples, see n. 309 below. Cf. however Picard 1979, 313: (B 252), for a return to commercial explanations of the circulation of Ptolemaic coinage in Euboea.

[128] E.g. Euergetes' payments to Aratus till 227 (Plut. *Arat.* 41.5, *Agis* and *Cleom.* 40(19).8).

[129] A survey of Seleucid gifts is given by Bikerman 1938, 125: (E 6); of Attalid gifts by Cardinali 1906, 199ff.: (E 120), and Robert 1937, 84 n. 4 and 201: (B 139); cf. in general Préaux 1978, 1.201ff.: (A 48).

[130] There is unfortunately very little systematic discussion of the magnitude and the economic effects of such violent transfers of specie in e.g. Ormerod 1924: (H 158), Launey 1949–50: (J 143), or Brulé 1978: (H 29), though the ranges and routes of displacement can be divined to some degree from evidence about piracy and ransom payments. Some references to booty and confiscation in Bikerman 1938, 120–1: (E 6); the list could be extended.

[131] Data collected and classified by Bikerman 1938, 106–20: (E 6); Préaux 1939, 61–435: (F 306); Jones 1940, 108–12: (A 25); Préaux 1978, II.438–41: (A 48).

[132] *Honoris causa* I single out Robert's pioneering detection of the trade-links of Histiaea with Macedon, the gulf of Pagasae, and Rhodes (n. 125 above), Le Rider's comments on foreign coinage in Crete as a reflection of mercenary service (Le Rider 1966, 267: (B 237)), and the lengthy and careful discussion by Hackens 1968(1): (B 226) of the reasons for the appearance of Seleucid and Ptolemaic coins in Peloponnesian hoards of the late third century.

[133] It is too simple to say with Robert 1951, 77 n. 8: (B 253), that 'bronze coins do not enlighten us about commerce and the movements of commodities, but about the journeys of men' (repeated in Robert 1966, 13: (B 254)). The remark has been acclaimed, but (a) account must be taken of the special role played by Ptolemaic bronze after the 220s, (b) the more the circulation of silver reflects mercenary service, the more it reflects human movement, (c) bronze does tell us about the movement of goods, but of different goods and on a smaller scale, and (d) bronze is probably less liable than silver to circulate by the mechanisms of seizure and taxation.

[134] *OGIS* 339 (=Austin 215) ll. 45ff. (Sestus, after 133 B.C., with Robert 1973: (B 150).

[135] Thus Newell 1919, 16–22: (E 88), but cf. Bellinger 1963, 78–9: (B 216).

[136] Bikerman 1938, 235: (E 6); Seyrig 1951(2), 213–14: (H 211); Préaux 1954, 73 and 130: (H 172); Seyrig 1958, 621: (E 97).   [137] Seyrig 1963, 19ff.: (B 261).

seen in the same light (see n. 113). Secondly, states could lay down what moneys were acceptable for particular purposes. Thus, for example, a Euboean law of 294–288 provides that performers at the *Demetrieia* should be paid in 'currency of Demetrius' (i.e. Attic standard, rather than the lighter local silver):[138] a treaty of 173/2 between Miletus and Heraclea-on-Latmus lays down that payments should be made in 'old Rhodian drachmas':[139] a treaty of the late third century between Attalus I and Malla states that payments to recruited mercenaries shall be made in Aeginetan (weight) drachmas:[140] inscriptions of Mylasa provide for payments in 'drachmas of light Rhodian silver':[141] and so on.[142] Thirdly, and more wide-rangingly, a state might be liberal or exclusive in prescribing which moneys could be used in its territory or markets. The Athenian coinage law of 375/4 provides for the acceptance of silver coins struck from the official die but not of 'silver coin bearing the same *charakter* as the Athenian' (i.e. of imitation owls if made of good silver).[143] Similarly, the Amphictyonic law of 124–100 B.C. enforces on all Greeks under penalty the acceptance of the Athenian (*sc.* New Style) tetradrachm.[144] Equally drastic were the regulations made earlier in Egypt, whereby from *c.* 300 B.C. foreign coins were not allowed to circulate within Ptolemaic territory:[145] a prohibition intensified for gold from 259/8 onwards by a decree (*prostagma*) providing for the compulsory surrender and reminting of all gold coin, foreign or local.[146] On the other hand, a fourth-century law of Olbia provides that gold and silver could be imported and exported freely, that buying and selling of currency had to be done in one specified place and in terms of the city's bronze or silver, and that apart from Cyzicene staters (for which a fixed exchange rate was laid down) exchange could be made at any mutually agreeable rate.[147] In the light of the other documentation it may be risky to claim that the Olbia decree 'points to commonly applied principles'.[148]

---

[138] *IG* XII.9.207 = *SIG* 348, l. 20, with Wallace 1956, 28 (B 274); Habicht 1970, 76–7: (I 29), and Picard 1979, 345: (B 252).

[139] Ducrey 1970, 638ff. no. 2, l. 23, with 656ff.: (E 121).

[140] *SIG* 633, ll. 96–7, with Rehm 1923, 11–21: (B 123), and Robert 1951, 173–4: (B 253).

[141] Robert 1951, 179: (B 253).

[142] E.g. *IG* XII.7.67–9 with Rostovtzeff 1953, I.223: (A 52).

[143] See T. V. Buttrey, 'The Athenian Currency Law of 375/4 B.C.', in *Greek Numismatics and Archaeology. Essays in honor of Margaret Thompson*, ed. O. Mørkholm and N. M. Waggoner (Wetteren, 1979) 33–46; *idem*, 'More on the Athenian Coinage Law of 375/4 B.C.', *Quad. Tic.* 10 (1981) 71–94; as against R. S. Stroud, 'An Athenian law on silver coinage', *Hesp.* 43 (1974) esp. 169ff and 186–7.

[144] *SIG* 729 = Pleket 1964, no. 13: (B 118), with Daux 1936, 387ff.: (D 77); Rostovtzeff 1953, I.743 and III.1503 n. 9: (A 52), and Giovannini 1978, 64–72: (B 224). [145] Jenkins 1967, 59: (B 230).

[146] *P. Cairo Zen.* 59021 = *SP* II.409: (F 89), with many commentaries: Préaux 1939, 271ff.: (F 306).

[147] *SIG* = Pleket 1964, no. 8: (B 118); Schmitz 1925: (B 259); Michell 1957, 228 n. 4: (H 143); Finley 1965, 21: (H 63). [148] Finley 1965, 21: (H 63).

All these factors can give any one currency a skewed distribution pattern. For example, that no Rhodian coins have been found in Hellenistic Egyptian hoards means nothing, in the light of the literary and papyrological evidence. Similarly their absence from S. Russia, Italy, Sicily, N. Africa and Spain[149] can hardly reflect a real absence of commercial contact, given the non-numismatic evidence for such contact.[150] Likewise, the heavy concentration of coins of Byzantium and Chalcedon in Thrace, W. Euxine, S. Russia and Asia Minor may reflect not just exchange relationships but Danegeld payments as well, while their rarity in Greece, Macedon, the Levant, Egypt and the West is striking and unexplained. We are on least unsafe ground if we take the distribution of Hellenistic Greek coins as a whole, and think of it as evidence of many mutually complementary flows and counterflows, some local,[151] some wide-reaching, but as an ensemble serving to define a 'Hellenistic world' at least as precisely and objectively as the evidence of the use of Greek.

Complementing the evidence of artefacts are some more indirect indices of economic interplay. Especially pertinent is the growth of certain institutions, of which three deserve specific mention.

(a) Perhaps first in importance, but still shamefully understudied, is the slave-trade. The skimpy evidence[152] suggests that though war, piracy, and brigandage contributed substantially to the supply of slaves, so also did more regular trading relationships, above all those which drew slaves from non-Greek peoples of the Black Sea littoral and took them past Byzantium (Polyb. IV.38.4 and 50.3) to points of sale or redistribution at e.g. Ephesus,[153] Rhodes, or later – and notoriously – at Side (Strabo XIV.3.2, p. 664) or Delos, with its facilities for receiving and despatching tens of thousands of slaves the same day.[154] Plainly, even before Roman demands for slaves became insatiable from the 160s onwards, this was no marginal trade. The quantities of Greek and later of Roman coin found in Bulgaria and Romania (436 Greek hoards in the Hellenistic period) must reflect it, at least in part, as of course does the ostentatious monumentality of post-166 Delos:[155] though not all so-

[149] Apart from a few strays reported from Spain (*IGCH* 2317, 2334).

[150] Cf. the wide distribution of Rhodian amphora handles in these areas, the exemption from dues (*ateleia*) given to Rhodian merchants at Syracuse in 227 (Polyb. V.88.7), and the nature of Roman–Rhodian relationships since 306 (Polyb. XXX.5.6, with Schmitt 1957, 1–49: (E 143)).

[151] E.g. the Achaean League coins found in 25 hoards, of which three are in Italy and three in Crete but otherwise all in Peloponnese or Central Greece.

[152] Mostly assembled by Rostovtzeff 1953, II.777–95 and 1258–63: (A 52), and by Finley 1962: (H 61), with Heinen 1976 and 1977: (H 93).

[153] Hdt. VIII.105; Front. *Strat.* III.3.7 = Polyaen. V.19 (287 B.C.); Menander fr. 195K; Varro, *Ling.* VIII.21.

[154] Strabo XIV.5.2. C. 668.

[155] See M. H. Crawford, 'Republican denarii in Romania: the suppression of piracy and the slave-trade', *JRS* 57 (1977) 117ff. at 121–2, and also the remarks of Stewart 1979, 65ff. and 142ff.: (B 319).

called Romans (*Rhomaioi*) – many were in fact Italians – at Delos will have been slave-dealers, many surely were. Nor should their suppliers be sought only among camp-followers and the *menu peuple*: some of the grossly wealthy men of the Greek Black Sea towns could well have derived part of their wealth from the slave-trade,[156] while there is good evidence that the kings themselves, at least after 166, saw advantage in supplying the market.[157]

(b) Another institution which spread gradually in the Hellenistic period, the association of traders and merchant-ship owners (κοινά or σύνοδοι ἐμπόρων καὶ ναυκλήρων) from one port established in another.[158] Egyptian and Tyrian groups were already attested (as cult groups) at Athens in the late 330s,[159] Sidonians by the late third century (*IG* ii².2946) and other groups a century later.[160] Delos similarly sees associations of men of Tyre from the third century onwards,[161] from Beirut (the later Poseidoniastai) by 175,[162] and from Alexandria by the 120s,[163] thereby largely predating the proliferation from the 140s onwards of Italian groups such as the Hermaistai, Apolloniastai, Poseidoniastai, etc.[164] That such groups took cult form and theophoric names not only reveals what sort of self-identification was most important (or most acceptable in the host town) but also suggests that many of the similarly named associations attested on Rhodes from the late third century onwards had comparable origins and functions.[165] Such associations have not yet been identified elsewhere, e.g. at Demetrias, Ephesus, or Miletus: their presence should be diagnostic of major long-term routes of exchange.

(c) The spread of certain other practices and institutions illustrative of naval trading can also be traced to some degree. The one document we

[156] For instance Protogenes of Olbia (*SIG* 495), Apollonius of Chersonese (*ISE* 132), or Dionysius of Istria (*ISE* 128).

[157] Strabo says as much of 'the kings of Cyprus and of Egypt' (xvi.5.2, p. 669), while *OGIS* 345 = *FD* iii.4.77 clearly shows Nicomedes III of Bithynia in 102/1 supplying Delphi with slaves (but as a favour, be it said, rather than as a commercial transaction). So too the injunction to the Eastern kings, in the Roman piracy law of 101/100 B.C., not to allow pirate bases in their territories, was presumably à propos (*FD* iii.4.37, B 10–11, with Rostovtzeff 1953, ii.774 and 784: (A 52), and Hassall *et al.* 1974: (H 88)).

[158] In general Ziebarth 1896, 26ff.: (H 249); Poland 1909, 106ff.: (H 168); Picard 1920, 264–70: (H 164); Ziebarth 1929, 90–9: (H 252); Fraser 1972, i.186–8: (A 15); I. Vélissaropoulos, *Les nauclères grecs* (Geneva–Paris, 1980), 91–124.

[159] *IG* ii².337 = Tod 189; we are not authorized to infer from *IG*ii².141 = Tod 139 that the Sidonians who came to Athens κατ' ἐμπορίαν already formed any such group in 367.

[160] *IG* ii².1012 = *SIG* 706 (112/11); *IG* ii².2952 (*c.* 97/6).

[161] *Insc. Délos* 50; Michel 998 = *Insc. Délos* 1519.

[162] *OGIS* 247 = *Choix* 72 = *IG*xi.4.114; Tod 1934: (B 167) = *Insc. Délos* 1520, with Robert 1973, 486ff.: (B 149); later references in Picard 1921: (H 165) and Mouterde 1964, 156ff.: (H 149).

[163] *Insc. Délos* 1528 (= *OGIS* 140 = *Choix* 108), 1529. Cf. also a group from Hieropolis in Syria in 128 B.C. (*Insc. Délos* 2226) and the 'voyagers to Bithynia' (καταπλέοντες ἐς Βιθυνίαν) (*Insc. Délos* 1705).

[164] Hatzfeld 1919, 31ff.: (H 90); Laidlaw 1933, 202ff.: (D 145).

[165] Pugliese Carratelli 1939–40, 165 no. 19 (earliest evidence), 176ff. (list), 187ff. (analysis): (E 141). Cf. also the Rhodian burial *koina* (Fraser 1977, 58ff.: (E 136)).

have of the Hellenistic period detailing a *bottomry loan*[166] shows indeed considerable change in format and legal background from fourth-century Athenian practice as attested in Dem. xxxv.10–13 but recognizably represents an extension of it, in this case to Red Sea trading financed and managed by men even more diverse in nationality than those known from fourth-century Athens. These and many other matters were reflected and regularized in the *Rhodian sea-law*,[167] which dates from A.D. 600–800 in its present form but may trace some part of its origin to Hellenistic practice as codified in Rhodian courts. So, too, the development of descriptive geography, as reflected in Polybius' great excursuses or in travellers' guides (*periploi* or *periodoi*), gave increasingly systematic guidance for such journeys by land or sea,[168] while the development of ports and harbour-installations[169] and the proliferation of grants of proxeny-status and *isopoliteia*[170] will have smoothed the path of many a traveller and his goods.

Not all of these phenomena were new or significant. Associations of foreign merchants were not a purely Hellenistic phenomenon;[171] *proxenoi* were appointed for many reasons other than commercial – political, judicial, athletic, cultural, or religious; Athens by the 420s was already importing goods to an extent and from within a radius very little different from anything the Hellenistic world can show; Phaselis by 429 (Thuc. II.69.1) was just as much the staging post of Graeco-Levantine trade as Rhodes was to be two centuries later, and so on. All that it is prudent to do is to register an impression, viz. that the economic interplay and exchange among the seaboard communities of the eastern Mediterranean did increase in intensity during the Hellenistic period and did go some way towards making one world out of what had been hitherto an assemblage of economic zones less intimately and more superficially connected: but that this increase took place on lines (geographical and institutional) already familiar in Alexander's lifetime,

---

[166] *P. Berl.* 5883 + 5853 = *SB* 7169, probably of the period 200–150 B.C. First edition by Wilcken 1925: (F 346), with subsequent discussions summarized by Bogaert 1965, 147ff.: (H 15); add Fraser 1972, I.187 and II.275 n. 216 and 321 n. 435; Ste Croix 1974, 53–4: (H 193).

[167] Ashburner 1909: (H 2); Kreller 1921: (H 122), Rostovtzeff 1953, II.688–9: (A 52), De Robertis 1953: (H 47).   [168] Rostovtzeff 1953, II.1035–41: (A 52).

[169] Rostovtzeff 1953, II.1041ff.: (A 52). Cf. Roehlig 1933, 61–2: (H 184), for Miletus.

[170] For proxeny-grants and *isopoliteia* see below, n. 324. Since the citations for proxeny-grants do occasionally specify services to traders and merchant shipowners (e.g. *IG* II².416 (Athens, *c.* 330)), their influence has been posited elsewhere, especially when a particular city predominates among the honorands (e.g. Rhodians at Olous in Crete, *IC* I xxii.4–5) or when a wide spread of ethnics mirrors otherwise attested trading relationships, as at Chios (Vanseveren 1937, 325ff. no. 6: (B 169)) or at Heraclea (Robert 1951, 179ff.: (B 253)). However, the absence of any such specification from the citations in the numerous proxeny-decrees of Samos is noticeable, while at Delphi honours to *theoroi* were a major component of *SIG* 585 (see ll. 3–6, note). Cf. also C. Marek, 'Der Geldumlauf der Stadt Histiaia und seine Bedeutung für die Verteilung seiner Proxenoi', *Talanta* 8–9 (1977), 72–9.   [171] Cf. *IG* II².337 = Tod 189 (Athens, 333/2 B.C.).

was at all times precarious and subject to much distortion and impediment for political reasons (above all fiscal), and was hampered by the limitations and fluctuations of effective demand. Apart from those few 'trunk-routes' which are reflected in the associations of merchants abroad, much movement must have been speculative and of rapidly fluctuating pattern, expressed as a strong need for *one* port of redistribution – be it Athens, Rhodes, Phaselis, Chalcis, Delos, or wherever – but not for much more than that at any one time.[172] Such study as there has been of price-movements encapsulates the problem of description. Glotz's studies of prices at Delos from 315 to 166[173] brought out clearly that their rise and fall were governed not by any supply–demand mechanism but by military events and political decisions; Heichelheim's study of 1930 on a wider canvas showed that the prices of a whole range of goods and services tended to rise and fall in unison through the same period and beyond throughout the eastern Mediterranean. Our difficulty is that both observations are true and pertinent.

IV. PIRACY AND ITS RAMIFICATIONS

Much of the activity described in the preceding section was affected by a phenomenon whose influence defined the life of the eastern Mediterranean no less than that of monarchy: piracy. There is indeed a link of a complex kind between piracy, monarchy, and Greek society at large. Because of that complex inter-penetration, piracy needs extended discussion at the levels both of description and of interpretation.

The descriptive framework is clear enough, and has often been sketched.[174] After the Social War of 357–355 Athens was unable to keep an effective patrol fleet at sea in the Aegean. Spasmodic expeditions in lieu were insufficient to prevent the development of piracy based on small islands such as Melos, Cythnos, Halonnesos, and Myonnesos.[175] Most known pirate leaders in the late fourth-century Aegean were local men, but incursions were also made by 'Tyrrhenians', i.e. Italians and Etruscans, who had gained greater freedom of action after the erosion of Dionysius' Syracusan empire in South Italian waters. The period of the Successors may have seen a remission in piratical activity, partly because they were themselves maintaining substantial fleets and partly because many pirates and pirate ships had been recruited into those very fleets.

---

[172] Thus rightly Picard 1979, 342–3: (B 252).
[173] Glotz 1913 and 1916: (H 79–80).
[174] See *imprimis* Ormerod 1924: (H 158); Ziebarth 1929: (H 252); Rostovtzeff 1953, I.195–200, 202–3, II.607–10, 679–82, 771–4, 783–6, and 948–55: (A 52); Trofimova 1963: (H 229); Brulé 1978: (H 29).   [175] Ormerod 1924, 116ff.: (H 158).

However, with the weakening of Ptolemaic power in the Aegean by the 250s and the subsequent gradual decay of the Macedonian fleet,[176] piracy began again in earnest, the main practitioners this time being Aetolians and Cretans, followed by Illyrians from the 230s onwards.[177] The responsibility for trying to deal with them gradually passed from the Ptolemies to the Rhodians, who are known to have been active in this capacity by c. 299 and onwards into the second century.[178] However, their ability to render the Aegean safe should not be overestimated in the light of the endless epigraphical documentation of piracy from the mid third century onwards. In any case, after 166 Rhodes did not have the revenues necessary to keep any kind of fleet at sea, and her failure even with Attalid help in the Second Cretan War of 155–153[179] left Aegean and eastern Mediterranean waters largely unpoliced and open to the organized and increasingly large-scale piracy which used Crete and the coast of Cilicia as its base of operations from the 140s till Pompey.

Implicit in such a sketch is a view of pirates and their landward counterparts in brigandage[180] as evil and marginal predators on settled society. That view is unsatisfactory, not so much because it reflects too Manichean a morality (though, such is the equivocation of our age, such doubts have justly been voiced)[181] as because piracy was too pervasive, and too firmly interwoven in the fabric of Greek society, to be dismissed as marginal. Two main aspects deserve comment.

The first is a matter of manpower and skill. The superior technology and seamanship evinced by the success of Illyrian *lemboi*, Black Sea *kamarai*, or Cretan *mydia* and *akatia*[182] put the pirates and their craft paradoxically far more in the vanguard of military progress than the great powers with their increasingly expensive and elephantine sevens, thirteens, and sixteens, etc.,[183] while the battle of the Paxi islands (Polyb. II.10) revealed all too clearly how helpless the traditional navies of minor powers could be. In consequence pirate ships and their crews were an asset worth neutralizing or harnessing. The major powers did both, by

[176] Walbank 1940, 13 n. 10: (D 43).

[177] Aetolians: Benecke 1934, 11ff.: (D 103); Cretans: Brulé 1978, 66–7: (H 29); Illyrians: Dell 1967(2): (D 10).

[178] See Blinkenberg 1938, 45 n. 2: (E 133), for a list of Rhodian campaigns against pirates.

[179] M. Segre, 'Κρητικὸς πόλεμος', *Riv. Fil.* 11 (1933) 365–92; Brulé 1978, 61–6: (H 29). The Rhodian fleet remained in being, as did those of Cos (Sherwin-White 1978, 208–10: (D 146)) and Athens; Rhodes also played some role in the events which precipitated the Roman pirate law of 101/100 B.C. (Hassall *et al.* 1974, lines 12–13: (H 88)), but that role may have been diplomatic only.

[180] Of whom in the Hellenistic period there has been less systematic study. Cf. however Robert 1937, 90–110: (B 139); Rostovtzeff 1953, 1514 n. 49: (A 52); and Briant 1976: (E 11); and for the Roman period MacMullen 1967, 192–241 and 255–68 (H 135).

[181] Brulé 1978, 46: (H 29); Garlan 1978, *passim*: (H 72).

[182] Casson 1971, 125ff.: (J 137); Strabo XI.2.12. C.495; Diod. XXXI.38.

[183] Tarn 1930, 132ff.: (J 153).

recruiting them for particular campaigns,[184] by retaining their leaders as admirals and commanders,[185] or by striking such treaties with piratically-inclined communities as siphoned off their surplus manpower[186] or as made it a *casus belli* for them to continue their depredations.[187] In this way the relationship between the military powers which needed and could pay mercenaries and the communities which nurtured pirates was not so much adversative as symbiotic. It has indeed been said that a pirate is an unemployed mercenary, but it is equally true that the more competent the pirate, the more he is worth employing. It is scarcely surprising that the monarchies (Egypt perhaps excepted) took no high moral tone towards the pirates whose skills they needed.

The second important aspect of piracy concerns the customs and the assumptions about its legitimacy which underpinned it. Since the practice of piracy requires a base, a command structure, and an initial investment in ship-building (time and resources) and supplies, it presupposes either the absence of effective state authority or its active connivance. Either way relationships are political, not purely criminal, and reflect a context of inter-communal custom the reverse of ours, whereby the right of seizure (συλᾶν) held good between the members of two communities unless outlawed by specific agreement. In this context, the basic structure of συλᾶν-procedure is triangular, viz, that [*a*], a citizen of State A, injured by [*b*¹], a citizen of State B, could forcibly exact recompense from a second citizen of State B, [*b*²], who could in turn recover it by legal process in B from [*b*¹] (as [*a*] could not, having no status and no access to legal process in B).[188] In theory, indeed, such seizure should be reprisal for an injury already suffered, but the boundary between reprisal and unprovoked attack was thin enough at the best of times and could easily be crossed, as Queen Teuta of the Illyrians did when challenged by the Coruncanii, by claiming that 'so far as concerned private activities it was not customary for Illyrian rulers to preclude their subjects from augmenting their fortunes at sea'.[189]

The effect of such a custom being to discourage movement on lawful as much as on unlawful occasions, Greek 'international law' from the

---

[184] E.g. by Demetrius against Rhodes in 305 (Diod. xx.82.4 and 83.1) and against Cassander in 302 (Diod. xx.110.4). [185] Ormerod 1924, 123: (H 158).

[186] E.g. Eumenes II's treaty with 30 Cretan cities (*SIG* 627 = *IC* iv.179, with *Bull. épig.* 1958, 406), or Antigonus' treaties with Hierapytna (*IC* iii.iii.1 = *SVA* 502) and Eleutherna (*IC* ii.xii.20 = *SVA* 501). Cf. in general Ducrey 1970, 643ff.: (E 121).

[187] The classic case is Rhodes' treaty of 205/4 with Hierapytna (*SIG* 581 = *IC* iii.iii.3 = *SVA* 551, §x, with Brulé 1978, 51ff.: (H 29)); cf. also her treaty of *c.* 203 with Olous (*SVA* 552, with Brulé 1978, 54ff.).

[188] On συλή/συλᾶν in general see Dareste 1889: (H 41); Gernet 1917, 264ff.: (H 78); Wilhelm 1911, 195–200: (B 173); Latte 1931: (H 126); Gauthier 1972, 209ff.: (H 74); Garlan 1978: (H 72).

[189] Polyb. ii.8.8, trans. M. Chambers.

archaic period onwards witnessed various attempts to obviate the need to invoke the right of seizure. (i) For example, specific outstanding rights against a foreign city or individual (B or [b^1]) might be taken over by State A, as the Chalcedonians did for urgent fiscal purposes:[190] or their activation might be made subject to State A's consent and to specific procedures, as in the late third-century agreement between Stymphalus and Aegira:[191] or, the inverse case, a citizen of a community vulnerable to such rights (State B) might take it upon himself to settle them, as Timagoras of Cyrene seems to have done in the late fourth century.[192] (ii) Alternatively, the evolution of proxeny-procedures allowed State A to appoint in B a citizen, [b^3], who could serve as sponsor in B in legal process for [a] or his fellow-citizens and who would himself have protected access to the courts of A. If we leave aside here the purely political role of *proxenoi*, it was probably this latter privilege of access which came to be the more important aspect and which led to the proliferation of such grants in the Hellenistic period.[193] (iii) Or, thirdly, A and B might agree *symbola* with each other, viz. bilateral judicial conventions envisaging access by citizens of A to the courts (or a court) of B (and vice versa) and specifying procedures, the composition of the court, etc., in some detail.[194]

(iv) Fourthly, a claim or grant of *asylia* might be made. These took various forms,[195] not all of which can be linked with the threat of piracy. However, it is convenient to set the various types out here, partly for convenience and partly because the uses of *asylia* as a social institution and as a diplomatic technique well illustrated how verbally similar phenomena may derive from very different economic or political contexts, fears, needs and ambitions. Freedom from σύλη attached in the first and foremost instance to a god and to his/her shrine,[196] and even in the Hellenistic period recognitions are occasionally couched in terms of the god rather than of the physical space of the shrine.[197] Claims for the

---

[190] [Arist.] *Oec.* II.1347b 20ff. with Van Groningen *ad loc.* and Gauthier 1972, 211–12: (H 74).

[191] *IG* v.2.357 = *SEG* XI.1105 = *SVA* 567, ll. 89–93, with Gauthier 1972, 238ff. and 295ff.: (H 74).

[192] Oliverio *et al.* 1961–2, 273 no. 103: (B 116), with *Bull. épig*, 1964, 565 and Gauthier 1972, 213: (H 74).

[193] E.g. the list of proxeny-grants made by Aetolia (Benecke 1934, 31ff.: (D 103)) in the third and early second centuries includes citizens of nearly all the major islands and seaboard states (Corinth and Athens being interesting exceptions). Cf. also n. 324 below.

[194] Gauthier 1972: (H 74) and Ziegler 1975: (H 234) are now the starting points of discussion.

[195] See especially Schlesinger 1933: (H 201), and also Gauthier 1972, 222–6, 242–4, 282–4: (H 74); Bravo 1974, 156–9: (B 54); Ziegler 1975, 167ff.: (H 254); Gawantka 1975, 115ff.: (H 76); Walbank 1981, 145ff.: (A 63).

[196] Hence of course the importance of altar and sanctuary for suppliants or for runaway slaves. This form of *asylia* is not our concern here, socially important though slave sanctuary was (cf. Tac. *Ann.* III.63).

[197] E.g. *OGIS* 333 = *RC* 68, l. 1; *SIG* 781, ll. 10–11.

explicit recognition of the inviolability of a particular shrine, hitherto sparse, became more frequent from the mid third century B.C. Thenceforward, stimulated either by convenient epiphanies of the deity in question, by emulation of neighbours, or by the ostentatious benevolence of a sovereign, many cities claimed *asylia* for a prominent shrine of theirs and went on later, if such claims were widely conceded, to make wider claims on behalf of their city and territory as well. Cities whose claims evoked widespread recognition[198] included Smyrna from 246 onwards, Cos from 242, Magnesia-on-the-Maeander from 207/6, Teos from 204/3, and Miletus. It is probably not chance that the best documented claims are those made by the coastal cities of Asia Minor, for the waning of Ptolemaic seapower, and their exposed position in a region accessible and attractive to all four major monarchies must have presented both an urgent need for protection and the opportunity to extract it by playing one power against another.

Inevitably most recognitions were formulaic (though flowery and elaborate on occasion), but did not thereby lack substance. Aetolia's recognition of Magnesia's *asylia* is business-like and explicit:

that the friendship towards them should be preserved, and that their city and land should be holy and free from pillage ($\mathring{a}\sigma\upsilon\lambda o\nu$), as their envoys proclaim: and that it should be permitted to no one of Aetolians or of those dwelling in Aetolia, whencesoever they may start as base, to carry off anyone ($\mu\eta\delta\acute{\epsilon}\nu a$) from the land of the Magnesians, neither by land nor by sea: if anyone should carry off, the (Aetolian) general in office shall recover the visible goods, and as for invisible goods, the *synedroi* are empowered to impose such penalty as they see fit, as against persons damaging the common weal, to exact the penalties and return them to those who are suffering injustice.[199]

The force of such recognitions emerges also from what we can occasionally detect, the refusal to accord them. Most of the documents in the Magnesia dossier grant the city's requests without further ado, but the letters of Antiochus III and Attalus I, and the decree of Chalcis drafted on Philip V's instructions, omit all reference to the *asylia* of city and land, thereby fuelling the reasonable presumption that the kings concerned did not want to tie their hands.[200]

Complementary to such recognitions of the inviolability of a place were those of the inviolability of persons. Such grants sometimes stood by themselves,[201] but since they were better adapted to the needs of

[198] Full list and documentation in Schlesinger 1933, 71–84: (H 201).

[199] *IG* IX².1.4, ll. 14–25. Other Aetolian *asylia*-decrees are closely similar (Benecke 1934, 17–31: (D 103)).

[200] Respectively *I. Magnesia* 18 (=*OGIS* 231=*RC* 31); 34 (=*OGIS* 282=*RC* 34); 47 (=*SIG* 561). *RC* p. 147; Walbank 1981, 147: (A 63).

[201] E.g. *SIG* 357, where Epidaurus' grant of *asylia* to the Astypalaeans as the former's colonists is linked only with *ateleia*.

travellers they were frequently linked via the formula 'the right of sailing in and out inviolably and without formal treaty' with the grant of *proxenos*-status, as in the innumerable such decrees from Delphi and elsewhere, whether they were given to individuals or to groups such as mercenaries or the *technitai* of Dionysus (see below p. 319). One should not overestimate their importance, for they tended to be granted by communities such as Delphi with little will or capacity for mischief, but that is not true of a further form, the bilateral treaty between two states which protected each other's nationals from *syle* 'by land or by sea, in war or in peace'.[202] A community thus protected was in a strong position.

Plainly, piracy was not the only precipitator of these diplomatic developments, for fear of royal encroachment and local ambitions for the prestige of a city's shrine and festivals also played some part. Yet the threat of piracy may well have been primary, as one more of the ways in which war and violence, together with the institutions they called into being, were basic determining factors of Hellenistic experience. Like formal war, too, piracy was used in an entirely rational fashion. We should not be seduced by Polybius' rude remarks about Aetolians and Cretans[203] into supposing that their public policy was the product of remoteness, primitiveness, or collective boorishness. Much more simply, it was in their interest to raise their nuisance value by allowing the age-old system of seizure to run its course. If it yielded no reaction from the victim (state or person), then Aetolians and Cretans were the wealthier by whatever proceeds their booty would fetch: if it did yield a reaction, then the *koinon* was that much better placed to make an advantageous treaty. The growth of the Aetolian League is testimony enough to the force of that logic.

V. CHANGE AND CONTINUITY

Piracy, and the reactions to it, provide a specific example of how the phrase 'Hellenistic Society' is a convenient but misleading label for a set of developing and *ad hoc* solutions to the very various immediate or longer-term needs and problems which had to be solved (or lived with) within certain boundary conditions by governments and individuals.[204]

---

[202] E.g. *IG* IX².1.136 = *SVA* 542   ʌetolia and Tricca in Thessaly, after 206).

[203] E.g. on Aetolians: 11.3.3, 4.6, ʌ5–9 *passim*; IV.3.1 and 5, 7.8, 16.4, 18.11, 67.4, 65.1ff.; V.9 and 11; IX.34, 35.6, 38.6; XVIII.34; On Cretans: IV.8, 11; VI.46–7; VIII.16.4–5: XXXIII.16.4–5.

[204] This is not the place for lengthy methodological disquisitions, but choices must be explicit. In these last and most general sections, which of course owe much to the lively debate of the last twenty years about Hellenistic society, I am deliberately adopting an empirical mode of analysis. I do so partly in order to avoid both the dangerous and largely futile language of 'East and West', 'heyday and decline', or 'crisis of the *polis*' and historicist analysis of Hellenistic society as 'the

Three of these boundary conditions need to be singled out. First and foremost, personal monarchy had shown itself repeatedly by 300 and often thereafter to be the only effective way of controlling large tracts of territory and revenue. Only *qua* monarch could one be a major power in contemporary Greek military conditions. Even the federal states were paper tigers, while the single *polis* as a power unit able to hold its own with the other eastern Mediterranean powers was dead: Sellasia proved it once again in 222 (as if it had not been clear since 500), and even at her peak of influence and prosperity Rhodes never acted alone.[205] Secondly, the monarchies were competitive, territorially unstable, and given to mutual spoiling. These characteristics had their roots in an idea-structure of monarchy which is explained elsewhere in this volume:[206] here we are concerned rather with what stems from them, such as the competition for soldiers, diplomats, client-scholars and primary resources of productive land, or the ingenious opportunism of cities (and would-be cities) everywhere in extracting concessions of status, or gifts of money, buildings and works of art from their suzerain or potentially suzerain kings. Thirdly, and obviously, no area or aspect of social life – especially indeed in the territories newly conquered and vulnerable to Greek culture – developed without reference to the past. On the contrary, there is increasing awareness that notwithstanding the innovations of kings and colonists, the types of settlement and land use, the forms of landowning and dependent labour, the patterns of cult, and the various ways (*polis*, temple-state, canton, principality, etc.) of structuring politico-administrative space – all themselves interlocking and reacting upon each other – represented far more of a continuity with the Achaemenid or local past than was once acknowledged. What follows here is therefore inevitably in part subdivided by region, since each region's experience and previous circumstances differed. However, no attempt is made to treat the several regions and kingdoms in the detail to be found in the relevant special chapters: the emphasis will instead be on common themes, especially on the changing and growing role of *polis*-style administrative ordering throughout much of the Hellenistic world.

That continuity is naturally most easily visible in mainland Greece and the Aegean. Here one can be confident that the pattern of major urban settlement changed very little. Synoecism had largely run its

linking member between slave-owning society and feudalism' (e.g. Jähne 1978, 140: (H 110)), and partly because we are dealing with institutions and practices created by decisions made through time within a framework of needs, ambitions, and possibilities.

[205] Her action against the Ptolemaic fleet at Ephesus (Polyaen. v.18) belongs somehow within the 'Second Syrian War' (Will 1979, 1.235ff.: (A 67)), while her action against Byzantium in 219 involved allied ships (Polyb. IV.50.5) and the co-operation of Prusias I of Bithynia.

[206] See ch. 3.

course,[207] and the only major town-foundation of note, that of Demetrias in Thessaly by Poliorcetes soon after 294,[208] did no more in effect than replace the existing urban centre of Pagasae. So too the restoration of Thebes in 316 (Diod. XIX.53–4) merely restored the *status quo*. The only lasting change, indeed, was the obliteration of Corinth in 146. Smaller-scale change, in towns or countryside, is harder to assess, since literary evidence tells us little which is reliable,[209] while the archaeological evidence for Hellenistic Greece has yet to be assembled and assessed.[210] However, the raw data from one area which has been seriously surveyed, Messenia, recording 96 habitation or burial sites from the classical period, 94 Hellenistic and 85 Roman,[211] suggest a stable population and settlement pattern and hardly confirm Strabo's comment on its depopulation in his time.[212]

Whether such imputed stability of population and settlement (if verified by future research) reflected stability in landownership and land use is harder to assess, for the evidence points both ways. On the one hand, as noted above (p. 268), the reduced need for citizen-soldiers had lowered one social barrier against the accumulation of land, and consistently enough documents from all corners of the Greek world attest not merely the existence of a small group of wealthy ruling families – as in Demetrias,[213] Larissa,[214] or notoriously pre-revolutionary Sparta, with its hundred or so possessors of land and *kleros*[215] – but also the existence of single individuals with predominant economic status vis-à-vis his or her (or another) city and fellow-citizens, in a position to give or to lend money to the city, to pay its debts, to build its walls, or to ransom its citizens from slavery.[216] True, the fact that the most spectacularly wealthy of these men are found in the cities of Pontus and western Asia Minor, and towards the end of our period rather than its beginning, may

---

[207] Cf. however the synoecism of the Acarnanians to Stratus and Sauria in 314, described by Diodorus (XIX.67.4) in terms which imply actual relocation of residence.

[208] Stähelin *et al.* 1934: (B 206); Meyer 1962, 24ff.: (H 141).

[209] For Polyb. XXXVI.17 see above, p. 268.

[210] See L. Gallo, 'Popolosità e scarsità di popolazione. Contributo allo studio di un topos', *Annali di Pisa*³ 10(1980)1233–70.

[211] Data counted off from W. A. McDonald and G. R. Rapp (eds.), *The Minnesota Messenia Expedition: Reconstructing a Bronze Age Environment* (Minneapolis, 1972), maps 8.17 and 8.18; uncertain sites excluded.

[212] Strabo VIII.4.11. c362. His note *ibid.* on the similar depopulation of Laconia appears to be merely an unsafe inference from the contrast between the 30 πόλιχναι of his own (i.e. Augustan) time and the epithet ἑκατόμπολις (elsewhere only of Crete, *Il.* II.6.649 and Strabo X.4.15.c479–480).

[213] Stähelin 1929, 203: (B 164).

[214] Stähelin 1924, 95: (D 86); pp. 268–9 above.

[215] Plut. *Agis* 5.6 (n. 64, above).

[216] Numerous examples in Maier 1959: (J 226), *ISE* I–II, Austin 1981, and elsewhere. See also Tarn and Griffith 1952, 108–9: (A 59), and Rostovtzeff 1953, II.805 with III.1521 n. 75, and II.819ff. with III.1527 n. 98: (A 52).

suggest that a different process was also under way, namely the attachment to Greek or hellenized cities of the great estates of western Asia Minor as they escaped from royal control (see below), but much of the evidence predates that emancipation and must be explained within a mainland frame of reference. Again, institutions and public offices were on occasion reordered so as to reflect the tenure of such preponderant wealth in a few hands. The most notable such change was probably Demetrius of Phalerum's abolition between 316 and 307 of the 100 or so festival liturgies at Athens. Instead a single person, the *agonothetes*, henceforth ran each festival, on the understanding that he held the position once only, had public funds to spend, but was also expected to contribute lavishly himself in a way that few fourth-century *choregoi* could have sustained.[217] So too when in Athens and elsewhere the state came to intervene more directly in education (see p. 308, below), the liturgical and administrative responsibilities for the *gymnasion* and the *epheboi* were concentrated in the person of the gymnasiarch (*kosmetes* at Athens and certain other places), whose personal outlay could be considerable.

Furthermore, we can detect another major component of change and concentration, the mutual counter-pressures of debtors and creditors. Cases known in detail usually involve a public body as the debtor,[218] and from them we can imagine the pressures which creditors could bring to bear upon individuals. There is indeed enough evidence of tension from the later fourth century and the Hellenistic period to suggest that the comparatively marginal role played (apart from bottomry loans) by interest-bearing debt in classical Athens cannot be predicated of Hellenistic Greece in general.[219] However, since Athens significantly remained free of such tensions until Athenion's régime in 88,[220] and since concentrations of such tensions can be seen e.g. in the Aegean islands in the mid third century[221] and in Central and Northern Greece in the 180s and 170s,[222] explanations need to be place- and time-specific rather than general. Moreover, such explanations as extravagance, wastefulness and love of pleasure,[223] offered by the literary sources, do less than justice to hints that debtors tended to be cultivators,[224] for

---

[217] Ferguson 1911, 55ff.: (D 89).

[218] E.g. the debts contracted by Orchomenus (Hennig 1977: (D 80)).

[219] See the data collected in Asheri 1969: (H 5); for Athens see Finley 1953: (H 60).

[220] Posidonius, *FGrH* 87F36, with Candiloro 1965, 145ff.: (H 34), but since Mithridates' propaganda was directed mainly at Asia Minor we should not infer much about Athens from it.

[221] Asheri 1969, 47ff.: (H 5) (examples from Carthaea, Naxos, Samos and Syros): add Amorgos in the 220s (*IG* XII.7.221–3).   [222] See Asheri 1969, 61ff.: (H 5).

[223] Polyb. xx.6 (Boeotia before 192, but see Hennig 1977: (D 80); Agatharchides, *FGrH* 86F16 (Arycanda in Lycia in 197), with Schmitt 1964, 285ff.: (E 51).

[224] As at Abydus ([Arist.] *Oec.* II.1349a3), and *imprimis* in the great debt moratorium law of Ephesus after 297, where creditors are τοκισταί or δανεισταί and debtors γεωργοί (*SIG* 364, ll. 2, 11,

whom foreclosure meant partial or (more likely) complete loss of land[225] in the absence of systems of collateral security: a consequence which underlay the repeated coupling of agitation for remission of debts (χρεῶν ἀποκοπή) with that for the redistribution of land (γῆς ἀναδασ-μός).[226] An increased alienability of land (*de jure* or *de facto*) must therefore be predicated, together perhaps with the breakdown of such prejudice against interest-bearing loans as may once have existed.[227] Even so, however, a gap in explanation remains, which only further detailed investigation will bridge. At present the best that can be offered is to note that the areas of north Greece most affected in the 180s and 170s were also those most affected by Roman abstraction of booty or reparations in the 190s.[228] The hypothesis of liquidity crisis, specific to area and period, would not only explain that correlation but would also explain why the worst tension between agrarian debtors and creditors occurred in just that region of Greece – Laconia – where the use and availability of coinage had made least headway by the 240s. It would also account for the occasions where partial or total remission of interest rates was reckoned to be enough to resolve the immediate crisis,[229] and could also explain why foreign judges, called in to resolve a 'difference' (διαφορά) or a 'disturbance' (ταραχή), were repeatedly able to restore 'unity of spirit' (ὁμόνοια) simply by processing equitably suits and contracted matters (συμβόλαια) which had been caught in a general seize-up of legal process (ἀκρισία) and had hence contributed to immobilizing such moneys as might otherwise have circulated.[230]

All the same, the scale of these movements, and of the social unrest they created, should not be exaggerated, as it sometimes has been. For example, evidence of the continued wide spread of property-holding

---

26, 34, with Asheri 1969, 44ff. and 108ff.: (H 5)) but implicit in any system of securing debts upon real property.

[225] Apart from the marginal use of collateral security via the *apotimema*-system (see above p. 261) in fourth-century Athens in pupillary and dotal contexts, Greek laws on security remained anchored to the concept of substitution (of the property pledged, *as a unit*, for the debt): otherwise e.g. the special procedures created at Ephesus in the 290s would have been unnecessary: see Finley 1952, 46–7 and 107ff.: (H 59).

[226] See Asheri 1966 and Asheri 1969: (H 4–5).

[227] Finley 1953, 257–8: (H 60).   [228] Larsen, *ESAR* IV.313–25.

[229] E.g. at Ephesus for certain debts (*SIG* 364, ll. 17ff.), or at Olbia, where at one point the *demos* hoped to arrange a moratorium on interest (ἐπιμηνιεῦσαι, *SIG* 495, l. 180, with Asheri 1969, 54–5: (H 5)).

[230] For this nexus of vocabulary see e.g. *OGIS* 43 = Austin 268, with Holleaux, *Études* III.27–37, and Sherwin-White 1978, 90ff.: (D 146) (Naxos *c.* 280); *IG* XI.4.1052 (Syros *c.* 250–240); *IG* XII.5.1065 (Carthaea on Ceos, *c.* 280); with Asheri 1969, 47ff. nos. xxiii, xxiv, and xxvi: (H 5). For the role of foreign judges see n. 355 below. This is not to deny that ἀκρισία was on occasion a deliberate suspension of court proceedings, adopted in debtors' interests so that creditors would have no legal judgements in their favour which they could proceed to enforce. This allegedly in Boeotia in the late third century (Polyb. xx.6.1: Heracleides Criticus 1.15–16 (*Geographi graeci minores* (Paris, 1885) 1.103), with Hennig 1977: (D 80) and Walbank 1979, III.72: (B 37)).

comes readily to hand. Festival-financing via the *choregia* continued in many places, and the gymnasiarchy itself was often split so as to share the expense. At Athens various subscription lists and records of voluntary contributions (ἐπιδόσεις) for various purposes continue through the Hellenistic period to suggest that a broad-based propertied class continued there much as before. Similar lists and records elsewhere, whether for fortification-building[231] or for other public purposes,[232] indicate a comparable picture, to be set against that of the overmasteringly wealthy individual. Again, though it is true that the pressures of debt did from time to time explode in revolution and tyranny,[233] equally salient are the efforts of kings or of neighbouring cities to reduce the pressures: it could well be argued that the kings performed no more helpful function than this vis-à-vis the cities they supervised, and that the violence at Cassandreia and Sparta was due respectively to the temporary absence of any effective Macedonian king and to the independence and remoteness of Sparta from Macedonian supervisory power. In any case, the appeal of the Spartan revolution did not spread beyond the Peloponnese, and that of Nabis not beyond Laconia. So too the shambles of public affairs in Boeotia, described with such misleading *parti pris* by Polybius, dissolves on examination into the mildly redistributive measures of a populist and unbellicose régime.[234] Again, the most strikingly violent surviving literary tract of the period against the extremes of wealth and poverty, Cercidas' fourth Meliamb, probably implies much less socially than it appears to do, having been written by a well-off politician whose presumed Cynic leanings did not prevent him from easing the rapprochement between Aratus and Antigonus Doson against Cleomenes.[235] Tyranny did indeed reassert itself as a mode of government in Greece from the late fourth century onwards, but it is essential to separate those few tyrants whose rise reflected serious social tensions from those whose position approximated more to that of

[231] See Maier 1961, 57ff.: (J 227).

[232] For examples see Kuenzi 1923, 67ff.: (H 124); *SEG* 1.367 (Samos, temple); Wilhelm 1932: (H 241) (corn supply); Robert 1933, 473–85: (B 135), and Robert 1935, 421–5: (B 137) (libraries); Béquignon 1935, 36–51: (B 49), with Tod, *JHS* 57 (1937) 189 (Crannon); Béquignon 1935: (B 184) (Pharsalus, stoa and buildings); Vanseveren 1937, 321ff.: (B 169) (Chios); Accame 1938, 228–9: (B 41) (religious purposes); Pugliese Carratelli 1939–40, 164ff. nos. 19–21: (E 141) (Rhodes); Rostovtzeff 1953, III.1463 n. 22: (A 52); Maier 1961, 18 n. 40 on p. 19: (J 227); and many more.

[233] To the Spartan revolutions add some others, such as those of Apollodorus at Cassandreia between 280 and 276 (references in Fuks 1974, 71 n. 23: (H 69)), or Molpagoras at Cius (*c.* 203–202: Polyb. xv.21), which may have been equally violent.

[234] Polyb. xx.6 with Feyel 1942, 273–83: (D 79), and Hennig 1977: (D 80).

[235] Text in Powell 1925, 203ff.: (B 28), with D. R. Dudley *A History of Cynicism from Diogenes to the Sixth Century A.D.* (London, 1937) 74–84, and other references *ap.* Walbank 1957, I.247–8: (B 37), Polyb. II.48ff. That the attitudes and values expressed *c.* 190 B.C. (Eissfeldt 1965, 597: (B 10)) by Jesus Ben Sira in *Ecclesiasticus* (see Tcherikover 1959, 142–51: (A 61)) bear some resemblance to those of Cercidas is hardly surprising.

strategos of a major king,[236] or from those like Lydiades of Megalopolis or the successive tyrants of Argos, whose government seems to have been stable and conducted without outrage. (Indeed, the need for re-election apart, the difference in power and accountability between a *strategos* of Achaea or Aetolia and many of the so-called tyrants was often subtle).[237] All in all, there is little justification for describing the social conditions of Hellenistic Greece in the apocalyptic terms which have sometimes been used.

VI. ROYAL POLICIES AND REGIONAL DIVERSITIES

The three boundary conditions noted above (p. 291) – the predominance of monarchy, its competitive characteristics, and continuity with the past – affected the wider canvas of the Hellenistic world with equal force. We must begin with the kings, and with the close interaction between the position and role of the king on the one hand and the pattern of land settlement and land tenure on the other. It is commonplace to observe that Ptolemies and Seleucids, and Antigonids in relation to land outside Macedonia, regarded their territories as spear-won land,[238] theirs by right of conquest and inheritance in an interpretation far-reaching enough to allow inheritance by will.[239] In this sense the land was the king's as beneficial landowner, and taxation on land was paid to him as rent to a landlord. In theory, therefore, absolute proprietorship bestowed absolute property-power, and the concentration of financial resources which it thereby permitted and their redistribution to courts, armies, cities, temples and artists, not only largely account for the patterns of Hellenistic patronage but also made any ruler who cared to use his opportunities into a power capable by itself of transforming economy and society. However, three qualifications must be borne in mind. First, such a theory was not new to Alexander or his successors. The Achaemenids had acted on the same principle in assigning lands to members of the royal family, to courtiers, to refugees such as Themistocles or to uprooted or transplanted

---

[236] Especially those in third- and second-century Asia Minor, for whom see Bikerman 1938, 166ff.: (E 6), Rostovtzeff 1953, III.1425 n. 230: (A 52), and Crampa 1969, 86ff.: (B 60).

[237] Cf. for example *SIG* 598E, Dicaearchus' letter as Aetolian *strategos* to Magnesia, which but for its casual reference to *synedroi* could easily have been written by an Attalid.

[238] δορίκτητος γῆ, Diod. XVIII.43.1 (Alexander), XIX.105.4 (general), XX.76.7 (Antigonus), XXI.1.5 (twice: general), XXI.2.2 (general), XXII.1.3 (Decius the Campanian at Rhegium). See Schmitthenner 1968: (I 64) and J. Hornblower 1981, 53: (B 21), but the concept was not confined to the successor generation: Antiochus III reckoned that Lysimachus' kingdom was his by right of conquest after Corupedium (Polyb. XVIII.51.4), and Antiochus IV claimed Coele-Syria and Palestine after Panium in the same way (Polyb. XXVIII.1.4). Cf. Bikerman 1938, 15: (E 6).

[239] As by Ptolemy VIII to Rome conditionally in 155 (*SEG* IX.7), and by Attalus III in 133.

populations,[240] as indeed the Chaldaean kings of Babylon may have done before them. Equally, Macedonian kings felt themselves entitled to make similarly wide-ranging gifts and dispositions in Europe, at least in respect of the new lands which came into their hands by conquest.[241] The uniformity and continuity of practice is striking. Secondly, there were practical and political limits on the exercise of such power. It could not be effectively wielded without upsetting traditional relationships or without eroding the king's own property-power. Thirdly, we need to distinguish the overriding royal ownership of land from its everyday beneficial ownership.[242] As the justification of taxation and of the king's ability to confer land by assignment (and to revoke such assignations), the former has fundamental residual importance, but it was the latter which affected social relationships more directly and immediately, since the beneficial landowner could be the king himself, a tenant-in-chief from the king, a temple, a city collectively, or an individual citizen of a city.

Herein lay one source of diversity outwith the areas of traditional Greek culture. Three others need to be singled out, the pattern of settlement, the extent and nature of local government, and the modes of production on the land and in crafts and trades.

(1) At the start of our period, in Asia and the Levant as in Greece and the Mediterranean generally, large urban agglomerations were rare and exceptional. Babylon, however, was certainly one until it was supplanted by Seleuceia-on-the-Tigris. Susa, Uruk, and Sippar may have been others,[243] and the existence of large cities elsewhere cannot be discounted.[244] However, there is little doubt that outwith the narrow band of Greek or semi-Greek coastal city-state settlement the predominant form of nucleated settlement all over the region was the so-called village, either on its own or (as often) grouped together in various

---

[240] For examples and references see Rostovtzeff 1953, III.1339 n. 8: (A 52); Dandamayev 1972, 29–33: (H 40); Briant 1973, 44ff.: (C 7); Wörrle 1978, 208–9: (B 179). For pre-Achaemenid practice see B. Oded, *Mass Deportations and Deportees in the Neo-Assyrian Empire* (Wiesbaden, 1979).

[241] Cf. again Rostovtzeff 1953, III.1339 n. 9: (A 52); add Theopompus, *FGrH* 115 F 225 b; *SIG* 302; *SIG* 332.

[242] Préaux 1939, 459ff.: (F 306); Kreissig 1978, 32ff.: (E 36).

[243] Estimates of population for these and other Mesopotamian cities in the Achaemenid and Hellenistic periods are very hard to come by (e.g. no estimate for Susa in Le Rider 1965, 28off.: (B 236)). For Uruk see Falkenstein 1941: (E 189); Sarkisian 1974: (H 200); Sarkisian 1974: (B 157); Doty 1977 and 1978: (B 63–4). Gaza in the fifth century was not much smaller than Sardis (Hdt. III.5) and was μεγάλη in 331 (Arr. *Anab.* II.26.1), but we have no idea how large Achaemenid Sardis may have been.

[244] However, the figure of 120,000 given for Jerusalem in Josephus' citation of Hecataeus (Jos. *C.Ap.* 1.197 = *FGrH* 264 F 21 (197)) must be treated with great reserve, since Josephus' source was not the late fourth-century Hecataeus of Abdera but a supposititious compilation probably of the early second century B.C. (Jacoby, *Comm. ad loc.* p. 62). For Tarsus see Welles 1962: (E 101); for Olbia see Knipovich 1956: (H 114).

ways.[245] The Greek terms used to denote such settlements vary considerably,[246] having in common only the reluctance to use the term 'polis' *tout court* without qualification. They are used to describe settlements in Asia Minor, in Egypt, in Babylonia, and in Palestine alike,[247] but the exact denotation of these terms in the minds of Greek colonialist authorities, as reflected in literary or epigraphical texts, is a matter of some difficulty. The size of settlement seems not to have been the primary consideration, nor the complete absence of local authority and government, for at least in Seleucid areas (including here Syria-Phoenicia) they, via local officials, were the basis for the collection of taxation.[248] Rather, the primary criteria, like those Pausanias (x.4.1) was much later to apply at Panopeus in Phocis, were probably negative, comprising the absence of physical institutions such as agora, gymnasia, theatre, walls, or temples, or of political institutions such as citizen assembly, elected magistrates, and law courts.

(2) Nevertheless, the Greek-style city, showing at least some of these institutions, was not so purely an imported phenomenon as has sometimes been implied. The Phoenician seaboard cities of Tyre, Sidon, Arad, and Byblus, for example, had certainly continued to enjoy some autonomy through the Achaemenid period.[249] The same was true for Babylon,[250] and in a complex sense for Xanthus, where the Greek and Lycian versions of the trilingual inscription of 358 or 337[251] use the phraseology of municipal autonomy even though the Aramaic version uses that of satrapal command. Yet, though there may have been other towns as yet unattested in the same position (Sardis, Damascus, and Tarsus are obvious possibilities), they plainly comprised only a minority of the communities which the Greeks encountered in their newly extended world. Other forms of local government were many and various. They ranged from quasi-independent and quasi-hereditary dynasties such as those of the Hecatomnids in Caria or the Hydarnes-Orontes family in Armenia, through tribal cantons, which might again be quasi-independent,[252] to areas with temple-oriented economies and/or

[245] Broughton 1938, 627ff.: (E 62), is still fundamental, with Tchalenko 1953–8: (H 224), Briant 1975: (E 10), and Kreissig 1978, 17ff.: (E 36).

[246] Broughton 1938, 628–9: (E 62); Briant 1975, 170: (E 10).

[247] Cf. *C.Ord.Ptol.* 21 = Austin 275(a), and the dossier from near Bet She'an published by Landau 1966: (B 101) ll. 11, 13, 22 and 29, with Fischer 1979: (B 72).

[248] Briant 1975, 177ff.: (E 10); *C.Ord.Ptol.* 21 = Austin 275(a), ll. 10ff.

[249] Bosworth 1981, 226 and 256: (B 5), Tod II.139 on Straton of Sidon.

[250] Sarkisian 1952 and 1953: (H 198–9).

[251] Metzger *et al.* 1974: (B 108); Badian 1977: (H 8); Wörrle 1978, 234 n. 174 and 236ff.: (B 179); Metzger *et al.* 1979 (166 n. 1 on Badian's date): (B 109). For the date see now Hornblower 1982, 46ff.: (E 73).

[252] Cf. in particular the Mardi, Uxii, Elymaei and Cassaei in the Zagrus mountains (Nearchus *FGrH* 133 F 1 (g) (= Strabo XI.13.6.C.524); Arr. *Anab.* III.17 with Bosworth *ad loc.* (Uxii): (B 5); *ibid.* VII.15 (Cassaei); Diod. XIX.17.3 (Uxii)).

priest-run institutions. Upper Egypt was plainly a case in point, and went on being so, as was Judaea and as were the many areas in Syria, Mesopotamia, and Asia Minor which looked primarily to a temple for a central place and to its priesthood-defined aristocracy for leadership.[253] That all these various forms continued throughout the Hellenistic period is a matter of elementary observation, confirmed by contemporary language.[254]

(3) There has been extensive recent debate about the third source of diversity, viz. the exact natures of the forms of dependence encountered by the Greeks in their newly extended dominions; a debate largely dependent on Marx's postulation of a specific 'Asiatic mode of production' as an identifiable stage in the development of productive relationships.[255] Here, as elsewhere in this chapter, an acknowledgement of great diversity of practice must be the starting point. This was true even in Greece itself, for though chattel slavery was and went on being normal in most areas,[256] it was of comparatively recent introduction in the remoter cantons,[257] serfdom continued in Crete well into the Hellenistic period,[258] and the status of helot continued in Laconia beyond the reforms of Agis, Cleomenes, and even Nabis 'until the supremacy of the Romans'.[259] Elsewhere, the diversity was at least as great. One the one hand, chattel slavery is well attested in some areas of the ex-Achaemenid empire, especially in Babylonia, Syria, and Egypt[260] (though it is questionable how many of the Persian-owned slave-worked estates attested in fifth-century Egypt had survived the

---

[253] E.g. those associated with Cybele at Pessinus, with Ma at Cappadocian Comana or at Pontic Comana, with Zeus at Venasa or with Anaitis at Zela, etc. See further: Rostovtzeff 1910, 269ff.: (H 185); Broughton 1938, 641ff. and 676ff.: (E 62); Magie 1950, I.181–2: (E 81); Rostovtzeff 1953, 503ff.: (A 52).

[254] Cf. Pol. VII.9.5 and *imprimis* OGIS 229 = *SVA* 492 = Austin 182, l. 11: 'Seleucus (II) wrote to the kings, the dynasts, the cities and peoples'. That the temple states tended to be seen as 'peoples' (*ethne*) rather than as a separate category is clear from the way in which Judaea was normally referred to (Bikerman 1938, 164: (E 6)).

[255] See Zel'in and Trofimova 1969: (E 56) and Kreissig 1978, 5ff.: (E 36), criticized by Ste Croix 1982, 155–6: (H 195).

[256] Westermann 1955, 28–57: (H 240); Rädle 1969: (H 178); Hopkins 1978, 133ff.: (A 24).

[257] Timaeus claims it as a phenomenon new in Locris and Phocis in the fourth century (*FGrH* 566 F 11).

[258] Dosiades, *FGrH* 485 F 3 (300–250 B.C.?); Sosicrates, *FGrH* 461 F 4 (*c.* 150 B.C.?); Willetts 1965, 95ff.: (D 148).

[259] Strabo VIII.5.4C.365, though the exact denotation of Strabo's phrase is unclear. Cf. Shimron 1966: (H 212); Oliva 1971, 281–2: (D 132).

[260] A. Cowley, *Aramaic Papyri of the Fifth Century B.C.* (Oxford, 1923) nos. 10, line 10, and 28 *passim*; Diakonov, I. M. 'Rabovladel'cheskie imeniya persidskick vel'mozh. Obeor dokumentov iedannych G. R. Draiverom, i sostoyane ieuchemiya parallel'nich istochnika' ('Slave states of Persian nobles. A survey of the documents published by G. R. Driver and the state of the study of parallel sources.') *VDI* 1959.4, 70–92; Dandamayev 1969, 301ff.: (E 18); Oelsner 1977: (H 156); Doty 1977 and 1978: (B 63–4).

period of Egyptian independence,[261] and there were few slaves in the work-force of Ptolemaic Egypt.[262] However, Syria and Judaea may have been rather sources of slaves than areas of use, while the predominant form of dependent labour in many contexts of Asia Minor were the *laoi* (λαοί),[263] subordinated peoples tied legally to a particular location and economically obliged to render a surplus of produce to their masters. This status was itself not uniform, for the identity and nature of the proximate, as of the ultimate, owner of the land (king, temple, temple-state, city-state, or individual), itself affected the position and title of the *laoi* as well as their chances of *de facto* or *de jure* emancipation. It is essential, for example, to distinguish between (i) the *laoi* known under various titles as dependent cultivators, on the lands of many Greek cities in Asia Minor,[264] (ii) the 'royal *laoi*' (βασιλικοὶ λαοί) attested, especially in three continually discussed inscriptions,[265] on lands in Asia Minor owned directly by the king, and (iii) the 'sacred slaves' (*hierodouloi*) known as cultivators of temple estates in many areas of Asia Minor.[266] Nevertheless, the statuses have so much in common that they are best seen as one. All the persons concerned seem to have been regarded by their superiors as attached to the land, in the triple sense (a) that the right to exploit their labour and to receive revenues from it could pass from one owner of the land to another, (b) that their physical absence from the land did not break the link or the obligation,[267] and (c) that a non-royal owner could not separate them from the estate, e.g. by selling them into chattel slavery.[268] They were emphatically not chattel slaves, for they were not displaced persons, their households and family relationships

---

[261] Still, *paradeisoi* in Syria seem to have survived till the Macedonian conquest (Tcherikover 1959, 432 n. 75: (A 61)), Apollonius' estate at Bet Anat being conceivably one of them.

[262] Bieżuńska-Małowist 1974, 140–1: (F 209).

[263] I deliberately do not translate. 'Peasants' is used by Austin 1981, 'serfs' often elsewhere, but comparisons with mediaeval *Leibeigene* and *adscripti glebae* are criticized as misleading (e.g. by Lotz 1959, 6off.: (H 133)), perhaps too puristically.

[264] E.g. the Mariandyni at Heraclea Pontica (Magie 1950, II.1192 n. 24: (E 81); Lotze 1959, 56–7: (H 113); Atkinson 1968, 41: (E 58)); Bithynians at Byzantium (Phylarchus, *FGrH* 81 F 8, Polybius IV.52.7, Lotze 1959, 57–8); Pedieis in Priene (*I. Priene* 3 = *IBM* III.1.415 with Atkinson 1968, 42ff.) and elsewhere (Rostovtzeff 1910, 259ff.: (H 165); Leleges in Caria (Philippus of Theangela, *FGrH* 741 F 2, with Hornblower 1982, 13 n. 60: (E 73)).

[265] (i) Donation of land between Ilium and Scepsis by Antiochus I to Aristodicides *c.* 275 (?) (*OGIS* = *RC* 10–13 = Frisch 1975, no. 33: (B 78) = Austin 180 [*RC* 13 only]; (ii) donation of land near Sardis by Antigonus to Mnesimachus, date disputed (Buckler and Robinson 1912: (B 55) = *idem* 1932, no. 1: (B 56) = Bogaert 1976, no. 36: (H 18) = Austin 181, with Atkinson 1972: (E 59)); (iii) sale of land near Zeleia and Cyzicus by Antiochus II to his ex-queen Laodice in 254/3 (*OGIS* 225 = *RC* 18–20 = *Didyma* II.492A–C = Austin 185, with Lockhart 1961: (B 105)).

[266] See the references in n. 253, with Welwei 1979: (E 55).

[267] Clearest in *RC* 18, ll. 11–13. Physical absence from the estate is explicitly envisaged in *RC* 11, ll. 22–5, but this was in the special circumstances of the disruption caused by the Gallic invasion (Wörrle 1975, 64: (B 177)).

[268] Whether kings could or did is debatable. Alexandria-on-Jaxartes was peopled partly by mercenaries and *apomachoi*, partly by locals, whether volunteer (thus Arr. *Anab.* IV.4.1) or bought

were not subject to dislocation, and their property rights seem to have been real even if restricted.[269]

In order to trace how these four diversities affected the development of the Hellenistic world, we must return to the kings and to the range of policy choices available to them. Either (a) they could leave traditional landholdings much as they were, or (b) they could abrogate traditional landholdings in order to limit the power of other holders and to maximize their own, or (c) they could confer part of their own holdings on others. Course (a) was most naturally followed by a conqueror or new ruler confirming landholdings or titles previously revoked or in dispute:[270] it created goodwill and cost little since it left his revenues untouched. Course (b) could only be adopted by a king in a very strong position vis-à-vis his subjects, as when Alexander revoked lands held by the hyparchs in the eastern satrapies or when the early Ptolemies took upon themselves the right to sell temple prebends, the administration of sacred land, and that of at least some cult taxes.[271] More often, course (b) was merely a preliminary to the re-assignation of land (course (c)) and to a consequent reordering of patronage relationships, as when a Ptolemy (IV?) threatened to confiscate Judaea in order to turn it into cleruchic holdings,[272] or when Apollonius in 167 and Lysias in 165 were ordered by Antiochus IV to execute a closely comparable transformation in Jerusalem.[273]

However, course (c) did not have to be punitive or violent, since it need not involve the revocation or confiscation of land. Instead, land already in royal hands could be alienated by gift (δωρεά). Three kinds of gift need to be distinguished. The first are *doreai* to individuals in the royal family, the court, the administrative hierarchy, or to other persons of influence and prestige with a claim on the king's goodwill. Instances in this group are mostly well known and due to special circumstances, such as the gifts of land to Aristodicides and Mnesimachus (n. 265 above), the sale of land for a nominal 30 talents to Laodice (*ibid.*)

back for the purpose by Alexander from the owners to whom he had sold them after their participation in the revolt of Sogdiana (thus Curt VII.6.27, not totally irreconcilable with Arrian). See Briant 1978, 75: (E 12).

[269] Buckler and Robinson 1932, no. 1, l. 13: (B 56); RC 18, ll. 8–9 and 26–7. For general discussions of the *laoi* see Rostovtzeff 1910, 258ff., 307ff.: (H 185); Rostovtzeff 1953, 1.341ff. and II.1103ff.: (A 52); Svenciskaya 1963: (H 223); Sarkisian 1953 in Diakonov 1969, 323ff.: (H 199); Kreissig 1978, *passim*: (E 36); Ste Croix 1982, 151–8: (H 195).

[270] E.g. Antiochus II to Erythrae (RC 15), or Seleucus II to Miletus (RC 22). Cf. also the use of βεβαιόω, διαφυλάσσω, διατηρέω in royal letters to cities (Préaux 1954, 91–2: (H 172)).

[271] Briant 1978, 71ff.: (E 12) (Alexander); Préaux 1939, 47ff. (general remarks) and 480–91 (Ptolemies): (F 306).

[272] Jos. *Ant. Jud.* XII.159, with Marcus *ad loc.* for the problems involved.

[273] For Apollonius: I *Macc.* 1.29–35, II *Macc.* v.24–6, Daniel XI.39 and Jos. *Ant. Jud.* XII.248ff. (garbled, see Abel on I *Macc.* 1.29), with Tcherikover 1959, 188–9: (A 61); for Lysias: I *Macc.* III.34–6, II *Macc.* XI.2–3, Tcherikover 1959, 211.

together with certain other gifts of land in Babylonia to her and to her sons Seleucus and Antiochus,[274] the revoked gift of Telmessus by Ptolemy II Philadelphus to an unidentifiable person,[275] its probable actual gift to Ptolemy son of Lysimachus by Ptolemy III Euergetes,[276] and certain other less certain examples.[277] In a second category come more institutionalized *doreai* to individuals or groups. The most prominent are the 'Ten Thousand Aroura' estates in Egypt of which Apollonius' at Philadelphia in the 250s is the classic[278] but by no means the only example,[279] but the *kleroi* given to Greek and to non-Greek military colonists by Ptolemies and Seleucids and other dynasts differed from the great *doreai* in size rather than in procedure and status.[280] A third category comprises gifts of land to temples, a matter of much complexity and controversy, at least in respect of Asia Minor. The older view, founded *imprimis* upon an inscription of A.D. 125/6 from Aezani in Phrygia,[281] was that much temple-land there was expropriated in order to provide land for military settlements,[282] but a further inscription from Aizani, by revealing donations of land to the temple by Attalus I and Prusias I, has so far demolished that view that the focus of attention has become instead the scale of donations of land *to* temples.[283] Seleucid gifts are not indeed attested in Asia Minor, but those of Attalids and others are,[284] as are Seleucid donations in Syria[285] and Babylonia,[286] not to

---

[274] Sarkisian 1953 in Diakonov 1969, 321ff.: (H 199).   [275] Wörrle 1978, 201ff.: (B 179).

[276] *OGIS* 55 = *Tituli Asiae Minoris* (ed. E. Kalinska and R. Heberdey) II.1 = Austin 271, with Segre 1938: (B 161), Bagnall 1976, 105–10: (F 204), and Wörrle 1978, 218–25: (B 179).

[277] Wörrle 1978, 207–8: (B 179).

[278] Rostovtzeff 1922: (J 164); Préaux 1947: (F 141); Pestman *et al.* 1981: (F 140). Separate affairs are his *dorea* near Memphis, which was not a single unified estate (Wipszycka 1961, 173: (F 347)) and need not have been of 10,000 arourai, and his estate at Bet Anat in Palestine.

[279] For other *muriarouroi* (and the ambiguity of the term) Criscuolo 1977: (F 243) and Clarysse 1979(2), 736ff.: (F 233); other major landholders and δωρεαί are listed by Préaux 1939, 20 n. 1: (F 306), and *Pros. Ptol.* IV.10061–108.

[280] The material for Ptolemaic cleruchies is surveyed by Préaux 1939, 468–80: (F 306), *Pros. Ptol.* IV.8551–10060, and Uebel 1968: (F 200); for Seleucid military settlements by Hansen 1971, 174–5: (E 122), and Cohen 1978: (E 16); for Attalid settlements (cf. *RC* 16 and 51) by Hansen 1971, 233; for other dynasts' settlements by Hansen 1971, 173, and Préaux 1978, 1.311: (A 48) with Funck 1978: (H 70).

[281] *OGIS* 502 = *Inscriptiones graecae ad res romanas pertinentes* IV.571; for the date, *PIR* A².1409.

[282] Rostovtzeff 1910, 26ff.: (H 185); Welles 1934, 282–3: (B 171); Broughton 1938, 641ff. and 676ff.: (E 62); Tarn and Griffith 1952, 138–41: (A 59): Rostovtzeff 1953, 1.492–3, 503–7, III.1440–1 n. 279–83: (A 52) (Seleucids); *ibid.* II.648–9 and III.1477–8 n. 62–3 (Attalids).

[283] Broughton 1951: (E 63); Zawadski 1952–3: (H 248); J. and L. Robert 1954, 296–7: (E 94); Musti 1966, 191ff.: (E 44); Atkinson 1968: (E 58); Laffi 1971: (E 75). Doubts about the older view already in Broughton 1934: (E 61).

[284] *RC* 62, with Robert 1930, 350–1: (B 134) (Attalus (II); *OGIS* 383 (Antiochus I of Commagene); Crampa 1969, 8, ll. 17–23: (B 60) (Olympichus to Zeus Osogoa, shortly after 240 B.C.).

[285] *RC* 70 = *IGLS* VII.4028 = Austin 178, with Seyrig 1951(2), 200ff.: (H 211), *Bull. épig.* 1955, 26 (Zeus of Baetocaece), and Rigsby 1980, 248–54: (E 47).

[286] Rostovtzeff 1953, 1.435, 494, and III.1427 n. 234: (A 52).

mention the donations made by the Ptolemies on an ever more substantial scale.[287]

In this way, and Old Greece and the islands apart, royal land policies helped to mould Hellenistic society. Every king had to reassign some land, since that was the only way to attract and retain men for the army and the administration and was also the best way of rewarding loyalty, because the beneficiary came to share an interest with his king in protecting possession of territory from third parties. To that degree, the immigration of privileged landholders of Greek culture was structurally essential for every royal régime (except perhaps Antigonid Macedonia). The areas of choice were rather (a) the extent of assignation, (b) the degree of permanency of tenure for each class or instance of assignation, and (c) the question whether lands once assigned to individuals could gravitate towards collectives (cities or temples). Choice (a) was a matter of need, determined above all by army requirements. It is notable, for example, how the Attalids managed to avoid large-scale re-assignations by using mercenaries from Crete and Mysia (later Galatia too) instead, thereby retaining in their own hands the disposition of royal land revenues, while Egypt found it more and more difficult to do so. Choice (b) depended on power relationships, since the interests of a king (in perpetuating precariousness of tenure) directly conflicted with that of the assignees (in converting it to permanency). The evolution towards permanency in Egypt is clear,[288] elsewhere much less so, but there can be little doubt that the right to alienate, an intrinsic element of permanency, was originally in Seleucid terms a privilege.[289] It was choice (c) which had the most far-reaching consequences. Ptolemaic reluctance to resign control of land to the extent and degree of permanence necessary to allow Greek-style *poleis* to consolidate themselves did indeed keep much power in royal hands. It is significant, as the treatment of Telmessus in 279[290] and again by 240 (*OGIS* 55) has revealed, that even outside Egypt they were prepared to subordinate the claims of cities to be treated as cities in favour of the administrative and political advantages of encompassing them within *doreai* to individuals. Yet the cost of so doing in Egypt was to leave unimpaired the power of temples and temple aristocracies, especially in Upper Egypt.[291] Greek culture was thereby robbed of the institutions essential for its long-term survival and extension outwith Alexandria. Seleucid policy, by contrast, largely leaned towards the other option. Granted, the fact that we can see

[287] See n. 291 below.
[288] Otto 1908, II.262ff.: (F 183); Préaux 1939, 464–80: (F 306).
[289] Explicitly so in the sale to Laodice (*RC* 18, line 16). Revocation by the king is equally explicitly envisaged in Mnesimachus' inscription from Sardis above, n. 265 (ii), col. 2, ll. 12–13).
[290] Wörrle 1978: (B 179).
[291] Meeks 1979: (F 179); Quaegebeur 1979: (F 312).

Antiochus I and Antiochus II explicitly permitting Aristodicides and Laodice to 'attach < the lands granted to them > to any city (s)he wishes in the *chora* and the *symmachia*'[292] shows that we must think in terms of specific decisions on individual occasions, not necessarily of an explicit long-term policy. Yet the combination of such decisions with Seleucid (and, later, Attalid) willingness both to recognize existing urban agglomerations as municipal entities and to increase their number substantially via their own military and civilian foundations coincided so harmoniously with existing local aspirations, inside the kingdoms as much as in Old Greece, as to amount to nothing less than the renaissance and re-institutionalization of the *polis*. Ironically, of course, that policy too damaged royal fiscal interests, though perhaps not substantially so until the collapse of Seleucid revenues after 188, and power after the 160s, left the royal administration in no position to resist the widespread demands for municipal autonomy which were successfully made from the 120s onwards.[293] It is significant that two late Hellenistic rulers could revert to the vocabulary of a much older world and refer to their capital cities as their πατρίδες; much though they had to lose by such identification, the pull of the *polis* was proving too strong.[294]

VII. THE POLIS TRANSFORMED AND REVITALIZED

In this way royal land policy impinges directly on the greatest cultural phenomenon of the Hellenistic world, the transformation and revitalization of the Greek *polis* in areas where it was long established, together with its relentless spread into area after area of erstwhile non-Greek lands.[295] So striking a movement will inevitably have been over-determined, and one can in fact see it as the product of no fewer than six converging interests. First, it was in the interest of the new Greek and Macedonian settlers in the conquered territories to continue to have access to, and status within, the sort of social structure that they were used to in the homeland. One may recall the 'New Macedonia' aspect of the settlements in Syria as revealed by the pre-dynastic city names, the survival of specifically Macedonian civic phraseology,[296] etc., quite apart

---

[292] *RC* 11, ll. 20–2; *RC* 18, l. 14.

[293] E.g *RC* 71=*OGIS* 257=Michel 149=Austin 173 (Seleuceia-in-Pieria, summer 109), and references in n. 136 above.

[294] *RC* 67=Austin 110(c), l. 6 (Attalus III to Pergamum, 135 B.C.), and *OGIS* 257=Michel 149=*RC* 71=Austin 173, l. 15 (Antiochus VIII(?) to Seleuceia-in-Pieria, 109 B.C.), with Welles 1934, 293: (B 171).

[295] For the general phenomenon cf. *imprimis* Préaux 1954 and 1955: (H 172–3), and Préaux 1978, II.401–60: (A 48), though the nuances of what follows here differ from hers.

[296] Cf. Pieria and Cyrrhestice as district names: Beroea (Strabo XVI.2, 7, c751); Larissa (Strabo IX.5.19.C.440); Pella (later Apamea, Strabo XVI.2.10.C.752); Bottiaea (later Antioch, Downey 1961, 54–5: (E 157)). For other references see Bikerman 1938, 79–80: (E 6), and for civic phraseology cf.

from the uniform Greek physical and governmental components of each new city. Secondly, it was in the interest of cities under the direct or indirect control of the kings to perpetuate traditional procedures as much as possible, if only because the diplomatic links thus engendered helped them to retain fully autonomous status within the network of the more independent *poleis*.[297] Thirdly and correspondingly, the interest and influence of the more independent leagues and city states such as Rhodes, Byzantium, Athens, Achaea, Aetolia, and Rome from the 220s onwards tended on the whole to favour republics against monarchs and dynasts. Fourthly, the interest of the existing non-Greek city states in Babylonia or Phoenicia lay in surviving with their privileges intact or enhanced under the new régimes even if that involved accommodation to the ideas and myths of the occupying power.[298] Fifthly, the upper classes of the *ethne* sometimes saw their interest as lying in a similar accommodation to the institutions of the dominant Greeks. The classic case in point is that of the hellenizers in Judaea in the early second century, after Judaea had come under a régime more sympathetic to such aspirations than the Ptolemies had been,[299] but others are revealed by the spread of Greek-language documents using the formulae of the city-state into areas not yet transformed into a *polis*.[300] Lastly, as we have seen, some of the kings some of the time saw their own interest in encouraging, or at least in allowing, such aspirations to come to fruition.

Yet inevitably, as it spread geographically, as time went on, and as the increasingly well-established monarchies set the tone and the limits of international diplomacy, the institution of the *polis* came to diverge from the classical city-state, to change its profile, and to drop some functions while assuming others. Since we have to deal here with an immensely complex historical phenomenon, reflecting the pressures of monarchic authority and the conflicting ambitions of rich and poor as much as more general cultural, religious, and economic change, it will beg fewest questions simply to identify and describe the separate components of change, affecting the cities of old Greece just as much as the new colonial territories, before seeking to assign any primacy to one or other of the interests and pressures listed above.

the *peliganes* at Laodicea-on-Sea (Roussel 1942–3: (B 154) (with *Bull. épig.* 1950, 208)=*IGLS* 1261, l. 22, 174 B.C.) and at Seleuceia-on-the-Tigris (Polyb. v.54.10, 220 B.C.), with Musti 1966, 123–4: (E 44), and Cohen 1978, 80: (E 16).

[297] The most extensive single illustration is the dossier of replies by numerous cities and leagues and four kings to the renewed invitation of Magnesia *c.* 206 to recognize their newly instituted festival for Artemis Leucophryene, references in Schlesinger 1933, 74–7: (H 201).

[298] As Diotimus of Sidon successfully did (p. 258 above). Other examples in Jones 1940, 47–50: (A 25). [299] Tcherikover 1959, 152–74: (A 61).

[300] Cf. the decree passed by the Neonteichitai and the Kiddioukometai of January 267 in the area which became Laodicea-on-the-Lycus some 6–14 years later (Wörrle 1975: (B 177)=Austin 142, Gagniers *et al* 1969, 2: (B 195). Other documents are cited by Wörrle 1975, 85.

(1) Rare exceptions apart, most Hellenistic cities had a government described as 'democratic'. The word has been argued to denote little more than republican self-government, since the Achaean federal constitution[301] and, in some contexts, the constitution of Rhodes[302] could be so described. However, since royal letters after Alexander noticeably avoid the term,[303] its use in third-century city documents should denote something more precise than that, as yet unclear.[304] In any case names are one thing, reality another, for there is little doubt that by and large in the Hellenistic period the participatory radicalism of the fifth and fourth centuries gave way to government by informal élites which knew how to exercise control through the forms of democratic institutions. Financial pressures will have assisted this development (see (4) below), for though large juries paid by *misthos* survived (ironically enough) at Rhodes[305] and though allotment *pinakia* are now quite widely attested,[306] *misthos*, whether for juries, magistrates, or attendance at assembly seems not to have survived the convulsions of the early third century in Athens and is only sparsely attested elsewhere.[307] Even more symptomatic were the tendencies for magistracies and liturgies to converge and for the various magisterial boards to coalesce into a single college with the power, or in some cases the exclusive right, to carry out probouleutic functions for the assembly.[308]

(2) Much of the activity of these assemblies must have been ceremonial and repetitive. The endless proxeny decrees of Samos or Delphi, or the ever more solemn and verbose decrees of Athens in praise of her own councillors will often have been purely ritual actions, gratifying minor

[301] Polyb. 11.38.6 with Walbank *ad loc.*; Holleaux, *Études* III.153 n. 1; Heuss 1937, 236–8: (A 22); Bikerman 1938, 135–6: (E 6); Larsen 1945, 88–91: (H 125); Aymard 1967, 94–5: (I 9); Crampa 1969, 82–5: (B 60).

[302] τὰν καθεστακυῖαν δαμοκρατίαν *SIG* 581 = *IC* III, p. 31 no. 3A = *SVA* 551 = Austin 95, l. 14, which should reveal Rhodian *Selbstgefühl*. Note however the pointed language of Strabo (or his source): δημοκηδεῖς δ᾽ εἰσὶν οἱ Ρόδιοι καίπερ οὐ δημοκρατούμενοι, (Strabo XIV.2.5.c.652 (= Austin 92). Polybius similarly avoids the word in Rhodian contexts, though he applies it to Epirus (II.7.11), Messene (VII.10.1), Thebes (VIII.35.6), and the magistracies of Crete (VI.46.4). Cf., however, O'Neil 1981: (E 140).

[303] Not in Polyperchon's *diagramma* of 319 (Diod. XVIII.56), though Diodorus himself summarizes it as τὰς δημοκρατίας ἀποκαταστήσειν ταῖς πόλεσι (55.4); not in Antigonus' proclamation of Tyre in 315 (Diod. XIX.61.3); not in the documents published in *RC*. For Alexander's own proclamations cf. Arr. *Anab.* 1.18.2, with Bosworth *ad loc.*, and 11.5.8 (Soli), but even then there can be no certainty that Alexander's own wording is preserved. Similarly, in *OGIS* 229 = *SVA* 492, l. 11, we have only Smyrna's word for it that Seleucus II promised the city democracy as well as autonomy. Note that Olympichus uses the word (Crampa 1969, 8, l. 14: (B 60).

[304] See Musti 1966, 138ff.: (E 44).   [305] Fraser 1972, 119–24: (E 135).

[306] Dow 1963: (B 289), Kroll 1972, 268–78: (B 300) (Myrina, Pamphylia, Rhodes, Sinope, Thasos, and perhaps elsewhere).   [307] Ste Croix 1975: (H 194) collects what evidence there is.

[308] Clear for Miletus (Müller 1976: (B 112)), detected also at Pergamum, Erythrae (Jones 1940, 166ff.: (A 25)), Cos (Sherwin-White 1978, 176–7: (D 146)), Rhodes (Touloumakos 1967, 129ff.: (H 228)), and elsewhere (in general Touloumakos 1967).

vanities in portentous phrases. Yet to dismiss all assembly business thus would be foolish, not just because decisions whom to honour, and how, could carry major diplomatic consequences but also because the cities did continue to concern themselves with much the same range of substantive business as in previous centuries. The running of festivals, the administration of justice, or the guardianship of boundaries (juridical and geographical) went on being normal preoccupations, as did the major worry of all, the corn supply and the means of financing it. Here the cities trod a delicate path. On the one side stood the reluctance of the kings to allow the free movement of corn, so as to be able to use its provision as a *philanthropon*[309] and its availability as a weapon. One may recall in particular the bland phrases of Antigonus to Teos *c*. 303:

Previously we were [unwilling] that [any] city should be given the right to import corn and that stocks of corn should be built up, [as we did not wish the] cities to spend unnecessarily large sums of money for this purpose; [we were still reluctant] to do this now, as the tributary [territory] is near by, [so that if there] is [need] for corn we believe it is easy to fetch [as much] as one wishes from [it].[310]

On the other side stood the complementary complications of tapping the resources of the rich, via loans to the state, liturgical magistracies, or foundations, in order to build up a corn-buying fund and of assigning scarce public revenues in order to provide corn in a cheaper and more regular way than the fluctuations of supply allowed.[311] It may well have been easiest, as it is certainly the best attested, to look rather to the goodwill of non-citizens, including the shippers themselves, and to accept the enhanced status within each city which their consequential honours conferred.

(3) In two areas of public life, indeed, we can see cities taking a larger role than formerly. One was medicine, where the spread of 'public physicians' (*iatroi demosioi* or *demosieuontes*) can be documented as men paid a retainer by the state to be available, whatever fees they might or

---

[309] Cf. gifts to Cos from Philadelphus or Euergetes (Maiuri 1925, no. 433: (B 106)), with Sherwin-White 1978, 99 n. 82: (D 146); to Athens from Lysimachus (*IG* II².657=*SIG* 374=Austin 43, ll. 10ff.), Ptolemy I (Plut. *Mor.* 851E) and Ptolemy II (Shear 1978: (C 62)=Austin 44, ll. 50ff.), Audoleon (*IG* II².654–5), and Spartocus (*IG* II².653 =*SIG* 370); to Rhodes from all sides after the 227 earthquake (Polyb. v.88–90), from Eumenes II *c*. 160 (Polyb. XXXI.31.1), and from Demetrius I in the same period or soon after (Diod. XXXI.36). Cleomenes' distributions from Cyrene in the 320s were closely similar in form and function (Tod 196). See also n. 127.

[310] *RC* 3 =*SIG* 344=Austin 40, ll. 80–5 (tr. Austin). Cf. also *SIG* 502=*IG* XII.8.156=Fraser 1960, pp. 39ff.: (B 76)=Austin 269 (Samothrace in Euergetes' time), and in general Heichelheim 1935, 875ff.: (H 92), and Moretti 1977, 329: (H 147). That Seleucus I provided grain silos for Antioch, his own capital city, is hardly counter-evidence (Downey 1961, 72: (E 157)), nor with Rostovtzeff (1910, 264 n. 1: (H 185)) should we see mercantilist considerations as applying.

[311] Wilhelm 1932: (H 241); Heichelheim 1935, 875ff.: (H 92); Hands 1968, ch. 7: (H 86).

might not then charge.[312] The second was education, where publicly sponsored training both altered its focus and spread much further through the age range than had been the case in the classical period.[313] As revealed by the re-invigorated Athenian *ephebeia* of the 330s onwards,[314] let alone by the Spartan *agoge*, state preoccupations were initially with military training and little else. This changed in two ways. Firstly, as the need for citizen militias declined, ephebic institutions as they spread outwards from Athens metamorphosed into sportive-cultural associations for 18–19-year olds, voluntary in membership (and therefore leisure-class) and eventually open even to non-citizens[315] – a development shared by the functionally similar groups of *neoi* (men in their twenties).[316] Secondly, the intense public debate in fourth-century Athens about the content of education yielded fruit in the form of the transformation of the *gymnasion* away from being purely a social-athletic club focussed on a *palaistra* towards being something far closer to a recognizable secondary school for *paides* (i.e. boys of 12–17). Founded and financed by gifts from kings[317] or private individuals,[318] supervised by public officials whose role might be primarily financial-liturgical (the *gymnasiarchos*, or the *kosmetes* at Athens and some other towns)[319] or primarily professional (the *paidonomos* or *ephebarchos*),[320] and linked to the life of the city by contests, prizes, and the participation of their members in festivals, the new-style *gymnasion* became architecturally and culturally the defining institution of Greek urban civilization, recognized as such alike by those who wished to exploit its opportunities and by those who saw in it a symbol of alien influence.[321]

[312] Cohn-Haft 1956: (H 36) (with previous literature); Hands 1968, 133–9: (H 86); Benedum 1977: (B 46); Sherwin-White 1978, 263–74: (D 146); *SIG* 528 = *IC* I, no. 7 = Austin 125; Habicht 1957, 233 no. 64: (B 81) = Austin 64.

[313] Excellent synopsis in Moretti 1977, 469ff.: (H 127); cf. also Ziebarth 1914: (H 250), Forbes 1933: (H 66), Jones 1940, 220–6: (A 25), Marrou 1965: (A 34), Nilsson 1955: (H 152), and Delorme 1960: (H 46).

[314] *Ath. Pol.* 42, Pélékidis 1962: (H 162), Reinmuth 1973: (B 124).

[315] In the 140s at Delos (*Insc. Délos.* 1922ff.); between 128/7 and 119/18 in Athens (Pélékidis 1962, 186ff.: (H 162), Davies 1977–8, 119: (H 43)). See Plates vol., pl. 175.

[316] Forbes 1933: (H 66).

[317] E.g. Eumenes II to Rhodes *c.* 160 (Polyb. xxxi.31.1) and to Delphi also *c.* 160 (*SIG* 672 = Austin 206, with Daux 1936, 686–92: (D 77), and Hansen 1971, 292ff.: (E 122), or Mithridates V and Ptolemy X at Delos (*Choix* 99 and 124). Other references in Ziebarth 1914, 45ff, and 73–7: (H 250), and in Holleaux 1924, 27–9: (B 92). In consequence royal cults were often located in gymnasia: Robert 1925 (3): (B 130), Delorme 1960, 342ff.: (H 46), Sherwin-White 1978, 135–6: (D 146).

[318] Most notably Eudemus at Miletus in 200/199 and Polythrus at Teos shortly afterwards (*SIG* 577–8 = Austin 119–20); Hands 1968, 120–7: (H 86), for other examples.

[319] Oehler 1912: (H 155); Delmorme 1960, *passim*: (H 46); Pélékidis 1962, 275–7: (H 162); Cormack 1977: (B 59) = Austin 118, with *Bull. épig.* 1978, 274. This last, the law of the gymnasiarchy at Beroea between 167 and 148, is the most informative single document, but cf. also *OGIS* 764 (honours for a gymnasiarch at Pergamum, 130s) and *SIG* 958 = Sokolowski 1969, no. 98: (H 218) (Coressus, third century).   [320] Roesch 1965, 231–3: (D 83) (in Boeotia).

[321] Both best illustrated by the Jewish hellenizing movement and the Maccabean reaction.

(4) There was also a complex change in the relationship of men and women, especially the wealthy, the intellectuals and the outsiders, to the *polis*. For one thing, the boundaries of the *polis* became more permeable. That Athens' envoys to Rome in 155 were Carneades from Cyrene, Diogenes from Seleuceia-on-the-Tigris, and Critolaus from Phaselis[322] would have been inconceivable before 300, but by the 150s was merely one of a series of developments which included, for example, the sale of citizenship for fiscal purposes,[323] the ever wider spread of potential dual citizenship via proxeny grants to individuals or *isopoliteia* treaties between communities,[324] royal pressure on cities to confer citizen or semi-citizen status upon soldiers, residents, or courtiers,[325] and honorary citizenships being lavished on successful athletes,[326] benefactors,[327] and royal officials.[328] By and large, though the citizen/non-citizen boundary still rigidly excluded slaves and non-Greeks,[329] and though attitudes of chauvinistic hostility towards neighbouring cities still persisted here and there, especially in Crete (where no one king had an interest in damping down such squabbles),[330] nonetheless changed attitudes and more receptive institutions did make the position of the foreigner that much easier.

[322] Polyb. XXXIII.2. Carneades was already a citizen (*Prosopographia Attica* 8257); we do not know about the others.

[323] M. Segre 1934, 267–8: (B 158); Robert, *Hellenica* I (1940) 37–41; Rostovtzeff 1953, III.1374 n. 71: (A 52); Robert 1967, 14–32: (B 147).

[324] The content, importance, and implications of each type of grant have been the subject of much recent discussion. For the debate whether proxeny-grants were mere formalities or valuable privileges see Wilhelm 1942, 11–86: (B 175); Huybrechs 1959: (H 109); Klaffenbach 1966, 80–5: (B 99); Gschnitzer 1974, 629–730: (H 84); and Gawantka 1975, 52ff.: (H 76), with further references. For *isopoliteia* Gawantka 1975, *passim*, whose distinction between the potentiality of such grants and their activation I follow.

[325] Examples are numerous, such as *ISE* 22 (*isoteleia* to soldiers at Rhamnus, on the initiative of Antigonus' general Apollodorus, 256/5), *OGIS* 229 = *SVA* 492 = Austin 182, ll. 39–40 (citizenship of Smyrna for the *katoikoi* and others at Magnesia, shortly after 243?), *SIG* 543 = *IG* IX.2.517 = *ILS* 217: cf. p. 268 above).

[326] E.g. *IG* II².3779. Other examples in Robert 1939, 230ff.: (B 141), and in Robert 1967, 14ff.: (B 147).

[327] E.g. *SIG* 354 = Austin 112; *SIG* 493 = *Choix* 50 = Austin 115; *SEG* 1.363 = Austin 135; and many others.

[328] E.g. *RC* 45 = *IGLS* 1183 = Austin 176; L. and J. Robert 1954, 285ff. no. 166: (E 94) = Austin 187; *OGIS* 329 = *IG* IV.1 = Austin 209; *SIG* 502 = *IG* XII.8.156 = Fraser 1960, p. 39: (B 76) = Austin 269; and many others.

[329] Cf. the μιξέλληνες as a separate group in Olbia (*SIG* 495 = Maier 1959, no. 82: (J 226) = Austin 97, l. 114), Smyrna's caution in granting citizenship 'to the other inhabitants of Magnesia who are free and Greek' (*OGIS* 229 = *SVA* 492 = Austin 182, l. 45), Miletus' grant of citizenship to the wives of Pidasans if they are Pidasans themselves or are πολιτίδες of a Greek city (*Milet* III.149, l. 10), or the careful grading of the rises in status accorded in Pergamum in 133 (*OGIS* 338 = Austin 211). Emancipation of slaves *en masse* such as those at Rhodes during the siege of 305/4 (Diod. XX.100.1) remained as rare as they had done during the classical period.

[330] Cf. *SIG* 527 = *IC* II.84, no. 1 = *SVA* 584 = Austin 91, ll. 35ff. (oath of Drerus *c.* 220), but one may also take into account the obstinate continuance as separate entities of tiny towns such as Heraclea by Amorgos (*ISE* 77, with Moretti *ad loc.*).

A second aspect of these relationships is also illustrated by Carneades and his colleagues. Philosophers, professional men, and royal officials had to learn to move with some ease in and between the world of their own city and the environment (city or court) where they exercised their talents. Their ranks will have been joined by those local politicians whom wealth, ambition, or social pressures made into diplomats and envoys. For these last one thinks, for example, of Hegesias of Lampsacus and his epic embassy in 196/5 to Lucius Flamininus in Greece, to Massilia and to Rome,[331] or of the repeated warm references in royal letters to the envoys who put their city's case to a king. Such men were as much hinges between king and city as were the officials whom they appointed to posts in or near their own native cities[332] or the intellectuals and professionals who served the kings as diplomats and administrators.[333] It is these men, whether moving primarily in civic, professional, military, or royal circles, who both provide a basis for traditional clichés about Hellenistic cosmopolitanism and help to put them in perspective. To the extent that we can indeed speak of them as a class, for whom more than anyone else Stoic theories of kingship and world government were pertinent, the clichés have substance, but it would be entirely misleading to see such international *déracinés* as more than a tiny though influential minority in a world which was still largely a long way behind them and which still moved in unchanging and traditional locally focussed ways.

A third aspect of change is financial. As politically, so also economically the *polis* could not do without its wealthy members, for whatever gifts (with strings attached) might come from kings, and whatever taxes had to go to kings, most public finance was still raised and spent locally. Regular revenues came *inter alia* from court fees, customs or harbour dues, market dues, trading licences, monopolies of salt or money-changing, rentals from fisheries and other state property, taxes on slaves, domestic animals, foodstuffs, gardens, or bee-hives, and (in Asia Minor) the sales of priesthoods,[334] many of these taxes being farmed out to the inevitably unpopular tax-farmers.[335] Often enough, it

[331] *SIG* 591 = Frisch 1978, no. 4: (B 79) = Austin 155.

[332] Demetrius of Phalerum most conspicuously, but also Apollodorus of Otryna (*ISE* 22) and Dicaearchus of Thria (*ISE* 25) in Attica, Epinicus of Samothrace (Bakalakis and Scranton 1939: (B 45), with *Bull. épig.* 1939, 298, Bengtson 1964–7, III.183 n. 1: (A 6), and Fraser 1960, 8 n. 30: (B 76)), Hagemonidas of Dyme (*ISE* 56–7), Callicrates of Samos (Hauben 1970: (F 198)), and Peisis of Thespiae (*ISE* 71).

[333] Besides Cephisodorus of Apamea (n. 10, above), cf. Stratius the physician with Eumenes II (Polyb. xxx.2.1) or Apollophanes the physician with Antiochus III (Polyb. v.56.1).

[334] The two most informative documents are *SEG* 11.579 = Pleket 1964. no. 22: (B 118) = J. and L. Robert 1976: (B 151) (Teos, *ateleia* decree for new citizens *c.* 300), and *SIG* 1000, with Rostovtzeff 1953, 1.241ff.: (A 52), and Sherwin-White 1978, 229–35: (D 146) (Cos, *c.* 100). In general see Robert 1933: (B 135), Laumonier 1934, 360ff.: (B 104), M. Segre 1937: (B 160) (with *Bull. épig.* 1938, 43), Jones 1940, 241–50: (A 25), Rostovtzeff 1953, III.1374 n. 71 and 1463 n. 22: (A 52), and Préaux 1978, II.435ff.: (A 48).

[335] On whom see W. Schwahn, 'τελῶναι', *PW* v.A (1934) cols. 418–25, and Herondas vi.63ff.

seems, these revenues were inadequate even for regular outgoings on *misthos*, public slaves, the upkeep of public buildings and services, festival expenses, and tribute to a suzerain. The creation of public banks on the model of the currently proliferating private banks[336] may have helped administratively, but empty treasuries are not far to seek, with consequential crises whenever extraordinary demands impinged, most notably for major public buildings, fortifications, the purchase of corn or the mounting of a military expedition. Expedients were various. Magistracies might be socially redefined so that the holder would be expected to pay some of the expenses of his area of administration:[337] he would receive public praise and honours for doing so, since he thereby displayed the key social quality of *philotimia* (conspicuous magnificence). Or citizens and others could be invited to make loans to the state, which the state might or might not be able to repay.[338] Or citizens and others could be invited to make outright voluntary gifts to the state (*epidoseis*), again in return for due public thanks and recognition.[339] Or a benefactor might set aside a substantial sum of money, to be held in trust by the state or private trustees with fierce stipulations against alienation or fraud, the annual income from which was to be used for specified public or charitable purposes.[340] These expedients all focus on the rich and on the choices available to them – whether to use their resources entirely on conspicuous consumption within the household (thereby redistributing such resources to the purveyors of foodstuffs, textiles, craftsman goods, slaves, grave monuments, horses, and so on),[341] or to make some resources available to the state in return for public honours. Plainly, so many rich were amenable to such appeals that most cities did get by without bankruptcy. What had altered was not so much the intensity of local patriotism as internal power relationships, since few civic assemblies were now in a position to coerce rich inhabitants without either losing more than they gained or bringing down upon themselves the attentions of a king or his *strategos*.

The fourth aspect of change concerned women,[342] where complex and

[336] Ziebarth 1924: (H 251), Bogaert 1968, 403–8: (H 17).

[337] 'Socially' rather than legally: the absence of any such stipulation in the gymnasiarchy law of Beroea (n. 319 above) is noticeable. Since it is incomplete, such a stipulation may have stood on side A, but note that the money for the weapons which the gymnasiarch was to provide at the Hermaea 'shall come from the existing revenues' (ll. 59–60).

[338] For the first contingency cf. *OGIS* 46=Pleket 1964, no. 26: (B 118)=Austin 100 (Halicarnassus, third century); for the second, *ISE* 130 (Istria, *c*. 200–150); uncertain which, *SIG* 544=*IG* VII.4263=Maier 1959, no. 26: (J 226)=Austin 101 (Oropus, third century).

[339] See nn. 230–2 above.   [340] See nn. 387–8 below.

[341] Hellenistic elegant living as a whole, in contrast to studies of single institutions or single artefact types, is a sadly understudied subject, in spite of scattered luminous remarks by Rostovtzeff and of party pieces such as Athenaeus' description from Hippolochus of the banquet given by Caranus (IV.128cff.); cf. however, Schneider 1969, II.3–69 and 208–21: (A 56).

[342] Macurdy 1932: (I 41); Préaux 1959; (H 174); Schneider 1967, 1.78–117: (A 56); Vatin 1970: (H 230); Pomeroy 1976: (H 170).

contrasting trends are visible. For all the abilities and political importance of some Hellenistic queens, and in spite of the occasional appearance of women making *epidoseis* or loans to the state,[343] receiving thanks and honours in public decrees,[344] or contributing creatively to intellectual and artistic life,[345] most women remained almost totally confined to the private and household domain. As in the classical period, they remained the transmitters of citizen status and rights without being able to exercise their privileges themselves, and in Greece and in all Greek-style documents from Egypt women continued to need their oldest adult male agnates to act as their guardian-representatives (*kyrioi*)[346] in all transactions of consequence. Yet there were signs of emancipation. Just as the convergence between magistracy and liturgy allowed gods to be named as magistrates (the implication being that the expenses of the office for the year were met from temple funds), so too women very occasionally appear as magistrates, no doubt for the same financial reasons.[347] Moreover, for much of the everyday business of existence and getting a living (contracts, sales, leases), the presence and authority of a male *kyrios* could be *de facto* purely nominal. Again, the legal format of marriage developed variations. In its classical Athenian form marriage was a relationship between two men, the husband and father of the bride, created by pledge (*engye*) and treating her solely as the object and transmitter of rights, transferred from one *kyrios* to another with the father retaining some residual rights for the bride's own protection. Egyptian evidence in contrast shows marriage first as a formal written contract between the husband and the parents of the bride, then as a relationship involving two contracts, one involving the bride's father but the other the spouses alone, and finally as a relationship wherein the spouses are the only contractual parties.[348] *Prima facie*, the emancipation involved is substantial, but qualifications are needed. The expectations which the contracts spell out remain unequal: marriages without contract (*agraphos gamos*) are well attested in Egypt and are presumed to represent the older Greek style;[349] marriage by *engye* certainly continued unchanged in Greece;[350] and the use of contracts

[343] Cf. Nicarete at Thespiae (n. 216 above), and Préaux 1959, 159 n. 2: (H 174).

[344] Pleket 1969, no. 3: (B 119), with *Bull. épig.* 1968, 444–5 (Archippe at Cyme, second century) and 6 (Polygnota at Delphi, 86 B.C.); *IG* IX.2.62 (Aristodama of Smyrna at Lamia).

[345] Examples listed by Schneider 1967, 1.94ff.: (A 56), and Pomeroy 1977: (H 171) (women as members of the guilds of *technitai*).

[346] Taubenschlag 1938: (F 370), Préaux 1959, 140ff.: (H 174).

[347] Pleket 1969, nos. 2: (B 119), with *Bull. épig.* 1963, 170 (Apollonis at Istria, second century) and 5 (=*I. Priene* 208; Phyle at Priene, first century).

[348] For this progression cf. *P. Eleph.* 1 (311: translation in Pomeroy 1976, 127–8: (H 170)); *P. Tebt.* III.815 (228) and 974 (early second century); *P. Freib.* III.26 and 29–30 (179); and *P. Giss.* 2 (173) and *P. Tebt.* 104, with Préaux 1959. 147ff.: (H 174), and Vatin 1970, ch. 4: (H 230).

[349] Montevecchi 1936: (F 361), Wolff 1939: (H 226), Modrzejewski 1956: (F 355).

[350] Vatin 1970, 145ff.: (H 230).

may have been due to the specific circumstances of a colonial context where relatives might be distant, spouses be of different cities, and social constraints less effective, so that a contract gave both parties more effective security. Most fundamental qualification of all, women's control over the basic decisions whether to marry or not, and whether to procreate or not, can at best have been patchy and precarious:[351] most women will have had no effective choice.

(5) There were two areas of life from which the cities withdrew, at least in part. One, from the aggressive or large-scale deployment of military force, needs little elaboration in a context of lack of financial reserves, the development of professional armies, and the scale of royal precautions against irredentist movements such as the Lamian War. The withdrawal was not complete, for Rhodes and Athens maintained naval squadrons of a sort, Aetolia and Achaea had armies of quality, Crete's internal wars were endemic, garrison duties and the manning of city defences are well attested, and some Pontic cities had to maintain forces in order to repel incursions from the hinterland.[352] It is noticeable, however, that such efforts as were made to keep military forces in good order applied particularly to cavalry – another symptom of altered power relationships – and that emergency calls for infantry could find a leader reduced to calling for volunteers.[353] It is as much against this background as against that of the presence of suzerain powers that we should see the growing resort to arbitration by a third power as a means of resolving territorial disputes without recourse to war.[354] Like the closely related practices of adopting a law or lawcode from elsewhere or of inviting foreign (and therefore more impartial) judges to preside over a city's own courts and to sort out a backlog of legal disputes,[355] and like them sometimes instigated by a king,[356] such expedients, as alternatives to violence, came more and more to consolidate into custom and to give substance to the old dream that war between Greeks was civil war.

---

[351] Unmarried free women, though attested, are rare, and methods of contraception were often medically unsound (K. Hopkins, 'Contraception in the Roman Empire', *CSSH* 8 (1965) 124–51; Pomeroy 1976. 166–8: (H 170).

[352] E.g. *ISE* 131 = Austin 98 (Istria, 200–150), with Pippidi 1963: (D 164), Pippidi 1971, 86, 89: (D 166), and Moretti *ad loc.*

[353] Thus e.g. Sotas at Priene against the Gauls in the 270s (*OGIS* 765, ll. 19ff.) or Agathocles at Istria against the Thracians (*ISE* 131, ll. 40ff.). The emphasis on cavalry is noticeable at Athens (cf. *ISE* 16, *IG* ii². 1264, *SEG* xxi. 435 and 526, with Habicht 1961: (B 82) and Kroll 1977: (H 123)), but also at Argos, with their loan of 100 tal. from Rhodes at the turn of the fourth and third centuries for the reconstruction of the walls and for the cavalry (Maier 1959, no. 33: (J 226) = *ISE* 40).

[354] Sonne 1888: (H 219); Raeder 1912: (H 179); Tod 1913: (H 226); Tod 1932, 39–68: (H 227); Marshall 1980, 633ff. (bibliographical surveys, 627 n. 1 and 633 n. 24): (H 136).

[355] Hitzig 1907(2), 236–243: (H 103); Robert 1924: (B 127); Robert 1925(1): (B 128); Robert 1925(2): (B 129); Robert 1926: (B 131); Robert 1927, 102ff.: (B 132); Robert 1928, 163ff.: (B 133); Larsen 1943, 249–55: (B 103); Robert 1973: (B 149). Cf. also n. 230 above.

[356] E.g. *SIG* 426 (a Teian at Bargylia at the instigation of Antiochus I) or *OGIS* 43 (Coans at Naxos at the instigation of the Ptolemaic nesiarch Bacchon).

The second partial withdrawal lay in the area of religion and association.[357] The late archaic and classical periods had seen strenuous efforts by many Greek states to bring all cults, whether foreign or indigenous, into a single national framework of reference wherein cults were publicly recognized and at least in part publicly financed, priests were public officials or under some public control, and amalgamated calendars of sacrifices imposed order and controlled innovation. Such efforts were probably not uniformly successful, but they represented the direction of flow: even major innovations such as the spread of Asclepius-worship or the tentative creation of hero-cults of living men were accommodated within the religious framework of the city. This flow certainly continued to be one of the major components of Hellenistic religious expression. Codifications of existing cult practice attested all over Greece[358] take the series on from classical Athens and her demes. Potentially disruptive cults such as that of Dionysus were publicly recognized and regulated,[359] gods were given new functions within civic space,[360] and especially after epiphanies, not infrequently reported in the period, new or existing deities were accommodated in city cult and accorded the appropriate honours and festivals.[361] The two best known instances are the Delphic *Soteria*, founded after the epiphany of Apollo and other deities against the Gauls in 279,[362] and the festival of Artemis Leucophryene at Magnesia, ultimately founded in 202 after her epiphany in 221/20.[363] It is not chance that in both cases the state authorities had good reasons of their own to promote such commemorations. The same was true for the foundations of festivals involving contests (athletic or musical), the effective promotion of which usually stemmed from the initiative of a city,[364] required recognition from other cities and rulers as 'equivalent to the Olympian' or 'Pythian' Games if they were to have more than regional significance, required such recognition to be widespread if they were to be effective or attract

[357] A proper account of Hellenistic religious developments is quite impracticable, but is fortunately the less necessary in view of Stewart's exemplary recent survey (Stewart 1977: (H 221)). See also Festugière 1972: (H 58); Schneider 1969, II.765–959: (A 56); Nilsson 1974 (first section-: (H 154); and Préaux 1978, II.637–60, with bibliography at I.72–4: (A 48).

[358] See Sokolowski 1955, Sokolowski 1962, and Sokolowski 1969, *passim*: (H 216–8).

[359] E.g. Sokolowski 1955, no. 48: (H 216) (Miletus, 276/5), with Quandt 1913: (H 177) and Nilsson 1957: (H 153).

[360] E.g. Sokolowski 1962, no. 45: (H 217) = *ISE* 59 (Apollo Actius as federal god of Acarnania, c. 216).

[361] E.g. *RC* 67 (Zeus Sabazius at Pergamum, 135 B.C.). Other examples are listed by Pfister 1924, 298–300: (H 163).

[362] For the problems involved see now Nachtergael 1977, 209ff.: (E 113).

[363] *I. Magnesia* 16 = *SIG* 557, with *SIG* 695 and Dunand 1978: (H 52).

[364] But not always: Alexander and some kings did the same (references in Moretti 1977, 492: (H 148)), as even did the occasional individual like Agathinus on Arcesine (*IG* XII.Suppl. 330, second century).

competitors, and were promoted for solidly rational reasons of trade, revenue, and prestige as much as to honour the god. The strength of the city-orientation of this custom is shown by the way in which kings who promoted such festivals had to behave like cities, appealing for recognition in exactly the same way.[365] Finally, it was also above all the cities who took the formal initiative in instituting cults in honour of kings and royal families:[366] whether the king was honoured as 'founder' (in many colonies, appropriately enough), as 'saviour' (like Antigonus and Demetrius in Athens), or as 'benefactor', the ideas involved all fitted with surprising ease, after the initial shock of the 320s, into Greek conceptual structures of the honours appropriate to god or hero,[367] all the more since the kings (after Alexander at least) carefully avoided requiring *proskynesis*, performing miracles or invoking divine status while addressing Greeks.

VIII. THE LIMITS OF THE POLIS

Thus far, then, the flow of traditional religiosity could be contained comfortably within the city-state frame of reference, perhaps even receiving some added impetus when, after the Roman takeover of Greece and western Asia Minor, such civic ceremonials took on the new role of symbolizing local or national identities and were revived or re-ordered accordingly.[368] Yet plainly that was not the whole story, for other currents of religious experience were moving in different directions. I single out three of the stronger ones.

First and foremost, Greek gods had their limits. For all the attractions (to Greeks) of the *interpretatio Graeca* of foreign gods, the initial acceptance of Jews or Brahmins as 'philosophers', the gradual and partial hellenization of some Anatolian and Syrian deities, or the export of Greek gods to the new colonial cities, the basic fact came to be that Greeks abroad were not numerous enough, and their religious culture not effervescent enough, for Greek gods to prevail in the long run. Rather, their spread eastwards was just one part of a gradual process of

---

[365] Cf. *ISE* 75, recognition of the *Ptolemaieia* by the Delphic Amphictyony in 266/5, and *SIG* 390 = Austin 218, its recognition *c.* 280 by the league of the Islanders. Or the dossier of documents concerning the reorganization of the *Nikephoria* at Pergamum in 182/1 (*RC* 49 (Iasus?); *RC* 50 with Sherwin-White 1978, 132 n. 265: (D 146) (Cos); *SIG* 629 = *IG* IX².1.179 (Aetolia); *SIG* 630 (Amphictyony), with Robert 1930, 332ff.: (B 134); M. Segre 1948: (H 207); Klaffenbach 1950: (E 126); Hansen 1971, 448ff.: (E 122) (but for the era-date C. P. Jones 1974: (E 125)).

[366] Habicht 1970, 37–126 and 253–62: (I 29), sets out the very considerable evidence; and see above, ch. 3, pp. 87–96.

[367] Nock 1930, 44ff.: (I 55); Robert 1945, 22ff.: (B 142); Nock 1951, 127ff.: (I 56); Cerfaux and Tondriau 1957: (I 18); Taeger 1957: (I 78); Fraser 1972, I.213ff.: (A 15); Nilsson 1974, II.132ff.: (H 154); Stewart 1977, 562ff.: (H 221).

[368] Some examples in Stewart 1977, 527: (H 221).

inter-penetration, as non-Greek populations and returning mercenaries in a corresponding movement brought their own gods with them along the major routes of communication. The latter process, of course, was long established and usually caused few tensions when the imported cult served only the cult's own nationals. Resentments were more likely once the cult gained adherents among the local population, and the fact that they did is evidence that some non-Greek gods or religious ideas might be meeting psychological and spiritual needs better than the traditional cults and gods. The spread of Sarapis,[369] and even more of Isis, are classic cases in point, though the latter in particular is hardly surprising in view of the heady combination of antiquity, exoticism, intensity, morality, superiority to Fate, confession, penitence, and miracles which Isis offered to her devotees.[370] Not that the miracles attributed to Isis in the numerous surviving aretalogies[371] were unique to her; no documents from the Hellenistic world are more revealing of the world of the individual of the *menu peuple*, and of his or her basic fears, preoccupations and irrational hopes, than the dossiers of miracle cures recorded as having been wrought in the sanctuaries of Asclepius at Cos or Epidaurus.[372] All are aspects of the growing importance of the notion of salvation, whether it be interpreted in the literal sense of salvation from death or disease, or in the more contemplative sense of serenity and freedom from the anxieties of mundane preoccupations which contemporary Stoic and Epicurean theories were at one in providing, albeit by very different intellectual routes.

Such anxieties are above all personal, and one can see, as a second current, a continued, perhaps enhanced, interest in forms of action which centred on the individual rather than on the collective action, and preoccupation with collective interests, which necessarily characterized all public religion.[373] Granted, not all such phenomena were new in the

---

[369] For the spread of Sarapis, and for the diffusion of cults by returning mercenaries, see Fraser 1960: (F 171) and Fraser 1967: (F 172), with Nilsson 1974, II.119ff.: (H 154) and J. E. Stambaugh, *Sarapis under the early Ptolemies*, Leiden, 1972. Opposition to him at Delos is attested *c.* 200 (*IG* XI.4.1299 = *SIG* 663 = *SEG* XXIV.1158 = Engelmann 1975: (H 55) = Austin 131, with Bruneau 1973: (B 187) (*Bull. épig.* 1974, 393)), and cf. also *SIG* 664 = *Choix* 77 = *Insc. Délos* 1510 = Sherk 1969, no. 5: (B 163), for political complications *c.* 164 involving Rome.

[370] The bibliography on the spread of Isis is endless. See particularly Schneider 1969, II.840ff.: (A 56); Witt 1971: (H 243); and Nilsson 1974, II.119ff. and 624ff.: (H 154), among many others.

[371] Assembled by Peek 1930: (H 161); for additions and amendments see Nilsson 1974, II.626 n. 5: (H 154), and Grandjean 1975: (H 83). The oldest extant texts appear to be that from Cyme (Peek 1930, 120ff., republished in *IG* XII.Suppl., p. 98, perhaps Augustan period) and that from Maronea (first century B.C., Grandjean 1975), but Müller 1961: (F 180) has argued that their Greek form was created *c.* 300.

[372] At Epidaurus Herzog 1931: (H 97) (= *SIG* 1168–9 and Austin 126 in part) (*c.* 300); at Lebena on Crete *IC* I.xviii.17–19 (= *SIG* 1171–2 in part) (first century B.C.). In general see Weinreich 1909: (H 233), Herzog 1931: (H 97), E. and L. Edelstein 1945: (H 54), Cohn-Haft 1956, 26ff.: (H 36), Nilsson 1974, II.222ff.: (H 154), and Sherwin-White 1978, 275ff.: (D 146).

[373] Nilsson 1974, II.218–22: (H 154); Stewart 1977, 530ff.: (H 221).

Hellenistic period. The practice of magic plainly continued much as it had done for centuries, attested in literature[374] and on the increasingly widespread curse-tablets.[375] All our documentation, especially the late Hellenistic curse-tablets from Cnidus,[376] reveals a world of purely personal occasions and crises. Similarly, the practice of consulting oracles continued much as before, though consultations by cities and kings were by now formalities or political ploys rather than genuine quests for guidance *in angustiis*. Yet individuals went on seeking help from them for personal and private anxieties, as shown both by attested consultations at Dodona and Delphi[377] and by the consultations of the specifically medical oracles at Epidaurus, Athens, and Oropus. That oracle-form also came to be used at the literary or sub-literary level to express prophecies, sometimes of a millennialist kind, on the political plane is not necessarily counter-evidence, for like later Jewish visions of the fall of Rome in *Revelation* or the *Sibylline Oracles*, the anti-Roman vision of Publius[378] or the anti-Greek Oracle of the Potter[379] were more substitutes for collective action than blueprints for it.

There were, however, at least two modes of relationship between individual and gods or cosmic powers which were either new, or took on renewed force, in the Hellenistic period. One was scepticism. Its manifold forms ranged from the ostentatious blasphemy of Philip V's admiral Dicaearchus, erecting altars to *Asebeia* (Impiety) and *Paranomia* (Lawlessness),[380] through Polybius' own view of religion as a tool of social control (VI.56.11) and his widely shared elevation of *Tyche* (Fortune) to the status of a deity in her own right,[381] to scepticism as a specific current in Hellenistic philosophy.[382] The other was astrology. Properly to delineate the intellectual and emotional background of its appeal would need a chapter to itself, but it needs notice here, however brief, because though barely known in classical Greece it gained increasing momentum throughout the period to become a serious challenge to orthodox organized religion at several levels.[383] First, though not originally or intrinsically concerned with the individual

---

[374] Theocr. II and Theophr. *Char.* 16 (*deisidaimonia*) are the most salient single texts.

[375] See Plates vol., pl. 230. References and discussions in Audollent 1904: (B 44), Kagarow 1929: (H 111), Nilsson 1967, I.800ff.: (H 154), Schneider 1969, II.916ff.: (A 56), and Nilsson 1974, II.221 n. 3: (H 154). [387] *GDI* 3536–48; three also in *SIG* 1178–80.

[377] Cf. Parke and Wormell 1956, II.133–45 and 173–8: (H 160) (Delphi); Parke 1967, 259–73: (H 159) (Dodona).

[378] Phlegon, *FGrH* 257 F 36 III (from Antisthenes of Rhodes), with Fuchs 1938, 5–6 and 29 n. 16: (H 67). [379] *P.Oxy.* XXII.2332; see ch. 5 n. 111. [380] Polyb. XVIII.54. 8–10.

[381] Schneider 1969, II.830–3: (A 56); Walbank 1972, 58–65: (B 38); and Nilsson 1974, II.200–10: (H 154).

[382] On which see Stough 1969, chs. 2–3: (H 222), and Long 1974, ch. 3: (H 132).

[383] Sketches in Boll 1931: (H 20), Cumont 1937, 13ff.: (F 170), Schneider 1969, II.907–12: (A 56), and Nilsson 1974, II.268–81: (H 154).

rather than the community, it had already become so in Achaemenid Babylonia,[384] and it was this aspect of it – the significance of the conjunctions of planets, stars, sun and moon at the time of birth or conception for the future life of the individual concerned – which was taken up. Secondly, since part of its appeal lay in the intellectual solidity of its foundations, i.e. the accurate observation of planetary movements and the everyday fact of the influence of sun and moon on events in the natural world, it could be, and was, taken seriously by critical and intelligent minds from Hipparchus to Posidonius. Moreover, the ordained inevitability of its imputed predictions put it within at least speaking distance of Stoic doctrines of the necessary connexion between all events in the universe[385] and of the 'fated' ($\epsilon i\mu\alpha\rho\mu\acute{\epsilon}\nu\eta$) as 'the cause of the things which are, or the principle in accordance with which the Universe is conducted' (Diog. Laert. VII.149); Panaetius (F74 van Straaten) was the only major Stoic figure who stood out against astrology. Such doctrines made the invocation of deities otiose unless, like Isis, they were claimed to be able to overmaster Fate. Thirdly, in proportion as it became possible to think of the sun, and to a lesser extent of the moon and planets, as deities, their challenge as literally universal entities to the power-radius of the local or regional gods and heroes of the Greek and other pantheons became a real one. That the stars were already important enough in the 160s to take a prominent role on the gods' side in the cosmic struggle represented on the frieze of the Great Altar at Pergamum tells its own tale.[386]

The third current which ran counter to city-based religion and society was the striving towards autonomy shown by associations which had religious functions or characteristics. Again, the phenomenon took many forms. One minor form, growing as traditional kinship structures weakened, was the creation of foundations which focussed purely on particular families and had as their prime purpose the commemoration, indeed heroization, of the benefactor by his descendants. The two best known cases are Diomedon's spectacularly egocentric dedication in the late fourth century of a *temenos* on Cos to Heracles Diomedonteius[387] and that created on Thera in the third century by the will of Epicteta,[388] but the commemorations provided for in the wills of philosophers were

---

[384] Sachs 1952: (H 191), with Nilsson 1974, II.270–1: (H 154).

[385] *SVF* II.944–5 (translations in Long 1974, 164: (H 132)).

[386] Plates vol., pls. 62–3. For the date of the Altar see Callaghan 1981: (E 119).

[387] In general Laum 1914: (H 127), with Kamps 1937: (H 112), Ziebarth 1940: (H 253), Hands 1968, 175ff.: (H 86), and Schneider 1969, II.526ff.: (A 56).

[388] Laum 1914, II.52 no. 45: (H 127) = *SIG* 1106 = Herzog 1928, 28 no. 10: (B 88), with Sherwin-White 1978, 363–4: (D 146) (Diomedon); Michel 1001 = *GDI* 4706 = Laum 1914, II.no. 43 = *IG* XII.3.330 = Sokolowski 1969, 135: (H 218) (partial), with Boyancé 1972, 330ff.: (H 22), and Nilsson 1974, II.113ff.: (H 154) (Epicteta).

similar in form and function[389] and serve to remind us that as institutions within Athenian society the philosophical schools were formally *thiasoi*, groups of persons owning property jointly, nominally as the adherents of a god but scarcely at all incorporated into the public structure of Athenian religion. Such groups, as they spread during the Hellenistic period at Athens and elsewhere, especially in Delos and Rhodes,[390] exemplified a second form of the phenomenon, for with their membership primarily composed of non-citizens of the host state and with their purposes as often as not social or commercial rather than devotional they exemplified forms of association which altogether escaped the city framework. The greatest of these associations, those of the *technitai* of Dionysus (the professional performing artists),[391] are a separate phenomenon in themselves. They were the product on the one hand of demand, for as the taste for Attic-style drama spread through the Greek culture area in the fourth and third centuries B.C. it transformed festivals, stimulated the building of theatres,[392] and thereby offered the means of existence to travelling actors, whether star players or whole companies. Since such travellers needed security of a kind which individual grants of proxeny or *asylia* could not provide, it was expedient for them to present themselves as a group, naturally under the divine protection of Dionysus, and to receive privileges and confer honours as such. The process had begun by *c.* 300 for the Athenian and the Isthmian-Nemean groups, by the mid third century for the Egyptian group, and by *c.* 235 for the group of Asia and the Hellespont,[393] and yielded entities so detached from the cities where they were based that they were virtually sovereign bodies in themselves, passing decrees which closely resembled city decrees, appointing city-style magistrates and envoys, and disputing with other cities (as well as with each other) on equal terms.[394] That Ptolemies and Attalids managed to exercise some control

---

[389] E.g. Theophrastus' (Diog. Laert. v.53–4) and Epicurus' (Diog. Laert. x.18).

[390] Poland 1909, 548ff.: (H 168) (lists); Tod 1932, 71–96: (H 227); Ferguson 1944: (II 57) (Athens); Pugliese Carratelli 1939–40: (E 141) (Rhodes); Laidlaw 1933, 201ff.: (D 145) (Delos).

[391] Poland 1934: (H 169); Welles 1934: 231ff.: (B 171); Sifakis 1967, 136–71: (H 214); Pickard-Cambridge 1968, 279–321: (H 166).

[392] Catalogues or special studies in Bulle 1928: (J 191); Pickard-Cambridge 1946: (J 240) (Athens); Neppi Modona 1961, 27–59: (J 235); Bieber 1961, 108ff.: (J 183); Mussche 1964, 21ff.: (J 233) (catalogue); Sifakis 1967, 42ff.: (H 214) (Delos) and 106ff. (Delphi); Lawrence 1973, 280ff.: (J 224).

[393] For the Athenian-based group, *SIG* 399=IG II².1132=*FD* III.2, no. 68 (279/8). For the Isthmian-Nemean group, *SIG* 460 (before 280, archon Aenesilas (F 27, Daux 1943: (B 62)); for the Egyptian group, Athen. v.198c and Fraser 1972, I.619 and II.870 n. 1: (A 15); for the Ionia–Hellespont group, *SIG* 507. See Pickard-Cambridge 1968, 279ff.: (H 166).

[394] For example, the Athenian group sends its own envoys to the Amphictyony in 279/8 (*loc. cit.*). For the language of decrees, see Pickard-Cambridge 1968, 308ff.: (H 166); for the quarrel between the Isthmian and Athenian guilds, *ibid.* 288ff.

and patronage over them[395] illustrates once again how cities could not be the only focus of social activity. So does one further form of the drift towards autonomy, the tendency for temples or temple-based groups to seek emancipation from the power or fiscal demands of a neighbouring *polis*. Such battles had mostly long been lost in Old Greece, though Delphi and Delos proved that they could be fought again with success if the vindicator of their autonomy was as powerful, but as geographically remote, as Rome. However, they were still to fight in the newly urbanizing or newly hellenizing areas of western Asia Minor, Syria and Egypt. In Egypt indeed, as we have seen, the fight was not against a *polis* but against the king, but Caria shows clear examples of resistance to a *polis*. The actions of Corris as priest of Zeus Labraundus vis-à-vis Mylasa illustrate it,[396] as does the protection offered by the Seleucid 'official in charge of the sanctuaries' in the third century to certain 'sacred villages' against what appears to have been pressure from Apollonia Salbace nearby.[397]

As this last example indicates, again and again in the Hellenistic period we have to analyse social relationships as being not between two parties but among three or more, at least one of whom may be a king or a royal official. That is one fundamental complexity confronting the social historian of the period. The second, already alluded to (p. 310, above) but requiring re-emphasis, is that while at the social level of the royal courts, the intellectuals, artists and writers, or the politically-minded large landowners we can speak of an increasingly uniform culture increasingly widely spread in Europe, Asia and the Levant, yet below that level we must speak of a multiplicity of societies, interacting little with each other and scarcely more with the culture of the courts. Though no one today would equate language with culture without many qualifications, the innumerable spoken languages of the Hellenistic East – twenty-two in the kingdom of Pontus alone – are a fair indication of that multiplicity, and are probably a better guide to the nature of 'Hellenistic society' than the Attic-based *koine* whose origin and diffusion has influenced – or misled – our vision of it for so long.

---

[395] For the Ptolemies, *OGIS* 50–1 and Fraser 1972, I.203, 232–3, and 619, II.870 n. 1: (A 15); for the Attalids, Hansen 1971, 460–4: (E 122).

[396] Crampa 1969, I.11–12: (B 60).

[397] L. and J. Robert 1954, 285ff. no. 166: (E 94) (cf. pp. 294–7)=Austin 187.

CHAPTER 9

HELLENISTIC SCIENCE: ITS APPLICATION IN PEACE AND WAR

9a HELLENISTIC SCIENCE

G. E. R. LLOYD

INTRODUCTION

Although there are marked continuities between classical and Hellenistic science,[1] the conditions and circumstances in which scientific investigations were conducted, and to some extent the nature of those investigations themselves, were, in certain respects, changed in the Hellenistic world. Four points that concern the different strands of scientific research to varying degrees are (1) the greater inter-penetration of Greek and non-Greek ideas, (2) the increasing specialization of the sciences, (3) the development of new centres of research (especially Alexandria) and of institutions (such as its Museum and Library), and (4), connected with the last point, the increase in kingly patronage.

First and most obviously, the science of the Hellenistic world is not a purely Greek phenomenon. The cross-fertilization between Babylonian and Greek astronomy, especially, is increasingly important from the fourth century B.C. onwards. Thus in the second century Hipparchus was able to draw extensively on Babylonian data, and the only astronomer we know to have followed Aristarchus of Samos in adopting the heliocentric theory was Seleucus, a Chaldaean or Babylonian from Seleuceia, who was active around 150 B.C.

Even in the classical period there were fairly well-defined distinctions between 'philosophers', 'mathematicians' and 'doctors'. Yet as practised, notably by Aristotle, philosophy embraced a wide range of what we should call scientific enquiries, both physical and biological, all of which were considered to make an important contribution to the

[1] The main sources for the aspects of Hellenistic science discussed in this and the next four sections are the substantial extant works of Theophrastus, Epicurus, Euclid, Aristarchus, Archimedes, Apollonius, Hipparchus, Strabo, Dioscorides and Hero of Alexandria, together with our chief ancient secondary sources, notably Ptolemy, Pappus, Proclus, Simplicius and Philiponus. For a number of important theorists we have to rely largely or exclusively on such secondary material. This applies to Strato, to the early Stoics, Zeno, Cleanthes and Chrysippus, to Eratosthenes, and especially to the medical writers. Although not a single complete treatise of Praxagoras, Herophilus or Erasistratus has survived, we can draw on the extensive reports and quotations in Celsus, Rufus, Soranus and especially Galen.

knowledge that the philosopher should attain. In the post-Aristotelian period, both Epicureanism and Stoicism certainly included 'physics' as one of the three branches of 'philosophy' (the other two being logic and ethics). Yet physical enquiry was, in their view, to be conducted with the narrower purpose of freeing the philosopher from fear and anxiety, and that enquiry consequently concentrated first on element theory – the ultimate constitution of material objects – and secondly on the explanation of strange or potentially frightening natural phenomena. No Epicurean and none of the early Stoics made, so far as we know, any significant original contribution to such sciences as astronomy or physiology, although both these subjects were being developed to quite high levels of sophistication in the fourth and third centuries. It is true that some scientists, such as Eratosthenes, had interests in a wide range of non-scientific subjects (though his ancient nicknames Pentathlos and **Beta** suggest that he was seen not just as a polymath but as not supreme in any field). But as the various sciences increased in technicality, so it generally became the pattern for individual scientists to focus their attention on one or a group of closely related disciplines. While this specialization brought benefits in the greater concentration of effort by particular individuals on particular problems, it was also accompanied by an increase in problems of communication and the fragmentation of studies that had all, under Aristotle, been considered parts of natural philosophy. Outside the Hellenistic philosophical schools, practising scientists rarely developed explicit, let alone original, philosophies of science, although the medical sects are something of an exception.

The founding, during the course of the fourth century, first of Plato's Academy and then of Aristotle's school, the Lyceum or Peripatos, had far-reaching significance not just for what may be called higher education, but also for scientific research. The Library and Museum at Alexandria, founded by Ptolemy Soter at the beginning of the third century, were modelled on and influenced by these predecessors – especially the Lyceum – but they take the development a step further. Like the Academy and the Lyceum, the Alexandrian Museum was a community of scholars working, and to some extent living, together. But the Museum differed first in that it was not – at least not primarily – a teaching institution, but one devoted rather to research and scholarship, and secondly in that whereas the Academy and Lyceum were mainly self-supporting, the Alexandrian Museum and Library were maintained entirely by funds provided by the Ptolemies.

The chief subject that benefited from the cultural policies of the Ptolemies was not science, but literature, including philology and literary criticism. But mathematics, the life sciences and even engineering were also, as we shall see, beneficiaries. It was thanks largely to this support that Alexandria became pre-eminent in many branches of scientific research in the third century, even though Athens remained supreme throughout antiquity in philosophy. Even Strato, who worked for a time in Alexandria, returned to Athens after Theophrastus' death to take up the headship of Aristotle's school. Some of the cultural ambitions of the Ptolemies were emulated by other rulers – notably by the Attalid dynasty at Pergamum – and Museums and Libraries were set up in other cities. Nevertheless, although the level of patronage available to scientists (among others) increased in the third century, it was still the case – as it was throughout antiquity – that the economics of scientific research were precarious, and many of the most eminent scientists were either men of independent means or earned their livings – or supplemented their incomes – by practising, for example, as doctors or as engineers.

In the four sections that follow, the emphasis will be on illustrating the distinctive features of Hellenistic science and on the question of the comparative successes and failures in the application of theoretical ideas to practical ends. Much of the complexity of Hellenistic science will thereby be omitted or glossed over, and for the details of the development of scientific thought in the period reference must be made to the books and articles specified in the bibliography.

I. PHYSICS

The Greek term *physike* ($\phi \upsilon \sigma \iota \kappa \acute{\eta}$) covers the whole of the study of nature and to deal, as we shall, with what we call physics together with aspects of mechanics and chemistry but in separation from the life sciences is to employ a distinction that the ancients would not have admitted.

Both Theophrastus and Strato, who in turn succeeded Aristotle as head of the Lyceum (in 322 and *c.* 287 respectively), made important and original contributions to several specific fields of enquiry which we shall be considering in due course. But although both were critical of Aristotle's element theory, Theophrastus' work stayed very much within its framework, and though Strato's physical doctrines were more eclectic (he assumed that the underlying structure of matter is particulate), he held that the fundamental principles are the two primary qualities, hot and cold, a view that clearly owes much to Aristotle.

Neither Theophrastus nor Strato, in fact, produced a comprehensive physical theory to rival Aristotle's, based on the primary qualities hot, cold, dry and wet, and the four simple bodies, earth, water, air and fire. The two main alternatives to Aristotle's theory available in the late fourth century were those of the Epicureans and the Stoics. On the fundamental question of the structure of matter, the Epicureans and

Stoics advanced in certain respects precisely antithetical positions, the Epicureans insisting that matter, as well as space and time, all consist of indivisibles, the Stoics maintaining that all three are continua. The arguments on either side are mainly abstract and dialectical: the empirical data that were deployed were mostly well-known facts or what passed as such, not the product of independent research. But, as we shall see later, research relevant to such questions as the existence of the void was carried out, though not by members of these philosophical schools.

How well known the treatises of the Aristotelian Corpus were in Athens at the end of the fourth century is disputed. It is likely that Aristotle was then known principally from his more literary works, now lost. Yet it seems clear that in taking over the atomic theory from its original fifth-century proponents, Leucippus and Democritus, Epicurus adapted it to meet some of the objections it had encountered, notably from Aristotle. On two points where the theory of Democritus may have been indefinite or open to attack, Epicurus suggested clarifications or modifications. (1) He distinguished clearly between physical and conceptual divisibility. The atoms are physical minima – the unsplittable units of which physical objects are composed – but they are conceptually divisible: the atom has size and parts. However, in addition to, but distinct from, the physical minima, he postulated ultimate conceptual indivisibles. (2) The primary properties of the atoms now definitely include not just shape, arrangement and position (specified by Aristotle as the primary differentiae in fifth-century atomism) but also weight. In the pre-cosmic state atoms all travel in the same direction ('downwards') in the void. Moreover, whereas Aristotle had held that the heavier the body the faster it falls, Epicurus maintained that in the void speed does not vary with weight. To effect the first collision between atoms and thus initiate the process that leads to the formation of worlds as we know them, Epicurus postulated the swerve: an atom deviates from the vertical by the smallest possible amount. There is no cause for this deviation: it is simply an effect without a cause. Moreover, this postulate had not just a cosmological, but also an ethical significance. Quite *how* by this means Epicurus secured free will is controversial: but *that* he did so is clear.

The ultimate ethical motivation of Epicurus' physics emerges clearly also in many of his discussions of particular natural phenomena. 'There is no other end to the knowledge of things in the sky . . . than peace of mind.'[2] Adopting a principle of plural explanations, he insisted that if several possible explanations of a single phenomenon suggest themselves, then so long as none of them is positively contradicted by the evidence all should be allowed to stand. Admirably undogmatic in

[2] Epicurus, *Letter to Pythocles* 85.

theory, and indeed in practice when applied to such obscure problems as the nature of thunder and lightning, this principle was sometimes invoked either to block further investigation or to dismiss the results his contemporaries or predecessors had obtained, as when he asserts that a plurality of explanations must be entertained for such phenomena as the phases of the moon. The unscientific, indeed anti-scientific, aspects of Epicureanism become evident when he dismisses further research as futile and accuses astronomers not just of dogmatism but of superstition and mythology because they sought single explanations.[3]

The underlying motive for the study of natural phenomena was the same for the Stoics as for the Epicureans, namely the attainment of peace of mind. Otherwise, however, the two schools were in fundamental disagreement on almost every important issue in physics. Whereas Epicurus held that atoms and the void alone exist, the Stoics denied that there is a void within the world, although outside it there is infinite void. They rejected the idea that the void is necessary to explain motion. The world is a plenum, but that does not prevent motion taking place within it. As fish move through water, so any object can move through the plenum conceived as an elastic medium.

In contrast to the essentially quantitative theory of the atomists, in which qualitative differences are reduced to differences in the shape, arrangement and position of atoms, the physics of the Stoics was fundamentally qualitative. The starting-point of their cosmology is a distinction between two basic principles, the active and the passive. The passive is quality-less substance or matter. The active is variously identified as cause, god, reason, πνεῦμα (breath or vital spirit) and fate. *Both* these principles are corporeal, and to describe the relation between them the Stoics used the idea of the total inter-penetration or mixture of substances – κρᾶσις δι' ὅλων. The active principle is thus thought of as inherent in the whole world and permeating every part of it.

The physics of Epicurus and the early Stoics (Zeno, Cleanthes and Chrysippus) were abstract systems based primarily on reflection on the problems of the ultimate constitution of matter. Although both schools proposed causal explanations of many astronomical, meteorological and biological phenomena, neither engaged in empirical research to any significant extent, though among the later Stoics Posidonius (*flor. c.* 80 B.C.) is something of an exception to this. Nevertheless, the late fourth-century debate brought into the open the issue between two fundament-ally opposed, but complementary, conceptions of matter: atomism and continuum theory. Either matter exists in the form of discrete particles, separated by void, or it is a continuum of inter-communicating parts. With each conception is associated a different doctrine of movement – a

[3] Epicurus, *Letter to Pythocles* 87.

particle, and a wave, theory: either motion is the transport of material particles through the void, or it is the transmission of a disturbance in an elastic medium. As so often in earlier Greek philosophy, cosmological debate of a highly speculative order thus generated ideas of considerable importance and lasting influence in physical theory.

The contrast between cosmological speculation and detailed empirical investigations into various branches of physics is marked. Yet contemporary with Epicurus and Zeno there were natural philosophers who engaged to good effect in the latter. In the Lyceum, especially, first Theophrastus (Epicurus' senior by some thirty years) and then Strato did so, and although after Strato's death (c. 269) the importance of the Lyceum declined, this tradition was carried on by others elsewhere, notably by Philo of Byzantium (around 200 B.C.) and Hero of Alexandria (probably first century A.D.).

Much of Theophrastus' work may be seen as a continuation of Aristotle's researches. He evidently collaborated closely with Aristotle in many areas of scientific enquiry and although we must certainly reject the extreme view that he was responsible for most of what appears in our Aristotelian Corpus, parts of the *Historia animalium* have plausibly been thought to owe as much to him as to Aristotle himself, and we shall be considering Theophrastus' undoubted botanical works later.

Two of his shorter treatises deal with physical problems. In *On Fire* he hits on a fundamental objection to Aristotle's doctrine of fire as a simple body. Unlike air, water and earth, fire requires a substratum. 'Everything that burns is always as it were in a process of coming-to-be and fire is a kind of movement.'[4] 'It seems absurd to call this a primary element and as it were a principle, if it cannot exist without matter.'[5] Yet although Theophrastus thus exposes an important weakness in Aristotle's doctrine, he attempts no new element theory himself. He does, however, provide some important data relevant to the investigation of what fire is, concerning, for example, the different ways in which fire may be made or extinguished, even if he draws back from the question of determining its nature.

In *On Stones*, too, the framework of Theophrastus' account is derived from Aristotle, in that he classifies 'things found in the earth' into two main groups, those (like the metals) in which water predominates, and those (the stones and earths) in which earth does. But within this framework he attempts an account of the different kinds of stones, distinguishing them by colour, hardness, smoothness, solidity, 'weight' (that is specific gravity) and their reactions to other substances or processes, especially fire and heat. The range of data his discussion encompasses is remarkable: thus he often gives detailed information

---

[4] Theophr. *On Fire* 51.24ff.   [5] Theophr. *On Fire* 51.30–1.

about the precise localities from which a particular kind of stone, earth or metal comes. He pays attention to – and provides us with interesting information concerning – contemporary technology. His description (section 16) of the mining of what is probably lignite contains our first extant Greek reference to the use of a mineral product as fuel. Sections 45–7 on the touchstone contain our first account of a method of determining the precise proportions of the constituents of an alloy. Among the processes which he describes as having recently been discovered are the production of red ochre and the extraction of cinnabar, and at the end of his brief account of how quicksilver is produced he remarks 'perhaps several other such things could be discovered'. The enquiry is certainly undertaken with theoretical, not practical, interests in mind: Theophrastus was no alchemist (cf. below, p. 330). There is no evidence of his attempting to conduct systematic experiments to advance the classification of stones and earths, let alone for technological motives. Nevertheless, within the limits of the aims he set himself, he collects and attempts to bring into systematic order a considerable body of mineralogical and petrological data. Again, whereas many ancient writers on stones and metals deal at length with their magical properties, especially their supposed therapeutic powers, Theophrastus' discussion is generally (though not entirely) free from such preoccupations.

The work of Theophrastus' successor, Strato, is much harder to reconstruct since we have no single complete treatise and have to rely on fragmentary reports and paraphrases in later writers. We know that he wrote on a wide variety of topics, including zoology, pathology, psychology and technology. Most of our information concerning his work relates to certain physical and dynamical investigations, notably in relation to the two problems of gravity (or as the Greeks called it the nature of the heavy and the light) and the void. Against Aristotle's view that there are two natural tendencies, one of heavy bodies towards the centre of the earth, and the other of light ones away from it, Strato argued that a single downward tendency can account for both movements, the upward movement of fire and air being explained by their being displaced by the downward motion of heavier bodies. More importantly, he is reported to have attempted to establish the phenomenon we call acceleration empirically, adducing the evidence of falling water and of the impact of stones dropped from different heights to support the conclusion that a falling body 'traverses each successive space more swiftly'.[6]

On the void, too, he attempted to deploy empirical, indeed experimental, evidence. It is generally agreed that an extended passage in the

[6] Simpl. *in Phys.* 916.18ff.

introduction to Hero's *Pneumatica* is derived partly from Strato. This contains first a simple test in which an empty vessel is inverted and pressed down into water in order to demonstrate the corporeality of air, and then a series of more striking experiments to show that a continuous vacuum can be produced artificially. A hollow metal sphere with a siphon let into it is used to show first that air can be forcibly introduced (this is taken to establish that a 'compression of the bodies in the sphere takes place into the interspersed vacua' in the air it contains[7]) and secondly that air can be forcibly withdrawn from the sphere (taken to show the artificial production of a continuous vacuum). As is often the case with ancient experiments, the tests are inconclusive. The results are interpreted already in terms of the theory they purport to demonstrate, and those who denied the void could, no doubt, have explained the phenomena described by appealing to the elasticity of air. Yet the attempt to adduce new empirical evidence relevant to the largely dialectical controversy on the existence of the void is notable and characteristic of Strato's approach.

The type of empirical investigations found in Strato continues in Philo and Hero. They too were interested in such problems as the existence of the void, but much of their discussion is devoted to the description of mechanical devices of various kinds, including some which involve the use of mathematics which we shall be considering later (pp. 336–7). Here we may concentrate on those that employ pneumatic or hydraulic principles. Many, even the majority, of these are gadgets explicitly designed to amaze or amuse. Hero's *Pneumatica*, for instance, describes more than two dozen gadgets constructed with secret compartments and interconnecting pipes and siphons that enabled strange effects to be produced – Magic Drinking Horns from which two different liquids can be poured, for example, or Magic Mixing Vessels that replenish themselves (from a hidden reservoir) as they are emptied. One toy even uses the power of steam: a hollow ball with bent tubes attached is made to rotate on a pivot over a cauldron of water which is heated to make steam – a primitive reaction turbine.

But some of the devices are meant not – or not just – 'to produce astonishment and wonder', but to 'supply the most necessary wants of human life' (as Hero puts it[8]) and some are of practical consequence. Several of the most interesting inventions are associated in our sources with the name of Ctesibius, an Alexandrian engineer active in the last quarter of the third century B.C. whose own mechanical treatise has not survived. Thus Vitruvius ascribes to him a force pump, incorporating a system of valves, cylinders and pistons to deliver water under pressure, and a development of the clepsydra, the constant-head water-clock.

[7] Hero, *Pneumatica* Proem 16.23–4.   [8] Hero, *Pneumatica* Proem 2.18ff.

Ancient technology, while essentially conservative, was not as totally stagnant as has often been claimed. The literary and archaeological records provide evidence of improvements in certain aspects of food technology and agriculture, in ships and sailing, in areas of metallurgy and in what we should call chemical technology, although such improvements are usually hard or impossible to date with any precision. These developments generally owe more to the trial and error adjustments of the craftsmen themselves than to the application of the theoretical investigations of those who studied mechanics. Nevertheless, the evidence of Philo and Hero especially shows that there was some limited interaction between theory and practice.

Moreover, an important text in Philo indicates that some of the research carried out or at least reported by the mechanical writers received state support. In his *Belopoeica* he describes the investigation of the construction and design of catapults incorporating the torsion principle to exploit the power of skeins of twisted hair or sinew (see further below, p. 358) and he contrasts the crude trial and error methods of earlier workers with the systematic experiments of their successors. Whereas some of the 'ancients' had begun to realize that the key factor in catapult construction was the diameter of the bore (the circle that receives the twisted skeins), their attempts to determine the correct size for different weights of shot had been haphazard. Only recently, Philo says, the right formula had been arrived at thanks to systematic trials increasing and diminishing the diameter of the hole and observing the results. This success, he continues, was achieved by Alexandrian engineers 'who received considerable support from kings who were eager for fame and well disposed to the arts and crafts'.[9]

The circumstances of this case were evidently exceptional. There were powerful motives for promoting research in military technology that did not apply elsewhere – not that we should suppose that the ancients were entirely lacking in ambition to improve technology in other fields as well, or that there was any general shortage of inventive talent (Ctesibius' work and Hero's gadgets show that). On the other hand that talent usually worked in some isolation and against a background of the largely conservative tendencies in the ancient arts and crafts. Throughout antiquity, and not just in the Hellenistic period, the ancients were slow to explore *as a matter of course* the practical applications of theoretical advances in science, and they more often saw theoretical work as an end in itself rather than as a means to be justified by its eventual practical applications. But if ancient values certainly did not favour systematic support of co-ordinated and methodologically sophis-

9 Philo, *Belopoeica* 50.37ff.

ticated technological research, Philo's text shows that in one instance, at least, such research was encouraged by the Ptolemies.

In the study of air and its effects the approach adopted by the Stoics and Epicureans contrasts with that of Strato and later mechanical writers. In our final topic in this section, chemical technology, the gap between practitioners with speculative tendencies and artisans is more marked still. Although on the question of the classification of natural substances little advance was made on Theophrastus' work, extensive proto-chemical literature exists from the late Hellenistic and Imperial periods, especially chemical papyri dating from the third century A.D. onwards, and a variety of alchemical texts going back some two centuries earlier.

We may distinguish broadly between two principal types of investigation, corresponding roughly to these two groups of texts. On the one hand there is what Needham has called aurifiction,[10] the production of imitations of gold – with or without an intent to deceive the customer – by men who were themselves under no illusions that what they were producing was gold. They could not afford to be under any illusions on the subject, for their profit depended on the difference between the real thing and the imitation, and they were usually, one presumes, in a position to test for gold, not just by the touchstone, but by cupellation.

On the other hand there is aurifaction, χρυσοποιία, the attempt to produce 'philosophers' gold', to transmute other substances into a gold that was meant to be indistinguishable from, as good as, or better than, natural gold. This was the aim of men who were influenced by philosophical, not to say mystical, beliefs, concerning, especially, the sympathies and antipathies between things. Unlike the artisans engaged in aurifiction, those who practised aurifaction remained, one must suppose, either ignorant of, or indifferent to, the test of cupellation. The appeal to that test would immediately have revealed that their products were not *ordinary* gold. Both types of investigation were practical in orientation in that they were each directed to obtaining certain endproducts. Moreover, both made important contributions to the development of chemical techniques and equipment – particularly in connexion with the processes of distillation and sublimation. At the same time they provide a striking illustration of the fragmentation of research and of the conceptual barriers between men working in the same or similar fields.

II. MATHEMATICS AND ITS APPLICATIONS

Already in the mid fourth century B.C. Plato and Isocrates distinguished between two main types of reasons for studying mathematics, that is

---

[10] Needham 1974, 10ff.: (J 103).

broadly the practical and the theoretical, though they differed radically in their evaluations of these two. That distinction is reflected in the extant sources for Hellenistic mathematics and it is echoed by later commentators, such as Pappus (early fourth century A.D.) and Proclus (fifth century A.D.). While the works of Euclid (*c.* 300 B.C.), Archimedes (287–212) and Apollonius (*c.* 210), especially, provide us with rich evidence for achievements both in what we would call 'pure' mathematics and in the applications of mathematics to the exact sciences, some of the works of Hero of Alexandria represent, as we shall see, a second, in many ways distinct, more practically oriented, strand of Greek mathematical work.

The problem of assessing Euclid's originality is severe. Almost all the work of his predecessors is lost, and although Plato and Aristotle offer valuable insights into fourth-century mathematics, the reconstruction of pre-Euclidean contributions otherwise depends very largely on what can be inferred from Euclid himself or from later commentators. Nevertheless, certain points are reasonably clear. First there can be little doubt that the vast majority of the theorems in the *Elements* were known before him. His debts to Theaetetus, for example in the study of incommensurables in Book x, and to Eudoxus, to whom is attributed the general theory of proportion in Book v, are particularly important, and the work of identifiable or unnamed predecessors underlies every book of the *Elements*. Secondly, we know that attempts to systematize parts of mathematics go back to Hippocrates of Chios in the late fifth century: he was the first to compose a treatise of *Elements*, this being the term used of the primary propositions from which others were derived. Moreover, between Hippocrates and Euclid we hear of a number of other writers, such as Archytas and Theaetetus, who, in Proclus' words, 'increased the number of theorems and progressed towards a more scientific arrangement of them.'[11]

Nevertheless, what no one before Euclid appears to have done is to have attempted so comprehensive a systematization of the whole of mathematical knowledge. The *Elements* begins with a statement of assumptions, distinguished into three kinds: 'definitions', 'common opinions' and 'postulates'. These three clearly bear a close resemblance to those that Aristotle identifies as the starting-points of demonstrations in his formal logic, namely definitions, axioms and hypotheses. How far Aristotle is drawing on pre-Euclidean mathematics, and how far Euclid in turn may be drawing on Aristotle, are controversial questions. But there is no definite evidence that any earlier mathematician had drawn clear distinctions between different kinds of starting-points, and what Plato has to say about the mathematicians' use of 'hypotheses' in the *Republic*[12] suggests that at that time there may have been some lack of determinacy in the notion. Moreover, among the particular assumptions that Euclid specifies is the famous parallel postulate, which states that non-parallel straight lines meet, and it is commonly and perhaps rightly thought that the inclusion of this among the postulates may be due to Euclid himself. His doing so was criticized extensively in antiquity on the grounds that the proposition should be proved. But in modern times, especially since the development in the nineteenth century of alternative geometries, the wisdom of his including as a postulate the fundamental assumption underlying what we call Euclidean geometry has received greater recognition.

After the statement of assumptions the *Elements* offers deductive proof of a wide range of theorems and the solution of a variety of problems of construction. Although judged by modern criteria some of the proofs presented have their shortcomings, in that, for example, they incorporate assumptions or intuitions that would now be deemed to require justification or defence, the rigour and economy achieved are, on the whole, remarkable. It was for this, pre-eminently, that the *Elements* subsequently became a model of method not just for mathematics but for science as a whole, and secured a place in mathematical education from which it has been displaced only in the present century.

Both Archimedes and Apollonius were creative mathematical geniuses of a far higher order than Euclid. Archimedes' interests were particularly wide-ranging. His extant treatises relate to arithmetic and geometry, statics and hydrostatics, but we know also of investigations in optics, astronomy and engineering. So far as his work in pure mathematics goes, *The Sand-Reckoner*, for instance, develops a new notation for expressing very large numbers. In the elementary treatise *Measurement of the Circle* he elaborates a method used by Euclid before him, based on Eudoxus' method of exhaustion. He determines the area of a circle by inscribing successively greater regular polygons within it and circumscribing successively smaller regular polygons outside it. These processes can be continued indefinitely – the difference between the areas of the polygons and that of the circle can be made as small as desired – not that the Greeks admitted the identification of either polygon with the circle.

A more strikingly original aspect of Archimedes' methods is his application of mechanical concepts to geometrical problems. Thus arguments based on principles in statics, in particular the law of the lever, are brought to bear on the problems of determining unknown areas or volumes, which can be thought of as *balanced* with known areas or volumes at particular distances from a fulcrum. Yet another even more important feature is one that he refers to himself in his *Method of Mechanical Theorems*. There he writes of a certain method by which certain problems can be investigated, even if the method in question does not, in his view, constitute a proof: the theorems discovered by the method have subsequently to be proved by rigorous geometrical methods. The method itself involves conceiving of a plane figure as composed of a set of parallel lines indefinitely close together and then thinking of these lines as balanced by corresponding lines of the same magnitude in a figure of known area. What Archimedes thereby performs is what we should call an integration, even if he lacks a general theorem for integration. It is, too, particularly remarkable that Archimedes is emphatic that his new method does not itself yield a demonstration. In the *Method* the illustration he gives is the proposition that the area of a segment of a parabola is four-thirds the triangle with the same base and the same height: but he follows the application of his method with a reference to the strict demonstration of the theorem that he had given in *Quadrature of the Parabola*.

In *On the Sphere and Cylinder*, *Quadrature of the Parabola*, and *Spirals* Archimedes adopts a Euclidean style of presentation, setting out, where necessary, his assumptions and definitions and proceeding in a rigorous deductive fashion. But he, like Apollonius after him, is now able to build on the *Elements* itself, taking many of its results as already demonstrated. Apollonius, in turn, takes a further area of mathematics forward in the one treatise of his that is extant, his masterpiece *Conics*, a comprehensive discussion of the three types of conic section, ellipse, parabola and hyperbola, including such questions as the construction of conics from certain data, tangents, focal properties, intersecting conics and the like.

Pure mathematics at the level at which it was practised by Archimedes and Apollonius was the concern of a tiny minority. But the prestige of mathematics depended rather on the appreciation of the rigour and certainty of its results – and that was easy enough to grasp even in elementary examples. It is likely that, like other scientists, mathematicians were the beneficiaries of royal patronage, though to what extent is a matter of guesswork. The evidence of Euclid's connexion with the Ptolemies is anecdotal, but we are reliably informed that the mathematician, geographer and polymath Eratosthenes was made head of the Library under Ptolemy Euergetes. Archimedes, however, was related to the ruling family at Syracuse, and his presence in the ranks of the foremost mathematicians may serve as a reminder that many of those who embarked on scientific enquiries were men of means and leisure.

This leads us towards the complex question of the applications of mathematics, a topic which can be discussed in two parts, first the applications of mathematics to the exact sciences (applied mathematics in this sense still being theoretical), and secondly the practical applications of mathematics in mechanical devices and in engineering.

Already in the fourth century Aristotle speaks of astronomy, optics and harmonics as the more physical of the mathematical studies and in all three cases the mathematical investigation of the subject-matter was well established by the end of that century. Later in the Hellenistic period other branches of enquiry were to be added to the list, especially statics and hydrostatics by Archimedes. Astronomy, together with mathematical geography, is important enough to be dealt with in a separate section (below, pp. 337–47). Euclid's *Optics* is our first extant treatise on the subject. Characteristically it begins with a statement of assumptions, which include such idealizations as that 'the figure contained by a set of visual rays is a cone of which the vertex is at the eye and the base at the surface of the subject seen'.[13] Again characteristically it proceeds by treating the subject-matter in purely geometrical terms.

Similarly in harmonics, where the Euclidean *Sectio canonis* is one in a long line of specialist treatises on the subject, though whether it was written by Euclid himself is disputed, the reduction of the audible concords to simple numerical relationships goes back at least to the fifth-century Pythagoreans, if not to Pythagoras himself, and work on the analysis of musical scales continues throughout the Hellenistic period. It is interesting, however, that at the end of the fourth century Aristoxenus reports an epistemological debate in which those who were for reducing harmonics to a purely mathematical subject, and who rejected the senses as inaccurate, were opposed by those who insisted rather that sense-perception is the ultimate criterion. Aristoxenus, for his own part, claims to steer a middle course, maintaining that the enquiry depends on the two faculties of hearing and the intellect and emphasizing that, unlike the geometer, who makes no use of sense-perception, the student of musical science must have a trained ear.[14]

It is in line with such reductions of physical phenomena to exact mathematical relationships that Archimedes investigates both statics, in *The Equilibrium of Planes*, and hydrostatics, in *On Floating Bodies*. The treatise *Mechanica* in the Aristotelian Corpus had already discussed a number of problems concerned with balances and the lever, often with, as we shall see, an emphasis on practical issues. What is quite new in Archimedes is the rigorous deductive proof of the basic propositions of statics. He begins by stating such postulates as that 'equal weights at equal distances are in equilibrium and equal weights at unequal distances are not in equilibrium but incline towards the weight which is at the greater distance',[15] and he then proceeds to demonstrate a series of simple propositions, including in proposition six and seven the law of the lever, first for commensurable and then for incommensurable

[13] Euc. *Optics* Def. 2.   [14] Aristox. *Harm.* II.32–3.
[15] Archimedes, *The Equilibrium of Planes* 124.3ff.

magnitudes. The rest of Book I and Book II deal with the problems of determining the centres of gravity of various plane figures such as a parallelogram or parabolic segments. The problems are, throughout, formulated in ideal, mathematical terms. Friction, the weight of the balance itself, every extraneous physical factor is discounted. The key physical assumptions (which Mach claimed already presuppose the law of the lever) are contained in the postulates. But these once assumed, the subsequent discussion is geometrical throughout. Archimedes, one may say, treats statics as a branch of geometry and the whole is an exercise in deductive proof on the model of Euclid's *Elements*.

Moreover, the same is true also of the hydrostatical treatise, *On Floating Bodies*. Again he begins with a postulate setting out the properties of fluids that have to be assumed. Again the proofs – including the proof of 'Archimedes' principle' itself in proposition seven – proceed deductively and again the development of the investigation is geometrical. After considering propositions concerning segments of a sphere in Book I, Archimedes turns, in Book II, to problems concerning paraboloids of revolution, investigating the conditions of stability of segments of paraboloids of varying shapes, and of varying specific gravities, in a fluid. It has been suggested that this focus on paraboloids reflects a practical interest in ship-building (the cross-section of the hull of a ship being, approximately, a parabola[16]). Yet Archimedes himself makes no such connexion and his idealized mathematical study is as far away as could be from matters of practical concern.

We find, then, that in a number of subjects Hellenistic scientists achieved notable successes in turning the enquiry into an exact science. These are among the most striking developments of Hellenistic, even of Greek, scientific endeavour. When we turn to the evidence for practical applications of mathematics, the record is a good deal thinner. First, as already noted, there is a strand of mathematical enquiry itself that overlaps, to be sure, with the Euclidean, but is often distinctly more practical in its concerns. Although Hero of Alexandria himself is now generally dated to the first century A.D., his writings – like Euclid's – evidently draw on a rich and long tradition, in some cases including aspects of Babylonian and Egyptian mathematics. Thus Hero's *Metrica* deals with problems of mensuration, for the solution of which geometry is certainly used, but which often have a practical significance, as when he discusses, for instance, the determinations of areas and volumes.

Our extant evidence for the practical investigation of mechanical problems begins a good deal earlier than Hero, with the Aristotelian *Mechanica*. The practical orientation of some of the discussions in this

[16] Cf. Landels 1978, 191. (J 94).

treatise is in marked contrast to Archimedes' *The Equilibrium of Planes.* The author (perhaps a pupil, certainly a follower, of Aristotle) considers such topics as why larger balances are more accurate than smaller ones, why longer bars are moved more easily than shorter ones round the same capstan, even why it is easier to extract teeth using a forceps than without, along with many other simple applications of the lever, the wedge, the pulley and the windlass.

Mechanica thus discusses four of the simple 'powers' known to the ancients. All four had been used in one form or another long before the fourth century. Yet the literature that begins with *Mechanica*, continues in Hero's mechanical treatises and goes on into late antiquity with such works as the eighth book of Pappus' *Mathematical Collection* is evidence of the interest shown both in the mathematical analysis of a number of mechanical problems and, conversely, in the practical applications of mathematical ideas to different fields. Thus both Hero and Pappus tackle the problem of the analysis of the forces acting on weights on an inclined plane. Several passages in Hero deal with the question of how to shift a weight of a given magnitude with a force of a given magnitude using either compound pulleys or levers, or toothed or cogged wheels.

The fifth 'power' treated in the mechanical writers, the screw, provides perhaps the most striking example of the application of mathematical knowledge. Far more than any of the other simple powers, the screw depends on working out and applying a mathematical construction. Moreover, unlike the other four, it appears to have been developed first, in its various ancient forms, during the Hellenistic period. It may have been used first in the water-lifting device still named after Archimedes (there is an ancient tradition that he invented this in Egypt[17]), but in Hero we also find it applied in presses, both the single- and the double-screw press, and in devices for lifting heavy burdens. Hero also provides evidence for ancient screw-cutting machines and discusses how to make a cog-wheel with a given number of teeth to fit a given screw.

Some of the devices in the mechanical literature are scarcely practicable. The frequent discounting of the effects of friction, especially, is in line with the simplification of physical problems which we have remarked on elsewhere, but it turns the discussion into a highly idealized one. Yet the point should not be exaggerated. The problem of confirming the use of cog-wheels, for example, in practice is severe, for most such devices would have been made in perishable materials. Yet the bronze Anticythera instrument shows that gear-wheels were incorporated into practical instruments, even if in this case they are not made to do much mechanical work: the object is a calendrical computer

[17] Diodorus 1.34: v.37; Athenaeus v.208f; Plates vol., pl. 260.

in which a system of differential gears is used to represent the sidereal motions of the sun and moon.[18]

When Plutarch, in a much quoted passage, reports that Archimedes despised technology and 'regarded the work of an engineer and every art that ministers to the needs of life as ignoble and vulgar',[19] this certainly represents attitudes that were common and influential among the educated cultural élite to which Plutarch himself belonged. Whether this correctly represents Archimedes' own views is another matter, since it would appear that his interest in mechanical devices was extensive and not confined merely to the domain of military technology and to his involvement in the construction of machines for the defence of Syracuse (cf. below, pp. 358–9). We must repeat that although the evidence for the interaction of theory and practice is limited, it is not negligible. That there were not greater practical results from the efforts of the mechanical writers is, once again, a matter to be referred to their comparative isolation and lack of systematic support, factors which, in turn, relate, as we have said, to the dominant values of ancient society.

III. GEOGRAPHY AND ASTRONOMY

Both geography and astronomy have on the one hand a descriptive and on the other a theoretical, mathematical aspect. In late antiquity Ptolemy,[20] for instance, explicitly distinguished what he called 'chorography' – descriptive geography dealing with the nature of lands, region by region – from geography proper, the mathematical study concerned principally with the problems of projection, although, like many other important ancient geographers, Ptolemy himself combined an interest in both fields. From the very beginning of Greek historical writing Hecatacus and Herodotus had concerned themselves with the description of countries as well as of events, and this tradition continued in, for example, the 'universal' historian Polybius. The most comprehensive extant treatise devoted primarily to descriptive geography is the work of Strabo (first century B.C. – first century A.D.), though his extensive references to his predecessors – especially Eratosthenes, Hipparchus and Posidonius (from the third, second and first centuries B.C. respectively) – enable us to reconstruct some of their contributions. These geographical studies were not just the product of individual curiosity and research, but were at least sometimes undertaken for reasons of state or stimulated by royal patronage. An incidental remark in Pliny tells us, for instance, that Dicaearchus, a pupil of Aristotle, undertook the measurement of the height of certain mountains charged by, and presumably with the

[18] See Price 1974: (J 116); Plates vol., pl. 261.
[19] Plut. *Marc.* 17.4.   [20] Ptol. *Geog.* 1.1.3.3ff.

support of, 'the kings',[21] though Pliny does not specify who these were.

Mathematical geography, too, goes back to the classical period. The sphericity of the earth was known before Aristotle, who demonstrates it in the *De Caelo*[22] partly from the shape of the earth's shadow in lunar eclipses and from the changes in the positions of the stars as observed from different latitudes, and who provides our first extant estimate of its circumference, namely 400,000 stades, although he does not specify how this figure was arrived at – nor is it certain which of several possible 'stades' of different lengths he was using. A division of the globe into zones ('arctic', 'temperate' and 'torrid') is also pre-Aristotelian, but not long after him was improved on. Even though none of Eratosthenes' books has survived, we know that his interests were extensive: they included philology and literature as well as mathematics, astronomy and geography. He appears to have been responsible for the first detailed map of the world based on a system of meridians of longitude and parallels of latitude. We are told by Cleomedes[23] not just the figure that Eratosthenes gave for the circumference (250,000 stades: again the 'stade' in question is disputed) but also how he arrived at it, namely on the basis of a comparison of the shadow cast at noon on the day of the summer solstice at two locations, Syene and Alexandria, assumed to lie on the same meridian circle. While at Syene the gnomon made no shadow, at Alexandria it gave one of seven and one fifth degrees. Given an estimate of the distance from Syene to Alexandria – which he took to be 5,000 stades – he could obtain the circumference of the earth by simple geometry.

The accuracy of the result depended on two factors. The first is the measurement of the gnomon's shadow. Ptolemy was later to note the difficulty of obtaining accurate solstice observations in the *Almagest*,[24] and it may be that it was for this reason that when Posidonius came to make his calculation of the circumference of the earth he adapted Eratosthenes' method and used comparisons not of solstice shadows, but of the observed altitude of the star Canopus.[25] The second, more important, factor was the accuracy of the estimate for the base-line Syene–Alexandria. Assessments of distances over land were notoriously unreliable, so much so that we find Ptolemy, for example, insisting that the locations of places on the earth's surface should, so far as possible, be determined from astronomical data rather than from the reports of travellers[26] – thereby rather reversing the procedure that Posidonius had

[21] Pliny, *NH* 11.162.
[22] Arist. *Cael.* 11.14, 297b24ff., 30ff., 298a15ff.
[23] Cleomedes 1.10.94.24ff. Elsewhere, however, a figure of 252,000 stades, giving a round figure of 700 stades per degree, is ascribed to Eratosthenes: Strabo 11.34.132; Theon Smyrnaeus 124.10ff.
[24] *Alm.* 111.1.196.21ff., 203.12ff.
[25] See Cleomedes 1.10.92.3ff.   [26] Ptol. *Geog.* 1.4.12.4ff.

used to determine the earth's circumference. Nevertheless, whether in Eratosthenes' version or in that of Posidonius, here was a notable application of mathematical principles to a geographical problem. Others were to involve more sophisticated mathematics. By the time we reach Ptolemy in the second century A.D. the problems of cartography – the projection of the sphere on to a plane surface – are discussed with considerable subtlety, the accuracy of different projections being assessed with some care.

It was, however, in astronomy that the greatest successes in the application of mathematics to physical problems were achieved. Two issues, one major, one minor, dominated theoretical astronomy from the fourth century B.C. onwards. The minor one, in the ancients' view – though it has been a dominant topic in some histories of astronomy – was the question of whether the earth or the sun is at the centre of the universe. We know from a report in Archimedes that Aristarchus of Samos, working around 280 B.C., produced a set of what Archimedes calls hypotheses that included the propositions that the fixed stars and the sun remain unmoved and that the earth is borne round the sun on the circumference of a circle.[27] The status of these hypotheses is a matter of some controversy. Plutarch contrasts Aristarchus' position, which he represents as the mere 'hypothesizing' of the idea of the earth's movement, with that of Seleucus who, Plutarch says, also 'asserted' it.[28] But Plutarch himself was no astronomer and his testimony is open to doubt. The report itself confirms, however, that one ancient astronomer at least maintained heliocentricity.

Moreover, we can be sure that whatever his own reservations about the physics of his hypotheses may have been – Aristarchus himself advanced his position in all seriousness as a possible mathematical model to account for the movements of the heavenly bodies. This is clear from the way the hypotheses are framed as a complete set and in particular from the care with which Aristarchus guards against one major objection to which the heliocentric theory was vulnerable, namely the apparent absence of stellar parallax – that is the shift in the relative positions of the stars as viewed from different points in the earth's orbit round the sun. Aristarchus evidently saw that this objection fails if the stars are sufficiently distant from the earth. He did not attempt to *prove* that they are. Rather he included as one of his initial assumptions, according to Archimedes, that the circle in which the earth revolves round the sun is as a point in relation to the sphere of the fixed stars, that is, that the stars may be thought of as at infinite distance.

Nevertheless, with the sole exception of Seleucus, no other ancient

<hr>

[27] Archimedes, *The Sand-Reckoner*, 1.4ff., 218.7ff.   [28] Plut. *Quaest. Plat.* VIII.1.1006c.

astronomer adopted Aristarchus' suggestion. The two greatest names in third- and second-century B.C. astronomy, Apollonius and Hipparchus, both retained the geocentric view, and so too did Ptolemy. If we may use Ptolemy as our chief source for the arguments that weighed with the astronomers in their rejection of heliocentricity, religion was not an important factor. It is true that the Stoic philosopher Cleanthes is reported by Plutarch to have thought that the Greeks ought to indict Aristarchus for impiety for putting the 'hearth of the universe' (that is, the earth) in motion.[29] But the discussions of the issue in astronomical authors are free from any such idea. Ancient astronomers had, in any case, no Church to contend with, and no Bible with the authority of revealed truth.

The objections to the earth's movement that Ptolemy mentions are partly physical and partly astronomical.[30] The Aristotelian doctrine of natural places starts from the idea that heavy objects, including earth, naturally move towards the centre of the universe. Applying this to the earth as a whole, we arrive at the conclusions that it is at rest in the centre of the world and that it could not be moved except by some immense force capable of overcoming its natural tendency. Secondly, there is the absence of any visible effects of the earth's rotation on solid objects, or even on the clouds, above the earth's surface. It is clear that the counter to this objection – that it is not only the earth, but also the surrounding air that rotates – had been suggested by Ptolemy's time, even if he himself is unimpressed by this defence. Thirdly, the chief astronomical difficulty, which Aristarchus had anticipated by suggesting that the stars may be thought of as infinitely distant, is the absence of stellar parallax. We might conjecture, though we cannot confirm, as a fourth factor, that ancient astronomers recognized that a simple circular movement was inadequate to account for the irregular movements of the sun and moon, where the issue between geocentricity and heliocentricity could be ignored as irrelevant. Given that either eccentric circles or epicycles had to be appealed to in those two cases, ancient astronomers may have assumed that a similar solution to planetary motion was also to be given.

These considerations are, to be sure, of very varying force, but their cumulative effect was felt to be decisive against any suggestion that the earth moves in space. We do not know how closely the opening chapters of Ptolemy's *Almagest* follow Hipparchus' thinking. But so far as Ptolemy himself is concerned, it is clear that he felt that the subsequent astronomical system he develops is securely founded on what he took to be well-established *physical* principles: that system is not just a mathematical construct without any basis in physical reality. His whole discussion betrays a confidence in the absurdity of the suggestion that

[29] Plut. *de Fac.* 6.923A.   [30] Ptol. *Alm.* 1.6.21.9ff.

the earth moves and he does not explore or even investigate the consequences of heliocentricity for the problems of planetary motion.

The major issue, in the eyes of ancient astronomers, was that of the explanation of the movements of the sun, moon and planets, especially the irregularities of planetary motion. The model of combinations of concentric spheres, proposed by Eudoxus and adapted by Callippus and Aristotle in the fourth century, failed – among other things – to account for the apparent variations in the distances of the moon and of the planets. The model that replaced this and was to last not only throughout antiquity but down to Kepler was the work of Apollonius of Perge, whose investigations of conic sections have already been mentioned (above, p. 333). He proposed that the motion of the sun, for instance, can be represented either as an eccentric circle (fig. 1), or as movement on the circumference of a circle (an epicycle) whose own centre moves round the earth (fig. 2). It is probable that Apollonius recognized that these two mathematical models can be made equivalent (fig. 3) and he no doubt appreciated that either model could give a simple explanation of the irregularity of the sun's movement, that is the inequality of the seasons, a fact discovered by Meton and Euctemon in the late fifth century B.C. but ignored by Eudoxus (see fig. 4).

It is, however, quite uncertain how far Apollonius applied these models to give detailed solutions to the movements of the sun, moon and planets. According to Ptolemy, not even Hipparchus succeeded in producing such solutions to the problems of planetary motion,[31] although his models for the sun and moon were accurate enough for Ptolemy to base his own theories on them – in the case of the sun with very little modification. Ptolemy himself, working long after Hipparchus, but relying very heavily on his results, provides us in the *Almagest* with the most elaborate example from the whole of extant ancient science of the application of pure geometry to the explanation of highly complex phenomena. It is true that there are points at which he gives us much less information about his data base than we should like; again there are others where his selectiveness of the data to be discussed is transparent, and yet others where he himself bewails the complexity of the hypotheses he has to develop in order to resolve the complexities of planetary motion. Yet the comparative success and exactness with which he produced models from which the positions of the main heavenly bodies could be deduced must rank as one of the most outstanding achievements of ancient science.

Although the elaboration of the epicycle-eccentric model was the chief problem of theoretical astronomy from the time of Apollonius, a great deal of attention was also paid to purely descriptive astronomy.

[31] Ptol. *Alm.* IX.2.210.8ff.

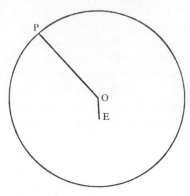

Fig. 1. Eccentric motion. The planet (P) moves round the circumference of a circle, whose centre (O) does not coincide with the earth (E). (From Lloyd 1973, fig. 6: (J 97).)

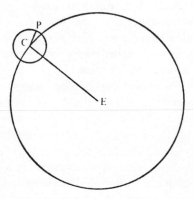

Fig. 2. Epicyclic motion. The planet (P) moves round the circumference of an epicycle, whose centre (C) itself moves round the circumference of the deferent circle, centre E, the earth. (From Lloyd 1973, fig. 5: (J 97).)

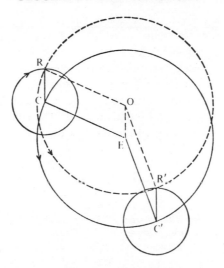

Fig. 3. The simplest case of the equivalence of eccentric and epicyclic motions. When the radius of the deferent circle (CE) is equal to that of the eccentric circle (RO) and the radius of the epicycle (RC) is equal to the eccentricity (OE), then if the angular velocities are regulated so that R and E remain the vertices of a parallelogram CROE, the two models give exactly equivalent results. (From Lloyd 1973, fig. 7: (J 97).)

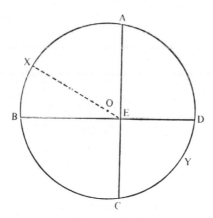

Fig. 4. The inequalities of the seasons explained by the eccentric hypothesis. If the sun moves regularly on a circle whose centre (O) does not coincide with the earth (E), it will not take the same time to traverse the four arcs AB, BC, CD and DA. X and Y are the positions of the sun at maximum, and at minimum, distance from the earth. (From Lloyd 1973, Fig. 8: (J97).)

Already in the fourth century B.C., Eudoxus, among others, had produced accounts of the main constellations, although, since he lacked the division of the celestial globe into 360 degrees, he identified and located individual stars generally rather imprecisely. A number of specific observations made by Timocharis and Aristyllus at Alexandria around the first third of the third century were thought accurate enough to be used by Hipparchus in his astronomical theories. By Hipparchus' own time various systems of spherical co-ordinates – ecliptic, equatorial

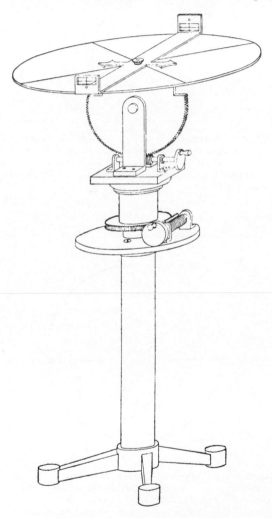

Fig. 5. Hero's dioptra, as reconstructed by H. Schöne. (From Schmidt and Schöne 1976, III.193: (J 34).)

and mixed – were employed: it was only later that the use of ecliptic co-ordinates came to predominate. Moreover, the bid for more precise observations led to certain developments in astronomical instruments. We hear of an improved dioptra named after Hipparchus, and Hero devoted a short treatise to the construction and use of the dioptra (see fig. 5), and it may be that Hipparchus also used the armillary astrolabe described at length by Ptolemy (see fig. 6).

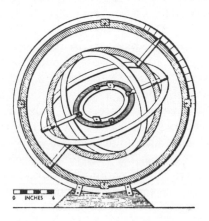

Fig. 6. The armillary astrolabe. (From *A History of Technology* III, ed. C. Singer et al. (Oxford 1957) 592.)

Hipparchus himself produced the first comprehensive star catalogue, giving the positions of an estimated 850 stars. This detailed analysis of star positions had at least one important result for theoretical astron-omy, for it led Hipparchus to the discovery of the phenomenon known as the precession of the equinoxes. The positions of the equinoctial points (where the ecliptic intersects the celestial equator) do not remain constant in relation to the 'fixed' stars, but are displaced from east to west at a rate that Hipparchus estimated as at least one degree in 100 years. Ptolemy tells us how Hipparchus first thought that the shift related only to the stars near the ecliptic, only later to assure himself that it was indeed a phenomenon that applied to the fixed stars in general.[32] We are also told that he wondered whether the tropical year itself (the period defined by the return of the sun to the same solstitial or equinoctial point) may not be a constant,[33] though Ptolemy believed that he realized that the evidence suggesting that it varied was quite inconclusive, that is, that it was within the margin of error of the observations on which it was based.

[32] Ptol. *Alm.* VII.1–3.2.3ff., 3.12ff., 12.7ff., 16.15ff.
[33] Ptol. *Alm.* III.1.191.15ff.

The investigation of the problems of planetary motion was a difficult, technical and specialized matter. But two aspects of the study of the heavens commanded very general interest. One important practical motivation for astronomical observation from early times in Greece had been the regulation of the calendar. In most Greek states the beginning of the new month depended in part on observations of the moon, though these were subject to conventional, not to say sometimes quite arbitrary, interpretation by the magistrates concerned.

The second aspect relates to the belief that the stars influence or even govern human affairs. There is no good evidence that astrological prediction was practised in Greece before the fourth century, and it has been thought likely that its origin owes much to the introduction of ideas from the East. While *some* knowledge of Babylonian astronomy may go back to the fifth century, a report in Simplicius[34] suggests that more detailed information concerning Babylonian ideas became available after the conquests of Alexander, and this, if true, would relate as much to Babylonian astrological beliefs as to their more purely astronomical data – not that the Babylonians themselves would have drawn such a distinction. We should, however, distinguish between quite general assumptions that heavenly phenomena such as eclipses or the conjunctions of planets influence events on earth, and the attempt to make detailed predictions of a man's destiny from the position of the heavenly bodies at his birth. The development of astrology in the latter sense – the casting of horoscopes or genethlialogy – into a universal system owes as much to Greek elaborations (not unrelated to the development of astronomical theory) as to original Babylonian beliefs.

How extensively the casting of horoscopes or other aspects of astrology were practised in Greece in the Hellenistic period can hardly be determined, but it is probable that – as in the Middle Ages and the Renaissance – the major astronomical theorists, including Hipparchus, were also practising astrologers. Once again our best evidence comes from Ptolemy, who wrote a four-book treatise on astrology, the *Tetrabiblos*. He is under no illusions either about the distinction between, on the one hand, the attempt to predict the positions of the heavenly bodies themselves (astronomy, in our sense) and, on the other, the attempt to predict their influence on human affairs (what we call astrology), or about the difference in reliability and exactness between the two studies.[35] Astrology is uncertain and conjectural, and he adds that many current ideas on the subject are absurd. Although the determination of the positions of the heavenly bodies can be exact, the interpretation of the powers of different planets was a matter of tradition

34 Simpl. *in Cael.* 506.11ff.   35 Ptol. *Tetrabiblos* 1.2.4.3ff.

and convention. Yet following tradition and – as it would no doubt have seemed to him – past experience, Ptolemy is prepared to try to establish a general framework for astrological predictions. There is no need to point out that the ambition to gain the ability to foresee the future must have been a powerful stimulus to many to engage, at least up to a point, in astronomical studies. Where we might be tempted to represent the relationship between what we might call the science and the pseudo-science as an entirely negative one, it is clear that the latter provided an important means of recruitment to the former.

IV. MEDICINE AND THE LIFE SCIENCES

The history of medicine and the life sciences in the Hellenistic period illustrates several of our principal themes, the increase in specialization, but also the fragmentation of scientific research, the role of royal patronage, and the patchy success in the application of scientific knowledge to practical ends. Already in the classical period those who practised medicine were clearly marked out from the natural philosophers, even though – firstly – some philosophers showed a considerable interest in medicine (Plato, even, saw fit to include a quite elaborate theory of the different causes of diseases in the *Timaeus*) and – secondly – the medical writers, for their part, varied greatly in their attitudes towards natural philosophy: some adopted or adapted much from the philosophers, especially in the matter of element theories, but others criticized the philosophers bitterly for producing untestable speculations irrelevant to the needs of the doctor faced with the task of trying to cure the sick.

In the Hellenistic period there are continuities with the various traditions represented in the Hippocratic writings, but also important developments. The continuities might well seem greater if we had more information about the work of such men as Diocles of Carystus (late fourth century) and Praxagoras of Cos (*flor. c.* 320), the latter of whom discovered the diagnostic value of the pulse and was, we are told, the teacher of Herophilus. Although none of the writings of Herophilus and Erasistratus themselves has survived, the critical reports of their work in such sources as Celsus, Rufus, Soranus and especially Galen enable us to reconstruct their ideas and interests, and the overwhelming impression we are left with is one of a high level of originality.

By comparison with either the Hippocratic writers or Aristotle, whose anatomical and physiological theories were often fanciful and naive, Herophilus and Erasistratus made massive advances in both these areas, and the principal reason for their successes lies in their use of dissection. Dissection had certainly been practised before, occasionally by some of the Hippocratic writers, and rather more systematically by Aristotle and his school. But we can confidently say that there had been no dissection of the adult human body for scientific purposes before the Hellenistic period. The truth of the reports that Herophilus and Erasistratus not only dissected but also vivisected human beings has, to be sure, often been contested. When the Christian writer Tertullian (*c.* A.D. 200) refers to Herophilus butchering hundreds of men,[36] he is open to the suspicion of exaggeration and distortion in his eagerness to vilify Greek scientific research, even though elsewhere, at least, he draws on a reliable source, the second-century A.D. medical writer Soranus, for some of his information. But other writers tend to confirm in general terms that human dissection (at least) was practised and Celsus, in particular, provides a circumstantial report that both Herophilus and Erasistratus carried out vivisections as well on 'criminals they obtained out of prison from the kings',[37] justifying themselves against the charge of inhumanity by claiming that the good outweighed the evil.

In Herophilus' case no one doubts that this took place in Alexandria – probably in the opening decades of the third century, that is under the first two Ptolemies. So far as Erasistratus goes, if, as has recently been argued,[38] he and his pupils worked at Antioch rather than at Alexandria, then this would mean, if we accept Celsus' evidence, that there was a second centre of human dissection and vivisection in the early third century. But it may be more likely – even in the absence of other evidence confirming that Erasistratus worked at Alexandria – that the usual assumption is correct, and that the kings referred to by Celsus are the Ptolemies alone. In any event, in one if not at two cities, Hellenistic monarchs appear not merely to have permitted but to have supported biological research on human subjects.

The outcome – not just of research on humans but also of more systematic animal dissection – was some spectacular advances in anatomy and physiology. Herophilus is credited with a whole range of anatomical discoveries, and in many cases the name by which the part is still known derives from him, as our 'duodenum' from the Latin word used to translate Herophilus' δωδεκαδάκτυλος, a term that refers to the length of this part of the intestine in man (twelve finger's breadths) and incidentally tends to confirm his working with human subjects. More important still, Herophilus and Erasistratus jointly can be said to have discovered the nervous system, distinguishing clearly between the sensory and the motor nerves and between them and other tissues – sinews, tendons, ligaments – which had all been referred to, and indeed continued to be referred to, indiscriminately as νεῦρα in Greek. The way

[36] Tert. *de Anim.* 10.13.4ff.   [37] Celsus, *Med.* Proem 23.21.15ff.
[38] Fraser 1969, 518ff.: (J 83); 1972, 1.347ff.: (J 84); cf. Lloyd 1975, 172ff.: (J 98).

was thus opened for the detailed investigation – such as was eventually to be undertaken by Galen in the second century A.D. – into the transmission of movement and sensation, replacing vague notions of ducts or pores connecting different parts of the body with far more definite, in some cases even experimentally established, links between nerve centres in the brain or spinal marrow on the one hand and the muscles or sense organs on the other.

Erasistratus was also responsible for developing a number of important, if sometimes highly speculative, physiological theories which Galen was later at pains to discuss, and usually to try to refute, at great length. In his theory of digestion Erasistratus emphasized the role of mechanical processes, rejecting the Aristotelian notion that digestion is the result of the action of 'innate heat'. He knew that food is propelled along the alimentary canal by the peristalsis of the gullet and the contractions of the stomach wall and he suggested that in the stomach it is subjected to further mechanical breaking down before being squeezed out as chyle into the blood-vessels. He also argued that nourishment is then absorbed by the tissues by being drawn out through the walls of the blood-vessels, a process he explained by appealing to the principle of *horror vacui*, suggesting that a partial vacuum is created in the tissues by the evacuation of certain residues and that the tissues then draw into themselves some of the contents of the blood-vessels themselves.

Even more influential was his development of an idea that is already found in some Hippocratic texts, namely that the arterial system normally contains air, not blood. Whereas several earlier writers, including Aristotle, had a fairly clear general grasp of the anatomical distinctions between arteries and veins (though they mostly continued to use the same term, φλέψ, indiscriminately for both types of blood-vessel), Erasistratus drew a clear physiological distinction between the two kinds of vessel. But even though the arteries, in his view, normally contain air, he supposed that in disease some blood entered from the veins, and he was evidently well aware that in lesions – when, for example, an artery is severed – blood flows from it. Here too, however, he explained these processes as the result of the creation of a partial vacuum. Blood is thereby drawn into the arteries from the veins through sub-sensible passages, ἀναστομώσεις or συναναστομώσεις, which have in common with the modern notion of capillaries that they act as communicating links between the two systems, the arterial and the venous, although in Erasistratus' theory the flow is not from arteries to veins but in the opposite direction.

Although Erasistratus also appreciated both that the heart acts as a pump and that each of the four principal valves of the heart allows material to pass through it in one direction only, he was not focussing on the problems that later came to be resolved, by Harvey, with the notion of the circulation of the blood. Greek biologists normally assumed that whatever was pumped from the heart or came from the liver was *consumed* by the various parts of the body it reached, and for Erasistratus in particular the arterial and venous systems were, as already explained, thought of as quite distinct in the healthy subject. It is more relevant to note that the recurrent appeal to the physical principle of *horror vacui* may be one of the comparatively rare Hellenistic examples where an investigator working in the life sciences was drawing on the work of a natural philosopher. Erasistratus is associated with the school of Aristotle by some of our sources,[39] and although he is generally critical of Aristotle's own ideas, he may well have been influenced by the investigations of the vacuum which we have seen were carried out by Strato.

As our last example indicates, Erasistratus' interests included pathology as well as physiology, and so too did those of Herophilus. Both were first and foremost medical men. Herophilus, in particular, developed the theory of the diagnostic value of the pulse which he had taken over from his master Praxagoras, and produced an elaborate classification of different types of pulse according to such criteria as their 'magnitude', 'speed', 'intensity', 'rhythm' and 'evenness'. But while the medical interests of the great Hellenistic biologists may be seen as a link connecting them with their Hippocratic predecessors, the extent to which they were able to engage in anatomical and physiological research was exceptional and reflects the kind of special royal patronage and support that Celsus' report suggests.

Herophilus and Erasistratus, along with Hippocrates and many others, figure in later histories of medicine as 'Dogmatists', though this label should not be taken to imply that the individuals in question held any specific pathological doctrines in common, let alone that they were particularly doctrinaire in their medical theories. But one of Herophilus' pupils, Philinus of Cos, led a break-away not just from the teachings of Herophilus, but from any view that engaged in speculation concerning 'hidden causes', particularly those relating to the constitution of man or to the origins of diseases. Against the Dogmatists, the so-called Empiricists argued that such speculation is neither legitimate nor necessary. The doctor's task is to treat individual cases and for this purpose he must avoid theorizing and attend to, and be guided by, the manifest symptoms of the patient and these alone. Experience will teach the doctor what treatment is beneficial in particular cases. He could and should engage in the comparison of particular sets of presented

---

[39] See Galen, *Nat. fac.* II.4.165.7ff. Helmreich; *An in arteriis* 7.IV.729.4ff. Kühn; Diog. Laert. v.57.

symptoms, but not in inferences concerning the hidden. 'Even students of philosophy', as Celsus puts it in reporting the Empiricist view, 'would have become the greatest medical practitioners if reasoning could have made them so; but as it is, they have words in plenty, but no knowledge of healing at all.'[40]

Positively, this assertion of the incomprehensibility of the invisible went with a fruitful emphasis on medical experience and on its practical application to secure cures. But negatively it was also accompanied by the denial of the usefulness of dissection. The internal parts of man are not just normally, for contingent reasons, hidden: they are in principle not investigable. Post mortem dissection can reveal only what is true of the dead, and vivisection, involving the injury of the living, besides being cruel, is no guide to the natural state of the normal subject either.

Nor were the Empiricists alone among the Hellenistic medical sects to reject dissection. Quite when the men who called themselves Methodists first formed themselves into a separate sect is disputed, but it is clear that there was a distinct school in the first century A.D., and they traced at least some of their ideas back to Themison in the previous century. The Methodists joined the Empiricists in abstaining from the Dogmatists' investigation of hidden causes, but they also rejected the Empiricists' own assertion of the incomprehensibility of nature as itself dogmatic. Like the Pyrrhonian Sceptics, the Methodists advocated the suspension of judgement on such questions. Their medical practice was based on the notion that there are three general types of physiological/pathological condition, the 'lax', the 'tense' and the 'intermediate', though it is clear from Soranus, the chief exponent of Methodism in the second century A.D., that the interpretation of these three states was the subject of some variation and disagreement. In view of the theoretical objections that were raised, it is not surprising, perhaps, that the practice of human dissection lost ground after the time of Herophilus and Erasistratus, although it may be that a more important factor inhibiting those later anatomists, such as Rufus and Galen, who might have wished to continue the tradition, was the lack of the kind of powerful support that the first Ptolemies were able to provide.

Ancient medicine, even at its most speculative and dogmatic, acknowledged a practical end, the healing of the sick. In other areas of the life sciences the application of knowledge in practice was far more haphazard. In zoology the Hellenistic period saw little advance on Aristotle's masterpieces, though it should be emphasized that these represented a corporate effort involving his associates in the Lyceum. Aristotle's zoological treatises in turn provided the model for Theophrastus' botanical studies, the *Inquiry Concerning Plants* and the *Causes of*

[40] Celsus, *Med.* Proem 29.22.11ff.

Plants. As with Aristotle's zoology, one of the chief interests, in Theophrastus, is in the classification of plants. But it is noteworthy that his descriptions of particular species often include information about distribution, favourable habitat, diseases and usefulness to man.

One context in which what may loosely be called experimentation with the parts of plants was well established is pharmacology. Our chief literary sources, including the famous works of Dioscorides in the first century A.D., presuppose a long tradition of popular curiosity about how substances occurring naturally – not just in plants or animals, but also as minerals – might prove efficacious as remedies. On the other hand the evidence for systematic experimentation with plants in order to achieve, for example, increased crop-yields is very limited (see further below, pp. 367–9). So far as the more theoretical writers are concerned, they show a lively curiosity about such special problems as artificial fertilization – for instance of the date-palm – but do not, in general, address themselves to giving guidance on how to improve horticultural performance. The specialist writers on agriculture (including horticulture and stock-rearing), such as the Latin authors Cato, Varro and Columella, were, for their part, certainly concerned with performance, but they were essentially repositories of knowledge, and not, or not often, themselves the sources of new ideas that might be tried out in the field. In practice horticultural techniques, while generally conservative, were not immune to development, as we can see from Varro's references to the recent introduction of a new method of grafting, for instance.[41] But the advances that occurred were rather the result of trial and error at the level of practice, than the product of the application of theoretical knowledge. The theoretical knowledge that was sought was not generally of a kind that might readily be given a practical application, and here, as elsewhere, a certain lack of adjustment between theoretical interests and practical concerns can be discerned.

[41] Varro, *RR* 1.40.6.

HELLENISTIC SCIENCE: ITS APPLICATION IN PEACE AND WAR

9b WAR AND SIEGECRAFT

YVON GARLAN

In the Hellenistic period, as in earlier periods, war was a presence always felt in the Greek world, not only because it happened but also because of its widespread impact upon modes of organization and expression. But clearly, we cannot possibly consider every aspect of war in a short section and shall have to confine our study here to the subject of the armies as they exercised their specifically military functions. We shall furthermore assume that the decisive changes brought about in the reigns of Philip and Alexander in this sphere are already familiar to the reader.[42]

In size the Hellenistic armies equalled those which had taken part in the conquest of the Persian kingdom. This was true at least in the kingdoms that had emerged following the break-up of Alexander's empire, although the old Greek cities usually found it hard to assemble forces comparable with those of the classical period. The sovereigns of the new kingdoms in effect went into decisive battles with about 60,000 men. Some were even in a position to raise 100,000: Antiochus III, for example, in the expedition that set out for central Asia. To these forces must be added 'those who were part of the baggage' (*aposkeue*), that is to say the heterogeneous assortment of non-combatants (women, children, slaves, merchants and entertainers of every kind) who must have swelled the numbers by an average of perhaps half as many again as the armed forces. This kind of town on the move clearly posed delicate logistic problems from the point of view of contemporary levels of productivity and means of transport, and these problems largely determined the course of military operations. The armies were incapable of sustaining themselves without any naval escort for more than four or five days so in their choice of itinerary and winter quarters they had to give top priority to the possibilities of revictualling, either through gifts or purchases more or less forced from peoples in the vicinity, or through pillage of the enemy territory. Another factor in the movement of armies was the prospect of booty which offered the soldiers their best hope of enrichment.

[42] For further reading see Bibliography, J(b).

Rather than the circulation of goods, however, it was the movement of men which was stimulated in the Hellenistic world by the formation of these large armies. In Greece itself, to be sure, military recruitment continued to rest more or less on the tradition of the soldier-citizen. It was a tradition that had become somewhat debased in several cities: in Athens, for example, the *ephebeia* took on above all the character of a cultural institution reserved for an élite. But elsewhere it was still healthy or was periodically revived when danger threatened (for example in the Aetolian or Achaean Leagues, in Rhodes, or during the third century in Boeotia, from which dozens of military catalogues have come down to us). Similarly, in Macedonia, where the aristocracy provided an officer class, the vigorous native peasantry continued to guarantee the military renown of the Antigonids despite overtures from all sides. In the newer Eastern kingdoms, however, the integration of the cream of the native forces (the Persians and Iranians) into the Graeco-Macedonian élite hardly survived the death of Alexander who had, not without causing some scandal, inaugurated the practice right at the end of his reign. Nearly all his successors and the monarchs of the early years of the Hellenistic period jibbed at such a policy, allowing native troops to serve at the very most in the naval or police forces (in Egypt) or as auxiliaries (in the Seleucid kingdom). Such monarchs were consequently compelled to draw heavily upon immigrants of Graeco-Macedonian origin, or at least of Greek culture, in order to maintain their power.

This increase in demand that was already making itself felt in the reign of Alexander had the effect of encouraging even further the phenomenon of mercenary soldiers. Inscriptions and, above all, Egyptian papyri, make it possible for us to gain some idea of the principal migratory routes in the various periods. These appear to be determined by a number of factors: at their point of origin by demographic surplus and the degree of cohesion in the community concerned, and their direction by their immediate geographical surroundings, the reputation of the employers available or the existence of political sympathies that sometimes led to the conclusion of employment agreements, similar to treaties of alliance, between one state and another. The statistical tables drawn up by M. Launey[43] reveal that 'in all the armies the proportion of Greeks, which in the third century was still considerable – being principally represented by natives of continental Greece and Cretans – decreased abruptly around 200 and virtually disappeared . . . The Balkan element, which had hitherto been quite vigorous, follows a similar downward curve although this is less steep. Asia Minor was also providing a high proportion of troops but this too progressively decreased . . . The second and first centuries, in Egypt at least, witnessed

[43] Launey 1949–50, 1.103: (J 143).

a startling rise in the number of Semites.' As for the troops of Macedonian origin, once the first days of the conquest were over, the number of these serving in the East was far lower than it appears to be, since all the members of the élite corps were automatically described as Macedonian.

Some of these emigrants set out with the intention of returning as soon as possible to their own countries, but in the meantime their chief interest was to hire themselves, either in groups or individually, to employers who would at least guarantee them the best pay. Pay was broken down into a number of forms: a certain sum was paid in cash (*opsonion, misthos*); then there were rations of wheat and other commodities (*sitos, metrema*), a part or all of which might be converted into cash; special allowances for the upkeep of horses, clothing or equipment; and to this were added hand-outs of an exceptional nature and the right to revictual at cut prices in the military markets. This, together with the conditions of service, clearly made for a permanent source of conflict between the employers and the employed. It engendered a lack of discipline that sometimes degenerated into open revolts which the kings and cities involved brought to an end by concluding official agreements identical to those they made with foreign powers as, for example, the famous agreements with their respective mercenaries made by Eumenes I of Pergamum (*OGIS* 1.266) and by the Carian cities of Iasus and Theangela (Austin 33). In their daily life these uprooted men also cultivated an *esprit de corps* within associations founded upon their common native origins, membership of the same fighting unit, attendance at the same gymnasium or worship of the same god, and they liked to present the external appearance of political communities by voting honorific decrees, by dedicating statues and by celebrating sacrifices. The painted stelai of Sidon and of Demetrias in Thessaly[44] and a number of funerary epigrams suggest that some of these mercenaries were figures of considerably greater dignity than the swaggerers depicted in New Comedy and its Roman imitations, such as Plautus' Pyrgopolinices, the 'Sacker-of-fortresses', or Terence's 'Thraso-the-Brave'.

Although mercenaries were much sought after for garrison service in the cities and whenever they were needed for some decisive battle or to stir up some revolt, they nevertheless constituted a labour force too unstable and costly to be considered satisfactory. Their eastern employers therefore tried to get some of them, preferably those of Greek or Macedonian origin, to settle, so as to provide a solid and lasting basis for the recruitment of the regular forces that were needed to contain the pressure exerted by both indigenous inhabitants and other rival powers.

[44] Launey 1949–50, 1.79–81: (J 143); Plates vol., pl. 242.

To this end they were everywhere assigned parcels of land (*kleroi*) the use of which entailed military obligations, although the organization of such arrangements varied from one system to another as can be seen from the chapters of the present work that are devoted to the various Hellenistic kingdoms. We would simply make two points in this connexion: first, that these colonists were more important in the Ptolemaic kingdom than in that of the Seleucids, who were never able to avoid recruiting virtually half their forces from amongst their Asiatic allies, semi-dependents or subjects; and, secondly, that while they proved to be powerful agents of hellenization, they at the same time fulfilled their principal function increasingly badly as the years passed so that, for example, the Ptolemies were compelled to draw heavily upon the Egyptians as early as the battle of Raphia (217 B.C.) and, throughout the Hellenistic world from the second century onwards, peoples such as the Mysians, the Galatians and the Jews played an increasingly important military role. So grave was the deficiency that even the recruitment of élite troops was affected.

These élite troops initially consisted of the phalanx. In Alexander's time this was composed purely of Macedonians but those who were admitted into it thereafter were given the pseudo-ethnic title of 'Macedonian'. The essential difference between this type of phalanx and the hoplite phalanx was its use of a spear known as the 'sarissa', the length of which appears to have originally been 12 cubits (about 5·30 m). According to Polybius, it was held in both hands in an inclined position, with the base stuck into the ground (Plates vol., Pl. 101). The manipulation of this spear, which was considerably longer and heavier than the hoplite one, made it possible or necessary (according to whether one favours a socio-economic or a technical explanation) to reduce the rest of the equipment. The members of the phalanx retained a short sword for hand-to-hand fighting, a helmet and metal greaves, but all they had for a breastplate was a leather jacket and their shield was a small round one about 50 cm in diameter, often ornamented in bronze (*chalkaspides*) or in gold (*chrysaspides*). The men were arranged in battalions (comprising about 1,500 men in Alexander's time), usually sixteen rows deep, the first five of which held their spears pointing forwards beyond the first line while the remainder held them upright so that they formed a kind of anti-missile screen. To their right would be stationed the royal guard of the hypaspists, apparently with similar equipment. Some of these were sometimes called the *argyraspides* (silver shields) or constituted an élite *agema*. This entire heavy infantry, forming the pivot of the battle order, was theoretically vulnerable only to attacks from the flanks or the rear.

It was accordingly on the flanks that the most mobile and effective forces would be stationed: the peltasts, bowmen, slingers, javelin throwers and light cavalry (frequently of local origin) and, most important, immediately to the right of the hypaspists, the heavy cavalry of 'Companions' (*hetairoi*) which gloried in the title of 'royal' and which, fictitiously at least, was described as Macedonian. To these 'Companions', who were equipped with metal helmets and breastplates, spears (shorter than those of the men of the phalanx), and a kind of scimitar, there usually fell the task of advancing in triangular formations to breach the enemy lines. Positioned in front or on the flanks would also be a number of special corps, a legacy of Eastern practice or devised by the fertile imagination of military theorists. These might include chariots of the Achaemenid type, with cutting blades attached to the wheels; camels carrying bowmen, from Arabia; soldiers equipped with oblong-shaped shields of Galatian origin; armoured horses and riders (cataphracts) on the Parthian model, and all kinds of mounted bowmen and javelin throwers often known by pseudo-ethnic names (such as the 'Tarentines'); and, most important of all, the combat elephants which were procured at great expense from India or the heart of Africa (Plates vol., pl. 110). These were used in their hundreds against enemy cavalry at the end of the fourth century B.C. (especially in the Seleucid kingdom) and thereafter with greater moderation once means had been found to diminish their effectiveness. Finally, behind the battle lines, with a purely defensive role, a number of reserve troops were positioned (used systematically for the first time, apparently, by Eumenes of Cardia) and the mass of non-combatants were encamped, the latter being the prime objective of the enemy when they broke through. The role of commander-in-chief (usually the king in person) consisted in co-ordinating the tactical deployment of the men who, in a somewhat imprecise hierarchy, were placed under his orders. To the great regret of military theorists such as Philo of Byzantium and Polybius, however, it was not long before the commander felt himself obliged to prove his 'valour' by putting himself personally at the head of his élite troops to make the decisive charge – although he would thereby often lose control of the subsequent course of the battle.

Nevertheless, the Hellenistic monarchs could not have achieved with such speed the conquests they did, had they not acquired the means to gain possession of fortified towns with the minimum of delay. On the basis of the advances already made by Dionysius of Syracuse and Philip and Alexander of Macedonia, siegecraft made spectacular progress in the fourth century, deeply impressing contemporaries and continuing to be regarded as a model for many years to come. The credit for this must go directly to the engineers who, either as professionals or for circumstantial reasons, became specialists in the construction of siege engines. Among these, for example, were the Athenian Epimachus who in 305/4 was at the side of Demetrius (who on that occasion won the title of 'sacker-of-cities') during his siege of Rhodes, or, in the enemy camp, the Rhodian Diognetus and Callias of Aradus; the Alexandrian Ctesibius, working for Ptolemy II; Archimedes at the end of the third century, tearing himself away from his theoretical studies to devote himself to the defence of Syracuse against the Romans; Philo of Byzantium, the author of a *Mechanical Collection*, whose books relating to siegecraft have come down to us; Bito, who dedicated his *Constructions of Engines of War and Projection* to a King Attalus of Pergamum,[45] not to mention Hero of Alexandria whose dates are now thought to be in the latter half of the first century A.D.[46]

Artillery was now regarded as an essential element in siege weaponry: catapults for arrows, known as *oxybeleis*, the invention of which went back to Dionysius of Syracuse, and – from the time of Alexander's siege of Tyre in 332 – catapults for cannon balls, known as *lithoboloi* or *petroboloi*. The composite bow had been superseded by rigid arms slotted into skeins of sinews or hair under torsion. Thanks no doubt to this recent improvement in the system of propulsion, both these kinds of catapult had reached their maximum potential by the end of the fourth century B.C. They could project over a distance of slightly more than a stade (177 m) projectiles possibly as long as 4 cubits (185 cm) and weighing as much as 3 talents (78 kg). It was discovered that the performance of these machines was directly related to the diameter of the holes used to secure the propelling skein into the wooden framework and it was this that determined the dimensions of the various pieces of wood used in the composition of the catapult. It can thus be deduced that the overall measurements of a *petrobolos* of one talent (the most common kind) were 7·75 m in length, 5 m in width, and about 6·35 m in height. Around 225 B.C. Philo introduced a distinction between 'euthytones' and 'palintones',[47] possibly on the basis of the angle given to the propelling arms by the disposition of the skeins that initiated the movement. This author is also the first to mention onagers, that is *petroboloi* with a single propelling arm which only came into general use in the fourth century A.D. Finally, in the course of the Hellenistic period a number of engines that were more complex or conceived on radically different lines were brought into operation on an experimental basis – for example Dionysius of Alexandria's repeating catapult and Ctesibius' catapults operated by bronze springs and compressed air.

The action of troops hurling themselves in successive waves against the enemy positions could only be successful, however, if recourse was also had to many other methods of destruction and of approaching

---

[45] Cf. Marsden 1971, II.78: (J 148).
[46] Cf. *idem* 1969, 1, 209: (J 148).   [47] Cf. *idem* 1969, 1.20–3.

walls. These, for the most part, had been invented much earlier but had never hitherto been used so systematically or on such a scale. They included mines and tunnelling; incendiary projectiles; access ramps similar to those that Alexander erected between Tyre and the mainland; wooden towers sometimes as high as 120 cubits (53 m), furnished with shooting embrasures, swing-bridges and steerable wheels, the most powerful and complex of which were given the name 'helepolis' ('the taker of towns') (Plates vol., pl. 113); large shelters for groups of soldiers, either fixed ('porches') or mobile ('tortoises'), some of which incorporated a wheeled borer or a suspended battering-ram that might measure as much as 120 cubits. There were also other innovations that enjoyed a varying success, such as the elephants known as 'wall-destroyers' which were used for the last time, apparently, by Antigonus Gonatas around 270 B.C.

The besieged would, of course, be employing similar procedures and others too that were peculiar to their position. In order to forestall or lessen the impact of the assault they adopted resolutely aggressive tactics by carrying the fighting outside the defences with numerous sorties, or by continuing it behind the main wall, and from the flanks of secondary walls built in the shape of a funnel. They countered the enemy machines with 'anti-machines' of their own that testify to the remarkable richness of their imagination. A whole gamut of these techniques is known to us, ranging from Diognetus of Rhodes tipping filth on to the path taken by Epimachus' *helepolis* to a questionable story of Archimedes setting fire to the Roman fleet by means of burning mirrors; they include the hurling of barbed tridents and body-trapping nets, the use of various scythes and grappling-irons ('crows' or 'cranes') that made it possible to shatter the frameworks of siege machines, the tipping of sand, oil or flaming missiles, and deadening the impact of projectiles by means of mattresses, screens or – on one occasion – revolving spoked wheels. In such circumstances the usual conservatism in Greek technical thought gave way under the pressure of danger – although it should be noted that most of these 'machines' still amounted to little more than stratagems and in any case did not involve the use of other than natural forces.

It is not surprising that this culmination in the development of siegecraft appears to have preceded that of the art of fortification by some decades, this being generally accepted to be the time of Philo of Byzantium (c. 225 B.C.). True, the second half of the fourth century B.C. already saw the invention or diffusion of devices whose purpose was obviously to counter the new techniques of attack. Flank defences were improved by 'toothed' or 'indented' fortifications, towers of various shapes (semi-circular, horseshoe-shaped, pentagonal or hexagonal), some of them large enough to accommodate artillery (Plates vol., pl. 114). Towers and the walks connecting them were roofed in to protect the firing positions set up there. Constructions were reinforced, for example curtain walls divided into sections by bond-stones and towers built architecturally independent of the walls. Outlying defences were improved with forecourts, trenches, outer walls and ramps. More postern gates were introduced, sometimes with low protective walls in front. But the most systematic and sophisticated devices date from the third century B.C. Particularly typical are those introduced at Apollonia in Cyrenaica, at the northern end of the acropolis of Selinus round about 270 B.C., or those of Epipolae at Syracuse, which appear to have been given their definitive form on the eve of the capture of the town by the Romans.

It is certainly no coincidence that the first Hellenistic monarchs also engaged in naval construction on a gigantic scale. The largest warships were admittedly in a minority among the two or three hundred vessels at the disposal of Demetrius and the first two Ptolemies, which did not include the transport ships for troops, horses and provisions and light craft of many kinds. But on the largest warships the number of 'rows' of oarsmen, which had not exceeded four or five in Alexander's time, was progressively increased first, with Demetrius, to sixteen, then with Antigonus Gonatas to eighteen and, under Ptolemy II, first to twenty

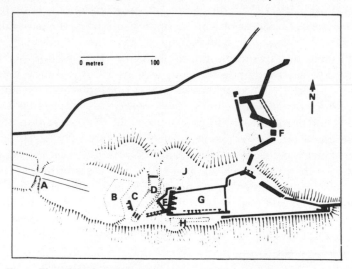

Fig. 7. Plan of the fort of Euryalus
Key   A Ditch   E Bastion

| Key | A | Ditch | | E | Epipolae gateway |

Fig. 7. Plan of the fort of Euryalus

Key   A Ditch   E Bastion
        B Ditch   F Epipolae gateway
        C Outwork   G Keep with five towers on
        D Ditch   western side
                                        H Ditch

(After A. Macadam, *Sicily* (Blue Guide, London 1981) 151.)

and then to thirty. The culmination was reached with forty rows, on a vessel built purely as a showpiece by Ptolemy IV, which could accommodate 4,000 oarsmen as well as 400 other sailors and nearly 3,000 soldiers. It is a startling increase and can only have been achieved by introducing superimposed layers of benches (three at the maximum) and increasing the number of oarsmen to each oar (eight at the maximum): with more than 24 rows this would imply a vessel with two hulls, like a catamaran. But, from the end of the third century B.C., this form of competition, which must have reduced naval warfare to a confrontation between floating fortresses, died away, and more modest designs came back into favour. Thus the Rhodian fleet, which ruled the seas in the second century B.C., was essentially composed of quadriremes and triremes or even lighter craft such as *trihemioliai* which were well suited for fighting pirates.

Greece itself, both through attachment to its glorious past and no doubt through lack of material means as well, introduced hardly any military innovations during this period. Certain specialized skills were maintained, however: the bow in Crete and wherever Greeks and barbarians were in contact with one another, the sling in Achaea and Rhodes, the javelin in the Balkans . . . and the art of generalship in Sparta. Infantry of the line remained in general composed of hoplites and peltasts, with their characteristic equipment tending to become confused since the former now sported only a light or half breastplate while the latter had in some cases exchanged their *pelte* for a Galatian *thyreos*. And it was only very late in the day that a number of cities, in the hope of finding victory once again, decided to yield to contemporary taste and adopt a panoply of the Macedonian type: the Boeotians in 250–245, Sparta in the reign of Cleomenes III and, to some extent, the Achaeans in the time of Philopoemen.

Apart from the archaic and decrepit nature of most of the citizen armies, it is the fossilization of the military art in the Hellenistic kingdoms that, from a strictly technical point of view, chiefly accounts for the difficulties they encountered when faced with Parthian horsemen in the East and the victorious Roman legions. It is a decline that should also, no doubt, be imputed to the dwindling of the treasures to be won in war, and to the increasingly inferior sources of recruitment, and also to the obsession with civil or dynastic wars that set the Greek states one against another. These factors account for the persistent mediocrity in military encampments which Polybius laments, for the reduction in initiatives taken both in siegecraft and in naval warfare and also for a diminishing manoeuvrability in pitched battles. The impressive – all too impressive – mathematical requirements assigned, with hindsight, to the Macedonian phalanx by the theoretician Asclepiodotus, who was a disciple of Posidonius, could not in practice counter the major criticism levelled at it by Polybius, who was a connoisseur of such matters: namely, that the phalanx disintegrated once contact was made with the enemy, especially on uneven ground (XVIII.28–32). The early users of the phalanx had sometimes sought to render it more manoeuvrable (Alexander the Great by replacing the central ranks by lightly-armed troops; and Pyrrhus, against the Romans, by arranging it in battalions that were interspersed with more mobile contingents). Nevertheless, its rigidity subsequently did nothing but increase, with the adoption of the longer sarissa spears (12 to 14 or even 16 cubits in length) and the battle formation of serried ranks (*synaspismos*). Meanwhile the cavalry, which had to varying degrees also become heavier, was proportionally less numerous than hitherto and was therefore incapable, as was the light infantry, of making any decisive impact (with the probable exception of that of the Bactrian kingdoms which were obliged to adapt to the modes of combat employed by the inhabitants of the steppes). The head-on assault of the phalanxes thus became crucial. Correspondingly, the art of generalship degenerated into stereotyped formulae. As for their encampments and their discipline, here too the Greeks were far inferior to the Romans. They were nevertheless reluctant to learn from their conquerors. There were only three partial exceptions to this: Philip V, from whom two sets of military regulations have survived, testifying to some effort at adaptation; Antiochus IV, who, at the review at Daphne in 165 B.C., produced 5,000 men 'equipped in the Roman style with coats of mail' (Polybius XXX.25.3); and Mithridates Eupator, who ended up by experimenting with the tactics of the maniple.

The Hellenistic states had their origins on the battle-field and that is where they met their doom. This outcome was not surprising and was altogether in line with the determining role played by violence in such societies.

HELLENISTIC SCIENCE: ITS APPLICATION IN PEACE AND WAR

9c AGRICULTURE

DOROTHY J. THOMPSON

Agriculture had always been, and was to remain, the basis of the ancient economy. The aim of this section is to consider the effect on agriculture of the very changed political, social and cultural conditions which followed Alexander's conquest of the East. In the new political world of Hellenistic kings and inter-connected Greek cities, in the context of royal patronage encouraging experimentation and the production of scientific and technical literature, how far were actual agricultural practices either developed or modified? What were the effects on agriculture of the changes in land-tenure brought by the arrival of new settlers? As so often, answers can only be partial, provisional and impressionistic. Egypt is the only country for which the surviving documents allow a more thorough investigation and here the pattern of irrigation-agriculture was always peculiar to the Nile valley, geographically and climatically divorced from the rest of the Mediterranean basin or the Hellenistic kingdoms of the East.

One of the most striking features of this period is the growth of scientific and practical manuals. When in 37 B.C., at the end of a productive literary life, the Roman writer Varro published his *de re rustica* he introduced his work (1.1.8 10) with a list of his predecessors and sources, more than fifty of them. His Latin predecessors, the two Sasernae and Cato, are mentioned later (1.2.22 and 28) and in an otherwise Greek context pride of place is here ascribed to the Carthaginian Mago, whose Punic handbook in twenty-eight books was translated into Greek and condensed into eight of the twenty books of Cassius Dionysius of Utica. Apart from this study, further usefully abridged to six books by Diophanes of Galatia, Varro lists forty-nine Greek experts (including the poets Hesiod and Menecrates of Ephesus), two of whom are kings, five described as philosophers, and of the others five are from Athens, three from the North Aegean coast, ten from Asia Minor and six from the larger Aegean islands; others are listed by name only. The Hellenistic legacy to Rome is inescapable and, whilst the listing of literary predecessors is conventional and unlikely to be either original or even to record Varro's direct sources, its very existence and the widespread origins of those included illustrate the extensive interest

in agriculture which characterized the period. The surviving literature
which may broadly be called agricultural falls into two main categories.
These are the scientific studies of Theophrastus, his investigations into
botany and his study of plants, in which practical knowledge and
observation are subordinated to a botanical classification, and the more
practical manuals in which agricultural processes are described and
advice given on a wide variety of country matters. Theophrastus was
well aware of matters of practical agriculture, of the importance of
manuring, for instance, or of the careful selection of seed corn,[48] but
Varro's view that such scientific studies were more suited to those
attending schools of philosophy than to those tilling the soil[49] was
probably widely shared by practising farmers. In the *Georgica* of the
Egyptian Bolus, on the other hand, practical advice on a wide range of
subjects (times for planting and harvest, arboriculture, market garden-
ing) was mixed with folklore.[50] Archibius' advice to Antiochus, king of
Syria, on how to prevent storm damage to crops by burying a toad in an
earthenware pot in the middle of the field[51] was one sort of advice
interspersed in these manuals. Such treatises together with those on
viticulture and apiculture[52] may be assumed, from the more strictly
practical nature of their contents, to have had a wide circulation, if not
influence.

The Hellenistic world was a world of kings and, just as earlier Persian
rulers had interested themselves in the agricultural development of their
kingdoms,[53] so their Hellenistic successors showed similar concerns.
Kings might sponsor scholarship or they might sponsor actual
agricultural experiment. Active in both areas, in neither were they alone.
Manuals might be written without royal patronage, others besides kings
might attempt improvement of crops and livestock. It is not known, for
instance, whether Bolus of Mendes wrote his *Georgica* around 200 B.C.
under sponsorship, though had this been the case he might not have
needed to take the pseudonym Democritus, a name assumed in a
(partially successful) attempt to identify himself with the earlier and
better known natural philosopher of Abdera. Innovation in agriculture
was also possible apart from royal sponsorship, as for example in the
planting of vines in Susis and Babylon introduced on a large scale by the
Greek settlers there.[54] Yet interest in agriculture, that is in the economic
basis of their new kingdoms, is a widely-documented feature of

---

[48] *Hist. Pl.* VIII.7.7.; 11.5; *Caus. Pl.* IV.3.4. Jardé 1925, 14: (J 162).

[49] RR 1.5.1–2.   [50] Wellman 1921, 42–58: (J 168).

[51] Pliny, *NH* XVIII.294.

[52] Rostovtzeff 1953, III.1618 n.144 and 1619 n. 148: (A 52), for bibliography. On *PSI* 624=
P. Lugd. Bat. xx.62 see Cadell 1969: (J 157).

[53] E.g. *SIG* 22.

[54] Strabo XV.3.11.C.731–2, modified by Rostovtzeff 1953, 1164–5: (A 52).

Hellenistic kings. Hiero II of Sicily and Attalus III Philometor of Pergamum head the list of Varro's experts and Attalus himself is mentioned elsewhere as the author of a work on plants and gardens; Diophanes sent his study to King Deiotarus of Galatia and Archibius addressed agricultural advice to Antiochus, king of Syria.[55] Theophrastus was approached by Ptolemy I Soter and his works were purchased by Ptolemy II Philadelphus for the Library at Alexandria.[56]

Besides their literary sponsorship Hellenistic kings played an active part in encouraging agricultural development and innovation. Alexander had shown interest both in the draining of Lake Copais in Boeotia and in the irrigation system of Babylon.[57] In Egypt large-scale reclamation projects in the Fayyûm, recorded both in the papyri and from archaeological excavation, as much as trebled land under cultivation in the area.[58] The Ptolemies' interest also in the techniques of improved cultivation is reflected in the appeal to the king of a Greek soldier settled in the Thebaid in the third century B.C. to support his demonstration of a water-raising machine which would counteract the effects of the recent drought: 'with its help the country-side will be saved . . . within fifty days of the time of sowing there will immediately follow a plentiful harvest throughout the whole Thebaid'.[59] The device mentioned here may be the sakia, the Persian wheel, which joined the long-established bucket-and-pole shadoof in making possible the cultivation of land irrigated perennially.[60] The Archimedes screw was also introduced in this period, bringing abundant harvests in the Delta.[61] Land reclamation and the techniques of improved agriculture were both the concern of Hellenistic kings.

Royal interest may also be charted in a variety of innovations, both in animal husbandry and in agriculture proper. As earlier Polycrates of Samos had attempted to improve livestock in his kingdom,[62] so Hellenistic kings experimented in stockbreeding. The notable strains of cows and sheep produced in Epirus by Pyrrhus in the fourth century were known by his name,[63] and in Egypt, under Ptolemy Philadelphus, Milesian and Arabian sheep were introduced to the Fayyûm on the 2,500 ha. gift-estate of his *dioiketes* Apollonius.[64] Philetaerus, perhaps typical of the Attalid kings, showed an interest in pasturage and

[55] Varro, *RR* 1.1.8; Pliny, *NH* xviii.22 (also Archelaus) and 294.

[56] Diog. Laert. v.37; Athen. 1.3b.

[57] Strabo ix.2.18.c.407 (cf. Diog. Laert. iv.23 (for Crates); xvi.1.9–11.c.740–1.

[58] Butzer 1976, 47: (j 156).   [59] *P. Edfou* 8.

[60] *P. Cornell* 5. On irrigation techniques: Crawford 1971, 107: (j 158).

[61] Diod. 1.34.2; see above, p. 336; Plates vol., pl. 260.

[62] Ath. xii.540c–d, hunting-dogs from Epirus, goats from Scyros, sheep from Miletus, pigs from Sicily.

[63] Arist. *HA* iii.21, 522b24–5; viii.7, 595b19 (early interpolations); Pliny, *NH* viii.176.

[64] *P. Cairo Zen.* 59195.3; cf. 59430.

stockbreeding in his kingdom[65] and the three hundred or more
Lycaonian flocks of Amyntas, the last ruler of Galatia, were well known
as a source of his wealth;[66] it is disappointing that Strabo has not
preserved more detail on the nature and size of these flocks. Some royal
experiments, such as the imported and exotic pheasants and guinea fowl
reared in the palace at Alexandria for the court of Ptolemy VIII
Euergetes II, might be of very limited importance,[67] but the new cultural
unity of the Hellenistic world combined with royal initiative to make
possible the spread of improved plants and animals within this world.

Most of the information on plants is again from Egypt where an
archive from Philadelphia in the Fayyûm, the papers of Zenon, manager
of the gift-estate of the *dioiketes* Apollonius, gives a detailed picture of
intensive agricultural activity in the mid third century B.C.[68] The
Fayyûm, or Arsinoite nome, was the centre of Ptolemaic reclamation
and experimentation. There were new owners to cultivate this land,
Greek soldiers settled as cleruchs in the countryside (in an attempt both
to reward them and to tie them to their new homes) and the recipients of
gift-estates such as Apollonius. This change in the pattern of Egyptian
land-tenure had important agricultural consequences, at least at the
outset. As in Babylonia, Greek settlers in Egypt brought new crop
strains or made changes to the balance of traditional agriculture. Land
brought under cultivation for the first time was planted with new crops
and orchards. A wide variety of crops is recorded, for example oil crops
on marginal lands at the edge of the irrigated area where salinity from
poor drainage remained a problem despite the extended canal system.
Such crops, however, whilst serving an agricultural purpose, might also
be planted for fiscal gain. In 259 B.C. Apollonius was himself responsible
for a lengthy decree on the organization of both the cultivation and
taxation of the major oil crops: sesame, castor-oil (*kroton* for *kiki*-oil),
kolokynthos (gourds), safflower and flax.[69] How effective this decree may
have been in monitoring oil production is open to dispute but it attests
both royal interest and interference in agriculture. The emphasis on oil
production is short-lived and the widespread cultivation of cash crops
seems to have been contrary to the traditional practices of Egyptian
agriculture.[70] Other innovations in the Fayyûm had a longer life. Vines
and olives (not covered by the Revenue Laws) were planted extensively
in the area, remaining through into the Roman period,[71] and the royal
garden of the palace at Memphis served as a nursery for the young trees
and seedlings to be transplanted in the neighbouring Fayyûm: figs,
walnuts, peaches, plums and possibly apricots.[72] Plants came to Egypt

[65] *OGIS* 748.
[66] Strabo XII.6.1.C.568.
[67] Ath. XIV.654c from Media.
[68] Rostovtzeff 1922: (J 164); Préaux 1947: (F 141).
[69] *P. Rev.* See above, pp. 148–9.
[70] Crawford 1973, 249–50: (J 159).
[71] Strabo XVII.1.35.C.809.
[72] Préaux 1947, 26–7: (F 141), for detailed references.

from all over the Hellenistic world: garlic from Tlos in Lycia,[73] chick-
peas from Byzantium,[74] the cystus from Carmania,[75] figs from Chios and
Syria,[76] wheat from Calymnos.[77] Diphilus of Siphnos describes an unsuccessful attempt to improve the quality of the Egyptian cabbage which was
somewhat bitter to Greek taste.[78] Seed was brought in from Rhodes to
Alexandria and for a year the quality of the vegetable improved; the
bitterness then returned, thereby illustrating the common belief that
within three years seeds would acquire the native characteristics of their
new home.[79]

The Zenon papyrus archive is full of enquiries, proposals and reports
on agricultural matters (Plates vol., pl. 119). The influx of Greeks to the
new city of Alexandria and as military settlers in the countryside meant
new demands and markets; Apollonius' estate was one of the areas
where attempts were made to satisfy them. It is reminiscent of the
attempts of Harpalus in Babylon to introduce a familiar flora to the
area.[80] But in considering the evidence from Apollonius' 10,000 aroura
(2,500 ha.) estate two points must be made. Firstly, there is the
exceptional and short-lived nature of the whole experiment. There is no
evidence that as a unified and organized agricultural concern the estate
survived the third century; the extreme experimentation and agricultural activity may not even have outlasted Zenon who, on losing his post
in 248–247 B.C., devoted himself to viticulture in the area.[81] Secondly,
even within the estate there is evidence for only a limited interest and
concern for the new commercial crops. Letters dealing with seed
purchases and enquiries about new crops are almost entirely confined to
those whose Greek names at this date probably still suggest an
immigrant origin. Apollonius, Zenon and their Greek and Carian
friends were only a small group within a more traditional peasant
population and in some matters they might lack the respect and co-
operation of the Egyptian peasants. Some Heliopolitan peasants for
instance, newly settled in the Fayyûm, complain to Apollonius in 257
B.C. that 'a large number of mistakes have been made in the 10,000
arouras since there is no one experienced in agriculture'.[82] The
organization of agriculture, the conditions of land-tenure and the
identity of the cultivators are all important factors in the impact of
agricultural innovation.

[73] PSI 433 = P. Cairo Zen. 59299 (250 B.C.); PSI 332 (257 B.C.).
[74] P. Cairo Zen. 59731 = P. Col. Zen. 69.14, 16, 21.
[75] Pliny, NH xii.76 (frutex).
[76] P. Cairo Zen. 59033.12; cf. 59839.6–8, Laconian and Libyan figs; PSI 499.6; 1313.10.
[77] Etym. Magn. 486.25 s.v. Κάλυμνος.   [78] Ath. ix.369ff.
[79] Theophr. Hist. Pl. viii.8.1; Caus. Pl. i.9.2.
[80] Theophr. Hist. Pl. iv.4.1; Pliny, NH xvi.144.
[81] P. Cairo Zen. 59832.4; PSI 439 (244 B.C.). The estate reverted to the crown before 243 B.C.,
Edgar in P. Mich. Zen. i. pp. 6–7.   [82] P. London vii 1954, 7–8.

It was not the new cash crops which the peasants chose to cultivate in their fields. A mid third-century B.C. papyrus from the north-west Fayyûm gives details for four villages of the annual crop order which was drawn up to check centrally the pattern of agriculture throughout the country.[83] Figures are given for the distribution of crops which have in fact been sown in contravention of the order together with official adjustments made to the original demands in the light of the present state of cultivation. The crops which had not been sown were the commercial oil crops, flax, safflower and poppy; in preference the peasants had planted subsistence crops, cereals (wheat, barley and *olyra*) and vetch for fodder. The evidence from land surveys of the end of the second century B.C. from the south Fayyûm village of Kerkeosiris shows a similar range of traditional subsistence crops. On the cultivated crown land between 121 and 110 B.C. wheat, barley and *olyra* accounted annually for between 57% and 65% of the area cultivated; lentils accounted for 13% to 20% and beans, garlic, black cummin, fenugreek, arakos, grass, pasturage and fodder crops made up the rest in varying quantities.[84] In spite of a fairly large settlement of military cleruchs in the area (accounting for 33% of the village land) this pattern of cultivation, with cereals and fodder crops predominating, was a traditional one and is more likely to be typical of the general agricultural picture of the country than is Apollonius' third-century gift-estate. Unless the peasants' preferences coincided with royal interests, agricultural experimentation was likely to be short-lived.

The one innovation in Egypt to which this combination of interests can be seen to apply is the acceptance of new wheat strains. Under Philadelphus attempts were made to increase cereal production by the introduction of a second crop of summer wheat, probably einkorn. During the third century Eratosthenes commented on summer and winter sowing in both India and Arabia[85] and in late December 256 B.C. a papyrus records instructions sent by Apollonius to Zenon to sow a three-month wheat on land irrigated artificially.[86] The wheat concerned may perhaps be identified with Syrian wheat, first recorded in Egypt in this period,[87] though this was only one of a wide variety of wheats grown on Apollonius' estate.[88] The practice of double-cropping is not recorded beyond the third century but the change of the main cereal grain in Ptolemaic Egypt from husked emmer wheat, *Triticum dicoccum*, the *olyra* recorded by Herodotus (II.77.3–5) as the staple crop of the country, to a

[83] *SB* 4369 a–b with Vidal-Naquet 1967, 25–36: (J 167).
[84] Crawford 1971, table XIII: (J 158).   [85] Strabo XV.1.20.C.693; XVI.4.2.C.768.
[86] *P. Cairo Zen.* 59155.   [87] Thompson 1930: (J 166).
[88] Persian wheat: *P. Ryl.* IV.571.4; native and dark summer wheat; *P. Cairo Zen.* 59731 = *P. Col. Zen.* 69.25–6.

naked tetraploid wheat, *Triticum durum*, was both popular and almost total. Within a hundred and fifty years *olyra*-cultivation had declined dramatically;[89] *Triticum durum* was, with barley, grown throughout the country and used for official rations, as the normal bread-flour and for export. Such a successful and far-reaching innovation as the replacement of the staple bread cereal could only take place in conditions in which royal interest (a fiscal concern for the country's main product for export) and the peasants' preferences combined.

Most of the agricultural change introduced in the Hellenistic world was internal to that world; the introduction of new species was often from countries in close political contact. Democritus Bolus of Mendes mentions the pistachio bush, recorded by Theophrastus in Bactria[90] and by Posidonius in Syria,[91] as grown in Egypt in his day,[92] and in the first century Paxamus was the first to describe in detail its cultivation in Greece.[93] But if the pistachio travelled from Syria to Egypt the Egyptian bean and lentil made the reverse journey.[94] Ptolemaic control of the area may have been the context in which these transfers took place. There is also, however, some evidence for the introduction of species from outside the Greek-speaking world. Alexander's expedition had opened up the spice trade from the East. Both the Ptolemies and the Seleucids attempted to acclimatize the frankincense tree to their countries and Seleucus I to grow cinnamon in Syria.[95] None of these experiments met with long-term success and their interest lies mainly in illustrating the far-reaching concerns of Hellenistic kings.

With Alexander's conquests a new world had been opened up to Greeks; Greek cities, settlers and kings might all provide a stimulus for change. New patterns of land-holding, whether military cleruchies or gift-estates, such as that of Apollonius at Philadelphia or Mnesimachus near Sardis, might affect the patterns of agriculture.[96] Some reclamation took place, there were improvements in irrigation techniques, as in the construction of wine- and olive-presses, and in Egypt, with the limited adoption of metal for plough-shares and some other tools,[97] some marginal improvement was made in agricultural implements. Writers such as Pliny record the introduction of new and exotic plants; the Zenon archive from third-century Egypt shows intensive agricultural

[89] Schnebel 1925, 94–9: (J 165). On the grains see Moritz 1958, xxii–xxv: (J 163).

[90] *Hist. Pl.*, IV.4.7. [91] Ath. XIV.649d.

[92] Wellmann 1921, 19: (J 168); Rostovtzeff 1953, III.1609 n. 98: (A 52), suggests an early Seleucid introduction to Syria.

[93] *Geop.* X.12.3.

[94] Heichelheim 1938, 130: (J 161).

[95] Pliny, *NH* XII.56–7; XVI.135.

[96] Buckler and Robinson 1932, no. 1: (B 56).

[97] *P. Cairo Zen.* 59782a; 59849; 59851; *PSI* 595, confined to Apollonius' estate and not found in excavation.

activity in one (rather exceptional) area of the country. But innovation is more notable, more likely to attract record than is no change, and for Egypt at least there is evidence showing a more traditional picture of agriculture in regular use. Although quantification is impossible, there was probably minimal change in the Hellenistic countryside. The constraints of climate and of the traditional attitudes of the peasants were strong. Without a change in these, significant and lasting changes in agriculture were unlikely to occur.

CHAPTER 9

HELLENISTIC SCIENCE: ITS APPLICATION IN PEACE AND WAR

9d BUILDING AND TOWNPLANNING

F. E. WINTER

In various forms the Hellenistic architectural tradition flourished over a very wide area, and many Hellenistic buildings and complexes survived relatively intact through later antiquity. Thus extant Hellenistic structures far outnumber those of earlier Greek periods; moreover, the body of known material is constantly growing as a result of new discoveries. Nevertheless, Hellenistic architectural chronology is often imprecise. In the Syro-Palestinian region few major monuments are firmly dated before the first century B.C.; and in Egypt, apart from a few important temple-complexes, and a series of Alexandrian tombs commencing not later than 300,[98] the record is fragmentary, and many dates uncertain. Students must therefore rely mainly on evidence from Greece, the Aegean and Western Anatolia, and on the Italo-Hellenistic style that flourished west of the Adriatic. The Western monuments are also important for their influence on Rome, and through Rome on the Italian Renaissance.

(a) Hellenistic townplanning

From the second quarter of the fourth century onward kings and local dynasts of the Eastern Mediterranean founded an unprecedented number of new cities with grid-plans of classical Hippodamian type.[99] Since urban traffic consisted mostly of pedestrians and pack-animals, ancient cities, regardless of terrain, required few main thoroughfares for wheeled traffic, and secondary lanes could be sloping ramps, or even stepped. Regular grids, however, facilitated both 'zoning' and division into blocks of uniform size and shape,[100] and thus occur in the vast majority of classical and Hellenistic foundations.[101]

---

[98] Plates vol., pl. 254.

[99] See Tcherikower 1927: (A 60); Martin 1974, 163–76: (J 231); Bean 1971, 135–52 (Cnidus), 101–14 (Halicarnassus): (J 179), both promoted by the Hecatomnid dynasts of Caria; Downey 1961, 70–1: (E 157); *Ancient Antioch* (Princeton, 1963) 28, on early Seleucid foundations in Syria. On Hippodamus, Arist. *Pol.* II. 1267b, Hsch. *Lexicon s.v.* Ἱπποδάμου νέμησις.

[100] Arist. *Pol.* II, 1267b 34–8; Martin 1974, 104–6: (J 231).

[101] See plans in Martin 1974: (J 231) and Ward-Perkins 1974: (J 256), Plates vol., pls. 47, 68.

Such plans were very convenient for the inhabitants, but had virtually no 'open spaces'. Moreover, the generally windowless façades flanking the long straight streets must have been quite monotonous. Slight changes in alignment of the grid provided little relief, being designed simply to avoid obstacles or help in circumventing excessively steep inclines.[102] Impressive architectural vistas did occur, but were generally confined to agoras and major sanctuaries; yet the backdrop of mountains, or sea, and sky lent interest to many townscapes (Plates vol., pls. 58, 64).

Radical departures from a uniformly oriented grid were rare. Ancient references to 'theatre-like' plans indicate, not a radial street-plan, but rather the relationship of a central agora, or agora and harbour (the 'orchestra' of the theatre), to the surrounding area (the auditorium). However, some changes in the grid may have occurred as the streets bent around the flanks of a harbour, e.g. at Halicarnassus.[103]

Even on sloping ground, as at Priene and Alinda, the Hellenistic agora was usually rectangular, with stoas on all four sides. Pergamon (Upper Agora) and Assus are notable exceptions; and the agora at Morgantina in Sicily was divided into two terraces connected by imposing stairways.[104]

There were apparently several regional schools of Hellenistic townplanning. For example, a series of known, or partly known, early Seleucid plans may indicate a theoretical model for complete settlements, with blocks of uniform size within an overall area of 220 to 250 ha.[105] In Pergamene cities the necessity of planning, or remodelling, settlements on irregular terrain encouraged effective integration of architecture and landscape. While the special character of Pergamum itself resulted largely from converting a military stronghold into a royal capital, the various elements were so skilfully fitted into the natural contours of the site, that the ensemble, even in ruins, remains extraordinarily impressive.[106]

(b) Hellenistic building materials and techniques

Perhaps the most significant development of the Italo-Hellenistic style of the Western Mediterranean was the replacement of fitted stone-

[102] E.g. at Selinus (Ward-Perkins 1974, fig. 31: (J 256)), Piraeus (Lenschau, *PW* XIX.1 (1938) 81–2, plan II), Olynthus (Martin 1974, 111, fig. 9: (J 231)), Cnidus (Martin 1974, pl. 31). At Miletus the slight change in orientation of the main N.–S. street south of South Agora was probably due to the location of the pre-existing Sacred Gate and Road.

[103] Vitr. *De Arch.* II.8.11 clearly uses the term 'theatre-like' of the *site*, rather than the street-grid, of Halicarnassus; and the Hippodamian grid of Rhodes (Kontis 1958: (J 221)) shows that Diod. XIX.45.3 must be interpreted in the same manner.   [104] Plates vol., pl. 97.

[105] Sauvaget 1934, esp. 108–9, fig. 11: (J 246), and 1941: (J 247) (Aleppo), 1949: (J 248) (Damascus); Downey 1961: (E 157) (Antioch and Laodicea); Balty 1969: (E 151) on Apamea.

[106] Cf. the similar effects at the Pergamene sites of Assus (Clarke *et al.* 1902–21: (J 194)) and Aegae (Bohn 1889: (J 185)). See Plates vol., pl. 58.

masonry[107] by various forms of mortarwork. Earlier Greek examples of stucco facings and of rubble masonry set in clay mortar, though more durable than mudbrick, and cheaper than ashlar, trapezoidal or polygonal masonry, were quite inferior to the genuine mortarwork developed in Italy, i.e. walls with a concrete core, consisting of a mixture of aggregate (*caementa* in Latin) with mortar, between facings of stone or baked brick set in mortar.

East of the Adriatic true mortared masonry was unknown before the later fourth century; perhaps Graeco-Macedonian architects were encouraged to experiment with this technique by encounters with actual examples during Alexander's Near Eastern campaigns.[108] Yet the use of mortarwork spread slowly among the Greeks, even in South Italy and Sicily, and was never really common in Hellenistic building.[109] Probably walls and columns constructed of soft stone and finished in stucco were equally convenient;[110] and Greek columnar façades in any event required massive stone beams above the columns.[111] Only when Greek post-and-lintel systems were replaced by Roman arches and vaults could mortarwork be used throughout entire buildings.

Alexander's eastern campaigns were probably also responsible for the introduction in Hellenistic architecture of true arch and vault construction, which appears after *c.* 325 in many contexts all over the Aegean.[112] West of the Adriatic the arch probably came into use even earlier. Here too it was doubtless imported; but on balance the evidence is against transmission from the Near East via the Aegean to Italy.[113]

Corbel arches and vaults had been familiar in Greece since Mycenaean times, but no pre-Hellenistic Greek examples rival the Lion Gate and the Treasury of Atreus at Mycenae. The great corbelled gateway at Assus, however, is quite as imposing as anything Mycenaean;[114] and Hellenistic combinations of voussoirs and corbelling are more sophisticated than any earlier Greek structures.[115] Yet Hellenistic architects apparently never considered seriously the merits of vaulted construction in

---

[107] See Plates vol., pls. 81, 114–16.

[108] Arrian (*Anab.* II.21.4) records that the walls confronting Alexander at Tyre in 332 were 'built of large stones laid in gypsum mortar'.

[109] Over a century after Alexander, Philo of Byzantium still recommends mortar only for facings, not for the fill (Philo 80.7–8, 81.6–8; cf. Winter 1971, 136: (J 259)).

[110] See Plates vol., pl. 67.

[111] See Plates vol., pls. 50, 54, 59, 86–7.

[112] See Boyd 1978: (J 188); Plates vol., pls. 71, 85, 115, 141.

[113] *Pace* Orlandos 1968, II.236: (J 237), and Napoli, 1966, 217–20: (J 234).

[114] See Plates vol., pl. 116; Winter 1971, 252, fig. 282: (J 259); Akurgal 1978, pl. 30a: (J 170); pre-Hellenistic according to A. W. Lawrence, in J. M. Cook, *The Troad* (Oxford 1973) 242–5. For a corbelled relieving arch, still standing in 1845 over the main gate of Assus, see Conybeare and Howson, *Life and Epistles of St Paul* II (London, 1881) 215 fig. and n. 1.

[115] E.g. the combination of corbel and keystone described by Philo of Byzantium (87.37–47); cf. Diels and Schramm 1919 (1920), 44 fig. 23: (J 27).

mortarwork,[116] or of arches framed by engaged columns (or pilasters) with horizontal entablature.[117]

While mudbrick construction occurs in all periods of Greek architecture, baked bricks are usually associated with Roman work. Yet here too there were some Hellenistic experiments, again perhaps inspired by firsthand experience of Near Eastern examples.[118]

In classical times free spans of slightly over 10–11 m, for example in the nave of the Parthenon, were doubtless near the maximum considered safe for wooden beams. Longer spans would have required triangular trusses, which were clearly still unknown *c.* 340, when Philo of Eleusis designed the new Piraeus arsenal (see fig. 8).[119] After *c.* 250 trusses must have been used in the porches of the Sardis temple and in the covered halls at Priene, Miletus, and perhaps Notium, for spans ranging from about 14 to (possibly) 20 m.[120] Yet Eastern Hellenistic builders never equalled the achievement of their Italo-Hellenistic counterparts, who, by the end of the first century B.C., routinely bridged spans up to 25 m.

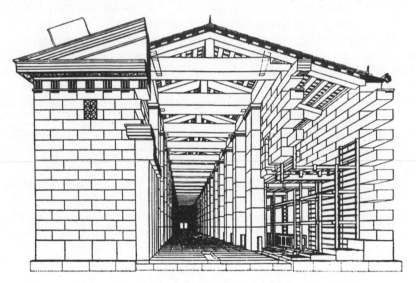

Fig. 8. Restoration of Philo's arsenal, Piraeus. (From Lawrence 1973, fig. 147: (J 224).)

[116] The cement vault of Upper Pirene on Acrocorinth, plausibly dated before 146, is quite unusual; see *Corinth* III.1 (1930) 31–44.

[117] Arched façades of *c.* 100 in Asia Minor should perhaps be attributed to the influence of the much more highly developed contemporary structures in Italy.

[118] Already observed by Herodotus (1.179) and Xenophon (*An.* II.4.12; III.4.7). On Greek examples Martin 1965, 1.63–4: (J 228); Orlandos 1966, 1.67–8: (J 237).

[119] On the Piraeus arsenal see below, p. 380 n. 150.

[120] See Plates vol., pl. 48 (Priene); Krischen 1941, pls. 1–20: (J 223), (Priene and Miletus); McDonald 1943, 217–19 and Pl. 6: (J 232), (Notium); Gruben 1961, 157, 166–7: (J 211) (Sardis). Coulton 1977, 157–8: (J 197), thinks that trusses may not have been fully appreciated even in Hellenistic times.

Hellenistic architectural writers constantly sought to provide a sound theoretical and technical basis for their practical activities, and to apply to inherited architectural forms new and coherent systems of exterior and interior proportions and ornament. Unfortunately most Hellenistic scientific and engineering treatises have perished, along with all their illustrative drawings. These works, however, were eagerly studied by Roman architects such as the Augustan writer Vitruvius, whose work *On Architecture* is easily our most important source for the history of Hellenistic architectural theory.[121] Yet few Hellenistic engineering specialists were also practising architects, or *vice versa*, whereas the Romans regarded mechanical and civil engineering as essential aspects of the architect's profession. Thus between the reigns of Nero and Hadrian Roman engineers produced a genuine architectural revolution, leaving little place for traditional Hellenistic forms except as decorative elements. If Vitruvius' book had not been written before the death of Nero, it might never have been written at all in its present form.

(c) *Hellenistic buildings*

Alongside conventional, though impressive, peripteral and dipteral temples, Hellenistic theorists also produced more original designs, with pseudo-dipteral, 'unfacial' prostyle or *in antis*, and circular plans.[122] While none of these plans was completely new, Hellenistic designers laid greater emphasis on the front, or entrance, of the temple, and blended temple, altar and court (increasingly often colonnaded) into a single coherent scheme.[123] Moreover, Hermogenes' pseudo-dipteral design at Magnesia, and the 'modified pseudo-dipteros' at Sardis, both represent unprecedentedly intricate arrangements of exterior and interior spaces.[124] Classical architecture had concentrated primarily on exterior (and later on interior) forms and their inter-relationships; the finest classical creations are 'really abstract sculpture'.[125] Hellenistic buildings were based on visual and spatial, rather than purely 'formal', relationships: roomy colonnades and porches; systematic ratios for base–diameter, taper, height and spacing of columns; emphatic widening of the central intercolumniation of the façades; contrasting plain and

---

[121] M. Vitruvius Pollio, *Ten Books on Architecture*, ed. F. Granger (Loeb edition), London and New York, 1934. About four-fifths of the architects, engineers and technical writers mentioned by Vitruvius, and about two-thirds of his Greek buildings, were probably later than *c.* 360.

[122] See Plates vol., pls. 38, 51, 74–5, 87.

[123] E.g. as at Magnesia: Humann 1904, pl. 2: (J 214); essential unity maintained over 150–200 years at Cos and Lindus, cf. Lawrence 1957 pl. 109A: (J 224), and Dyggve 1960, 43, pl. 2A: (J 203).

[124] Despite their size and fame, the great Ionic dipteroi at Ephesus and Didyma, and the Corinthian dipteros of Zeus at Athens, all followed an Archaic pattern, with none of the originality of Magnesia and Sardis.

[125] Lawrence 1957, 293: (J 224).

carved or painted surfaces. Even the façades of uncanonical temples, at sites outside the mainstream of Greek religious architecture, often followed normal principles of Hellenistic design (fig. 9).[126]

Fig. 9. Restoration of the Hieron, Samothrace. (From Lehmann 1969, III.3, fig. CX: (J225).)

Hellenistic stoas were often two-storeyed, and effectively defined the borders of large open areas, e.g. the Athena precinct at Pergamum, or the Athenian Agora (Stoa of Attalus II).[127] The Sacred Stoa at Priene provided a unifying colonnaded façade for the disparate forms of civic offices, public banquet rooms, assembly-hall and prytaneum; at Athens the Middle Stoa formed an imposing visual link between the Agora proper and the South Square. The East Stoa of the Milesian South Agora housed inward- and outward-facing shops placed back-to-back; at Alinda and Aegae the storerooms and shops, accessible only from the street outside, lay beneath the two-aisled colonnade on the downhill side of the agora.[128] Delian inscriptions even describe the Hypostyle Hall as a stoa;[129] and its relationship to more conventional

[126] E.g. the Hieron on Samothrace: Lehmann 1969, pls. 102, 108, 110: (J 225). Hellenistic theories of visual and spatial relationships surely underlie much of Vitruvius' Books III–IV.

[127] Pergamum: Akurgal 1978, pl. 33a: (J 170); Stoa of Attalus: Plates vol., pl. 86; Thompson and Wycherley (1972) 103–7 and pls. 54–7 (J 251). Cf. Assus, North Stoa: Lawrence 1957, 266 fig. 151: (J 224); Plates vol., pls. 47, 72, 182a.

[128] Bohn 1889, 28 figs. 27–8 (Alinda), 14–27 and figs. 15–16 (Aegae): (J 185).

[129] Vallois and Poulsen 1914, 27–39, 49–54: (J 254).

stoas is certainly clear. Yet the concentric rectangles of interior columns and the small central clerestory make this building at least a collateral ancestor of the Roman basilica;[130] like many basilicas, it was evidently a commercial exchange.[131]

The small upper order (usually Ionic) of two-storeyed stoas presented special problems of design. The spans, the same as those of the large lower order, required sturdy supports; yet short thick columns would have been most unattractive. Half-columns attached to rectangular piers more than doubled the strength of the supports, while keeping the columnar element very slender. Such 'composite' members perhaps originated in the late fourth century.[132] Pergamene architects used columnar elements on both sides of the piers; the parapet was mounted between the piers, the 'columns' continuing down to floor-level on both faces.[133]

In general Hellenistic columnar orders display a remarkable richness and flexibility. After *c.* 440 interior columns in Doric structures were increasingly often non-Doric;[134] in the fourth century these interior orders were frequently half-columns, as at Tegea and in the Philippeum at Olympia. Even the freestanding interior orders at Nemea (Ionic placed above Corinthian, probably copying Tegea[135]) were essentially decorative. After 300 superimposed engaged orders also appeared on façades, e.g. the Gate of Zeus and Hera at Thasos and the Great Tomb at Lefkadhia in Macedonia.[136] The Ptolemaeum on Samothrace even had an outer Ionic and an inner Corinthian façade sharing a common 'Ionic-Corinthian' entablature.[137] In the hypaethral court of the Ionic Didymaeum Corinthian half-columns framed the central doorway to the oracle-room, while piers with 'Corinthianizing' sofa-capitals decorated the remaining wall-surfaces; and three types of column were employed in the Stoa of Attalus at Athens and the Milesian council-house.[138]

This Milesian building, a gift of the Seleucid king Antiochus IV Epiphanes, exemplified the spirit of the new secular architecture: prominent dedicatory inscription, Corinthian propylon, plain Doric for the courtyard, richly ornamental engaged Doric on the exterior of the

[130] Antedating by 20 to 25 years the earliest basilica at Rome, the Porcia, built in 184 (Livy XXXIX.44.7; Plut. *Cat. Mai.* 19.3, *Cat. Min.* 5.1). Cf. Plates vol., pl. 130.

[131] On commercial transactions in basilicas see Vitr. v.1.4–5 and 8.

[132] Coulton's (1964, 100–31: (J 195)) date for the L-shaped Stoa at Perachora.

[133] Cf. Travlos 1971, 512–13, 519, figs. 644–5, 656: (J 253); Plates vol., pl. 86.

[134] The new Argive Heraeum, of the late fifth century, was the last important Doric temple to have Doric interior columns.

[135] On the relationship of the Nemea to the Tegea temple see Hill and Williams 1966: (J 212); on Ionic above Corinthian at Tegea Naomi Norman, *AJArch.* 84 (1980) 225.

[136] Martin 1968, fig. 1: (J 229); 1973, 56 fig. 53: (J 230); Plates vol., pl. 67.

[137] J. M. McCredie in U. Jantzen, 1976, 93–5 and fig. 3: (J 215).

[138] Didyma sofa-capitals: Knackfuss 1941, 1.2 pls. 112–32, 1.3 pls. 32–5: (J 219); Miletus council-house, *idem* 1908: (J 218), Krischen 1941: (J 223). Cf. Plates vol., pls. 86, 210.

council-chamber, freestanding Ionic columns inside (fig. 10). Such buildings served as models for many later bouleuteria and odea.[139] In smaller towns assembly-halls were often plainer, unless they faced a courtyard, the agora, or major streets.[140]

Fig. 10. Restoration of the Bouleuterion, Miletus. (From Knackfuss 1908, I.2, pl. xiv: (J 218).)

The Corinthian propylon of the Milesian council-house was probably typical of Seleucid decorative architecture; for Corinthian was much more popular in Syria and Egypt than in the Aegean world. The Athenian Olympieum and the contemporary temple of Zeus at Uzuncaburç (Olba) in Cilicia, both begun c. 170 by Antiochus IV, are the earliest major Corinthian temples; and the Corinthian capitals from Hermopolis Magna (Upper Egypt) and Aï Khanum (Afghanistan) are among the most impressive Hellenistic examples discovered through excavation.[141]

Corinthian leaf-capitals reached Tarentum soon after 400, and proved instantly popular in Italy.[142] After c. 300 Italic developments were strongly influenced by Seleucid and Ptolemaic models, doubtless often imported directly through the Campanian ports. By 150–100 Corinthian was firmly established in Latium, especially for circular

[139] Seleucid connexions of Miletus dedicatory inscription: Knackfuss 1908, 95–100: (J 218). Cf. Milesian building with later buildings, e.g. at Troy and Nysa-ad-Maeandrum, Akurgal 1978, 62, 234–5, and pl. 59b: (J 170). The date of the final remodelling of the 'New Bouleuterion' at Athens (Thompson and Wycherley 1972, 33: (J 251)) is quite uncertain; it may in fact have been based on the Seleucid model.

[140] Quite plain at Priene (Plates vol., pl. 48), more ornamental at Termessus and Alabanda (Akurgal 1978, 243, 327, and pls. 75a, 95a: (J 170)), and at Latmian Heraclea.

[141] Olympieum: Plates vol., pl. 87; Vitr. VII. Praef. 15, 17; Uzuncaburç temple: Williams 1974, 405–14: (J 258); Hermopolis Magna: A. J. B. Wace, Hermopolis Magna (Alexandria 1959), colour-plate; Aï Khanum: Bernard 1968, fig. 4 and pls. 13, 14: (J 181).

[142] For Corinthian at Tarentum see Ronczewski 1927 and 1934: (J 242–3), and Roux 1961, 376, 381–2: (J 244).

temples.[143] Later Roman 'normal Corinthian' was also indebted to Seleucid work, i.e. the capitals of the Athenian Olympieum sent to Rome by Sulla.[144]

Hellenistic artists and architects frequently borrowed earlier forms and ideas. For example, Pergamene leaf-capitals were evidently derived from archaic palm-capitals, while the Doric half-capitals of the Miletus bouleuterion copied those of the Erechtheum Caryatids (fig. 11). While Ionic ornament already appears in sixth-century Doric, Hellenistic mixing of the orders is much more conspicuous and thoroughgoing. The Italo-Hellenistic style produced the unorthodox 'Italian Temple' at Paestum, and probably also the 'Corinthian-Doric' Inner Propylaea at Eleusis;[145] Seleucid and Anatolian designers successfully combined Attic and 'Asiatic' Ionic bases and entablatures;[146] and 'mixed orders' appear in stoas and elsewhere (fig. 11).[147] Indeed Hellenistic architects

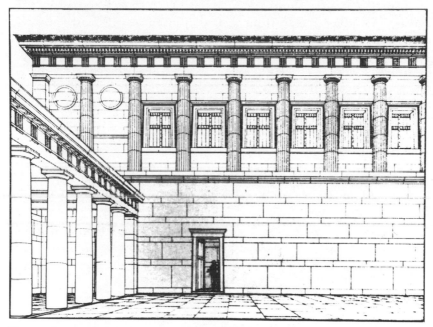

Fig. 11. Restoration of the interior of the Bouleuterion, Miletus. (From Krischen 1941, pl. 4: (J 223).)

[143] E.g. Temple B in the Largo Argentina at Rome (mid second century) and the round temple at Tivoli (early first century); cf. Boethius 1970, pls. 76 and 83: (J 184).   [144] Pliny, *HN* xxxvi.45.
[145] Paestum: Krauss and Herbig 1939: (J 222); Eleusis: Hörmann 1932, pl. 35: (J 213).
[146] Attic-Ionic bases on plinths: Corinthian half-columns at Didyma, Corinthian columns of the Belevi mausoleum; combination of frieze-band and dentils: Belevi and the new *naiskos* at Didyma. Seleucid involvement is possible in all these examples. Plates vol., pl. 243.
[147] Pergamum, Athena precinct: Lawrence 1957, 209 fig. 115: (J 224); Priene, North Stoa of agora: Martin 1973, 38 fig. 34: (J 230).

increasingly treated the orders as a single repertoire of architectural ornament, permitting many different combinations. By liberating essentially ornamental details from rigid rules based on the assumption that the forms in question were still structural, they avoided the frequent awkwardness of archaic and classical work.[148]

Sometimes even utilitarian storage-buildings achieved the visual effectiveness recommended by Aristotle for city-walls.[149] The Piraeus arsenal, planned by Aristotle's contemporary Philo of Eleusis, who also wrote a treatise on temple-design, was famous for its harmony and elegance (fig. 8).[150] Storehouses also illustrate the technical proficiency of Hellenistic architecture. Thus Philo of Byzantium describes granaries with floors suspended on transverse arches or on barrel-vaults;[151] and the Pergamene arsenals were plain wooden sheds erected over intricate stone basements that ensured good ventilation.[152]

Large-scale commemorative buildings of Greek style were originally created for non-Greek patrons, e.g. at Xanthus (early fourth century) and Limyra (perhaps c. 360) in Lycia,[153] and the gigantic tomb of the Carian dynast Mausolus at Halicarnassus, begun c. 360–355.[154] Purely Greek examples, e.g. the Philippeum at Olympia, the choragic monument of Lysicrates at Athens, and the Lion Tomb at Cnidus, all post-date 350. Commemorative monuments of the 'temple-tomb-on-podium' type are important descendants of the classical temple, often using the columnar orders in new contexts. Moreover, the superstructures of built tombs, like the earth-mounds of Macedonian tumulus-burials, were sometimes supported on vaulted chambers, e.g. in the Charmyleum on Cos.[155]

If the tholoi at Delphi and Epidaurus were also 'commemorative' buildings, their fame might explain the circular plan of the Philippeum and the tholos crowning the Monument of Lysicrates.[156] Curvilinear and rectilinear forms were again combined in the great lighthouse, the

[148] Cf. Coulton 1977, 139: (J 197).

[149] Arist. *Pol.* VII.1331a.

[150] Building described at length in *IG* II².1668; treatise by the architect, Vitr. VII. *Praef.* 12, cf. Cic. *De Or.* 1.14.62.

[151] Philo 87.9.31 and Diels and Schramm 1919 (1920), 42 fig. 22: (J 27).

[152] See Szalay and Boehringer 1937: (J 250).

[153] Nereid Monument: Demargne and Coupel (1969): (J 201); Limyra: Borchhardt 1970 and 1976: (J 186–7).

[154] On the Mausoleum see Jeppesen 1976: (J 217); Hornblower 1982, 223–74: (E 73). The monument was obviously commissioned by Mausolus some time before his own death, though work was still continuing after Artemisia's death in 351 (Pliny, *HN.* XXXVI.30–1).

[155] For Lefkadhia, Great Tomb: Martin 1973, 353 figs. 396–7: (J 230); Charmyleum: P. Schazmann, 'Das Charmyleion', *JDAI* 49 (1934) 110–27, S. M. Sherwin-White 1978, 365–6 with notes: (D 146).

[156] Tholoi: Berve and Gruben 1978, 96: (J 182) (Delphi), but see also Chr. Le Roy, *Études Delphiques* (Paris 1977) 247–71, esp. 250–1; Berve and Gruben 1978, and Roux 1961, 131–200: (J 244) (Epidaurus).

Pharos, at Alexandria,[157] and in many later Hellenistic and Roman memorials.

As architectural types, gymnasia and stadia were also Hellenistic creations. Again the columnar orders played important decorative roles, e.g. in the porticos of gymnasia or palaestrae, the entrance to the 'ephebeum' of the Lower Gymnasia at Priene, and the starting-gates of stadia.[158] Furthermore, Hellenistic engineers evidently designed, for palaestrae and related structures, the first hot baths with the sub-floor system of heating from which Roman hypocausts later developed.[159]

Until *c.* 350 Athenian dramas were probably performed on a low wooden platform slightly above orchestra-level, in front of a wooden stagehouse (*skene*).[160] The high Hellenistic stage seems to have developed *c.* 350–325 from Athenian experiments in staging later Middle Comedy. These experimental wooden *skenai* were two-storeyed; the stage was a flat-roofed, single-storeyed *proskenion* (= part in front of the *skene*), with the *episkenion* (upper storey of the *skene*) serving as backdrop.[161] The *proskenion* was provided with practicable doors, and was used as backdrop for performances at or near orchestra-level, in the older manner. Current views notwithstanding, the earliest *skene–proskenion* in stone was most probably built at Athens no later than *c.* 300; Athenian New Comedies were all produced on this stone *proskenion*-stage or its wooden predecessors. By *c.* 300–280 stone *proskenia* were being built elsewhere, doubtless under Athenian influence.[162]

Stone *proskenia* with colonnaded façades, and practicable doors of adequate width, required sturdy supports. Here again, Hellenistic designers substituted slender half-columns, attached to piers, for freestanding columns. These composite members were structurally sound as well as visually attractive, and door-frames and painted scene-

[157] Pharos: Dinsmoor 1950, pl. 68: (J 202).

[158] Courts of the gymnasia at Delphi and Epidaurus: Jannoray 1953: (J 216) and Dinsmoor 1950, 320–1 and fig. 116: (J 202); Priene gymnasium and stadium: M. Schede, *Die Ruinen von Priene* (Berlin 1934) fig. 99. Cf. Plates vol., pls. 54, 72, 182a.

[159] The discovery of simple hypocausts of middle and late Hellenistic date, in the Asclepieum baths of Arcadian Gortys (Ginouvès 1959: (J 209)), suggests that the Romans used Greek terms such as *thermae* and *hypocaustum* because the basic development work had been Greek. The 'Greek hypocaust bath' at Olympia should probably be regarded as an early example of Italic influence (Plates vol., pl. 183).

[160] In one form or another this view is espoused by almost all recent students of Greek drama; see Arnott 1971, 23–5: (J 173); Webster 1970, 7: (J 257); Baldry 1971, 44–5: (J 175).

[161] See Plates vol., pls. 193a–b.

[162] E.g. at Thasos (Salviat *et al.* 1968), 50–4 and figs. 18–19: (J 245)), and despite the objections of some scholars, also at Epidaurus, where von Gerkan's arguments for an early Hellenistic *proskenion* have yet to be shaken (Gerkan 1961, 45–83, esp, 77–80: (J 208)). The stone *proskenion* of the deme-theatre at Trachones, near Athens, whatever its exact date, presumably copied the first stone *proskenion* in the theatre of Dionysus at Athens; cf. Winter, 'The stage of New Comedy', *Phoenix* 37 (1983) 38–47. Cf. Plates vol., pls. 195a–b.

panels (*pinakes*) could easily be mounted between them.[163] The *episkenion* façade had few fixed elements in stone, usually consisting of three or more large openings (*thyromata*) between stone piers. These openings could accommodate painted scenery; alternatively, a set just inside the *thyroma* might represent an interior.

Greeks west of the Adriatic early developed a tradition of acting on a wooden stage of medium height, against a backdrop of wooden architecture. By *c.* 300 some stagehouses had two tiers of columns crowned by a pediment.[164] The Western stagehouse was combined with a high Aegean *proskenion* in the late Italo-Hellenistic theatre at Segesta in Sicily, but was taken over unchanged for the wooden theatres of Republican Rome.[165] These in turn inspired the permanent masonry *scenae frons*, first encountered at Rome in Pompey's theatre. Despite some experiments, both in theatres and in stadia, with seating-areas suspended on stone vaults,[166] there are no real Hellenistic antecedents for Pompey's auditorium, entirely supported on vaulted underpinnings.

Few examples of Hellenistic palace and villa architecture are known from the Eastern Mediterranean. Nevertheless, the impressive Macedonian complex at Palatitsa, above Vergina, is the first genuine palace extant in mainland Greece since the Mycenaean age (Plates vol., pl. 69); both this palace and the Hellenistic villa, or palace, overlooking the sea at Samos offer typically Hellenistic vistas of land- and seascape.[167] The stepped, multi-level design of the House of the Hermes on Delos is virtually unique before the Roman period; and the Delian 'Granite Building' and block of the House of the Comedians were apparently both responses to the need for extensive rental accommodation within a relatively small area. These two units are thus Aegean relatives of the Roman Republican *insula*.[168] Moreover, while Pergamum and Antioch evidently produced little or no real palace architecture, the Alexandrian literary evidence indicates that Italic and Roman palaces and villas borrowed heavily from Ptolemaic Egypt. The lavish symposium-tent of Ptolemy II, described by Callixeinus of Rhodes, was clearly a temporary version of the Ptolemaic *basilikai aulai* (royal halls) that were the chief ancestors of Roman civil and residential basilicas;[169] and Callixeinus'

---

[163] See the cuttings for mounting *pinakes* in the *proskenion*-piers at Priene, Wiegand and Schrader 1904, fig. 246: (B 212); also Coulton 1977, 137: (J 197).

[164] As in the Naples plaque: Bieber 1961, 130 fig. 480: (J 183). See Plates vol., pl. 208.

[165] Bieber 1961, 170 figs. 600–1: (J 183); Boethius 1970, 166–9: (J 184).

[166] Alinda: Boyd 1978, 96 and 111.4: (J 188); Letoon theatre near Xanthus: Martin 1973, 43 fig. 39: (J 230); stadia: Boyd 1978, 91 and n. 32, 100: (J 188).

[167] Palatitsa: Andronikos *et al.* 1961: (J 172); Samos: Tölle-Kastenbein 1974: (J 252).

[168] Comedians, Bruneau *et al.* 1970: (J 190); Hermes: Bruneau and Ducat 1966, 134–7: (J 189); Plates vol., pl. 137; 'Granite Building': Gallet de Santerre 1959, 73–107 and esp. 104–5: (B 196).

[169] Ath. *Deipn.* II.196b – 197c on the symposium-tent; cf. with Vitr. VI.3.9 (Egyptian *oikoi*) and VI.5.2 ('residential' basilicas).

account of the basilican dining-halls and other appointments of the river-barge of Ptolemy IV vividly reflects the splendour of polychrome masonry, luxurious wood-panelling, and gilded ivory decoration employed in Ptolemaic palace-architecture. Ptolemaic palaces in fact remained unrivalled until the time of Nero and the Flavians; yet both in Alexandria and at Vergina and Samos, Greek, or Graeco-Egyptian, columnar orders formed the basis of most of the designs.[170]

In sum, from the later fourth century onward Hellenistic architects made great strides in many areas. They created a third complete order out of late classical experiments with the Corinthian capital; reshaped all three orders into a rich and flexible idiom adaptable to many different contexts; devised new types of temples and of monumental tombs and other commemorative structures; gave clear architectural form to Greek stagehouses and gymnasia; worked out effective designs for warehouses and covered halls, including prototypes of the Roman basilica; exploited the potential of the stoa for monumental definition of the borders of agora and sanctuary complexes; developed the first hypocaust heating-systems; and produced both the first examples of Greek palace-architecture since the Bronze Age, and some of the prototypes of later Roman villas and *insulae*. Probably no other period, either of Greek or of Roman architecture, can advance as impressive a claim to originality as the centuries from *c.* 350 to 100.[171]

[170] River-barge: Ath. *Deipn.* II.205a–206c; gardens in the Alexandria palaces: Strabo XVII.794.
[171] Adriani 1963, 290–311, and esp. 290, 'General Characteristics': (J 169).

CHAPTER 10

AGATHOCLES*

K. MEISTER

I. AGATHOCLES' RISE AND SEIZURE OF POWER

At the time of Timoleon's death in 337 B.C. the situation in Sicily seemed quite stable: the tyrannies had been removed and replaced by democratic systems, the Carthaginians had been decisively defeated in the battle at the Crimisus, the Greek cities of the island had been drawn together into a *symmachia* under the hegemony of Syracuse and a generous settlement programme had been carried through that seemed to promise the island a new period of prosperity. In reality, however, Timoleon's work was not of long duration. Soon after his death bitter party struggles and social unrest broke out, particularly in Syracuse, where Timoleon had established a moderate form of democracy. This constitution proved to be very short-lived, for as early as about 330 power fell into the hands of an oligarchic coterie of 600 men from the noble and wealthy families under the leadership of Sosistratus and Heracleides. The constitutional battles reflected not only the long-standing antagonism between oligarchs and democrats but above all the contrast between old and new citizens. In addition, an important role in the factional struggle was played by the 'radicals', that is to say the many people without property who were hostile to the ruling oligarchy. The Sicels, in so far as they were politically and economically dependent on Syracuse, also constituted a source of unrest. These sharp political and social contrasts

* The question of sources for the history of Agathocles is fraught with problems. Only a few fragments by contemporary historians have survived, such as the apologetic work by Agathocles' brother Antander (*FGrH* 565), the panegyric portrayal by Agathocles' protégé Callias (*FGrH* 564), the vitriolic description by Timaeus, whom the tyrant banished (*FGrH* 566 T 8, F 34–5, 120–4) and the sensationally exaggerated narrative by Duris (*FGrH* 76 F 16–21, 56–9). The only piece of contemporary historiography to come to us seems to be a newly discovered Oxyrhynchus papyrus (*P. Oxy.* vol. XXIV, no. 2399), whose author is unknown. Among the surviving historical works, that of Diodorus is the most important; he describes the history of Agathocles in fair detail up to 302 B.C. (XIX.1–XXI.17), at which point the surviving part of his account breaks off. For his sources he drew mainly on Timaeus and to a lesser extent on Duris (cf. Meister 1967, 130–65: (G 8)). Thus Timaeus' distorted picture of Agathocles recurs frequently here (e.g. in XIX.5.4–8, 65, 70–2, 102–4, 106–10; XX.4, 9–14, 43–4, 54–5, 65, 70–2, 101; XXI.16), as does on occasion the sensationally over-inflated portrayal by Duris (e.g. XIX.2–3.2; XX.5–7, 16, 33–4, 63, 66–7). Several of Polybius' comments on Agathocles are important (VIII.12; IX.23.2; XII.15; XV.35.6). A large part of Justin's brief account (XXII.1–XXIII.2) is based ultimately on Timaeus; Polyaenus (V.3.1–8) is also relevant.

explain how it was that one man was able to assert himself in the struggle against the ruling oligarchy and to seize absolute power in the form of a typical military monarchy. That man was Agathocles. While in the East the Diadochi were creating vast territorial empires and taking the title of king, in the West Agathocles succeeded in establishing absolute rule and, by proclaiming himself king, demonstrated his equality with the Diadochi. This was happening at the same time as the Romans were expanding over central Italy in the course of their successful confrontation with the Samnites and were themselves becoming an important factor in the power struggle.

Agathocles was the dominant figure in the western Greek world for about thirty-five years and also the last Sicilian ruler to play an independent role in the power politics of the Mediterranean. He was born in 361/60 in Thermae, a Greek town in the Carthaginian *epikrateia* of Sicily, where his father Carcinus had settled and married a native woman after his banishment from Rhegium. Carcinus was a trained potter, a trade that Agathocles also practised initially. Hostile accounts like to dwell on his lowly origins and great poverty, but under an oligarchic régime working potters would not become officers (as Agathocles later did) and certainly not *strategoi* (as Agathocles' brother Antander became). Hence in reality he must have come from a family of wealthy entrepreneurs who appointed a slave overseer to run their pottery and directed their own energies to activities more befitting their status.

The history of Agathocles' childhood and youth on the one hand abounds in legends, which tend to grow up around the youth of many a future ruler,[1] and, on the other, is characterized by the slur cast upon him by Timaeus, who called Agathocles a common prostitute.[2] After the battle at the Crimisus – Agathocles was then 18 years old – his family moved to Syracuse and were among those who received Syracusan citizenship from Timoleon. Agathocles already distinguished himself as a file-leader under Timoleon in the battle against the Campanians of Aetna in 339 and later attained the rank of chiliarch in a campaign against Acragas through the patronage of the wealthy Syracusan Damas. After Damas' death Agathocles married his widow, thus becoming one of the richest men of Syracuse. As a result, he could subsequently bring considerable financial resources to bear in his attempt to win a leading position in the state. In about 330, when the Bruttians resumed their attacks on the Greek cities of southern Italy after the death of Alexander the Molossian, the oligarchic government of beleaguered Croton appealed to the Syracusan Six Hundred for assistance. In this campaign

[1] For example, in Diod. XIX.2.1–7 (based on Duris) we read of the exposure and miraculous rescue of the new-born child, a story derived from the Cypselus legend.   [2] *FGrH* 566 F 124 b.

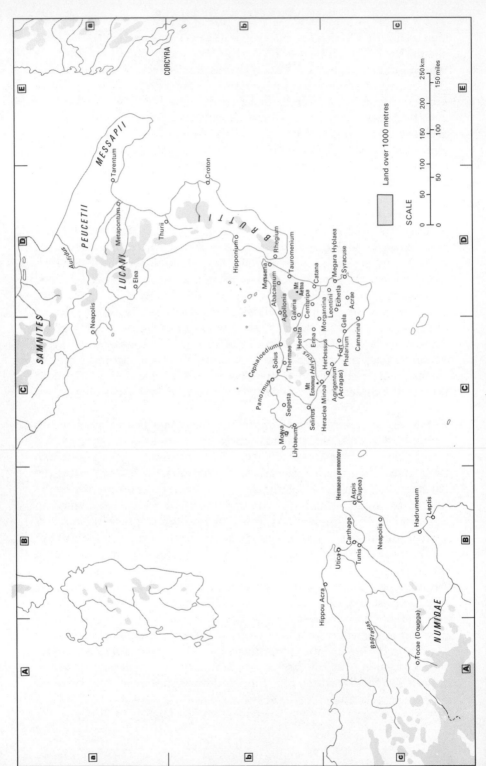

Map 6. South Italy, Sicily and North Africa.

Antander held the office of *strategos*, while Agathocles occupied the rank of chiliarch. Although he distinguished himself by great bravery in battle and played a decisive part in the defeat of the barbarians, he did not receive his due reward. Because of this rebuff Agathocles immediately took up cudgels against the Six Hundred and accused Sosistratus and Heracleides before the people on a charge of aiming at tyranny. He did not win the day and, indeed, after their return from Croton the oligarchs asserted their power to the full: Agathocles had to leave Syracuse, and his first attempt to bring down the régime had thus failed.

Agathocles then attempted to create a power base as a condottiere in southern Italy and continued his struggle against the ruling oligarchies. Around the year 325 B.C. he tried unsuccessfully to take the city of Croton; he subsequently entered the service of the Tarentines, but they soon dismissed this ambitious and presumptuous man. He met with unqualified success, however, in the battle for Rhegium, his father's home town; in about 322 the Syracusan oligarchs attacked the town with the object of introducing an oligarchic constitution in place of democracy. Agathocles came to the aid of Rhegium with a great many mercenaries and exiled democrats from other cities in southern Italy and brought the oligarchs' plans to nought. The failure of this enterprise had serious consequences for the Six Hundred: Heracleides, Sosistratus and many other leaders were banished from Syracuse and the Demos once again came to power. Agathocles was allowed to return to the city, but he did not gain a position of influence, for it is said that the adroit demagogue was already suspected of aiming to establish a dictatorship. The banished oligarchs won support from the Carthaginians, who had reappeared in eastern Sicily. This link between the Syracusan oligarchs and the Carthaginian arch-enemy was unprecedented in the history of the island. By intervening in the struggle between the factions at Syracuse the Carthaginians no doubt hoped to extend their influence in eastern Sicily. Nothing more is known of the course of these conflicts. We only learn that Agathocles served with particular distinction, sometimes as an officer and sometimes even as a simple soldier. In accordance with a law passed under Timoleon for resolving state crises, the Syracusans finally requested the mother-city Corinth to send a *strategos* to settle the factional strife. From the outset Acestorides – such was the general's name – was set upon reconciliation between moderate democrats and oligarchs: the banished oligarchs were permitted to return and they again won influence in the political life of the city; peace was also made with the Carthaginians. On the other hand, Agathocles, the bitter enemy of the oligarchs and staunch champion of the 'radicals',

had to leave Syracuse a second time. It is even alleged that Acestorides
wanted to have him secretly killed.

In these circumstances Agathocles could only hope to obtain a leading
position in Syracuse by exerting strong pressure from outside. Hence he
used his great wealth to raise a private army among the discontented
Sicels in the interior and stood up against Syracusans and Carthaginians
alike. He must have already had a large following in Syracuse itself, as
many of his supporters were banished or executed at the instigation of
Sosistratus and even prisoners from the quarries were drafted into the
Syracusan army. Meanwhile, Agathocles took Leontini and actually
attacked Syracuse. Admittedly he could achieve nothing here at first, as
the Carthaginian Hamilcar had brought up an army to protect the city.
However, with diplomatic skill Agathocles mastered this difficult
situation. He succeeded in establishing contact with Hamilcar and
persuaded him to withdraw. Hamilcar obviously aspired to a position of
power in Carthage just as Agathocles did in Syracuse and was thus keen
to have good relations with him. The withdrawal of the Carthaginians
left the oligarchs of Syracuse in a much weaker position and Agathocles,
for his part, could return to the city. On this occasion he had to swear to
the Syracusans 'to do nothing against the democratic order'. This oath
shows clearly that the authorities were already taking seriously the
possibility that he would establish a dictatorship, so that it is not without
irony that he of all people should be immediately appointed 'general and
protector of the peace until such time as real harmony might be
established among those who had come together in the city'. In view of
his political past, his implacable enmity towards the oligarchs and his
staunch commitment to the cause of the Demos, he was not the man to
bring about a compromise among the various factions. In fact,
Agathocles took the first opportunity to seize absolute power.

A great many 'rebels', which should probably be taken to mean
oligarchs who had fled Syracuse rather than rebellious Sicels, were
arming against Syracuse at Herbita in the interior of the island. In view
of this, Agathocles was appointed 'general plenipotentiary in command
of the fortified positions in Sicily' (319/18 B.C.), in other words the
position he had previously usurped in the Sicel areas was legalized. He
now had full official power to enlist a body of men totalling 3,000 in
Morgantina and other Sicel towns who were fully devoted to him from
the earlier battles and, furthermore, were hostile towards Syracusan
democracy. He also took many poor Syracusans into his units. Instead of
fighting the 'rebels' in the interior, however, he soon called his troops
out for the decisive blow against the oligarchs in Syracuse. According to
the dramatic account of Diodorus,[3] who has certainly drawn upon

---

[3] Diod. XIX.5.4–8.

Timaeus, Agathocles also invited the members of the Six Hundred to a discussion of 'matters of common interest' in the Timoleonteum, and indeed about forty of the Six Hundred attended, including the leaders of the time, Peisarchus and Diocles. As Peisistratus had earlier done in Athens, Agathocles claimed that his life had been threatened because of his sympathy for the people. This declaration had the desired effect; the enraged throng immediately seized the forty oligarchs present and demanded the punishment of all the guilty persons. Agathocles thereupon ordered the Six Hundred and their supporters to be killed and their property to be confiscated. There then followed a bloody settlement of accounts with the opposing faction; the two-day rampage of Agathocles' rabble and his supporters is described in detail by Diodorus. It is claimed that more than 4,000 oligarchs were murdered and that a further 6,000 managed to escape or were banished, most of them seeking refuge in Acragas. Agathocles then called a public assembly and justified his action on the grounds that he had purged the city of those elements that had been striving for a dictatorship. He was now giving back to the people its full liberty and wanted to withdraw to private life. This gesture of refusing power was certainly not meant seriously and its effect was just as certainly the calculated one: from the *ekklesia* came the unanimous demand for him to 'accept the general administration of the state'. Like Dionysius I before him, Agathocles proclaimed himself ready to do so on condition that he should have no colleagues as he did not wish to accept responsibility for their illegal actions. The assembly then granted him sole command and elected him 'general plenipotentiary' and 'governor (*epimeletes*) of the city'. With the granting of this mandate, which was subject to no time-limit, Agathocles received almost unrestricted power in the military and civil fields. At the age of about forty-five he had thus achieved his objective. For the year 316/15 the Parian Chronicle notes succinctly 'Agathocles became tyrant of the Syracusans'.

As far as assessing Agathocles' seizure of power is concerned, some modern historians have stressed the legality of his election. In reality, it is a question of only formal pseudo-legality. Let us remind ourselves again of the circumstances of his election. First came the elimination of most of his political opponents by murder or banishment. After that the oligarchs and their adherents in Syracuse had every reason to refrain from vociferous opposition. The assembly was thus composed predominantly of Agathocles' supporters and members of the lower classes. In addition, Agathocles' militia stood threateningly in the background. In these circumstances there can be no talk of a free and legal election. Like the coup d'état of Peisistratus or the seizure of power by Dionysius the Elder, the putsch of 316/15 has all the hallmarks of a typical tyranny.

Immediately, Agathocles introduced many measures to secure the favour of the people. For example, he promised the cancellation of debts and land redistribution and certainly translated these revolutionary proposals into deeds. In addition, he created employment by expanding the fleet, manufacturing weapons and erecting buildings in Syracuse and elsewhere, resumed the city's expansionist policy and pursued an astute financial policy. His personal life style was simple and even later as king he boasted of his humble origins. Furthermore, he behaved affably and knew how to please the simple man by means of jokes, mimicry, demagogic skill, a friendly approach and many promises. He restored discipline and order in the army and was a model of courage and bravery to his soldiers. He dispensed with the bodyguard and the diadem, in Syracuse the hated symbols of absolute authority; instead he wore a priest's head-band and paid great reverence to Demeter and Kore, the folk patron goddesses of Sicily. All this undoubtedly gave him initial popularity with the people. Nevertheless, it would be wrong to see him as the prototype of the 'tyran populaire' or to deny the tyrannical nature of his rule from a constitutional point of view. However, we shall come to that later.

11. DEVELOPMENTS IN SICILY BETWEEN 316/15 AND 310

Once he had secured his position in Syracuse Agathocles attempted to extend his rule over other parts of Sicily. From the very beginning this attempt met with the bitter opposition of the exiles from Syracuse and other cities. It has been emphasized quite rightly that driving these people from their homes ultimately only shifted the conflict from within to without – between 316/15 and 306 the exiles were the driving force in Sicilian history. They goaded the Greek city states to resist Agathocles, mobilized the Carthaginians to fight him and finally led the battle against him on their own initiative.

In his endeavour to extend Syracusan power Agathocles won 'most of the places and towns in the interior'; Messana and Acragas, on the other hand, became the centres of the refugee movement. In 315/14 Agathocles made two unsuccessful attacks on Messana. On the second occasion, in particular, he came to know the bitter opposition of the exiles. The Carthaginians also intervened and warned Agathocles to respect the existing treaties, by which was meant the agreements concluded under Timoleon guaranteeing the freedom of the Greek cities lying outside the Carthaginian *epikrateia*.[4] Moreover, the Carthaginian intervention came not from Hamilcar but from a delegation sent direct

---

[4] See Bengtson, *SVA* II, no. 344.

from Carthage. This is the first indication of a more energetic Sicilian policy on the part of Carthage since the seizure of power by Agathocles. In the meantime the exiles did not slacken in their activities. In their main refuge, Acragas, they drew the attention of the city's leading men to the danger from Agathocles: it would be better to wage a preventive war now, while he was still relatively weak, they said, than to put off the decision to fight until he had reached his full strength. The events around Messana lent conviction to their words. Hence in 314 the Demos of Acragas voted for war and at the same time made an alliance with Gela and Messana to present a united front to Agathocles. It was decided to bring in a general from outside, probably out of mistrust towards their own citizens, who not infrequently used the office of *strategos* as a springboard to tyranny. The crown prince of Sparta, Acrotatus, declared his readiness to take supreme command. As the ephors would not hear of the adventure in view of the political uncertainty, Acrotatus equipped a few ships at his own expense and Tarentum, Sparta's colony, contributed a further twenty ships to the expedition. Acrotatus took command upon his arrival in Acragas but he subsequently made no move against Agathocles. He certainly had good reason not to venture onto the battlefield with the army he found at his disposal. Furthermore, as he had already aroused hatred in Sparta because of his excessive severity, it is easy to imagine that he was even more detested by the Sicilians. In particular Sosistratus, the former leader of the Six Hundred, came out against Acrotatus, who therefore put his rival to death. The general indignation about the Spartan and his alleged excesses now burst into the open: he was relieved of his command and only escaped the wrath of the mob by fleeing secretly. As a result the Tarentines left the alliance and recalled their ships. Having lost their leader, the exiles saw themselves compelled to treat for peace with Agathocles, which was attained in the late summer of 314 on the basis of the *status quo* as a result of Hamilcar's mediation. The Greek city states east of the Halycus (the Platani) were granted autonomy, but they had to acknowledge Syracusan suzerainty. Carthage, for its part, obtained confirmation of its possession of the west Sicilian cities of Heraclea Minoa, Selinus and Thermae.[5] Messana obviously did not accept the peace and thus became the main rallying point of the refugees. This circumstance soon led to another attack on the city by Agathocles (312/11), and this time he was successful, as in the hope of a peaceful solution to the conflict the people of Messana went so far as to admit Agathocles and his army into the city and to expel the refugees. Agathocles nevertheless had his most bitter opponents from Messana and Tauromenium executed, 600 men

---

[5] See Schmitt, *SVA* III, no. 424.

altogether. It was probably on this occasion that the historian Timaeus was banished, and thenceforward persecuted the tyrant with fanatical hatred through his work.

The peace of 314 brought advantage to neither the refugees nor Carthage; it only benefited Agathocles, for recognition of Syracusan supremacy implied *de facto* recognition of Agathocles' rule. It is therefore understandable that in Carthage Hamilcar was held responsible for the setback and action was taken against him; he was accused of collaboration with Agathocles and even of aiming at tyranny. Secret proceedings were opened against him, but he died before the sentence was pronounced.

The action against Hamilcar also signalled a change in Carthage's policy towards Sicily. Recognizing that the military monarchy established by Agathocles might become no less a threat than the rule of Dionysius had once been, the Carthaginians decided to restore the balance of power on the island by conducting a vigorous campaign against Agathocles. The refugees' appeals for help were a major factor in bringing this change about. Under the leadership of Deinocrates, whom Agathocles had spared in the coup d'état because of their personal friendship, they called on the Carthaginians to intervene 'before Agathocles subdues all Sicily'. Agathocles, for his part, realized that the peace with Carthage could no longer be maintained and decided to steal a march on his adversary. He increased his army of mercenaries to 10,000 infantry and 3,500 cavalry, to which must be added the Syracusan citizen levy and allied contingents. While both sides were arming heavily the refugees were active as an independent military unit and tried to persuade several towns in the interior to break with Agathocles. However, an attack on Centuripa failed and although the refugees initially took Galaria they were unable to hold it against the enemy; the refugees had clearly overestimated their strength. They therefore ceased to engage in independent action and soon combined with the Carthaginian army. Meanwhile Agathocles began to besiege Acragas in flagrant breach of the treaty of 314 but had to break off, as sixty Carthaginian ships came to the aid of the city. He violated the treaty yet again by invading the Carthaginian *epikrateia* and brought many towns over to his side 'partly by force, partly by persuasion'. These occurrences stimulated the resistance of Carthage: while a fleet of fifty Carthaginian ships even sailed into the Great Harbour of Syracuse – though without indeed achieving anything – a Carthaginian army occupied a fortified position on the strategically important Mt Ecnomus on the west bank of the southern Himera. Agathocles tried to bring the Carthaginians to action, but they refused to join battle in the expectation of greater reinforcements. In the spring of 311 B.C. another Hamilcar, the son of Gisgo, put to sea from Carthage with a fleet of 130 ships and an army of about 14,000 men. He suffered heavy losses in the storm during the crossing, but was reputedly able to muster a total of about 40,000 infantry and 5,000 cavalry on the island by uniting the remnants of his army with the troops already stationed on Mt Ecnomus, enlisting mercenaries and welcoming the arrival of new allies. The majority of the refugees also joined his army at this stage; Hamilcar acknowledged their political claims by appointing Deinocrates leader of the cavalry. One event that occurred at this time illustrates the superiority of the Carthaginian fleet – twenty Syracusan ships and their crews fell into the hands of the enemy in the straits. In view of the concentration of Carthaginian troops on Mt Ecnomus, talk of revolt began to spread in nearby Gela, which had remained neutral thus far, but Agathocles managed to take the town by surprise. Once again he treated the inhabitants cruelly: citizens suspected of treason, said to be more than 4,000 men, were executed and a heavy contribution was imposed on the remaining townsfolk. Agathocles then marched against the Carthaginians and pitched camp at Fort Phalarium across the Himera directly opposite the enemy. Minor clashes soon developed into a battle. The Greek army's attempt to storm the Punic camp was only just driven off by the Balearic slingers. However, a further attempt to take the camp was thwarted by the timely arrival of reinforcements from Carthage, who fell upon the Greek rear from seaward and forced a retreat. The retreat soon developed into a headlong flight over a distance of 40 stadia, however, in which the Greeks suffered heavy casualties in the midday heat – it was the season of the Dog Star (July 311). A total of 7,000 Greeks fell on the battlefield, whereas losses on the Carthaginian side came to only 500 men. Agathocles assembled his remaining troops in Gela, which had excellent fortifications. Hamilcar first besieged Gela but soon recognized the futility of the exercise and turned his attention to conquests in the interior of the island. As he cast himself everywhere as the liberator from the tyrant's yoke, one town after another fell to him – first Camarina, Leontini, Catana and Tauromenium, then Messana, Abacaenum and many other towns. Faced with this situation, Agathocles hurried back to Syracuse, where there had still been time to bring in the harvest and prepare the defence of the city. Soon afterwards Syracuse was cut off to landward and to seaward by the Carthaginians.

III. THE AFRICAN CAMPAIGNS (310–307)

Agathocles was in a desperate situation mainly because no help could be expected from overseas. For the powers in the east of the Greek world were too occupied with their own problems to be able to concern themselves with events in the west. He thus resolved on a course of action that in audacity was on a par with the boldest ventures of the Diadochi, an offensive in Africa. Diodorus[6] rightly explains this strategic diversion as follows:

For he hoped that, if he did this, those in Carthage, who had been living luxuriously in long-continued peace and were therefore without experience in the dangers of battle, would easily be defeated by men who had been trained in the school of danger; that the Libyan allies of the Carthaginians, who had for a long time resented their exactions, would grasp an opportunity for revolt; most important of all, that by appearing unexpectedly, he would plunder a land which had not been ravaged and which, because of the prosperity of the Carthaginians, abounded in wealth of every kind; and in general, that he would divert the barbarians from his native city and from all Sicily and transfer the whole war to Libya (tr. R. M. Geer).

Agathocles quickly took various measures to raise an effective army, safeguard Syracuse during his absence and finance the forthcoming war. He enlisted a great number of mercenaries, called up many Syracusans from as many families as possible and even drafted slaves into his units. With customary treachery, he had numerous oligarchic opponents put to death and their property confiscated. In this way he purged the town of his enemies and at the same time obtained the bulk of the resources needed for the war. In addition, he appropriated offerings from the temples and women's jewellery, raised compulsory loans and had trustees pay trust moneys over to him. He sought to conceal the war preparations from the Carthaginians and even kept his own army in the dark about the objective of the expedition. He transferred the administration of Syracuse to his brother Antander and appointed the Aetolian Erymnon as his adviser. With sixty ships and about 13,500 men, predominantly mercenaries, he then waited for a favourable moment to sail. This finally came when the approach of a convoy of grain-ships distracted the Carthaginians' attention. The following day, 15 August 310, there occurred a total solar eclipse. Calculations of its course have shown that Agathocles did not take the normal southern route to Africa but sailed along the northern coast of Sicily in order to deceive the Carthaginians about his true plans.[7] After six days at sea the Greek army landed safely near the so-called Latomiae on the Hermaean promontory (Cape Bon) about 110 km from Carthage.

It was the first time that European armed forces had invaded North Africa. As Agathocles could not spare a detachment of troops to guard the ships and certainly did not wish them to fall into the hands of the enemy, he decided to burn the fleet and justified this to his army with a

[6] Diod. xx.3.3   [7] See Schoch, *Sirius* (1926) 248–50.

skilful psychological trick – he declared that during the crossing he had dedicated the ships to Demeter and Kore, the two patron goddesses of Sicily, for a successful voyage and was now obliged to honour his promise. The Greek army then marched through a very fertile region of plantations, plundering as it went, took the towns of Megalopolis (Soliman) and White Tunis (Tunis) and finally pitched camp in open country not far from Carthage. The arrival of the Greek army caused great terror in the city, as there was a firm conviction that Hamilcar had lost both army and fleet in Sicily. Only later did the truth emerge. As always in times of greatest tribulation, the population was called to arms, thus reportedly assembling 40,000 infantry-men and 2,500 horsemen, although admittedly in comparison with the Greeks they were completely untried. Hanno and Bomilcar, whose families were enemies, were elected generals. The rivalry between these men was seen as the best protection against a possible coup, but this was a delusion, as Bomilcar was probably already plotting treason. In the ensuing battle Hanno fell after a valiant fight, but Bomilcar ordered his wing to retreat prematurely, thus deliberately – according to Diodorus[8] – causing a disastrous defeat that he considered propitious to the realization of his monarchic ambitions. The Carthaginians suffered very heavy losses, abandoned their camp and withdrew behind the city walls. A curious situation had thus arisen in which Carthage had a Syracusan army before its gates while at the same time Syracuse was encircled on land and sea by Carthaginian troops. The dismay among the Carthaginians was so great that a rite was revived that had not been practised for decades: allegedly 500 children from the noblest families were offered as a holocaust to Moloch. In addition, precious offerings were made to placate Melkart, the principal god of the mother-city Tyre. At the same time messengers were sent to Sicily instructing Hamilcar to send a contingent of 5,000 men from the siege force outside Syracuse back to Carthage.

In the meantime, Agathocles had a free hand in Africa. He captured numerous towns in the environs of Carthage and others surrendered willingly out of hatred for the Carthaginians. Agathocles set up a fortified camp near Tunis, where his headquarters were situated for the entire African campaign, captured Neapolis (Nabeul) and other towns, besieged Hadrumetum (Sousse) and made an alliance with the Libyan king Elymas. It is thought that in the course of this campaign he took more than 200 places on the eastern coast of present-day Tunisia and then advanced into the interior. During his absence the Carthaginians made an attempt to relieve Tunis. The newly-discovered Oxyrhynchus papyrus is instructive in this regard; it states that the Carthaginians

<hr />

[8] Diod. xx.12.5ff.

placed the Greeks in dire straits, cut their lines of communication with Neapolis and the east and also subdued many of the inland Libyans who had defected.[9] Elymas was among those who went over to them again and they even succeeded in taking the Greek camp outside Tunis. Agathocles therefore hurried back to Tunis, set upon the troops scattered before their camp and drove them back; more than 2,000 Carthaginians are said to have been killed and the disloyal Elymas was executed. The Greek victory was all the more significant as the Punic reinforcements that had arrived from Sicily had taken part in the battle. Hence in the first year of the war Agathocles won a firm foothold in Africa, whereas the Carthaginians again had to withdraw behind the city walls.

These successes did not, however, lead to a final outcome; on the contrary, at the beginning of the following year (309 B.C.) Agathocles found himself in a predicament as a result of a mutiny in his army over arrears of pay that cast one of the main problems of the war into sharp relief. Agathocles would have jeopardized his credibility with Carthage's former Libyan subjects if he had imposed heavy levies on them. This would undoubtedly have led them to feel that they had only exchanged one master for another. On the other hand, consideration for the newly-won allies inevitably meant that payment of the soldiers' wages came to a standstill. So the problem remained, even though Agathocles managed to quell this mutiny with psychological skill – a theatrically staged suicide attempt led to a spontaneous change of mind on the part of the soldiery that Agathocles exploited to launch a surprise attack on the Carthaginians.

That year – 309 – the war shifted more to the interior, as the Carthaginians tried to reconquer the rebellious Numidians. Agathocles left his son Archagathus in Tunis and took the best part of his army in pursuit of the enemy. Initially, at least, the Carthaginians achieved their objective, as a large proportion of the Numidian Zuphones once again swore them allegiance. Battle was soon joined, probably in the valley of the Bagradas; Agathocles was victorious, in spite of being out-numbered, and drove the Punic forces back. The Greeks were deprived of a complete victory, however, as Numidians had meanwhile been plundering Agathocles' camp, which had been set up far from the battlefield.

A decisive turning-point in the African campaign seemed to be developing when Agathocles offered an alliance to Ophellas of Cyrene (spring of 309?). He was a former comrade and officer of Alexander the Great who had taken part in the Asian campaign and had governed

[9] *P. Oxy.* 2399, col. I.

Cyrenaica since 322, nominally under the suzerainty of Ptolemy I but *de facto* as an independent ruler. His country was thus immediately adjoining Punic territory. Agathocles offered Ophellas Carthage's African possessions, while claiming for himself dominion over all Sicily. If he – Agathocles – should later entertain higher ambitions, then it would be towards Italy that he would extend his rule, not towards Africa, whither he had now come by force of circumstance. Ophellas willingly accepted this proposal, which opened the prospect of founding a great African empire and thus accorded with his own plans. He had coins struck showing the medicinal plant silphium, the symbol of Cyrene, and the date palm, the emblem of Carthage. Ophellas used his great influence in Greece to persuade entire families to take part in the expedition. As Greece at that time was plagued by incessant wars and internal unrest, many colonists joined him in the hope of finding a new home in the fertile region of Africa. Ophellas finally left Cyrene in the summer of 308 with more than 10,000 infantry, 600 cavalry and 100 chariots; besides this there were about 10,000 non-combatants, including many women and children. The Cyrenaic border town of Automala (near the altars of the Philaeni) was reached in a few days; after a further two months' extremely arduous march through the desert of Tripolis most of the emigrants reached the Syracusan headquarters, where Agathocles gave them a friendly reception. For reasons that are not apparent, however perhaps over the question of the supreme command – the two leaders soon disagreed. Agathocles felt threatened and resolved to forestall Ophellas. While most of the troops from Cyrene were out searching for provisions their camp was captured and Ophellas himself was murdered. It cannot be accepted that Agathocles had been playing a treacherous game from the outset, as is sometimes claimed in ancient accounts and modern histories. Such a desperate step as an attack on an allied army within sight of the enemy is generally taken only out of dire necessity. The now leaderless army of Ophellas entered the service of Agathocles; the colonists who were no use as soldiers and the women and children were to be sent to Sicily, but most of them died during the crossing. The grand colonization plan of the Cyrenean ruler was thus a complete failure (October/November 308 B.C.).

The incorporation of Ophellas' soldiers into Agathocles' army almost doubled the latter's strength. The Carthaginians, on the other hand, were verging on civil war at about this time as a result of an attempt by Bomilcar to seize absolute power. The moment seemed propitious, as the Punic forces were on campaign against the Numidians. In any conflict between the Carthaginian government and a general it is difficult to say who first showed disloyalty towards the other. In the present case we do not know whether Bomilcar had cause for grievance or was spurred by sheer ambition. However that may be, the coup that should have given him a position similar to that which Agathocles had won in Syracuse failed owing to the armed opposition of the Carthaginians. While the 500 citizens and 1,000 mercenaries involved in the putsch were spared, Bomilcar himself was executed. That he entertained treasonable relations with Agathocles, as modern scholars sometimes assume on the authority of Justin,[10] is certainly not true. Indeed, our main source, Diodorus,[11] states that although the murder of Ophellas by Agathocles and Bomilcar's revolution occurred at the same time, there was no connexion between the two events. This attempt to usurp power was not without effect on the morale and discipline of the Punic army. That is the reason why Agathocles enjoyed significant successes at that very time and captured numerous ports in northern Tunisia – Utica, the most important town after Carthage, was taken after long resistance, as was Hippou Acra (Bizerta), which possessed the best natural harbour in the region. He had a naval port constructed there and had shipyards, arsenals and ships built. A naval base was also established at Aspis. By this means Agathocles wanted to establish a permanent line of communication with Sicily and cut the supply route to Carthage. In the long run he could have even considered a naval blockade of Carthage, for no attack by land had any prospect of success in view of the heavy fortification of the city and its position on a peninsula connected to the mainland only by a narrow isthmus, easy to defend. Several of the towns in the interior once again sided with him, so that he controlled almost all of Punic Libya. However, just at the moment when developments in Africa were becoming critical for the Carthaginians and the shortage of food in the capital was growing serious, events in Sicily took a turn that urgently required Agathocles' presence. He therefore transferred the African command to his son Archagathus and set sail for Sicily with about 2,000 men. His departure was to be the turning-point of the African war. At first, however, things continued to go in the Greeks' favour; an expedition led by Eumachus into southern Tunisia and the capture of Tocae (Dougga) and other towns not only led to the subjugation of Numidian tribes but also brought in rich booty. A second expedition by Eumachus further into the interior was only a partial success, however. Again several towns were taken, it is true, but when he learnt that the tribes in the area were advancing against him he had to retreat. The fact that the situation now swung round at a stroke to the detriment of the Greeks is to be ascribed partly to a change in Carthaginian tactics and partly to the incompetence of Archagathus. Spurred on by an extreme

[10] Justin XXII.2.5ff.   [11] Diod. XX.43.7.

shortage of food and emboldened by the absence of Agathocles, the
Carthaginians decided to launch a new offensive and sought primarily to
enforce obedience upon the peoples that had rebelled. This time,
however, the Carthaginians took care not to send the entire army – that
had only led to heavy defeats in the past – but decided instead to
despatch the forces in three divisions of 10,000 men, each with a specific
area of operation; one was to operate along the coast, another inland and
the third still further into the interior. Faced with this situation,
Archagathus committed two serious errors. First he let the rules
governing action be dictated to him and decided that he too would
divide the army into three columns – Eumachus, Aeschrion and
Archagathus himself were the commanders – in addition to which a
garrison had to be left in Tunis. In this way he scattered his forces,
thereby doing precisely what Agathocles had consciously avoided up to
then. Secondly, he either did not wait for Eumachus to return or did not
adequately co-ordinate his own actions with those of his general. As a
result, disaster quickly overtook the Greeks. In the interior Aeschrion
was lured by Hanno into an ambush in which he was killed, along with
more than 4,000 infantry and 200 cavalry; those of the survivors who
were not captured marched 500 stades to join Archagathus' army.
Further inland, the booty-laden army under Eumachus, while on its way
back to Archagathus, also fell into an ambush and was cut to pieces; only
thirty out of 8,000 foot-soldiers escaped, along with forty of the 800
horsemen. After these disasters Archagathus returned to Tunis and
assembled the remaining troops there. Many of his allies again went over
to the Carthaginians, who set up two fortified camps a short distance
from Tunis and shut the Greeks in the city. A desperate call for help was
then sent to Agathocles. With the support of an allied flotilla from
Etruria he succeeded in raising the Punic blockade of the Great Harbour
at Syracuse and soon afterwards, in the summer of 307, he was able to
return to Africa. Together with the reinforcements he brought with
him, his army still numbered about 13,500 men; on top of this there were
some 10,000 Libyans, although no reliance could be placed upon them.
Agathocles staked everything on an attempt to induce the Carthaginians
to leave their camp, which was in an excellently protected position on
high ground, and to fight in the open, but they refused to do battle,
seeking instead to wear the Greeks down and starve them out. In these
circumstances Agathocles decided to take the offensive against the
enemy fortifications; this action was not only a failure but it ended with
the complete retreat of the Greek army and a loss of about 3,000 men.
Agathocles' cause was now finally lost, particularly as all the Libyans
now went over to the Carthaginians. Agathocles recognized that the
Carthaginians would scarcely be ready to make peace after their present

successes or, if they were, would certainly demand that he be handed over. Moreover, he saw that there were far from enough ships to evacuate the army and that in any case Carthage once again had full mastery of the seas, and so decided to escape secretly. After one abortive attempt he managed to get away at the setting of the Pleïades (October/November 307). He was accompanied by only a small band of followers; even his two sons had to stay behind. The soldiers were thus left to their fate in an unscrupulous manner, for which they exacted vengeance at once by murdering his sons. They soon reached an agreement with the Carthaginians; in exchange for a payment of 300 talents they were obliged to evacuate the positions they occupied and were given the choice of either entering the service of Carthage at the same pay as under Agathocles or settling in Solus in Sicily.[12] The majority of the soldiers accepted these terms; the few garrisons that remained loyal to Agathocles were soon defeated.

The one and only Greek anabasis into Africa thus ended in a complete fiasco. It should not be forgotten, however, that in spite of the failure of the expedition Agathocles succeeded in maintaining his position in Sicily against the Carthaginians, and this was indeed the primary objective of the African venture. The African campaign was important not least from the point of view of world history, for Agathocles had shown the way in which Carthage could be defeated. It is certainly no accident that when asked who were the 'greatest statesmen combining courage and wisdom', Scipio the Elder, who towards the end of the Second Punic War carried the struggle over to Africa, and there won the decisive victory over Hannibal, replied: 'Agathocles and Dionysius'.[13]

IV. EVENTS IN SICILY (310–304)

When Agathocles set off for the African campaign Syracuse was besieged on land and water by the Carthaginians. Soon after his arrival in Africa and the burning of the fleet Hamilcar tried a ruse to persuade Syracuse to surrender. He had the news spread that Agathocles had lost the entire fleet and army in Africa. As proof he brought with him the plundered bronze fittings of the burned ships. As the newly-discovered Oxyrhynchus papyrus shows,[14] a lively debate developed in the Syracusan Assembly, in the course of which a certain Diognetus nicknamed Phalaeneus stood up and recommended surrendering the town to the Carthaginians. Antander had Diognetus arrested and taken away in order to prevent a possible commotion. This papyrus, which gives a lively and probably contemporary description, is important for

[12] See Schmitt, *SVA* III, no. 436.
[13] Polyb. xv.35.6.   [14] *P. Oxy.* 2399, cols. II–IV.

our judgement of Antander, among other things. Whereas according to Diodorus[15] Antander was conspicuous for his cowardice and was inclined to accede to the demand to capitulate, the papyrus shows clearly that this was not the case. As would soon emerge, the Syracusans did well to reject Hamilcar's demand, for a dispatch boat arrived soon afterwards with news of what had really happened in Africa. In order to make up for this diplomatic defeat Hamilcar decided to storm an unprotected part of the city wall, but without success. These two failures were soon joined by a third — after the crushing defeat of the Carthaginians in Africa Hamilcar was obliged to send 5,000 of his men to Carthage, so that he had to abandon the siege of Syracuse by land. However, Antander then conducted another purge of opposition elements; the accounts state with wild exaggeration that 8,000 men had to leave the city.

Hamilcar subsequently captured many towns in the interior of Sicily and strengthened his ranks mainly with the great numbers of refugees from Syracuse and other cities, who were under the leadership of Deinocrates. He wanted to raise a vast army and along with the refugees to resume the landward siege of Syracuse the following year (309). To this end he proposed to occupy the area around the Olympieum outside the city walls to the west of Syracuse, where on several earlier occasions the Carthaginians had established their operational base against the city. However, his intention was betrayed to the Syracusans, who promptly stationed about 3,000 infantry and 400 cavalry up at Euryalus on the plateau of Epipolae. The Punic general was cautious enough to begin the march through the Anapus valley under cover of darkness, but the fact that the cumbersome baggage train had been brought along on an exercise that demanded the greatest speed and discipline was to have fateful consequences, as the narrowness of the path soon caused congestion and turmoil. For the Syracusans, who knew the lay of the land, this was a favourable moment to attack. They swooped on the disorganized column from their high positions and quickly decided the battle in their favour. The Punic army finally fled in utter rout, while Hamilcar himself was captured and executed, and his head was sent to Agathocles in Africa. A long time was to pass before the Carthaginians recovered from this disaster, so that in the years that followed the struggle in Sicily was not primarily between Carthaginians and Greeks but between rival Greek armies; soon after the battle of Epipolae the refugees under Deinocrates separated from their Punic ally and continued the war on their own initiative. Acragas also gave up the alliance with Carthage and, under the leadership of Xenodicus, instigated a liberation movement whose real objective was to give

[15] Diod. xx.16.1.

Acragas hegemony over the island but whose propagandist slogan 'Autonomy for all Greek cities' was likely to mobilize all parties on the island who were hostile to both Agathocles *and* the Carthaginians. The Acragantines made a promising start by expelling Agathocles' garrison from Gela and a Carthaginian garrison from Herbessus. Enna, Echetla, Leontini, Camarina, Heraclea Minoa and other towns joined the new league, which soon encompassed the entire south of the island. The Syracusans could only watch impotently; their lands had been laid waste, the Great Harbour was blockaded by the Carthaginian fleet and the problems of supply were growing daily worse. An attempt to end the food shortage by means of a naval expedition misfired; twenty triremes that had put out to escort an expected supply convoy into the Great Harbour were attacked near Megara by thirty Carthaginian ships and half of them were captured.

The Acragantines' sweeping successes induced Agathocles to leave for Sicily in the summer of 308 B.C. His absence from Africa was to prove fatal; his presence in Sicily added little. Even before his arrival his precarious position on the island had improved considerably. Xenodicus had taken the field with an army of over 10,000 infantry and about 1,000 cavalry. Leptines and Demophilus, Agathocles' generals, had a total of 8,200 foot-soldiers and 1,200 horsemen to oppose them. Contrary to expectations, they won a decisive victory in which Xenodicus lost 1,500 men and had to retreat to Acragas. Agathocles landed in Selinus shortly afterwards and combined his own troops with the victorious army of his two generals. As initially no enemy dared meet him in a pitched battle, he achieved a series of successes and even conquered part of the Carthaginian *epikrateia*; he took Heraclea Minoa, concluded an alliance with Segesta and a treaty with Thermae and, reaching over into non-Carthaginian territory, captured Cephaloedium. An attempt to take Centuripa failed, but he managed to conquer Apollonia.

Now that the Acragantines had had to bury their dreams of hegemony on the island it was the turn of Deinocrates and the refugees. Deinocrates appointed himself 'Champion of the common liberty' and thus established a new programme for the refugees' campaign. Whereas hitherto they had striven mainly for their restoration, Deinocrates hoped that the slogan of common freedom would draw a great following among the Greeks. Indeed, his army did increase considerably in size, so that it finally numbered almost 20,000 infantry and 1,500 cavalry. In view of his great numerical inferiority Agathocles did not dare offer battle, but tamely fell back upon Syracuse. Hence his return to Sicily did not lead to the pacification of the island, while developments in Africa made his presence there urgently required, for news of the crushing defeats of the Greeks had just arrived. Agathocles immediately equipped seventeen warships and, with the aid of eighteen Tyrrhenian ships that had arrived at the auspicious moment, he lifted the Carthaginian sea blockade of Syracuse and thus assured the city's continued supply of food. At about the same time his general Leptines defeated the Acragantines under Xenodicus a second time; he thus finally re-established Agathocles' dominance in the south of the island, while the Acragantine liberation movement collapsed entirely. After allegedly putting another 500 opponents to death in Syracuse, Agathocles returned to Africa. As we have already seen, he was no longer able to restore his fortunes there and suffered a devastating defeat.

The African debacle had far-reaching effects in Sicily, where Agathocles tried to maintain his shaky position by extreme brutality. His action against Segesta and the measures taken by Antander in Syracuse are symptomatic in this regard. As his greatest lack was resources to recruit new mercenaries, Agathocles imposed a heavy contribution on the allied city of Segesta that fell primarily on the rich. Since the city was unwilling to meet his demands he ordered drastic sanctions. A large part of the male population was put to death and the women and children were sold into slavery. He even stripped the city of its name, re-naming it Dicaeopolis ('City of Justice'), and gave it as a dwelling to deserters. Meanwhile, in Syracuse Antander ordered the mass execution of those Syracusans who were related to the soldiers of the African campaign and the murderers of Agathocles' sons. This brutal behaviour, which struck down rich and poor alike, could by no means be justified on the grounds of political necessity. Since the complete miscarriage of the African campaign, the unscrupulous abandonment of his entire army and the above-mentioned events in Segesta and Syracuse Agathocles must have lost much of his popularity with the common man and his rule must have been felt to be more and more oppressive. It is therefore no coincidence that his own general Pasiphilus and the entire army under his command chose this moment to defect to the refugees. This created a critical situation for Agathocles, but he was able to overcome it with diplomatic skill. He made contact with Deinocrates, the leader of the refugees, and declared that he was prepared to restore the freedom of Syracuse and the other towns; his only condition was that the towns of Thermae and Cephaloedium should remain in his possession. This offer, which was tantamount to an almost complete abdication of power, could hardly have been meant seriously and Deinocrates had every reason to doubt the sincerity of the tyrant. He therefore rejected the offer and made much more onerous counter-proposals: Agathocles should leave Sicily entirely or at least deliver his children as hostages. This could, however, create the impression that Deinocrates was more concerned with the leading position he had won than with the restoration of Syracusan freedom. This was exactly what Agathocles hoped to achieve. He thus succeeded in discrediting his opponent and shaking the faith of many of Deinocrates' adherents. As a confrontation with his rival was now inevitable, Agathocles decided to make peace with Carthage by offering substantial concessions, thus securing freedom of action on that front. The settlement restored the *status quo ante*, that is to say the situation prevailing before the beginning of the war in 312/11 B.C.; Agathocles evacuated the towns of the Carthaginian *epikrateia* that he had occupied – primarily Heraclea Minoa, Selinus, Segesta and Thermae – and received in exchange 200,000 bushels of grain and gold to the value of 150 Greek silver talents.[16] In the same year (306 B.C.) the so-called Philinus treaty between Carthage and Rome was signed whereby the Romans were barred from all Sicily and the Carthaginians from all Italy. The historicity of this treaty was unjustly challenged by Polybius;[17] its content proves that Rome was now a significant factor in the power equation and was recognized as such by Carthage.

Having made peace with the Carthaginians, Agathocles could concentrate entirely on the conflict with Deinocrates. Once again, he was far inferior in numbers. We are told that his 5,000 infantry and some 500 cavalry were ranged against more than 25,000 foot-soldiers and 3,000 horsemen. The deciding battle was fought at Torgium, whose location is unknown. Its outcome was determined to a large extent by the fact that more than 2,000 men from Deinocrates' army rallied to Agathocles during the engagement. This led to panic in the refugee army, which prematurely assumed all was lost and took flight. The cavalry under Deinocrates retreated to a town called Ambicae, while part of the infantry – by one account 7,000, by another 4,000 – took positions on a hilltop. Agathocles agreed peace terms with these soldiers, assured them that they could return home and persuaded them to leave the hill; then, we are told, he had them put to death nevertheless. This information is undoubtedly a gross exaggeration. Agathocles probably had only his most stubborn opponents killed but allowed the remaining refugees to return to their home towns. Most of them doubtless accepted this offer after the years of war and exile. They clearly recognized the futility of further opposition and seem to have reached an arrangement with Agathocles somehow or other. At any rate, in the years that follow we hear of neither any active opposition to Agathocles nor the tyrant's customary reprisals against the oligarchs and their adherents. Instead, the sources[18] state that once he had finally con-

---

[16] See Schmitt, *SVA* III, no. 437.
[17] Polyb. III.26; the treaty had been recorded by the historian Philinus (*FGrH* 174F 1). Cf. K. Meister, 'Der sogenannte Philinosvertrag', *Riv. Fil.* 98 (1970) 408–23.   [18] Polyb. IX.23.2.

solidated his rule Agathocles displayed leniency, a fact that doubtless relates primarily to his behaviour towards the oligarchs. Furthermore, Deinocrates was spared a second time and even received a position of command. In exchange, he handed over the fortified positions that were still in his possession and even had his colleague Pasiphilus murdered in Gela. Shortly afterwards Agathocles attacked the island of Lipara without warning and exacted a heavy contribution (304 B.C.).

After the peace with Carthage and the defeat of the refugees Agathocles was master of the entire eastern half of Sicily and held roughly the same area of territory as Dionysius I had ruled. Only Acragas seemed to have maintained its autonomy. At this time (304 B.C.) he followed the example of the Diadochi in taking the title of king, the first Sicilian ruler to do so, 'since he thought that neither in power nor in territory nor in deeds was he inferior to them (i.e. the Diadochi)'.[19] Like the Diadochi, Agathocles bore the title of king without the addition of any country's or people's name, meaning that like them he recognized no power or law above himself in the area he had conquered or would yet conquer. By taking the royal title Agathocles was ostentatiously displaying his equality with the Diadochi; for the same reasons, he was at pains to establish good relations with a number of them. This will be discussed later.

V. AGATHOCLES' REIGN AS KING (304–289/8). HIS POLICIES TOWARDS ITALY AND THE EAST. HIS PLAN FOR A NEW CARTHAGINIAN WAR

At the beginning of his political career Agathocles had been active in southern Italy, where he had supported the struggle of the democrats against the oligarchs. After an interlude of several years occupied by the fighting in Sicily and the war with Carthage he now once more turned his attention to Italy, where the rise of the Romans was no less disquieting than the threat to the Italiote Greeks from the Bruttians and Lucanians. While Agathocles was waging war against the Carthaginians, the Romans were driving the Samnites back. The Italiote Greeks could have played an important role in this twenty years' war if they had combined their forces and fought under an energetic leader such as Alexander the Molossian. After the death of the latter in 334 B.C., however, their history is essentially passive; they figure as the prey of

[19] Diod. xx.54.1. According to Aalders 1955, 321ff.: (G 19), this occurred in Africa as early as 309, according to Consolo Langher 1964, 311: (G 14), in 307/6. Diodorus places the taking of the royal title in 308/7, but at the same time declares that Agathocles was thus following the example of the Diadochi. As it can be proved that they took the title of king in 306 and 305, in the case of Agathocles we thus arrive at a date of 304, which is also the most probable for historical reasons. In this connexion, see especially O. Müller 1973, 122ff.: (C 51).

Italic tribes and 'protectors' from mainland Greece. At about the same time as Agathocles was making peace with the Carthaginians and the Carthaginians were concluding the so-called Philinus treaty with Rome the Romans were bringing the Samnite War to a successful conclusion. In the course of this confrontation they had extended their power as far as northern Iapygia and had already crossed the Aufidus (Ofanto). This expansion led to war with Tarentum, a conflict in which the Lucanians engaged as allies of Rome. The Tarentines alone were no match for this coalition, so that in 303/2 they appealed to their mother city, Sparta. The Spartans sent Cleonymus, the brother of Acrotatus, who soon engaged in ambitious undertakings outside Italy – for example, he captured the island of Corcyra – but achieved very little in Italy itself,[20] while the Italians renewed their attack on Tarentum, which then called on Agathocles for help. Thus began the second phase of his Italian policy, and the question arises as to his objectives there. Ancient sources give a wholly unsatisfactory reply, in that Diodorus' account breaks off at the year 302 B.C. and consists of only fragmentary notes for the period that followed. It would certainly be false to conclude on the basis of the scanty sources available that only 'occasional forays' were made and that 'Agathocles did not attempt any extensive conquests'.[21] In fact, a carefully considered plan lay behind the Syracusan ruler's Italian policy – he clearly aimed to consolidate the entire forces of the western Greek world under his hegemony for the planned new confrontation with Carthage.

Agathocles went to Italy in about 300 B.C. in response to the Tarentines' appeal. He overcame the Bruttians in a battle and forced them to ally with him. He then became involved in the strife and struggles of mainland Greece for a brief moment. After Cleonymus had been driven from Corcyra, probably by the islanders themselves, Cassander saw his chance to take the island, as Demetrius Poliorcetes was fully occupied in the East after his defeat at Ipsus. Cassander had already surrounded the island by land and by water when Agathocles intervened in the struggle at the request of the Corcyraeans. He did not want to let a mighty foreign power gain a foothold on this important island at the entrance to the Adriatic Sea and thus use it as a stepping stone to the West. For his own part, Agathocles sought to imitate Dionysius by extending his influence in the Adriatic and controlling the sea route to Greece. He won a victory over the Macedonian blockade fleet and forced Cassander to evacuate the island, which now passed into his possession. He held it for only a few years and then gave it to his daughter Lanassa as her dowry upon her marriage to King Pyrrhus in

---

[20] On Cleonymus see *CAH* vii.2².   [21] Cf. Cary in *CAH* vii¹, 634.

295 B.C. Agathocles thus avoided overstretching his forces and yet had the assurance that a friendly power represented his interests there. Pyrrhus, who had regained control of Epirus shortly before with the help of Agathocles' father-in-law Ptolemy I, could also provide valuable support for Agathocles' Italian policy.

During his absence from Italy a mutiny had broken out among some of his mercenaries, chiefly Ligurians and Etruscans, over arrears of pay. Agathocles crushed the revolt and allegedly had about 2,000 men put to death. On these grounds the Bruttians again broke with him and defeated him heavily in a night ambush; 4,000 of his troops are said to have been killed. Agathocles was thus obliged to leave Bruttian territory and return to Sicily. As we have already said, in 295 he married his daughter to King Pyrrhus. He escorted her personally to her husband with a war fleet and used this opportunity to make a surprise attack on Croton, which he plundered and occupied. He also formed an alliance with the Iapygians and Peucetians at that time; nothing is known about the content of the treaty and it is very doubtful whether it was directed primarily against Rome. As far as Agathocles' relations with the Romans or their relations with him are concerned, it may be assumed *a priori* that Agathocles was as aware of the Romans' progressive expansion over central Italy as they were of Agathocles' attempts to gain a firm position in the south of the peninsula. Just because their aims and spheres of interest were different, however, there appear to have been no diplomatic or even military conflicts between the two powers. Agathocles later made a fresh attempt to secure the Bruttian peninsula; in about 293 he launched a new campaign against the Bruttians with an army of 30,000 infantry and 3,000 cavalry. At the same time his admiral, Stilpo, plundered the Bruttian coast, but lost the greater part of his fleet in a storm. On the other hand, Agathocles did manage to conquer Hipponium, thus winning an important base in the struggle with the Bruttians. His opponents now agreed to provide hostages and to recognize Syracusan sovereignty, but no sooner had Agathocles returned to Sicily than the rebellion flared up again. The Syracusan troops stationed there were overpowered and the hostages freed. Hence the Bruttians regained their independence, although Hipponium and the southern part of the Bruttian peninsula obviously remained in Agathocles' possession. Literary sources provide no answer to the question how far Agathocles did in fact extend his rule over southern Italy. There is nothing in the numismatic evidence to suggest that Agathocles engaged in 'commercial imperialism', as has been claimed in modern literature.[22]

Agathocles had been at peace with the Carthaginians since 306/5, but

---

[22] Cf. Consolo Langher 1979, 319: (G 28).

from his point of view this was no more than a pause in the battle, for he had forgotten neither the African catastrophe nor the far-reaching concessions he had had to make to the Carthaginians in the treaty of 306/5 in view of the impending decisive struggle with Deinocrates; the entire west of Sicily had been ceded to the Carthaginians on that occasion. He therefore soon began to rearm on a large scale for a new confrontation, the object of which was to drive the Carthaginians from the island entirely. As the Carthaginians had won the previous war mainly on account of their naval superiority, he had a sizeable fleet of 200 warships built. While Agathocles' Italian policy was motivated primarily by the idea of uniting all the forces of the western Greek world under his hegemony for the struggle against Carthage, the prime object of his eastern policy was to win allies for the forthcoming war. It was probably for this reason that in about 300 Agathocles married Theoxena, a daughter or step-daughter of Ptolemy I, who was a direct neighbour of the Carthaginians as overlord of Cyrene and no doubt saw this marriage as a guarantee for the security of his rule there. Moreover, it was the first time that a Syracusan ruler had married a foreign princess. However, Ptolemy obviously had neither the time nor the inclination to become involved in ambitious ventures in the West, so that Agathocles soon established contact with another of the Diadochi who not only possessed a large fleet but was also more favourably disposed towards expeditions in the West, that is to say Demetrius Poliorcetes. In about 291 Agathocles' daughter Lanassa separated from Pyrrhus, returned to her island of Corcyra and married Demetrius, who thus succeeded Pyrrhus not only as husband of Lanassa but also as the ruler of Corcyra. This marriage, which cannot have taken place without the consent of the bride's father, marks the change of political allegiance on the part of Agathocles, who sided with the stronger party in the conflict that was brewing between Pyrrhus and Demetrius and at the same time abandoned the alliance with Egypt in favour of one with Poliorcetes. Soon afterwards Agathocles sent his son of the same name to Demetrius to conclude a treaty of friendship with him. Demetrius gladly accepted, received the young man with royal honours and had him accompanied on his return by one of his confidants, Oxythemis of Larissa, in order to have the treaty ratified in Syracuse and at the same time to examine the situation in Sicily. It is not known what the treaty contained, but it is fair to assume that therein Agathocles secured the support of the ruler of the seas for the impending Carthaginian war.

Agathocles was not able to realize his ambitious plans aimed against Carthage, however, for just when the preparations for the war were complete he contracted a serious illness to which he soon succumbed. While the king lay dying, the battles for the succession had already broken out. His two sons by his first wife, the widow of Damas – that is to say, Archagathus and Heracleides – had been murdered by the troops in Africa; the children of his third wife, Theoxena, were still minors. By his second wife, Alcia, he had a daughter, Lanassa, and a son called Agathocles. Hence it was mainly on this son that the dying king pinned his hopes and he even recommended him to the Syracusan people as his successor. However, Agathocles' grandson Archagathus, son of the Archagathus murdered in Africa, contested the succession. At the time he commanded an army on Aetna. When the younger Agathocles came to him on his father's orders to take over the supreme command, Archagathus killed him and threw his body into the sea. Agathocles, who was not willing to make his son's murderer his successor, thereupon gave Syracuse back its liberty. He died soon afterwards at the age of 72, probably of cancer of the jaw (289/8 B.C.).

VI. GENERAL ASSESSMENT

The overall assessment of Agathocles was hotly debated even by contemporary historians; whereas Callias[23] claims that he far surpassed others in piety and humanity, Timaeus[24] saw him as a tyrant without equal in terms of brutality. Modern historians also disagree in their appraisal of Agathocles. The excessively favourable judgement of some scholars,[25] who positively glorify Agathocles' ability as a statesman and general, contrasts with the condemnation of others,[26] who point to the endless series of political murders in the first part of his rule and portray Agathocles as one of the most cruel tyrants in the annals of history. Yet another group of scholars[27] take an intermediate position in so far as they lay stress on both positive and negative aspects. Indeed, in assessing Agathocles it is well to adopt a middle course. Tribute can be paid to his personal courage and audacity and his qualities of leadership in military and civil affairs. It was these attributes that enabled him to rise from modest beginnings to be ruler of a state that later encompassed a large part of Sicily and certain areas in southern Italy and which, significantly, collapsed immediately upon his death. The fact that he knew how to act at the crucial moment is shown not least by his bold decision to transfer the war to Africa; although this campaign ultimately failed, it did succeed in its primary object, which was the maintenance of his rule in Sicily. Moreover, Agathocles initially understood how to win favour with the

[23] *FGrH* 564T3.
[24] *FGrH* 566F124.
[25] See in particular Beloch 1925–7: (A 5) and most recently Consolo Langher 1979: (G 28).
[26] See especially Cary in *CAH* VII[1] and Scaturro 1943: (G 49).
[27] See for instance Berve 1952 and 1967: (G 21–2), and Aalders 1955: (G 19).

common man by the various measures mentioned above. On the other hand, it remains a fact that his rule was marked by an endless series of political murders which were not by any means always 'class based', in other words directed against 'the wealthy and oligarchically minded', as has been claimed.[28] On several occasions Agathocles also struck with full vigour at the poorer people, particularly after the failure of the African campaign, when he had the families of the soldiers and relatives of his sons' murderers killed in Syracuse. This brutal behaviour in particular, the total fiasco of the African campaign and the unscrupulous abandonment of the entire army dealt a severe blow to his popularity with the common people. The Syracusans were also indignant about the return of the banished oligarchs as they were about the granting of citizenship to mercenaries, not to mention the tyrant's heavy financial impositions. In short, the people eventually came to view Agathocles' rule as oppressive. The ancient sources[29] tell us that immediately after the death of the tyrant the Syracusans confiscated his property, pulled down his statues and conducted a thorough *damnatio memoriae*, so that it seems quite absurd to describe his rule in general as a 'tyrannie populaire'[30] or even to speak of the 'boundless popularity' that he is supposed to have enjoyed.[31] It is also incorrect to claim that from a constitutional point of view Agathocles' rule was not a tyranny and to see him as the legally elected custodian of state affairs, emphasizing his conformity with the constitution, as does, above all, Berve[32] in his important examination of Agathocles. In reality, his election as general-plenipotentiary and governor of Syracuse should be seen not as a legal process but as a prime example of a tyrannical usurpation scantily embellished with constitutional trimmings. It is true that under his rule the Syracusan *ekklesia* and probably also the *boule* continued to exist, but it would be wrong to see this as proof of his constitutionality, for these institutions were stripped of their true functions and became merely instruments for the implementation of the sovereign's will; the newly discovered Oxyrhynchus papyrus,[33] among other sources, shows clearly that freedom of expression was not possible in the Syracusan assembly. Agathocles' rule also bears many other hallmarks of a typical tyranny; take, for instance, his harsh action against political opponents (particularly the oligarchs and their adherents), involving innumerable murders, banishments and confiscations in the early years of his rule, or his endeavour to win favour with the common people in a variety of ways. It is also true of the continuous spying on his

---

[28] By Finley 1968, 103: (G 34).   [29] Diod. xxi.18.1.
[30] According to Mossé 1969: (G 44).   [31] So Beloch 1925–7, 1.209: (A 5).
[32] Berve 1952, also 1967: (G 21–2).   [33] *P. Oxy.* 2399, cols. ii–iv.

subjects,[34] the use of mercenary armies and his expansionist foreign policy. In addition, Berve's study with its one-sided concentration on the formal aspect of constitutionality makes a distinction that is difficult to sustain. He describes Agathocles' *basileia* as a personal monarchy that related not to the city of Syracuse, where Agathocles continued to hold the office of general-plenipotentiary or governor of the city, but to the territory in Sicily and elsewhere that he had conquered in his own name. According to this view, Agathocles therefore made conquests in the name of the *polis* of Syracuse as its highest executive officer but then, as ruler, added them to his personal property as 'land won by the spear'. As a logical consequence of this, according to Berve, he gave the plenipotentiary's powers and governorship of the city back to the people shortly before his death but did not abdicate as king. This distinction is artificial and unfounded. As historical probability would let us suppose and as numismatic finds clearly prove,[35] the title of king did indeed also relate to Syracuse. This also invalidates the other conclusions drawn by Berve.

Agathocles' life-work collapsed upon his death; Sicily reverted to chaotic confusion until the Romans established their dominion over the island a few decades later. This reveals the historical importance of Agathocles, who stood, so to speak, at the turning-point between Sicily's Greek past and its Roman future; he was one of the last significant representatives of the Greek world and also a celebrated model for the Romans. We have only to think of the above quoted dictum of Scipio Africanus, who followed in Agathocles' footsteps in Africa and thus won the decisive victory over Hannibal.

[34] See, for example, Diod. xx.63.6.

[35] The coinage of Syracuse is of the utmost importance for following and appraising the development of Agathocles' rule. The following four stages can be identified: (1) The first coins to be struck after his election as general plenipotentiary or governor of the city acclaim Agathocles as victor, as the type with the adjective *ΑΓΑΘΟΚΛΕΙΟΣ (sc. ΝΙΚΗ)* = 'Agathoclean (sc. victory)' proves, but they still name the Syracusans as the actual minting authority. (2) The name of the Syracusans soon disappears entirely from the coins, which now refer only to Agathocles and his victories. (3) After the crossing to Africa and the great successes against the Carthaginians the coins bear the name of Agathocles in the genitive. That implies that the coining prerogative is attributed to him alone. During his absence from Syracuse it was exercised by his representative Antander. (4) After the adoption of the title of king the coins bear the inscription *ΑΓΑΘΟΚΛΕΟΣ ΒΑΣΙΛΕΟΣ*, i.e. (coins) 'of King Agathocles'. For details see Giesecke 1923, 89ff.: (G 15) (with much documentation and literature) and P. R. Franke and M. Hirmer, *Die griechische Münze*[2] (Munich, 1972) 54.

CHAPTER 11

THE SYRIAN-EGYPTIAN WARS AND THE NEW KINGDOMS OF ASIA MINOR

H. HEINEN

I. INTRODUCTION

This chapter describes the wars between the Ptolemies and the Seleucids from the end of the eighties to the battle of Raphia (217 B.C.).[1] These conflicts, which scholars term the Syrian Wars, were to continue in the second century; they run like a scarlet thread through the history of the Ptolemies and the Seleucids. The virtually incessant enmity between the two neighbouring kingdoms was not restricted to the wars for possession of the border areas of Phoenicia and Palestine but came to assume far greater proportions; in the third century the Syrian Wars also encompassed the western and southern coasts of Asia Minor and helped create the conditions that led to a new configuration of states in that area. The Jewish people was caught up in the centre of the conflict through the fact that Palestine was under Ptolemaic rule throughout the third century. This link with Egypt had brought large numbers of Jews to Alexandria. In the second century B.C. the growing hellenization of the Alexandrian Jews made it necessary to translate the Scriptures into Greek (the Septuagint) but it also gave rise to anti-semitism, which would reach its bloody climax in Roman Alexandria. This hellenization also ranks as one of the historical consequences of the link between Ptolemaic Egypt and the Phoenician-Palestinian region, no less than the intervention of the Romans in the Near East from the beginning of the second century onwards, which was invited by the conflicts between the Ptolemies and the Seleucids.

The root cause of the Syrian Wars can be traced back to the battle of Ipsus in 301 B.C. Ptolemy I did not relinquish the territories in Phoenicia and Coele-Syria[2] that he then occupied and the Seleucids, for their part,

---

[1] Fundamental reading: Will 1979: (A 67), with reference to sources and bibliography. 'Syrian War of Succession': Will, 1.139–42; First Syrian War: Will, 1.144–50; Second and Third Syrian Wars: Will, 1.234–61; Fourth Syrian War: Will 1982, II.26–44: (A 67).

[2] Coele-Syria (meaning 'hollow Syria') is really the name given to the long depression stretching from the Lebanon and Antilebanon through the valleys of the Litani and Jordan to the Dead Sea and beyond to Aqaba on the Red Sea. Designations frequently vary, however, so that Coele-Syria can also mean, *inter alia*, southern Syria including Palestine and the coast. I have used it in the latter sense to denote Ptolemaic possessions in this region. Coele-Syria is also used by many authors to mean the entire area between Egypt and Cilicia.

missed no opportunity of trying to change that state of affairs. The account that follows describes the course of the conflict chronologically and relates developments in the theatres of war from Syria to the Aegean Sea. A separate section is devoted to the smaller states that sprang up in Asia Minor in the shadow of the competing Hellenistic powers. The chapter concludes with an investigation of the aims and principles behind Ptolemaic policy towards the Seleucids.

The whole history of the Greek East in the third century B.C. is very poorly documented and this includes the Syrian Wars. There are practically no detailed accounts of this period by ancient historians. The preserved part of Diodorus' history is interrupted in the year 302 B.C. and Polybius does not take up the narrative until the last few decades of the third century; his description of the Fourth Syrian War (221–217 B.C.) is of particular importance for this chapter.[3] The gaps can be filled, rather sketchily, on the basis of scattered literary references, of inscriptions and, to a lesser degree, the evidence provided by coins. In isolated cases papyri also throw light on the 'great' events of history in Egypt and elsewhere.

II. PTOLEMY II AND THE FIRST SYRIAN WARS (282–246)

The beginning of the period covered by this chapter was wholly dominated by the tremendous historical consequences of the battle of Corupedium (near Sardis) in 281 B.C., at which Lysimachus was defeated and killed. A large number of cities in western Asia Minor that had until then been firmly under the rule of Lysimachus now vowed allegiance to the victor, Seleucus I. In the same year, however, Seleucus was assassinated by Ptolemy Ceraunus.[4] Whereas the assassin looked to Macedonia for support, Seleucus' successor, his son and co-regent Antiochus I, was facing the task of securing his inheritance. He succeeded in this, but only with great difficulty. Antiochus, who was then in the eastern provinces of the Seleucid empire, first had to put down a revolt in Seleucis, in the heart of his kingdom, before he could begin to consolidate his power in Asia Minor.

A little earlier there had also been a change of rule in the Ptolemaic empire; Ptolemy I Soter had died in 283/2 B.C. and had been succeeded by his son, Ptolemy II, later to receive the title of Philadelphus. He had been co-regent with his father since 285 B.C., so his future seemed assured. He removed all further obstacles by brutally eliminating his rivals within the royal house itself. His elder half-brother Ptolemy

---

[3] Essential reading: Walbank 1957, 1967 and 1979: (B 37), in particular 1957, 1.585ff. (on the Fourth Syrian War); see also Pédech 1964, 140ff.: (B 26) ('Les guerres de Coelé-Syrie') and for a general treatment of Polybius and Egypt see Walbank 1979: (F 151).

[4] Heinen 1972, 3–94: (A 21). See above, p. 113.

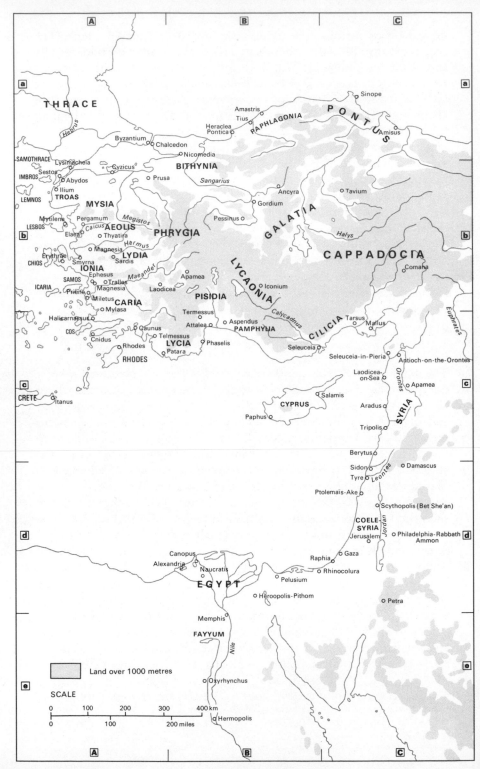

Map 7. The Syrian–Egyptian wars.

Ceraunus, mentioned above, had already been excluded from the Egyptian succession and driven into exile abroad. The empire inherited by Ptolemy II comprised not only Egypt as its nucleus, but also the lands in Syria and Phoenicia occupied earlier by Ptolemy I (Coele-Syria), Cyprus and parts of the coast of Asia Minor. Ptolemaic sovereignty also extended over a series of Aegean islands and Cyrenaica, where Magas, another half-brother of Ptolemy II, represented Ptolemaic rule.

Although initially the Syrian Wars focus attention on Coele-Syria, the point where the two hostile empires meet, it should not be forgotten that the oriental Hellenistic states themselves, the empires of the Ptolemies and the Seleucids, were strongly drawn, as though by a magnet, towards Greece, the Aegean Sea and the Greek coastal cities in western Asia Minor. These regions continued to be sources of energy for the Hellenistic world and it was here that the Ptolemies and the Seleucids also attempted to exert their influence. We shall examine the reasons for this attitude later; at this stage it is sufficient to acknowledge the westward orientation of these Hellenistic states in order to understand that the collapse of Lysimachus' kingdom and the sudden death of Seleucus I not only threw western Asia Minor into turmoil and brought Antiochus I upon the scene but also provoked the intervention of the Ptolemaic realm.

Since the time of J. G. Droysen historians have frequently spoken of the Syrian War of Succession (about 280/279 B.C.) in this connexion, meaning thereby the campaign conducted by Antiochus I both in his homeland and in Asia Minor for possession of his inheritance. Ptolemy II is depicted as the main opponent of the Seleucids, who drove his rival back as far as Seleucis. There is no evidence to support the latter view, although there are many indications that Ptolemy exploited the temporary weakness of Antiochus to acquire or extend Ptolemaic possessions in western and southern Asia Minor. However, the exact extent of Ptolemaic acquisitions cannot be ascertained; historical sources do not show clearly how much of these areas was conquered during the Syrian War of Succession. The success of Antiochus I in western Asia Minor is better documented; here Sardis became a western secondary residence of the Seleucids. On the other hand, he encountered great difficulties with the tribes and cities on the northern coast of Asia Minor, particularly at Heraclea Pontica, which continued to oppose the Seleucids for many decades. The situation in Asia Minor was further complicated by the incursion of the Celts (also termed Galatians in the Hellenistic East), who fought a devastating campaign through Macedonia and Greece and crossed the Hellespont in 278/7. The newcomers plagued their neighbours for a long time until they gradually found their place in the constellation of states in Asia Minor (see below, pp. 422–5).

In about 275 or perhaps a little later – around 270[5] – Antiochus I defeated them soundly in the so-called elephant battle, but even then the danger was far from removed. It was in the struggle against the Galatians and the Seleucids that Pergamum rose to greatness, but this belongs in another section (see below, pp. 423–4).

It is possible, but not certain, that this first clash between Ptolemy II and Antiochus I was ended by a formal peace, but the root cause of the conflict – the rivalry between the Ptolemies and the Seleucids – was not resolved. Grounds for the next confrontation were supplied by Magas, half-brother of Ptolemy Philadelphus and the representative of Alexandria in Cyrene. His wife was Apame, the daughter of Antiochus I. It was possibly the murders within the house of Ptolemy II and perhaps also the latter's marriage to Arsinoe II that drove Magas to rebel against Ptolemy and led him to take the title of king. The army of invasion that he led to Egypt had to withdraw without achieving its purpose, however, as Libyan nomads raised a revolt in his rear. Ptolemy himself, who was preparing to defend his sovereignty, was detained by an uprising at home – a mutiny among Celtic mercenaries – and prevented from giving chase to the fleeing Magas, who was now able to rule Cyrenaica free from serious threat until the middle of the third century.

What is really astonishing is that Magas encouraged his father-in-law Antiochus to wage war on Ptolemy but that the two allies were not able to co-ordinate their military operations. It would appear that Magas' troops had already withdrawn – probably in 275 – before the actual outbreak of war between Ptolemy II and Antiochus I (the so-called First Syrian War, 274–271). This may have been due to the fact that Magas' plans were upset by the nomads' uprising and that Antiochus was tied down in Asia Minor by the Galatians.[6] Our knowledge of the campaigns in the First Syrian War is based on scattered and totally isolated references; the discovery of any new source could lead to a thorough amendment of the hypotheses proposed hitherto. As far as we can tell, this war did not lead to any serious change in the *status quo ante*, so that basically it represented failure for Antiochus I, who was interested in revising the state of affairs. Ptolemy, on the other hand, was obviously able to confirm his position, as otherwise Theocritus' *Idyll* xvii with its panegyric on the Alexandrian ruler would be difficult to understand; the idyll lays great stress on the extensive ring of Ptolemaic external possessions in Phoenicia and Arabia, in Syria, Libya and Ethiopia, in Pamphylia and Cilicia, in Lycia and Caria and in the Cyclades.

Ptolemy II held magnificent displays to underline his success, or what

[5] See below p. 423 n. 26.
[6] New angles on the relationship between Alexandria and the western territories, in particular Cyrenaica, in Bagnall 1976, 195–209: (F 204).

was claimed as success, in this war. A hieroglyphic stele in Pithom (the Greek Heroopolis, in the eastern Delta) records that in his campaign against the Seleucid empire the king brought back to Egypt statues of gods that had been carried away by the enemy.[7] This does admittedly rank as one of the more frequently documented actions of an Egyptian ruler, especially in the third century, but it should not be rejected on these grounds as a worthless cliché. Instead, the entire episode recorded on the Pithom stele demonstrates that the repatriation of Egyptian deities actually occurred and was celebrated with due ceremony by the native priesthood. No less important is the clear indication it gives of the extent to which the Ptolemaic ruler acknowledged the traditions of the Egyptian monarchy. By respecting the traditions of the country the Ptolemies consolidated their positions in Egypt. The quarrel between the Ptolemies and the Seleucids was therefore more than just a conflict between two Hellenistic dynasties. From the point of view of native Egyptians Ptolemaic foreign policy could be perceived as the continuation of their age-old traditions in the struggle against 'the foreign lands', against the enemies of Egypt and its gods. This was the beginning of the line of thought that later would lead naturally to the much commented upon participation of native Egyptians in the battle of Raphia in 217 B.C.[8] Just as the repatriation of Egyptian deities was arranged for its calculated effect at home, so Ptolemy II wooed the Greeks in Egypt and the Hellenistic world with a triumphal procession (*pompe*) of unheard-of splendour, which was possibly held in 271/70 in connexion with the festival in Alexandria known as the *Ptolemaieia*.[9] A vivid description of at least part of the splendour displayed at this *pompe* is to be found in a report by the Rhodian Callixeinus contained in Athenaeus v.196a 203b. If the attribution of this procession to the year 271/70 is correct, then it is fair to regard it as a triumphal celebration to mark the victorious end of the First Syrian War.[10]

Arsinoe II, the sister and wife of Ptolemy Philadelphus, died in 270 B.C. Modern portrayals often emphasize her influence on Ptolemaic

[7] For the text of this Pithom stele cf. Sethe 1904–16, 81–105 (no. 20): (F 126). Mahaffy 1895, 138–9: (F 137), offers a partial translation of this text into English. Complete German translation in Roeder 1959, 108–28: (F 119). Further information in the Bibliography, F(c).

[8] The same sentiment is already expressed in the tenor of the so-called satrap's stele (311 B.C.) after the victory of Ptolemy I at Gaza in 312 B.C. which, incidentally, was achieved with the help of native Egyptian units (Diod. XIX.80.4). This is a hieroglyphic inscription from the temple of Buto in the Delta recording the deeds of Ptolemy I and his services to the temple. Original text in Sethe 1904–16, 11–22 (no. 9): (F 126), and Kamal 1905, I.168–71 (text no. 22182); II, pl. 56 (photograph): (F 117); English translation in Bevan 1927, 28–32: (F 127).

[9] For the dating of the *Ptolemaieia* and its initial celebration in 279/8 B.C. see Shear 1978, 33–6: (C 62), based on a newly found Athenian inscription. See also ch. 5, p. 138.

[10] The link between the *pompe* and the *Ptolemaieia* in 271/70 is contested by Fraser 1972, 1.231–2: (A 15).

foreign policy, although it is difficult to recognize her hand in individual instances. The importance of Arsinoe in monarchic representation and in the ruler cult is quite clear. She must have been an extraordinary woman in many respects, but we should be very cautious about stressing any specific role that she may have played in Ptolemaic foreign policy.[11]

In the following decade, the sixties of the third century, the disputes between the Ptolemies and the Seleucids do not occupy the front of the stage to the same extent. Attention is concentrated more on happenings in Greece and the Aegean, in particular on the Chremonidean War (267–261?), in which Ptolemy II allied with Athens and Sparta in an unsuccessful attempt to counteract Macedonian influence in Greece.[12] It is possible that the decline of the Ptolemies' naval power in the Aegean also began in the sixties. Greater certainty in this regard can be obtained only by first establishing a firm date for the Macedonian victory over the Ptolemaic fleet at Cos. It is conceivable that this battle formed part of the Chremonidean War, but there is as little certainty over this as in dating the no less elusive battle of Andros (see ch. 7, pp. 239–40, 248–9). For the purposes of this chapter it is regrettable that the involvement of the Seleucids in the disputes between the Macedonian king Antigonus Gonatas and the Ptolemaic kingdom is not clear. The direct participation of Antiochus I in the Chremonidean War cannot be easily proved, but it is quite conceivable that he might have exploited Ptolemy's involvement and difficulties in the war to curb Ptolemaic influence in Asia Minor. Here too, however, historical sources provide very sparse indications, for even the best and most detailed inscriptions cannot compensate for the loss of a continuous account from the pen of a historian. Nonetheless, the fact that something was happening with regard to the Ptolemaic possessions in Asia Minor in the sixties is shown by the turbulent history of Ephesus, which fell under Ptolemaic rule in about 262/1. This could only have been the result of a conflict with the Seleucids, who were then able to bring Ephesus back into their sphere of influence, probably around 258.[13]

This action places us already mid-way through the Second Syrian War (260–253?).[14] It was probably triggered by the death of Antiochus I in 261 and the accession of Antiochus II, a state of affairs that Ptolemy II no doubt wished to exploit. We know practically nothing of the details or chronology of this war. Ptolemaic rule in Ephesus and Miletus was

---

[11] Longega 1968: (F 136) goes too far in this regard.
[12] Heinen 1972, 95–213: (A 21).
[13] Regarding these events and their dates see Orth 1977, 130–2: (A 46).
[14] This numbering of the Syrian Wars has been retained purely for the sake of convention. If the so-called War of Succession were also counted, this would already be the third major war between the Ptolemies and the Seleucids. We know far too little, however, to separate the individual wars with any precision.

shaken by revolts (led by Ptolemy 'the Son' in Ephesus[15] and Timarchus in Miletus); even Rhodes, which had previously enjoyed good relations with Egypt, now temporarily joined the opponents of the Ptolemies and inflicted a defeat on them in a naval battle off Ephesus (see below, p. 433). Nothing is known about hostilities in Syria-Phoenicia; the Eleutherus river (now called Nahr al-Kebīr, north of Tripolis) obviously continued to form the boundary between the Ptolemaic and Seleucid empires.[16]

If we assess the separate items of evidence available, we see that Antiochus II emerged the victor in this struggle. In certain areas – specifically in Ionia, Cilicia and Pamphylia – he certainly succeeded in gaining new territory. In addition, Ptolemy II lost part of his thalassocracy in the Aegean to Antigonus Gonatas and, in particular, to Rhodes, whose real ascent was now beginning in parallel with the growing importance of Pergamum on the mainland of Asia Minor. We do not know the details of the peace settlement between the Ptolemaic and Seleucid empires (253 or earlier[17]) apart from the interesting fact that Antiochus II repudiated his wife Laodice to marry Berenice, the daughter of Ptolemy II. We can only speculate about the intentions behind this dynastic link that was supposed to seal the peace and about the hopes and fears that the two parties may have harboured. Although at the time of their conclusion such political marriages could contribute to the reconciliation of competing powers, through their offspring they also promoted reciprocal claims to the throne and probably created more problems than they solved, at least between the Ptolemies and the Seleucids.

Until the deaths of Ptolemy II and Antiochus II – both died in 246 B.C. – peaceful relations could be maintained between the two kingdoms. Ptolemy II also managed to restore good relations with Magas of Cyrene; Berenice, Magas' only daughter, became engaged to Ptolemy's son, the future Ptolemy III Euergetes. This ensured the reincorporation of Cyrenaica into the Ptolemaic empire – in the face of unsuccessful resistance from Apame, the widow of Magas and daughter of Antiochus I (see above, p. 243 n. 62). Ptolemy II's policy of dynastic marriages has also earned him a reputation among historians as an adroit diplomatist, no doubt with good reason, but it never displaced war as an instrument of policy. Although there was a *de facto*, albeit precarious, balance of power

---

[15] Ptolemy of Ephesus was probably a son of Ptolemy II; cf. Will 1979, 1.236: (A 67).

[16] An ostracon from Karnak that recently came to light relates to the beginning of 258/7 and mentions that the king (Ptolemy II) went to war in Syria: Bresciani 1978: (F 222). Contrary to the opinion of the editor, this should perhaps be seen as a reference to the Second Syrian War rather than a reminiscence of the First. See further ch. 5, pp. 135–6.

[17] The summer of 253 is the *terminus ante quem* for the peace treaty, according to Clarysse on the basis of new views regarding papyrological sources: Crawford *et al.* 1980, 83–9: (F 241).

between the great Hellenistic states, there was no policy of equilibrium in the sense of a mutually accepted principle. It was a battle of each against the rest that was played out not only in the border regions of the rival kingdoms but was often aimed at the heart of the adversary, whenever this was possible (see below, p. 445).

III. PTOLEMY III AND THE THIRD SYRIAN WAR (246–241)

The truth of this statement is well illustrated by the Third Syrian War, also known as the Laodicean War. We have more numerous and better sources of information about this war than about the previous ones between the Ptolemies and the Seleucids, but even these data are mostly isolated and often contradictory, so that modern reconstructions of the Third Syrian War frequently diverge from one another.

Yet again it was a change of sovereign that provided the grounds for the military conflict. Antiochus II had died in Ephesus in 246 in mysterious circumstances in the residence of his former queen, Laodice. The latter claimed, whether truthfully or not is difficult to ascertain, that on his death-bed Antiochus had named their son, later to become Seleucus II, as his heir. For Laodice this was a belated victory over the Ptolemaic princess Berenice – the second wife of Antiochus – and her son, whose name is not recorded. Whereas Seleucus II was recognized in large parts of Seleucid Asia Minor but nowhere else, Berenice had her son proclaimed king and appealed for help to her brother Ptolemy III, who had ascended the Egyptian throne shortly before. While Seleucus was still in Asia Minor, Ptolemy advanced on Syria, obviously meeting with no resistance as he could present himself as the champion of Berenice and her son. This explains the friendly reception he received in the central imperial cities of Seleuceia and Antioch-on-the-Orontes. So, at any rate, the matter is represented in a report preserved on papyrus and originating in the entourage of Ptolemy III.[18] Unfortunately this fragmentary source tells us nothing about the decisive peripeteia of this war, the murder of Berenice and her son. However, Ptolemy kept up the fiction that both were still alive and advanced to the Euphrates and from there to Mesopotamia. These successes, obviously gained with ease, are, however, difficult to interpret. Ptolemy was probably not seen as a foreign, Egyptian conqueror but rather as the champion of one of the two claimants to be the legitimate successor to Antiochus II. We cannot be absolutely certain about this point.

Ptolemy was recalled from this triumphal progress to deal with a rising in Egypt.[19] Shortly afterwards, in the summer of 245, we find

[18] The so-called Gurob papyrus, reproduced e.g. in Jacoby, *FGrH* 160, and elsewhere.

[19] Reference to this is also found in *P. Haun.* 6 (now an improved reading by Bülow-Jacobsen 1979, 91ff. and pl. 3: (E 13); see also Huss 1978, 151–6: (F 268)).

Seleucus II recognized in Babylonia. The successes of Ptolemy III in the East were thus of short duration. Once again the native Egyptians acclaimed their ruler for the return of statues of the gods that had been carried away by the Persians.[20] Ptolemy III thus set alongside the dynastic policy that was his first priority that other, ancient and continuous aspect of the Pharaoh going to war against the Persians, the arch-enemy of Late Period Egypt. Nothing certain can be said about Ptolemy's military objectives. Initially everything appeared clear; he wanted to intervene in defence of the rights of his sister Berenice and those of her son. Their murder invalidated this aim. How Ptolemy intended to proceed in the eastern parts of the Seleucid kingdom is impossible to tell, since his campaign there was interrupted by the insurrection in his own country.

This did not, however, signal the end of the Third Syrian War in all theatres. When Seleucus II left Asia Minor to assert his power in the Syrian heartland and in the eastern part of the kingdom his brother Antiochus, nicknamed Hierax (the Hawk) on account of his rapacious nature, was made co-regent of the area west of the Taurus. Between 245 and 241 Ptolemaic forces must have been operating successfully along the southern and western coast of Asia Minor; there can be no other explanation for the territorial gains in Cilicia, Pamphylia and Ionia and on the Hellespont as far round as Thrace which remained in the hands of the Ptolemies after the end of the war in 241 B.C.[21] It is particularly interesting to note that Seleuceia-in-Pieria, the port of the Seleucid capital Antioch-on-the-Orontes, remained a Ptolemaic possession. We do not know the background to this quite astonishing situation, but it can only be explained on the assumption that the Ptolemaic fleet still exerted a decisive influence in the area.

IV. THE RISE OF THE STATES OF ASIA MINOR

The Seleucid empire, which stretched from the western coast of Asia Minor to the Hindu-Kush, was the largest of all the great Hellenistic kingdoms. As the true heirs to the Achaemenid empire the Seleucids had also inherited the problems which afflicted this vast and disparate land mass exposed to forces pulling it towards the west and the east. However, whereas the Achaemenids governed their empire from a centre further to the east (Babylonia, Media, Persis), the Seleucids clung to the Mediterranean, as did the other great Hellenistic dynasties. It was

[20] See *inter alia* the Monumentum Adulitanum (*OGIS* 54, ll. 20ff.) and the Canopus decree (*OGIS* 56, ll. 10ff.); English translation of the latter in Bevan 1927, 208–14: (F 127). Further information in the Bibliography, F (c).

[21] Good surveys of the scattered evidence are to be found in Huss 1976, 188ff.: (F 133), and in Will 1979, I.259ff.: (A 67).

here, after the death of Alexander the Great, that the decisive battles over the division of his empire were fought, here too that in the third century the great rivals, with the Ptolemies chief among them, took their stand, and here that various regional dynasts strove to achieve independence and threatened the cohesion of the western territories of the Seleucid empire. The Seleucids' attention remained concentrated on the West, whether they liked it or not. Nonetheless, they made immense efforts to keep the eastern part of their empire under control, but the secession of entire provinces and the rise of the Parthians from the middle of the third century B.C. onwards increasingly frustrated these attempts. This cannot be described in detail here; it needed to be emphasized only to demonstrate the extent to which the centrifugal forces in the west and east of the empire and the constant wars with the Ptolemies compelled the Seleucids to disperse their forces. They became the victims of the sheer dimensions of the area they governed. In the shadow of these difficulties independent states could emerge in Asia Minor and pursue their own policies. In the second century B.C. these policies led to the intervention of Rome and thus contributed decisively to the fall of the Seleucid empire. The purpose of this section is to sketch briefly the rise of these states in Asia Minor in as far as this is necessary for an understanding of the conflict between the Ptolemies and the Seleucids.

The collapse of Achaemenid rule, the break-up of Alexander's empire and finally the conflicts among the Diadochi created a new framework for the political development of the Greek cities of Asia Minor and Anatolia. While the Greek cities caught between the pressures of the political rulers attempted to retain as much as possible of their freedom and autonomy, individual enterprising dynasts managed to forge kingdoms of their own from former satrapies, modelling their constitution and life style largely on the Hellenistic monarchies and on Greek culture. The pushing back of Seleucid rule and the rise of dynasts in Asia Minor was also partly due to the Celtic invasion of 278/7. We shall therefore begin this section by looking at the Celts.

(a) The Celts[22]

Whereas the Thraco-Macedonian empire of Lysimachus had managed to resist the pressure of the Celts thrusting down from the north, the fall of Lysimachus at the battle of Corupedium (281 B.C.) ushered in new developments in this area, too. The residual Thraco-Macedonian state of Ptolemy Ceraunus gave way under the pressure of the Celts, who

[22] Still fundamental, although superseded in many details, is Stähelin 1907: (E 116); see also the Bibliography, E(c) on the Celts.

marched through Macedonia and Thrace in 280/79 and invaded Greece, where one of their hordes was repulsed before the sanctuary of Delphi in 279. While one section of the Celtic invaders settled in Thrace and there founded the kingdom of Tylis (which was to last until *c.* 212) – much to the detriment of the Greek coastal cities – other groups under the leadership of Lutarius and Leonnorius crossed over to Asia Minor in 278/7, some of them at the invitation of Nicomedes of Bithynia.[23] Nicomedes used them successfully in his fight against the pretender Zipoetes. The Celts then seized their independence, however, and overran the Greek cities and the countryside of Asia Minor. They were not just military formations but complete tribal groups (Tolistoagii, Tectosages, Trocmi) that had migrated with wives, children and chattels. As a migratory people they initially had no permanent home in Asia Minor either, but ranged about, plundering as they went. Cities and dynasts often knew no alternative but to pay tribute to keep the barbarians off their backs.[24] On the other hand, we also read of acts of determined opposition.[25] Defence against the Celts was, of course, particularly in the interest of the Seleucids, who had come into possession of Lysimachus' dominions and sphere of influence in Asia Minor as a result of the battle of Corupedium. But Antiochus I (281–261 B.C.) had his hands tied by the disputes with Ptolemy II, so that it is quite possible that Antiochus' notorious victory over the Celts, the so-called elephant battle, took place not as early as 275 but shortly before 270 or even somewhat later, in other words immediately after the First Syrian War (with regard to the date, see above, p. 416). A newly discovered inscription and its interpretation by M. Wörrle have shown, however, that this victory did not have the lasting effect that was earlier supposed.[26] It would now appear that the Celts were in a position to undertake large scale military operations in the sixties as well, rather than being incapacitated until the fifties, as was commonly held previously. The Celts also appear with increasing regularity as allies or mercenaries in Hellenistic armies; for example, they played a decisive role in the victory of Antiochus Hierax over his brother Seleucus II at Ancyra, present-day Ankara, in 240 or 239(?).

The Celts met with firm resistance, however, from Attalus I (241–197 B.C.), who is reputed to have been the first to refuse them tribute.[27] In a series of battles that he was compelled to wage either against the Celts alone or against the Celts in alliance with Antiochus Hierax he gained

[23] Survey of the activities of the Celts in Asia Minor in Livy xxxviii.16 (based upon Polybius).
[24] Cf. *SIG* 410 (Erythrae).
[25] *OGIS* 765 (Priene, honouring Sotas).
[26] Wörrle 1975, 59–87 (B 177). For the date of the battle see in particular p. 72. The inscription was found close to Denizli, near Laodicea-on-the-Lycus, about 200 km south-east of Smyrna.
[27] Liv. xxxviii.16.14.

mastery over them and at the same time greatly extended his own sovereignty.[28] These battles have an importance that reaches beyond the purely military and political sphere, since they prompted the famous representations of the victories over the Celts and thus led to the birth of Pergamene art. In the sacred enclosure of the Pergamene city goddess Athena Attalus had works of sculpture erected which were intended to portray Pergamum as a centre of Hellenistic culture and Attalus himself as its champion against the barbarians.[29] In the centre of the grand square before the temple of Athena stood a round plinth, which probably supported not a group of Galatians but the statue of Athena. The sculptures of the Galatians stood on two long bases bordering the sacred way to the temple. The bronze originals of these sculptures are lost; all that remains are marble copies dating from the time of the Roman empire. The attribution of individual sculptures to the Galatian monument of Attalus I is arguable in many cases, but the famous representation of the Dying Gaul and the Gaul killing himself and his wife certainly formed part of it. There is also debate about the positioning of the individual figures and the part played by the sculptor Epigonus in the overall conception of the monument. The Celts and their opponents are depicted as individuals and not woven into a mythological setting, as was later the case on the 'Pergamum altar'. The appearance of these statues gives some idea of the effect that the wild barbarians from the north must have had on their contemporaries. Despite the fact that their subject conforms to the tradition of portraying barbarians, the sculptors working for Attalus succeeded in depicting the full awe of the suffering and death of the defeated Celts.[30]

The confinement of the Celts to a permanent place of settlement in the north of Greater Phrygia (subsequently called Galatia) was obviously a very long process in which their defeat at the hands of Antiochus I in the elephant battle probably did not play as decisive a role as has frequently been assumed hitherto. Archaeological evidence for the presence of the Celts in the third century B.C. has been found mainly in the western coastal area of Asia Minor; not until the second century is there a body of material from central Anatolia.[31] The settlement of the Celts in these partly desolate areas was certainly not entirely voluntary; the successful

[28] Important in this regard above all the evidence of inscriptions: *OGIS* 269ff.

[29] See the recent work by Künzl (1971: (E 110)) and Wenning (1978: (E 117); pl. 20 gives a reconstructed plan of the enclosure of Athena with the Galatian monument of Attalus I). Regarding the accentuation of the barbarian theme in the Galatian wars of Attalus I see Cardinali 1906, 23–39: (E 120). See Plates vol., pls. 59–60.

[30] R. Özgan, 'Bermerkungen zum großen Gallieranathem', *AA* 1981, 489–510, offers new views about the positioning and interpretation of this group. In his opinion, marble, not bronze, would have been the material of the original.

[31] Polenz 1978, 181–220: (E 115). The fact that there is so little archaeological evidence for the presence of the Celts in central Anatolia in the third century is, however, surprising.

raids conducted by the Attalids and others must increasingly have driven them out of the coastal regions, a process that was completed by the campaign of Cn. Manlius Vulso in 189 B.C. The Celts retained their tribal divisions even in the interior of Asia Minor; the Tolistoagii settled in the west around Pessinus and Gordium, the Tectosages to the east around Ancyra and finally the Trocmi yet further east on the banks of the River Halys. The assimilation of the Celts into the Phrygian way of life and the slow hellenization of their upper classes did not begin until the second century, however, and thus fall outside the scope of this section. By contrast, the third century B.C. was the great age of the Celtic mercenary;[32] the campaign waged by Cn. Manlius Vulso marked a break in this respect too. In the third century B.C. we come across Celts as mercenaries or allies in many Hellenistic armies, particularly those of the Seleucids. However, the Celts were not truly integrated into these armies but generally fought in their own closed bands with their characteristic equipment (the long shield) and in their typical fighting style – physically impressive and feared for their reckless courage but rather lacking in discipline and tenacity.

(b) Bithynia

Bithynia was one of the areas on the north coast of Asia Minor that the Achaemenids had not fully brought under control and Alexander the Great too had not really subjugated. After 301 B.C. even Lysimachus had been unable to make headway against the valiant Thracian population of Bithynia and their dynasts. The successful resistance to Lysimachus emboldened Zipoetes to take the royal title. The Bithynian royal era began in the year 297/6 (rather than in 298/7). A further important step was taken by Nicomedes I (279 250 B.C.), the successor to Zipoetes. Around the year 264 he founded Nicomedia on the Propontis as the capital of his kingdom, thus orienting Bithynia towards the sea and at the same time opening the door to an accelerated hellenization of the country. In about 255/4 Ziaelas managed to win control of Bithynia, against the testamentary wishes of his father Nicomedes, and extended his kingdom eastwards. In an inscription from Cos[33] probably dating from the period between 246 and 242 Ziaelas boasts of his friendship with the Ptolemies; he doubtless regarded this as a counterweight against his powerful Seleucid neighbour and the latter's ally Pontus. Whether and to what extent Ziaelas intervened in the War of the Brothers between Seleucus II and Antiochus Hierax (see below, pp. 429–30) cannot be ascertained. Around 230 B.C. he met his death at the hands of the Galatians.

[32] Launey 1949–50, I.490–534: (J 143).   [33] SIG 456.

(c) *Pontus*

The history of Pontus in the third century B.C. is even less well known than that of Bithynia. It is true that the Pontic royal era also began in 297/6, the same year as in Bithynia, but actually this is a case of backdating, as it was not until 281 that Mithridates I was proclaimed king, either following the fall of Lysimachus in that year or after the slightly later victory over a Seleucid army. Subsequently, however, we find the royal house of Pontus on the side of the Seleucids. Mithridates II married Laodice, the sister of Seleucus II, probably around 245. It seems likely that Seleucus was seeking in this way to protect his rear for the Third Syrian War. Whereas the Seleucids still possessed land between Bithynia and the kingdom of Pergamum which could be a source of conflict, there was no common border between Pontus and Seleucid territory, as they were separated by the Galatians and Cappadocia. These geo-political factors doubtless also contributed to the community of interests between the Pontic and Seleucid royal houses.

(d) *Cappadocia*

Cappadocia, a mountainous region situated between Pontus in the north, the Taurus in the south, Lycaonia in the west and the upper Euphrates in the east, occupied a key position for the Seleucids as the overland route between Syria and the Seleucid possessions in western Asia Minor passed through Cappadocian territory. Cappadocia was ruled by an Iranian dynasty that had regained a large degree of independence for the country after the turmoil experienced during the age of the Successors. The royal era in Cappadocia began around the year 255 B.C., when Ariarathes III took the title of king. Neighbourly relations subsequently developed between Cappadocia and the Seleucids through the mutual agreement of interests. Ariarathes III married Stratonice, a daughter of Antiochus II, a dynastic link the political significance of which may perhaps be viewed in the light of the special situation in the Second Syrian War.[34]

(e) *Pergamum*[35]

(i) *Philetaerus and Eumenes I*

After the battle of Ipsus in 301 B.C. all of western Asia Minor with the exception of Bithynia and Pontus came under the rule of Lysimachus.

---

[34] See Seibert 1967, 56ff.: (A 57).   [35] The best recent treatment is Hansen 1971: (E 122).

The latter entrusted a man from Asia Minor – the Paphlagonian Philetaerus, son of an Attalus – with command of the important fortress of Pergamum and protection of the treasure of 9,000 talents deposited there.[36] Relations between Philetaerus and Lysimachus grew increasingly strained, however, as a result of the intrigues of the king's wife, Arsinoe (the sister and later wife of Ptolemy II Philadelphus). The murder of Lysimachus' son Agathocles in about 283/2 was the signal for a dangerous shift of allegiance from Lysimachus to Seleucus I,[37] a movement in which Philetaerus joined. For Pergamum, as for Pontus, the fall of Lysimachus at the battle of Corupedium constituted the great turning-point, the prerequisite for its future rise. At first the state was closely dependent on the Seleucids. Philetaerus carried over the good relations he had enjoyed with Seleucus I to his son Antiochus I and negotiated the return of Seleucus' body to Antiochus after his assassination by Ptolemy Ceraunus a few months after the battle of Corupedium. Philetaerus subsequently attempted, with the utmost caution, to adopt a position as an independent dynast, but not as king. Some time around 275/4 he began to have coins struck in his own name but it was not his likeness that they bore – the obverse showed Seleucus and the reverse Athena, the goddess of the city of Pergamum. The arrival of the Celts in Asia Minor from 278/7 onwards led the Seleucids to take military countermeasures, but at this time of great danger the cities and dynasts of Asia Minor were largely left to fend for themselves. In this situation Philetaerus did not neglect to give aid to Hellenic cities such as Cyzicus.[38]

Under Philetaerus began the systematic development of Pergamum as a Greek city-state and simultaneously as a royal residence in the Hellenistic style.[39] On the soil of the former satrapy of Mysia now arose a city that steadily developed into a centre of Greek art and intellectual life. The same objective lay behind Philetaerus' endowments for Greek cities in Asia Minor and temples on the Greek mainland; in this way he sought to present himself to the outside world too as the protector of Hellenism. His own sovereignty was limited, however, to little more than the central portion of the Caïcus valley. Any further expansion would have threatened Seleucid positions; the Pergamene dynast clearly wanted to avoid conflict with such a powerful neighbour.

[36] The origins of Philetaerus are an open question in ancient sources and in modern literature. The opinion that he was a eunuch of servile origin has recently been reasserted by P. Guyot, *Eunuchen als Sklaven und Freigelassene in der griechisch-römischen Antike* (Stuttgarter Beiträge zur Geschichte und Politik 14) (Stuttgart, 1980) 219–20.

[37] Regarding the facts and their chronology see Heinen 1972, 3–20: (A 21).

[38] On Cyzicus see *OGIS* 748 and Launey 1944, 217–36: (E 111); for a critical view of the latter see Wörrle 1975, 64: (B 177).

[39] A good recent map: *Altertümer von Pergamon*, Deutsches Archäologisches Institut (ed.) XII (Appendix: topographic map of Pergamum, 1:2,500). Berlin, 1978.

Things were different under his successor, Eumenes I (263–241 B.C.), who was his nephew and adopted son. Perhaps it was the influence of the Ptolemies in Asia Minor that encouraged Eumenes to take bolder action; it remains uncertain, however, whether co-operation between the Pergamene ruler and Ptolemy II may be assumed. Anyway, there was soon a military conflict between Eumenes and Antiochus I, in the course of which the latter was defeated at Sardis. Eumenes went a step further than Philetaerus and put the latter's effigy on the Pergamene coinage. He did not, however, assume the title of king.

He succeeded in expanding considerably Pergamum's territory, adding not only the upper Caïcus valley but also the lower reaches of the river and hence the important access to the sea and the port of Elaea. The southern slopes of Mt Ida were also incorporated into the kingdom of Pergamum at that time. The forests of this region supplied wood, pitch and tar and were a significant gain for the Pergamene economy. The Caïcus valley itself was predominantly agricultural, with pasture, arable land and gardens, and its pattern of settlement consisted of villages, temple lands and large estates. The Greek coastal settlements with their harbours, olive groves and vineyards constituted a third economic region. Like the Ptolemies, the Attalids were very cautious in the founding of Greek cities. Under Eumenes we hear of the newly established towns of Philetaereia under Mt Ida and Attalea,[40] but they probably marked the limits of Eumenes' rule and must therefore have been rather more military in character. Finally, the rest of the country, in contrast to Pergamum and the Greek coastal cities, constituted the *chora* and was subject to central administration from the capital.

The closing years of Eumenes' rule were influenced by the Third Syrian War (246–241 B.C.; see above, pp. 420–1), in the course of which Asia Minor also became a theatre for the military conflict between the Ptolemies and the Seleucids. In order to come to grips with the dangers facing him Seleucus II felt obliged around 242/1 to make his brother Antiochus Hierax co-regent and to grant him the lands west of the Taurus.

(ii) *Attalus I (241–197 B.C.) and the 'War of the Brothers'*

This then was the state of affairs in 241 B.C. when Attalus, the son of Attalus and Antiochis, succeeded his adoptive father Eumenes. The situation was characterized by the growing strength of the dynasts and kings of Asia Minor, the fickle allegiance of the Greek cities and not least by the ever wakeful preparedness of the Ptolemies to intervene. This conjunction of circumstances would have demanded the very close

[40] *OGIS* 266.

concentration of Seleucid forces. The opposite happened, however – at the end of the Third Syrian War Seleucus and Antiochus Hierax quarrelled (the so-called War of the Brothers). Antiochus Hierax rebelled, demanding sole dominion over the Seleucid empire, and reinforced his troops with Galatian mercenaries. The traditionally pro-Seleucid Mithridates II of Pontus and Ariarathes III of Cappadocia had to decide where they stood, and sided with the usurper, while Attalus I of Pergamum (241–197) hesitated at first. Seleucus took the offensive and marched into Asia Minor, but after initial successes he suffered a crushing defeat at the hands of his brother near Ancyra, probably in 240 or ?39, and hurriedly retreated to Cilicia. We do not know precisely when peace was made between the warring brothers, but it must have occurred before 236. Antiochus Hierax retained Asia Minor while Seleucus was called to the east of the empire to deal with the invasion of the Parni in Hyrcania and Parthyene – after which the Parni were known as Parthians – and the secession of Bactria. This forced activity in the east prevented Seleucus from exploiting the difficulties that were soon to beset his brother and from reimposing his sovereignty over Asia Minor.

The most determined exploiter of this situation proved to be Attalus of Pergamum. In the fight against Antiochus Hierax Attalus made Pergamum the most important state in Asia Minor. The precise course and chronology of the conflict are uncertain in the extreme; the sources permit only a very broad reconstruction.[41] After his defeat of Seleucus II near Ancyra Antiochus Hierax allies with the Galatians and attacks Attalus. Antiochus is defeated and the Galatians succumb to the Pergamene troops in several battles. As a consequence Attalus takes the title of king, receives the cognomen Soter (Saviour) and adopts the traditional Greek stance of the warrior victorious over barbarians. While these battles give Attalus possession of the Seleucid lands in Asia Minor as far as the Taurus, Hierax withdraws eastwards and turns against the troops of his brother Seleucus. Success is denied him, however, and he returns to the west. His subsequent movements are difficult to reconstruct – we hear of his links with Ariarathes III and Ptolemy III, but these pieces of information defy accurate classification. In 226 Antiochus Hierax is murdered in Thrace. At almost the same time – 226 or 225 – his brother Seleucus dies, having been engaged in fighting in the east of the empire ever since his defeat at Ancyra.

Our sources do not permit us to trace clearly the position adopted by Ptolemy III in the War of the Brothers and the actions between Attalus

---

[41] According to Will 1979, 1.298: (A 67) (based partly on E. Bickermann), the first war between Attalus and Hierax should be placed as early as 238/7, as Attalus already bore the royal title before 236, which would presuppose decisive military achievements. Will believes there was another war between these two antagonists around 229–227, after which Hierax supposedly turned eastward.

and Hierax. The Adulis inscription[42] gives the impression that Ptolemy won territory on the west coast of Asia Minor, on the Hellespont and in Thrace as early as the Third Syrian War. It is hardly conceivable that these Ptolemaic possessions were not affected by the War of the Brothers and the battles between Attalus and Hierax or that from these footholds Ptolemy did not attempt to seize his own opportunities for intervention in the ebbing and flowing affairs of Asia Minor. Indeed, isolated references, some of them difficult to interpret, do point to such Ptolemaic intervention. Further than that we cannot go. That Ptolemy had an interest in controlling maritime cities and coastal regions in Asia Minor is quite clear. It is on the contrary very doubtful whether he could have been interested in penetrating deep into the mainland of Asia Minor and thus attracting opposition not only from the Seleucids but also, and especially, from the kings and dynasts, who were jealous of their independence. The Macedonian ruler Antigonus Doson also exploited the collapse of Seleucid sovereignty in Asia Minor. It was in this connexion that he conducted his Carian campaign in 227, an operation of surprising scope at that time, whereby the Macedonians established their presence in south-western Asia Minor, the highly explosive meeting point of various spheres of influence where the interests of Rhodians and Pergamenes, Ptolemies and Seleucids mingled and clashed (see ch. 12, pp. 459–61). The inscriptions from the temple of Zeus in Labraunda (near Mylasa), published a few years ago, give insight into the interweaving of local relationships in this part of Caria with the great political events of the time. In particular, light is thrown on the difficult position of the local *strategos* and dynast Olympichus, who through great effort managed to retain his position in the face of the alternating intervention of the great powers.[43]

Seleucus III (226/5–223 B.C.), the short-lived successor to Seleucus II, tried in vain to reconquer Asia Minor. During the campaign against Attalus I he fell victim to a conspiracy in 223. At his side we find Achaeus, another member of the Seleucid house. His father, Andromachus, must at some time have fallen captive to Ptolemy III, although we do not know the precise circumstances. Nor do we know of any direct military engagement between Ptolemaic and Seleucid troops during the reign of Seleucus III. W. Huss has recently offered an interesting explanation of the circumstances on the basis of *P. Haun.* 6.[44] He

---

[42] *OGIS* 54.

[43] Edition of the inscriptions by Crampa 1969. Part 1: *Period of Olympichus:* (B 60); cf. J. and L. Robert, *Bull. épig.* 1970, nos. 542–53, Bengtson 1971: (B 48), and Habicht, *Gnomon* 44 (1972), 162–70.

[44] Huss 1977, 187ff.: (E 163) (now partly confirmed by the new reading of *P. Haun.* 6 in *ZPE* 36 (1979) 91ff.). On Magas' position see also the interpretation of Habicht 1980, 1–5: (E 28), based on a new reading.

suggests that after the death of Seleucus III his successor Antiochus III directed Achaeus to reconquer Asia Minor and that Ptolemy III sent his son Magas to oppose him in support of Attalus. The Ptolemaic intervention could not, however, prevent the Seleucid troops from driving Attalus back to the confines of Pergamum in 223/2. As K. J. Beloch surmised, the Ptolemaic support for Attalus may have been one of the grounds on which Antiochus III launched the Fourth Syrian War.

Before we turn our attention to this conflict, however, let us take another look at the situation of Attalus I. These were years of dramatic fluctuations in his fortunes. Pergamum emerged strengthened from the clash with Antiochus Hierax and the Galatians. The period from 226 to 223 B.C. marked one of the high points of Attalus' reign. He presented his victories over the Galatians as an important achievement and posed as the champion of Greek civilization against barbarism (see also above, pp. 423–5). The latter Attalids emulated him in this regard; the Galatian monuments and the figures for the 'Pergamum altar' (first half of the second century B.C.) present this view in an artistically striking manner (Plates vol., pls. 60–3). In the Pergamene kings' conception of themselves the Galatians came to occupy the place that had once been filled by the Persians in the political thought and art of Athens. This is not simply proof of the power of attraction of Hellenic culture, which the half-Greek Attalids espoused with missionary zeal; it is also a delicately calculated play on the barbarian theme. The ideology that found such an impressive manifestation in art should not blind us to the fact that the dynasts of Asia Minor, such as Antiochus Hierax and not least of all the Attalids, themselves took Galatian troops into their service.

The successes of Attalus I in battle first against Antiochus Hierax and the Galatians and then against Seleucus III were short-lived, however. We have seen how swiftly Achaeus destroyed Attalus' dream of becoming a major power.

The tying down of Seleucid forces first in the upper satrapies and then in the Fourth Syrian War (221–217 B.C.) gave Achaeus a free hand as far as his position and activities in Asia Minor were concerned. In the autumn of 220 he had himself proclaimed king in Laodicea in Phrygia, thus finalizing the break with Antiochus III. At the same time there was clearly a rapprochement between Achaeus and Attalus, for both emerged as allies of Byzantium in the war that broke out between Rhodes and Byzantium in 220 (see below, pp. 433, 440). This arrangement lasted only a short time, however, as in 218 Attalus took advantage of Achaeus' commitments in Pisidia to regain lost territory. At that time he took the Greek cities of northern Ionia, Aeolis and Troas and the

Mysian lands as far east as the Megistos river (=Makestos or Mekestos).[45] Although Pergamene sovereignty was not restored in all the areas west of the Taurus that had been won before 223 and then lost, the campaign of 218 once again established the Attalid kingdom as the most important political force in Asia Minor. Having thus consolidated his base, Attalus could play a part in the great political events of his time, and particularly in the First Macedonian War (215–205 B.C.). This development and its consequences do not, however, fall within the scope of this chapter.

(f) Rhodes[46]

No treatment of relationships in Asia Minor within the context of the conflicts between the Ptolemies and the Seleucids is complete without casting at least a swift glance at Rhodes. It is true that Rhodes does not belong directly to Asia Minor even though the mainland coast can be seen from its shores; in Hellenistic times, however, it was linked to the mainland and its fate by many threads. Rhodes possessed territories on the coast of Asia Minor (the Rhodian Peraea)[47] and was drawn into the disputes between the Ptolemies and the Seleucids on Asian soil.

In contrast to the great Hellenistic monarchies and the rising dynasts of Asia Minor, Rhodes was and remained a distinctly Greek *polis*. It emerged strengthened from the era of the Successors; it had repulsed the assaults of Antigonus Monophthalmus on its independence and pursued a policy of neutrality wherever possible, largely in view of its trade interests. The Rhodians maintained particularly good relations with Ptolemaic Egypt from the end of the fourth century onwards, but without committing themselves to a treaty. This 'special relationship' was supported by close economic ties between the island state and the country on the Nile. After southern Russia Egypt was probably the main source of Rhodes' vital supply of grain. No less important for the relationship with Alexandria was Rhodes' position as the most important reshipment centre and clearing house for trade in the eastern Mediterranean, functions that it was able to perform thanks to its extremely favourable geographic situation, its powerful fleet, its far-ranging trade relations and its enterprising and wealthy merchant class.[48] The community was structured accordingly; it was led by a financial aristocracy who pursued a markedly paternalistic welfare

---

[45] On this campaign see above all Polyb. v.77; cf. Robert 1937, 185–98: (B 139), and Walbank 1957, 1.601–5 (including a map of the area of Attalus' operations in 218): (B 37).

[46] The earlier standard work by van Gelder 1900: (E 137) is long since out of date but as yet there is no substitute. For an initial survey of Hellenistic Rhodes see Préaux 1978, II.489–96: (A 48), and the Bibliography, E(e).

[47] Fraser and Bean 1954: (E 134).   [48] Fraser 1972, 1.162–9: (A 15).

policy that allowed the lower classes to share at least some of the economic rewards.[49]

Egypt was important to Rhodes not only as a supplier of grain. In the third century the Ptolemies controlled large areas along the coast of Syria and Phoenicia and the seaboard of southern and western Asia Minor. Good relations with Alexandria and free access to the Ptolemaic ports were thus vital to Rhodes' sea trade. We also find references to a military conflict between Rhodes and the Ptolemaic empire, but the reasons behind it and its precise date remain shrouded in mystery in spite of the efforts of modern research. This clash may have occurred during the Second Syrian War, that is to say in the 250s.[50] It seems that the dispute had no lasting ill-effects on relations between the island state and Egypt. At any rate, Ptolemy III was one of the rulers who gave Rhodes generous aid after the devastating earthquake of 227/6 B.C.[51]

The decline in Ptolemaic maritime influence was compensated by a corresponding rise in that of Rhodes. This is demonstrated not only by the leading role that the island played in the toll war against Byzantium (220 B.C.),[52] but also by the fact that from the last few decades of the third century onwards it is possible to speak of a Rhodian thalassocracy.[53] Rhodes had thereby won decisive influence over the islands of the Aegean but had also assumed the obligation to combat piracy. The conflict between the Ptolemies and the Seleucids had given Rhodes latitude to pursue policies of its own, as it had in the case of Pergamum. By the end of the third century these two states had emerged as the most important political factors in the region of the Aegean and Asia Minor. They were therefore destined to play a leading role in the conflict between Rome and the Hellenistic monarchies that was just beginning.

V. ANTIOCHUS III, PTOLEMY IV AND THE FOURTH SYRIAN WAR[54]

The fall of Seleucus III, the accession of Antiochus III, the Seleucid operations in the west (Asia Minor) and in the east of the empire and finally the Fourth Syrian War (221–217 B.C.) are so closely interwoven that the relations between the Ptolemies and the Seleucids can only be understood if the events are viewed as a whole. Our knowledge of these

[49] See primarily Strab. XIV.652–3.
[50] The evidence and recent literature are discussed by Seibert 1976, 45–61: (E 172); a divergent opinion is to be found in Orth 1977, 130–1: (A 46).
[51] Polyb. V.88–9.   [52] See below, p. 440.
[53] See, for example, Polyb. IV.47.1 and Strab. XIV.652–3.
[54] Cf. especially Huss 1976, 20–87 (with detailed discussion of sources and older literature): (F 133). For the Seleucid side see Schmitt 1964: (E 51) and Bar-Kochva 1976, 117–41: (J 136), particularly for military operations and questions concerning their location.

years rests upon a sounder foundation, as from this time onwards the historical work of the Achaean politician Polybius is available as a source. He offers not only details but an overall perspective. For all his sobriety, however, Polybius was not an entirely unbiassed observer, so that caution must be exercised in evaluating his narrative and, in particular, his interpretations.

At the time of the assassination of Seleucus III his younger brother Antiochus was in the upper satrapies in the eastern part of the empire. The diadem was offered first to Achaeus, a member of the Seleucid family (see above, p. 430), but he turned it down in favour of Antiochus. When Antiochus III, later to be called Antiochus the Great, came to power in 223 Molon was appointed governor-general of the eastern satrapies; Achaeus, on the other hand, continued his operations in Asia Minor against Attalus and succeeded in driving him back to the territory of Pergamum in 222 B.C.

Antiochus, who was then aged about twenty, was at first completely under the influence of the Carian Hermeias, who directed the Seleucid civil and financial administration. Hermeias provoked resistance, so that it is fair to assume that the great revolts that shook the Seleucid kingdom in the next few years were directed as much against Hermeias as against the king in person. The first great threat came from Molon, who rebelled against the central authority as early as 222. Upon the advice of Hermeias, however, Antiochus entrusted his generals with the campaign against Molon while he himself set off to reconquer Coele-Syria. This decision has often been criticized by historians, but it must be realized how close the Ptolemaic positions were to the heart of the Seleucid empire. The Ptolemaic occupation of Seleuceia in particular, more or less at the gates of the capital Antioch, must have appeared to the Seleucids as a constant provocation. Hence in 221 B.C. Antiochus himself took command of the war against the Ptolemaic kingdom. Success was denied him at first, however, as his troops could not pass the Ptolemaic positions in Lebanon and Antilebanon that were defended by the Aetolian Theodotus. Meanwhile in the east Molon had managed to defeat the generals sent against him. He occupied the important city of Seleuceia-on-the-Tigris and coins show that he was proclaimed king. Only now did Antiochus see the need to campaign personally against Molon. The rebel was defeated and committed suicide. The hour had struck for Hermeias too; he had begun to arouse the king's suspicions and was eliminated on his orders.

Even while Antiochus was returning westwards in the autumn of 220 he learnt of the insurrection of Achaeus in Asia Minor. What is of particular interest for the subject of this chapter is the question whether

Achaeus acted in collusion with Alexandria. According to Polybius[55] Hermeias forged a letter in which Achaeus informed Antiochus that Ptolemy had encouraged him to revolt and to usurp the Seleucid throne. The authenticity of this letter is questioned by historians, but even Polybius admits that Antiochus feared collaboration between Achaeus and Ptolemy. However that may be, Antiochus was able to conduct the Fourth Syrian War without being harried in any way by Achaeus.

Meanwhile a change had also occurred on the Alexandrian throne – in 221 Ptolemy IV Philopator had succeeded upon the death of Ptolemy III. Polybius describes the government of the new ruler as a striking break in the history of the Ptolemies and says that with the accession of Ptolemy IV began the decline of the Ptolemaic empire.[56] Polybius' adverse assessment of the fourth Ptolemy no doubt also reflects the negative attitude of conservative Greek aristocrats towards a pattern of monarchy that was increasingly characterized by Dionysian *tryphe*, that is opulent living and ecstatic worship of Dionysus.[57] Indeed, we know of Ptolemy IV that he established a real Dionysian community at his court. Whether Polybius' unfavourable portrayal of the foreign policy of Ptolemy IV is justified is another matter. Such an assessment encompasses events and developments that fall beyond the scope of this chapter. The heavy Ptolemaic losses in the Fifth Syrian War (202–200 B.C.?), in particular, have swayed the consensus of learned opinion in favour of Polybius' judgement. W. Huss has contested it, claiming that Ptolemy IV was entirely successful in maintaining the *status quo*.

This section must focus on the Fourth Syrian War, however, a war that was a success for the Ptolemaic kingdom. Initially it appeared that Antiochus III was in the better position in 220: Molon's revolt had been crushed, the removal of Hermeias had given Antiochus freedom of action and Achaeus posed no immediate threat. Ptolemy, on the other hand, had only begun his reign in 221, and that under great difficulties. The leading men at the Alexandrian court were Sosibius and Agathocles; at the succession of Ptolemy IV they had safeguarded their influence by committing a series of murders and had also eliminated Magas, the king's younger brother. Even the queen mother, Berenice II, became a victim of these intrigues. The confusion in the Ptolemaic capital seemed to offer Antiochus a favourable opportunity for a fresh attack on the enemy positions in Coele-Syria.

In 219 Antiochus first succeeded in taking Seleuceia-in-Pieria which had been in Ptolemaic possession since the Third Syrian War. During the next stage of the war the tensions at the Alexandrian court proved to

<hr>

[55] v.42.7–8. [56] Polyb. v.34.
[57] See Préaux 1965, 364–75: (F 310).

be a true stroke of luck for the Seleucids. The opposition towards the king and his advisers drove Theodotus, the Ptolemaic commander in Coele-Syria, to betray his master by surrendering the cities of Ptolemaïs (Ake) and Tyre. The Ptolemaic front that Theodotus had successfully held in 221 was thus breached at important points. The Seleucid army could now advance southwards, albeit slowly as numerous strongholds in Coele-Syria still offered resistance and obliged Antiochus to mount lengthy sieges. Meanwhile Sosibius and Agathocles, who had obviously not expected the Seleucid to achieve such success, hastened to organize the defence of Egypt. By means of skilful delaying tactics they won Antiochus' agreement to negotiations and a four-months' truce in the winter of 219/18. It is possible that Antiochus underestimated his Alexandrian opponents and was too sure of his success; he probably also feared that Achaeus might attack him from the north.[58] In the meanwhile Alexandria was hectically trying to establish a new front after the partial loss of Coele-Syria and to raise a new army. Pelusium, the north-eastern gateway to Egypt, was put on a defensive footing, troops were recalled to Egypt from Ptolemaic possessions abroad and additional mercenaries were enlisted. This was clearly insufficient to bring the army to the necessary numerical strength, and therefore 20,000 native Egyptians were also recruited. All these troops were assembled as secretly as possible and trained near Alexandria while the Ptolemaic government conducted the negotiations with Antiochus from Memphis in order to keep the enemy in the dark about the war preparations.

In the spring of 218 Antiochus resumed his advance through Coele-Syria. He succeeded in taking a series of fortified cities by surprise or by besieging them into submission, particularly after the Seleucid army had defeated Ptolemaic forces under the command of Nicolaus and Perigenes in a combined land and sea battle fought slightly north of Berytus and south of the mouth of the Damuras (Nahr Damur). As a result of these successes some Ptolemaic officers and their troops went over to Antiochus. The king's systematic approach in Coele-Syria clearly indicates that he intended to place Seleucid rule there on a firm footing, but his slow advance also shows that there was still strong resistance. The fact that Ptolemaic rule in Coele-Syria did not collapse more quickly in spite of Antiochus' successes proves that it was not merely upheld by Ptolemaic lances but was also supported by significant sections of the native population.[59] Antiochus moved to quarters in Ptolemaïs for the winter of 218/17.

In the spring of 217 the preparations began for the decisive engagement of the opposing armies. Then in the summer the Ptolemaic

[58] Polyb. v.66.3 and 67.12–13.
[59] Cf. Polyb. v.86.10–11 and Walbank 1957, 1.615–16: (B 37).

troops advanced north-eastwards beyond Pelusium and met with the army of Antiochus III near Raphia in the extreme south of Palestine. It was here that the war was decided on 22 June 217.[60] The Ptolemaic army was numerically superior, with 75,000 men (rather than 55,000) ranged against the 68,000 soldiers on the Seleucid side. Its superiority was not only numerical, however; after initial Seleucid successes the Ptolemaic phalanx managed to breach that of Antiochus and the Ptolemaic right wing under Echecrates put the Seleucid left to flight.

Antiochus thereupon surrendered Coele-Syria and withdrew to his capital Antioch. He now had to fear not only the pursuit of the Ptolemaic army but also the unreliability of his own troops.[61] In addition, he was greatly concerned that Achaeus might seize the opportunity created by the battle of Raphia to take the offensive. In this situation the Seleucids were fortunate that Ptolemy did not wish to crown his victory by destroying the enemy. He has been criticized for this lack of severity and determination,[62] but we must ask ourselves what realistic alternatives were, in fact, open to him. Annexation of the Seleucid empire would probably not have lasted long and would certainly have overtaxed Alexandria's strength. The overthrow of Antiochus III and his replacement by Achaeus, who might have collaborated with Ptolemy, would have brought Asia Minor back under central Seleucid administration; whether Achaeus would have continued to co-operate with Alexandria and, if so, for how long would have been completely unpredictable in any case. It was therefore in the interests of both belligerents to proclaim a year's truce.

In the meantime Ptolemy had regained possession of Coele-Syria and, as victor, was received with due jubilation. The reorganization cannot have presented any particular problems, as Ptolemy left Coele-Syria after three months and returned to Egypt. Admittedly at this point there is one more piece of information to insert that is not reported in Polybius' account and has survived only in the demotic version of the Raphia decree (lines 23–5).[63] Both the text and the translation are unclear at this point, however, and tell us less than some interpreters wish to read into it. This much seems clear: Ptolemy invaded Seleucid territory

[60] For accounts of the battle see primarily Galili 1976/7 (with new points of view): (E 160), and also Bar-Kochva 1976, 128–41 (with a map of the battlefield): (J 136); but I cannot accept all the hypotheses of the latter. Conversion of the date, which is preserved only according to the Egyptian calendar (10 Pachons), creates difficulties. Thissen 1966, 53: (F 123), considers 25 March a possible alternative to 22 June, but this is less probable.

[61] The Seleucid infantry had admittedly suffered heavy losses, but on the other hand the battle had given Antiochus numerical superiority in cavalry. As Galili 1976/7, 60–1: (E 160), remarks, probably correctly, this must have made direct pursuit very risky for the Ptolemaic troops.

[62] Polyb. v.87.3. But see also Huss 1976, 69: (F 133).

[63] Cf. Thissen 1966, 19 (translation) and 60–3 (commentary): (F 123). Further information on the Raphia decree in the Bibliography, F (c).

and conducted a kind of punitive expedition, which apparently lasted twenty-one days. Only after this did he come to an understanding with Antiochus. However interesting this information may be, no particular importance should be attached to this action on the part of Ptolemy, for otherwise Polybius would not have omitted it and, what is more, he could hardly have reproached Ptolemy for not having exploited his victory at Raphia with sufficient energy.

The peace treaty signed after the Fourth Syrian War largely restored the *status quo ante*. Seleuceia-in-Pieria was captured by Antiochus III at the beginning of the war. The fact that it was still in the hands of the Seleucids after the victory of Ptolemy IV is probably due to the peace settlement, but this is not certain. Were it so, then Ptolemy really did concede Antiochus very lenient peace terms and Polybius' reproach would be more understandable. If Ptolemy actually did forgo Seleuceia-in-Pieria at that time, the most likely reason was the realization that this advanced and isolated outpost could be held only at great military expense and was bound to be a constant impediment in his relations with the Seleucids.

In dealing with the consequences of the battle of Raphia modern historians continually emphasize the damaging effects of the participation of native Egyptian soldiers in the campaign against Antiochus III, claiming that the part they played in the victory filled them with pride and encouraged them to offer increasing resistance to the Ptolemaic regiment in Alexandria. They quote in this regard a passage from Polybius in which he does in fact present this development as an adverse consequence of the battle of Raphia.[64] W. Peremans has rightly pointed out, however, that an exact interpretation of the relevant passages in Polybius does not conclusively point to a direct link between the battle of Raphia and the outbreak of fighting between natives and Greeks in Egypt.[65] Nonetheless, the fact remains that Upper Egypt rose against Alexandria in 207/6 B.C. and was ruled by a rebel-king from 205/4 onwards.[66] There was probably a wide variety of reasons for this: economic pressure, social and political tensions and patriotic and religious separatism. The link that Polybius claims to see between the battle of Raphia and the Egyptian autonomy movement is probably a very one-sided Greek view of affairs.

The above-mentioned Raphia decree – a resolution published in hieroglyphs, demotic and Greek by the Egyptian priesthood assembled in Memphis – illuminates the proceedings from a different angle.[67]

[64] Polyb. v.107.1–3; cf. also Polyb. xiv.12.4.
[65] Peremans 1975, 393–402: (F 297).
[66] Survey and bibliography in Walbank 1979, iii.203: (B 37); regarding the date see Pestman 1967, 41ff.: (F 398), and for the names of the native rebel-kings see Clarysse 1978, 243–53: (F 231).
[67] See the Bibliography, F(c).

Ptolemy IV is treated fully in the pharaonic tradition. The Egyptian deities accompany him in combat against the foreign land. Just like Horus, the son of Isis (Harsiesis) and avenger of his father, so the king smites his enemy. Along his triumphal route he attends to the Egyptian idols and has them brought home from the enemy's land. Ptolemy celebrates his victorious return to Egypt at the festival of lamps held to mark the birthday of Horus, undoubtedly a deliberate choice. On his journey through Egypt he is warmly welcomed by the native priests, who respond to his good deeds for the Egyptian temple with cultic honours and festivals in his name. They also decide to have statues of Ptolemy IV and his sister-wife Arsinoe III made in the Egyptian style and erected in the temples of the land.

Modern historians have frequently regarded the terms of the Raphia decree as proof of a decisive breakthrough of Egyptianizing tendencies and have interpreted the artistic representation of the king in the Egyptian style as an indication of this development. Such an interpretation goes much too far, however. It ignores the fact that Ptolemy IV's attitude is part of a long-term trend that began with Ptolemy I and can also be observed in the reigns of Ptolemy II and Ptolemy III.[68] From the very beginning the Ptolemies presented themselves in the pharaonic tradition with regard to their native subjects, whereas they displayed the Graeco-Hellenistic side of their kingship to the Greek world. This accommodating attitude towards Egyptian traditions, which is often interpreted as a sign of weakness or as a concession, may better be regarded as an intelligent attempt to bind the mass of native Egyptians to the Ptolemaic dynasty. The benefactions of Ptolemy IV to the temples of Egypt, on the one hand, and the conferring of honours on the king after Raphia by the priests assembled in Memphis, on the other, show that both sides were acting in their mutual interests. Such a policy of compromise naturally found opponents in both the Greek and Egyptian camps; this is demonstrated by Polybius' criticism of the participation of Egyptian soldiers in the struggle against Antiochus III and, on the other side, by the temporary defection of the Thebaid from Alexandria that began in 207/6. Nevertheless, this policy of balance was ultimately successful; the Ptolemaic dynasty was never seriously endangered by opposition from the native population and survived until 30 B.C., when it was destroyed by the Romans. Hence the participation of Egyptian soldiers in the battle of Raphia should not be overestimated and should not, above all, be represented one-sidedly as an adverse stage in the development of Ptolemaic rule.

While the Ptolemies and Seleucids were fully occupied with the

---

[68] Regarding the artistic representation see the recent work of Kyrieleis 1975: (F 135). See also the archaeological and egyptological contributions in the collective volume: *Das ptol. Aegypten.*

conduct of their dispute, there was a stirring among the smaller powers in Asia Minor. In 220 a war broke out between Byzantium and Rhodes over tolls; Bithynia, Pergamum and Achaeus were drawn into the conflict. Eventually peace was concluded. The truly significant aspect of this affair was the fact that none of the large Hellenistic powers intervened in a matter of such importance as the freedom of the Straits and that this task was undertaken by the rising maritime power Rhodes. Attalus also profited from the occasion; he recovered from the low point to which he had sunk in 222 and managed to bring north-western Asia Minor back under his control by means of the campaign of 218 B.C. (see above, pp. 431–2). We have already stated that Achaeus did not intervene against Antiochus III in the Fourth Syrian War. He was fully occupied fighting in Asia Minor, in such areas as Pisidia and Pamphylia. The direction of his actions leads us to suppose that Ptolemaic spheres of influence were affected. It can be proved, at any rate, that after the death of Ptolemy III a series of Pamphylian cities loosened their ties with the Ptolemaic empire; this is shown by issues of coins bearing dates calculated from the beginning of local autonomy. The bell tolled for Achaeus, however, when Antiochus III crossed the Taurus in 216 and reached an understanding with Attalus. Achaeus was systematically cornered and finally driven back to Sardis. There he was betrayed and captured in 213 and executed by Antiochus as a traitor.

VI. PTOLEMAIC RULE IN COELE-SYRIA[69]

The reconquest of Coele-Syria by Ptolemy IV in the Fourth Syrian War opened the last phase of Ptolemaic presence in this region. In the Fifth Syrian War (202–200?) Coele-Syria fell to the Seleucids and thereafter the Ptolemies were never again able to gain a foothold there, apart from short episodes under Ptolemy VI in the second century and under Cleopatra VII in the first century B.C. It is therefore appropriate at this point to review briefly the exercise of Ptolemaic sovereignty in this area (for the broader context see also below, pp. 442–5). The importance of Coele-Syria – or in the official Ptolemaic phraseology 'Syria and Phoenicia' – lay primarily in the military field as far as the Ptolemies were concerned; it formed a buffer zone between Egypt and the Seleucid empire and a glacis that protected the north-eastern approach to Egypt. It is therefore highly likely that this region was governed by a single *strategos* with both military and civil powers.[70] There were Ptolemaic

---

[69] For a general survey see Tscherikower 1937, 9–90: (F 334); Avi-Yonah 1973, cols. 351–6: (E 150); Hengel 1973: (E 31) (fundamental); Hengel 1976, 35–51: (E 32); Bagnall 1976, 11–24: (F 204). New material is provided by a recently published inscription containing a list of Ptolemaic soldiers in Coele-Syria: Rey-Coquais 1978, 313–25: (B 126).

[70] Bengtson 1967, III.166–71: (A 6).

garrisons in the most important cities, including Jerusalem. In addition, there were numerous military colonists who had been settled in Coele-Syria and the areas beyond the Jordan, for example in Bet She'an, which was perhaps colonized by Scythian mercenaries and thus received the name Scythopolis. Dynastic names such as Ptolemaïs for Ake/Akko on the Phoenician coast or Philadelphia for Rabbath-Ammon (present-day Amman) beyond the Jordan underlined the links between these territories and the Ptolemaic empire.

Besides the military factors there were economic considerations that made possession of Coele-Syria very attractive to the Ptolemies.[71] Egypt was poorly endowed with timber for building, so that the cedars of Lebanon were very welcome, especially for the fleet, the backbone of the Ptolemaic maritime empire. The caravan trade that brought the products from the east and the south to the Phoenician coastal towns was also important. By levying tolls the Ptolemaic kings shared in the profits from this flow of goods. The crown obtained further revenue from an efficient system of taxation. Taxes were farmed out, as in Egypt; the tax farmers generally came from the native ruling class of Coele-Syria and found opportunities to share in the profits while the mass of the population bore the brunt of taxation. The economic take-over by Alexandria was not restricted to the field of state finances. Besides military settlers, we also know of large private estates in Coele-Syria that were acquired by powerful subjects of the Ptolemaic kingdom, such as Apollonius, the well-known *dioiketes* ('finance minister') of Ptolemy Philadelphus (see above, pp. 142–4). Through the correspondence of his agent Zeno we are relatively well informed about the financial transactions that were carried out on his behalf.[72] Apollonius owned, for example, a large wine-growing estate at Bet Anat, close to Ptolemaïs-Ake which he had inspected by one of his agents.[73]

Alexander the Great's wars of conquest had exposed Coele-Syria to the influence of Greek language and culture. Naturally there was no change under the Ptolemies, but during their era hellenization did not provoke the opposition that the Jews were to mount in the second century B.C. against the Seleucids, the successors to the Ptolemies as masters over Coele-Syria. In the third century the leading classes in particular were receptive towards the influence of the Hellenistic way of life in as far as they could profit from the new order. This was true primarily of the Phoenician coastal cities, whose merchants had been oriented towards the Mediterranean since time immemorial, but it also applies to the

[71] Survey in MacLean Harper 1928, 1–35: (H 134), and Rostovtzeff 1953, 1.340–51: (A 52); with special reference to wine and spices see Walser 1970: (E 177).

[72] Cf. Tscherikower 1937, 9–90: (F 334); for the chronology of Zeno's activities in Coele-Syria (259/8 B.C.) see W. J. Tait in Pestman 1980, 137–41: (F 18).

[73] *P. Lond.* VII.1948: (F 59).

hinterland, as we know from the partly fictitious account of the house of Tobias in the lands beyond Jordan.[74] The lower classes will have been the least accessible to foreign influences; they were also the ones to suffer the most under the new civilization and its representatives. It is revealing to find that the slave trade predominates in Zeno's transactions in Coele-Syria; even more significant is a decree issued by Ptolemy II between 262 and 260 expressly forbidding the enslavement of free members of the native population except for the non-payment of debts to the exchequer.[75] The Greeks may have attempted to reduce sections of the rural bond population to a state of slavery, that is, to deprive them completely of their freedom. Ptolemy II counteracted such a change in the social structure, no doubt in order to prevent the build-up of dangerous tensions and in the interest of settled working relations, which were more profitable for the exchequer.

VII. THE AIMS OF PTOLEMAIC POLICY TOWARDS THE SELEUCID EMPIRE

After many attempts, Ptolemy I succeeded in establishing his dominion over Coele-Syria in 301 B.C. The Ptolemies held sway there for a full century before Antiochus III won the region for the Seleucid empire at the battle of Panium (200 B.C.) in the Fifth Syrian War. What importance did Coele-Syria hold for the rival Ptolemaic and Seleucid powers that it should be the subject of at least five wars within the space of a century? The same question may be asked about the other territories outside Egypt that the Ptolemies won in the course of the third century. In this instance it was principally the Ptolemaic possessions and spheres of influence on the southern and western coasts of Asia Minor that affected Seleucid interests to some degree or other.

In order to understand the force behind this expansion we must say a word about the aims of Ptolemaic foreign policy. Historians have discussed these aims at length, but the ancient sources that might solve the problem are very scant and uncertain. Hence we shall first isolate one element of the problem that is better documented, although not as well as we might wish – the forms of Ptolemaic rule in external territories, that is to say lands other than Egypt.[76] This may permit a better approach to the greater problem of the aims of Ptolemaic foreign policy. We shall not, however, stray too far afield, but shall remain within the

[74] See especially Jos. *Ant. Jud.* xii.160–236; cf. Hengel 1973, 51–3 and 489–503: (E 31), and Fischer 1980, 11–13 (with extensive bibliography): (E 159).

[75] Text and bibliography in *C. Ord. Ptol.*, no. 22: (F 8).

[76] Fundamental reading: Bagnall 1976: (F 204).

confines set by the subject of this chapter, the wars between the Ptolemies and the Seleucids.

The determining factor for the development that concerns us lies outside the chronological limits of our contribution, namely in the time of the first Ptolemy. It was Ptolemy I who opposed all attempts to restore the unity of Alexander's empire and concentrated on Egypt as his power base. On the other hand, he was also the one who surrounded Egypt with a ring of external possessions – Coele-Syria, Cyprus and Cyrenaica – as well as territories and spheres of influence on the southern and western coasts of Asia Minor and in the Aegean (the Island League). Ptolemy II inherited this power structure from his father and it remained intact under the subsequent Ptolemies until the dismemberment of the Ptolemaic empire began at the end of the third century. Research has long since established that certain of the external territories of the empire occupied a prominent position; these were Coele-Syria, Cyprus and Cyrenaica. Together with Egypt they formed the nucleus of the empire and were administered in a very similar fashion to Egypt itself. Their ties with the central government in Alexandria were generally closer than those of the other territories. They formed a relatively closed monetary area based on the use of Ptolemaic currency, were subject to direct taxation, were administered direct by Ptolemaic officials and were covered by a network of garrisons. The adaptation of the administration in these regions to that in Egypt can be seen particularly clearly in the development of the office of *strategos* from the last quarter of the third century onwards.[77] Of course, many of these elements are also to be found in the other territories of the Ptolemaic empire, albeit to varying degrees depending on local or regional requirements and traditions. In spite of its centralism the Ptolemaic administration displayed a high degree of flexibility. The combination of these two principles – centralism and flexibility – proved its worth and gave the Ptolemaic empire strong cohesion throughout the third century. Although some variation in the Ptolemies' possessions on the periphery of the empire is evident in the third century, the fact stands out that possession of the regions forming the nucleus was defended tenaciously. This is most clearly demonstrated in the case of Coele-Syria.

This brings us back to our question concerning the importance of the inner ring: Coele-Syria, Cyprus and Cyrenaica. Ancient texts contain practically nothing with regard to the principles of Ptolemaic foreign policy.[78] One of the exceptions occurs in Polybius v.34.2–9; here he

[77] The standard work on this subject is Bengtson, 1964–7: (A 6).
[78] The best discussion of the principles of Ptolemaic foreign policy in the third century B.C. is to be found in Will 1979, I.153–208: (A 67).

expounds the idea that the deep cordon of external possessions surrounding Egypt allayed all fears the Ptolemies might otherwise have had about the possession of Egypt. It was not until the time of Ptolemy IV that the situation is said to have changed. Thus an important politico-strategic aspect is already named: the external possessions as a glacis to protect the true heartland, Egypt – in a way, expansion as the basis of defence. While the possession of Cyrenaica denied overland access to Egypt from the west, Coele-Syria blocked the much more dangerous line of attack from the north-east. Possession of Cyprus gave Egypt protection from the sea. This was only possible with a strong fleet; Egypt lacked the necessary raw materials, in particular wood, but these were available in Coele-Syria and Cyprus. Polybius' explanation is thus immediately evident as far as the inner ring of states is concerned. The question is whether it also applies to the Ptolemaic possessions on the coasts of Asia Minor and in the Aegean. If we take first only the politico-strategic aspect, then it is certainly true that Ptolemaic presence in Asia Minor and the Aegean enabled Alexandria better to observe and if necessary to counteract the activities of the Antigonids of Macedonia and the Seleucids. However, this entailed costs and risks that must have been hard to justify from the point of view of strategic defence alone. Modern historians have therefore proposed other considerations, each with its own nuances.[79]

U. Wilcken has emphasized the imperialistic nature of Ptolemaic foreign policy and its close association with trade interests. M. Rostovtzeff, on the other hand, has stressed that all that mattered to the Ptolemies was Egypt itself. For the defence of its independence they naturally needed a fleet and money, which in turn created the need to acquire territories that were able to provide raw materials and revenue. E. Will has analysed all these aspects and concluded, without doubt correctly, that politico-strategic interests predominated in Ptolemaic foreign policy and that the mercantile policy of Alexandria merely played a supporting role. Sources hitherto available do not support the opposite theory, that politico-strategic action was determined by the Ptolemies' economic interests. Commercial interests could have been pursued without exercising direct political control. Little can be added to Will's observations. We shall merely point out that, except for the inner ring of external possessions, the Ptolemies strove to establish their influence mainly along the edge of their rivals' areas of interest – in the Peloponnese, Crete, the Aegean and along the coasts of Asia Minor. These regions had the advantage that the political and military risk could be kept under watch and, in addition, they opened up interesting

---

[79] Documentation in Will, *loc. cit.*

markets and opportunities for direct and indirect taxation. In the early decades the Ptolemies probably also set great store by attracting the necessary skilled workmen from these regions for the creation of a Hellenistic state in Egypt. In any event, Greece, the Aegean and western Asia Minor continued to form the centre of the Greek world. There were doubtless not only strategic, political and economic reasons but also psychological motives that made it seem unthinkable, at least in the first century of Hellenism, for the Ptolemies to cut the link with the centre of the Greek world and forgo influence there.

If one is dealing with the relations between the Ptolemies and the Seleucids the question easily arises whether there was a policy of equilibrium between the two powers. The third great Hellenistic power, Macedonia, should be included in this examination, but that is not the subject of this chapter. In spite of the bitter struggle for Coele-Syria the empires of the Ptolemies and Seleucids never destroyed one another. Did they lack the will or the ability? There is no consistent answer, as it depends on situations and the leading personalities. In general, each of the two rivals was too strong to be destroyed by the other, in other words neither of the two dynasties was normally in a position to eliminate the other and to incorporate its territory into its own empire by 'unification'. It is possible, but not certain, that Ptolemy III wanted to make a move in this direction in the Third Syrian War; in any case, his intervention came to nothing in this regard. How far Antiochus III and Antiochus IV intended to go in the Fifth Syrian War (202–200?) and the Sixth Syrian War (170–168) respectively remains unclear; on both occasions the Romans hindered further action by the Seleucids. On the other hand, Ptolemy IV deliberately refrained from completely crushing his opponent in the Fourth Syrian War after his victory at Raphia (217), an attitude that Polybius is known to have criticized. Although in practice equilibrium was largely maintained between the Ptolemies and the Seleucids in the third century, no evidence can be found that this balance of power was the result of a durable political principle mutually accepted and applied.[80]

---

[80] For a different view see Klose 1972, in particular pp. 91–2: (A 29). The problem is set in a wider context in Schmitt 1974, 65–93 (discussion on pp. 94–102): (A 55).

CHAPTER 12

MACEDONIA AND THE GREEK LEAGUES

F. W. WALBANK

I. THE REIGN OF DEMETRIUS II

On his death in 239 Antigonus II was succeeded without challenge by his son Demetrius II, who had shouldered much of the administration during his last years, perhaps with a special responsibility for the northern frontiers, and had indeed been co-regent at least since 257/6.[1] His accession was followed almost at once by several major changes in areas affecting Macedonia. About the time of Antigonus' death Alexander of Epirus had also died, leaving his widow Olympias as guardian to their two sons, Pyrrhus and Ptolemy. This moment of weakness for the Epirote kingdom offered an opportunity for aggrandisement which the Aetolians could not resist and in 239 they invaded western Acarnania, which Epirus had received as its share in the agreed dismemberment of that state.[2] In reply Olympias asked for help from the new king of Macedonia, offering him her daughter Phthia (also called Chryseis)[3] in marriage to seal an alliance, and Demetrius accepted,[4] thereby effecting an open breach with the Aetolians. His motives can only be surmised. It has been suggested that a strong Epirus bound closely to Macedonia would be a bulwark against the Illyrians; but it was the Dardanians rather than the Illyrians of the Adriatic region who had posed the greatest threat to Macedonia and Demetrius may have had his eyes on the Aetolians themselves. Realizing that they were already edging towards an agreement with Achaea, he may well have decided to jettison any hope of retaining their goodwill as the price of establishing a friendly and, with luck, subservient Epirus on his western frontier.

It was in this situation that Aratus joined the Aetolian leader

---

[1] *SEG* xii.314 = *ISE* ii.109 mentions Demetrius' twenty-seventh year; this could be Demetrius I only if there was posthumous dating and the inscription was later re-engraved (so Errington 1977, 115–22: (B 69)).

[2] See above, ch. 7, p. 251.

[3] The identity of Philip V's mother is problematical. Tarn's solution (1940, 403–501: (D 40)) that Chryseis was a by-name for Phthia, daughter of Alexander II of Epirus, seems the most likely; for bibliography see Will 1979, 1.360: (A 67); add Bohec 1981, 34–46: (D 4).

[4] Stratonice fled to the Seleucid court (Just. *Epit.* xxviii.1.1–3, dating this, however, to the reign of her brother Antiochus II), failed to arrange a marriage with her nephew Seleucus II and after attempting to raise a revolt under Antiochus Hierax (Agatharchides, *FGrH* 86 F 20) was executed.

Pantaleon in converting the existing peace into an alliance.[5] Though it cannot be established with certainty which agreement came first, the likelihood is that the one between the leagues followed that between Demetrius and Olympias. It suited both parties. From Aratus' point of view it was a means of assuring Aetolian pressure on Macedonia while he took the offensive against her outposts in the south, and the Aetolians, though more at risk from an effective compact between Macedonia and Epirus, drew the correct conclusion that useful collaboration with Macedonia had reached its limits and hoped to gain more from a joint war against the new king.

Evidence for the details of the war is scanty and not easy to date. The war probably began in 239/8.[6] Despite Plutarch's assertion (*Arat.* 33.1) that at the outset the Achaeans were being threatened on every side, it must for them be regarded as a continuation of Aratus' aggressive policy against Argos, Athens and Arcadia. Demetrius sent what help he could. Argos received reinforcements from Macedonian troops, certainly mercenaries, and there were also Macedonian forces present in Attica. An inscription found at Gortyn in Crete (*SVA* 498), which is dated to Demetrius' third year, records a treaty of friendship and alliance between the king and Gortyn and her allies (who had opposed Macedonia in the Chremonidean War) and probably provided for the sending of Cretan troops to assist Demetrius. Aratus launched several attacks over the Isthmus against Attica, in one of which he dislocated his leg while fleeing through the Thriasian plain towards Eleusis; but in addition Attica was now subjected to Aetolian piratical raids, like those of Bucris, who carried off prisoners to be sold in Crete (where some were ransomed by Eumaridas of Cydonia).[7] Despite these attacks the Athenians were determined not to acquiesce in a 'liberation' which would have led to their submersion in the Achaean League.

Argos was also a target for Achaean attacks, and here too 'liberation' seems not to have been wholly popular, for when in 235 Aratus effected a night entry into the city, the Argives 'as though it were not a battle to secure their liberties, but a contest in the Nemean games of which they were the judges, sat as just and impartial spectators of what was going on, without lifting a finger' (Plut. *Arat.* 27.2). The water supply ran out and Aratus, wounded in the thigh, was compelled to withdraw. Later in the year he attempted an open attack by day but was twice driven off by the tyrant Aristippus. Aratus' failure on this occasion causes no surprise, for throughout his career he was completely lacking in the temperament

---

[5] Polyb. 11.44.1; Plut. *Arat.* 33.1 (linking the alliance too closely with the earlier peace).

[6] *SIG* 485, l. 57: the war began in the Attic archonship of Lysias, but this cannot be dated with certainty; see on this Meritt 1938, 123–36, no. 25: (B 107); Meritt 1977, 161–91 (D 95); Klaffenbach, *PW s.v.* 'Polyeuktos (6)'; Habicht 1979, 137–46 (D 91).   [7] *SIG* 535.

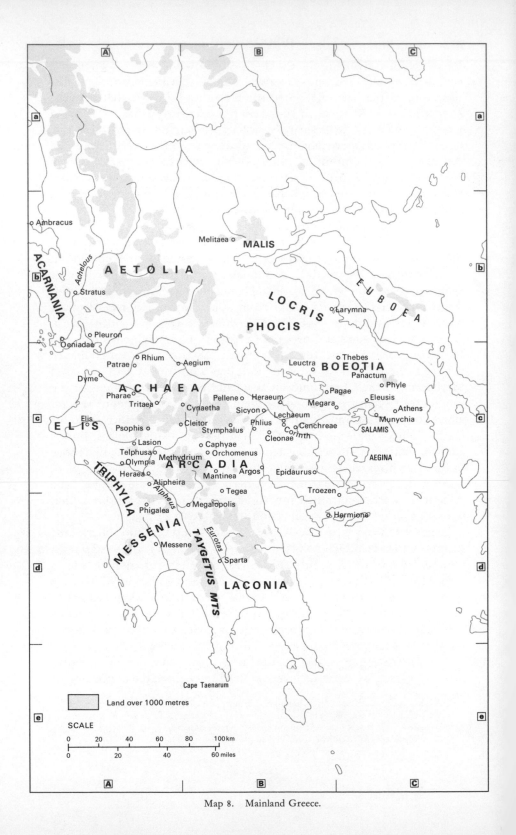

Map 8. Mainland Greece.

or the skills of the field general. His speciality was the ruse, the sudden attack, the unexpected diversionary raid or coup; but in the regular battle line he lost his nerve, and his alleged cowardice and the physical symptoms which it provoked were the frequent object of popular ribaldry. On this occasion he withdrew his forces but shortly afterwards, after taking Cleonae (and holding rival Nemean games there), he managed to kill Aristippus, having tricked him into attacking the town. But Aristippus' brother Aristomachus took over the tyranny and with the aid of Macedonian troops kept Argos firmly aligned with Demetrius.

Aratus combined these campaigns against Attica and the Argolid with a steady advance in Arcadia. The capture of Heraea in 236 in Dioetas' generalship[8] implies that Achaea already held Cleitor and Telphusa – though Triphylia and Alipheira were still under the control of Elis (see above, ch. 7, p. 250). The Achaeans were thus gradually creeping up on Megalopolis, where Lydiades must have been alarmed at the violent death of Aristippus. Accordingly in 235 he negotiated an amnesty, abandoned his tyranny and united Megalopolis with the Achaean League. It was a wise move, which recognized the inability of Macedonia to maintain indefinitely its outposts of power in the Peloponnese without the possession of Corinth; and for the ex-tyrant it opened up a career inside the Achaean League. For the Achaeans the accession of Megalopolis was a mixed blessing. It brought a large increase of territory but also the influence of a large city whose interests and enmities were not those of Achaea. In particular the League inherited along with Megalopolis a tradition of hostility towards Sparta; and it was an unfortunate coincidence that in the year that Lydiades resigned his tyranny a new king, Cleomenes III, succeeded to the Agiad throne on the death of his father Leonidas, for Cleomenes' ambitions were soon to reinforce Megalopolitan hostility in setting Sparta and Achaea on a course for collision. Meanwhile the risks implicit in Lydiades' accession to the Achaean League became evident in 234 when, having at once been elected general, he attempted to proclaim an expedition against Sparta; this move was probably thwarted by Aratus.

Demetrius' movements in the first half of the war against the leagues are somewhat obscure. No source attests his bringing help to Epirus in order to resist the Aetolian attack on western Acarnania; and the title 'Aetolicus' recorded in Strabo (x.2.4c. 451) probably refers to Demetrius Poliorcetes, who is known to have ravaged the area around Pleuron.[9] But western Acarnania continues to be independent of Aetolia, and this suggests that some help had reached Epirus; and since it was to obtain such help that Olympias had made the alliance with Macedonia, it may

[8] Polyaenus, *Strat.* II.36.

[9] Beloch 1927, IV.2.136–7: (A 5); cf. Ehrhardt 1978, 251–3: (D 15), who argues that Demetrius II is probably meant.

be assumed that Demetrius' first action in the war was in support of Epirus. His next recorded move, this time in central Greece, was to invade Boeotia, a successful venture which caused that state to swing over from Aetolia to Macedonia.[10] The date of the invasion is not certain, but it probably fell after 235, when the Boeotians still had two representatives on the Amphictyonic Council (and so were still closely aligned with Aetolia), and when the decision of the people of Rhamnus (in the archonship of Ecphantus, 236/5) to send their flocks over into Macedonian-held Euboea for safety is best explained on the assumption that north-eastern Attica was still afraid of being attacked by land from a hostile Boeotia associated with the Aetolians.[11] It has been argued that when Demetrius seized Boeotia he also occupied Megara;[12] but the King Demetrius mentioned in several Megarian proxeny decrees (upon which this argument rests) is almost certainly Demetrius Poliorcetes, who controlled Megara for many years, and there is no other evidence for a break in the Achaean control of Megara between 243 (see above, ch. 7, p. 251) and 224, when it was made over to Boeotia (see below, p. 467). Thus Aratus was still able to continue his raids over the Isthmus into Attica. Indeed, when in 233 Demetrius' general Bithys, having shipped an army to Argos, invaded Achaean territory by land and inflicted a defeat on Aratus at a place which Plutarch (*Arat.* 34.2) calls Phylacia – it is perhaps to be located at Phylace some ten miles south of Tegea – Aratus, the false report of whose death in battle had led to premature rejoicing at Athens, at once followed up his discomfiture with one of the raids on Attica of which he was now a past master, and got as far as the Academy before retiring.

For the Aetolians the war brought few advantages. True, at some date in the late thirties – in the Delphic archonship of Herys, which probably fell between 234 and 230[13] – the rise from nine to eleven in the number of votes in the Amphictyonic Council controlled by the Aetolians indicates an extension in the territory of their league; this has been identified as that of Malis and northern Phocis.[14] But this gain was in some degree offset by the loss of Opuntian Locris, which went over to Macedonia after 235 when Demetrius seized Boeotia;[15] from then until about 228 (see below, p. 455) Boeotia controlled this area. Elsewhere too the

---

[10] Polyb. xx.5.3.

[11] Pouilloux 1954, 129ff. insc. no. 15: (B 205)=*ISE* 1.25; that Rhamnus was guarding against piratical attacks is less likely.

[12] So Feyel 1942, 85ff.: (D 79); the refutation by Urban 1979, 66ff.: (D 117) is decisive.

[13] See Flacelière 1937, App. 1 no. 32: (D 105); for the various suggested dates see Will 1979, 1.348: (A 67).

[14] Flacelière 1937, 247: (D 105). Klaffenbach 1939, 200: (D 107) suggested Malis and Phthiotic Achaea.

[15] Cf. Beloch 1925, IV.1.631 n. 4: (A 5); Étienne and Knoepfler 1976, 331–41: (D 78).

Aetolians had little success. Their attack on western Acarnania had failed, whether through Demetrius' intervention or some other cause; and they cannot have viewed with equanimity the extension of Achaean power into Arcadia, where the accession of Megalopolis had, it seems, been followed by the Achaean acquisition of the eastern cities of Tegea, Mantinea, Orchomenus and Caphyae.

The evidence concerning these cities, which were successively in the hands of Achaea, Aetolia and, from 229 onwards, Sparta, is far from unambiguous. It seems likely, though it cannot be proved, that they all four shared the same fortunes. Against the hypothesis that they were annexed by the Aetolians at the time of their raids into the Peloponnese in 241[16] is the fact that Mantinea, at least, is known to have been a member of the Achaean League before joining Aetolia, and it is unlikely that this was the case before 241.[17] Furthermore, the treaty of accession made when Orchomenus joined the Achaean League has survived (*SVA* 499) and its terms demonstrate that the union took place after the accession of Megalopolis to the League in 235 and that at the time of the union Orchomenus was governed by a tyrant, Nearchus. This rules out the possibility that the agreement in question is one made in winter 199/8, when Philip V restored Orchomenus to the Achaean League. The most likely solution to the problem of the change of allegiance of these cities is to suppose that they acceded to the Achaean League in the footsteps of Megalopolis in 235, not through friendship towards that city – the Orchomenian agreement proves the opposite – but through fear that their own turn to be absorbed would come next. Soon afterwards, however, they left Achaea for Aetolia for reasons that can only be guessed at. One possibility is that their sympathies were really with Sparta and that in consequence they were wholly opposed to Lydiades' anti-Spartan policy,[18] but judged that a transfer to Achaea's ally Aetolia would seem less provocative than a direct alignment with Sparta. The link established with Aetolia was probably one of *isopoliteia* such as many cities geographically separate from Aetolia enjoyed. The Achaeans, however great their resentment – it was to show itself later in the case of Mantinea – could hardly take immediate action without breaking with their Aetolian allies. But the incident clearly generated bad feeling, which was not assuaged when, in 229, after the Aetolian alliance had virtually lapsed, the four cities were swallowed up, probably with Aetolian connivance, by Sparta (see below, p. 456).

---

[16] On this see Will 1979, 1.322: (A 67); Urban 1979, 79ff.: (D 117).

[17] Polyb. II.57.1. That the four cities joined Achaea as early as 251 in the wake of Sicyon and went over to Aetolia in 241 before the Achaean-Aetolian peace (cf. Will 1979, 1.322, 337: (A 67)) seems less probable.

[18] So De Sanctis 1966 [1894], 1.392: (D 51).

Aetolia thus obtained some immediate compensation for her general lack of success in the war; and she gained further advantages from the events which took place from 234 onwards in Epirus. There Olympias had handed over the kingdom to her elder son Pyrrhus upon his coming of age, and he having died prematurely had been succeeded by his brother Ptolemy, who in turn died very soon afterwards, followed by Olympias herself; and it was probably in 233 that the only surviving member of the royal house, the princess Deidamia,[19] took refuge at the altar of Artemis in Ambracia and was there murdered. Her death brought the Epirote royal family to an abrupt extinction and a federal republic was set up, though with diminished territory, since western Acarnania seems now to have asserted its independence, and the Aetolians seized Ambracia, Amphilochia and the remaining land to the north of the Ambracian Gulf. The new Epirote capital was therefore established at Phoenice in place of Pyrrhus' capital Ambracia. The reasons for the swift fall of the Aeacid dynasty were probably complex. Aetolian pressure must have played a part, and the Macedonian alliance may have been unpopular; in addition there were perhaps social tensions such as appear in other parts of the Greek world (though the sources have nothing to say on this). Finally, the growth of federal states in Aetolia and Achaea probably awakened a desire for emulation in the strongly centralized Epirote alliance, which had developed out of the Molossian *koinon*, and exercised a power that was no doubt resented in some of the other tribes of Epirus.

The political revolution in Epirus had consequences as significant for Rome as they were for Greece and Macedonia. Confronted with an ultimatum to join the Aetolian League, the Acarnanians in Medeon sent an appeal to Demetrius to which, probably owing to trouble on his northern frontiers, he was unable to respond. He therefore hired Agron, the king of the powerful Illyrian tribe of the Ardiaei centred on the bay of Kotor, to intervene instead, and this he did successfully, defeating the Aetolians when they believed that Medeon was theirs for the taking. Soon afterwards Agron died and his wife Teuta, who succeeded him, promptly sent out further raiding parties. One of these, in 230, after attacking Elis and Messenia, put in at Phoenice and seized the town with the help of treacherous Gaulish mercenaries, while another band led by Scerdilaidas advanced by land and defeated the Epirotes near Antigoneia (mod. Jerme). The Epirotes appealed for help to the Achaean and Aetolian Leagues, but just as this arrived the Illyrians were suddenly recalled on account of a revolt in the northern part of Teuta's kingdom.

[19] Her sister Nereis had married Gelon, son of Hiero II of Syracuse. Polyb. VII.3.5 makes them both daughters of Pyrrhus; but the genealogy of Pyrrhus' descendants is controversial. See Cabanes 1976, 39–65: (D 5); Ehrhardt 1975, 176–82: (D 14).

Despondent at their losses the Epirotes now came to terms with the Illyrians, a switch of allegiance which in effect brought them back into the Macedonian camp. Illyrian attacks on Epidamnus (which they failed to take) and on Corcyra led to further action by the Achaeans and Aetolians. Fighting alongside the Acarnanians they were heavily defeated in a naval battle off Paxos (229); it was their last joint action. Meanwhile however Illyrian attacks on Italian traders furnished a pretext for Roman intervention and so sparked off the First Illyrian War (see vol. VIII).

These events had brought no response from Macedonia, where Demetrius had been obliged to march north to repel an invasion of his northern frontiers by the Dardanians. Of this fighting no details survive; but in spring 229, about the time the Romans were crossing over into Illyria, Demetrius died.[20] His reign is shadowy, thanks to the inadequacy of the sources, and his aims cannot be clearly apprehended, though his seizure of Boeotia suggests that his ultimate object was to restore Macedonian domination in southern Greece. His policy in Epirus had collapsed ruinously, and the Dardanian invasion seems to have imposed a serious strain on the resources of the realm. Worst of all, however, Demetrius' death left Macedonia in the hands of an eight-year-old boy, his son Philip by the Epirote princess Phthia.

II. ANTIGONUS DOSON: THE FIRST YEARS

The situation in Macedonia demanded a strong ruler, not a boy, and the leading Macedonians agreed to appoint Antigonus, the son of Deme-Trius the Fair (see above, p. 243 n. 62) and the late king's cousin, as general (*strategos*)[21] and guardian to the boy Philip; and after a little time he acquired the full title of king. Antigonus' nickname Doson ('he who is about to give'?) was taken in ancient times to refer to his guardianship of Philip, but its meaning is in fact obscure. Antigonus married Philip's mother but declined, it is alleged, to raise any of their children so as to safeguard Philip's claim to the throne.

Almost at once Antigonus had to face a Thessalian revolt,[22] which he successfully suppressed. It seems likely that this rebellion was stirred up by the Aetolians, over whom Antigonus won a considerable victory;[23] and the Aetolian annexation of much of Thessaly may account for the increase in the number of Aetolian votes on the Amphictyonic Council

---

[20] Polyb. 11.44.2. Bengtson 1971, 33ff.: (B 48) dates Demetrius' death at the end of 230 (and that of Antigonus III in consequence at the end of 222).

[21] Plut. *Aem.* 8.

[22] Trogus, *Prol.* 28; Just. *Epit.* XXVIII.3.14.

[23] Frontin. *Str.* 11.6.5. The Aetolians received unspecified help from Ptolemy III; see *P. Haun.* 6 fr. 12, l. 18, with the comments of Habicht 1980, 1ff.: (E 28).

during the years 229 and 227 from eleven to fourteen. These three additional votes have been variously identified as those of Thessaliotis, Hestiaeotis and either Perrhaebia or the residue of Phthiotic Achaea (see above, ch. 7, p. 241). Against this hypothesis is the lack of any convincing evidence that the Aetolians occupied these districts, other than Phthiotic Achaea, for any length of time; on the other hand it is hard to point to any other territories whose occupation at this time might explain the increased number of Aetolian Amphictyonic votes. There seems in fact little doubt that Antigonus very quickly recovered Thessaly; and this being so, the continued exercise of the three votes by Aetolia requires some explanation. One suggestion is that on over-running Thessaly the Aetolians claimed its votes and after being expelled continued to exercise them through exiles; but against this is the fact that the Aetolians did not normally exercise the votes of the various states incorporated in the League through delegates coming from those states, but treated the delegates representing the Aetolian block as a single panel, to which citizens from any part of the League could be appointed; hence there was no need of Thessalian exiles to exercise the Thessalian votes. Alternatively Antigonus may have left some peripheral areas in the hands of the Aetolians, thus giving them a claim of sorts to votes which the Thessalians would be in no position to challenge since, following the Macedonian lead, they took no part in the proceedings of the Amphictyony. The matter remains obscure, and is complicated by the increase in the number of Aetolian votes to fifteen in 226 and a drop to thirteen by 223. None of these dates, it should be noted, is absolutely firm.[24] At present no wholly satisfactory explanation is available of this fluctuation in the Amphictyonic voting.

The success of the Aetolians in their invasion of Thessaly was perhaps due to the fact that at the time Antigonus was occupied on the northern front by the same Dardanian inroad which seems to have cost Demetrius his life. Here Antigonus was victorious over the invaders and recovered the valley of the Axius, probably as far north as the pass of Demir Kapu, but he left the Paeonians, who held the area north of that point, in Dardanian hands, where they remained until Philip V took Bylazora in 217. There was thus an element of compromise in Antigonus' settlements in both Thessaly and the north. Whether in fact the Thessalian or the Dardanian campaign came first is not recorded but the likelihood is that the northern frontier claimed precedence.

The crisis in Macedonian fortunes did not go unnoticed in southern Greece where the Athenians seized the opportunity to assert their independence. Under Eurycleides they swallowed their pride and called

[24] Flacelière 1937, 254–5, 285ff.: (D 105); Will 1979, 1.362–3: (A 67); Fine 1932, 130ff.: (D 19); Ehrhardt 1975, 124–38: (D 14).

in Aratus, who helped to negotiate an agreement with Diogenes, the commander of the Macedonian garrisons in Piraeus, Munychia, Salamis and Sunium, as a result of which the Athenians paid off his troops and he handed over the fortresses to them. A subscription list, to which Aratus contributed twenty talents, produced the 120 talents necessary for the purpose and by the summer of 228 Athens was at long last free. Honours were voted to Eurycleides and Micion, who had sponsored the operation,[25] and Diogenes was rewarded with a cult, the *Diogeneia*, and a gymnasium was called after him.[26] But Aratus' hopes of coaxing Athens into the Achaean League were disappointed and under the conservative leadership of Eurycleides and Micion the city embarked on a cautious neutrality which enjoyed the favour of Ptolemy; it was probably a few years later that a new tribe, Ptolemais, and a festival, the *Ptolemaieia*, were instituted.[27] In addition to this new and valuable patronage the Athenians took steps to heal the breach and open friendly relations with Pella; an embassy undertaken by the philosopher Prytanis of Carystus to Antigonus in 226/5 (archon Ergochares) may well have been concerned with this.[28]

To the north of Attica Boeotia, occupied a few years earlier by Demetrius, now asserted its independence of Macedonia, and once more aligned itself with Achaea and Aetolia against Antigonus, who was in no position to reimpose Macedonian domination there, though he succeeded in getting control of Opuntian Locris,[29] which had been Boeotian since shortly after 235 (see above, pp. 450–1). This switch in allegiance by Boeotia is reflected in loans made by the cities of Thespiae and Thebes to Athens, which have been plausibly interpreted as contributions towards the fund to pay off Diogenes. In addition both Boeotia and Phocis made alliances with the Achaean League, and deposited hostages as an assurance of loyalty; an Achaean inscription from Aegium (*SIG* 519) records honours later voted to these hostages.[30]

For the Achaean League the crisis which attended the accession of Antigonus had brought opportunities for progress and expansion. Though Aratus had failed to attract Athens into the League, he experienced greater success with Argos, where the tyrant Aristomachus, recognizing the weakness of Macedonia, consented to follow the example of Lydiades of Megalopolis and resign his tyranny, if the Achaeans could find fifty talents to pay off his mercenaries. There was a

---

[25] *SIG* 497.   [26] *IG* ii².1011, l. 14.

[27] *ISE* I.30; a gymnasium called the Ptolemaeum may date from now or from the time of Ptolemy VI (cf. Thompson 1964, 122ff.: (B 269)).   [28] *ISE* I.28.

[29] Cf. Etienne and Knoepfler 1976, 331–41: (D 78).

[30] Loans: *IG* vii.1737–8, 2405–6; Feyel 1942, 19ff.: (B 71). The alliance was probably preceded by one between Boeotia and Phocis, now free from Aetolia: *IG* ix.1.98 = *ISE* ii.83; Roesch 1982, 359–64: (D 85).

brief hitch in the proceedings when, in the early months of 229, Lydiades, who was then general, tried to make political profit from the operation. Aratus had the issue postponed and early in his own generalship for 229/8 proposed the admission of Argos. About the same time Xenon, the tyrant of Hermione, and Cleonymus, the tyrant of Phlius, laid down their powers and joined Achaea; and Aegina also became a member of the League. These accessions added to the size and wealth of Achaea, but at the same time they brought political complications, since Aristomachus (who following Lydiades' precedent was elected general for 228/7) also brought his influence to bear in support of the anti-Spartan policy already pressed by his fellow ex-tyrant. Furthermore, later events were to show that the loyalty of many cities towards the League was dubious. As Polybius admits (11.38.7), some states had been forced in, and it is clear that his claim that they suddenly saw the light and became reconciled to their position is exaggerated. However it required outside pressures to expose these fundamental weaknesses.

Such pressures were soon to be felt as a result of events at Sparta. There the young king Cleomenes III was of a very different stamp from his father Leonidas. According to Plutarch, having been married by Leonidas to Agis' rich widow, Agiatis, he had become fired with enthusiasm for Agis' ideas and revolutionary aims; but this romantic theme may be overstated, for there is no evidence of any initiative taken by Cleomenes during the first five years of his reign – perhaps as a young man he was still dominated by the ephors – and all the impulse towards a clash between Sparta and Achaea came from the other side, where Aratus had had to check Lydiades from invading Laconia in his first generalship. In 229, but not necessarily on Cleomenes' initiative, the Spartans took over the Arcadian cities of Tegea, Mantinea, Orchomenus and Caphyae, perhaps at their own request.[31] The Aetolians were scarcely in a position to do anything about these outlying parts of their federation, the less so if at the time they were occupied in Thessaly (see pp. 453–4); but the Achaeans, whose relations with the Aetolians were by this time wearing thin, blamed them for consenting to this transfer, which confronted the Achaean League with a potentially hostile salient interposed between Arcadia and the Argolid. About the same time the ephors sent Cleomenes to occupy the Athenaeum (a fortress of disputed ownership which stood on the borders of Arcadia in Belbinatis, controlling the route over into the Eurotas valley) and Aratus retaliated with an unsuccessful night attack on Tegea and Orchomenus. So far hostilities had been limited in scope, perhaps because both Achaea and

[31] Polyb. 11.46.2; Caphyae is not mentioned here, but probably went along with the other three cities.

Sparta were reluctant to endanger the support and goodwill of Ptolemy III which both enjoyed; but after the Spartan seizure of the Athenaeum the Achaeans, in autumn 229 or early in 228, declared war on Sparta.[32] Soon afterwards, and before his ninth generalship ended in May 228, Aratus attacked and captured Caphyae.

Feeling at Sparta was against extending the war and shortly before the fall of Caphyae the ephors had recalled Cleomenes from an expedition into Arcadia. But now, provoked by Aratus' action, they sent the king out once more, this time into the heart of Arcadia where he seized Methydrium, a town belonging to Megalopolis, and thence into the Argolid, which he ravaged. The Achaeans, under their new general Aristomachus, marched out against Cleomenes with an army which Plutarch puts at the exaggerated figure of 20,000 foot and 1,000 horse, and the two sides met at Pallantium somewhat to the west of Tegea. Cleomenes had only 5,000 men but despite the Achaean superiority, Aratus succeeded in persuading Aristomachus to decline battle; he perhaps still hoped to avoid a complete breach with Sparta and the possible implications for the Egyptian subsidies.

The following spring (227), having been re-elected general for the tenth time, Aratus led an Achaean army against Elis, but was brought to battle by Cleomenes on the slopes of Mt Lycaeum in Arcadia, evidently while on his way back to Megalopolis, and he sustained a serious defeat; but he repaired the damage by a quick march over the mountains to take Mantinea (where he installed 300 Achaean settlers and a garrison of 200 mercenaries) and began the siege of Orchomenus. Meanwhile at Sparta Cleomenes, who had been recalled by the ephors from Arcadia, tried to reinforce the royal position by inviting back Archidamus, the brother of Agis IV, from his voluntary exile in Messenia, to occupy the Eurypontid throne. But Archidamus' murder soon afterwards at the hands of the same group who had killed Agis was held against Cleomenes, who was accused of either organizing or consenting to the crime.[33] His embarrassment and his weakened position after these events may have encouraged him to carry out the violent coup which he was already planning against the ephors, who represented the constitutional obstacle to his seizure of absolute power. For the present he persuaded them to send him out again into Arcadia and, after taking the fortress of Leuctra, about 10 km south of Megalopolis, he advanced to the walls of the city, whence Aratus drove him back; but when Aratus checked his forces from pursuit, Lydiades, unable to restrain himself, led the cavalry –

---

[32] Polyb. 11.46.6.
[33] The responsibility for Archidamus' murder was much debated. Polybius (V.37.1; cf. IV.35.13: VIII.35.5) blamed Cleomenes; but Phylarchus (Plut. *Cleom.* 5; *Comp. of Agis and Cleomenes and the Gracchi* 5) thought others were responsible, though Cleomenes knew of the plot and took no steps to prevent it. See Walbank 1957, I.568–9: (B 37); Oliva 1971, 234–44: (D 132).

perhaps that of Megalopolis – after the Spartan army and was killed near a village called Ladoceia. His indiscipline involved the Achaeans in heavy losses, but rid Aratus of a dangerous rival. Lydiades' death aroused some anger in Achaea since his supporters accused Aratus of responsibility for the catastrophe and an assembly angrily voted to suspend all moneys for the war – a decision which seems not to have been implemented.

Cleomenes now set out on yet a third campaign. He seized Heraea on the Alpheus, and from there marched round in a broad circle to introduce food into Orchomenus and besiege Mantinea. Finally, after extended marches in Arcadia he left his citizen-army there and returned to Sparta with a force of mercenaries.

III. CLEOMENES' REVOLUTION

Cleomenes had planned his coup well in advance with the collaboration of a small group of sympathizers, including his step-father Megistonous, a rich landowner. Returning to Sparta one evening he fell upon the ephors at supper, killing four of them and ten of their chief supporters, and seized power. Eighty opponents were proscribed. Cleomenes then proceeded to carry out the same revolutionary programme which had led to the downfall of Agis. All landed property was put into a common pool, debts were cancelled, and the land was divided into 4,000 Spartan lots. The citizen body was made up to perhaps 5,000 from the metics and *perioikoi*,[34] but in the reassignment of the land lots were reserved for the proscribed, whose eventual reconciliation and return was evidently envisaged – or at least that was the impression Cleomenes sought to convey. Equally important for his aims, the traditional Spartan *agoge*, with military training, age-groups for boys and common messes for adults, was now re-introduced. But Cleomenes' measures were not simply backward-looking. Now at last, a century after Alexander, he introduced the Macedonian type of phalanx at Sparta and spent the winter drilling his troops in the use of the long pike, the *sarissa*. Constitutionally, he weakened the council and abolished the ephorate, which he condemned as an excrescence on the 'Lycurgan constitution', a move which led his opponents to brand him as a tyrant. According to Pausanias (II.9.1), he established a new board of magistrates, the *patronomoi*, evidently to protect the laws – it is otherwise attested only from Roman times, and Pausanias may be wrong here – and in an attempt to disguise the illegality of his measures he set his brother Eucleidas on the other throne (though he was not of course a

---

[34] Cf. Shimron 1972, 39ff., 151–2: (D 140).

Eurypontid). The tradition going back to Phylarchus attributed a role in Cleomenes' plans to the Stoic Sphaerus; but there is nothing in what is reported of his measures which can be explained as specifically Stoic. His aims were practical and straightforward – to re-impose the ancient Spartan hegemony on Southern Greece – and his social measures were intended both to restore the kind of Sparta which had enjoyed domination in the past and to secure this once again in his own time.

The Spartan revolution carried out in the autumn of 227 and consolidated during the following winter increased the manpower available to Cleomenes and clearly rendered him a more formidable opponent to the Achaean League. It thus gave a fillip to those in Achaea, particularly but not exclusively in Argos and Megalopolis, who advocated an active and provocative programme against Sparta. Aratus was well aware of the internal weakness in the League; its military potential was limited, it commanded insufficient loyalty in many cities, and particularist interests were still strong in a federal state which had perhaps expanded too rapidly. He also recognized the danger to Achaea should Antigonus choose to take advantage of the clash with Sparta, perhaps even by making a compact with Cleomenes; a Peloponnese disunited was always an incentive for Macedonia to try to recover her hegemony. The Aetolians too, though technically still Achaean allies, had let the Arcadian cities go without any protest, and since the failure of their inroad into Thessaly they might well revert to the kind of understanding with Macedonia which had served them very well in the reign of Antigonus Gonatas.[35] Faced with these various dangerous possibilities and alarmed at the growth in Spartan man-power, especially now that Cleomenes was in sole command, Aratus decided in the winter of 227/6 to sound out Antigonus III with a view to ensuring at least that he should not give active help to Cleomenes.

IV. THE CARIAN EXPEDITION

Antigonus' position inside Macedonia was by this time incomparably stronger than at the time of his succession. The Dardanians and Aetolians had been defeated and expelled from most of the areas they had occupied; and in the winter of 227/6 Antigonus had just returned from an expedition in Asia Minor. Originally appointed 'general and

[35] Polybius (11.45.1–5) argues that out of greed and envy the Aetolians united with Cleomenes and Antigonus in an alliance against Achaea. This theme, which probably derives from a Megalopolitan source (for it seems to have figured neither in Aratus' *Memoirs* nor in Phylarchus) cannot be reconciled with Cleomenes' fear of having Aetolia as an enemy (Plut. *Cleom.* 10.6) nor with Aratus' appeal to Aetolia for help in 225 (Plut. *Arat.* 41.3), and since this 'triple alliance' plays no further part in the sequence of events it should most likely be rejected as unreal (cf. Urban 1979, 131ff.: (D 117)).

guardian to Philip' he now exercised full authority as king, and this status had been endorsed when, confronted by a mutiny in Pella, his firm attitude and threat to hand back the purple and diadem had sufficed to suppress the disorder and had left him stronger than before.[36] The naval expedition which Antigonus led against Caria in the spring or summer of 227 was a striking reaffirmation of Macedonian naval interests, dormant since the reign of Antigonus II. According to a brief mention in Trogus (*Prol.* 28) Antigonus conquered Caria; and an inscription recording a Rhodian arbitration between Samos and Priene indicates that Priene accepted Macedonian authority about this time and mentions both 'king Antigonus' and 'the heir to the kingdom, Phi . . .', who must be Philip.[37] Furthermore several inscriptions throw light on the career of a minor dynast, Olympichus of Alinda, originally a representative of Seleucus II in Caria about 240, later an independent ruler making benefactions to Rhodes at the time of a great earthquake *c.* 227. Thereafter Olympichus was closely aligned with Antigonus and, after his death, with Philip V, in the early part of whose reign he held a Macedonian generalship in Caria, receiving instructions from Philip concerning the treatment of Mylasa and Iasus.[38] One of these inscriptions refers to Antigonus' presence in Mylasa.

Antigonus' purpose in mounting the Carian campaign is not recorded and since so few details survive speculation is hazardous. There is however no evidence to suggest that it was directed against Ptolemy. Indeed, unless the battle of Andros can be shown to belong to the reign of Antigonus Doson (see above, ch. 7, p. 249), there is no sign of direct hostility between Pella and Alexandria during his reign. More probably, then, Antigonus was influenced by the opportunities presented in Caria following the recent defeat and expulsion of Antiochus Hierax by Attalus I of Pergamum (see ch. 11, p. 429). Whether Antigonus was acting independently of Attalus, against him or – though this is unlikely – with some collusive agreement to share Seleucid possessions in Asia Minor must, however, remain uncertain. In putting forward a claim to territories in Asia Minor he was of course recalling Antigonid pretensions not in evidence since the death of Demetrius Poliorcetes, and this may not have been without its advantages if, as Polybius (XX.5.7) seems to suggest, he was still Philip's guardian and not yet recognized as king in his own right. The scope of Antigonus' ambitions cannot be assessed since he may well have planned to go beyond the

[36] Just. *Epit.* XXVIII.3.10; cf. Errington 1978, 93 n. 54: (D 17). Eusebius assigns a reign of twelve years to Antigonus, and Dow and Edson (1937, 172ff.: (D 12)) argue that this arises from his having added Antigonus' three years as *strategos* to nine years' reign as a whole.

[37] *I. Priene* 37, ll. 136ff.

[38] Polyb. v.90.1; cf. Walbank 1957, I.621–2; 1967, II.645; 1979, III.70–1: (B 37), for references, especially Crampa 1969: (B 60).

conquest of Caria, but have jettisoned these schemes once he was confronted with the prospect of an alternative line of advance in southern Greece.

The start of the Carian expedition was marked by a curious incident. On its way south from Demetrias through the Euripus Antigonus' fleet ran aground on the frontier of Boeotia, near Larymna in Opuntian Locris. It was a politically delicate region since Antigonus had only recently acquired this part of Locris when Boeotia broke with Macedonia (above, p. 455); and some hostile action on Antigonus' part (perhaps in Larymna, though the details escape us) was intended and may indeed have been expected, since the Boeotian cavalry was in the neighbourhood. Neon, its commander, decided however not to take advantage of Antigonus' plight and the king was able to refloat his ships and continue his voyage to Asia. Neon's family later appear as warm supporters of the Antigonid house; but the incident illustrates the hostility towards Macedonia prevalent at this time in Boeotia.

The Carian expedition remains a curious and apparently irrelevant incident in Antigonus' reign. Apart from this his activities are divided between the northern frontier and southern Greece. That he undertook it at least indicates that Illyria and Epirus were not among his serious preoccupations. It had little aftermath beyond an overseas possession in Caria which did not remain very long in Macedonian hands, though the recent memory of its possession may have been one factor in Philip's invasion of that region in 201. Antigonus' sudden loss of interest in Caria is probably to be attributed to the arrival in Pella of emissaries from Megalopolis.

V. THE ACHAEAN APPROACH TO MACEDONIA

It was towards the end of 227 that Nicophanes and Cercidas of Megalopolis, the city most at risk from Cleomenes' sudden accession of military strength, obtained permission to go as envoys to Antigonus to sound him about the sending of help from Macedonia. Such a move was facilitated by the death of Lydiades, whose earlier desertion of the Macedonian cause might have made an approach to Antigonus difficult. Polybius and Phylarchus both recorded the sending of this embassy and were in agreement that Aratus, who had family ties with the two Megalopolitans, was himself behind it; indeed Polybius regards it as a crafty measure taken to outwit his enemies.[39] Aratus on the other hand explained his eventual calling in of Antigonus (at the end of 225) as a desperate step to preserve Achaea when all else had failed; and the Megalopolitan embassy, or at least his own part in it, seems to be one of

[39] Polyb. 11.48.

those things which, according to Polybius, Aratus did not mention in his *Memoirs*.[40] Polybius' account, which he derived from an oral tradition at Megalopolis rather than from Phylarchus,[41] presents some difficulties. It does not explain very clearly whether Nicophanes and Cercidas went to Pella as Megalopolitan or as Achaean envoys. Furthermore it describes the danger which led Aratus to encourage this approach to Antigonus as that of a triple alliance of Macedonia, Aetolia and Sparta, and in the envoys' speech to Antigonus, as recorded in Polybius, the emphasis is laid entirely on the threat to Achaea should Aetolia and Cleomenes join arms against her; against Cleomenes alone they could hold out.

The weight which Polybius lays on the danger from Aetolia is largely to be discounted; it is built up of vague accusations and apprehensions and cannot be confirmed from any overt Aetolian act of hostility – indeed at one critical moment the Achaeans appealed to Aetolia for help, and at the time of his coup Cleomenes spoke of the Aetolians as possible enemies.[42] But the agreed opinion of Polybius and Phylarchus that Aratus stood behind the Megalopolitans in their approach to Antigonus must take precedence over Aratus' silence, for his *Memoirs* were written with an apologetic purpose. The move was in fact far-sighted. Aratus was aware that a full-scale war in the Peloponnese must present opportunities to Macedonia and his main aim in making soundings through Nicophanes and Cercidas must have been to ensure that Antigonus did not send help to Cleomenes. The Megalopolitans had therefore two objects. Openly they were concerned to secure for Megalopolis immediate assistance of such limited kind as would not by Greek custom involve Macedonia in a state of belligerency against Sparta;[43] but secretly Antigonus was to be asked if he would agree to provide major intervention should the war develop in such a way as to make this necessary.

Antigonus was a realist. By giving such a promise he had everything to gain and nothing to lose. The envoys received an open letter promising the help they asked for, provided the Achaeans consented to their receiving it; and, secretly, Aratus was sent assurances on the more important issue. Upon the return of the envoys the Megalopolitans were all for calling on the proffered aid at once, but to safeguard his own reputation Aratus, who now knew where he stood, persuaded the Achaean assembly to postpone any appeal to outside powers and for the time being to carry on the war alone.

[40] Plut. *Arat.* 38.11–12; Polyb. 11.47.11.
[41] Urban 1979, 126ff.: (D 117); Pédech 1964, 160: (B 26); against Gruen 1972, 609–25: (D 59).
[42] Plut. *Arat.* 41.3; *Cleom.* 10.5.
[43] Cf. Bikerman 1943, 287–304: (D 47) on the so-called *epimachia*, the right of a state to send help to the victim of an attack without itself becoming a belligerent.

VI. THE ACHAEAN DISINTEGRATION

In deciding on his answer to Aratus' secret appeal Antigonus was no doubt influenced in part by his assessment of the military capacity of the Achaean League to hold out alone. The events of the next two years fully justified his decision, for in that space of time the League was brought to a point of virtual collapse.

Early in 226 Aratus ended his tenth *strategia* (227/6) with a victory over a Spartan force at Orchomenus, taking prisoner Megistonous, Cleomenes' step-father (he was later ransomed); but more significant perhaps was a demonstration by Cleomenes, who led his newly-trained forces against Megalopolis, ravaged its territory and held theatrical performances on Megalopolitan territory as a mark of his contempt for both the city and the League. Early in the generalship of Hyperbatas (226/5) Cleomenes marched on Mantinea by night and seized the city, helped by a pro-Spartan party within; the Achaean mercenary garrison was expelled and the Achaean settlers were put to death. Thence, after a brief visit to Tegea, Cleomenes set out on a new offensive directed against the oldest cities of Achaea, his object being to disrupt the league and attract the support of Elis, whose 5,000 hoplites could be an invaluable supplement to his own forces. At the Hecatombaeum near Dyme Hyperbatas challenged him to battle but the result was a resounding victory for Cleomenes, who seized the border fortress of Lasion and handed it over to Elis. At this point the two sides entered into negotiations, a truce was arranged and, evidently under pressure from a peace party in Achaea, Cleomenes was invited to a conference to discuss the question of hegemony (winter 226/5).

What hegemony meant is not entirely clear. In all likelihood the Achaeans envisaged something like the position enjoyed by Ptolemy III (and later by Antigonus Doson), that is the office of *hegemon* held by a prominent figure outside the League rather than a permanent general-ship held within it, an innovation which would have transformed the federal constitution. But Cleomenes was seized with a haemorrhage which caused a postponement of the conference, and Aratus was thus able to work secretly against the envisaged settlement; and when the elections for the generalship of 225/4 approached, Aratus stood down in favour of a supporter, Timoxenus. His reasons are not recorded. Seeing the league torn between pro- and anti-Spartan factions he perhaps hoped to evade the responsibility of office; but more probably he wanted to be free of routine business in order to follow up his earlier negotiations with Antigonus. Macedonian help now seemed the only alternative to capitulating to Cleomenes and a direct appeal to Antigonus was essential, not only as a result of the Spartan victories, but also because Aratus had learnt that Ptolemy III, evidently persuaded that money paid to a disintegrating Achaea would henceforth be wasted, had transferred his subsidies to Sparta,[44] probably upon hearing of the Megalopolitan embassy to Pella. There is also evidence of close relations between Ptolemy and the Aetolian League at this time, when Lamius, an Aetolian, set up a line of statues representing the royal family of Egypt at Delphi under Ptolemy Euergetes, though it cannot be assumed that Ptolemy's move towards Cleomenes was accompanied by any formal arrangement with Aetolia.[45]

The postponed conference with Cleomenes was reconvened in the summer of 225 at Argos, but at once broke down over the conditions which Aratus sought to impose. The details are variously reported. According to one version Cleomenes was required to bring only 300 men to the meeting, and was offered Achaean hostages if he was distrustful of Aratus, but according to another he was to receive 300 Achaean hostages and enter Argos alone, or alternatively the conference would be held outside at the Cyllarabium gymnasium.[46] Whatever the precise details, there can be little doubt that Aratus was determined at all cost to prevent control of the League passing into the hands of Cleomenes, and had not sufficient confidence in his ability to direct the Achaean decision in the way he wanted, if the meeting took place. On his side Cleomenes was not so committed to attaining his end by peaceful means to be willing to make the concession demanded; he no doubt by now had full confidence in his troops and in his own ability as a general. Presumably he did not yet know of the negotiations with Antigonus.

Had it not been for that, his assessment was correct, for the breakdown of negotiations at Argos was speedily followed by the disintegration of the Achaean League. This cannot be explained solely in terms of Spartan military superiority. It is clear that the confederation was rent by internal divisions, in which Aratus was opposed by several groups. These included his personal opponents – and he must have had many throughout the cities of Achaea – and those who had hitherto supported him but who, as the approach to Macedonia became known, refused to follow him into the Macedonian camp. There were also those who positively supported Cleomenes, either through ancient ties with Sparta or as an exponent of radical social change, which some, quite

[44] Hackens 1968, 69–96: (B 226) suggests that Ptolemaic bronze coins from this period found in the Peloponnese represent subsidies to Cleomenes III. A dedication made on behalf of Cleomenes by Ptolemy III at Olympia (*I. Olympia* 309) evidently dates to this time.

[45] Cf. Flacelière 1937, 268 n. 3: (D 105). A monument erected at Thermum honouring Ptolemy III and his family may belong to this period or, more probably, during or just after the reign of Demetrius II (*IG* IX².1.1.56=*ISE* II.86); see Huss 1976, 105 n. 7: (F 133); 1975, 312–20: (F 267); Will 1979, 1.378: (A 67).   [46] Plut. *Arat.* 39.2; *Cleom.* 17.1.

mistakenly, expected to see introduced in the cities of the League. Amid the clamour of these different voices it is not surprising that so many cities failed to offer effective resistance when Cleomenes approached.

No sooner was the conference cancelled than Cleomenes marched over the mountains to seize Pellene, Pheneus and the adjacent citadel of Penteleium; and Caphyae too went over. These acquisitions brought Cleomenes to the Corinthian Gulf, splitting the Achaean League into two parts – Arcadia and the older Achaean cities to the west and to the east the larger cities of Sicyon, Corinth, Megara and Argos with the Argolid. Internal divisions began to surface, but at an assembly Aratus was still sufficiently in command to get himself appointed general with supreme powers (*strategos autokrator*) and provided with a Sicyonian bodyguard. By virtue of this office he was invested with special judicial authority to investigate alleged cases of disaffection in Sicyon and Corinth.[47]

Aratus had put down the trouble at Sicyon and was already in Corinth when news arrived that Cleomenes, defying the sacred truce, had taken advantage of the Nemean games and the fact that Argos was crowded with visitors to enter the city by night. The later treatment of Aristomachus by the Achaeans suggests that he was involved in the secession. This news rendered Aratus' position at Corinth untenable and he managed to escape with his bodyguard to Sicyon, leaving the Corinthians to summon Cleomenes, who came by way of Hermione, Troezen and Epidaurus, taking over these cities en route; since his seizure of Argos he had already captured Phlius and Cleonae. Before occupying Corinth he made one further attempt to reach an agreement with Aratus, but to no purpose; nor had he any greater success with a second offer sent after he had entered Corinth and was investing the citadel. He therefore surrounded Sicyon and held Aratus virtually imprisoned in his own city for three months. At the end of this time – it was probably about April 224[48] – Aratus escaped to attend a meeting of the Achaeans at Aegium.

Already in the summer of 225 the Achaeans had been persuaded to despatch an embassy, including Aratus' son of the same name, to Pella to ascertain Antigonus' terms for immediate help.[49] The situation foreseen by Aratus in his earlier negotiations through the Megalopolitans had now come about, and it can be assumed that Cleomenes' desperate

---

[47] Plut. *Arat.* 41.1–2. According to Plutarch Aratus was made *strategos autokrator*, general with full powers, after Corinth fell to Cleomenes; but this probably took place earlier and was the basis of the power by virtue of which he carried out his judicial duties in Sicyon and Corinth; see Walbank 1957, II.252: (B 37).

[48] Will 1979, I.386: (A 67) dates this meeting late in 225; on the chronology see below, n. 54.

[49] Polyb. II.51.5; the decision had probably followed further (secret?) negotiations between Aratus and Antigonus since the battle of Hecatombaeum.

efforts to persuade Aratus to come to terms were made in the knowledge that this emba ;sy had been sent to Pella. At the meeting now called to Aegium Ant zonus' terms were announced – the surrender of Achaean hostages and the handing over of Acrocorinth. By this time the Achaeans had explored all alternatives, including an appeal to Athens and even Aetolia,[50] but with no success; they had therefore no alternative but to acquiesce, and the younger Aratus therefore returned to Pella, this time as one of the hostages.[51] Already, it seems, Antigonus had anticipated the answer and was on his way south with an army of 20,000 infantry and 1,300 cavalry.

The decision to call in Macedonian help was violently debated at the time and has been so ever since. It was clearly caused by the weakness of the Achaean League and its inability to resist Cleomenes; but the trouble went deeper. At least part of Cleomenes' support came from those who expected him to apply to the cities of Achaea the principles of social revolution and land-redistribution which had had such remarkable success in Sparta; and this implies considerable discontent among the population of the Achaean towns and countryside. Indeed in a somewhat rhetorical passage (*Cleom.* 16.5) Plutarch asserts that it was to avoid the most dreadful of evils – the abolition of wealth and the restoration of poverty – that Aratus handed over the fortress of Corinth to the Macedonians. The social aspect of the clash should not however be exaggerated. There was indeed at this time a certain amount of theorizing about wealth and poverty in society; the Cynic poet Cercidas, for example, has a good deal to say against the unjust accumulation of landed property.[52] But that did not prevent his going as one of the Megalopolitan envoys to Pella in 227. Cleomenes will hardly have commanded much support based on ideological grounds, though no doubt the poor and landless were attracted, misguidedly, by his reforms at Sparta. More important will have been the positive opposition to Macedonia in cities with a long tradition of Spartan control or more especially in those like Argos whose rulers had consciously abandoned Macedonia for Achaea and therefore saw the Macedonian alignment as fraught with personal danger. Many no doubt were also weary of the war; and, as usual, the smaller cities followed the lead of their larger neighbours. These will have been among the reasons for the Achaean collapse – together with sheer military inadequacy. But in the end it was Aratus' influence that counted. He had already made his decision, preferring a distant overlord to the Spartan king, who would have ousted him from his leadership. For Aratus, if not necessarily for Achaea

---

[50] Plut. *Arat.* 41.2.   [51] Plut. *Arat.* 42.3; *Cleom.* 19.9 (confused).
[52] On Cercidas see Tarn and Griffith 1952, 279: (A 59); D. R. Dudley, *A History of Cynicism from Diogenes to the Sixth Century* A.D. (London 1938) 80; Africa 1961, 20: (D 118); Gabba 1957, 19: (B 13).

and Greece, it was a prudent choice and was to result in his continued domination in Achaea almost without interruption until his death.

On learning of the Achaean decision, which of course completely changed the military balance of forces, Cleomenes abandoned his siege of Sicyon to take up a defensive position at the Isthmus, with his lines running over Mt Oneium and including the defences of Corinth and the walls of Lechaeum; the gap between Oneium and the Acrocorinth was secured by a palisade and trench. Meanwhile Antigonus, who had followed the usual Macedonian route south through Euboea to avoid any clash with Aetolia, met Aratus at Pagae and good personal relations were quickly established between the two men. Among various provisions made was the transfer of Megara – now cut off from the rest of Achaea by Cleomenes' lines at Corinth – to Boeotia,[53] probably under pressure from Antigonus, but apparently with Achaean consent; there was probably little choice.

Cleomenes held a strong defensive line and the Macedonians failed to pierce it. Faced with a problem of supplies Antigonus tried to outflank Cleomenes' system by night at Lechaeum, but without success, and eventually he had to envisage marching to Heraeum (mod. Perachora) and ferrying his army over to Sicyon. But at that moment fortune intervened to produce what was perhaps the decisive event of the war: led by one Aristoteles, Argos revolted from Cleomenes. Aratus sailed at once with 1,500 men to Epidaurus, but already Aristoteles had risen and attacked the citadel, helped very soon by Achaean troops sent from Sicyon under Timoxenus. Megistonous was despatched with a relief force but was killed, and Cleomenes, fearing for Sparta, now that there was a hostile army in his rear capable of occupying the passes south, abandoned his lines – and Corinth – and marching south tried to win back Argos. But Antigonus pursued him and he had no alternative but to retreat to Sparta.[54]

VII. CLEOMENES' DEFEAT. THE HELLENIC LEAGUE. THE DEATH OF ANTIGONUS DOSON

The collapse of Cleomenes' power was as sudden and as striking as that of Achaea had been the previous summer, yet it is not at all inexplicable. The defection of Argos typifies his dilemma. Until he was actually in

[53] Polyb. xx.6.7.

[54] The chronology is uncertain. Polyb. 11.53.2 says that when Timoxenus brought Achaean troops to assist at Argos he was general (μετὰ Τιμοξένου τοῦ στρατηγοῦ). Since Timoxenus' *strategia* was in 225/4, this implies that Argos revolted before May 224 and that Timoxenus had kept his office despite Aratus' appointment as *strategos autokrator*. But this chronology leaves 224 almost devoid of events after the recovery of Argos. An alternative is to assume that Timoxenus was

power he could make his appeal to many different elements in the population; but once in control he must either satisfy or disappoint the expectations he had aroused. Plutarch (*Cleom*. 20.6) mentions the disillusionment felt at Argos at Cleomenes' failure to cancel debts; but any step in that direction would have lost him the support of the rich, many of whom looked to him not as a social reformer but as an alternative to Aratus and the Macedonians. In any case, he was hardly likely to adopt measures calculated to strengthen a city which, with a slight change of fortune, might become a rival to Sparta.

Before marching over to Argus Antigonus had already brought Acrocorinth under his control; and Cleomenes' other cities quickly surrendered to him. At Argos Aristomachus was taken prisoner and paid for his vacillation with death, being drowned in the sea off Cenchreae; there was also a massacre of his supporters, once Antigonus had left.[55] Without much delay he had gone on into Arcadia, where he annexed the Athenaeum and along with Aegytis presented it to Megalopolis, no doubt seeking to build on that city's goodwill and on its ancient ties with the Macedonian royal house. After that he returned to Aegium where, probably at the autumn meeting of 224, he was elected *hegemon*, or commander-in-chief, of all the allied forces. It may have been on this occasion too that the Achaeans passed a law enjoining the magistrates to summon an assembly whenever they were required to do so by the king of Macedonia. Antigonus then went into winter quarters in the neighbourhood of Corinth and Sicyon.

It was probably at this meeting at Aegium that Antigonus also elaborated his plans for a new Hellenic alliance, the *symmachia*, envisaged as a League of Leagues (not cities) which would be the instrument to crush Sparta, but (as soon became clear) would have great potential as a union of states opposed to Aetolia. Whether Antigonus had thought this out in the time between the original Achaean approach and the invitation to march south is unknown. It is at least possible that Aratus had some part in the planning of an organization so well designed to favour Achaean interests.

The original membership of the Symmachy consisted of the Achaeans, Macedonians, Thessalians, Epirotes, Acarnanians, Boeotians and Phocians. The Macedonians were perhaps only nominally members.[56] A dedication made to Apollo on Delos after the battle of Sellasia

holding a *de facto* command during the absence with Antigonus on the other side of Cleomenes' lines of Aratus, the general for 224/3. The recovery of Argos then occurs after May 224; and indeed the account of Antigonus' desperation (Plut. *Cleom*. 20) suggests that the kings confronted each other for some time at the Isthmus. This second chronology has been followed above; it implies that the meeting at Aegium (above, n. 48) was the Achaean spring *synodos* of 224.   [55] Polyb. v.16.6.

[56] See Polyb. 11.54.4; IV.9.4, 15.1; XI.5.4; Livy XXIX.12.14; *SVA* 507. Polyb. XI.5.4 includes the Euboeans and Opuntian Locrians, but in a speech by a Rhodian ambassador which extends the

(*SIG* 518) by 'King Antigonus and [the Macedonians] and the allies' (see above, Ch. 7, p. 226) suggests that there was a distinction between the Macedonians and the other allies, and this indeed was to be expected for, despite their occasional independent role, the Macedonians could hardly function in the decision-taking except through their king. The same was true of the Thessalians; but both people will have exercised a convenient vote in the *synedrion*, or council, of the Symmachy, which was summoned by the king of Macedonia in his capacity as commander-in-chief or president (*hegemon*) and had the power to decide questions of war and peace, the voting of supplies and the admission of new members. The Symmachy possessed no separate treasury for it was an alliance, not a super-state. All decisions were subject to ratification by the executive bodies of the separate leagues, which thus maintained a considerable measure of political independence. The resolution founding the Symmachy may have guaranteed the freedom and autonomy of the member-states, but this is not recorded. The Symmachy was a loose organization which though useful could not by itself give the king of Macedonia the full power and authority which he sought in central and southern Greece. That could only be secured as before by garrisoning chosen strong points, of which the Acrocorinth was the chief. The Symmachy however provided Antigonus and later Philip with a means of harnessing goodwill and securing collaboration; it could also be exploited to the advantage of its members.

The inclusion of Acarnania, Epirus and Phocis in the alliance brought together under the aegis of Macedonia a group of states all potentially hostile to Aetolia; but whether the alignment of Acarnania and Epirus with Antigonus also had implications for the Macedonian attitude towards Rome, whether in fact the creation of the Symmachy is to be regarded as in any way directed against Rome, is another matter. The main evidence adduced as pointing towards such a purpose is the presence of Demetrius of Pharos in Antigonus' entourage in 223 and at the battle of Sellasia in 222; and according to Appian (*Illyr.* 8) it was at this time, when the Romans were occupied with the Gallic wars (225–222), that Demetrius first broke his treaty commitments by sailing south of Lissus and engaging in piracy. This was all no doubt noted by the Romans. But that is not to say that Antigonus, by enrolling Demetrius as his ally, was consciously planning future hostilities against Rome. There is on the contrary no evidence at all that Antigonus was interested in Rome at this time. Events since his accession had given him little opportunity to concern himself with the Illyrian coast, and the

notion of allies for a rhetorical purpose. The Euboeans were in fact directly under Macedonia and Opuntian Locris under Macedonia or Boeotia; neither figures in the list of members in Polyb. IV.9.4. See Picard 1979, 274: (B 252).

Carian expedition suggests that without the unforeseen opportunities provided by the Achaean collapse his ambitions would have developed in quite another direction. The situation after the Second Illyrian War and Demetrius' defeat and expulsion from his kingdom was of course very different (see below, p. 478); and by then another king was sitting on the Macedonian throne.

On his return to Sparta Cleomenes sent an urgent appeal for aid to Ptolemy. His only hope of standing up to the combined forces ranged against him lay in hiring mercenaries, and for this Egyptian money was essential. Ptolemy agreed to help him but only on condition that he sent his mother and children to Alexandria as hostages; his experience with Aratus had rendered him cautious, and indeed he was himself already in secret communication with Antigonus. In spring 223 Cleomenes opened the campaigning season with an unsuccessful attack on Megalopolis, at which Antigonus emerged from winter quarters to seize Tegea and then, deferring his advance into Laconia, returned to take Orchomenus and after it Mantinea. There Achaean vengeance was cruel. The killing of the Achaean settlers when the city went over to Cleomenes in 226 had not been forgotten and Mantinea was now sacked and its population massacred or enslaved. This reversion to the harsher rules of war which had been in abeyance for a century created a shock throughout Greece; and the renaming of Mantinea as Antigoneia was held against Aratus by his opponents. From Mantinea Antigonus advanced into western Arcadia, where he received the surrender of Heraea and Telphusa. Significantly he put Macedonian garrisons in Orchomenus and Heraea,[57] where they were to remain until 199/8, and then sent his Macedonian troops home for the winter. The season's warfare had not been particularly impressive. Antigonus was evidently counting on wearing Cleomenes down or perhaps relying on the outcome of his negotiations with Ptolemy.

If Phylarchus can be believed, Cleomenes now took the desperate step of liberating 6,000 helots capable of paying five minae each for their freedom, thus raising 500 talents and acquiring additional heavy troops, since 2,000 of these were armed in the Macedonian fashion, that is, as phalangites. Though not recorded elsewhere,[58] the story is not impossible, though the possession of five minae by so many helots would imply a considerable development of a money economy in Laconia.[59] But in any case it was an emergency measure and formed no part of Cleomenes' original social programme. The same autumn (223)

[57] Aymard 1938, 25–7 n. 5, 59 n. 53: (D 102) argues that Philip V garrisoned Heraea; against this see Walbank 1940, 17 n. 2: (D 43).   [58] Except in an exaggerated form in Macrob. *Sat.* 1.11.34.
[59] Cf. Oliva 1971, 259–60: (D 132).

Cleomenes seized on the absence of the Macedonian army to surprise and capture Megalopolis; and after he had failed to persuade the population, most of whom escaped to Messenia, to join him, he razed the rival city to the ground and carried off its main contents to Sparta. Early the following spring (222) he led his forces into the Argolid and there he ravaged the countryside up to the walls of Argos, Antigonus' winter quarters, before returning in a side sweep, plundering Arcadia. It was an impressive demonstration, but it had no effect other than to make even more clear that Cleomenes had to be defeated in a pitched battle.

The Macedonian army returned to Greece in the early summer of 222 and in June or July Antigonus advanced into Laconia with forces amounting to nearly 29,000 men, of whom 13,300 were Macedonians; the remaining 14,000 consisted of Galatians, Agrianians and other mercenaries together with troops provided by the allies, among whom the 4,300 Achaeans (including 1,000 Megalopolitans) formed the largest contingent. The mercenaries may have come in part from Crete, where Antigonus had recently made treaties with the cities of Eleutherna and Hierapytna which seem to make provision for the recruitment of Cretan troops.[60] It was a predominantly infantry force, for it contained only 1,200 cavalry in all. Only ten days before the final battle Cleomenes learnt that Ptolemy had suspended all further aid and bade him now make peace with Antigonus.[61] Despite the plunder from Megalopolis, which may have amounted to 300 talents, this news put Cleomenes in a hopeless position in which he must either follow Ptolemy's counsel or fight. The Egyptian volte-face signifies the success of Antigonus' diplomacy. Whether Ptolemy received a *quid pro quo* from Macedonia is not recorded; but one reason for his decision was probably the recent accession of Antiochus III to the Seleucid throne (223) and the successful campaign initiated soon afterwards by Antiochus' general Achaeus against Ptolemy's protégé, Attalus of Pergamum.[62] Asia may well have seemed to demand his attention and his resources; and in any case Cleomenes was now a broken reed. This was shown by his inability to muster more than 20,000 troops, including Spartiates, *perioikoi*, liberated helots, mercenaries and such allies as he still possessed (from the Peloponnesian towns, or even pro-Spartan contingents from pro-Achaean towns). The battle which was to settle the war was fought near Sellasia on the northern borders of Laconia. It was a mainly infantry encounter in which a Macedonian ambush played an important part in dislodging the Lacedaemonian left wing commanded by Cleomenes' brother and fellow-king Eucleidas, but the main decision took place on

[60] *SVA* 501–2. Huss 1976, 139–40: (F 133) attributes these treaties to Antigonus Gonatas.
[61] Polyb. 11.63.1 quoting Phylarchus.   [62] Cf. Will 1979, 1.400: (A 67).

the Lacedaemonian right where, in the clash of the two phalanxes, the superior weight of Macedonian numbers eventually proved decisive.[63] Cleomenes' losses were heavy, including Eucleidas; but he himself escaped with a handful of men to Sparta, and thence to Gytheum, where they embarked for Egypt. Antigonus followed on to take Sparta.

Cleomenes' political reforms were now cancelled and the ephorate was restored; the kingship was in effect left vacant. The fate of the social and economic measures is less certain.[64] The cancellation of debts clearly could not be reversed; but returning exiles probably got back some if not all their land. The heavy casualties at Sellasia will have left many lots ownerless and this may have helped in adjudicating between various claims. It seems on the whole likely that in this field Cleomenes' measures were not wholly abrogated but that some sort of compromise was reached. To solve these and other problems Antigonus appointed the Boeotian Brachylles, the son of Neon (see above, p. 461), as military governor (*epistates*). Whether or no Sparta joined the Symmachy is problematical. The evidence for the question in Polybius is ambiguous;[65] but despite some passages which describe Sparta's relationship to the Symmachy in vague terms, it seems likely that she was accepted as a member, though not immediately. Sparta was penalized territorially, the area of Denthaliatis on the western slopes of Taygetus being now awarded to Messenia.

Soon after reaching Sparta Antigonus was called home by news of an invasion of Macedonia by Illyrian tribes akin to the Dardanians. On his way north he paused at Tegea to make constitutional changes and attended the Nemean games at Argos, which had been postponed from 223 because of the war. In Greece he left Taurion as his representative, probably charged with similar responsibilities towards the new Symmachy to those assigned to Antipater by Alexander in relation to the League of Corinth.[66] Antigonus defeated the Illyrians, but following the strain and excitement of the battle he began vomiting blood and fell into a decline, probably caused by a tubercular infection. He most likely lived into the next year (221)[67] and in the meantime he appointed guardians for the young Philip, Demetrius' son, whom he had always treated as his

[63] See on the battle Polyb. 11.65.1–69.11; Plut. *Cleom.* 28; *Phil.* 6. Plutarch draws on Phylarchus (in *Cleom.*) and on Polybius' *Life of Philopoemen* (in *Phil.*). Polybius used a Megalopolitan source, perhaps Philopoemen himself; see Walbank 1957, 1.272–3: (B 37). On the battle-site see Pritchett 1965, 1.59–70: (A 49), with criticism of earlier reconstructions.

[64] Shimron 1972, 53ff.: (D 140) argues that Cleomenes' social and economic changes were left intact; against this see Oliva 1971, 264–5: (D 132), Walbank in Badian 1966, 303–12: (A 4), and Mendels 1978, 161–6: (D 130).

[65] For references and discussion see Shimron 1972, 66–8: (D 140); Ehrhardt 1975, 265–72: (D 14). Polyb. IV.9.6, 23.6, 24.4 and IX.36.9 seem decisive for Spartan membership.

[66] Cf. Bengtson 1964–7, 11.358: (A 6).

[67] Bengtson 1971, 57: (B 48) dates his death to late in 222; see above, n. 20.

heir, and whom he despatched to the Peloponnese to make the acquaintance of Aratus (and no doubt other leading Achaeans) in preparation for his role as president of the Symmachy.

In his short reign of a little over eight years Antigonus had some remarkable achievements to his credit. By suppressing the Thessalian revolt, expelling the Aetolian and Illyrian invaders and recovering most of the territories they had seized (though not Phthiotic Achaea) he had restored Macedonian morale and consolidated the realm; and by exploiting an opportunity given him through the rise of Cleomenes, he had put Macedonia back in her position of dominance in central Greece and the Peloponnese and had created an organization with some novel features to foster Greek loyalty or at least acquiescence in the new hegemony. But not everything had turned out to the advantage of Macedonia. Athens and Attica were irretrievably lost. The Carian expedition had brought vestigial gains and must be regarded as part of a programme which Antigonus deliberately jettisoned at the prospect of greater gains in an area more vital to Macedonian interests; and since then Macedonian naval strength had been allowed to decline. The Aetolians too, though they had met with some setbacks, were still a threat to the kingdom. Antigonus (and after him Philip) would hardly forget that they had closed Thermopylae to the Macedonian forces in 224. It was no doubt partly with the Aetolians in mind that Antigonus had organized the Symmachy. Meanwhile in Greece his supporters, from conviction or expediency, loaded him with honours. In Achaea Aratus instituted an *Antigoneia* festival in his honour and a similar festival is recorded from Histiaea in Euboea. When Mantinea was refounded as Antigoneia, Aratus acted as *oikistes* and Antigonus as 'founder'; he was also celebrated as 'saviour and benefactor', both at Mantinea and at Sparta. At Olympia the Eleans set up a statue representing Antigonus and Philip, crowned, and at Epidaurus the Epidaurians raised an altar to him.[68] Upon Philip's accession much of this goodwill was inherited by the new king.

VIII. THE SOCIAL WAR

By a coincidence the one hundred and fortieth Olympiad (220–216) – the point selected by Polybius to begin the main narrative of his *Histories* – saw three new rulers on the thrones of the greater Hellenistic kingdoms, in Syria Antiochus III (in 223), in Egypt Ptolemy IV (in 221) and in Macedonia Philip V (in 221); and in 221 Hannibal also succeeded Hasdrubal as the Carthaginian general-in-chief in Spain. It was, as

[68] Cf. Polyb. 11.70.5; v.9.9–10; references in Walbank 1957, 1.290–1: (B 37); add *ISE* 1.46 (Epidaurus); *SEG* XI.1089 (Mantinea); *IG* v.1.1122 (Geronthrae in Laconia).

Polybius recognized, a moment when various separate historical threads were about to become inextricably combined; but for a year or two at least Macedonia and Greece continued to go their own way. Philip was only seventeen. He was to prove intelligent, resilient in every sort of crisis, but quick to anger and perhaps over-ready to be influenced by advisers who were not always wisely chosen. In view of his youth Antigonus had left him a group of guardians, officially his Friends, consisting of Apelles, Leontius, captain of the peltasts, Megaleas, the secretary of state, Taurion, the general over the Peloponnese, and Alexander, the commander of the bodyguard. If these men represented the element of continuity in Macedonian policy, in his relations with Greece the young king looked more readily to Aratus; and it was with Greece that he was to be first concerned and in particular with war against the Aetolian League.

The allied victory at Sellasia had been a source of alarm to the Aetolians, who saw themselves hemmed in by the new Symmachy and their outlying territories under threat from both Macedonia and Achaea. Their economy and their national traditions combined to make raiding for plunder an integral part of their way of life and they naturally resisted the implied constraints. The simplest way to put pressure on Achaea was through her neighbours in Messenia, Elis and Phigalea, until recently Aetolian allies. But already Messenia was controlled by a group favourable to Achaea; and the erection at Olympia of statuary representing Antigonus and Philip by the Eleans could indicate a move towards the Symmachy by that state.[69] So in 221 the Aetolian Dorimachus launched raids into Messenia from a base in Phigalea, where he was present on public business – perhaps the organizing of an alliance to embrace Elis, Messenia and Sparta. The raids on Messenia, besides their obvious use as a source of plunder, were a way of putting pressure on that state. The seizure of a Macedonian ship and the selling of its crew was, however, a typically Aetolian indiscretion and a serious miscalculation.

The next year saw a stepping-up of Aetolian aggression. The raids from Phigalea continued under Dorimachus and Scopas, who marched across Achaea from Rhium; and complaints poured in to Aegium. The outgoing general Timoxenus was reluctant to act, so Aratus assumed office for 220/19 five days early and while attempting to usher the Aetolian freebooters out of the Peloponnese was completely routed at Caphyae. These incidents, though militarily disconcerting, provided excellent material for a diplomatic campaign. The Achaeans had every interest in preventing the war spreading to the other Peloponnesian

[69] Paus. VI.16.3.

states; and it was Aratus' intention to enlist Philip and the Symmachy behind Achaea, preferably by persuading them to attack the Aetolians on their own ground. At the same time the potential enemies near home must if possible be turned into friends and allies. In fact the Messenians were already negotiating to join the Symmachy, and before marching out against Dorimachus and Scopas Aratus had persuaded the Achaean assembly to accept their hostages and to forward their application with approval to the other allies; in the meantime he sponsored the swearing of an alliance between Messenia and Achaea.

The Aetolians replied to these diplomatic moves with a declaration that they proposed to remain at peace with all parties; but for inclusion in this the Achaeans must abrogate their treaty with Messenia. This attempt to isolate Achaea was based on a shrewd suspicion that Philip would be unwilling to be drawn into war; and in fact the allied response to the Messenian application, inspired no doubt from Macedonia, was to accept Messenia as a member of the Symmachy but to remain at peace with Aetolia. At this point the Aetolians, whose diplomacy was usually clumsy and badly co-ordinated, made a serious mistake. The two Illyrian princes, Scerdilaidas and Demetrius of Pharos, had sailed south of Lissus in defiance of the terms of the treaty made with Teuta, and joined in a plundering expedition on the Messenian coast; they had then split up, Demetrius going on to pursue his piratical activities in the Aegean while Scerdilaidas now joined a prominent Aetolian, Agelaus, in a raid on the Arcadian city of Cynaetha, which was rent between pro-Achaean and pro-Aetolian factions, though at this time held by Achaea. The inhabitants, whatever their political complexion, were massacred and the city burnt. The incident could hardly be ignored when shortly afterwards Philip and the allied representatives assembled at Corinth to hear complaint after complaint of Aetolian outrages against various cities and temples in all parts of Greece.

The Aetolians had thus played into Aratus' hands. It was unanimously resolved to make war on Aetolia, and the better to encourage this policy a series of war-aims were now sketched out. The allies pledged themselves to recover all cities and territories occupied by the Aetolians since the death of Demetrius II, to restore their traditional forms of government to all states thus coerced and finally to free Delphi and the Amphictyonic Council from the Aetolian yoke. Aratus, it must be assumed, had shown considerable dexterity in pressing for what was primarily an Achaean war. The marshalling of complaints had been well organized; and there was sufficient in the list of war aims to win over Philip and his advisers, for the expulsion of the Aetolians from Phthiotic Achaea and the transfer of control over the Amphictyony from Aetolia to Macedonia (for this was surely implied) would amount to substantial gains. Philip was not content, however, to function simply as the *hegemon* of the Symmachy. In anticipation of fighting in the south he took steps to strengthen his northern frontiers and, conveniently ignoring the outrage at Cynaetha, he boldly arranged a meeting with Scerdilaidas and bought the support of the pliant Illyrian for twenty talents. A little earlier Taurion had made an agreement with Demetrius of Pharos, who had reached Corinth in flight before the Rhodians, to give help against the Aetolians in the Corinthian Gulf; but little had come of this. Philip also welcomed an approach from Crete. There the rival cities of Cnossus and Gortyn, in an unusual alliance, had attempted to enforce their joint hegemony on the whole island and had been successful in destroying the city of Lyttus, their main opponent. Now the group of cities allied to Lyttus sent a request for help from Macedonia and Achaea. Philip had them admitted, presumably as a league, into the Symmachy, and Illyrian, Achaean and Phocian troops were sent to their assistance. The help was not all on one side, however. If a dedication by Cretan soldiers found at Hermione in the Argolid (*SEG* xi.380) belongs to the Social War, the Achaeans in turn recruited mercenaries from Crete.

The declaration of war was a success for Aratus; but before the campaign of 219 could open he suffered a serious setback in the Peloponnese. There Sparta was inclining strongly towards Aetolia. Even before the meeting at Corinth Philip had visited the city and administered a reproof and fresh oaths following a clash within the ephorate and the assassination of some supporters of Achaea. But in spring 219 the arrival at Sparta of the news that Cleomenes had died leading a futile revolt in Alexandria precipitated a revolution; the ephors were assassinated and Lycurgus and Agesipolis made kings; and an alliance was contracted with Aetolia. The Spartan example was enough to persuade Elis to adopt the same course; and Messenia, despite its application to join the Symmachy, remained deeply split and failed to ratify the declaration of war on Aetolia. Thus the alignment of forces in the Peloponnese in the spring of 219 was very much what it had been during the Cleomenean War; it was a situation that could bring little comfort to Achaea.

The general pattern of fighting in 219 was also of small help to Achaea; for while the League cities found themselves under attack from three directions, Philip opted to campaign in the north-west, in Epirus and Acarnania. The details may be considered briefly. From Sparta Lycurgus attacked the Argive towns east of Parnon and seized the Athenaeum, while the Aetolians attacked Aegeira from across the Corinthian Gulf and the cities of western Achaea from Elis. This pressure was so effective that the cities of Dyme, Pharae and Tritaea, which had perhaps from early times been accustomed to form a separate grouping (*synteleia*) within the League, decided to withhold their taxes and use them to hire their own private mercenaries. Philip meanwhile remained in Epirus. His hesitation to come further south and to attack Aetolia directly was probably caused to some extent by events in Illyria, where the Romans had sent two consular armies to punish Demetrius of Pharos for sailing south of Lissus. Understandably Philip was reluctant to move south while forces on this scale were operating in Illyria and the Adriatic; but with an army containing 16,000 Macedonians, the Epirote levy, and Cretan and Achaean light-armed troops, he attacked and after a siege captured Ambracus (which he presented to Epirus) before advancing to take various Aetolian frontier towns, ravage the area around Stratus and seize and fortify Oeniadae at the mouth of the Achelous. He was then recalled to Pella by a threatened Dardanian invasion, which never in fact took place, and from there marched south to winter at Larissa in Thessaly. Besides their raids in the Peloponnese the Aetolians attacked Dium in southern Macedonia and Dodona in Epirus; both possessed temples containing valuable plunder, and this as much as the effect on enemy morale shaped Aetolian policy in planning these attacks.[70]

The campaign of 219 had placed a strain on Achaea and it was to bring some relief there that Philip undertook an unexpected campaign in the winter of 219/18. Around the time of the winter solstice he appeared with 6,000 men at Corinth and, after defeating an Aetolian raiding party near Stymphalus, marched on to a rendezvous with the Achaean army at Caphyae. He first seized the strong fortress of Psophis on the Erymanthus and then penetrated southern Elis and Triphylia, which he conquered in a lightning campaign lasting six days. The rich plain of Elis furnished much booty to replenish his war-chest. The Achaeans received Psophis but Triphylia was placed under a Macedonian *epimeletes*, Ladicus of Acarnania, and its towns were garrisoned. This resumption of Antigonus III's policy, as exemplified in his occupation of Orchomenus and Heraea, may reflect the pressure of his Macedonian advisers against the policy of Aratus, whose influence now fell into eclipse.

The acquisition of Triphylia was a positive gain for Philip; but he and probably even more his counsellors were aware of the expense of campaigning to save the Achaeans from the penalty of their military weakness. Apelles aimed at forcing Achaea into a position of dependence and to that end used the rest of the winter, which Philip spent at Argos, cultivating Aratus' enemies and pressing them upon Philip's notice. Recognizing the threat, Aratus declined to stand for the

[70] The booty may have gone towards minting the silver tetradrachms issued by the Aetolian League, if these indeed date to the Social War; cf. de Laix 1973, 47–75: (B 235).

generalship of 218/17 (as he had done in 225) and let Timoxenus go forward in his place. But Philip arranged to be at Aegium during the election and this was a factor in the success of Eperatus of Pharae, the candidate of the western cities which harboured many of Aratus' opponents; once this coup had been engineered, Philip carried out a swift and rewarding campaign in Elis on behalf of these very cities. He soon discovered, however, that the new general commanded no solid support and Aratus, as a private citizen, once more emerged as the one man able to speak for Achaea. It was therefore with Aratus that Philip made an important agreement.[71]

This was a financial arrangement by which Philip was to receive compensation in pay and corn for the whole of any period during which he campaigned in the Peloponnese. Though costly to the Achaeans, it carried political implications which were welcome, since it was tantamount to an acknowledgement that the Peloponnese was an Achaean sphere of interest and to that extent a defence against Apelles' campaign to undermine Achaean independence; but it meant that Aratus would now think twice before soliciting Macedonian aid. For this financial agreement Philip had special reasons which he now disclosed to his Friends. He had decided on a new policy which would eat up all the money he could lay hands on, namely the resuscitation of the fleet, which had been allowed to decay since 227, and its exploitation to effect rapid movement across the Corinthian Gulf, to strengthen Macedonian influence in Epirus and Acarnania and to cut the communications of the enemy in Sparta, Elis and Aetolia. The origins of this plan are uncertain: perhaps Philip had been struck by the potentialities of Oeniadae when he decided to fortify it the previous summer. The campaign of 219 had opened up a western coast route through Epirus, western Ambracia and Acarnania; to carry that route through to the Peloponnese he needed a port and a navy. He now had the one and was determined to acquire the other.

There was, however, another element in Philip's decision, the influence of a new figure at Philip's court. After his defeat by the Romans in summer 219 Demetrius of Pharos had fled to Philip and was henceforth to play a prominent part in his counsels. A naval policy was not in itself anti-Roman, nor is there any reason to suppose that Philip saw it in that light; but it indicates an interest in western waters which, when translated into action, must necessarily attract the attention of the Romans, who will in any case have noted with displeasure the asylum

---

[71] Polyb. v.1.10–11; the text is ambiguous and may mean that Philip was now compensated retrospectively for the winter campaign of 219/18 or that payments were reckoned from the time of the agreement onwards, depending on how one translates the phrase εἰς τὴν πρώτην ἀναζυγήν. See Walbank 1957, I.538–9: (B 37).

granted to Demetrius. Thus Philip's new policy had in it the seeds of a clash with Rome – as Demetrius was no doubt well aware.

Philip saw his fleet as a contribution to mobility, not as a fighting force. No new ships were built but several old Macedonian and Achaean craft were assembled and put into commission at Patrae in June 218. The first operation, an assault on Cephallenia, was a fiasco; but it was followed by a far more effective campaign, which illustrates Philip's rapid growth and maturity as a tactician and a general. Landing at Limnaea he invaded the heart of Aetolia as far as Thermum, and in revenge for the plundering of Dium and Dodona, devastated the sacred buildings and colonnades. This demonstration, remarkable for its precision, speed and ruthlessness, was followed by an equally impressive move against Sparta. Fourteen days after leaving Thermum Philip and his army were standing on the hills overlooking Sparta to the east; he had sailed round to Corinth and sent out mobilization orders to the Peloponnesians, and with an army of 10,000 he ravaged the Laconian plain as far as Taenarum and Malea. The Spartans, perhaps weakened by an abortive rising by one Cheilon the previous winter, offered no effective resistance, and Philip withdrew unharmed to sell his booty at Tegea.

During this summer (218) Philip rid himself of his now unwanted council of guardians. According to Polybius, their opposition to his naval policy had developed into sabotage and high treason, but his picture is undoubtedly coloured by their hostility to Aratus, which is made to occupy the centre of the picture. Soon after the invasion of Aetolia Megaleas and a friend Crinon had been arrested for their defiance of Philip following an after-dinner brawl in which they had stoned Aratus. It was the culminating episode in a series of obstructive actions by Megaleas and Leontius who were, according to Polybius, in a conspiracy with Apelles to sabotage the naval policy. Megaleas was fined and released on bail provided by Leontius, Apelles meanwhile had gone to Chalcis, where he had used his authority to hold up supplies from that base. Upon his returning to court and receiving a cold reception, his instrument, Megaleas, took fright and fled to Athens and, having been rebuffed, from there to Thebes.

At this point Philip made an expedition to Phocis, taking Apelles with him. The purpose of this is obscure, but he may have been scheming to tighten Macedonian control over this state, perhaps partly with a view to developing more direct communications with the new naval base at Corinth via Elatea. The project, whatever it was, proved unsuccessful; but by the next year Phocis was directly under a Macedonian commander and was to remain so until 198.[72]

[72] Polyb. v.96.4–8; x.42.2, 42.7; cf. Paus. x.34.3.

On his return to Sicyon Philip sent Apelles to Corinth and dispatched Leontius' troops to Triphylia. Leontius, who had earlier tried to lead the peltasts and the crack regiment, the *agema*, to mutiny, was now arrested to meet Megaleas' bail and despite appeals by the army he was executed. Shortly after this, alleging new evidence of Megaleas' treachery which had turned up in a letter from Phocis, Philip also executed Apelles and his son. Megaleas forestalled a similar fate by suicide. This story contains much that is unsatisfactory. How far was there really a conspiracy? The Phocian letters alleging complicity with Aetolia may have been forged to answer any opposition from the army; or Megaleas may have sought to stiffen Aetolian resistance so as to tempt Philip back into the Peloponnese to the detriment of Achaea; or finally long-rankling jealousy of Aratus and fear of losing their hold on Philip may have turned Antigonus' trusted counsellors into traitors. But Polybius' account obscures the fact that Demetrius, not Aratus, benefited from the elimination of the older men. Meanwhile peace negotiations initiated by the Rhodians and Chiotes came to nothing. The Aetolians postponed the conference and Philip, who was clearly not anxious for peace, withdrew from participation. The year ended indecisively. The Aetolians had raided Thessaly, and Messenia, having at last come down firmly on the allied side, had been attacked from Sparta. But there was no immediate prospect of an end to the war.

In the winter of 218/17 an Elean invasion of western Achaea once again demonstrated the military weakness of the League, and faced with the renewed threat of disintegration Aratus, elected general for 217/16, carried through measures to establish a mercenary force of 8,000 foot and 500 horse and an élite corps of citizens amounting to 3,000 foot and 300 horse, of whom 500 foot and 50 horse each were to be furnished by Argos and Megalopolis; and three ships were to cruise off the Argolid and three in the Corinthian Gulf. This reorganization brought a few successes but not enough to break a stalemate punctuated with minor raids, especially on the front between Aetolia, Epirus and Acarnania. Philip's own interest seemed to have reverted to Macedonia. In a campaign up the Axius he completed Antigonus' work by seizing Bylazora (modern Titov Veles) in Paeonia, and from there moved against Phthiotic Achaea. There he failed to take Melitaea but after a fifteen-day siege and assault he captured Phthiotic Thebes, enslaved its population and resettled it with Macedonians. Only the report that the turncoat Scerdilaidas had seized four Macedonian ships hindered his conclusion of the conquest of Phthiotic Achaea. Setting off in pursuit of the Illyrian he dragged his light ships over the Isthmus of Corinth and sent a handful of decked ships round the Peloponnese for action against him and, no doubt, the Aetolians; but on the way west he turned aside to Argos for the Nemean games.

It was at these games that Philip received a report which led him to a sudden and complete change of policy. Hannibal, he learnt from a message forwarded from Macedonia, had just won a sensational victory over the Romans at Lake Trasimene (June 217). Clearly Philip had arranged to be well posted on developments in the Hannibalic War. At first, Polybius records, he showed the message only to his new adviser,[73] Demetrius, who at once urged him to end the Aetolian war and concentrate on the reduction of Illyria; he might then hope to invade Italy – and in due course conquer the world. These inflated prospects were welcome to the young man, already tiring of the indecisive war with Aetolia and her allies. He quickly made contact with the Aetolians, but at the same time seized Zacynthos, which was likely to be useful in any western policy. A conference was called to Naupactus and it was here that Agelaus from the Aetolian side made a famous speech[74] calling upon the Greeks to compose their differences before the 'cloud in the west' settled over Greece and advising Philip to adopt a policy of defensive alertness; the clear implication was that he should not plunge into a war against Rome.

Peace was now made on the basis of the *status quo*. The war had brought the Symmachy few gains. The Epirotes and Acarnanians had had some advantage and Achaea had acquired Psophis and Phigalea. But the sanguine and ambitious programme of 220 had been abandoned and Delphi remained under Aetolian control. Philip had come out of it best with the acquisition of Triphylia, Phthiotic Achaea and Zacynthos, with garrisons in Orchomenus and Heraea, and with Phocis under a Macedonian commander, as Euboea had been since Antigonus' reign; all this gave him a firmer control over Greece and Thessaly. To the north he now held Bylazora controlling Paeonia; and across the sea he was recognized as president (*prostates*) throughout much of Crete, and through his representative Olympichus still exercised authority in parts of Caria. His personal prestige was high; the inscription beneath his statue at Epidaurus hailed him as 'the glorious leader of the Greeks' and Polybius likewise calls him 'the darling of the Greeks' at this time.[75] In Macedonia he had rid himself of Antigonus' counsellors nor did he depend any longer on the advice of Aratus. His apprenticeship was over and he was ready to lead his country onto the larger stage where Rome and Carthage were already locked in conflict. The consequences were to be disastrous for Greece and ultimately for his own kingdom and dynasty.

[73] Polyb. v.101.7.
[74] Polyb. v.104; its authenticity has been questioned, but unnecessarily (cf. Walbank 1979, III.774: (B 37) for references).
[75] Polyb. VII.11.8; *ISE* 1.47.

HELLENISTIC DYNASTIES

1. THE PTOLEMIES

Ptolemy I Soter	305–283
Ptolemy II Philadelphus	283–246
Ptolemy III Euergetes I	246–221
Ptolemy IV Philopator	221–204
Ptolemy V Epiphanes	204–180
Ptolemy VI Philometor	180–145
with Ptolemy VIII Euergetes II and	
Cleopatra II	170–164
with Cleopatra II	163–145
Ptolemy VIII Euergetes II (restored)	145–116
Cleopatra III and Ptolemy IX Soter II	
(Lathyrus)	116–107
Cleopatra III and Ptolemy X Alexander I	107–101
Ptolemy X Alexander I and Cleopatra	
Berenice	101–88
Ptolemy IX Soter II (restored)	88–81
Cleopatra Berenice and Ptolemy XI	
Alexander II	80
Ptolemy XII Neos Dionysus (Auletes)	80–58
Berenice IV (at first with Cleopatra	
Tryphaena)	58–56
Berenice IV and Archelaus	56–55
Ptolemy XII Neos Dionysus (restored)	55–51
Cleopatra VII Philopator	51–30

2. THE SELEUCIDS

Seleucus I Nicator	305–281
Antiochus I Soter	281–261
Antiochus II Theos	261–246
Seleucus II Callinicus	246–226/5
Seleucus III Soter	226/5–223
Antiochus III Megas	223–187
Seleucus IV Philopator	187–175
Antiochus IV Epiphanes	175–164
Antiochus V Eupator	164–162
Demetrius I Soter	162–150
Alexander Balas	150–145
Demetrius II Nicator	145–140
Antiochus VI Epiphanes	145–142/1 or 139/8
Antiochus VII (Sidetes)	138–129
Demetrius II Nicator (restored)	129–126/5
Cleopatra Thea	126/5–123

Antiochus VIII Grypus	126/5–96
Seleucus V	126
Antiochus IX Philopator (Cyzicenus)	114/13–95
Seleucus VI	95
Antiochus X Eusebes Philopator	95
Demetrius III Philopator Soter	95–88 (at Damascus)

twins
{
    Antiochus XI Epiphanes Philadelphus   95
    Philip I   95–84/3
}
} (in Cilicia)

Antiochus XII Dionysus	87 (at Damascus)
Philip II	84/3

3. RULERS OF MACEDONIA BEFORE ANTIGONUS GONATAS

Philip III Arrhidaeus	323–317
Olympias	317–316
Cassander (king from 305)	316–297
Philip IV	297
Antipater	297–294
Alexander V	297–294
Demetrius I Poliorcetes	294–288
Lysimachus	288–281
Ptolemy Ceraunus	281–279

4. THE ANTIGONIDS

Antigonus I (Monophthalmus)	306 301
Demetrius I (Poliorcetes)	307–283
Antigonus II (Gonatas)	283–239
Demetrius II	239–229
Antigonus III (Doson)	229–221
Philip V	221–179
Perseus	179–168

5. THE ATTALIDS

(Philetaerus	283–263)
(Eumenes I	263–241)
Attalus I Soter	241–197
Eumenes II Soter	197–159/8
Attalus II	159/8–139/8
Attalus III	139/8–133
(Eumenes III (Aristonicus)	133–129)

GENEALOGICAL TABLES

THE FAMILY OF LYSIMACHUS

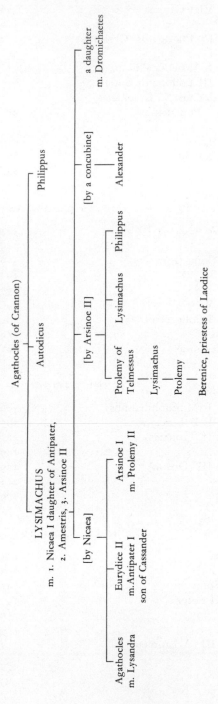

THE ATTALIDS

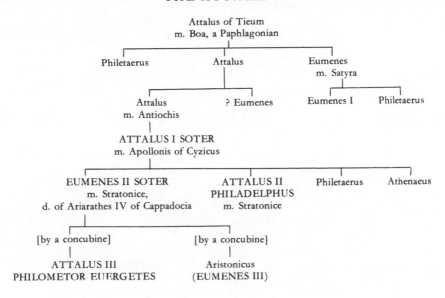

THE KINGS OF EPIRUS

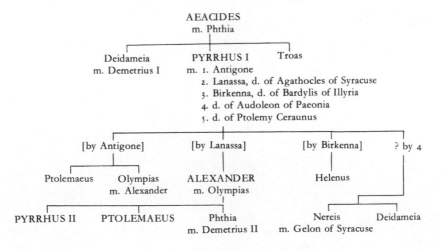

THE FAMILY OF ANTIPATER

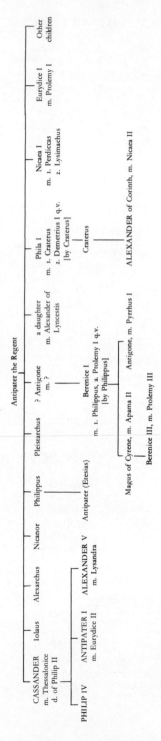

487

THE ANTIGONIDS

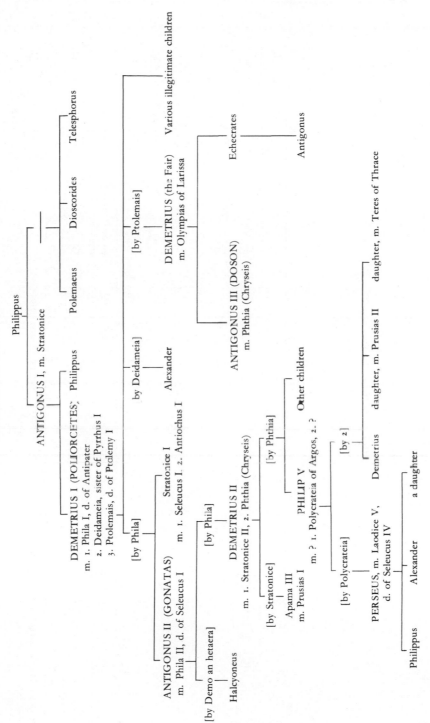

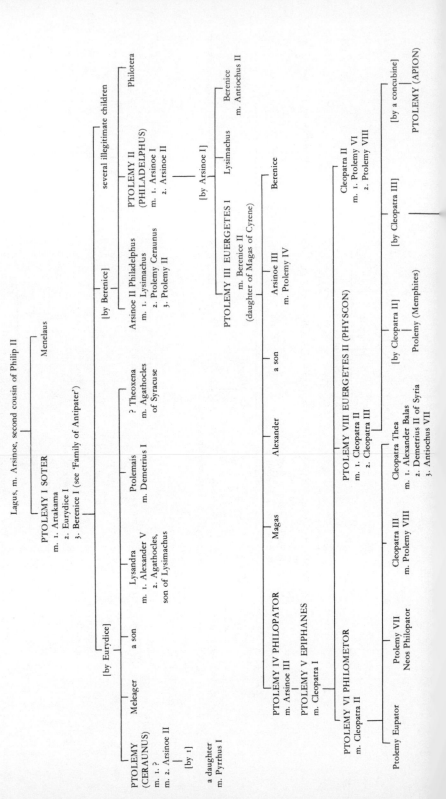

THE PTOLEMIES

489

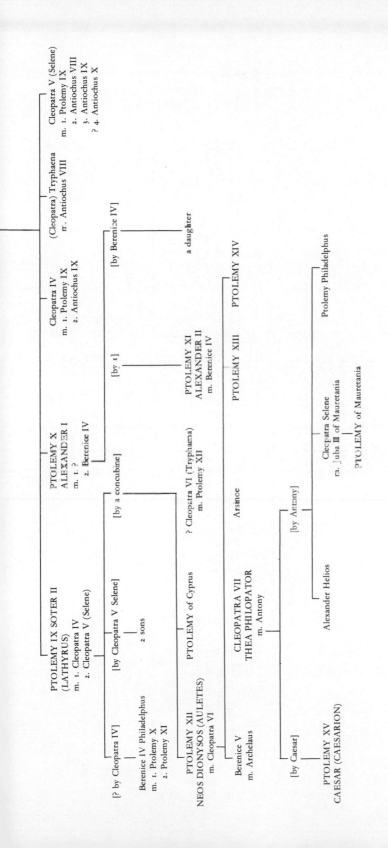

THE SELEUCIDS

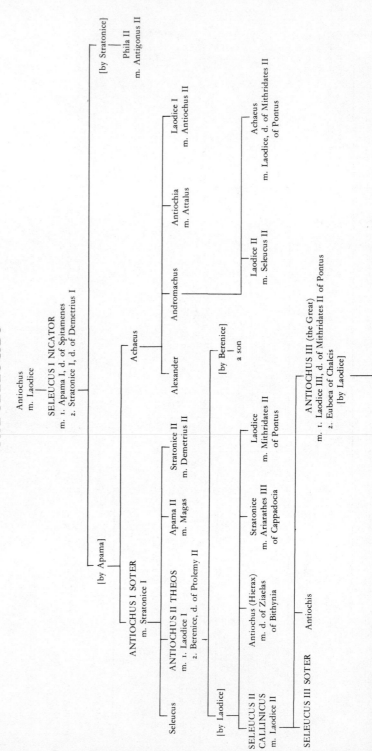

Antiochus
m. Laodice

SELEUCUS I NICATOR
m. 1. Apama I, d. of Spitamenes
2. Stratonice I, d. of Demetrius I

[by Stratonice]
Phila II
m. Antigonus II

[by Apama]
ANTIOCHUS I SOTER
m. Stratonice I

Seleucus

ANTIOCHUS II THEOS
m. 1. Laodice I
2. Berenice, d. of Ptolemy II

Apama II
m. Magas

Stratonice II
m. Demetrius II

Achaeus

Alexander

Andromachus

Antiochia
m. Attalus

Laodice I
m. Antiochus II

Laodice II
m. Seleucus II

Achaeus
m. Laodice, d. of Mithridates II of Pontus

[by Laodice]
SELEUCUS II CALLINICUS
m. Laodice II

Antiochus (Hierax)
m. d. of Ziaelas of Bithynia

Stratonice
m. Ariarathes III of Cappadocia

Laodice
m. Mithridates II of Pontus

[by Berenice]
a son

SELEUCUS III SOTER

Antiochis

ANTIOCHUS III (the Great)
m. 1. Laodice III, d. of Mithridates II of Pontus
2. Euboea of Chalcis

[by Laodice]

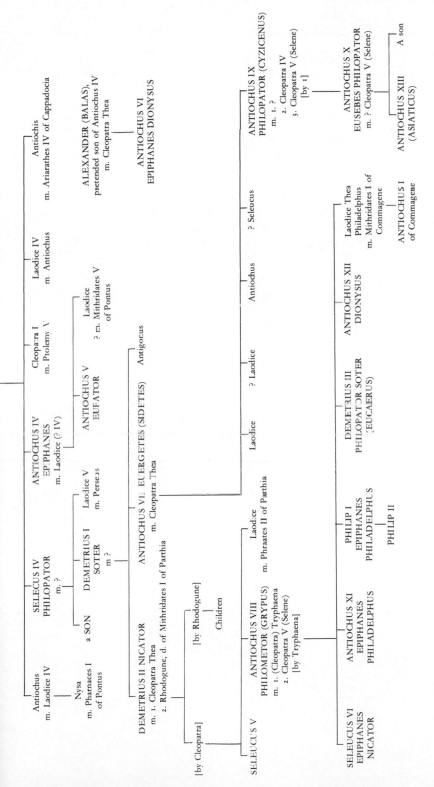

CHRONOLOGICAL TABLE (323–217 B.C.)

Sicily, South Italy, Carthage	Greece and Macedonia	Aegean, Egypt, Cyrene, Asia	Literature, Philosophy, Science, Art
	323 Lamian War breaks out. Athens and Aetolia allied. Antipater shut up in Lamia.	June 323 Death of Alexander at Babylon. Organization of succession. Division of the satrapies.	
c. 322 Return of Agathocles from S. Italy to Syracuse.	322 Athenian naval defeats. Aug. Battle of Crannon. Oligarchic government set up at Athens.	323/2 Revolt of the Greeks in Bactria.	322 Hypereides' Funeral Oration. Deaths of Aristotle, Demosthenes and Hypereides. Theophrastus succeeds Aristotle as head of the Peripatetic School.
	321 Polyperchon organizes Greece.	322 Spring. Perdiccas conquers Cappadocia: Eumenes as satrap.	321 First production of Menander.
		322/1 Ptolemy conquers Cyrenaica.	c. 371–c. 287 Theophrastus.
		321 Campaign and death of Perdiccas in Egypt. Defeat of Craterus in Asia Minor. Conference at Triparadisus. Antipater declared regent.	341–281 Epicurus.
320 c. 320 Agathocles forced to leave Syracuse again.	319 Polyperchon regent. War between Polyperchon and Cassander. Execution of Demades.	319 Death of Antipater. Ptolemy's first invasion of Syria-Phoenicia.	c. 320 Praxagoras flor. Hecataeus of Abdera writing in Egypt before 315.
319/18 Agathocles appointed general and guardian of the peace at Syracuse.	318 Execution of Phocion. 317 Polyperchon declares the Greeks free. Athens, controlled by Demetrius of Phalerum, makes a treaty with Cassander. Polyperchon restricted to the Peloponnese. Cassander regent of Macedonia. Autumn. Philip III assassinated.	318 Coalition of Cassander and Antigonus against Polyperchon. Eumenes makes gains in Asia at the expense of Ptolemy and Antigonus.	

Sicily, South Italy, Carthage	Greece and Macedonia	Aegean, Egypt, Cyrene, Asia	Literature, Philosophy, Science, Art
	316 Cassander takes Pydna and has Olympias executed. Foundation of Cassandreia and Thessalonica. Thebes rebuilt by Cassander.	316 Eumenes defeated, captured by Antigonus and executed.	
316/15 Agathocles elected *strategos autokrator* at Syracuse. 316/15–306/5 Struggle of the exiles in Sicily against Agathocles.			*c.* 315 Death of Aeschines.
315		315 Seleucus, expelled from Babylon by Antigonus, takes refuge with Ptolemy. Lysimachus, Ptolemy and Cassander present an ultimatum to Antigonus. Antigonus' proclamation at Tyre: war on Cassander, freedom for the Greeks. Ptolemy proclaims the freedom of the Greek cities. 315/14 Foundation of *koinon* of the Nesiotes by Antigonus. 313 Capital of Egypt moved from Memphis to Alexandria. 312 Victory of Ptolemy and Seleucus over Demetrius Poliorcetes at Gaza. Return of Seleucus to Mesopotamia-Babylonia. Beginning of the 'Seleucid Era'.	314 Death of Xenocrates, head of the Academy; succeeded by Polemon.

312/11 Outbreak of war against Carthage in Sicily.			
311 June. Carthaginians defeat Agathocles on the southern Himera, and blockade Syracuse by sea and land.		311 Peace between Antigonus, Ptolemy, Lysimachus and Cassander.	312/11 Zeno comes to Athens.
		311-301 Seleuceia-on-the-Tigris capital of the Seleucid kingdom.	
310	310 Cassander assassinates Alexander IV.	310 Menelaus, Ptolemy's brother, made *stratēgos* of Cyprus, which Ptolemy had annexed. Breach between Ptolemy and Antigonus.	
Aug. 310-Oct./Nov. 307 Agathocles' African expedition; parts of Punic Libya annexed. Antander represents Agathocles in Syracuse.			
309 Syracusans defeat Carthaginians under Hamilcar. Land blockade of Syracuse abandoned.	309 (or 308) Reconciliation between Cassander and Polyperchon.	309/8 (?) Antigonus expelled from Iran by Seleucus.	
309/7 Liberation movement in Acragas.			
309 Spring (?). Alliance between Agathocles and Ophellas of Cyrene.			
308 Oct./Nov. Murder of Ophellas.	308 Temporary reconciliation between Ptolemy and Antigonus. Ptolemy in Greece.	308 (or 305)-303 War between Seleucus and Chandragupta.	
307 Oct./Nov. Agathocles' catastrophe in Africa; he returns to Syracuse leaving his army in Africa. Nov. Treaty between Carthage and the Syracusan army.	307 Demetrius Poliorcetes takes Athens from Cassander. Demetrius of Phalerum expelled. Cassander's offensive against Ptolemy in Greece.		

Sicily, South Italy, Carthage	Greece and Macedonia	Aegean, Egypt, Cyrene, Asia	Literature, Philosophy, Science, Art
			307/6 Theophrastus exiled from Athens.
306/5 Peace between Agathocles and the Carthaginians: the Halycus to be the boundary of the Punic dominion in Sicily.		306 Antigonus and Demetrius take Cyprus from Ptolemy. The Antigonids assume the royal title.	306 Epicurus opens a school in Athens.
305 Agathocles' victory over the exiles under Deinocrates.		305/4 Demetrius fails to take Rhodes. Ptolemy, Lysimachus, Seleucus and Cassander take the title of King.	
304 Agathocles takes the title of King.			
303/2–293 Agathocles in S. Italy; struggle with the Bruttii.	303 Demetrius expels Cassander from the Isthmus.	303 Agreement between Seleucus and Chandragupta.	
303/2 Cleonymus at Tarentum. Tarentine appeal to Agathocles.	302 New 'League of Corinth' founded by Antigonus and Demetrius. Pyrrhus expelled from Epirus.	301 Coalition against Antigonus: his defeat and death at Ipsus. Partition of his kingdom: Ptolemy occupies Coele-Syria.	
300 c. 300 Agathocles takes Corcyra. Marriage of Agathocles to		c. 300 Alliances between Ptolemy and Lysimachus and between Demetrius and Seleucus.	c. 300 Euclid *flor.*

			c. 297 Demetrius of Phalerum in Alexandria. Foundation of the Museum and Library at Alexandria.
		300–297 Demetrius as ally of Ephesus makes war on Priene.	
		300/299 Foundation of Seleuceia-in-Pieria and Antioch.	
	298 (or 297) Death of Cassander and of his son, Philip IV. Pyrrhus back in Epirus.	297/6 Beginning of the Bithynian era. Pontic era subsequently back-dated to this year.	
c. 295 Marriage of Agathocles' daughter Lanassa to Pyrrhus.	295 Demetrius Poliorcetes in Greece.	295/4 Ptolemy recovers Cyprus.	
295	295 Lachares seizes power at Athens.	294 Antiochus I co-regent with Seleucus; in Iran.	
	294 Demetrius recovers Athens.		293/2 Death of Menander.
	294–287 Oligarchic government in Athens. Demetrius king in Macedonia.		
	293 Demetrius founded. Lysimachus briefly a prisoner of the Getae.		
	291/2 Boeotia in alliance with Aetolia rises against Demetrius. Demetrius fighting against Aetolia and Pyrrhus.	291 and in the following years. Ptolemy establishes a protectorate over the Aegean islands.	
c. 291 Lanassa marries Demetrius Poliorcetes.	291/90 Pyrrhus receives Corcyra as dowry from Agathocles.		

	Sicily, South Italy, Carthage	Greece and Macedonia	Aegean, Egypt, Cyrene, Asia	Literature, Philosophy, Science, Art
290	c. 290 Alliance between Agathocles and Demetrius: plan for a new Punic war. 289/8 Death of Agathocles. Syracuse free.			
		288/7 Invasion and partition of Macedonia by Lysimachus and Pyrrhus. 287 Athens under Olympichus revolts from Demetrius, who retains Piraeus.	288/7 Ptolemy takes Tyre and Sidon from Demetrius.	c. 287 Death of Theophrastus: Strato of Lampsacus succeeds him as head of the Lyceum. c. 287–212 Archimedes.
			286 Demetrius captured by Seleucus in Asia.	
285		285 Lysimachus seizes Pyrrhus' share of Macedonia. 284/3 (or 283/2) Dynastic crisis in court of Lysimachus.	285 March/April. Ptolemy II co-regent with Ptolemy I. 283 Death of Demetrius Poliorcetes. Death of Ptolemy I. Ptolemy II reigns as sole king. 282/1 Seleucus invades Asia Minor: death of Lysimachus at Corupedium (c. Feb. 281). 281 Mithridates I king of Pontus. Antiochus I sole king in Seleucid kingdom.	283 onwards. Callimachus, Apollonius, Theocritus, Herondas and the Tragic Pleiad active at Alexandria under Ptolemy II.
280	280–275 Pyrrhus' campaigns in Italy and Sicily.	281 Sept. Seleucus assassinated by Ptolemy Ceraunus, who becomes king of Macedonia after defeating Antigonus Gonatas. 280 Gauls invade Thrace and Macedonia: defeat and death of Ceraunus. Achaean League refounded.		c. 280 Zenodotus and Lycophron active. c. 280–245 Aristarchus of Samos flor.

c. 276–c. 196 Eratosthenes.
276/5 Aratus of Soli at court of Antigonus Gonatas.

c. 275 Theocritus' *Idyll* XVII.

280/79 Syrian war of succession between Antiochus I and Ptolemy II.
279 *Ptolemaieia* celebrated at Alexandria. Nicomedes I succeeds Zipoetes in Bithynia.
278/7 Gaulish invasion of Asia Minor under Lutarius and Leonnorius.

275 (?) Magas of Cyrene attacks Egypt.
c. 275 Antiochus I grants land to Aristodicides.
275/4 Philetaerus begins to strike coins at Pergamum.
Before 274 Ptolemy II marries Arsinoe.
274–271 First Syrian War between Ptolemy II and Antiochus I.

280/79 Decree honouring Demosthenes proposed by Demochares.
The Aetolians and other Greeks repel the Gauls from central Greece.
279 The Gauls establish the kingdom of Tylis in Thrace.
278 Reconciliation of Antiochus I and Antigonus Gonatas.

277 Antigonus II defeats the Gauls at Lysimacheia and becomes king of Macedonia.
Spring, Delphi: two Aetolian *hieromnemones* at the Amphictyony; Thessalians preside.
Aetolians gain control of the Amphictyony.
276/5 (or 275/4) Aegium joins the Achaean League.
276 Aetolians seize Dolopia. Thessalians disappear from Amphictyonic lists with Gonatas master of Thessaly.

274 Pyrrhus conquers Macedonia.

Sicily, South Italy, Carthage	Greece and Macedonia	Aegean, Egypt, Cyrene, Asia	Literature, Philosophy, Science, Art
	273 Pyrrhus' son Ptolemy defeats Gonatas.		
	272 Spring. Pyrrhus invades Peloponnese.		
	Delphi: five Aetolian *hieromnemones*. Aeniania absorbed.		
	Summer. Pyrrhus at Sparta. Autumn. Death of Pyrrhus at Argos.		
	Aristippus tyrant at Argos.		
	(?) Aristodamus tyrant at Megalopolis.		
	(?) Athenian–Aetolian treaty. Aristotimus, tyrant of Elis, murdered.	272/1 Arsinoe and Ptolemy II receive divine honours.	
		271 End of First Syrian War.	
	271 (?) Gonatas recovers Chalcis.	271/70 (?) Procession of Ptolemy II in Alexandria.	
270	271/70 Athens passes a decree honouring Demochares.		
		270 Death of Arsinoe (July).	270 Death of Epicurus.
		c. 270 Antiochus I defeats Gauls in the 'elephant-battle'.	*c.* 270 Ctesibius *flor.*
	270/69 Athenian decree for Callias of Sphettus.		
	268/7 Peithidemus archon at Athens. Decree of Chremonides (autumn 268).		*c.* 269 Death of Strato.
	267–261 Chremonidean War.		*c.* 268–265 Death of Polemo: succeeded briefly by Crates and then by Arcesilaus as head of the Academy.
	267 Rhamnus held by Athens and allies. Athenian traitors helping pirates allied to Gonatas.		

265

264–241 First Punic War between Rome and Carthage.

260

Gonatas and Patroclus in Attica.
First Spartan expedition: reaches Isthmus.
266 Second Spartan expedition checked at Isthmus.
Gonatas suppresses Galatian mercenaries at Megara.
Siege of Athens.
266/5 Nicias 'Otryneus' archon at Athens.
265 Third Spartan expedition: Areus defeated and killed near Corinth.
265–262 Athens holds out.
264 Cleinias murdered at Sicyon: Aratus in Argos.
264/3 Diognetus archon at Athens.

262/1 Antipater archon at Athens.
261 Alexander of Epirus invades Macedonia and is expelled from Epirus.
Renewed siege of Athens which falls to Gonatas.
Amphictyons accept the Alexandriar Ptolemaïeia.
Peace between Gonatas and Athens.
(?) Aetolian–Acarnanian treaty.
Alexander restored in Epirus.

267 Inscription from Denizli honours Achaeus, a Seleucid functionary.

c. 264 Nicomedia founded.

263 Eumenes I succeeds Philetaerus at Pergamum (without royal title).
c. 262/1 Ephesus under the Ptolemies.
261 Death of Antiochus I: Antiochus II succeeds him.
c. 261 Apollonius becomes dioiketes of Ptolemy II.
Zeno of Caunus arrives in Egypt.
(?) Battle of Cos: 'peace in the Aegean'.
Gonatas attacks Miletus.

260–253 Second Syrian War: Ptolemy II against Antiochus II.
c. 260 Bilingual edict of Aśoka (Greek and Aramaic) at Kandahar.

262 Reclamation work in the Fayyûm.
261 Death of Zeno: succeeded by Cleanthes of Assus as head of the Stoa.

c. 260 Erasistratus flor.
c. 260/250 Death of Herophilus (330/320–260/250).

Sicily, South Italy, Carthage	Greece and Macedonia	Aegean, Egypt, Cyrene, Asia	Literature, Philosophy, Science, Art
			c. 260 Apollonius Rhodius head of the Library at Alexandria.
	c. 257 Demetrius becomes co-regent with Gonatas.	259 Revenue Laws promulgated in Egypt.	
	256/5 'Liberty restored' at Athens.	258 Ephesus once more Seleucid.	
	255 One general substituted for two in Achaea.	256–250 Beginning of the Parthian breakaway.	c. 255 Death of Timaeus (c. 350–c. 255).
255	c. 255 Argos free of Macedonia.	c. 255 Beginning of the Cappadocian royal era.	
		c. 255/4 Ziaelas gains control of Bithynia.	
		253 (?) End of Second Syrian War.	
		253 Gonatas founds the *Antigoneia* and *Stratoniceia* at Delos.	
	c. 251 Megalopolis freed: death of Aristodamus.	c. 253–251 Ptolemy II re-establishes good relations with Magas of Cyrene.	
	251 Jan. Nicocles tyrant at Sicyon: Aratus' attack fails. May. Aratus frees Sicyon. Sicyon joins the Achaean League.	252 Antiochus II marries Berenice II.	
	251/50 Aratus visits Egypt. Ptolemaic subsidy for Achaea.		
250	c. 250 Death of Craterus governor of Corinth.	250 Death of Magas of Cyrene. Demetrius the Fair called in: murdered by Berenice. Cyrenaica falls to Ptolemy. Death of Nicomedes I of Bithynia.	
	250–248 Aristomachus I tyrant of Argos. Aratus attacks Alexander, governor of Corinth.		

Alexander revolts from Gonatas and makes a treaty with Achaea.
Gonatas attacks Corinth from Athens and Argos.
Peace between Gonatas and Alexander.

246 Aetolians make the *Soteria* quadrennial

245 May, Aratus first generalship in Achaea.
? Death of Alexander of Corinth.
Autumn. Aetolians defeat Boeotians at Chaeronea. Gonatas recovers Corinth. Beginning of his 'system of tyrants'.
Suppression of the Euboean League.
245/4 First performance of new Delphic *Soteria*.
244 (?) *Isopoliteia* between Messenia and Phigalea.
Lydiades tyrant at Megalopolis.
(or later) Elis acquires Triphylia.
(or 243) Agis IV ascends the throne at Sparta.

c. 250–237 Secession of Bactria and Parthia from the Seleucids.

247 Beginning of Parthian era.
246 Deaths of Ptolemy II and Antiochus II: succeeded by Ptolemy III and Seleucus II. Revolt in Egypt.
246–241 Third Syrian (Laodicean) War: Ptolemy III against Seleucus II.
246 Ptolemy III reaches Ephesus and goes thence to the Euphrates and Mesopotamia: Antiochus Hierax in charge in Asia Minor.
(?) Battle of Andros: Gonatas defeats Sophron.
245 Gonatas institutes *Paneia* and *Soteria* at Delos.
Seleucus II recognized in Babylon.
245–241 Ptolemaic forces active on the southern and western shores of Asia Minor.

c. 246 Erastosthenes head of the Library at Alexandria.

246 Callimachus' *Coma Berenices*.

Sicily, South Italy, Carthage	Greece and Macedonia	Aegean, Egypt, Cyrene, Asia	Literature, Philosophy, Science, Art
	243 May. Aratus general for second time. Summer. Aratus seizes Corinth. Megara, Troezen and Epidaurus join the Achaean League. (?) Gonatas and the Aetolians agree to partition Achaea. (?) Alexander of Epirus and the Aetolians agree to partition Acarnania. Autumn. Lysander ephor at Sparta.		
	242 Spring. Aratus invades Attica and Salamis. Leonidas in exile at Tegea. Spartan reforms (debts cancelled). Achaeo-Spartan alliance. Autumn. Agesilaus ephor at Sparta.	242/1 Antiochus Hierax, co-ruler with Seleucus II, controls lands west of the Taurus Mountains.	
241 End of the First Punic War.	241 May. Aratus general for third time. Autumn. Aratus and Agis at the Isthmus. Agis is sent back: Aetolian defeat at Pellene. Fall of Agis and Agesilaus at Sparta.	241 End of Third Syrian War. Death of Eumenes I. Accession of Attalus I.	
	241/40 (?) Aratus seizes Cynaetha. Peace between Aetolia, Gonatas and Achaea.		241/40 Death of Arcesilaus: Lacydes succeeds him as head of the Academy.
	240 Aratus' regular attacks on Athens begin.	240/39–c. 237 War of the Brothers: Seleucus II against Antiochus	

240–237 Carthaginian Mercenary War.

Aristomachus and later Aristippus of Argos.

c. 240 Death of Alexander II of Epirus: Olympias regent.

240/39 Death of Antigonus Gonatas: Demetrius II succeeds.

239 Aetolian attacks on Epirote Acarnania.

Achaean attacks on Athens and Argos continue.

Alliance between Macedonia and Epirus: Demetrius marries Phthia.

(?) Aetolo-Achaean alliance between Aratus and Pantaleon.

May. Aratus' fourth generalship.

239/8 (?) Outbreak of Demetrian War (in the archonship of Lysias at Athens).

237 May. Aratus' fifth generalship.

(?) Demetrius invades Boeotia.

237/6 (or before 228/7) Opus leaves Aetolia and joins Boeotia.

236 Dioetas Achaean general: Achaeans take Heraea.

235 May. Aratus' sixth generalship. Aratus' attacks on Argos. Aratus' seizure of Cleonae.

Death of Aristippus: Aristomachus tyrant of Argos.

Lydiades abandons his tyranny. Megalopolis joins the Achaean League.

(?) Tegea, Mantinea, Orchomenus and Caphyae join the Achaean League.

Cleomenes III king at Sparta.

240 (or 239) Seleucus defeated by Hierax: retires to Cilicia.

c. 240 Foundation plaques of the great Serapeum of Alexandria.

239 Attalus defeats Antiochus Hierax and takes the royal title.

Canopus decree.

(?) Diodotus of Bactria takes royal title.

c. 237 End of the War of the Brothers.

237/6 Demetrius II's alliance with Gortyn.

c. 236 Dedications by Attalus I using sculptors of the First Pergamene School. Apollonius of Perge flor.

Sicily, South Italy, Carthage	Greece and Macedonia	Aegean, Egypt, Cyrene, Asia	Literature, Philosophy, Science, Art
	234 May. Lydiades' first generalship. Attempted expedition against Sparta. (?)Deaths of Ptolemy of Epirus and of Olympias.		
	233 May. Aratus' seventh generalship. Battle of Phylacia; Bithys defeats Aratus. Aratus attacks Athens up to the Academy. (?) Demetrius invades Boeotia. Collapse of the Epirote royal house: Deidamia murdered.		
	232 May. Lydiades' second generalship. Arcanania independent of Epirus.		c. 232 Death of Cleanthes (c. 331–c. 232): succeeded by Chrysippus as head of the Stoa.
	231 May. Aratus' eighth generalship. Demetrius occupied against the Dardanians. Autumn. The Illyrian Ardiaei relieve Medeon, besieged by Aetolians. Death of Agron, king of the Ardiaei.		
	230 May. Lydiades' third generalship. Illyrian privateering: seizure of Phoenice. Achaeans and Aetolians send help to Epirus against the Illyrians. Epirotes ally themselves with	c. 230 Ziaelas killed by Galatians.	

229 Corcyra appeals to Achaea and
Aetolia.
Battle of Paxos: death of
Margus.
229/8 First Illyrian War.
Lydiades tries to bring Argos
into the Achaean League.
Death of Demetrius II.
Thessaly revolts from
Macedonia: Aetolians invade
Thessaly
Antigonus III Doson succeeds
Demetrius: he recovers
Thessaliotis, Hestiaeotis and
Perrhaebia; Aetolians retain
Achaea Phthiotis.
Boeotia and Phocis allied to
Achaea.
May. Aratus' ninth generalship.
Argos, Hermione, Phlius and
Aegina join Achaean League.
Sparta acquires Tegea,
Mantinea, Orchomenus and
Caphyae from Aetolia.
Cleomenes takes the
Athenaeum.
Aratus attacks Tegea and
Orchomenus.
Achaea declares war on Sparta.
Athens declares her
independence: negotiations
with Diogenes.
228 Aratus seizes Caphyae.
May. Aristomachus general.
Summer. Athens finally free.
c. 228 Doson takes Opuntian Locris
from Boeotia.

228 Attalus' victory over Hierax at
Lake Coloe; further victory
on R. Harpasus.

228 Spring, Romans admitted to
Isthmian games.

Sicily, South Italy, Carthage	Greece and Macedonia	Aegean, Egypt, Cyrene, Asia	Literature, Philosophy, Science, Art
	227 Mutiny at Pella. Antigonus now takes royal title. May. Aratus' tenth generalship. Battle of Mt Lycaeum. Aratus takes Mantinea. Battle of Ladoceia: death of Lydiades. Hierax killed by the Gauls of Tylis. Cleomenes captures Alea and Heraea. Cleomenes' *coup* at Sparta: social reforms carried. 227/6 Megalopolitan embassy to Pella. 226 Jan./Feb. Achaean success at Orchomenus. May. Hyperbatas general. Cleomenes takes Mantinea and invades north-west Achaea. Autumn. Battle of Hecatombaeum. Cleomenes approaches the Achaean League. 225 May. Timoxenus general. Conference between Cleomenes and the Achaeans breaks down. Cleomenes takes Pellene, Pheneus, Argos, Cleonae, Phlius, Hermione, Troezen, Epidaurus, Corinth. Aratus *strategos autokrator*. Achaean embassy to Antigonus Doson.	227 Carian expedition of Antigonus Doson. 227/6 Earthquake seriously damages Rhodes. *c.* 227/5 Doson makes treaties with Eleutherna and Hierapytna. 226/5 Death of Seleucus II: Seleucus III succeeds. 226–223 Attalus master of western Asia Minor.	*c.* 225 Rhianus *flor.*

225/4 Aratus besieged in Sicyon. 224 Achaean alliance with Macedonia. Doson comes south. May. Aratus' eleventh generalship Argos abandons Cleomenes. Antigonus enters the Peloponnese and takes Aegytis and Belbinatis. Sept. Antigonus appointed *hegemon* of the allied forces. 224/3 Foundation of the Hellenic Symmachy. 223 Cleomenes attacks Megalopolis. Antigonus takes Tegea, Orchomenus, Mantinea, Heraea and Telphusa. Cleomenes takes Megalopolis. 222 Cleomenes invades the Argolid. May. Aratus' twelfth generalship. July. Battle of Sellasia. Cleomenes flees to Egypt. Antigonus marches north to meet the Illyrians. 222/1 Philip in the Peloponnese. 221 May. Timoxenus general. c. July. Death of Antigonus: accession of Philip V. Dorimachus in Messenia. Autumn. Aetolian aggression at Clarium, in Epirus and on the high seas. 221/20 Winter. Aetolian inroads into Messenia.	223 Death of Seleucus III. Accession of Antiochus III. Molon put in charge of the eastern satrapies. 223/2 (?) Seleucid troops under Achaeus drive Attalus back to Pergamum. 222 Revolt of Molon. 221 Feb. Death of Ptolemy III: accession of Ptolemy IV. Molon defeated and commits suicide.

	Sicily, South Italy, Carthage	Greece and Macedonia	Aegean, Egypt, Cyrene, Asia	Literature, Philosophy, Science, Art
220		220 May. Aratus' thirteenth generalship. Battle of Caphyae. Demetrius of Pharos sails south of Lissus. Sack of Cynaetha. Philip at Corinth. War declared by the Symmachy on Aetolia. 220–217 Social War. 220/19 Philip allied to Scerdilaidas. Spartan alliance with Aetolia. Second Illyrian War: Rome against Demetrius of Pharos. 219 Spring. Lycurgus attacks the Argolid and seizes the Athenaeum. Summer. Philip in Epirus and Acarnania. Aetolians raid Aegeira, Dium and Dodona. Demetrius of Pharos joins Philip. Philip at Larissa. 219/18 Winter. Philip's winter expedition: Psophis, southern Elis and Triphylia subdued. 218 May. Eperatus general. Campaign in north Elis. Financial agreement between Philip and the Achaeans. Philip's naval policy. Apelles at Chalcis. Summer. Philip attacks Cephallenia. Philip invades Aetolia and sacks Thermum.	220 War of Rhodes and Prusias against Byzantium over tolls. War of Cnossus and Gortyn against Lyttus. Troops sent by the Symmachy to help Lyttus. Autumn. Achaeus proclaimed king in Phrygia: rapprochement with Attalus. 220–213 Usurpation of Achaeus. 219 Fourth Syrian War (219–217) begins: Antiochus III against Ptolemy IV. Antiochus takes Seleuceia-in-Pieria. Theodotus deserts to Antiochus, bringing Ptolemais and Tyre. Death of Cleomenes in Egypt. 219/18 Four months truce between Antiochus and Ptolemy. 218 Attalus seizes the Greek cities of northern Ionia, Aeolis and Troas and Mysia to the Macestus, breaking with Achaeus. Antiochus advances south in Coele-Syria.	c. 220 Euphorion of Chalcis *flor.* Starting point for the main theme of Polybius' *Histories.*
	218–202 Second Punic War.			

217 June. Battle of Lake Trasimene.	Aetolians attack Messenia and Thessaly. Megaleas condemned. Autumn. Philip in Phocis. Execution of the Apelles group. 218/17 Elean invasion of western Achaea. 217 Summer. Philip takes Bylazora and Phthiotic Thebes. Macedonian preparations against Scerdilaidas. July. Nemea. News of Trasimene. Sept. Peace of Naupactus. Philip's first letter to Larissa on filling the citizen-body.	218/17 Antiochus winters in Ptolemais. 217 June. Battle of Raphia. Ptolemy recovers Coele-Syria: expedition into Seleucid territory. Peace between Ptolemy IV and Antiochus III.	217 Nov. 15. Synod at Memphis (Pithom stele).

BIBLIOGRAPHY

ABBREVIATIONS

For abbreviations of papyrological publications, etc., see Bibliography F(b)

A Arch. Syr.   *Annales archéologiques syriennes* (Damascus)

Abh. Akad. Berlin   *Abhandlungen der preussischen Akademie der Wissenschaften,* Berlin, phil.-hist. Klasse (later '*der deutschen Akademie der Wissenschaften zu Berlin,* Klasse für Sprache, Literatur und Kunst' or 'Klasse für Philosophie, Geschichte etc.)

Abh. Akad. Mainz   *Abhandlungen der Akademie der Wissenschaften und der Literatur, Mainz,* geistes- und sozialwissenschaftliche Klasse

Abh. Sächs. Akad.   *Abhandlungen der sächsischen Akademie der Wissenschaften in Leipzig,* phil.-hist. Klasse

Act. ant.   *Acta antiqua academiae scientiarum Hungaricae*

Actes Besançon   *Actes du colloque sur l'esclavage (Besançon),* 1971: Paris, 1972; 1973: Paris, 1976

Actes VII congrès épig. 1977   *Actes du VIIe congrès international d'épigraphie grecque et latine, Costantza 9–15 Sept. 1977.* Bucharest–Paris, 1979

Actes X congr. intern. papyrolog.   *Actes du Xe congrès international de papyrologues, Varsovie-Cracovie, 1961,* sous la rédaction de J. Wolski (Académie polonaise de Sciences, Comité des sciences de la culture antique). Warsaw, 1964

Actes XV congr. intern. papyrolog.   *Actes du XVe congrès international de papyrologie (Pap. Brux.* 16–19), ed. J. Bingen and G. Nachtergael. 4 vols. Brussels, 1978–9

AHDO   *Archives d'histoire du droit oriental*

AHR   *American Historical Review*

AJAH   *American Journal of Ancient History*

AJArch.   *American Journal of Archaeology*

AJPhil.   *American Journal of Philology*

Ancient Macedonia   *Ancient Macedonia,* ed. B. Laourdas, C. Makaronas and others. 3 vols. Thessalonica, 1970, 1977 and 1983

Anc. Soc.   *Ancient Society*

Annali di Pisa   *Annali della scuola normale superiore de Pisa.* Classe di lettere e filosofia

Ann. Serv. Ant. Égypte   *Annales du Service des Antiquités de l'Égypte*

Annuario   *Annuario della regia scuola archeologica di Atene e delle missioni italiane in oriente*

ANRW   *Aufstieg und Niedergang der römischen Welt: Geschichte und Kultur Roms im Spiegel der neueren Forschung*, ed. H. Temporini and W. Haase. Berlin-New York, 1972–

ANSMN   *American Numismatic Society: Museum Notes*

ANSNNM   *American Numismatic Society, Numismatic Notes and Monographs*

Ant. class.   *L'Antiquité classique*

Antike, Die   See *Neue Jahrbücher*

Arch. Anz.   *Archäologischer Anzeiger* (supplement to *JDAI*)

Arch. Pap.   *Archiv für Papyrusforschung*

Ath. Mitt.   *Mitteilungen des Deutschen Archäologischen Instituts, Athenische Abteilung*

Atti Acc. Torino   *Atti dell' Accademia delle Scienze di Torino*

Austin   M. M. Austin, *The Hellenistic World from Alexander to the Roman Conquest: A Selection of Ancient Sources in Translation.* Cambridge, 1981

BAR   *British Archaeological Reports* (Oxford)

BASP   *Bulletin of the American Society of Papyrologists*

BCH   *Bulletin de correspondance hellénique*

BICS   *Bulletin of the Institute of Classical Studies* (London)

BIFAO   *Bulletin de l'Institut français d'archéologie orientale*

BM   Inventory no., unpublished cuneiform inscriptions in the British Museum

BSA   *Annual of the British School at Athens*

BSAAlex.   *Bulletin de la société archéologique d'Alexandrie*

Bull. épig.   *Bulletin épigraphique* (by L. & J. Robert in *Rev. Ét. Gr.*)

Bull. Hist. Med.   *Bulletin of the History of Medicine*

CAH   *The Cambridge Ancient History*

Choix   F. Durrbach, *Choix d'inscriptions de Délos avec traduction et commentaire* 1.1–2. Paris, 1921–3

Chron. d'Égypte   *Chronique d'Égypte*

C. Ord Ptol.   See Bibliography: F8

Corinth   *Corinth.* Results of excavations conducted by the American School of Classical Studies at Athens. Vols. by various authors, 1929–

CPhil.   *Classical Philology*

CQ   *Classical Quarterly*

CR   *Classical Review*

CRAcad. Inscr.   *Comptes rendus de l'Académie des inscriptions et belles lettres*

CSCA   *California Studies in Classical Antiquity*

CSDIR   *Centro studi e documentazione sull'Italia Romana, Atti* (Milan-Varese)

CSSH   *Comparative Studies in Society and History*

Das Ptol. Aegypten   *Das Ptolemäische Aegypten. Akten des internationalen Symposions 27–29 September 1976 in Berlin*, ed. H. Maehler and V. M. Strocka. Mainz, 1978

Délos   *Exploration archéologique de Délos.* Vols. by various authors. 1902–

DHA   *Dialogues d'histoire ancienne* (Paris)

Didyma   T. Wiegand and others, *Didyma.* I (Buildings): Berlin, 1941; II (Inscriptions, by A. Rehm): Berlin, 1958

Edson Studies   *Ancient Macedonian Studies in Honor of Charles F. Edson*, ed. H. Dell. Thessalonica, 1981

EHR   *Economic History Review*

Entretiens Hardt   *Entretiens sur l'antiquité classique*. Fondation Hardt. Vandoeuvres-Geneva

ESAR   *Economic Survey of Ancient Rome*, ed. T. Frank. 6 vols. Baltimore, 1933–40 (reprint New York, 1975)

Fairman Studies   *Glimpses of Ancient Egypt. Studies in Honour of H. W. Fairman*, ed. J. Ruffle, G. A. Gaballa and K. A. Kitchen. Warminster, 1979

FD   *Fouilles de Delphes*. Vol III: Inscriptions, ed. G. Colin, E. Bourguet, G. Daux and A. Salac. Paris, 1909–

FGrH   F. Jacoby, *Fragmente der griechischen Historiker*. 3 parts in 15 vols. (Part 1, ed. 2). Berlin-Leiden, 1923–58

FHG   C. Th. Müller, *Fragmenta historicorum graecorum*. 5 vols. Paris, 1841–70

GDI   *Sammlung der griechischen Dialekt-Inschriften*, ed. H Collitz and F. Bechtel. Göttingen, 1884–1915

Gött. Anz.   *Göttingische gelehrte Anzeigen*

GRBS   *Greek Roman and Byzantine Studies*

Harv. Theol. Rev.   *Harvard Theological Review*

Hesp.   *Hesperia. Journal of the American School of Classical Studies at Athens*

Holleaux, *Études*   M. Holleaux, *Études d'épigraphie et d'histoire grecques*, ed. L. Robert. 6 vols. Paris, 1938–68

HSCP   *Harvard Studies in Classical Philology*

IBM   *The Collection of Ancient Greek Inscriptions in the British Museum*. London, 1874–1916

IC   *Inscriptiones Creticae*, ed. M. Guarducci. 4 vols. Rome, 1935–50

IEJ   *Israel Exploration Journal*

IG   *Inscriptiones Graecae*

IG²   *Inscriptiones Graecae*, editio minor

IGB   G. Mihailov, *Inscriptiones Graecae in Bulgaria repertae*. Sofia. I^2 (1970), II (1958), II.1 (1961), III.2 (1964), IV (1966)

IGCH   O. Mørkholm, C. M. Kraay and M. Thompson, *An Inventory of Greek Coin Hoards*. New York, 1973

IGLS   *Inscriptions grecques et latines de la Syrie*, ed. L. Jalabert, R. Mouterde and J. P. Rey-Coquais. Paris, 1929–

ILS   *Inscriptiones latinae selectae*, ed. H. Dessau

I. Magnesia   *Die Inschriften von Magnesia-am-Mäander*, ed. O. Kern. Berlin, 1900

Insc. Délos   *Inscriptions de Délos:* nos. 1–88, ed. A. Plassart, Paris, 1950; nos. 290–371, 372–509, ed. F. Durrbach, Paris, 1926 and 1929; nos. 1400–96, ed. F. Durrbach and P. Roussel, Paris, 1935; nos. 1497–2879 (2 parts), ed. P. Roussel and M. Launey, Paris, 1937

I. Olympia   W. Dittenberger and K. Purgold, *Olympia: die Ergebnisse . . . der Ausgrabung.* v: *Die Inschriften*. Berlin, 1896

I. Priene   F. Hiller von Gaertringen, *Die Inschriften von Priene*. Berlin, 1906

ISE   L. Moretti, *Iscrizioni storiche ellenistiche*. 2 vols. Florence, 1967 and 1975

Istanb. Forsch.   *Istanbuler Forschungen*

Istanb. Mitt.   Mitteilungen des deutschen archäologischen Instituts, Istanbuler Abteilung

JCS   Journal of Cuneiform Studies

JDAI   Jahrbuch des (kaiserlichen) Deutschen Archäologischen Instituts

JEA   Journal of Egyptian Archaeology

JHS   Journal of Hellenic Studies

JJP   Journal of Juristic Papyrology

Journ. asiatique   Journal asiatique

Journ. Econ. Bus. Hist.   Journal of Economic and Business History

Journ. Sav.   Journal des savants

JRS   Journal of Roman Studies

Kuml   Kuml. Årbog for Jysk Arkaeologisk Selskab (Århus)

Lindos   Lindos: Fouilles de l'Acropole, 1902–14. I and II, by Ch. Blinkenberg. *Le Sanctuaire d'Athéna Lindia et l'architecture lindienne,* with catalogue of V. Poulsen; III, by E. Dyggve and others. Berlin-Copenhagen, 1931–60

MAAR   Memoirs of the American Academy in Rome

Mélanges Dussaud   Mélanges syriens offerts à René Dussaud par ses amis et ses élèves. 2 vols. Paris, 1939

Mélanges Glotz   Mélanges Gustave Glotz. 2 vols. Paris, 1932

Mélanges Holleaux   Mélanges Holleaux. Recueil de mémoires concernant l'antiquité grecque, offert à Maurice Holleaux en souvenir de ses années de direction a l'École française d'Athènes (1904–1912). Paris, 1913

Mélanges Préaux   Le monde grec: pensée, littérature, histoire, documents. Hommages à Claire Préaux, ed. J. Bingen, G. Cambier, G. Nachtergael. Brussels, 1975

Mélanges Thomas   Mélanges Paul Thomas: recueil de mémoires concernant la philologie classique. Bruges, 1930

Mél. USJ   Mélanges de l'Université St Joseph, Beyrouth

Michel   Ch.Michel, *Recueil d'inscriptions grecques.* Brussels, 1900 (with suppl. 1912 and 1927)

Milet   Th. Wiegand, *Milet: Ergebnisse der Ausgrabungen und Untersuchungen seit dem Jahr 1899.* 3 vols., each in several parts, by various authors. Berlin, 1906–29

Miscellanea Rostagni   Miscellanea di studi alessandrini in memoria di Augusto Rostagni. Turin, 1963

Mitteis, *Grundzüge* and *Chr.*   See Mitteis, 1912: (F 92)

ML   R. Meiggs and D. Lewis, *A Selection of Greek Historical Inscriptions.* Oxford, 1969

Mnemos.   Mnemosyne

Momigliano, *Contributo* I–VI   The various volumes of his *Contributi,* listed in Bibliography (A 35–9, 42)

Münch. Beitr. Papyr.   Münchener Beiträge zur Papyrusforschung und antiken Rechtsgeschichte

Mus. Helv.   Museum Helveticum

[*Neue*] *Jahrbücher*   (1) [*Neue*] *Jahrbücher für Philologie und Pädagogik* (1826–97) (2) *Neue Jahrbücher für das Klassische Altertum und für Pädagogik* (1898–1925)

(3) *Neue Jahrbücher für Wissenschaft und Jugendbildung* (1925–36)
(4) *Neue Jahrbücher für deutsche Wissenschaft* (1937)
(5) *Neue Jahrbücher für Antike und deutsche Bildung* (1938–42)
(6) *Die Antike: alte Sprachen und deutsche Bildung* (1943–   )
Num. Chron.   Numismatic Chronicle
Num. Stud.   American Numismatic Society: Numismatic Studies
OGIS   Orientis graeci inscriptiones selectae, ed. W. Dittenberger. 2 vols. Leipzig, 1903
Op. Ath.   Opuscula Atheniensia. Skrifter utgivna av Svenska Institutet i Athen
Philol.   Philologus
PIR   Prosopographia imperii Romani saec. I, II, III, ed. E. Klebs, H. Dessau, P. von Rohden. 3 vols. Berlin, 1897–8
    New edition: ed. E. Groag, A. Stein, L. Petersen. Berlin-Leipzig, 1933–
Pol. Sci. Quart.   Political Science Quarterly
PP   La parola del passato
Proc. Brit. Acad.   Proceedings of the British Academy
Proc. IX Intern. Congr. Papyrolog.   Proceedings of the ninth International Congress of Papyrology, Oslo 1958 (Association internationale de Papyrologues. Univ. i Oslo, Klassisk Inst.), ed. L. Amundsen and V. Skånland. Oslo, 1961
Proc. XII Intern. Congr. Papyrolog.   Proceedings of the twelfth International Congress of Papyrologists. (Organised by the American Society of Papyrologists and held at the University of Michigan, 1968), ed. D. H. Samuel. (American Society of Papyrologists. American Studies in Papyrology, 7.) Toronto, 1970
Proc. XIV Intern. Congr. Papyrolog.   Proceedings of the fourteenth International Congress of Papyrologists (Oxford 1974). London, 1975
Proc. XVI Intern. Congr. Papyrolog.   Proceedings of the sixteenth International Congress of Papyrologists (New York, 1981), ed. R. S. Bagnall. Chico, 1981
Proc. Int. Num. Symp. Warsaw-Budapest 1976   Proceedings of the International Numismatic Symposium, Warsaw and Budapest 1976, ed. I. Gedai and K. Biro-Sey. Budapest, 1980
Pros. Ptol.   W. Peremans, E. van't Dack and others, Prosopographia Ptolemaica. 8 vols. (1950–75); vols. I–V, reprinted 1977; VI (1968); VII, VIII (1975) (*Studia Hellenistica* 6, 8, 11, 12, 13, 17, 20, 21). Louvain.
PW   Pauly, Wissowa and others, Real-Encyclopädie der classischen Altertums-Wissenschaft
Quad. Tic.   Quaderni ticinesi di numismatica e antichità classiche (Lugano)
RBPhil.   Revue belge de philologie et d'histoire
RC   C. B. Welles, Royal Correspondence in the Hellenistic Period: A Study in Greek Epigraphy. New Haven, Conn., 1934
Rend. Ist. Lomb.   Rendiconti del Istituto Lombardo di scienze e lettere
Rend. Linc.   Rendiconti dell'Accademia dei Lincei
Rev. Bibl.   Revue biblique
Rev. Ét. Anc.   Revue des études anciennes
Rev. Ét. Gr.   Revue des études grecques
Rev. Hist.   Revue historique

Rev. Num. Revue numismatique
Rev. Phil. Revue de philologie
RGVV Religionsgeschichtliche Versuche und Vorarbeiten
Rh. Mus. Rheinisches Museum für Philologie
RIDA Revue internationale des droits de l'Antiquité
Riv. Fil. Rivista di filologia e d'istruzione classica
Robert, *Hellenica* L. Robert, *Hellenica. Recueil d'épigraphie, de numismatique et d'antiquités grecques.* 13 vols. Paris, 1940 (I), 1946 (II–III), 1948 (IV–VI), 1949 (VII), 1950 (VIII–IX), 1955 (X), 1960 (XI–XII), 1965 (XIII)
Robert, *OMS* L. Robert, *Opera minora selecta*
Robinson Essays Essays in Greek Coinage presented to Stanley Robinson, ed. C. M. Kraay and G. K. Jenkins. Oxford, 1968
SEG Supplementum epigraphicum graecum
SIG W. Dittenberger, *Sylloge inscriptionum graecarum.* 4 vols. Ed. 3. Leipzig, 1915–24
Sitz. Bayer. Akad. Sitzungsberichte der Bayerischen Akademie der Wissenschaften, phil.-hist. Abteilung
Sitz. Berlin Sitzungsberichte der Preussischen (Deutschen) Akademie der Wissenschaften, Berlin, phil.-hist. Klasse (from 1973: *Sitzungsberichte der Akademie der Wissenschaften der DDR*)
Sitz. Wien Sitzungsberichte der Akademie der Wissenschaften in Wien, phil.-hist. Klasse
Studi Arangio-Ruiz Studi in onore di Vincenzo Arangio-Ruiz nel xlv anno del suo insegnamento, ed. M. Lauria. 4 vols. Naples, 1951–3
Studi Calderini-Paribeni Studi in onore di A. Calderini e R. Paribeni, ed. S. Pagani. 3 vols. Milan, 1956–7
Studi class. e orient. Studi classici e orientali (Pisa)
SVA Die Staatsverträge des Altertums II: *Die Verträge der griechisch-römischen Welt von 700 bis 338 v. Chr.,* ed. H. Bengtson. Ed. 2, 1975; III: *Die Verträge der griechisch-römischen Welt von 338 bis 200 v. Chr.,* ed. H. H. Schmitt. Munich, 1969
SVF H. Diels and W. Kranz, *Fragmente der Vorsokratiker.* 3 vols. Ed. 6. Berlin, 1951–2
TAPA Transactions of the American Philological Association
Tod M. N. Tod, *Greek Historical Inscriptions* I, ed. 2, 1946; II, 1948. Oxford
UPZ U. Wilcken, *Urkunden der Ptolemäerzeit.* 2 vols. Berlin-Leipzig, 1922–7 and 1957
VDI Vestnik drevnej istorii
Verhandelingen v. d. Kon. Acad. Belgie Verhandelingen van der Koninklijke Academie voor Wetenschappen Letteren en Schone Kunsten van Belgie, Klasse de Letteren
Welles Essays Essays in Honor of C. Bradford Welles (American Studies in Papyrology 1). New Haven, 1966
Wilcken, *Grundzüge* and *Chr.* See Wilcken 1912: (F 91)
YCS Yale Classical Studies
ZAeS Zeitschrift für ägyptische Sprache und Altertumskunde
ZPE Zeitschrift für Papyrologie und Epigraphik
ZSS Zeitschrift der Savigny-Stiftung für Rechtsgeschichte, Romanistische Abteilung

BIBLIOGRAPHY

A. GENERAL

1. Austin, M. M. *The Hellenistic World from Alexander to the Roman Conquest.* Cambridge, 1981
2. Aymard, A. *Études d'histoire ancienne.* Paris, 1967
3. Badian, E. *Studies in Greek and Roman History.* Oxford, 1964
4. Badian, E. (ed.) *Ancient Society and Institutions. Studies presented to Victor Ehrenberg.* Oxford, 1966
5. Beloch, K. J. *Griechische Geschichte* IV.1 and 2. Ed. 2. Berlin-Leipzig, 1925–7
6. Bengtson, H. *Die Strategie in der hellenistischen Zeit. Ein Beitrag zum antiken Staatsrecht (Münch. Beitr. Papyr.* 26, 32, 36). Ed. 2 Munich, 1964–7
7. – *Griechische Geschichte von den Anfängen bis in die römische Kaiserzeit* (Handbücher der Altertumswissenschaft III.4). Ed. 5. Munich, 1977
8. Berve, H. *Die Tyrannis bei den Griechen.* 2 vols. Munich, 1967
9. Bury, J. B., Barber, E. A., Bevan, E. and Tarn, W. W. *The Hellenistic Age.* Cambridge, 1923
10. Cary, M. *A History of the Greek World from 323 to 146 B.C.* Ed. 2. London-New York, 1951 (issued with new bibliography by V. Ehrenberg, 1963)
11. Corradi, G. *Studi ellenistici.* Turin, 1929
12. De Sanctis, G. *Scritti minori* I, ed. S. Accame. Rome, 1966
13. Ehrenberg, V. *Der griechische Staat* II: *Der hellenistische Staat.* Leipzig, 1958. Translated as V. Ehrenberg, *The Greek State.* Ed. 2. London, 1969
14. Errington, R. M. 'Alexander in the Hellenistic world', *Entretiens Hardt* 22 (1976) 137–79
15. Fraser, P. M. *Ptolemaic Alexandria.* 3 vols. Oxford, 1972
16. Gelzer, M. *Kleine Schriften.* 3 vols. Wiesbaden, 1962–4
17. Giovannini, A. *Untersuchungen über die Natur und die Anfänge der bundesstaatlichen Sympolitie in Griechenland* (Hypomnemata 33). Göttingen, 1971. (*Contra* see Walbank 1976/7: (A 62))
18. Glotz, G., Cohen, R. and Roussel. P. *Histoire grecque* IV.1: *Alexandre et le démembrement de son empire.* Paris, 1945
19. Goukowsky, P. *Essai sur les origines du mythe d'Alexandre* I: *Les origines politiques.* Nancy, 1978
20. Hampl, F. *Die griechischen-Staatsverträge des 4. Jhts. v. Chr.* Leipzig, 1938
21. Heinen, H. *Untersuchungen zur hellenistischen Geschichte des 3. Jahrhunderts v. Chr. Zur Geschichte der Zeit des Ptolemaios Keraunos und zum Chremonideischen Krieg (Historia* Einzelschr. 20). Wiesbaden, 1972
22. Heuss, A. *Stadt und Herrscher des Hellenismus in ihren staats- und völkerrechtlichen Beziehungen (Klio* Beiheft 39). Leipzig, 1937
23. Holleaux, M. *Rome, la Grèce et les monarchies hellénistiques au IIIe siècle av. J.-C.* (*273–205*). Paris, 1921
24. Hopkins, K. *Conquerors and Slaves.* Cambridge, 1978
25. Jones, A. H. M. *The Greek City from Alexander to Justinian.* Oxford, 1940

26. – *The Cities of the Eastern Roman Provinces.* Ed. 2. Oxford, 1971

27. Jouguet, P. *L'impérialisme macédonien et l'hellénisation de l'Orient.* Paris, 1926

28. Kaerst, J. *Geschichte des Hellenismus.* Leipzig, 1927 (I, ed. 3); 1926 (II, ed. 2)

29. Klose, P. *Die völkerrechtliche Ordnung der hellenistischen Staatenwelt in der Zeit von 280–168 v. Chr. Ein Beitrag zur Geschichte des Völkerrechts (Münch. Beitr. Papyr.* 64). Munich, 1972

30. Kromayer, J. and Veith, G. *Antike Schlachtfelder. Bausteine zu einer antiken Kriegsgeschichte.* 4 vols. Berlin, 1903 (I); 1907 (II); 1912 (III.1); 1912 (III.2); 1924–31 (IV)

31. Larsen, J. A. O. 'Representative government in the panhellenic leagues', *CPhil.* 20 (1925) 313–29; 21 (1926) 52–71

32. – *Representative Government in Greek and Roman History.* Berkeley-Los Angeles, 1955

33. – *Greek Federal States, their Institutions and History.* Oxford, 1968

34. Marrou, H. I. *Histoire de l'éducation dans l'antiquité.* Ed. 6. Paris, 1965

35. Momigliano, A. *Contributo alla storia degli studi classici.* Rome, 1955 (= *Contributo* I)

36. – *Secondo contributo alla storia degli studi classici.* Rome, 1960 (= *Contributo* II)

37. – *Terzo contributo alla storia degli studi classici e del mondo antico.* 2 vols. Rome, 1966 (= *Contributo* III)

38. – *Quarto contributo alla storia degli studi classici e del mondo antico.* Rome, 1969 (= *Contributo* IV)

39. – *Quinto contributo alla storia degli studi classici e del mondo antico.* 2 vols. Rome, 1975 (= *Contributo* V)

40. – *Alien Wisdom: The Limits of Hellenization.* Cambridge, 1975

41. – *Essays in Ancient and Modern Historiography* (Blackwells Classical Studies). Oxford, 1977

42. – *Sesto contributo alla storia degli studi classici e del mondo antico.* 2 vols. Rome, 1980 (= *Contributo* VI)

43. Mossé, C. *La tyrannie dans la Grèce antique.* Paris, 1969

44. Niese, B. *Geschichte der griechischen und makedonischen Staaten seit der Schlacht bei Chaeronea.* 3 vols. Gotha, 1893–1903

45. Olshausen, E. *Prosopographie der hellenistischen Königsgesandten* I: *Von Triparadeisos bis Pydna (Studia Hellenistica* 19). Louvain, 1974

46. Orth, W. *Königlicher Machtanspruch und städtische Freiheit (Münch. Beitr. Papyr.* 71). Munich, 1977. (Review by D. Musti, *Gnomon* 52 (1980) 525–9.)

47. Pöhlmann, R. von *Geschichte der sozialen Frage und des Sozialismus in der antiken Welt.* Ed. 3 by F. Oehrli. Munich, 1925

48. Préaux, C. *Le monde hellénistique. La Grèce et l'Orient de la mort d'Alexandre à la conquête romaine de la Grèce (323–146 av. J.-C.) (Nouvelle Clio* 6 and 6 bis). 2 vols. Paris, 1978

49. Pritchett, W. K. *Studies in Ancient Greek Topography.* 3 vols. Berkeley-Los Angeles, 1965 (I), 1969 (II: *Battlefields*), 1980 (III: *Roads*)

50. Ranowitsch, A. B. *Der Hellenismus und seine geschichtliche Rolle.* Berlin, 1958

51. Rizzo, F. P. *Studi ellenistico-romani.* Palermo, 1974

52. Rostovtzeff, M. *The Social and Economic History of the Hellenistic World*. 3 vols. Ed. 2. Oxford, 1953

53. Samuel, A. *Greek and Roman Chronology, Calendars and Years in Classical Antiquity* (Müllers Handbücher der Altertumswissenschaft 1.7). Munich, 1972

54. Schmitt, H. H. *Die Staatsverträge des Altertums* III: *Die Verträge der griechisch-römischen Welt von 338 bis 200 v. Chr.* Munich, 1969

55. – 'Polybios und das Gleichgewicht der Mächte', in O. Reverdin (ed.), *Entretiens Hardt* 20 (1974) 65–93 (discussion: 94–102)

56. Schneider, C. *Kulturgeschichte des Hellenismus*. 2 vols. Munich, 1967–9

57. Seibert, J. *Historische Beiträge zu den dynastischen Verbindungen in hellenistischer Zeit* (*Historia* Einzelschr. 10). Wiesbaden, 1967

58. Tarn, W. W. *Alexander the Great*. 2 vols. Cambridge, 1948

59. Tarn, W. W. and Griffith, G. T. *Hellenistic Civilisation*. Ed. 3. London, 1952

60. T(s)cherikower, V. *Die hellenistischen Städtegründungen von Alexander dem Grossen bis auf die Römerzeit* (*Philol.* Suppl. B.XIX.1). Leipzig, 1927

61. – *Hellenistic Civilisation and the Jews*. Philadelphia-Jerusalem, 1959

62. Walbank, F. W. 'Were there Greek federal states?', *Scripta Classica Israelica* 3 (1976/7) 27–51

63. – *The Hellenistic World*. London, 1981

64. Welles, C. B. *Alexander and the Hellenistic World*. Toronto, 1970

65. Welskopf, E. C. (ed.) *Hellenische Poleis: Krise-Wandlung-Wirkung*. 4 vols. Berlin, 1974

66. Will, Ed. 'Comment on écrit l'histoire hellénistique . . . (Notes critiques)', *Historia* 27 (1978) 65–82

67. – *Histoire politique du monde hellénistique*. 2 vols. Nancy, 1967 (II); 1979 (I, ed. 2); 1982 (II, ed. 2)

68. Will, Ed., Mossé, C. and Goukowsky, P. *Le monde grec et l'Orient* II: *Le IVe siècle et l'époque hellénistique*. Paris, 1975

B. SOURCES

a. ANCIENT AUTHORS AND WORKS ON THESE

See also G(a) on Agathocles and J(a) on Hellenistic science

1. Abel, F. M. *Les Livres des Maccabées*. Paris, 1949

2. Badian, E. 'Lionel Pearson: The lost histories of Alexander the Great', *Gnomon* 33 (1961) 666–7 = *Studies in Greek and Roman History*, 250–61: (A 3)

3. Bendinelli, G. 'Cassandro di Macedonia nella vita plutarchea di Alessandro Magno', *Riv. Fil.* 43 (1965) 150–64

4. Bizière, F. 'Comment travaillait Diodore de Sicile?', *Rev. Ét. Gr.* 87 (1974) 369–74

5. Bosworth, A. B. *A Historical Commentary on Arrian's History of Alexander* I: *Commentary on Books I–IV*. Oxford, 1981

6. Braccesi, L. 'L'epitafio di Iperide come fonte storica', *Athenaeum* 48 (1970) 276–301

7. Brown, T. S. *Timaeus of Tauromenium* (University of California Publications in History 55). Berkeley-Los Angeles, 1958

8. Burton, A. *Diodorus Siculus, Book I: A Commentary*. Leiden, 1972

9. Dancy, J. C. *A Commentary on I Maccabees*. Oxford, 1954

10. Eissfeldt, O. *The Old Testament. An introduction*, tr. P. R. Ackroyd. Oxford, 1965

11. Engel, R. 'Zum Geschichtsbild des Hieronymos von Kardia', *Athenaeum* 50 (1972) 120–5

12. Errington, R. M. 'The chronology of Polybius' *Histories* Books I and II', *JRS* 57 (1967) 96–108

13. Gabba, E. 'Studi su Filarco. Le biografie plutarchie di Agide e di Cleomene', *Athenaeum* 35 (1957) 3–55, 193–239

14. – *Appiani bellorum civilium liber primus*. Florence, 1958

15. Gallo, I. *Frammenti biografici da papiri* I: *La biografia politica*. Rome, 1975

16. Gelzer, M. 'Die hellenische *ΠΡΟΚΑΤΑΣΚΕΥΗ* im zweiten Buche des Polybios', *Hermes* 75 (1940) 27–37, reprinted in *Kleine Schriften* III, 111–22: (A 16)

17. – 'Die Achaica im Geschichtswerk des Polybios', *Abh. Akad. Berlin* 1940 no. 2, reprinted in *Kleine Schriften* III, 123–54: (A 16)

18. Gozzoli, S. 'Etnografia e politica in Agatarchide', *Athenaeum* 56 (1978) 54–79

19. Gutschmid, A. von 'Trogus und Timagenes', *Rh. Mus.* 37 (1882) 548–55 = *Kleine Schriften* V (1894) 218–27

20. Helm, R. *Die Chronik des Hieronymos*. Ed. 2. Berlin, 1956

21. Hornblower, J. *Hieronymus of Cardia*. Oxford, 1981

22. Jacoby, F. *Atthis: The Local Chronicles of Ancient Athens*. Oxford, 1949

23. Kebric, R. B. *In the Shadow of Macedon. Duris of Samos* (*Historia* Einzelschr. 29). Wiesbaden, 1977

24. Merkelbach, R. *Die Quellen des griechischen Alexanderromans*. Munich, 1954

25. Momigliano, A. D. 'Atene nel III secolo a.C. e la scoperta di Roma nelle storie di Timeo di Tauromenio', *Rivista Storica Italiana* 71 (1959) 529–56 = *Contributo* III 1.23–53: (A 37)

26. Pédech, P. *La méthode historique de Polybe*. Paris, 1964

27. Peremans, W. 'Diodore de Sicile et Agatharchide de Cnide', *Historia* 16 (1967) 432–55

28. Powell, J. V. *Collectanea Alexandrina*. Oxford, 1925

29. Reekmans, T., Dack, E. van't and Verdin, H. (eds.) *Historia Antiqua. Commentationes Lovanienses in honorem W. Peremans septuagenarii editae* (Symbolae 6). Louvain, 1977

30. Rosen, K. 'Political documents in Hieronymus of Cardia', *Acta Classica* 10 (1967) 41–94.

31. Russell, D. A. *Plutarch*. London, 1973

32. Schubert, R. *Die Quellen zur Geschichte der Diadochenzeit*. Leipzig, 1914 (repr. Aalen, 1964)

33. Schwab, G. *De Livio et Timagene*. Stuttgart, 1834

34. Simpson, R. H. 'Abbreviation of Hieronymus in Diodorus', *AJPhil.* 80 (1959) 370–9.

35. Stadter, P. A. *Arrian of Nicomedia*. Chapel Hill, N.C., 1980
36. Urban, R. '"Historiae Philippicae" bei Pompeius Trogus: Versuch einer Deutung', *Historia* 31 (1982) 82–96
37. Walbank, F. W. *A Historical Commentary on Polybius*. 3 vols. Oxford, 1957 (I); 1967 (II); 1979 (III)
38. – *Polybius*. Berkeley, Los Angeles and London, 1972
39. – 'Polybius' last ten books', *Historia Antiqua*, ed. T. Reekmans and others (1977), 139–62: (B 29)
40. – 'Livy, Macedonia and Alexander', in *Edson Studies*, 335–56

b. EPIGRAPHY

See also E(g) (Asoka) and items listed in Abbreviations: Holleaux, *Études*; IC, IG, IG², IGB, I. Magnesia, Insc. Délos, I. Olympia, I. Priene

41. Accame, S. 'Un nuovo decreto di Lindo del V sec. a.C.', *Clara Rhodos* 9 (1938) 209–29
42. Altheim, F. and Stiehl, R. 'Die Seleukideninschrift aus Failaka', *Klio* 46 (1965) 273–81
43. Andronikos, M. *Ἀρχαῖαι Ἐπιγραφαὶ Βεροίας*. Thessalonica, 1950
44. Audollent, A. *Defixionum tabellae quotquot innotuerunt tam in graeci orientis quam in totius occidentis partibus praeter atticas* (diss. Paris, 1904)
45. Bakalakis, G. and Scranton, R. L. 'An inscription from Samothrace', *AJPhil.* 60 (1939) 452–8
46. Benedum, J. 'Inschriften aus Kos', *ZPE* 27 (1977) 229–40
47. Bengtson, H. 'Randbemerkungen zu den Koischen Inschriften', *Historia* 3 (1955) 456–63
48. – 'Die Inschriften von Labranda und die Politik des Antigonos Doson', *Sitz. Bayer. Akad.* 1971 no. 3
49. Béquignon, Y. 'Études thessaliennes VII: Inscriptions de Thessalie', *BCH* 59 (1935) 36–77
50. Bikerman, E. 'Sur une inscription grecque trouvée à Sidon', *Mélanges Dussaud* 1.91–9. Paris, 1939
51. Bousquet, J. 'Nouvelles inscriptions de Delphes', *BCH* 62 (1938) 332–69
52. – 'L'acceptation des Ptolemaieia', *BCH* 82 (1958) 77–82
53. Brashinsky, J. B. 'The progress of Greek ceramic epigraphy in the U.S.S.R.', *Eirene* 11 (1973) 111–44
54. Bravo, B. 'Une lettre sur plomb de Berezan: colonisation et modes de contact dans le Pont', *DHA* 1 (1974) 111–87
55. Buckler, W. H. and Robinson, D. M. 'Greek inscriptions from Sardis I', *AJArch.* 16 (1912) 11–82
56. – *Sardis* VII.1: *The Greek Inscriptions*. Leiden, 1932
57. Buckler, W. H. 'Documents from Phrygia and Cyprus', *JHS* 55 (1935) 71–8
58. Cameron, A. 'Inscriptions relating to sacral manumission and confession', *Harv. Theol. Rev.* 32 (1939) 143–79
59. Cormack, J. M. R. 'The gymnasiarchal law of Beroea', in *Ancient Macedonia* II (1977).139–50

60. Crampa, J. *Labraunda. Swedish Excavations and Researches* III.1–2: *The Greek Inscriptions* (Acta Instituti Atheniensis Regni Sueciae, Series in 4°, v). Lund, 1969 and Stockholm, 1972. (Critical review of III.1: Chr. Habicht in *Gnomon* 44 (1972) 162–70.)

61. Cumont, F. 'Nouvelles inscriptions grecques de Suse', *CR Acad.Inscr.* 1931, 233–50, 278–92; 1932, 271–86

62. Daux, G. *Fouilles de Delphes* III: *Épigraphie (fascicule hors série). Chronologie delphique.* Paris, 1943

63. Doty, L. T. *Cuneiform Archives from Hellenistic Uruk* (diss. Yale, 1977)

64. – 'The archive of the Nanaiddin family from Uruk', *JCS* 30 (1978) 65–90

65. Dow, S. 'The first enneëteric Delian Pythaïs. *IG* II².2336', *HSCP* 51 (1941) 111–24

66. Drew-Bear, Th. 'Deux décrets hellénistiques d'Asie Mineure', *BCH* 96 (1972) 435–71

67. Edson, C. F. 'Macedonica. A dedication of Philip V', *HSCP* 51 (1941) 125–6

68. Engelmann, H. and Merkelbach, R. (eds.) *Die Inschriften von Erythrai und Klazomenai* I. Bonn, 1972

69. Errington, R. M. 'An inscription from Beroea and the alleged co-rule of Demetrius II', in *Ancient Macedonia* II (1977).115–32

70. Étienne, R. and Piérart, M. 'Décret du koinon des Hellènes à Platées en l'honneur de Glaucon, fils d'Etéoclès, d'Athènes', *BCH* 99 (1975) 51–75

71. Feyel, M. *Contribution à l'épigraphie béotienne* (Publications de la faculté des lettres de l'Université de Strasbourg 95). Le Puy, 1942

72. Fischer, Th. 'Zur Seleukideninschrift von Hefzibah', *ZPE* 33 (1979) 131–8

73. Fränkel, M. *Die Inschriften von Pergamon.* Berlin, 1890

74. Fraser, P. M. 'Two Hellenistic inscriptions from Delphi', *BCH* 78 (1954) 49–67

75. – 'Inscriptions from Cyrene', *Berytus* 12 (1956–8) 120–7

76. – *Samothrace* II.1: *The Inscriptions on Stone.* New York, 1960

77. – 'Greek-Phoenician bilingual inscriptions from Rhodes', *BSA* 65 (1970) 31–6

78. Frisch, P. *Die Inschriften von Ilion.* Bonn, 1975

79. – *Die Inschriften von Lampsakos.* Bonn, 1978

80. Geagan, D. J. 'Inscriptions from Nemea', *Hesp.* 37 (1968) 381–5

81. Habicht, Chr. 'Samische Volksbeschlüsse der hellenistischen Zeit', *Ath. Mitt.* 72 (1957 [1959]) 152–274

82. – 'Neue Inschriften aus dem Kerameikos', *Ath. Mitt.* 76 (1961) 127–43

83. – 'Epigraphische Zeugnisse zur Geschichte Thessaliens unter der makedonischen Herrschaft', in *Ancient Macedonia* I (1970).265–79

84. – 'Hellenistische Inschriften aus dem Heraion von Samos', *Ath. Mitt.* 87 (1972) 191–228

85. Herrmann, P. 'Antiochos der Grosse und Teos', *Anadolu (Anatolia)* 9 (1965) 29–159

86. – 'Neue Urkunden zur Geschichte von Milet im 2. Jahrh. v. Chr.', *Istanb. Mitt.* 15 (1965) 71–117

87. Herrmann, P. and Polatkan, K. Z. *Das Testament des Epikrates und andere neue Inschriften aus dem Museum von Manisa (Sitz. Wien* 265.1). Vienna, 1969

88. Herzog, R. 'Heilige Gesetze von Kos', *Abh. Akad. Berlin* 1928 no. 6

89. Herzog, R. and Klaffenbach, G. 'Asylieurkunden aus Kos', *Abh. Akad. Berlin* 1952 no. 1

90. Heuss, A. 'Die Freiheitserklärung von Mylasa in den Inschriften von Labranda', in *Mélanges Préaux*, 403–15

91. Hiller von Gaertringen, F. *Die Inschriften von Priene*. Berlin, 1906

92. Holleaux, M. 'Inscription trouvée à Brousse', *BCH* 48 (1924) 1–57 = *Études* 1 (1938) 73–125

93. Ihnken, T. H. *Die Inschriften von Magnesia am Sipylos*, Bonn, 1978

94. *Inschriften griechischer Städte aus Kleinasien* (Kommission für die archäologische Erforschung Kleinasiens bei der Österreichischen Akademie der Wissenschaften. Institut für Altertumskunde der Universität Köln). 1–. Bonn, 1972–

95. Jacobsen, T. W. and Smith, P. M. 'Two Kimolian dikast decrees from Geraistos in Euboia', *Hesp.* 37 (1968) 184–99

96. Jalabert, L., Mouterde, R. and Rey-Coquais, J. P. *Inscriptions grecques et latines de la Syrie*. Paris, 1929–

97. Kennedy, D. A. *Cuneiform Texts from Babylonian Tablets in the British Museum* XLIX: *Late-Babylonian Economic Texts*. London, 1968

98. Klaffenbach, G. 'Bemerkungen zum griechischen Urkundenwesen', *Sitz. Akad. Berlin* 1960 no. 6

99. – *Griechische Epigraphik*. Ed. 2. Gottingen, 1966

100. Landau, Y. H. 'A Greek inscription from Acre', *IEJ* 11 (1961) 117–26

101. – 'A Greek inscription found near Hefzibah', *IEJ* 16 (1966) 54–70

102. Langdon, M. K. and Watrous, L. V. 'The farm of Timesios: rock-cut inscriptions in South Attica', *Hesp.* 36 (1977) 162–77

103. Larsen, J. A. O. '*TAM* II, 508. Part 1: Introduction, text, and commentary. Part II: Discussion', *CPhil.* 38 (1943) 177–90 and 246–55

104. Laumonier, A. 'Inscriptions de Carie', *BCH* 58 (1934) 291–380

105. Lockhart, P. N. 'The Laodice inscription from Didyma', *AJPhil.* 82 (1961) 188–92

106. Maiuri, A. *Nuova silloge epigrafica di Rodi e Cos*. Florence, 1925

107. Meritt, B. D. 'Greek inscriptions', *Hesp.* 7 (1938) 75–159

108. Metzger, H., Laroche, E. and Dupont-Sommer, A. 'La stèle trilingue récemment découverte au Létôon de Xanthos', *CRAcad.Inscr.* 1974, 82–93 (H. Metzger: Le texte grec), 115–25 (E. Laroche: Le texte lycien), and 132–49 (A. Dupont-Sommer: Le texte araméen)

109. Metzger, H., Laroche, E., Dupont-Sommer, A., and Mayrhofer, M. *Fouilles de Xanthos* VI: *La stèle trilingue du Létôon*. Paris, 1979

110. Moretti, L. *Iscrizioni agonistiche greche*. Rome, 1953

111. – *Iscrizioni storiche ellenistiche*. 2 vols. Florence, 1967 and 1976

112. Müller, H. *Milesische Volksbeschlüsse. Eine Untersuchung zur Verfassungsgeschichte der Stadt Milet in hellenistischer Zeit* (Hypomnemata 47). Göttingen, 1976

113. Musti, D. 'Osservazioni in margine a documenti delle cancellerie ellenistiche', *Annali di Pisa*[2] 26 (1957) 267-84

114. – 'Sui nuovi testi relativi al culto di Antioco I di Commagene', *Rend. Linc.* 21 (1966) 57-70

115. Oelsner, J. 'Eine Rechtsurkunde aus dem seleukidischen Uruk in der Hilprecht-Sammlung Vorderasiatischer Altertümer', *Wissenschaftliche Zeitschrift der Friedrich-Schiller Universität Jena*, Gesellschaftliche und Sprachwissenschaftliche Reihe 19 (1970) 905-12

116. Oliverio, G., Pugliese Carratelli, G. and Morelli, D. 'Supplemento epigrafico cirenaico', *Annuario* N.S. 39-40 (1961-2 [publ. 1963]) 219-375

117. Pippidi, D. M. (Histria and Callatis in the 3rd and 2nd centuries B.C. à propos of an unpublished inscription). *Studi și cercetari de istorie veche* 4 (1953) 487-514 (in Rumanian) = Pippidi 1962, 11-34: (D 163)

118. Pleket, H. W. *Epigraphica* I: *Texts on the Economic History of the Greek World* (Textus minores XXXI). Leiden, 1964

119. – *Epigraphica* II: *Texts on the Social History of the Greek World* (Textus minores XLI). Leiden, 1969

120. Pouilloux, J. and Verdélis, N. M. 'Deux inscriptions de Démétrias', *BCH* 74 (1950) 33-47

121. Préaux, C. 'Sur l'inscription de Cyrène *SEG* ix, 1 no. 5', *Chron. d'Égypte* 37 (1941) 148

122. Pugliese Carratelli, ˙G. 'Supplemento epigrafico di Iasos', *Annuario* N.S. 29-30 (1967-8) 437-86

123. Rehm, A. 'Zur Chronologie der milesischen Inschriften des II. Jhdts, v. Chr.', *Sitz. Bayer. Akad.* 1923 no. 8

124. Reinmuth, O. *The Ephebic Inscriptions of the Fourth Century* B.C. Leiden, 1973

125. Rey-Coquais, J.-P. *IGLS* VII: *Arados et régions voisines.* Paris, 1970

126. – 'Inscription grecque découverte à Ras Ibn Hani: stèle de mercénaires lagides sur la côte syrienne', *Syria* 55 (1978) 313-25

127. Robert, L. 'Notes d'épigraphie hellénistique. Inscriptions relatives à des juges étrangers', *BCH* 48 (1924) 331-42 = *OMS* I (1969) 1-12

128. – 'Notes d'épigraphie hellénistique V-XII', *BCH* 49 (1925) 219-38 = *OMS* I (1969) 13-32

129. – 'Lesbiaca I. Décrets de Methymna et d'Erésos en l'honneur de juges milésiens', *Rev. Ét. Gr.* 38 (1925) 29-43 = *OMS* II (1970) 721-35

130. – 'Lesbiaca II. Décret d'Erésos', *Rev. Ét. Gr.* 38 (1925) 423-6 = *OMS* II (1970) 736-9

131. – 'Notes d'épigraphie hellénistique XIII-XXIII', *BCH* 50 (1926) 469-522 = *OMS* I (1969) 33-86

132. – 'Études d'épigraphie grecque I-VI', *Rev. Phil.* 53 (1927) 97-132 = *OMS* II (1970) 1052-87

133. – 'Notes d'épigraphie hellénistique XXIV-XXVIII. Décrets de Delphes

pour des médecins', *BCH* 52 (1928) 158–78 = *OMS* 1 (1969) 87–107

134. – 'Notes d'épigraphie hellénistique xxxvi–xxxix', *BCH* 54 (1930) 322–51 = *OMS* 1 (1969) 141–70

135. – 'Inscriptions d'Erythrai', *BCH* 57 (1933) 467–84 = *OMS* 1 (1969) 455–72

136. – 'Sur des inscriptions de Chios', *BCH* 57 (1933) 505–43 = *OMS* 1 (1969) 473–511

137. – 'Notes d'épigraphie hellénistique xli–xlv', *BCH* 59 (1935) 421–37 = *OMS* 1 (1969) 178–94

138. – 'Études d'épigraphie grecque xl–xlviii', *Rev. Phil.* 62/10 (1936) 113–70 = *OMS* 11 (1970) 1192–249

139. – *Études anatoliennes. Recherches sur les inscriptions grecques de l'Asie Mineure.* Paris, 1937

140. – 'Hellenica i–xix', *Rev. Phil.* 65/13 (1939) 97–217 = *OMS* 11 (1970) 1250–370

141. – 'Inscriptions grecques d'Asie Mineure', in *Anatolian Studies presented to W. H. Buckler*, ed. W. M. Calder and J. Keil, 227–48. Manchester, 1939

142. – *Le sanctuaire de Sinuri près de Mylasa* i: *Les inscriptions grecques* (*Mém. Inst. fr. arch. Stamboul* 7). Paris, 1945

143. – *Noms indigènes dans l'Asie Mineure gréco-romaine* i. Paris, 1963

144. – *Nouvelles inscriptions de Sardes* i (Archaeological Exploration of Sardis). Paris, 1964

145. – *Documents de l'Asie Mineure méridionale. Inscriptions, monnaies et géographie.* Geneva-Paris, 1966

146. – 'Encore une inscription grecque de l'Iran', *CR Acad.Inscr.* 1967. 281–97

147. – 'Sur des inscriptions d'Éphèse: fêtes, athlètes, empereurs, épigrammes', *Rev. Phil.* 93/41 (1967) 7–84

148. – 'De Delphes à l'Oxus. Inscriptions grecques nouvelles de la Bactriane', *CR Acad.Inscr.* 1968, 414–57

149. – 'Sur des inscriptions de Délos', *Études déliennes* (*BCH* Suppl. 1) 435–89. Paris, 1973

150. – 'Les monétaires et un décret hellénistique de Sestos', *Rev. Num.* 15 (1973) 43–53

151. Robert, L. and J. 'Une inscription grecque de Téos en Ionie. L'union de Téos et de Kyrbis', *Journ. Sav.* 1976, 153–235

152. Rostovtzeff, M. 'A parchment contract of loan from Dura Europus on the Euphrates', *YCS* 2 (1931) 1–77

153. Roussel, P. 'Un nouveau document relatif à la guerre démétriaque', *BCH* 54 (1930) 268–82

154. – 'Décret des Péliganes de Laodicée-sur-mer', *Syria* 23 (1942–3) 21–32

155. Rutten, M. *Contrats de l'époque séleucide conservés au Musée du Louvre.* Paris, 1935

156. Salviat, F. and Vatin, Cl. 'Le cadastre de Larissa', *BCH* 98 (1974) 247–62

157. Sarkisian, G. Kh. 'New cuneiform texts from Uruk of the Seleucid period in the Staatliche Museen zu Berlin', *Forschungen und Berichte: Staatliche Museen zu Berlin* 16 (1974) 15–76

158. Segre, M. 'Decreto di Aspendos', *Aegyptus* 14 (1934) 253–68
159. – 'Osservazioni epigrafiche sulla vendita di sacerdozio', *Rend. Ist. Lomb.* 69 (1936) 811–30
160. – 'Osservazioni epigrafiche sulla vendita di sacerdozio', *Rend. Ist. Lomb.* 70 (1937) 83–105
161. – 'Iscrizioni di Licia i–ii', *Clara Rhodos* 9 (1938) 181–208
162. Seyrig, H. 'Décret de Séleucie et ordonnance de Séleucus IV', *Syria* 13 (1932) 255–8
163. Sherk, R. K. *Roman Documents from the Greek East*. Baltimore, 1969
164. Stähelin, F. 'Zur Chronologie und Erklärung der Inschriften von Magnesia und Demetrias', *Ath. Mitt.* 54 (1929) 201–26
165. Tarn, W. W. 'The date of Milet i, iii, no. 139', *Hermes* 65 (1930) 446–54
166. Taslikioğlu, Z. and Frisch, P. 'New inscriptions of the Troad', *ZPE* 17 (1975) 101–14
167. Tod, M. N. 'Greek inscriptions at Cairness House', *JHS* 54 (1934) 140–62
168. – 'A Greek inscription from the Persian Gulf', *JHS* 63 (1943) 112–13
169. Vanseveren, J. 'Inscriptions d'Amorgos et de Chios', *Rev. Phil.* 63/11 (1937) 313–47
170. Vidman, L. *Sylloge inscriptionum religionis Isiacae et Sarapiacae*. Berlin, 1969
171. Welles, C. B. *Royal Correspondence in the Hellenistic Period: A Study in Greek Epigraphy*. New Haven, 1934 (= RC)
172. Wiegand, Th. and Rehm, A. *Didyma* ii; *Die Inschriften*. Berlin, 1958
173. Wilhelm, A. 'Die lokrische Mädchen-inschrift', *Jahreshefte des Österreichischen Instituts in Wien* 14 (1911) 163–256
174. – 'Zu Inschriften aus Delphi', *Anzeiger der Akademie der Wissenschaften in Wien* 1922, 5–28
175. – 'Proxenie und Euergesie', in *Attische Urkunden* v (*Sitz. Wien* 220.5) 11–86. Vienna, 1942
176. Woodhead, A. G. *The Study of Greek Inscriptions*. Ed. 2. Cambridge, 1981
177. Wörrle, M. 'Antiochos I., Achaios der Ältere und die Galater. Eine neue Inschrift in Denizli', *Chiron* 5 (1975) 59–87
178. – 'Epigraphische Forschungen zur Geschichte Lykiens i, *Chiron* 7 (1977) 43–66
179. – 'Epigraphische Forschungen zur Geschichte Lykiens ii: Ptolemaios II. und Telmessos'. *Chiron* 8 (1978) 201–46 and Table 2
180. – 'Epigraphische Forschungen zur Geschichte Lykiens iii: Ein hellenistischer Königsbrief aus Telmessos', *Chiron* 9 (1979) 83–111 and Table 3

c. EXCAVATION REPORTS: DESCRIPTIONS OF SITES

See also J(d); E 181–3, 194, 201; and items listed in Abbreviations: *Corinth*, *Délos*, *FD*, *Lindos*, *Milet*
181. *Altertümer von Pergamon* (Königliche Museen zu Berlin and Deutsches Archäologisches Institut). Berlin, 1885– (12 volumes so far published)

182. Bakhuizen, S.C. *Salganeus and the Fortifications on its Mountains*. Groningen, 1970

183. Benoit, F. *Fouilles sous-marines: L'épave du Grand Congloué à Marseille* (*Gallia* Suppl. 14). Paris, 1961

184. Béquignon, Y. 'Études thessaliennes VIII: La stoa de Pharsale et les Leonidaia', *BCH* 59 (1935) 514–19

185. Bingen, J. 'Le trésor monétaire Thorikos 1969', in H. F. Mussche and others, *Thorikos 1969: Rapport préliminaire sur la sixième campagne de fouilles*, 7–59. Brussels, 1973

186. Braun, K. 'Der Dipylos-Brunnen B1. Die Funde', *Ath. Mitt.* 85 (1970) 129–269

187. Bruneau, Ph. 'Le quartier d'Inopos à Délos et la fondation du Sarapieion A dans un "lieu plein d'ordures"', *Études déliennes* (*BCH* Suppl. 1) 111–36. Paris, 1973

188. Callaghan, P. J. 'KRS 1976. Excavations at a shrine of Glaukos, Knossos', *BSA* 73 (1978) 1–30

189. Colt, H. D. (ed.) *Excavations at Nessana* 1. London, 1962

190. Crowfoot, J. W., Crowfoot, G. M., Kenyon, K. M. and others. *Samaria-Sebaste. Reports of the work of the joint expedition in 1931–1933 and of the British expedition in 1935* III: *The objects from Samaria*. London, 1957

191. Cumont, F. *Fouilles de Doura-Europos*. Paris, 1926

192. Diest, W. von *Nysa ad Maeandrum* (*JDAI* Ergänzungsheft 10). Berlin, 1913

193. Dörner, F. K. and Goell, Th. *Arsameia am Nymphaios* (*Istanb. Forsch.* 23). Berlin, 1963

194. Dunbabin, T. J. (ed.) *Perachora* II. Oxford, 1962

195. Gagnière, J. des, Devambez, P., Ginouvès, R., Kahil, L., Robert, L. and De Planhol, X. *Laodicée du Lycos: le nymphée* (*Campagnes 1961–63*). Quebec Paris, 1969

196. Gallet de Santerre, H. *Délos* XXIV: *La Terrasse des Lions, le Létoon, le Monument de Granit*. Paris, 1959

197. Geirafi, F. and Kirichian, A. 'Recherches archéologiques à Ayin-Dara au n.-o. d'Alep', *AArch.Syr.* 15 (1965) 3–20

198. Goldman, H. (ed.) *Excavations at Gözlü Kule, Tarsus* I: *The Hellenistic and Roman Periods*. Princeton, 1950

199. Gullini, G. 'First report of the results of the first excavation campaigns at Seleucia and Ctesiphon (1st October–17th December 1964)', *Sumer* 20 (1964) 63–5

200. Hanfmann, G. M. A. and Waldbaum, J.C. *A Survey of Sardis and the Major Monuments outside the City Walls* (Archaeological Exploration of Sardis, Report 1). Cambridge, Mass., 1975

201. Hood, S., Smyth, D. and Roberts. N. *Archaeological Survey of the Knossos Area* (*BSA* Suppl. 14). Ed. 2. Athens-London, 1981

202. Jordan, J, *Uruk-Warka*. Berlin, 1928

203. Litvinskiy, D. A. and Pichikiyan, I. R. 'The temple of the Oxus', *Journal of the Royal Asiatic Society* 1981, 133–67

204. Milojčić, V. and Theocharis, D. *Demetrias* I. Bonn, 1976
205. Pouilloux, J. *La Forteresse de Rhamnounte. Étude de topographie et d'histoire.* Paris, 1954
206. Stähelin, F., Meyer, E. and Heidner, A. *Pagasai und Demetrias. Beschreibung der Reste und Stadtgeschichte.* Berlin-Leipzig, 1934
207. Stroud, R. S. 'An ancient fort on Mount Oneion', *Hesp.* 40 (1971) 127–45
208. Vanderpool, E., McCredie, J. R. and Steinberg, A. 'Koroni: A Ptolemaic camp on the east coast of Attica', *Hesp.* 31 (1962) 26–61
209. Vanderpool, E., McCredie, J. R. and Steinberg, A. 'Koroni: The date of the camp and the pottery', *Hesp.* 33 (1964) 69–75
210. Welles, C. B., Fink, R. O., Gilliam, J. F. *Antioch-on-the-Orontes* II: *The Excavations, 1933–1936*, ed. R. Stillwell. Princeton, 1938
211. Welles, C. B., Fink, R. O., Gilliam, J. F. (eds.) *The Excavations at Dura-Europos, Final Report* V.1: *The Parchments and Papyri.* New Haven, 1959
212. Wiegand, Th. and Schrader, H. *Priene: Ergebnisse der Ausgrabungen und Untersuchungen in den Jahren 1895–1898.* Berlin, 1904
213. Young, R. S. 'The 1963 campaign at Gordion', *AJArch.* 68 (1964) 279–92

d. NUMISMATIC PUBLICATIONS

See also F(k) on Egypt and G(a–ii) on Agathocles; E 118, 132; H 202; *IGCH*

214. Akarca, A. *Les monnaies grecques de Mylasa.* Paris, 1959
215. Bellinger, A. R. *Troy Supplementary Monographs* II: *The Coins.* Princeton, 1961
216. – *Essays on the Coinage of Alexander the Great* (*Num. Stud.* 11). New York, 1963
217. Boehringer, Chr. *Zur Chronologie mittelhellenistischer Münzserien, 220–160 v. Chr.* Berlin, 1972
218. Casey, J. and Reece, R. (eds.) *Coins and the Archaeologist* (BAR 4). Oxford, 1974
219. Chantraine, H. 'Der Beginn der jüngeren achäischen Bundesprägung', *Chiron* 2 (1972) 175–90
220. Davis, N. and Kraay, C. M. *The Hellenistic Kingdoms. Portrait coins and history.* London, 1973
221. Dodson, O. H. and Wallace, W. P. 'The Kozani hoard of 1955', *ANSMN* 11 (1964) 26–8
222. Franke, P. R. *Die antiken Münzen von Epirus* I: *Poleis, Stämme und Epeirotischer Bund bis 27 v. Chr.* Wiesbaden, 1961
223. Fritze, H. von *Die Münzen von Pergamon* (*Abh. Akad. Berlin*). Berlin, 1910
224. Giovannini, A. *Rome et la circulation monétaire en Grèce au IIe siècle avant J.-C.* Basel, 1978
225. Hackens, T. 'Trésor hellénistique trouvé à Délos en 1964, 1: Les monnaies', *BCH* 89 (1965) 503–34
226. – 'A propos de la circulation monétaire dans le Péloponnèse au IIIe siècle

av. J.-C', *Antidorum W. Peremans oblatum (Studia Hellenistica* 16), 69–96. Louvain, 1968

227. – 'Monnaies d'Italie et de Sicile circulant en Grèce', *Revue Belge de Numismatique* 114 (1968) 119–29

228. – 'La circulation monétaire dans la Béotie héllenistique: trésors de Thèbes 1935 et 1965', *BCH* 93 (1969) 701–29

229. Jenkins, G. K. 'A note on Corinthian coins in the West', *American Numismatic Society Centennial Volume*, ed. H. Ingholt, 367–79. New York, 1958

230. – 'The monetary systems in the early Hellenistic time with special regard to the economic policy of the Ptolemaic kings', *Proceedings of the International Numismatic Convention, Jerusalem 1963*, ed. A. Kindler, 53–74. Tel Aviv-Jerusalem, 1967

231. Kleiner, F. S. and Noe, S. P. *The Early Cistophoric Coinage (Num. Stud.* 14). New York, 1977

232. Kleiner, F. S. 'Further reflections on the early cistophoric coinage', *ANSMN* 25 (1980) 45–52

233. Kleiner, G. *Alexanders Reichmünzen.* Berlin, 1949

234. Kraay, C. M. *Greek Coins and History: Some Current Problems.* London, 1969

235. Laix, R. A. de 'The silver coinage of the Aetolian League', *CSCA* 6 (1973) 47–75

236. Le Rider, G. *Suse sous les Séleucides et les Parthes: les trouvailles monétaires et l'histoire de la ville (Mémoires de la mission arch. en Iran* 38). Paris, 1965

237. – *Monnaies crétoises du IVe au 1er siècle.* Paris, 1966

238. Lewis, D. M. 'The chronology of the Athenian new-style coinage', *Num. Chron.*[7] 2 (1962) 275–300

239. May, J. M. F. *The Coinage of Damastion and the Lesser Coinages of the Illyro-Paeonian Region.* London, 1939

240. Merker, I. L. 'The silver coinage of Antigonus Gonatas and Antigonus Doson', *ANSMN* 9 (1960) 39–52

241. Mørkholm, O. 'Greek coins from Failaka', *Kuml* 1960, 199–207 (in Danish; English summary, 205 7)

242. – 'Studies in the coinage of Antiochus IV of Syria', *Historisk-filosofiske Meddelelser udg. af det kgl. Danske Videnskabernes Selskab* 40 no. 3 (1963)

243. – 'New coin finds from Failaka', *Kuml* 1979, 219–36 (in Danish; English summary, 230–6)

244. – 'Some reflections on the early cistophoric coinage', *ANSMN* 24 (1979) 47–61

245. – 'Chronology and meaning of the wreath coinage of the early second century B.C.', *Quad. Tic.* 9 (1980) 145–58

246. Newell, E. T. *Alexander hoards* III: *Andritsaena (ANSNNM* 21) New York, 1923.

247. – *The Coinages of Demetrius Poliorcetes.* Oxford, 1927

248. – *The Pergamene Mint under Philetaerus (ANSNNM* 76). New York, 1936

249. – *The Coinage of the Eastern Seleucid Mints (Num. Stud.* I). New York, 1938

250. – *Late Seleucid Mints in Ake-Ptolemais and Damascus* (*ANSNNM* 84). New York, 1939

251. – *The Coinage of the Western Seleucid Mints from Seleucus I to Antiochus III*, with a summary of recent scholarship by O. Mørkholm (*Num. Stud.* 4). Ed. 2. New York, 1977

252. Picard, O. *Chalcis et la confédération eubéenne. Étude de numismatique et d'histoire (IVe–Ier siècle).* Paris, 1979

253. Robert, L. *Études de numismatique grecque.* Paris, 1951

254. – *Monnaies antiques en Troade* (Centre de Recherches d'Histoire et de Philologie de la IVe Section de l'École Pratique des Hautes Études, Hautes Études Numismatiques 1.1). Geneva-Paris, 1966

255. – *Monnaies grecques. Types, légendes, magistrats monétaires et géographie* (Hautes Études Numismatiques 1.2). Geneva-Paris, 1967

256. Robinson, E. S. G. 'Cistophori in the name of King Eumenes', *Num. Chron.*[6] 14 (1954) 1–8

257. Scheers, S. 'Les imitations en Gaule du statère de Philippe II de Macédoine', *Proc. Int. Num. Symp., Warsaw–Budapest 1976*, 41–53

258. Scheu, F. 'The coinage system of Aetolia', *Num. Chron.*[6] 20 (1960) 37–52

259. Schmitz, H. *Ein Gesetz der Stadt Olbia zum Schutze ihres Silbergeldes. Studie zur griechischen Währungs-Geschichte des IV. Jhdts v. Chr.* Freiburg in Baden, 1925

260. Schönert-Geiss, E. *Die Münzprägung von Byzantion.* 2 vols. Berlin, 1970

261. Seyrig, H. 'Monnaies hellénistiques', *Rev. Num.*[6] 6 (1963) 7–64

262. – 'Monnaies hellénistiques de Byzance et de Chalcédoine', *Robinson Essays* (1968), 183–200

263. – *Trésors du Levant anciens et nouveaux. Trésors monétaires séleucides* II (Inst. fr. arch. Beyrouth. Bibl. arch. hist. 94). Paris, 1973

264. Shelov, D. B. *Coinage of the Bosporus VI–II Centuries* B.C. (*BAR* Suppl. 46). Oxford, 1978

265. Thompson, M. 'A hoard of Greek federal silver', *Hesp.* 8 (1939) 116–54

266. – 'A countermarked hoard from Büyükçekmece', *ANSMN* 6 (1954) 11–34

267. – *The New-Style Silver Coinage of Athens* I–II (*Num. Stud.* 10). New York, 1961

268. – 'Athens again', *Num. Chron.*[7] 2 (1962) 301–33

269. – 'Ptolemy Philometor and Athens', *ANSMN* 11 (1964) 119–29

270. – 'The mints of Lysimachus', *Robinson Essays* (1968), 163–82

271. – *The Agrinion Hoard* (*ANSNNM* 159). New York, 1968

272. Troxell, H. A. 'The Peloponnesian Alexanders', *ANSMN* 17 (1971) 41–94

273. Varoucha-Christodoulopoulou, I. 'Les témoignages numismatiques sur la guerre chrémonidéenne (265–262 av. J. C.)' *Atti del congresso internazionale di numismatica, Roma 1961*, 225–6. Rome, 1965

274. Wallace, W. P. *The Euboean League and its Coinage* (*ANSNNM* 134). New York, 1956

275. Wuilleumier, P. *Le trésor de Tarente.* Paris, 1930

276. Youroukova, J. *Coins of the Ancient Thracians* (*BAR* Suppl. 4). Oxford, 1976

277. – 'Imitations de monnaies antiques au IVe siècle av. n.è. faites en Bulgarie', *Proc. Int. Num. Symp., Warsaw-Budapest 1976*, 63–8

e. ART, MONUMENTS, CERAMICS, JEWELLERY AND OTHER OBJECTS

See also H 98–9
278. Andronikos, M. 'Ancient Greek paintings and mosaics in Macedonia', *Balkan Studies* 5.2 (1964) 287–302.
279. Arvanitopoulos, Th. A. '*Θεσσαλικὰ μνημεῖα*', *Polemon* 5 (1952–3) 5–18
280. Atzler, M. 'Ein ägyptischer Reliefbruchstück des Königs Alexanders IV.', *Antike Kunst* 15 (1972) 120–1
281. Baur, P. V. C. 'Megarian bowls in the Rebecca Darlington Stoddard collection of Greek and Italian vases in Yale University', *AJ Arch.* 45 (1941) 229–48
282. Bon, A.-M. and Bon, A. with Grace, V. R. *Études thasiennes* IV: *Les timbres amphoriques de Thasos*. Paris, 1957
283. Callaghan, P. J. 'Macedonian shields, shield bowls, and Corinth. A fixed point in Hellenistic ceramic chronology?', *Athens Annals of Archaeology* 11 (1978) 53–60
284. – 'The trefoil style and second-century Hadra vases', *BSA* 75 (1980) 145–59
285. Cook, B. F. *Inscribed Hadra Vases in the Metropolitan Museum of Art (Metropolitan Museum of Art Papers* 12). New York, 1966
286. Cook, R. M. *Greek Painted Pottery*. London, 1960
287. Courby, F. *Les vases grecs à reliefs*. Paris, 1922
288. Dow, S. 'Panathenaic amphorae of the Hellenistic period', *Hesp.* 5 (1936) 50–8
289. – 'Dikasts' bronze pinakia', *BCH* 87 (1963) 653–87
290. Edwards, G. R. *Corinth* VII.3: *Corinthian Hellenistic Pottery*. Princeton, 1975
291. Eftimie, V. 'Imports of stamped amphorae in the lower Danubian regions and a draft Rumanian corpus of amphora stamps', *Dacia* N.S. 3 (1959) 195–215
292. Grace, V. R. 'Stamped amphora handles found in 1931–1932', *Hesp.* 3 (1934) 195–310
293. – 'Standard pottery containers of the ancient Greek world', *Hesp.* Suppl. 8 (1949) 175–89
294. – 'The eponyms named on Rhodian amphora stamps', *Hesp.* 22 (1953) 116–28
295. Hausmann, U. *Hellenistische Reliefbecher aus attischen und böotischen Werkstätten. Untersuchungen zur Zeitstellung und Bildüberlieferung*. Stuttgart, 1959
296. Hellström, P. *Labraunda. Swedish Excavations and Researches* II.1: *Pottery of Classical and Later Date, Terracotta Lamps and Glass*. Lund, 1965
297. Hoffmann, H. and Davidson, P. F. *Greek Gold: Jewelry from the Age of Alexander*. Mainz, 1965
298. Invernizzi, A. 'Bulles de Séleucie du Tigre', *A Arch. Syr.* 21 (1971) 105–8
299. Kleiner, G. *Tanagrafiguren. Untersuchungen zur hellenistischen Kunst und Geschichte* (diss. phil. Munich). Berlin, 1942

300. Kroll, J. H. *Athenian Bronze Allotment Plates.* Cambridge, Mass., 1972
301. Lapp, P. W. *Palestinian Ceramic Chronology, 200 B.C.–A.D. 70.* New Haven, 1961
302. Laumonier, A. *Exploration archéologique de Délos* XXIII: *Les figurines de terre cuite.* Paris, 1956
303. – *Exploration archéologique de Délos* XXXI: *La céramique hellénistique à reliefs* I: *Ateliers 'ioniens'.* Paris, 1977
304. Leroux, G. *Lagynos: recherches sur la céramique et l'art ornemental hellénistique.* Paris, 1913
305. McDowell, R. H. *Stamped and Inscribed Objects from Seleucia on the Tigris.* Ann Arbor, 1935
306. Metzger, I. R. *Eretria, Ausgrabungen und Forschungen* II: *Die hellenistische Keramik in Eretria.* Bern, 1969
307. Nilsson, M. P. *Exploration archéologique de Rhodes* V: *Timbres amphoriques de Lindos.* Copenhagen, 1909
308. Papanikolaou-Christensen, A. and Friis-Johansen, Ch. *Hama, fouilles et recherches 1931–1938* III.2: *Les poteries hellénistiques et les terres sigillées orientales.* Copenhagen, 1971
309. Parlasca, K. 'Das Verhältnis der megarischen Becher zum alexandrinischen Kunsthandwerk', *JDAI* 70 (1955 [1956]) 129–54
310. Peters, K. *Studien zu den panathenäischen Preisamphoren* (diss. phil. Köln). Berlin, 1942
311. Petsas, Ph. M. 'Mosaics at Pella', in *La mosaïque gréco-romaine* (Colloques internationaux du Centre National de la Recherche Scientifique) 41–50. Paris, 1965
312. Robertson, M. 'Greek mosaics', *JHS* 85 (1965) 72–89
313. – 'Greek mosaics: a postscript', *JHS* 87 (1967) 133–6
314. Säflund, M.-L. *Labraunda* II.2: *Stamped Amphora Handles.* Istanbul, 1980
315. Schäfer, J. *Pergamenische Forschungen* II: *Hellenistische Keramik aus Pergamon.* Berlin, 1968
316. Scheurleer, C. W. Lunsingh, *Grieksche Cerameik.* Rotterdam, 1936
317. Schwabacher, W. 'Hellenistische Relief-keramik im Kerameikos', *AJArch.* 45 (1941) 182–228
318. Sinn, U. *Die homerischen Becher: hellenistische Reliefkeramik aus Makedonien.* Berlin, 1979
319. Stewart, A. F. *Attika. Studies in Athenian sculpture of the Hellenistic age* (*JHS* Suppl. Paper 14). London, 1979
320. Strong, D. E. *Greek and Roman Gold and Silver Plate.* London, 1966
321. Talcott, L., Philippaki, B., Edwards, G. R. and Grace, V. R. *Small Objects from the Pnyx* II (*Hesp.* Suppl. 10). Princeton, 1956
322. Thompson, D. B. 'Three centuries of Hellenistic terracottas I.A. (coroplast's dump)', *Hesp.* 21 (1952) 116–64
323. – 'Three centuries of Hellenistic terracottas I.B. (the hedgehog well) and C (the Demeter-cistern)', *Hesp.* 23 (1954) 72–107
324. – 'Three centuries of Hellenistic terracottas II.A: the early third century B.C.', *Hesp.* 26 (1957) 108–28
325. – 'Three centuries of Hellenistic terracottas II.B: the altar well', *Hesp.* 28 (1959) 127–52

326. – 'Three centuries of Hellenistic terracottas II.C: the satyr cistern', *Hesp.* 31 (1962) 244–62

327. – 'Three centuries of Hellenistic terracottas III: the late third century B.C.', *Hesp.* 32 (1963) 276–92

328. – 'Three centuries of Hellenistic terracottas IV: the second century B.C.', *Hesp.* 32 (1963) 301–17

329. – 'Three centuries of Hellenistic terracottas V: the mid second century B.C. VI: Late second century B.C. to 86 B.C.', *Hesp.* 34 (1965) 34–71

330. – 'Three centuries of Hellenistic terracottas VII–VIII', *Hesp.* 35 (1966) 1–19 and 252–67

331. Thompson, H. A. 'Two centuries of Hellenistic pottery', *Hesp.* 3 (1934) 311–480

332. Trendall, A. D. 'A new polychrome vase from Centuripe', *Bulletin of the Metropolitan Museum of Art, New York*[2] 13 (1955) 161–6

333. Waagé, F. O. (ed.) *Antioch-on-the-Orontes* IV.1: *Ceramics and Islamic Coins.* Princeton, 1948

334. Watzinger, C. 'Vasenfunde aus Athen', *Ath. Mitt.* 26 (1901) 50–102

335. Zahn, R. 'Hellenistische Reliefgefässe aus Südrussland', *JDAI* 23 (1908) 45–77

C. THE DIADOCHI AND THE ESTABLISHMENT OF THE KINGDOMS

1. Adams, W. L. and Borza, E. N. (eds.) *Philip II, Alexander the Great and the Macedonian Heritage.* Washington, D.C., 1982

2. Andreades, A. 'L'administration financière du roi Lysimaque', *Mélanges Thomas* (1930), 6–15

3. Aucello, E. 'La politica dei Diadochi e l'ultimatum del 314 av. Cr.', *Riv. Fil.* 35 (1957) 382–404

4. Barron, J. 'The tyranny of Duris of Samos', *CR* 12 (1962) 189–92

5. Bayer, E. *Demetrios Phalereus der Athener (Tübinger Beiträge zur Altertumswissenschaft* 36). Stuttgart-Berlin, 1942 (repr. Darmstadt, 1963)

6. Bosworth, A. B. 'The death of Alexander the Great: rumour and propaganda', *CQ* 21 (1971) 112–36

7. Briant, P. 'D'Alexandre le Grand aux Diadoques: le cas d'Eumène de Kardia', *Rev. Ét. Anc.* 74 (1972) 32–73; 75 (1973) 43–81

8. – *Antigone le Borgne. Les débuts de sa carrière et les problèmes de l'assemblée macédonienne.* Paris, 1973

9. Chamoux, F. 'Le roi Magas', *Rev. Hist.* 216 (1956) 18–34

10. Cloché, P. 'Les dernières années de l'Athénien Phocion', *Rev. Hist.* 144 (1923) 161–86; 145 (1924) 1–41

11. – 'Remarques sur la politique d'Antigone le Borgne à l'égard des cités', *Ant. class.* 17 (1948) 101–18

12. Cohen, G. M. 'The Diadochi and the new monarchies', *Athenaeum* 52 (1974) 177–9

13. Colombini, A. 'Su alcuni tratti dell'opera politica e culturale di Demetrio Falereo', in *Miscellanea greca e romana*, 177–94. Rome, 1965

14. Cozzoli, U. 'La Beozia durante il conflitto tra l'Ellade e la Persia', *Riv. Fil.* 36 (1958) 264–87
15. Daux, G. 'Adeimantos de Lampsaque et le renouvellement de la ligue de Corinthe par Démétrios Poliorcète', Ἀρχαιολογικὴ Ἐφημερίς 92/3 Part 1 (1953–4, published 1955) 245–54
16. Deprado, A. 'La liberazione di Atene nel 286 a.C.', *Riv. Fil.* 31 (1953) 27–42
17. De Sanctis, G. 'Lacare', *Riv. Fil.* 6 (1928) 53–77 = *Scritti Minori* (Rome, 1966) 349–69
18. – 'Atene dopo Ipso e un papiro fiorentino', *Riv. Fil.* 14 (1936) 134–52, 253–73
19. Durrbach, F. 'Antigoneia-Demetrieia: les origines de la Confédération des Insulaires', *BCH* 31 (1907) 208–27
20. Elkeles, G. *Demetrios der Städtebelagerer* (diss. Breslau, 1941)
21. Engel, R. 'Polyäns Stratagem IV, 6, 8 zur "Seeschlacht am Hellespont"', *Klio* 55 (1973) 141–5
22. Errington, R. M. 'From Babylon to Triparadeisos: 323–320 B.C.', *JHS* 90 (1970) 49–77
23. – 'Samos and the Lamian War', *Chiron* 5 (1975) 51–7
24. – 'Diodorus Siculus and the chronology of the early Diadochoi 320–311 B.C.', *Hermes* 105 (1977) 478–504
25. Ferguson, W. S. 'Demetrios Poliorcetes and the Hellenic League', *Hesp.* 17 (1948) 112–36
26. Fortina, M. *Cassandro, re di Macedonia.* Turin, 1965
27. Funck, B. 'Zur Innenpolitik des Seleukos Nikator', *Act. ant.* 22 (1974) 505–20
28. Gauthier, Ph. 'La réunification d'Athènes en 281 et les deux archontes Nicias', *Rev. Ét. Gr.* 92 (1979) 348–99
29. Gehrke, H. J. *Phokion. Studien zur Erfassung seiner historischen Gestalt.* Munich, 1976
30. Gesche, H. 'Nikokles von Paphos und Nikokreon von Salamis', *Chiron* 4 (1974) 103–25
31. Geyer, F. 'Lysimachos', *PW* XIV.1 (1928) 1–31
32. Guggenmos, A. T. *Die Geschichte des Nesiotenbundes bis zur Mitte des III. Jhdts v. Chr.* (diss. Würzburg, 1929)
33. Habicht, Chr. 'Literarische und epigraphische Überlieferung zur Geschichte Alexanders und seiner ersten Nachfolger', *VI Internationales Kongress für griechische und lateinische Epigraphik*, 367–77. Munich, 1973
34. – 'Der Beitrag Spartas zur Restitution von Samos während des lamischen Krieges', *Chiron* 5 (1975) 45–50
35. Hauben, H. 'On the chronology of the years 313–311 B.C.', *AJPhil.* 94 (1973) 256–67
36. – 'A royal toast in 302 B.C.', *Anc. Soc.* 5 (1974) 105–17
37. – *Het Vlootbevelhebberschap in de vroege Diadochentijd* (Verhandelingen v.d. Kon. Acad. Belgie 37). Brussels, 1975
38. – 'Antigonos' invasion plan for his attack on Egypt in 306 B.C.', *Orientalia Lovaniensia Periodica* 6/7 (1975/6) 267–71
39. – 'Rhodes, Alexander and the Diadochi from 333/2 to 304 B.C.', *Historia* 26 (1977) 307–39

40. – 'The first war of the Successors (321 B.C.)', *Anc. Soc.* 8 (1977) 85–120
41. Heuss, A. 'Antigonos Monophthalmos und die griechischen Städte', *Hermes* 73 (1938) 133–94
42. Laronde, A. 'Observations sur la politique d'Ophellas à Cyrène', *Rev. Hist.* 245 (1971) 297–306
43. – 'La date du diagramma de Ptolémée à Cyrène', *Rev. Ét. Gr.* 85 (1972) xiii–xiv
44. Lenschau, Th. 'Phokion (2)', *PW* xx.1 (1941) 458–73
45. Lepore, E. 'Leostene e le origini della guerra lamiaca', *PP* 10 (1955) 161–85
46. Lévèque, P. *Pyrrhos*. Paris, 1957
47. Machu, J. 'Cyrène: la cité et le souverain à l'époque hellénistique', *Rev. Hist.* 205 (1951) 41–55
48. Manni, E. *Demetrio Poliorcete*. Rome, 1951
49. – 'Arconti eponimi ateniesi 292/1–141/0 a.C.', *Historia* 24 (1975) 17–32
50. Merker, I. M. 'The Ptolemaic officials and the League of the Islanders', *Historia* 19 (1970) 141–60
51. Müller, O. *Antigonos Monophthalmos und "das Jahr der Könige"*. Bonn, 1973
52. Nederlof, A. B. *Pyrrhus van Epirus. Zijn achtergronden – zijn tijd – zijn leven (historie en legende)*. Amsterdam, 1978
53. Nenci, G. *Pirro, Aspirazioni egemoniche ed equilibrio mediterraneo*. Turin, 1953
54. Osborne, M. J. 'Kallias, Phaidros and the revolt of Athens in 287 B.C.', *ZPE* 25 (1979) 181–94
55. Pagliaro, A. 'Osservazioni sul *diagramma* di Cirene', in *Studi Calderini-Paribeni* 1.101–9. Milan, 1956
56. Robert, L. 'Adeimantos de Lampsaque et la ligue de Corinthe sur une inscription de Delphes', *Hellenica* 11 (1946) 15–36
57. Saitta, G. 'Lisimaco di Tracia', *Kokalos* 1 (1955) 62–154
58. Schachermeyr, F. *Alexander in Babylon und die Reichsordnung nach seinem Tode (Sitz. Wien 268.3)*. Vienna, 1970
59. Schaefer, H. 'Pleistarchos (2)', *PW* xxi.1 (1951) 197–9
60. Schlumberger, D. 'Triparadisos', *Bulletin du Musée de Beyrouth* 22 (1969) 147–9
61. Seibert, J. 'Philokles, Sohn des Apollodoros, König der Sidonier', *Historia* 19 (1970) 337–51
62. Shear, T. L., Jr *Kallias of Sphettos and the Revolt of Athens in 286 B.C.* (*Hesp.* Suppl. 17). Princeton, 1978
63. Simpson, R. H. 'The historical circumstances of the peace of 311 B.C.', *JHS* 74 (1954) 25–31
64. – 'Polemaeus' invasion of Greece in 313 B.C.', *Mnemos.*[4] 8 (1955) 34–7
65. – 'Antigonos the One-Eyed and the Greeks', *Historia* 8 (1959) 385–409
66. Smith, L. C. 'The chronology of Books 18–22 of Diodorus Siculus', *AJPhil.* 82 (1961) 283–90
67. – 'Demochares of Leuconoe and the dates of his exile', *Historia* 11 (1962) 114–18
68. Tarn, W. W. 'The heritage of Alexander', *CAH* vi, pp. 461–504. Cambridge, 1927
69. Traill, J. S. *The Political Organization of Attica* (*Hesp.* Suppl. 14). Princeton, 1975

70. Treves, P. 'Demade postumo', *Rend. Ist. Lomb.* 92 (1958) 327–80
71. Vezin, A. *Eumenes von Kardia: ein Beitrag zur Geschichte der Diadochenzeit* (diss. Tübingen). Münster, 1907
72. Vitucci, G. 'Il compromesso di Babilonia e la prostasia di Cratero', *Miscellanea Rostagni* (1963) 63–7
73. Vogt, J. 'Kleomenes von Naukratis, Herr von Ägypten', *Chiron* 1 (1971) 153–7
74. Volkmann, H. 'Ptolemaios', *PW* XXIII.2 (1959) 1592–1691
75. Wehrli, C. *Antigone et Démétrios.* Geneva, 1969
76. Westlake, H. D. 'Eumenes of Cardia', *Bulletin of the John Rylands Library, Manchester* 37 (1954) 309–27
77. Will, Ed. 'La Cyrénaïque et les partages successifs de l'empire d'Alexandre', *Ant. class.* 29 (1960) 369–90
78. – 'Ophellas, Ptolémée, Cassandre et la chronologie', *Rev. Ét. Anc.* 66 (1964) 320–33

D. GREECE, MACEDONIA, THE BALKANS, THRACE AND THE BLACK SEA

a. MACEDONIA, EPIRUS AND ILLYRIA

See also I 9 and, on p. 602 (Addenda), D 17a, D 35a

1. Alexander, J. A. 'Cassandreia during the Macedonian period: an epigraphical commentary', in *Ancient Macedonia* I (1970). 127–46
2. Bettingen, W. *König Antigonos Doson von Makedonien (229–220 v. Chr.)* (diss. Jena). Weida-in-Thüringen, 1912
3. Bikerman, E. 'Sur les batailles navales de Cos et d'Andros', *Rev. Ét. Anc.* 40 (1938) 368–83
4. Bohec, S. le 'Phthia, mère de Philippe V', *Rev. Ét. Gr.* 94 (1981) 34–46
5. Cabanes, P. *L'Épire de la mort de Pyrrhus à la conquête romaine (272–167 av. J.-C.).* Besançon-Paris, 1976
6. Chambers, M. 'The first regnal year of Antigonus Gonatas', *AJPhil.* 75 (1954) 385–94
7. Cross, G. N. *Epirus: A Study in Greek Constitutional Development.* Cambridge, 1932
8. De Francisci, P. *Arcana Imperii.* 4 vols. Esp. vol. II.345–495, 'Il regno di Macedonia: Alessandro e gli stati ellenistici'. Milan, 1947–8
9. Dell, H. J. 'Antigonus III and Rome', *CPhil.* 62 (1967) 94–103
10. – 'The origin and nature of Illyrian piracy', *Historia* 16 (1967) 344–58
11. – 'The western frontier of the Macedonian monarchy', in *Ancient Macedonia* I (1970) 115–26
12. Dow, S. and Edson, C. F. 'Chryseis. A study of the evidence in regard to the mother of Philip V', *HSCP* 48 (1937) 127–80
13. Edson, C. F. 'The Antigonids, Heracles and Beroea', *HSCP* 45 (1934) 213–46
14. Ehrhardt, C. T. H. R. *Studies in the Reigns of Demetrius II and Antigonus Doson* (diss. SUNY at Buffalo, 1975; microfilm)

15. – 'Demetrius ὁ Αἰτωλικός and Antigonid nicknames', *Hermes* 106 (1978) 251–3

16. Errington, R. M. 'Macedonian royal style and its historical significance', *JHS* 94 (1974) 20–37

17. – 'The nature of the Macedonian state under the monarchy', *Chiron* 8 (1978) 77–133

18. Fellmann, W. *Antigonos Gonatas, König der Makedonier und die griechischen Staaten* (diss. Würzburg, 1930)

19. Fine, J. V. A. 'The problem of Macedonian holdings in Epirus and Thessaly in 221 B.C.', *TAPA* 63 (1932) 126–55

20. Franke, P. R. *Alt-Epirus und das Königtum der Molosser*. Kallmünz-Opf., 1954

21. – 'Zur Geschichte des Antigonos Gonatas und der Oitaioi', *JDAI* 73 (1958), *Arch. Anz.* cols. 38–62

22. Giovannini, A. 'Le statut des cités de Macédoine sous les Antigonides', in *Ancient Macedonia* 11.465–72

23. Granier, F. *Die makedonische Heeresversammlung: ein Beitrag zum antiken Staatsrecht*. Munich, 1931

24. Grilli, A. 'Zenone e Antigono II', *Riv. Fil.* 91 (1963) 287–301

25. Hammond, N. G. L. 'The kingdom of Illyria *c.* 400–167 B.C.', *BSA* 61 (1966) 239–53

26. – *Epirus. The geography, the ancient remains, the history and the topography of Epirus and adjacent areas*. Oxford, 1967

27. – 'Illyria, Rome and Macedon in 229–205 B.C.', *JRS* 58 (1968) 1–21

28. – *A History of Macedonia* I: *Historical Geography and Prehistory*. Oxford, 1972

29. Hammond, N. G. L. and Griffith, G. T. *Id.* II: *550–336* B.C. Oxford, 1979

30. Hampl, F. *Der König der Makedonen*. Leipzig, 1934

31. Heinen, H. Review of Sofman, *Istorija antičnoj Makedonii* (1960–3), *Makedonika* 9 (1969) 349–53

32. Manni, E. 'Antigono Gonata e Demetrio II, punti fermi e problemi aperti', *Athenaeum* 34 (1956) 249–72

33. Mikroyiannakis, E. L. '*ΤΟ ΠΟΛΙΤΙΣΤΙΚΟΝ ΕΡΓΟΝ ΤΟΥ ΚΑΣΣΑΝΔΡΟΥ*', in *Ancient Macedonia* II (1977). 225–36

34. Momigliano, A. D. and Fraser, P. M. 'A new date for the battle of Andros? A discussion', *CQ* 44 (1950) 107–18

35. Momigliano, A. 'Re e popolo in Macedonia prima di Alessandro Magno' in *Contributo* V (1975). 1.445–64: (A 39)

36. Piraino, M. T. 'Antigono Dosone, re di Macedonia', *Atti dell' Accademia di Scienze Lettere e Arti di Palermo* 13.3 (1952–3), Part 2, 301–75

37. Šofman, A. S. *Istorija antičnoj Makedonii*. 2 vols. Kazan, 1960–3

38. Tarn, W. W. *Antigonos Gonatas*. Oxford, 1913

39. – 'Philip V and Phthia', *CQ* 18 (1924) 17–23

40. – 'Phthia-Chryseis', in *Athenian Studies presented to W.S. Ferguson*, 403–501. Cambridge, Mass., 1940

41. Treves, P. 'La tradizione politica degli Antigonidi e l'opera di Demetrio II', *Rend. Linc.* 8 (1932) 168–205

42. – 'Studi su Antigono Dosone', *Athenaeum* 12 (1934) 381–411; 13 (1935) 22–56

43. Walbank, F. W. *Philip V of Macedon*. Cambridge, 1940

44. – 'Olympichus of Alinda and the Carian expedition of Antigonus Doson', *JHS* 62 (1942) 8–13

45. – 'Sea-power and the Antigonids', in Adams and Borza 1982, 213–36: (c 1)

46. Welwei, K.-W. 'Das makedonische Herrschaftssystem in Griechenland und die Politik des Antigonos Doson', *Rh. Mus.* 110 (1967) 306–14

b. GREECE AND THE WARS WITH MACEDONIA

47. Bikerman, E. 'Notes sur Polybe, II. Les négotiations entre Aratos et Antigonos Doson', *Rev. Ét. Gr.* 56 (1943) 287–304

48. Briscoe, J. 'The Antigonids and the Greek States, 276–196 B.C.', in *Imperialism in the Ancient World*, edd. P. D. A. Garnsey and C. R. Whittaker, 145–77. Cambridge, 1978

49. Daubies, M. 'Un chasse-croisé diplomatique dans le Péloponnèse au IIIe siècle av. J.-C.', *Ant. class.* 42 (1973) 123–54

50. De Sanctis, G. 'Contributi alla storia ateniese della guerra lamiaca alla guerra cremonidea', *Studi di storia antica* 2 (1893) 3–62 = *Scritti minori* 1 (Rome, 1966) 249–302

51. – 'Questioni politiche e riforme sociali. Saggio su trent'anni di storia greca (258–228)', *Rivista internazionale di scienze sociali* 4 (1894) 50–63, 229–38 = *Scritti minori* 1 (Rome, 1966) 371–92

52. – 'La ribellione d'Alessandro figlio di Cratero', *Klio* 9 (1909) 1–9 = *Scritti minori* 1 (Rome, 1966) 393–403

53. Errington, R. M. 'Philip V, Aratus and the conspiracy of Apelles', *Historia* 16 (1967) 19–36

54. – *Philopoemen*. Oxford, 1969

55. Ferrabino, A. *Il problema della unità nazionale nella Grecia* 1: *Arato di Sicione e l'idea federale*. Florence, 1921

56. Fine, J. V. A. 'The background of the Social War of 220–217 B.C.', *AJPhil.* 61 (1940) 129–65

57. Golan, D. 'Aratus' policy between Sicyon and Argos: an attempt at Greek unity', *Rivista storica dell'antichità* 3 (1973) 59–70

58. Grace, V. and Kroll, J. H. 'Revisions in early Hellenistic chronology', *Ath. Mitt.* 89 (1974) 193–203

59. Gruen, E. 'Aratus and the Achaean alliance with Macedon', *Historia* 21 (1972) 609–25

60. Habicht, Chr. 'Aristeides, Sohn des Mnesitheos, aus Lamptrai', *Chiron* 6 (1976) 7–10

61. Kougeas, S. B. "Ὁ Δημητριακὸς πόλεμος καὶ αἱ 'Αθῆναι.' *Ἑλληνικά* 3 (1930) 281–95

62. Laix, R. A. de 'Polybius' credibility and the triple alliance of 230/229 B.C.', *CSCA* 2 (1969) 65–83

63. Larsen, J. A. O. 'Phocis and the Social War of 220–217', *Phoenix* 19 (1965) 116–28

64. Launey, M. 'Études d'histoire hellénistique. L'exécution de Sotadès et l'expédition de Patroklos dans la mer Égée (266 av. J.-C.)', *Rev. Ét. Anc.* 47 (1945) 33–45
65. Mendels, D. 'Polybius, Philip V and the socio-economic question in Greece', *Anc. Soc.* 8 (1977) 155–74
66. Osborne, M. J. 'Kallias, Phaidros, and the revolt of Athens in 287 B.C.', *ZPE* 35 (1979) 18–94
67. Peek, W. 'Diomedes von Troizen', in *Studies presented to D. M. Robinson* (St Louis, 1953) ii.318–25
68. Petrakos, B. Chr. 'Νεαὶ πηγαὶ περὶ τοῦ Χρεμωνιδείου πολέμου', *Ἀρχαιολογικὸν Δελτίον* 22.1 (1967) 38–52
69. Schwartz, J. 'Athènes et l'Étolie dans la politique Lagide (à la lumière de *P. Haun.* 6)', *ZPE* 30 (1978) 95–100
70. Tarn, W. W. 'The Arcadian League and Aristodemus', *CR* 39 (1925) 104–7
71. – 'The new dating of the Chremonidean War', *JHS* 54 (1934) 26–39
72. Treves, P. *Euforione e la storia ellenistica*. Milan-Naples, 1955
73. Walbank, F. W. *Aratos of Sicyon*. Cambridge, 1933
74. – 'Aratos' attack on Cynaetha', *JHS* 56 (1936) 64–71
75. Welles, C. B. 'Gallic mercenaries in the Chremonidean War', *Klio* 52 (1970) 477–90 (cf. J. and L. Robert, *Bull. épig.* 1971, no. 415)

C. THESSALY, BOEOTIA AND CENTRAL GREECE

See also B 252, 274
76. Cloché, P. *Thèbes de Béotie des origines à la conquête romaine*. Paris, n.d.
77. Daux, G. *Delphes au IIe et au Ier siècle jusqu'à la paix romaine*. Paris, 1936
78. Étienne, R. and Knoepfler, D. *Hyettos de Béotie et la chronologie des archontes fédéraux entre 250 et 171 av. J.-C.* (*BCH* Suppl. 3). Paris, 1976
79. Feyel, M. *Polybe et l'histoire de Béotie au IIIe siècle av. notre ère*. Paris, 1942
80. Hennig, D. 'Der Bericht des Polybios über Boiotien und die Lage von Orchomenos in der 2. Hälfte des 3. Jhdts v. Chr.', *Chiron* 7 (1977) 119–48
81. Klaffenbach, G. 'Zur Geschichte von Ost-Lokris', *Klio* 20 (1926) 68–88
82. Lerat, L. *Les Locriens de l'ouest*. 2 vols. Paris, 1952
83. Roesch, P. *Thespies et la confédération béotienne*. Paris, 1965
84. – 'Les lois fédérales béotiennes', *Teiresias* Suppl. 1 (1972) 66–7
85. – *Études béotiennes*. Paris, 1982
86. Stähelin, F. *Das hellenische Thessalien*. Stuttgart, 1924

D. ATHENS

See also H 42–3, 48–9, 59, 138
87. Dinsmoor, W. B. *The Archons of Athens in the Hellenistic Age*. Cambridge, Mass., 1931
88. – *The Athenian Archon List in the Light of Recent Discoveries*. New York, 1939 (repr. 1977)

89. Ferguson, W. S. *Hellenistic Athens. An historical essay.* London, 1911 (repr. 1974)

90. – *Athenian Tribal Cycles in the Hellenistic Age* (Harvard Historical Monographs 1). Cambridge, Mass., 1932

91. Habicht, Chr. *Untersuchungen zur politischen Geschichte Athens im 3. Jahrhundert (Vestigia 30).* Munich, 1979. (Review by H. Heinen, *Gött. Anz.* 233 (1981) 175–207.)

92. Klaffenbach, G. 'Polyeuktos (6)', *PW* XXI.2 (1952) 1623–9

93. McCredie, J. R. *Fortified Military Camps in Attica (Hesp.* Suppl. 11). Princeton, 1966

94. Meritt, B. D. *The Athenian Year.* Berkeley-Los Angeles, 1961

95. – 'Athenian archons 347/6–48/7 B.C.', *Historia* 26 (1977) 161–91

96. Pélékidis, Chr. 'L'archonte athénien Polyeuktos (247/6)', *BCH* 85 (1961) 53–68

97. Pouilloux, J. 'Antigone Gonatas et Athènes après la guerre de Chrémonidès', *BCH* 70 (1946) 488–96

98. – 'Glaucon fils d'Éteoclès d'Athènes', in *Mélanges Préaux* (1975), 376–82

99. Pritchett, W. K. and Meritt, B. D. *The Chronology of Hellenistic Athens.* Cambridge, Mass., 1940

100. Rhodes, P. J. *The Athenian Boule.* Oxford, 1972

101. Sartori, F. 'Cremonide: un dissidio fra politica e filosofia', in *Miscellanea Rostagni* (1963), 117–51

e. ACHAEA AND AETOLIA

102. Aymard, A. *Les Assemblées de la confédération achaienne. Étude critique d'institutions et d'histoire.* Paris, 1938 (repr. 1967)

103. Benecke, H. *Die Seepolitik der Aitoler.* Hamburg, 1934

104. Daux, G. 'L'expansion étolienne vers le nord à la fin du IIIe siècle av. J.-C.', in *Studia antiqua A. Salac septuagenario oblata*, 35–9. Prague, 1955

105. Flacelière, R. *Les Aitoliens à Delphes. Contribution à l'histoire de la Grèce centrale au IIIe siècle av. J.-C.* Paris, 1937

106. Giovannini, A. 'Polybe et les assemblées achéennes', *Mus. Helv.* 26 (1969) 1–17

107. Klaffenbach, G. 'Zur Geschichte Aitoliens und Delphis im 3. Jahrhundert', *Klio* 32 (1939) 189–219

108. – 'Die Zeit des ätolisch-akarnanischen Bündnisvertrages, Δεύτεραι φροντίδες', *Historia* 4 (1955/6) 46–51

109. Larsen, J. A. O. 'The assembly of the Aetolian League', *TAPA* 83 (1952) 1–33

110. – 'The Aetolians and the Cleomenic War', in *The Classical Tradition: Literary and Historical Studies in Honor of Harry Caplan*, ed. L. Wallach, 43–57. Ithaca, 1966

111. – 'The rights of cities within the Achaean confederacy', *CPhil.* 76 (1971) 81–6

112. – 'The Aetolian–Achaean alliance of *c.* 238–220 B.C.', *CPhil.* 70 (1975) 159–72

113. Levi, M. A. 'La cronologia degli strateghi etolici degli anni 221–168 a.C.', *Atti Acc. Torino* 57 (1921–2) 179–85
114. – 'Arato e la liberazione di Sicione', *Athenaeum* 8 (1930) 508–18
115. Nachtergael, G. 'L'archonte athénien Polyeuctos et la périodicité des Sôtéria étoliennes', *Historia* 25 (1976) 62–78
116. Niccolini, G. *La confederazione achea.* Pavia, 1914
117. Urban, R. *Wachstum und Krise des achäischen Bundes: Quellenstudien zur Entwicklung des Bundes von 280 bis 222 v. Chr.* (*Historia* Einzelschr. 35). Wiesbaden, 1979

f. SPARTA AND MESSENIA

118. Africa, T. W. *Phylarchus and the Spartan Revolution.* Berkeley-Los Angeles, 1961
119. – 'Cleomenes III and the helots', *CSCA* 1 (1968) 1–11
120. Bernini, U. 'Studi su Sparta ellenistica. Da Leonida II a Cleomene III', *Quaderni urbinati di cultura classica* 27 (1978) 29–59
121. Chrimes, K. *Ancient Sparta. A re-examination of the evidence.* Ed. 2. Manchester, 1952
122. Cloché, P. 'Remarques sur les règnes d'Agis IV et Cléomène III', *Rev. Ét. Gr.* 65 (1943) 53–71
123. – 'La politique extérieure de Lacédémone depuis la mort d'Agis III jusqu'à celle d'Acrotatos fils d'Areus I', *Rev. Ét. Anc.* 47 (1945) 218–42; 48 (1946) 29–61
124. Daubies, M. 'Cléomène III, les hilotes et Sellasie', *Historia* 20 (1971) 665–95
125. De Sanctis, G. 'Areo II di Sparta', *Atti Acc. Torino* 47 (1911/12) 267–77 = *Scritti minori* 1 (Rome, 1966) 461–71
126. Fuks, A. 'The non-Phylarchean tradition of the programme of Agis IV', *CQ* 12 (1962) 118–21
127. – 'Agis, Cleomenes and equality', *CPhil.* 57 (1962) 161–6
128. – 'The Spartan citizen-body in the mid-third century B.C. and its enlargement proposed by Agis IV', *Athenaeum* 40 (1962) 244–63
129. Marasco, G. 'Nuove testimonianze sul regime di Agide IV', *Prometheus* 7 (1981) 35–42
130. Mendels, D. 'Polybius, Cleomenes III and Sparta's *Patrios Politeia*', *PP* 180 (1978) 161–6
131. Oliva, P. 'Die Auslandspolitik Kleomenes III.', *Act. ant.* 16 (1968) 179–85
132. – *Sparta and her Social Problems.* Amsterdam-Prague, 1971
133. Ollier, F. 'Le philosophe stoicien Sphairos et l'oeuvre réformatrice des rois de Sparte Agis IV et Cléomène III', *Rev. Ét. Gr.* 49 (1936) 536–70
134. – *Le mirage spartiate: étude sur l'idéalisation de Sparte dans l'antiquité grecque.* 2 vols. Paris, 1933, 1943
135. Pozzi, F. 'Le reforme economico-sociali et le mire tiranniche di Agide IV e Cleomene III, re di Sparta', *Aevum* 42 (1968) 383–402
136. Roebuck, C. *A History of Messenia from 369 to 146 B.C.* Chicago, 1941

137. Roussel, P. *Sparte*. Paris, 1939
138. Shimron, B. 'Spartan policy after the defeat of Cleomenes III', *CQ* 14 (1964) 232–9
139. 'Polybius and the reforms of Cleomenes III', *Historia* 13 (1964) 147–55
140. – *Late Sparta. The Spartan revolution 243–146 B.C.* Buffalo, 1972
141. Tigerstedt, E. N. *The Legend of Sparta in Classical Antiquity* II. Stockholm, 1974
142. Walbank, F. W. 'The Spartan ancestral constitution in Polybius', in Badian 1966, 303–12: (A 4)

g. THE AEGEAN, CRETE AND CYPRUS

See also C 32, H 189
143. Effenterre, H. van *La Crète et le monde grec de Platon à Polybe*. Paris, 1948
144. Hill, G. *A History of Cyprus* I. Cambridge, 1940
145. Laidlaw, W. A. *A History of Delos*. Oxford, 1933
146. Sherwin-White, S. M. *Ancient Cos. An historical study from the Dorian settlement to the imperial period* (Hypomnemata 51). Göttingen, 1978
147. Spyridakis, S. *Itanos and Hellenistic Crete*. Berkeley, 1970
148. Willetts, R. F. *Ancient Crete: A Social History from Early Times until the Roman Occupation*. London, 1965

h. THRACE AND THE BLACK SEA

149. Belin de Ballu, E. *L'histoire des colonies grecques du littoral nord de la mer noire*. Ed. 2. Paris, 1965
150. – *Olbia, cité antique du littoral nord de la mer noire*. Leiden, 1972.
151. Bengtson, H. 'Neues zur Geschichte des Hellenismus in Thrakien und in der Dobrudscha', *Historia* 11 (1962) 18–28
152. – 'Bemerkungen zu einer Ehreninschrift der Stadt Apollonia am Pontos', *Historia* 12 (1963) 96–104
153. Condurachi, Em. 'Problèmes économiques et sociaux d'Histria à la lumière des dernières recherches', in *Nouvelles études historiques présentées au Xe congrès des sciences historiques de Rome* (Bucarest, 1955) 121–37
154. – 'Les villes pontiques et leur importance pour l'histoire ancienne du Sud-Est européen', *Bulletin de l'Association internationale d'Études du Sud-Est européen* (Bucharest) 3.1 (1965) 19–30
155. Danoff, Chr. M. 'Thracian penetration into the Greek cities on the west coast of the Black Sea', *Klio* 38 (1960) 75–80
156. – 'Pontos Euxeinos', *PW* Suppl. B.IX (1962) cols. 1062–1151, 1912–20
157. – *Altthrakien*. Berlin-New York, 1976
158. Mihailov, G. 'La Thrace aux IVe et IIIe siècles av. notre ère', *Athenaeum* 39 (1961) 33–44
159. 'Documents épigraphiques de la côte bulgare et de la mer noire', in *Actes VII Congrès Épig. 1977* (1979), 265–71
160. Minns, E. H. *Scythians and Greeks*. Cambridge, 1913

161. Pippidi, D. M. 'Nouvelles informations sur la constitution d'Histria préromaine', in *Nouvelles études historiques présentées au Xe congrès des sciences historiques de Rome* (Bucarest, 1955) 85–102

162. – 'Zur Geschichte Histrias im 3. bis 2. Jhdt. v. u. Z.', *Klio* 37 (1959) 119–34

163. – *Epigraphische Beiträge zur Geschichte Histrias in hellenistischer und römischer Zeit.* Berlin, 1962

164. – 'Note sur l'organisation militaire d'Istros à l'époque hellénistique', *Klio* 41 (1963) 158–65

165. – 'Les colonies grecques de Scythie Mineure à l'époque hellénistique', *Balkan Studies* 6 (1965) 95–118

166. – *I greci nel basso Danubio dall'età arcaica alla conquista romana.* Milan, 1971

167. Pippidi, D. M. and Popescu, E. M. 'Les relations d'Istros et d'Apollonie du Pont à l'époque hellénistique', *Dacia* 3 (1959) 235–58

168. Popescu, E. 'Die Inschriften aus Kleinskythien', in *Actes VII Congrès Épig. 1977* (1979), 274–92

169. Rostovtzeff, M. I. *Iranians and Greeks in South Russia.* Oxford, 1922

170. Vinogradov, J. G. 'Griechische Epigraphik und Geschichte des nördlichen Pontosgebietes', in *Actes VII Congrès Épig. 1977* (1979), 293–316

171. Wasowicz, A. *Olbia pontique et son territoire* (Annales littéraires de l'Université de Besançon, Centre de Recherches d'histoire ancienne, 168). Paris, 1975

E. THE SELEUCID KINGDOM, ASIA MINOR, THE MIDDLE EAST, THE FAR EAST, THE WARS OF SYRIA AND EGYPT

a. GENERAL

1. Altheim, F. *Weltgeschichte Asiens im griechischen Zeitalter.* 2 vols. Halle, 1947

2. Aymard, A. 'Du nouveau sur la chronologie des Séleucides', *Rev. Ét. Anc.* 57 (1955) 102–12 = *Études d'histoire ancienne*, 263–72: (A 2)

3. Bengtson, H. 'Die Bedeutung der Eingeborenenbevölkerung in den hellenistischen Oststaaten', *Die Welt als Geschichte* (1951) 135–42

4. Bertrand, J. M. 'Sur les hyparques de l'Empire d'Alexandre', in *Mélanges d'histoire ancienne, offerts à W. Seston.* 25–34. Paris, 1974

5. Bevan, E. *The House of Seleucus.* 2 vols. London, 1902

6. Bikerman, E. *Institutions des Séleucides.* Paris, 1938

7. – 'Notes on Seleucid and Parthian chronology', *Berytus* 8 (1944) 73–83

8. – 'The Seleucids and the Achaemenids', *Atti Convegno: La Persia e il mondo greco-romano 1965* (*Acc. Lincei*), 87–117. Rome, 1966

9. Bouché-Leclercq, A. *Histoire des Séleucides (232–64 avant J.-C.).* 2 vols. Paris, 1913–14

10. Briant, P. 'Villages et communautés villageoises d'Asie achéménide et hellénistique', *Journal of the Economic and Social History of the Orient* 18 (1975) 165–88

11. – 'Brigandage, dissidence et conquête en Asie achéménide et hellénistique', *DHA* 2 (1976) 163–280

12. – 'Colonisation hellénistique et populations indigènes; la phase d'installation', *Klio* 60 (1978) 57–92

13. Bülow-Jacobsen, A. '*P. Haun.* 6: an inspection of the original', *ZPE* 36 (1979) 91–100

14. Bunge, J. G. 'Die Feiern Antiochos' IV Epiphanes in Daphne 166 v. Chr.', *Chiron* 6 (1976) 53–71

15. Chesneaux, J. 'Le mode de production asiatique. Quelques perspectives de recherches', in *Sur le ' mode de production asiatique'*, 13–45. Paris, 1969

16. Cohen, G. M. *The Seleucid Colonies. Studies in founding, administration and organization (Historia* Einzelschr. 30). Wiesbaden, 1978

17. Cracco Ruggini, L. 'Nuclei immigrati e forze indigene in tre grandi centri commerciali dell'impero', in *The Seaborne Commerce of Ancient Rome (MAAR* 36), edd. J. H. D'Arms and E. C. Kopff, 55–76. Rome, 1980

18. Dandamayev, M. 'Achaemenid Babylonia'. English version in Diakonov 1969, 296–311: (E 188)

19. Edson, C. 'Imperium Macedonicum: the Seleucid Empire and the literary evidence', *CPhil.* 53 (1958) 153–70

20. Ferrary, J. L. 'Rome, les Balkans, la Grèce et l'Orient au deuxième siècle av. J.C.', in *Rome et la conquête du monde méditerranéen* II. *Genèse d'un empire*, ed. C. Nicolet, 729–88. Paris, 1978

21. Fischer, H. 'Zu einigen Fragen von Kontinuität und Weiterentwicklung orientalischer Vorbilder im Hellenismus und im römischen Reich', *Klio* 60 (1978) 35–44

22. Frezouls, E. 'Observations sur l'urbanisme dans l'Orient syrien', *AArch.Syr.* 21 (1971) 231–43

23. Funck, B. 'Die Wurzeln der hellenistischen Euergetes-Religion im Staat und in den Städten des Seleukos Nikator', in Welskopf 1974, III.1290–334: (A 65)

24. Furlani, G. and Momigliano, A. D. 'La cronaca babilonese sui Diadochi', *Riv. Fil.* 10 (1932) 462–84

25. Goukowsky, P. 'Le roi Poros, son éléphant et quelques autres', *BCH* 96 (1972) 474–502

26. Gruen, E. J. 'Rome and the Seleucids in the aftermath of Pydna', *Chiron* 6 (1976) 73–95

27. Günther, W. *Das Orakel von Didyma in hellenistischer Zeit. Eine Interpretation von Stein-Urkunden (Istanb. Mitt.* Beiheft 4). Tübingen, 1971. (Critical review by J. Seibert, *Gött. Anz.* 226 (1974) 186–212.)

28. Habicht, Chr. 'Bemerkungen zum *P. Haun.* 6', *ZPE* 39 (1980) 1–5

29. Hadley, R. A. 'Royal propaganda of Seleucus I and Lysimachus', *JHS* 94 (1974) 50–65

30. Hahn, I. 'Königsland und königliche Besteuerung im hellenistischen Osten', *Klio* 60 (1978) 11–34

31. Hengel, M. *Judentum und Hellenismus. Studien zu ihrer Begegnung unter*

besonderer Berücksichtigung Palästinas bis zur Mitte des 2. Jahrhunderts v. Chr. Ed. 2. Tübingen, 1973

32. — *Juden, Griechen und Barbaren. Aspekte der Hellenisierung des Judentums in vorchristlicher Zeit* (Stuttgarter Bibelstudien 76). Stuttgart, 1976
33. Horain, C. M. *L'identité de l'Antioche Epidaphné.* Ghent, 1963
34. Kahrstedt, U. *Syrische Territorien in hellenistischer Zeit* (*Abh. Göttingen,* philol.-hist. Klasse, N.S. xix.2). Berlin, 1926
35. Kreissig, H. 'Tempelland, Katoiken, Hierodulen im Seleukidenreich', *Klio* 59 (1977) 375–80
36. — *Wirtschaft und Gesellschaft im Seleukidenreich. Die Eigentums- und Abhängigkeitsverhältnisse.* Berlin, 1978
37. Liebmann Frankfort, Th. *La frontière orientale dans la politique extérieure romaine depuis le traité d'Apamée jusqu'à la fin des conquêtes asiatiques de Pompée (189/8–63).* Brussels, 1969
38. Lorton, D. 'The supposed expedition of Ptolemy II to Persia', *JEA* 57 (1971) 160–4
39. Marinoni, E. 'La capitale del regno di Seleuco I', *Rend. Ist. Lomb.* 106 (1972) 579–631
40. Meyer, Ed. 'Die makedonischen Militärcolonien', *Hermes* 33 (1898) 643–7
41. — *Blüte und Niedergang des Hellenismus in Asien.* Berlin, 1925
42. Momigliano, A. 'Honorati amici', *Athenaeum* N.S. 11 (1933) 136–41
43. Mørkholm, O. *Antiochus IV of Syria.* Copenhagen, 1966
44. Musti, D. 'Lo stato dei Seleucidi. Dinastia popoli città da Seleuco I ad Antioco III', *Studi class. e orient.* 15 (1966) 61–197
45. 'Antioco il Grande', in *I Protagonisti,* ii.393–420. Milan, 1968
46. Otto, W. *Beiträge zur Seleukidengeschichte des 3. Jahrhunderts v. Chr.* (*Abhandlungen der Bayerischen Akademie der Wissenshaften,* Phil.-hist. Abteilung, xxxiv.1). Munich, 1928
47. Rigsby, K. J. 'Seleucid notes', *TAPA* 110 (1980) 233–54
48. Rostovtzeff, M. 'Syria and the East', *CAH* vii, 155–96. Cambridge, 1928
49. Sachs, A. J. and Wiseman, D. J. 'A Babylonian king-list of the Hellenistic period', *Iraq* 16 (1954) 202–12
50. Schalit, A. 'The letter of Antiochus III to Zeuxis regarding the establishment of Jewish military colonies in Phrygia and Lydia', *Jewish Quarterly Review* 50 (1960) 289–318
51. Schmitt. H. H. *Untersuchungen zur Geschichte Antiochos' des Grossen und seiner Zeit* (*Historia* Einzelschr. 6). Wiesbaden, 1964
52. Schulten, A. 'Die makedonischen Militärcolonien', *Hermes* 32 (1897) 523–37
53. Seyrig, H. 'Séleucos I et la fondation de la monarchie syrienne', *Syria* 47 (1970) 290–311
54. Tarn, W. W. 'The first Syrian War', *JHS* 46 (1926) 154–62
55. Welwei, K. W. 'Abhängige Landbevölkerungen auf "Tempel-territorien" im hellenistischen Kleinasien und Syrien', *Anc. Soc.* 10 (1979) 97–118
56. Zel'in, K. K. and Trofimova, M. K. *Formy zavisimosti v vostočnom sredizemnomor'e ellinističeskogo perioda.* Moscow, 1969

b. ASIA MINOR

See also B 178–80

57. Archi, A. 'Città sacre d'Asia minore', *PP* 30 (1975) 329–44
58. Atkinson, K. T. M. 'The Seleucids and the Greek cities of western Asia Minor', *Antichthon* 2 (1968) 32–57
59. – 'A Hellenistic land-conveyance: the estate of Mnesimachus in the plain of Sardes', *Historia* 21 (1972) 45–74
60. Briant, P. 'Remarques sur "laoi" et esclaves ruraux en Asie Mineure hellénistique', *Actes Besançon 1971* (1972), 93–133
61. Broughton, T. R. S. 'Roman landholding in Asia Minor', *TAPA* 65 (1934) 207–39
62. – 'Roman Asia Minor', *ESAR* IV (1938). 499–916
63. – 'New evidence on temple-estates in Asia Minor', in *Studies in Roman Economic and Social History in honor of Allan C. Johnson*, ed. P. R. Coleman-Norton and others, 236–50. Princeton, 1951
64. Cadoux, C. J. *Ancient Smyrna*. Oxford, 1938
65. Calder, W. M. 'A Hellenistic survival at Eucarpia', *Anatolian Studies* 6 (1956) 49–51
66. Dupont-Sommer, A. and Robert, L. *La déesse de Hierapolis Castabala (Cilicie)*. Paris, 1964
67. Errington, R. M. 'Rom, Antiochos der Grosse und Teos', *ZPE* 39 (1980) 279–84
68. Fleischer, R. *Artemis von Ephesos und verwandte Kultstatuen*. Leiden, 1973
69. Habicht, Chr. 'Prusias I, II, III', *PW* xxiii.1 (1959) cols. 1086–128
70. – 'Ziaelas', *PW* x.a (1972) cols. 387–97
71. – 'Zipoites I', *PW* x.a (1972) cols. 448–55
72. Haussoullier, B. *Études sur l'histoire de Milet et du Didymeion*. Paris, 1902
73. Hornblower, S. *Mausolus*. Oxford, 1982
74. Hunt, D. W. S. 'Feudal survivals in Ionia', *JHS* 67 (1947) 68–76
75. Laffi, U. 'I terreni del tempio di Zeus ad Aizanoi', *Athenaeum* N.S. 49 (1971) 3–53
76. Lenschau, Th. *De rebus Prienensium* (Leipziger Studien zur Classischen Philologie 12) 111–220. Leipzig, 1890
77. Levi, M. A. 'Au sujet des *laoi* et des inscriptions de Mnésimachos', *Actes Besançon 1973*, 257–79
78. Levick, B. *Roman Colonies in Southern Asia Minor*. Oxford, 1967
79. Machu, J. 'Milet et les grandes monarchies hellénistiques', in *Atti X congresso internazionale di scienze storiche (Roma, 4–11 Settembre 1955)*, 241–4, Rome, 1957
80. Magie, D. 'The political status of the independent cities of Asia Minor in the Hellenistic period', in *The Greek Political Experience. Studies in honor of W. K. Prentice*, 173–86. Princeton, 1941
81. – *Roman Rule in Asia Minor to the End of the Third Century after Christ*. 2 vols. Princeton, N.J., 1950
82. Mastrocinque, A. 'Osservazioni sull'attività di Antioco III nel 197 e nel 196 a.C.', *PP* 31 (1976) 307–22

83. – *La Caria e la Ionia meridionale in epoca ellenistica (323–188 a.C.)*. Rome, 1979
84. McDonald, A. H. and Walbank, F. W. 'The treaty of Apamea (188 B.C.): the naval clauses", *JRS* 59 (1969) 30–9
85. Meyer, Ed. *Geschichte des Königreichs Pontos*. Leipzig, 1879
86. Meyer, Ernst *Die Grenzen der hellenistischen Staaten in Kleinasien*. Zürich-Leipzig, 1925
87. Musti, D. 'Aspetti dell'organizzazione seleucidica in Asia Minore nel III sec. a.C.', *PP* 20 (1965) 153–60
88. Newell, E. T. *Tarsos under Alexander*. New York, 1919
89. Olshausen, E. 'Zeuxis', *PW* X.A. (1972) cols. 381–5
90. Radet, G. *De coloniis a Macedonibus in Asiam cis Taurum deductis*. Paris, 1892
91. Ramsay, W. M. *The Historical Geography of Asia Minor*. London, 1890
92. – *The Cities and Bishoprics of Phrygia*. Oxford, 1895–7
93. Reinach, Th. *Trois royaumes de l'Asie Mineure: Cappadoce, Bithynie, Pont.* Paris, 1888
94. Robert, J. and L. *La Carie. Histoire et géographie historique avec le recueil des inscriptions antiques*. II: *Le plateau de Tabai et ses environs*. Paris, 1954
95. Robert, L. *Villes d'Asie Mineure. Études de géographie ancienne*. Ed. 2. Paris, 1962
96. Schuchhardt, C. 'Die makedonischen Kolonien zwischen Hermos und Kaikos', *Ath. Mitt.* 13 (1888) 1–17
97. Seyrig, H. 'Parion au IIIe siècle avant notre ère', in *Centennial Volume of the American Numismatic Society*, ed. H. Ingholt, 603–24. New York, 1958
98. Virgilio, B. *Il 'tempio stato' di Pessinunte fra Pergamo e Roma nel II–I secolo a.C. (C.B. Welles, Royal Corr., 55–61)*. Pisa, 1981
99. Vitucci, G. *Il regno di Bitinia*. Rome, 1953
100. Waldmann, H. *Die kommagenischen Kultreformen unter König Mithridates I. Kallinikos und seinem Sohne Antiochos I.* Leiden, 1973
101. Welles, C. B. 'Hellenistic Tarsus', *Mél. USJ* 38 (*Mélanges R. Mouterde* II) 43–75. Beirut, 1962
102. Zawadzki, T. *Z zagadnien struktury agrarno-społecznej krajów małoazjatyckich w epoce hellenismu*. Poznan, 1952
103. – 'Quelques remarques sur l'étendue et l'accroissement des domaines des grands temples en Asie Mineure', *Eos* 46 (1953/4) 86–96

C. THE CELTS (GALATIANS)

See also Launey 1949, 1.490–534: (J 143)
104. Anderson, J. G. C. 'Exploration in Galatia cis Halym. Part II', *JHS* 19 (1899) 52–134, 280–318
105. Bar-Kochva, B. 'On the sources and chronology of Antiochus I's battle against the Galatians', *Proceedings of the Cambridge Philological Society* 119 (1973) 1–8
106. Bienkowski, P. *Die Darstellungen der Gallier in der hellenistischen Kunst.* Vienna, 1908

107. — *Les Celtes dans les arts mineurs gréco-romains avec des recherches iconographiques sur quelques autres peuples barbares.* Cracow, 1928
108. Bittel, K. *Kleinasiatische Studien (Istanb. Mitt.* 5). Istanbul, 1942
109. Dressel, W. 'Galatisches mit Exkursen zu Lenition und britannischen Rix-Namen', in *Beiträge zur Indogermanistik und Keltologie Julius Pokorny zum 80. Geburtstag gewidmet*, 147–54. Innsbruck, 1967
110. Künzl, E. *Die Kelten des Epigonos von Pergamon* (Beiträge zur Archäologie 4). Würzburg, 1971
111. Launey, M. 'Un épisode oublié de l'invasion galate en Asie Mineure (278/7 av. J.-C.)', *Rev. Ét. Anc.* 46 (1944) 217–36
112. Moraux, P. 'L'établissement des Galates en Asie Mineure', *Istanb. Mitt.* 1957, 56–75
113. Nachtergael, G. *Les Galates en Grèce et les Sôtéria de Delphes. Recherches d'histoire et d'épigraphie hellénistiques* (Acad. royale de Belgique. Mémoires de la Classe des Lettres[2] LXIII.1). Brussels, 1977
114. Özgan, R. 'Bemerkungen zum grossen Gallieranathem', *Arch. Anz.* 1981, 489–510
115. Polenz, H. 'Gedanken zu einer Fibel vom Mittellatèneschema aus Kayseri in Anatolien', *Bonner Jahrbücher* 178 (1978) 181–220 (with a comprehensive survey of Celtic finds in Asia Minor)
116. Stähelin, F. *Geschichte der kleinasiatischen Galater.* Ed. 2. Leipzig, 1907
117. Wenning, R. *Die Galateranatheme Attalos' I. Eine Untersuchung zum Bestand und zur Nachwirkung pergamenischer Skulptur* (Pergamenische Forschungen 4). Berlin, 1978

d. PERGAMUM

See also H 186
118. Bauslaugh, R. A. 'The date of the unique portrait tetradrachm of Eumenes II', *AJArch.* 85 (1981) 185–6
119. Callaghan, P. J. 'On the date of the Great Altar of Zeus at Pergamon', *BICS* 28 (1981) 115–21
120. Cardinali, G. *Il regno di Pergamo. Ricerche di storia e di diritto pubblico.* Rome, 1906
121. Ducrey, P. 'Nouvelles remarques sur deux traités attalides avec des cités crétoises', *BCH* 94 (1970) 637–59
122. Hansen, E. V. *The Attalids of Pergamon* (Cornell Studies in Classical Philology 36). Ed. 2. Ithaca-London, 1971
123. Hoffmann, W. 'Philetairos (1)', *PW* XIX.2 (1938) cols. 2157–61
124. Holleaux, M. *Études d'épigraphie et d'histoire grecques.* II: *Études sur la monarchie attalide.* Paris, 1938
125. Jones, C.P. 'Diodoros Pasparos and the Nikephoria of Pergamon', *Chiron* 4 (1974) 183–205
126. Klaffenbach, G. 'Die Nikephorien von Pergamon', *Ath. Mitt.* 65 (1950) 99–106
127. Laurenzi, L. 'Pergamo', in *Enciclopedia dell' arte antica classica e orientale* VI, 36–51. Rome, 1965

128. McShane, R.B. *The Foreign Policy of the Attalids of Pergamum* (Illinois Studies in the Social Sciences 53). Urbana, 1964
129. *Pergamenische Forschungen*. Deutsches Archäologisches Institut (ed.). Berlin (4 vols. so far published).
130. Segre, M. 'L'institution des Niképhoria de Pergame', in L. Robert, *Hellenica* v (1948) 102–28
131. Van Looy, H. 'Apollonis reine de Pergame', *Anc. Soc.* 7 (1976) 151–65
132. Westermark, U. *Das Bildnis des Philetairos von Pergamon. Corpus der Münzprägung*. Uppsala, 1961

e. RHODES

See also Fraser 1972, 1.162–9: (A 15); Holleaux, *Études* i, esp. 381–462
133. Blinkenberg, Ch. 'Trihemiolia: étude sur un type de navire rhodien', *Arkaeologisk-Kunsthistoriske Meddelelser udg. af det kgl. Danske Videnskabernes Selskab*. II.3 (1938) 59ff. (*Lindiaka* VII)
134. Fraser, P. M. and Bean, G. E. *The Rhodian Peraea and Islands*. Oxford, 1954
135. – 'Notes on two Rhodian institutions', *BSA* 67 (1972) 113–24
136. – *Rhodian Funerary Monuments*. Oxford, 1977
137. Gelder, H. van *Geschichte der alten Rhodier*. The Hague, 1900
138. Hiller von Gaertringen, F. 'Rhodos', *PW* Suppl. v (1931) 731–840
139. Kruškol, J. S. 'Osnovnye punkty i napravlenija torgovli Severnogo Pričernomor'ja s Rodosom v ellinističeskuju epochu', in Russian; 'The most important points and directions of trade between the northern Black Sea area and Rhodes in Hellenistic times', *VDI* 1957(4) 110–15
140. O'Neil, J. L. 'How democratic was Hellenistic Rhodes?', *Athenaeum* 59 (1981) 468–73
141. Pugliese Carratelli, G. 'Per la storia delle associazioni in Rodi antica', *Annuario* N.S. 1–2 (1939–40 [1942]) 147–200
142. Rostovtzeff, M. 'Alexandrien und Rhodos', *Klio* 30 (1937) 70–6
143. Schmitt, H. H. *Rom und Rhodos* (*Münch. Beitr. Papyr.* 40). Munich, 1957
144. Segre, M. 'Il culto rodio di Alessandro e dei Tolomei', *BSA Alex* 34 (1941) 29–39
145. Sippel, D. V. *Rhodes and the Nesiotic League* (diss. University of Cincinnati, 1966)
146. Ziebarth, E. 'Zur Handelsgeschichte der Insel Rhodos', in *Mélanges Glotz* (1932) II.909–24

f. SYRIA, PALESTINE, MESOPOTAMIA, THE SYRIAN-EGYPTIAN WARS

See also F 120–3, H 198
147. Abel, F.-M. 'Les confins de la Palestine et de l'Égypte sous les Ptolémées', *Rev. Bibl.* 48 (1939) 207–35, 530–48; 49 (1940) 55–75, 224–39
148. – *Histoire de la Palestine depuis la conquête d'Alexandre jusqu'à l'invasion arabe*. 2 vols. Paris, 1952
149. Avi-Yonah, M. 'Scythopolis', *IEJ* 12 (1962) 123–34

150. – 'Palaestina', *PW* Suppl. XIII (1973) cols. 321–454

151. Balty, J.-Ch. (ed.) *Apamée de Syrie: Bilan de recherches archéologiques 1965–68.* Brussels, 1969

152. – 'Nouvelles données topographiques et chronologiques à Apamée de Syrie', *A Arch.Syr.* 21 (1971) 131–5

153. Bikerman, E. 'La charte séleucide de Jérusalem', *Revue des Études Juives* 197–8 (1935) 4–35

154. – 'La Coelé-Syrie. Notes de géographie historique', *Rev. Bibl.* 54 (1947) 256–68

155. Cumont, F. 'The population of Syria', *JRS* 24 (1934) 187–90

156. Downey, G. 'The water supply of Antioch on the Orontes in antiquity', *A Arch.Syr.* 1 (1951) 171–87

157. – *A History of Antioch in Syria from Seleucus to the Arab Conquest.* Princeton, 1961

158. Dussaud, R. *Topographie historique de la Syrie antique et médiévale.* Paris, 1927

159. Fischer, Th. *Seleukiden und Makkabäer. Beiträge zur Seleukidengeschichte und zu den politischen Ereignissen in Judäa während der 1. Hälfte des 2. Jahrhunderts v. Chr.* Bochum, 1980

160. Galili, E. 'Raphia, 217 B.C.E., revisited', *Scripta Classica Israelica* 3 (1976/7 [1978]) 52–156. (Also published separately with corrigenda.)

161. Honigman, E. 'Historische Topographie von Nordsyrien im Altertum', *Zeitschrift des deutschen Palästina-Vereins* 47 (1923) 149–93; 48 (1924) 1–64

162. Hörig, M. *Dea Syria.* Leiden, 1979

163. Huss, W. 'Eine ptolemäische Expedition nach Kleinasien', *Anc. Soc.* 8 (1977) 187–93

164. Jaehne, A. 'Die syrische Frage, Seleukeia in Pierien und die Ptolemäer', *Klio* 56 (1974) 501–19

165. Klengel, H. *Syria antiqua.* Leipzig, 1971

166. Koch, W. *Ein Ptolemaeerkrieg.* Stuttgart, 1923

167. Kraeling, C. H. 'The Jewish community at Antioch', *Journal of Biblical Literature* 51 (1932) 130–60

168. Leuze, O. *Die Satrapieneinteilung in Syrien und im Zweistromlande von 520–320.* Halle, 1935

169. Mahaffy, J. P. 'The army of Ptolemy IV at Raphia', *Hermathena* 10 (1898–9) 140–52

170. Otto, W. 'Zu den syrischen Kriegen der Ptolemäer', *Philol.* 86 (1931) 400–18

171. Segal, J. B. *Edessa, 'the Blessed City'.* Oxford, 1970

172. Seibert, J. 'Die Schlacht bei Ephesos', *Historia* 25 (1976) 45–61

173. Seyrig, H. 'Aradus et sa Pérée sous les rois séleucides', *Syria* 28 (1951) 206–17

174. – 'Seleucus I and the foundation of Hellenistic Syria', in *The Role of the Phoenicians in the Interaction of Mediterranean Civilizations*, ed. W. A. Ward, 53–63. Beirut, 1968

175. Tchalenko, G. *Villages antiques de la Syrie du Nord.* 3 vols. Paris, 1953–8

176. Vidal-Naquet, P. *Il buon uso del tradimento. Flavio Giuseppe e la guerra giudaica.* Rome, 1980

177. Walser, J. G. III. *A Study of Selected Economic Factors and their Contribution to the Understanding of the History of Palestine during the Hellenistic Period* (diss. Duke University, 1969; publ. 1970)

178. Welles, C. B. 'The constitution of Edessa', *YCS* 5 (1935) 121–42

179. Wirth, E. *Syrien. Eine geographische Landeskunde.* Darmstadt, 1971

g. IRAN, PARTHIA, THE PERSIAN GULF, BACTRIA, INDIA

For Aï Khanum see also, on p. 602 (Addenda), E 191a, E 197a

180. Benveniste, E. 'Édits d'Asoka en traduction grecque', *Journ. asiatique* 252 (1964) 137–57

181. Bernard, P. Account of the excavations of Aï Khanum in *CR Acad.Inscr.* 1966–72, 1974–6, 1978

182. – 'Aï Khanum on the Oxus. A Hellenistic city in central Asia', *Proc. Brit. Acad.* 53 (1967) 71–95

183. – *Fouilles d'Aï Khanoum: Campagnes 1965, 1966, 1967, 1968.* Paris, 1973

184. – 'Aï Khanoum ville cononiale grecque', *Les dossiers de l'archéologie Dijon* 5 (1974) 99–114

185. Bloch, J. *Les inscriptions d'Asoka, traduites et commentées.* Paris, 1950

186. Colledge, M. A. R. *The Parthians.* London, 1967

187. Debevoise, N. C. *A Political History of Parthia.* Chicago, 1938

188. Diakonov, I. M. (ed.) *Ancient Mesopotamia.* Moscow, 1969

189. Falkenstein, A. *Topographie von Uruk* I: *Uruk zur Seleukidenzeit.* Leipzig, 1941

190. Gentelle, P. *Étude géographique de la plaine d'Aï-Khanoum et de son irrigation depuis les temps antiques.* Paris, 1978

191. Ghirshman, R. *L'Iran, des origines à l'Islam.* Paris, 1964

192. Gutschmid, A. von *Geschichte Irans und seiner Nachbarländer von Alexander dem Grossen bis zum Untergang der Arsaciden.* Tübingen, 1888

193. Jeppesen, K. 'A royal message to Ikaros; the Hellenistic temples of Failaka', *Kuml* (1960) 153–98 (in Danish; English summary, 187–98)

194. Marshall, J. *Taxila: An Illustrated Account of Archaeological Excavation.* 3 vols. Cambridge, 1951

195. Masson, V. M. 'Demetrij Batrijskij i zavoievanie Indii', *VDI* 76 (1961) 39–45

196. Narain, A. K. *The Indo-Greeks.* Oxford, 1957 (with excellent bibliography)

197. Pugliese Carratelli, G. and Garbini, G. *A Bilingual Graeco-Aramaic Edict by Asoka.* Rome, 1964

198. Schlumberger, D. 'The excavations at Surkh Kotal and the problem of Hellenism in Bactria and India', *Proc. Brit. Acad.* 47 (1961) 77–95 with Pls. I–XXIV

199. – 'Une nouvelle inscription grecque d'Asoka', *CR Acad.Inscr.* 1964, 126–40

200. Schlumberger, D., Dupont-Sommer, A., Robert, L. and Benveniste, E.
     'Une bilingue gréco-araméenne d'Asoka', *Journ. asiatique* 246 (1958)
     1–48. (For the Greek part of the text see *SEG* 20 (1964) no. 326.)
201. Schlumberger, D. and Bernard, P. 'Fouilles d'Ai Khanoum', *BCH* 89
     (1965) 590–637
202. Schneider, U. *Die grossen Felsen-edikte Asokas: Ausgabe, Übersetzung und
     Analyse der Texte* (Freiburger Bände zur Indologie 11). Wiesbaden,
     1978
203. Schwarz, F. F. 'Mauryas und die Seleukiden, Probleme ihrer gegen-
     seitiger Beziehungen', *Studien zur Sprachwissenschaft und Kulturkunde.
     Gedenkschrift für W. Brandenstein*, 181–90. Innsbruck, 1968
204. Simonetta, A. M. 'A new essay on the Indo-Greeks, the Šakas and the
     Pahlavas', *East and West* 9 (1958) 154–83
205. Tarn, W. W. 'Seleucid-Parthian studies', *Proc. Brit. Acad.* 16 (1930) 1–33
206. – *The Greeks in Bactria and India.* Ed. 2. Cambridge, 1951
207. Thapar, R. *Asoka and the Decline of the Mauryas.* Oxford, 1961
208. Tucci, G., Scerrato, U., Pugliese Carratelli, G. and Levi della Vida, G. *Un
     editto bilingue di Asoka.* Rome, 1958
209. Welles, C. B. 'The Hellenism of Dura-Europos', *Aegyptus* 39 (1959) 23–8
210. Wolski, J. 'L'effondrement de la domination des Séleucides en Iran au IIIe
     siècle av. J.C.', *Bulletin international de l'Académie polonaise des Sciences et
     des Lettres; classe de philologie, histoire et philosophie* Suppl. 5, 13–70.
     Cracow, 1947
211. – 'The decay of the Iranian Empire of the Seleucids and the chronology
     of the Parthian beginnings', *Berytus* 12 (1956–8) 35–52
212. – 'L'historicité d'Arsace I', *Historia* 8 (1959) 222–38
213. – 'Les Iraniens et le royaume gréco-bactrien', *Klio* 38 (1960) 110–21
214. – 'Arsace II ou la généalogie des premiers Arsacides', *Historia* 11 (1962)
     136–45
215. – 'L'origine de la relation d'Arrien sur la paire des frères Arsacides,
     Arsace et Tiridate', *Act. ant.* 24 (1976) 65–70
216. – 'Untersuchungen zur frühen parthischen Geschichte', *Klio* 58 (1976)
     39–57
217. Woodcock, G. *The Greeks in India.* London, 1966

F. EGYPT

a. BIBLIOGRAPHIES OF EGYPTOLOGISTS

Note the bibliographies in the following:

1. Peremans, W. *Antidorum W. Peremans sexagenario ab alumnis oblatum* (*Studia
   Hellenistica* 16), xiii–li. Louvain, 1968. Continued in *Historiographia
   Antica* (Louvain, 1977) 336–41: (A 29)
2. Préaux, Cl. Bibliography by M.-Th. Lenger (Éditions de l'Université de
   Bruxelles). Brussels, 1980
3. Rostovtzeff, M. Bibliography compiled by C. B. Welles in *Historia* 5 (1956)
   358–81
4. Turner, E. G. Bibliography in *P. Turner*, xiii–xx: (F 84)
5. Welles, C. B. Bibliography compiled by K. Rigsby in *Welles Essays*, ix–xxii

b. PAPYRI AND OSTRACA

Papyri

Publications are not recorded unless they contain papyri of the Ptolemaic period and form volumes obtainable separately. (An exception is listed under *P. Berl. inv. no.*)

6. *Actenstücke* U. Wilcken, *Actenstücke aus der Königlichen Bank zu Theben* (*Abh. Akad. Berl.*) Berlin, 1886 (now republished in *UPZ* II.198–229)

7. *BGU Aegyptische Urkunden aus den Staatlichen Museen zu Berlin, Griechische Urkunden.* Berlin, 1895–

I–IV, quarto size, lithographed, consisting of the fascicles in which they were issued. 1895

V: *Der Gnomon des Idios Logos,* ed. W. Schubart. 1919

VI: *Papyri und Ostraka der Ptolemäerzeit,* ed. W. Schubart and E. Kühn. 1922

VII: *Papyri, Ostraka und Wachstafeln aus Philadelphia,* ed. P. Viereck and F. Zucker. 1926

VIII: *Spätptolemäische Papyri,* ed. W. Schubart and D. Schäfer. 1933

X: *Papyrusurkunden aus ptolemäischer Zeit,* ed. W. Müller. 1970

XIV: *Ptolemäische Urkunden aus Mumienkartonage,* ed. William M. Brashear. 1980

[W. Müller] *Festschrift zum 150-jährigen Bestehen des Berliner ägyptischen Museums,* esp. pp. 343–462. 1974

8. *C. Ord. Ptol.* M.-Th. Lenger, *Corpus des ordonnances des Ptolémées.* Brussels, 1964; revised ed., 1980

9. *CPJ Corpus Papyrorum Judaicarum,* ed. V. A. Tcherikover and A. Fuks. Cambridge, Mass., I (1957); II (1960); III (1964)

10. *P. Aberd.* E. G. Turner, *Catalogue of Greek and Latin Papyri and Ostraca in the Possession of the University of Aberdeen.* Aberdeen, 1939

11. *P. Achmîm Les Papyrus grecs d'Achmîm,* ed. P. Collart. Cairo, 1930

12. *P. Adler The Adler Papyri,* Greek texts ed. by E. N. Adler, J. G. Tait and F. M. Heichelheim; Demotic ed. F. Ll. Griffith. Oxford, 1939

13. *P. Alex. Papyrus grecs du Musée gréco-romain d'Alexandrie,* ed. Anna Swiderek and Mariangela Vandoni. Warsaw, 1964

14. *P. Alex. Giss Papyri variae Alexandrinae et Gissenses (Pap. Brux. 7),* ed. J. Schwartz. Brussels, 1969

15. *P. Amb. The Amherst Papyri . . . of . . . Lord Amherst of Hackney,* ed. B. P. Grenfell and A. S. Hunt. 2 vols. London, 1900, 1901

16. *Pap. Brux. Papyrologica Bruxellensia,* a series published in Brussels, 16 vols. in 1978

17. *Pap. Colon. P. Köln.* III, ed. B. Kramer and others. Cologne, 1980

18. *Pap. Lugd. Bat. Papyrologica Lugduno-Batava.* Leiden XIX: *Textes grecs, démotiques et bilingues,* ed. E. Boswinkel and P. W. Pestman. 1978

XX: *Greek and Demotic Texts from the Zenon Archive,* ed. P. W. Pestman. 1980

XXI: *A Guide to the Zenon Archive,* compiled by P. W. Pestman and others, two Parts: XXI.A, *Lists and Surveys*; XXI.B, *Indexes and Maps.* 1981 [XXIII (in the press), ed. P. W. Pestman and others, is a re-edition and commentary on the Greek and Demotic texts of the Hermopolite Law Code.]

19. *P. Baden   Veröffentlichungen aus den badischen Papyrus-Sammlungen.*
Pt 2: *Griechische Papyri*, ed. F. Bilabel. Heidelberg, 1923
Pt 4: *Griechische Papyri*, ed. F. Bilabel. Heidelberg, 1924

20. *P. Berl. inv. no.*   Berlin papyri cited by inventory number

21. *P. Berl. Zilliacus   14 griechische Berliner Papyri*, ed. H. Zilliacus. Helsingfors, 1941

22. *P. Bour.   Les Papyrus Bouriant*, ed. P. Collart. Paris, 1926

23. *P. Cairo Zen.   Catalogue général des antiquités égyptiennes du Musée du Caire: Zenon Papyri*, ed. C. C. Edgar, Cairo, 1925–31. 4 vols; vol. v published by the Société Fouad I de Papyrologie and edited from Edgar's materials by O. Guéraud and P. Jouguet, 1940

24. *P. Col. inv. 480 (P. Col.* 1)   W. L. Westermann, *Upon Slavery in Ptolemaic Egypt.* New York, 1929

25. *P. Col.* 11   *Tax Lists and Transportation Receipts from Theadelphia*, ed. W. L. Westermann and C. W. Keyes. New York, 1932

26. *P. Col. Zen.   Zenon Papyri: Business Papers of the Third Century* B.C. *dealing with Palestine and Egypt* 1, ed. W. L. Westermann and E. S. Hasenoehrl, New York, 1934; 11, ed. W. L. Westermann, C. W. Keyes and H. Liebesny. New York, 1940. (These volumes are counted as *P. Col.* 111 and 1v.)

27. *P. Coll. Youtie   Collectanea Papyrologica. Texts published in honor of H. C. Youtie*, by various hands, ed. A. E. Hanson, 1 (nos. 1–65), 11 (nos. 66–126) (*Papyrologische Texte und Abhandlungen* xix and xx). Bonn, 1976

P. Copenhagen see P. Haun.

28. *P. Cornell   Greek Papyri in the Library of Cornell University*, ed. W. L. Westermann and C. J. Kraemer, Jr. New York, 1926

29. *P. Dura   The Excavations at Dura-Europos . . . Final Report.* v.1: *The Parchments and Papyri*, ed. C. Bradford Welles, Robert O. Fink, J. Frank Gilliam. New Haven, 1959

30. *P. Edfou   papyri published in Fouilles Franco-polonaises.* Rapport 1: *Tell Edfou 1937*, ed. B. Bruyère, J. Manteuffel, K. Michalowski, J. Sainte Fare Garnot. Cairo, 1937
Rapport 11: *Tell Edfou 1938*, ed. K. Michalowski, I. de Linage, J. Manteuffel, J. Sainte Fare Garnot. Cairo, 1938
Rapport 111: *Tell Edfou 1939.* Cairo, 1950

31. *P. Eleph.   Elephantine Papyri*, ed. O. Rubensohn. Berlin, 1907

32. *P. Ent. ΕΝΤΕΥΞΕΙΣ: Requêtes et plaintes adressées au roi d'Égypte au IIIe siècle avant J.-C.*, ed. O. Guéraud. Cairo, 1931–2

33. *P. Fay.   Fayûm Towns and their Papyri*, ed. B. P. Grenfell, A. S. Hunt and D. G. Hogarth. London, 1900

34. *P. Flor.   Papiri greco-egizii*, ed. D. Comparetti and G. Vitelli. 3 vols. Milan, 1906–15 (photographic reprint, 1962)

35. *P. Fouad   Les Papyrus Fouad I* (Publ. de la Société Fouad I de Papyrologie, Textes et Documents 111), ed. A. Bataille, O. Guéraud, P. Jouguet and others. Cairo, 1939

36. *P. Frankf.* *Griechische Papyri aus dem Besitz des Rechtswissenschaftlichen Seminars der Universität Frankfurt*, ed. H. Lewald. Heidelberg, 1920

37. *P. Freib.* *Mitteilungen aus der Freiburger Papyrussammlung*, ed. W. Aly and M. Gelzer, J. Partsch and U. Wilcken.
Pt I includes *Ptolemäische Kleruchenurkunden*, ed. M. Gelzer. Heidelberg, 1914
Pt III: *Juristische Urkunden der Ptolemäerzeit*, ed. J. Partsch. Heidelberg, 1927

38. *P. Fuad I Univ.* *Fuad I University Papyri*, ed. D. S. Crawford. Alexandria, 1949

39. *P. Giss.* *Griechische Papyri im Museum des oberhessischen Geschichtsvereins zu Giessen*, ed. O. Eger, E. Kornemann and P. M. Meyer. Leipzig-Berlin, 1910–12. Pt I (nos. 1–35); Pt II (nos. 36–57); Pt III (nos. 58–126)

40. *P. Giss. Univ.-Bibl.* *Mitteilungen aus der Papyrussammlung der Giessener Universitätsbibliothek*, ed. H. Kling and others.
Pt I: *Griechische Papyrusurkunden aus ptolemäischer und römischer Zeit* (*P. Bibl. Univ. Giss.* 1–16). Giessen, 1924

41. *P. Gradenwitz* *Griechische Papyri der Sammlung Gradenwitz*, ed. G. Plaumann. Heidelberg, 1914

42. *P. Grenf.* I *An Alexandrian Erotic Fragment and other Greek Papyri chiefly Ptolemaic*, ed. B. P. Grenfell. Oxford, 1896

43. *P. Grenf.* II *New Classical Fragments and other Greek and Latin Papyri*, ed. B. P. Grenfell and A. S. Hunt. Oxford, 1897

44. *P. Gurob* *Greek Papyri from Gurob*, ed. J. G. Smyly (Royal Irish Academy: Cunningham Memoirs 12). Dublin, 1921

45. *P. Hal.* *Dikaiomata: Auszüge aus Alexandrinischen Gesetzen und Verordnungen in einem Papyrus des philologischen Seminars der Universität Halle mit einem Anhang weiterer Papyri derselben Sammlung*, ed. by the Graeca Halensis. Berlin, 1913

46. *P. Hamb.* *Griechische Papyrusurkunden der Hamburger Staats- und Universitätsbibliothek* I (in 3 parts), ed. P. M. Meyer. Leipzig-Berlin, 1911–24
A new series begins with *Griechische Papyri der Hamburger Staats- und Universitätsbibliothek, mit einigen Stücken aus der Sammlung Hugo Ibscher*, ed. B. Snell and others. Hamburg, 1954

47. *P. Harris* *The Rendel Harris Papyri of Woodbrooke College, Birmingham*, ed. J. E. Powell. Cambridge, 1936

48. *P. Haun.* *Papyri Graecae Haunienses* I, ed. T. Larsen. Copenhagen, 1942

49. *P. Hawara* W. M. Flinders Petrie, *Hawara, Biahmu and Arsinoe*, 24–36. London, 1889. (Further publication of some texts by J. G. Milne, *Arch. Pap.* 5 (1913) 378–97.)

50. *P. Heidelberg* *Veröffentlichungen aus der Heidelberger Papyrussammlung* N.S. 3: *Griechische Papyrusurkunden und Ostraka der Heidelberger Papyrussammlung*, ed. P. Sattler. Heidelberg, 1963

51. *P. Hib.* *The Hibeh Papyri.*
Pt I, ed. B. P. Grenfell and A. S. Hunt. London, 1906
Pt II, ed. E. G. Turner and M. T. Lenger. London, 1955

52. *PIFAO*   *Papyrus grecs de l'Institut français d'archéologie orientale.* Cairo. I, ed.
J. Schwartz, 1971; II, ed. G. Wagner, 1971; III, ed. J. Schwartz and
G. Wagner, 1975

53. *P. Jena*   *Jenaer Papyrus-Urkunden,* ed. F. Zucker and F. Schneider. Jena,
1926

54. *P. Köln   Sonderreihe Papyrologica Coloniensia* Kölner Papyri, Cologne.
I, ed. B. Kramer and R. Hübner, 1976; II, ed. B. Kramer and D.
Hagedorn, 1978; III, ed. B. Kramer, M. Erler, D. Hagedorn, R.
Hübner, 1980

55. *P. Kroll   Eine ptolemäische Königsurkunde,* ed. L. Koenen. Wiesbaden, 1957

56. *P. Kronion*   D. Foraboschi, *L'archivio di Kronion.* Milan, 1971

57. *P. Laur.*   [Biblioteca Medicea Laurenciana] IX: Paola Pruneti, *I Centri
abitati dell' Ossirinchite.* Florence, 1981

58. *P. Lille   Papyrus grecs* (Institut papyrologique de l'Université de Lille),
ed. P. Jouguet, P. Collart, J. Lesquier, M. Xoual. Paris, vol. I in 4
fasc. (1907–28); II (1912)

59. *P. Lond.   Greek Papyri in the British Museum* (now the British Library), ed.
F. G. Kenyon and H. I. Bell. London, 1893–
I, Catalogue with texts, ed. F. G. Kenyon. 1893
II, item. 1898
III, Catalogue with texts, ed. F. G. Kenyon and H. I. Bell. 1907
VII: *The Zenon Archive,* ed. T. C. Skeat. 1974
Vols. I–III reprinted Milan, 1974

60. *P. Merton   The Greek Papyri in the Collection of Wilfred Merton*
I, ed. H. I. Bell and C. H. Roberts. London, 1948
II, ed. B. R. Rees, H. I. Bell, J. W. B. Barns. Dublin, 1959
III, ed. J. D. Thomas. London, 1967

61. *P. Meyer   Griechische Texte aus Ägypten* I: *Papyri des Neutestamentlichen
Seminars der Universität Berlin;* II: *Ostraka der Sammlung Deissmann,* ed.
P. M. Meyer. Berlin, 1916

62. *P. Mich.   Papyri in the University of Michigan Collection.* Ann Arbor, 1931–
I: *Zenon Papyri* (nos. 1–120), ed. C. C. Edgar. 1931
III: *Miscellaneous Papyri* (nos. 131–221), ed. J. G. Winter and others.
1936
VIII: *Papyri and Ostraca from Karanis,* Second Series (nos. 464–521), ed.
J. G. Winter and H. C. Youtie. 1951
P. Mich. Zen. see *P. Mich.* I

63. *P. Mil.   Papiri Milanesi.* Milan. I, fasc. I, ed. A. Calderini, 1928; fasc. 2,
ed. S. Daris, 1966
*Papiri documentari dell'Univ. Cattolica di Milano, presentato all'XIV
Congresso Int. di Papirologia* ... (= *Aegyptus* 54 (1974) 1–20)

64. *P. Mil. R. Univ.   Papiri della R. Università di Milano* I, ed. A. Vogliano.
Milan, 1937 (repr. 1966)

65. *P. Mil. Vogliano   Papiri della Università degli Studi di Milano* (continuation
of *P. Mil. R. Univ.*). Milan. III, ed. I. Cazzaniga, M. Vandoni and
others, 1965; IV, ed. D. Foraboschi, M. Vandoni and others, 1967; VI:
(nos. 258–300), ed. C. Gallazzi and M. Vandoni, 1977

66. *P. Osl.* *Papyri Osloenses,* ed. S. Eitrem and L. Amundsen. 3 vols. The plates are in separate fascicles. Oslo, 1925–
    II: *Literary Texts, Documents, Private Correspondence,* ed. S. Eitrem and L. Amundsen. 1931
    III: *Literary Texts, Documents (official and private), Private Correspondence, Horoscopes, Short Texts and Fragments,* ed. S. Eitrem and L. Amundsen. 1936
67. *P. Oxford Wegener* *Some Oxford Papyri,* ed. E. P. Wegener. Leiden, 1942 (= *Papyrologica Lugd.-Bat.* III)
68. *P. Oxy.* *The Oxyrhynchus Papyri,* ed. B. P. Grenfell, A. S. Hunt, and others. London, 1898–. In progress, 50 vols. in 1983. There are not many Ptolemaic papyri in this celebrated collection.
69. *P. Par.* *Notices et textes des papyrus grecs du Musée du Louvre et de la Bibliothèque impériale* (Notices et extraites des manuscrits de la Bibliothèque impériale et autres bibliothèques 18.2), ed. A. J. Letronne and W. Brunet de Presle. Separate volume of plates. Paris, 1865
70. *P. Petrie* *The Flinders Petrie Papyri,* ed. J. P. Mahaffy and J. G. Smyly. Dublin, 1891–1905
    I (Royal Irish Academy, *Cunningham Memoirs* 8), + Pt 2 (Plates), 1891
    II (*Cunningham Mem.* 9), + Plates, 1893;
    III (*Cunningham Mem.* 11) + Plates, 1905
71. *P. Princ.* *Papyri in the Princeton University Collections,* by A. C. Johnson, H. B. van Hoesen, E. H. Kase Jr. and S. P. Goodrich. 3 vols. Baltimore and Princeton, 1931–42
72. *P. Rein.* *Papyrus grecs et démotiques recueillis en Égypte,* ed. T. Reinach, W. Spiegelberg and S. de Ricci. Paris, 1905. *Les Papyrus Théodore Reinach* II, ed. P. Collart. Cairo, 1940
73. *P. Rev.* *Revenue Laws of Ptolemy Philadelphus,* ed. B. P. Grenfell. Oxford, 1896. Re-edited by J. Bingen in *SB,* Beiheft 1. Göttingen, 1952
74. *P. Ross. Georg.* *Papyri russischer und georgischer Sammlungen* II: *Ptolemäische und frührömische Texte,* ed. O. Krüger. Tiflis, 1929
75. *P. Ryl.* *Catalogue of the Greek Papyri in the John Rylands Library, Manchester,* by A. S. Hunt, J. de M. Johnson, V. Martin, C. H. Roberts and E. G. Turner. 4 vols. Manchester, 1911–52
76. *PSA Athen.* *Papyri Societatis Archaeologicae Atheniensis,* ed. G. A. Petropoulos. Athens, 1939
77. *PSI* *Papiri greci e latini* (Pubblicazioni della Società Italiana per la ricerca dei Papiri greci e latini in Egitto), ed. G. Vitelli, M. Norsa, and others. 14 vols. Florence, 1912–
78. *P. Sorb.* *Papyrus de la Sorbonne.* Part 1, nos. 1–68, ed. H. Cadell. Paris, 1966
79. *P. Strasb.* *Papyrus grecs de la bibliothèque de Strasbourg* (continuation of *Griechische Papyrus der Universitäts- und Landesbibliothek zu Strassburg).* In progress
    III, ed. P. Collomp and pupils. Paris, 1948
    IV, ed. J. Schwartz and pupils. Strasbourg, 1963
80. *P. Tebt.* *The Tebtunis Papyri,* by B. P. Grenfell, A. S. Hunt, J. G. Smyly,

E. J. Goodspeed and C. C. Edgar. London, 1902–38
  I, ed. B. P. Grenfell, A. S. Hunt, J. G. Smyly, 1902
  III, ed. A. S. Hunt and J. G. Smyly, assisted by B. P. Grenfell, E. Lobel, and M. Rostovtzeff, 1933
  III.2, ed. A. S. Hunt, J. G. Smyly and C. C. Edgar, 1938
  IV, ed. J. G. Keenan and J. C. Shelton, 1976
81. *P. Tebt. Tait*   Papyri from Tebtunis in Egyptian and Greek, ed. W. J. Tait. London, 1977
82. *P. Tor.*   'Papyri graeci R. Musei Aegyptii Taurinensis', in *Memorie della R. Accademia delle scienze di Torino* 31 (1826) 9–188; 33 (1827) 1–80, ed. A. Peyron
83. *P. Tsoukalas* ἀνέκδοτοι φιλολογικοὶ καὶ ἰδιωτικοὶ πάπυροι by M. G. Tsoukalas. (**Βιβλ.** τῆς ἐν Ἀθηναῖς φιλεκπαιδευτικῆς ἑταιρείας 17). Athens, 1962
84. *P. Turner*   Papyri Greek and Egyptian edited by Various Hands in Honour of Eric Gardner Turner (EES Graeco-Roman Memoirs 68). London, 1981 (esp. no. 15)
85. *P. Vars.*   Papyri Varsovienses, ed. G. Manteuffel. Warsaw, 1935. Vol. II in *JJP* (1948) 81–110
86. *P. Würzb.*   Mitteilungen aus der Würzburger Papyrussammlung, ed. U. Wilcken. Berlin, 1934
87. *P. Yale*   Yale Papyri in the Beinecke Rare Book and Manuscript Library, ed. J. F. Oates, A. E. Samuel, C. B. Welles. New Haven, 1967
88. *SB*   Sammelbuch griechischer Urkunden aus Ägypten. (Collection of papyri and inscriptions published in journals, or unindexed catalogues. Begun by F. Preisigke in 1915, continued by F. Bilabel and E. Kiessling.) 12 vols. in 1978. In progress
89. *SP*   Select Papyri I–II, ed. A. S. Hunt and C. C. Edgar. Loeb ed. London-Cambridge, Mass., 1932–4
90. *UPZ*   Urkunden der Ptolemäerzeit (ältere Funde), ed. U. Wilcken (republication of texts published in the nineteenth century, up to but not including the Petrie papyri).
  I: *Papyri aus Unterägypten.* Berlin-Leipzig, 1922–7
  II: *Papyri aus Oberägypten.* 1957
91. Wilcken, *Gdz.* and *Chr.*   U. Wilcken, *Grundzüge und Chrestomathie der Papyruskunde* I: Historischer Teil. 2 vols. Leipzig-Berlin, 1912
92. Mitteis, *Gdz.* and *Chr.*   L. Mitteis, *Grundzüge und Chrestomathie der Papyruskunde* II: Juristischer Teil. 2 vols. Leipzig-Berlin, 1912

Ostraca

93. *O. Amst.*   Ostraka in Amsterdam Collections, ed. R. S. Bagnall, P. J. Sijpesteijn and K. A. Worp. Zutphen, 1976
94. *O. Bruss.-Berl.*   Ostraka aus Brüssel und Berlin, ed. P. Viereck. Berlin-Leipzig, 1922
  O. Edfou see *P. Edfou*

95. *O. Leiden Insinger* *Griechischen Ostraka aus dem Rijksmuseum van Oudheden in Leiden (Oudheidkundige Mededelingen uit het Rijksmuseum van Oudheden te Leiden* 44 (1963) and 49 (1968)), ed. by P. J. Sijpesteijn. Republished in *SB* x.10309–10377
   O. Meyer see *P. Meyer*

96. *O. Mich.* *Greek Ostraca in the University of Michigan Collection*, ed. L. Amundsen. Ann Arbor, 1935. See also *P. Mich.* viii, ed. J. G. Winter and H. C. Youtie

97. *O. Osl.* *Ostraca Osloënsia*, ed. L. Amundsen. Oslo, 1933

98. *O. Pr. Joachim* *Die Prinz-Joachim-Ostraka*, ed. F. Preisigke and W. Spiegelberg. Strasbourg, 1914

99. *O. ROM* *Ostraka in the Royal Ontario Museum, Toronto*
   i: *Death and Taxes*, ed. A. E. Samuel, W. K. Hastings, A. K. Bowman, R. S. Bagnall. 1971
   ii: *Ostraka in the Royal Ontario Museum*, ed. R. S. Bagnall and A. E. Samuel. 1976

100. *O. Strassb.* *Griechische und griechisch-demotische Ostraka der Universitäts- und Landesbibliothek zu Strassburg in Elsass*, ed. P. Viereck. Berlin, 1923

101. *O. Tait* *Greek Ostraca in the Bodleian Library at Oxford and various other collections*. London
   i. ed. J. G. Tait. 1930
   ii. ed. J. G. Tait and C. Préaux. 1955
   iii. Indexes to vols. i and ii, ed. J. Bingen and M. Wittek. 1964

102. *O. Theb.* *Theban Ostraca*. (Ostraca in Hieratic, Demotic, Greek, and Coptic. The Greek ostraca edited by J. G. Milne.) London-Oxford, 1913

103. *O. Wilb.* *Les ostraca grecs de la collection Charles-Edwin Wilbour au Musée de Brooklyn*, ed. C. Préaux. New York, 1935

104. *Wadi Sarga* *Wadi Sarga: Coptic and Greek Texts*, ed. W. E. Crum and H. I. Bell. (Papyri and ostraca, in Coptic and Greek; Greek texts edited by H. I. Bell.) Copenhagen, 1922

105. *WO* *Griechische Ostraka aus Aegypten und Nubien*, ed. U. Wilcken. 2 vols. Leipzig-Berlin, 1899

Demotic texts

106. Boswinkel, E. and Pestman, P. W. *Textes grecs, démotiques et bilingues (Pap. Lugd. Bat.* 19). Leiden, 1978

107. Bresciani, E. *L'archivio demotico del tempio di Nesos* (Testi e documenti per lo studio dell'antichità). Milan, 1975

108. Mond, R. and Myers, O. H. *The Bucheum* ii: *The Inscriptions* (EES Memoir 41), especially the chapter on 'The hieroglyphic inscriptions', by H. W. Fairman. London, 1934

109. Pestman, P. W., with the collaboration of J. Quaegebeur and R. L. Vos. *Recueil de textes démotiques et bilingues.* 3 vols. i: *Transcriptions*; ii: *Traductions*; iii: *Index et Planches*. Leiden, 1977

c. INSCRIPTIONS

See also F 281

Canopus Inscription (OGIS 56)

110. Bayoumi, A. and Guéraud, O. 'Un nouvel exemplaire du décret de Canope', *Ann. Serv. Ant. Égypte* 46 (1947) 373–82
111. Bernand, A. *Le Delta égyptien d'après les textes grecs* I: *Les confins libyques*, 3 (Greek text), 989–1036 (French translation and commentary). Cairo, 1970
112. Daumas, F. *Les moyens d'expression du Grec et de l'Egyptien comparés dans les décrets de Canope et de Memphis* (Supplement to *Ann. Serv. Ant. Égypte* 16). Cairo, 1952
113. Onasch, Chr. 'Zur Königsideologie der Ptolemäer in den Dekreten von Kanopus und Memphis (Rosettana)', *Arch. Pap.* 24/5 (1976) 137–55
114. Sauneron, S. 'Un cinquième exemplaire du décret de Canope: la stèle de Boubastis', *BIFAO* 56 (1957) 67–78
115. Spiegelberg, W. *Der demotische Text der Priesterdekrete von Kanopus und Memphis (Rosettana) mit den hieroglyphischen und griechischen Fassungen und deutscher Übersetzung nebst demotischem Glossar.* Heidelberg, 1922

Pithom Stele (Ptolemy II)

116. Brugsch, H. and Erman, A. 'Die Pithomstele. Eine hinterlassene Arbeit von Heinrich Brugsch', *ZAeS* 32 (1894) 74–87
117. Kamal, A. *Stèles ptolémaïques et romaines* (Catalogue général des antiquités égyptiennes du Musée du Caire 20, nos. 22001–8) I.171–7 (text, no. 22183); II, pl. 57 (photograph). Cairo, 1905
118. Naville, E. 'La stèle de Pithom', *ZAeS* 40 (1902/3) 66–75, Tables III–V
119. Roeder, G. *Die ägyptische Götterwelt*, 108–28. Zürich, 1959

Raphia Inscription

120. Gauthier, H. and Sottas, H. *Un décret trilingue en l'honneur de Ptolémée IV.* Cairo, 1925
121. Spiegelberg, W. *Beiträge zur Erklärung des neuen dreisprachigen Priesterdekretes zu Ehren des Ptolemaios Philopator (Sitz. Bayer. Akad. 1925 no. 4).* Munich, 1925
122. Spiegelberg, W. and Otto, W. *Eine neue Urkunde zu der Siegesfeier des Ptolemaios IV. und die Frage der ägyptischen Priestersynoden (Sitz. Bayer. Akad. 1926 no. 2).* Munich, 1926
123. Thissen, H.-J. *Studien zum Raphiadekret (Beiträge zur klassischen Philologie 23).* Meisenheim am Glan, 1966
124. Bernand, A. *De Koptos à Kosseir.* Leiden, 1972
125. Fraser, P. M. 'Inscriptions from Ptolemaic Egypt', *Berytus* 13 (1960) 123–61
126. Sethe, K. *Hieroglyphische Urkunden der griechisch-römischen Zeit.* Leipzig, 1904–16. (Texts without translation or commentary.)

d. GENERAL

See also H 77; items listed in Abbreviations: *Das Ptol. Aegypten, Pros. Ptol.*

127. Bevan, E. *A History of Egypt under the Ptolemaic Dynasty.* London, 1927
128. Bouché-Leclercq, A. *Histoire des Lagides.* 4 vols. Paris, 1903–7
129. Butzer, K. W. 'Physical conditions in Eastern Europe, Western Asia and Egypt before the period of agricultural and urban settlement', in *CAH³* 1.1, esp. 62–9. Cambridge, 1970
130. Calderini, A. *Dizionario geografico.* In progress. Milan, 1936–
131. Fritze, M. L. *Die ersten Ptolemäer und Griechenland* (diss. Halle, 1917)
132. Heinen, H. 'Die politischen Beziehungen zwischen Rom und dem Ptolemäerreich von ihren Anfängen bis zum Tag von Eleusis (273–168 v. Chr.)', *ANRW* 1. 633–59
133. Huss, W. *Untersuchungen zur Aussenpolitik Ptolemaios' IV.* (*Münch. Beitr. Papyr.* 60). Munich, 1976
134. Kolbe, A. 'Die griechische Politik der ersten Ptolemäer', *Hermes* 51 (1916) 530–53
135. Kyrieleis, H. *Bildnisse der Ptolemäer.* Berlin, 1975
136. Longega, G. *Arsinoe II* (Università degli Studi di Padova. Pubblicazioni dell'Istituto di storia antica 6). Rome, 1968
137. Mahaffy, J. P. *The Empire of the Ptolemies.* London, 1895
138. Montevecchi, O. *La Papirologia.* Turin, 1973
139. Moser, E. *Untersuchungen über die Politik Ptolemaios' I. in Griechenland* (diss. Leipzig, 1914)
140. Pestman, P. W. and others. *A Guide to the Zenon Archive.* Leiden, 1981
141. Preaux, C. *Les grecs en Égypte d'après les archives de Zénon.* Brussels, 1947
142. – 'Réflexions sur l'entité hellénistique', *Chron. d'Égypte* 40 (1965) 129–39
143. – 'Graeco-Roman Egypt', ch. 12 of *The Legacy of Egypt*, ed. J. R. Harris, 323–54. Ed. 2. Oxford, 1971
144. Schnebel, M. *Die Landwirtschaft im hellenistischen Ägypten* (*Münch. Beitr. Papyr.* 7). Munich, 1925
145. Seibert, J. *Untersuchungen zur Geschichte Ptolemaios I.* Munich, 1969
146. – 'Ptolemaios I. und Milet', *Chiron* 1 (1971) 159–66
147. – 'Nochmals zu Kleomenes von Naukratis', *Chiron* 2 (1972) 99–102
148. Smith, H. S. *A Visit to Ancient Egypt: Life at Memphis and Saqqara (c. 500–30 B.C.).* Warminster, 1974
149. Turner, E. G. *Greek Papyri.* Ed. 2. Oxford, 1980
150. Volkmann, H. *PW* XXIII (1959) 1600–1761. *s.v.* Ptolemaios
151. Walbank, F. W. 'Egypt in Polybius', in *Fairman Studies* (1979), 180–9
152. Witkowski, S. *Epistulae privatae Graecae.* Leipzig, 1911
153. Zauzich, K. *Die ägyptische Schreibertradition in Aufbau, Sprache und Schrift der demotischen Kaufverträge aus ptolemäischer Zeit.* Wiesbaden, 1968

e. PRE-PTOLEMAIC EGYPT

154. Breasted, J. *Ancient Records of Egypt.* 5 vols. Chicago, 1905 (repr. New York, 1962)

155. Bresciani, E. 'La satrapia d'Egitto', *Studi class. e orient.* 7 (1958) 132–88
156. Curtis, J. W. 'Coinage of Pharaonic Egypt', *JEA* 43 (1957) 71–6
157. Gardiner, A. *The Wilbour Papyrus* I: Plates; II: *Commentary*; III: *Translation.*
     Oxford, 1941, 1948 (for the Brooklyn Museum)
158. – *Ramesside Administrative Documents.* Oxford, 1948 (prov. ed. 1941)
159. Kienitz, F. K. *Die politische Geschichte Ägyptens vom 7. bis zum 4. Jahrhundert
     vor der Zeitwende.* Berlin, 1953
160. Menu, B. *Recherches sur l'histoire juridique, économique, et sociale de l'ancienne
     Égypte.* Paris, 1982
161. Menu, B. and Harrari, I. 'La notion de propriété privée dans l'Ancien
     Empire égyptien', *Cahiers de Recherches de l'Institut de Papyrologie et
     d'Égyptologie de Lille* 2 (1974) 125–54
162. Mooren, L. 'Die angebliche Verwandtschaft zwischen den ptolemäischen
     und pharaonischen Hofrangtiteln', *Proc. XIV Intern. Congr. Papy-
     rolog.*, 233–40. London, 1975
163. Pfluger, K. 'The edict of King Haremhab', *Journal of Near Eastern Studies* 5
     (1946) 260–76
164. Posener, G. 'L''*Αναχώρησις* dans l'Égypte pharaonique', in *Mélanges
     Préaux* (1975), 663–9
165. Seidl, E. *Ägyptische Rechtsgeschichte der Saiten- und Perserzeit.* Ed. 2.
     Glückstadt, 1968
166. Smith, H. S. 'A note on amnesty', *JEA* 54 (1968) 209–14

f. RELIGION

167. Bianchi, U. *Mysteria Mithrae a cura di Ugo Bianchi: Atti del seminario
     internazionale sulla specificità storico-religiosa dei Misteri di Mithra con
     particolare riferimento alle fonti documentarie.* Leiden, 1979
168. Bivar, A. D. H. 'Mithraic images of Bactria', in *Mysteria Mithrae*, ed. U.
     Bianchi (1979), 741–52: (F 167)
169. Crawford, D. J. 'Ptolemy, Ptah and Apis in Hellenistic Memphis', *Studia
     Hellenistica* 24 (1980) 1–42: (F 241)
170. Cumont, F. *L'Égypte des astrologues.* Brussels, 1937
171. Fraser, P. M. 'Two studies on the cult of Sarapis in the Hellenistic world',
     Op. Ath. 3 (1960) 1–54
172. – 'Current problems concerning the early history of the cult of Sarapis',
     Op. Ath. 7 (1967) 23–45
173. Gardiner, A. ''*Οννῶφεις*', in *Miscellanea Academica Berolinensia*, 44–53.
     Berlin, 1950
174. Geraci, G. 'Ricerche sul Proskynema', *Aegyptus* 51 (1971) 1–211
175. Grimm, G. 'Die Vergöttlichung Alexanders des Grossen in Ägypten und
     ihre Bedeutung für den ptolemäischen Königskult', in *Das Ptol.
     Aegypten* (1978), 103–12
176. Koenen, L. 'Prophezeiungen des "Töpfers"', *ZPE* 2 (1968) 178–209
177. – 'Bemerkungen zum Text des Töpferorakels und zu dem Akaziensym-
     bol', *ZPE* 13 (1974) 313–19
178. Lauer, J.-Ph. and Picard, Ch. *Les statues ptolémaiques du Sarapieion de*

Memphis (Publ. de l'Institut d'art et d'archéologie de l'Université.de Paris 3). Paris, 1955

179. Meeks, D. 'Les donations aux temples dans l'Égypte du 1er millénaire av. J.-C.', in Lipinski 1979, II.605–88: (H 131)

180. Müller, D. 'Aegypten und die griechischen Isis-Aretalogien', *Abh. Sächs. Akad.* 53.1. Berlin, 1961

181. Nachtergael, G. 'La chevelure d'Isis', *Ant. class.* 50 (1981) 584–606

182. – 'Bérénice II, Arsinoé III et l'offrande de la Boucle', *Chron. d'Égypte* 55 (1980) 240–53

183. Otto, W. *Priester und Tempel in Hellenistischen Ägypten.* 2 vols. Leipzig and Berlin, 1905 and 1908

184. Quaegebeur, J. 'The genealogy of the Memphite High Priest family in the Hellenistic period', in *Studia Hellenistica* 24 (1980) 43–82: (F 241)

185. Reymond, E. A. E. and Barns, J. W. B. 'Alexandria and Memphis: some historical observations', *Orientalia* 46 (1977) 1–33

186. Ronchi, G. *Lexicon Theonymon Rerumque Sacrarum et Divinarum ad Aegyptum pertinentium quae in papyris ostracis titulis Graecis Latinisque in Aegypto repertis laudantur.* 5 vols. Milan, 1974–7

187. Sauneron, N. *Temples ptolémaiques et romains d'Égypte: études et publications parues entre 1939 et 1954.* Cairo, 1956

188. Sauneron, S. *Les prêtres de l'ancienne Égypte.* Paris, 1957

189. Skeat, T. C. and Turner, E. G. 'An oracle of Hermes Trismegistos at Saqqara', *JEA* 54 (1968) 199–208

190. Welles, C. B. 'The discovery of Sarapis and the foundation of Alexandria', *Historia* 11 (1962) 273–4

191. Winter, E. *Untersuchungen zu den ägyptischen Tempelreliefs der griechisch-römischen Zeit.* Vienna, 1968

192. – 'Der Herrscherkult in den aegyptischen Ptolemäertempeln', *Das Ptol. Aegypten* (1978), 147–60

193. Youtie, H. C. '*ΙΣΙΣ ΤΡΙΧΩΜΑΤΟΣ*', *Harv. Theol. Rev.* 39 (1946) 165–7 = *Scriptiunculae* I (Amsterdam, 1973) no. 23, pp. 483–5

194. – 'Questions to a Christian oracle', *ZPE* 18 (1975) 253–7

195. Zuntz, G. 'Once more: the so-called "Edict of Philopator on the Dionysiac Mysteries" (*BGU* 1211)', *Hermes* 91 (1963) 228–39

g. ARMY AND NAVY

196. Fraser, P. M. and Roberts, C. H. 'A new letter of Apollonius', *Chron. d'Égypte* 24 (1949) 289–94

197. Geraci, G. 'L' ὁ πρὸς τῆι συντάξει: Note sull'amministrazione militare nell'Egitto tolemaico', *Proc. XVI Intern. Congr. Papyrolog.* (1981) 267–76

198. Hauben, H. *Callicrates of Samos. A contribution to the study of the Ptolemaic admiralty (Studia Hellenistica* 18). Louvain, 1970

199. Lesquier, J. *Les institutions militaires de l'Égypte des Lagides.* Paris, 1911

200. Uebel, F. *Die Kleruchen Ägyptens unter den ersten sechs Ptolemäern (Abh. Akad. Berlin* 3). Berlin, 1968

h. ADMINISTRATION, SOCIETY, ECONOMIC STRUCTURE

See also H 187, J 158, J 164–7

201 Bagnall, R. S. 'Some notes on *P. Hib.* 198', *BASP* 6 (1969) 73–118
202. – 'The toparch Leon and his archive', *GRBS* 15 (1974) 215–20
203. – 'Ptolemaic foreign correspondence', *JEA* 61 (1975) 168–80 and pl. 24
204. – *The Administration of the Ptolemaic Possessions outside Egypt.* Leiden, 1976
205. – 'Archagathos son of Agathocles Epistates of Libya', *Philol.* 120 (1976) 195–209
206. – 'The date of the foundation of Alexandria', *AJAH* 4 (1979) 46–9
207. Barns, J. W. B. *Egyptians and Greeks* (Oxford Inaugural lecture, 25 September 1966, privately printed 1973; reprinted without alteration as *Pap. Brux.* 14). Brussels, 1978
208. Bengtson, H. 'Die ptolemäische Staatsverwaltung im Rahmen der hellenistischen Administration', *Mus. Helv.* 10 (1953) 161–77
209. Bieżuńska-Małowist, I. *L'esclavage dans l'Égypte gréco-romaine* I: *Période ptolémaïque.* Wroclaw-Warsaw-Krakow-Gdansk, 1974
210. Bingen, J. 'Grecs et Égyptiens d'après *PSI* 502', *Proc. XII Intern. Congr. Papyrolog.* (1970), 35–40
211. – 'Présence grecque et milieu rural ptolémaique', in *Problèmes de la terre en Grèce ancienne*, ed. M. I. Finley, 215–22. Paris-The Hague, 1973
212. – 'Le milieu urbain dans la chôra égyptienne à l'époque ptolémaïque', *Proc. XIV Intern. Congr. Papyrolog.* (1975) 367–73
213. – 'Économie grecque et société égyptienne au IIIe siècle', in *Das Ptol. Aegypten* (1978), 211–19
214. – 'Le papyrus Revenue Laws – Tradition grecque et adaptation hellénistique', *Rheinisch-Westfälische Akademie der Wissenschaften*, Vorträge G 231. Opladen, 1978
215. – 'The third-century B.C. land-leases from Tholthis', *Illinois Classical Studies* 3 (1978) 74–80
216. Boerner, E. *Der staatliche Korntransport im griechisch-römischen Ägypten* (diss. Hamburg, 1939)
217. Bonneau, D. *La Crue du Nil, divinité égyptienne à travers mille ans d'histoire.* Paris, 1964
218. – *Le fisc et le Nil.* Paris, 1971
219. Bouché-Leclerq, A. 'L'ingénieur Cléon', *Rev. Ét. Gr.* 21 (1908) 121–52
220. Braunert, H. 'Auswärtige Gäste am Ptolemäerhofe: zu den sogennanten Hadra-Vasen', *JDAI* 65/66 (1951/2) 231–63
221. – *Die Binnenwanderung: Studien zur Sozialgeschichte Ägyptens in der Ptolemäer- und Kaiserzeit (Bonner historische Forschungen* 26). Bonn, 1964
222. Bresciani, E. 'La spedizione di Tolomeo II in Siria in un ostrakon demotico inedito da Karnak', *Das Ptol. Aegypten* (1978), 31–7
223. Cadell, H. 'La γεωργία en Égypte: genèse d'un thème économique et politique', in *Mélanges Préaux* (1975), 639–45
224. Casson, L. 'The grain trade of the Hellenistic world', *TAPA* 85 (1954) 168–87
225. – 'Rome's trade with the East: the sea voyage to Africa and India', *TAPA* 110 (1980) 21–36

226. – '*Periplus maris Erythraei*: three notes on the text', *CQ* 30 (1980) 495–7

227. – 'The location of Adulis (*Periplus maris Erythraei* 4)', in *Coins, Culture and History in the Ancient World* (*Numismatic and other Studies in Honor of Bluma L. Trell*), ed. L. Casson, 113–21. New York, 1981

228. Caton-Thompson, G. and Gardner, E. *The Desert Fayum*. London, 1934

229. Cenival, F. de 'Deux papyrus inédits de Lille avec une révision du *P. dem. Lille* 31, *Enchoria* 7 (1977) 1–49

230. Černý, J. 'Consanguineous marriages in Pharaonic Egypt', *JEA* 40 (1954) 23–9

231. Clarysse, W. 'Hurgonaphor et Chaonnophris, les derniers pharaons indigènes', *Chron. d'Égypte* 53 (1978) 243–53

232. – 'Ptolemaic papyri from Lycopolis', in *Actes XV Congr. Intern. Papyrolog. (= Pap. Brux.* 19), 101–6. Brussels, 1979

233. – 'Egyptian estate-holders in the Ptolemaic period', in Lipinski 1979: (H 131)

234. – 'A royal visit to Memphis and the end of the Second Syrian War', *Studia Hellenistica* 24 (1980) 83–90: (F 241)

235. – 'Philadelphia and the Memphites in the Zenon archive', *Studia Hellenistica* 24 (1980) 91–122: (F 241)

236. – 'Aratomenes, brother of Komanos', *Chron. d'Égypte* 56 (1981) 347–9

237. Cockle, W. E. H. and Turner, E. G. 'Complaint against a policeman', *JEA* 68 (1982) 272–6

238. Coles, R. A. 'The Naucratites and their ghost-names: *P. Oxy.* 2338 revisited', *ZPE* 18 (1975) 199–204

239. Crawford, D. J. '*Skepe* in Soknopaiou Nesos', *JJP* 18 (1974) 169–75

240. – 'The good official of Ptolemaic Egypt', in *Das Ptol. Aegypten* (1978), 195–202

241. Crawford, D. J., Quaegebeur, J. and Clarysse, W. *Studies on Ptolemaic Memphis* (*Studia Hellenistica* 24). Louvain, 1980

242. Criscuolo, L. 'Ricerche sul *Komogrammateus* nell'Egitto tolemaico', *Aegyptus* 48 (1978) 3–101

243. – 'I miriarori nell'Egitto tolemaico: note sull'amministrazione dell'Arsinoite nel III secolo a.C.', *Aegyptus* 57 (1977) 109–22

244. Dack, E. van't 'La toparchie dans l'Égypte ptolémaïque', *Chron. d'Égypte* 23 (1948) 147–61

245. – 'Recherches sur les institutions du village en Égypte ptolémaïque', *Studia Hellenistica* 7 (1951) 1–59

246. – 'Notes concernant l'epistratégie', *Aegyptus* 32 (1952) 437–50

247. – 'Sur l'évolution des institutions militaires lagides', in *Armées et fiscalité dans le monde antique* (Colloques Nationaux du CNRS 936), 77–105. Paris, 1977

248. – *Reizen, expedities en emigratie uit Italië naar Ptolemaeïsch Egypte* (*Mededelingen van de Koninklijke Vlaamse Academie voor Wetenschappen, Letteren en Schone Kunsten van Belgie* 42 no. 4) Brussels, 1980

249. Déléage, A. 'Les cadastres antiques jusqu'à Dioclétien', *Études de papyrologie* 2 (1934) 73–228

250. Foraboschi, D. and Gara, A. 'L'economia dei crediti in natura (Egitto)', *Athenaeum* N.S. 60 (1982) 69–83

251. Fuks, A. 'Dositheos son of Drimylos: a prosopographical note', *JJP* 7/8 (1953–4) 205–9

252. Funck, B. 'Zu den Landschenkungen hellenistischer Könige', *Klio* 60 (1978) 45–55

253. Gorteman, C. 'Médecins de cour dans l'Égypte du IIIe siècle av. J.-C.', *Chron. d'Égypte* 32 (1957) 313–36

254. Grier, E. *Accounting in the Zeno Papyri*. New York, 1934

255. Groningen, B. A. van 'De Cleomene Naucratica', *Mnemos.* N.S. 53 (1925) 101–30

256. Harmatta, J. 'Zur Wirtschaftsgeschichte des frühptolemäischen Ägyptens', in *Sozial-ökonomische Verhältnisse im Alten Orient und im klassischen Altertum*, ed. H. J. Diesner *et al.*, 119–40. Berlin, 1961

257. Harper, G. M. Jr. 'Menches, komogrammateus of Kerkeosiris', *Aegyptus* 45 (1934) 14–32

258. Hauben, H. 'An annotated list of Ptolemaic naukleroi', *ZPE* 8 (1971) 259–75

259. – 'Kalikratou Meris and Kallikratous Kome in Middle Egypt', *Arch. Pap.* 26 (1978) 51–6

260. – 'Nouvelles remarques sur les nauclères d'Égypte à l'époque des Lagides', *ZPE* 28 (1978) 99–107

261. – 'Le transport fluvial en Égypte ptolémaïque: les bateaux du roi et de la reine', in *Actes XV Congr. Intern. Papyrolog.* (*Pap. Brux.* 19), 68–77. Brussels, 1978–9

262. Heinen, H. 'Ägyptische und griechische Traditionen der Sklaverei im ptolemäischen Ägypten', in *Das Ptol. Aegypten* (1978), 227–37

263. Henne, H. 'Sur la titulature aulique des stratèges de nomes à l'époque ptolémaïque', *Rev. Ét. Anc.* 42 (1940) = *Mélanges G. Radet*, 172–86

264. Herrmann, J. 'Zum Begriff γῆ ἐν ἀφέσει', *Chron. d'Égypte* 30 (1955) 93–106

265. Hohlwein, N. *Le Stratège du Nome*. Ed. 2 = *Pap.Brux.* 9. Brussels, 1969

266. Hopkins, K. 'Brother–sister marriage in Roman Egypt', in *CSSH* 22.3 (July 1980) 303–54

267. Huss, W. 'Die zu Ehren Ptolemaios III. und seiner Familie errichtete Statuengruppe von Thermos (*IG* ix² 1.1, 56)', *Chron. d'Égypte* 50 (1975) 312–20

268. – 'Eine Revolte der Aegypter in der Zeit des 3. Syrischen Krieges', *Aegyptus* 58 (1978) 151–6

269. Ijsewijn, J. *De Sacerdotibus Sacerdotiisque Alexandri Magni et Lagidarum Eponymis*. Brussels, 1961

270. Johannesen, R. 'Ptolemy Philadelphus and scientific agriculture', *CPhil.* 18 (1923) 156–61

271. Jouguet, P. 'La politique intérieure du premier Ptolémée', *BIFAO* 30 (1930/1) 513–36

272. Kaimio, M. 'On the sureties of tax-contractors in Ptolemaic Egypt', *Proc. XVI Intern. Congr. Papyrolog.* (1981), 281–7

273. Koenen, L. *Eine ptolemäische Königsurkunde* (*P. Kroll*) (Klassisch-philologische Studien 19). Wiesbaden, 1957

274. – '*ΘΕΟΙΣΙΝ ΕΧΘΡΟΣ*: ein einheimischer Gegenkönig in Ägypten (132/1ᵃ)', *Chron. d'Égypte* 67 (1959) 103–19

275. – *Eine agonistische Inschrift aus Ägypten und frühptolemäische Königsfeste.* Meisenheim am Glan, 1977
276. Kooh, P. *De Phylakieten in Grieks-Romeins Egypte* (diss. Leiden, 1954)
277. Kornemann, E. 'Die Satrapenpolitik der ersten Lagiden', in *Raccolta di scritti in onore di Giacomo Lumbroso (1844–1925)*, 235–45. Milan, 1925
278. Kortenbeutel, H. *Der ägyptische Süd- und Osthandel in der Politik der Ptolemäer und römischen Kaiser* (diss. Berlin, 1931)
279. Lewis, N. *Inventory of Compulsory Services in Ptolemaic and Roman Egypt* (American Studies in Papyrology 3). New Haven-Toronto, 1968 (revised pages 1975)
280. Martin, V. *Les épistratèges.* Geneva, 1911
281. Masson, O. *Carian Inscriptions from North Saqqara and Buhen.* London, 1978
282. Michurski, C. 'Avances aux semailles et les prêts de semences dans l'Égypte gréco-romaine', *Eos* 48 (1956) [= *Symbolae R. Taubenschlag dedicatae* III] 105–38
283. Miller, J. I. *The Spice Trade of the Roman Empire 29 B.C. to A.D. 641.* Oxford, 1969
284. Modrzejewski, J. 'Régime foncier et statut social dans l'Égypte ptolemaïque', in *Terre et paysans dépendants dans les sociétés antiques* (Colloque CNRS Besançon 1974) 163–88. Paris, 1979
285. Mooren, L. 'Über die ptolemäischen Hofrangtitel', in *Antidorum W. Peremans* (*Studia Hellenistica* 16), 161–80. Louvain, 1968
286. – *The Aulic Titulature in Ptolemaic Egypt. Introduction and prosopography.* Brussels, 1975
287. – 'La hiérarchie du cour ptolémaïque: contribution à l'étude des institutions et des classes dirigeantes à l'époque hellénistique', *Studia Hellenistica* 23. Louvain, 1977
288. – 'Macht und Nationalität', in *Das Ptol. Aegypten* (1978), 51–7
289. – 'Die diplomatische Funktion der hellenistischen Königsfreunde', *Antike Diplomatie* 1979, 256–90
290. – 'Ptolemaic families', in *Proc. XVI Intern. Congr. Papyrolog.* (1981) 289–301
291. Oertel, F. 'Das Problem des antiken Suezkanals', in *Spiegel der Geschichte: Festgabe für Max Braubach*, 18–51. Münster, 1964
292. Orrieux, C. 'Les archives d'Euclès et la fin de la *dôréa* du dioecète Apollonios', *Chron. d'Égypte* 55 (1980) 213–39
293. – 'Les comptes privés de Zénon à Philadelphie', *Chron. d'Égypte* 56 (1981) 314–40
294. Packman, Z. M. *The Taxes in Grain in Ptolemaic Egypt: A Study of the Receipts issued from the Granary of Diospolis Magna during the years 164–88 B.C.* (American Studies in Papyrology 4). New Haven, 1968
295. Perdrizet, P. *Les terres cuites grecques d'Égypte de la Collection Fouquet.* Nancy-Paris-Strasbourg, 1921
296. Peremans, W. 'Sur la titulature aulique en Égypte au IIe et Ier siècle av. J.-C.', in *Symbolae Van Oven*, 129–59. Leiden, 1946
297. – 'Ptolémée et les Egyptiens', in *Mélanges Préaux* (1975), 393–402
298. – 'Les révolutions égyptiennes sous les Lagides', in *Das Ptol. Aegypten* (1978), 39–50

299. Pestman, P. W. 'Harmachis et Anchmachis, deux rois indigènes du temps des Ptolémées', *Chron. d'Égypte* 40 (1965) 157–70

300. Piatowska, M. *La ΣΚΕΠΗ dans l'Égypte ptolémaïque* (*Archiwum filologiczne* 32). Warsaw, 1975

301. Pikous, N. N. *Carskie zemledel'cy (neposreds van-nye proizvoditeli) in remeslanniki v Egipte III v. de n.e. Issledovanija social' no-abonomičeskikh otnesenij* (= *Paysans royaux (producteurs immédiats) et artisans en Égypte au IIIe s. av. n.è. Recherches sur les relations socio-économiques*). In Russian. (Éditions de l'Univ. de Moscou 1972, 255 pp. Summary in a brochure of 36 pp. of Univ. of Moscow of same title, pub. 1969)

302. – 'À propos de la διαγραφὴ τοῦ σπόρου', in *Proc. XII Intern. Congr. Papyrolog.* (1974) 405–10

303. – 'L'esclavage dans l'Égypte hellénistique', in *Actes X Congr. Intern. Papyrolog.* (1964) 97–107

304. Plaumann, G. *Ptolemais in Oberägypten: ein Beitrag zur Geschichte des Hellenismus in Ägypten.* Leipzig, 1910

305. Poethke, G. *Epimerismos* (= *Pap. Brux.* 8). Brussels, 1969

306. Préaux, C. *L'économie royale des Lagides.* Brussels, 1939

307. – 'Sur les communications de l'Éthiopie avec l'Égypte hellénistique', *Chron. d'Égypte* 53 (1952) 257–81

308. – 'De la Grèce classique à l'Égypte hellénistique. La banque-témoin', *Chron. d'Égypte* 33 (1958) 243–55

309. – 'L'économie lagide: 1933–1958', in *Proc. IX Intern. Congr. Papyrolog.*, 200–32. Oslo, n.d. [1961]

310. – 'Polybe et Ptolémée Philopator', *Chron. d'Égypte* 40 (1965) 364–75

311. Pruneti, P. 'I κλῆροι del nomo Ossirinchite', *Aegyptus* 55 (1975) 159–244

312. Quaegebeur, J. 'Documents égyptiens et rôle économique du clergé en Égypte hellénistique', in Lipinski 1979, II.707–30: (H 131)

313. Raschke, M. G. 'Papyrological evidence for Ptolemaic and Roman trade with India', in *Proc. XIV Intern. Congr. Papyrolog.* (1975) 241–6

314. Reekmans, T. 'Economic and social repercussions of the Ptolemaic copper inflation', *Chron. d'Égypte* 48 (1949) 324–42

315. – *La sitométrie dans les archives de Zénon* (= *Pap. Brux.* 3). Brussels, 1966

316. Reekmans, T. and Dack, E. van't 'A Bodleian archive on corn transport', *Chron. d'Égypte* 53 (1952) 149–95

317. Samuel, A. E. 'The internal organisation of the nomarch's bureau in the third century B.C.', in *Welles Essays* (1966), 213–30

318. – 'The Greek element in the Ptolemaic bureaucracy', *Proc. XII Intern. Congr. Papyrolog.* (1970) 443–53

319. Scherer, J. 'Reçu de loyer délivré à un nauclère pour la location d'un bateau (*P. Sorb.* inv. 2395)', *BASP* 15 (1978) 95–101

320. Segré, A. 'Note sull'economia dell'Egitto ellenistico nell'età tolemaica', *BSA Alex.* 8.29 (1934) 257–305

321. Shelton, J. C. 'Ptolemaic land ἐν ἀφέσει: an observation on the terminology', *Chron. d'Égypte* 46 (1971) 113–19

322. – 'Land and taxes in Ptolemaic Egypt: three technical notes', *Chron. d'Égypte* 50 (1975) 263–9

323. Skeat, T. C. 'A forthcoming catalogue of nome strategi', *Mizraim* 2 (1936) 30–5

324. – 'A letter from Philonides to Kleon revised', *JEA* 34 (1948) 80–1

325. – 'The date of the *dioiketes* Theogenes', *Anc. Soc.* 10 (1979) 159–66

326. Swarney, P. R. *The Ptolemaic and Roman Idios Logos*. Toronto, 1970

327. Świderek, A. 'Hellénion de Memphis – la rencontre de deux mondes', *Eos* 51 (1961) 55–63

328. – 'La société grecque en Égypte au IIIe siècle av. n.è. d'après les archives de Zénon', *JJP* 9–10 (1955–6) 365–400

329. Thierfelder, H. *Die Geschwisterehe im hellenistisch-römischen Ägypten*. Münster, 1980

330. Thomas, J. D. *The Epistrategos in Ptolemaic and Roman Egypt* I: *The Ptolemaic Epistrategos*. Opladen, 1975

331. – 'Aspects of the Ptolemaic Civil Service: the *dioiketes* and the nomarch', in *Das Ptol. Aegypten* (1978), 187–94

332. Tomsin, A. *Étude sur les πρεσβύτεροι des villages de la χώρα égyptienne*. Brussels, 1953

333. Trindl, M. *Ehrentitel im Ptolemäerreich* (diss. Munich, 1942)

334. Tscherikower, V. 'Palestine under the Ptolemies (a contribution to the study of the Zenon Papyri)', *Mizraim* 4–5 (1937) 9–90

335. Turner, E. G. 'The hanging of a brewer', in *Welles Essays* (1976), 79–86

336. 'A C-in-C's order from Saqqara', *JEA* 60 (1974) 239–42

337. 'Four obols a day men at Saqqara', in *Mélanges Préaux* (1975), 573–5

338. Uebel, F. 'Ταραχὴ τῶν Αἰγυπτίων', *Arch. Pap.* 17 (1962) 147–52

339. – 'Μονοπωλία φακῆς: ein bisher unbezeugtes Handelsmonopol frühptolemäischer Zeit in einem Jenaer Papyrus (*P. Jen.* inv. 900)', in *Actes X Congr. Intern. Papyrolog.* (1964) 165–81

340. Vandoni, M. *Gli epistrategi nell'Egitto*. Milan, n.d. [1970]

341. Viereck, P. *Philadelpheia: die Gründung einer hellenistischen Militärkolonie in Ägypten*. Leipzig, 1928

342. Warmington, E. H. *The Commerce between the Roman Empire and India*. Cambridge, 1928

343. Welles, C. B. 'The Ptolemaic administration in Egypt', *JJP* 3 (1949) 21–48

344. – 'The role of the Egyptians under the first Ptolemies', in *Proc. XII Intern. Congr. Papyrolog.* (1970) 505–10

345. Westermann, W. L. *Upon Slavery in Ptolemaic Egypt*. New York, 1929

346. Wilcken, U. 'Puntfahrten in der Ptolemäerzeit', *ZAeS* 60 (1925) 86–102

347. Wipszycka, E. 'The Δωρεά of Apollonios the Dioiketes in the Memphite nome', *Klio* 39 (1961) 153–90

348. Wörrle, M. 'Epigraphische Forschungen zur Geschichte Lykiens. II: Ptolemaios II. und Telmessos', *Chiron* 8 (1978) 201–46

349. Zauzich, K. T. 'Neue Namen für die Könige Harmachis und Anchmachis', *Göttinger Miszellen* 29 (1978) 157–8

i. LAW AND THE ADMINISTRATION OF JUSTICE

See also H 142

350. Bresciani, E. 'Annotazioni demotiche ai Πέρσαι τῆς ἐπιγονῆς', PP 27 (1972) 123-8

351. Brecht, C. H. *Zur Haftung der Schiffer im antiken Recht* (*Münch. Beitr. Papyr.* 45.1). Munich, 1962

352. Lenger, M.-Th. 'Prostagma dans les archives de Zénon', *Chron. d'Égypte* 56 (1981) 311-13

353. Mattha, G. *The Demotic Legal Code of Hermopolis West*. Preface, additional notes and glossary by G. R. Hughes. (Institut français d'archéologie orientale du Caire, Bibliothèque d'étude 45). 2 vols. Cairo, 1975

354. Meyer-Termeer, A. *Die Haftung der Schiffer im griechischen und römischen Recht* (= *Studia Amstelodam*. 13). Zutphen, 1978

355. [Mélèze-] Modrzejewski, J. 'Note sur *P. Strasb.* 237. Une contribution au problème de l'agraphos et eggraphos nomos', *Eos* 48 (1956) [= *Symbolae Taubenschlag* III] 139-54

356. – 'Zum Justizwesen der Ptolemäer', *ZSS* 93 (1962) 42-82

357. – 'La règle de droit dans l'Égypte ptolémaïque', in *Welles Essays* (1966), 125-73

358. – 'Note sur la législation royale des Lagides', in *Mélanges d'histoire ancienne offerts à William Seston*, 365-80. Paris, 1974

359. – 'Papyrologie et droits de l'antiquité', in *Annuaires 1977/8 de l'École pratique des Hautes Études* (IVe Section), 351-67

360. – 'Régime foncier et statut social dans l'Égypte ptolémaïque', in *Terres et paysans dépendants dans les sociétés antiques*, 163-88. Paris, 1979

361. Montevecchi, O. 'Ricerche di sociologia nei documenti dell'Egitto greco-romano II: Il contratto di matrimonio e gli atti di divorzio', *Aegyptus* 16 (1936) 3-83

362. Müller, B. J. *Ptolemaeus II. Philadelphus als Gesetzgeber* (diss. Cologne, 1968)

363. Oates, J. F. 'The status designation Πέρσης τῆς ἐπιγονῆς', *YCS* 18 (1963) 1-129

364. Rupprecht, H.-A. *Untersuchungen zum Darlehen im Recht der graeco-ägyptischen Papyri der Ptolemäerzeit* (*Münch. Beitr. Papyr.* 51). Munich, 1967

365. Schmidt, W. *Der Einfluss der Anachoresis im Rechtlebens Ägyptens zur Ptolemäerzeit* (diss. Cologne, 1966)

366. Seidl, E. *Der Eid im Ptolemäischen Recht* (diss. Munich, 1929)

367. – *Ptolemäische Rechtsgeschichte*. Ed. 2. Gluckstadt, 1962

368. – *Bodennutzung und Bodenpacht nach den demotischen Texten der Ptolemäerzeit* (Sitz. Wien 291, 2). Vienna, 1973

369. Stern, M. and Murray O. 'Hecataeus of Abdera and Theophrastus on Jews and Egyptians', *JEA* 59 (1973) 159-68

370. Taubenschlag, R. 'La compétence du κύριος dans le droit gréco-égyptien', *AHDO* 2 (1938) 293-314

371. Wolff, H. J. *Das Justizwesen der Ptolemäer* (*Münch. Beitr. Papyr.* 44). Munich, 1962

372. – 'Law in Ptolemaic Egypt', in *Welles Essays* (1966), 67–77
373. – *Das recht der griechischen Papyri Ägyptens in der Zeit der Ptolemäer und des Prinzipats* II: *Organisation und Kontrolle des privaten Rechtsverkehrs.* Munich, 1978
374. – *Opuscula dispersa.* Amsterdam, 1974

j. ART AND LITERATURE

375. Adriani, A. *Repertorio d'arte dell'Egitto greco-romano* (Series A). 2 vols. Palermo, 1961
376. Breccia, E. *Monuments de l'Égypte gréco-romaine* II: *Terrecotte figurate greche e greco-egizie del Museo di Alessandria.* Bergamo, 1934
377. Hackin, J. *Mémoires de la délégation française en Afghanistan* XI. Paris, 1954
378. Lefebvre, G. *Le Tombeau de Petosiris* I: *Description*; II: *Les textes*; III: *Vocabulaire et planches.* Cairo, 1923–4
379. Parlasca, K. 'Hellenistische und römische Mosaiken aus Ägypten', in *La mosaïque gréco-romaine* (Colloques internationaux du CNRS), 363–9. Paris, [1965]
380. Pfeiffer, R. *History of Classical Scholarship from the Beginnings to the End of the Hellenistic Age.* Oxford, 1968
381. Roeder, G. 'Die Ausgrabungen in Hermopolis im Frühjahr 1939', *Ann. Serv. Ant. Égypte* 39 (1939) 727–65
382. Thompson, D. B. *Ptolemaic Oinochoai and Portraits in Faience: Aspects of the Ruler-cult.* Oxford, 1973
383. – 'The Tazza Farnese reconsidered', in *Das Ptol. Aegypten* (1978), 113–27 with pls. 97–109
384. – 'A faience fellah', in *Studies in Classical Art and Archaeology. A tribute to Peter von Blanckenhagen*, ed. G. Kopcke and M. B. Moore, 175–8, pls. xlix–lx. Locust Valley, N.Y., 1979
385. Wace, A. J. B., Megaw, A. H. S. and Skeat, T. C. (with the assistance of Samy Shenouda) *Hermopolis Magna, Ashmunein: The Ptolemaic Sanctuary and the Basilica.* Alexandria, 1959
386. Weber, W. *Die ägyptisch-griechischen Terrakotten.* 2 vols. Berlin, 1914
387. Youtie, H. C. 'Callimachus in the tax rolls', *Proc. XII Intern. Congr. Papyrolog.* (1970) 545–51
388. Ziegler, K. *Das hellenistische Epos: ein vergessenes Kapitel griechischer Dichtung.* Leipzig-Berlin, 1934

k. COINS

389. Buttrey, T. V. 'Pharaonic imitations of Athenian tetradrachms', in *Actes du IX Congrès International de Numismatique, Berne, Septembre 1979*, ed. T. Hackens and R. Weiller, 137–40. Louvain-la-Neuve, 1982.
390. Jenkins, G. K. 'An early Ptolemaic hoard from Phacous', *ANSMN* 9 (1960) 17–37
391. Milne, J. G. 'The currency of Egypt under the Ptolemies', *JEA* 14 (1938) 200–7

392. Mørkholm, O. 'Cyrene and Ptolemy I: some numismatic comments', *Chiron* 10 (1980) 145–59

393. Nash, D. 'The Kuft hoard of Alexander III tetradrachms', *Num. Chron.* [7] 14 (1974) 14–30

394. Reekmans, T. 'The Ptolemaic copper inflation', *Studia Hellenistica* 7, 61–120. Leiden, 1951

395. Segré, A. 'The Ptolemaic copper inflation, ca. 230–140 B.C.', *AJPhil.* 63 (1942) 174–92

396. Svoronos, J. N. *Τὰ Νομίσματα τοῦ Κράτους τῶν Πτολεμαίων.* 4 vols. Athens, 1904–8 (vol. 4 is a German translation of vol. 1 by W. Booth *et al.*)

397. Zervos, O. H. 'The early tetradrachms of Ptolemy I', *ANSMN* 13 (1967) 1–16

l. CHRONOLOGY

398. Pestman, P. W. *Chronologie égyptienne d'après les textes démotiques 332 av. J.-C. à 453 ap. J.-C. (Pap. Lugd. Bat.* 15). Leiden, 1967

399. Samuel, A. E. *Ptolemaic Chronology (Münch. Beitr. Papyr.* 43). Munich, 1962

400. Skeat, T. C. 'The Macedonian calendar during the reign of Ptolemy Euergetes I', *JEA* 34 (1948) 75–9

401. – *The Reigns of the Ptolemies (Münch. Beitr. Papyr.* 39). Munich 1954, reissued 1969

402. – 'Notes on Ptolemaic chronology II: "The twelfth year which is also the first": the invasion of Egypt by Antiochus Epiphanes', *JEA* 47 (1961) 107–12

403. – 'Notes on Ptolemaic chronology IV: the 16th year of Ptolemy Philopator as a terminus ad quem', *JEA* 39 (1973) 169–74

404. Smith, H. S. 'Dates of the obsequies of the mothers of Apis', *Revue d'Egyptologie* 24 (1972) 176–87

405. Uebel, F. 'Die drei Jahreszählwesen in den Zenonpapyri', in *Proc. XIV Intern. Congr. Papyrolog.* (1975) 313–23

406. Walbank, F. W. 'The accession of Ptolemy Epiphanes: a problem in chronology', *JEA* 21 (1936) 20–34

G   AGATHOCLES

a. SOURCES

(i) *Literary sources*

Diodorus XIX.1–XXI.17
Justinus XXII.1–XXIII.2
P. Oxy. XXIV, no. 2399: Anonymus (Duris?), 'History of Sicily under Agathocles'.
Polyaenus V.3.1–8
Polybius VIII.12, IX.23.2, XII.15, XV.35.6

Recent publications on the literary sources:

1. Cavallaro, M. A. 'Un "tendency" industriale e la tradizione storiografica su Agatocle', *Historia* 26 (1977) 33–66
2. De Sanctis, G. *Ricerche sulla storiografia siceliota.* Palermo, 1958
3. Dolce, C. 'Diodoro e la storia di Agatocle', *Kokalos* 6 (1960) 124–66
4. Grimal, P. 'Échos plautiniennes d'histoire sicilienne', *Kokalos* 14/15 (1968/9) 228–42
5. Huss, W. 'Neues zur Zeit des Agathokles. Einige Bemerkungen zu P. Oxy. XXIV.2399', *ZPE* 39 (1980) 63–71
6. Manni, E. 'Timeo e Duride e la storia di Agatocle', *Kokalos* 6 (1960) 167–73
7. – 'Un frammento di Antandro?', *Kokalos* 12 (1966) 163–71
8. Meister, K. *Die sizilische Geschichte bei Diodor von den Anfängen bis zum Tod des Agathokles.* Munich, 1967 (with full bibliography)
9. Orlandi, T. 'Duride in Diodoro XIX–XXI', *PP* 19 (1964) 216–26
10. Walbank, F. W. 'The historians of Greek Sicily', *Kokalos* 14/15 (1968/9) 476–97
    See also Kebric 1977, 68–80: (B 23)

(ii) *Coins*

11. Buda, V. 'Le emissioni siracusane negli ultimi due decenni del sec. IV. a.C. ed il significato della riforma monetaria di Agatocle', *Helikon* 9/10 (1969/70) 193–231
12. Burnett, A. 'The coinages of Rome and Magna Graecia in the late fourth and third centuries B.C.', *Swiss Numismatic Review* 56 (1977) 119–20
13. Buttrey, T. V. 'The earliest representation of an eclipse?', *ZPE* 22 (1976) 248–52
14. Consolo Langher, S. *Contributo alla storia della monetazione del bronzo in Sicilia.* Milan, 1964
15. Gieseccke, W. *Sicilia Numismatica.* Berlin, 1923
16. Jenkins, G. K. 'Electrum coinage at Syracuse', in *Robinson Essays* (1968), 145–62
17. Tusa Cutroni, A. 'I Καμπανοί ed i Τυρρηνοί in Sicilia attraverso la documentazione numismatica', *Kokalos* 16 (1970) 250–67

(iii) *Archaeological material*

18. Talbert, R. J. A. *Timoleon and the Revival of Greek Sicily*, especially 214–29 (comprehensive survey of the more recent excavations in Sicily). Cambridge, 1974

b. GENERAL

See also Roussel in Glotz *et al.*, 375–99: (A 18); Seibert 1979, 1.258ff. and 11.569ff.: (H 208) and, on p. 602 (Addenda), G 38a
19. Aalders, G. H. D. 'Studien over Agathokles', *Tijdschrift voor Geschiedenis* 68 (1955) 315–66

20. Berve, H. *PW* xviii (1939) cols. 632–5 *s.v.* Ophellas (1)
21. – 'Die Herrschaft des Agathokles', *Sitz. Bayer.* phil.-hist. Klasse 1952 no. 5
22. – *Die Tyrannis bei den Griechen.* 1.441–57, 11.728–31. Munich, 1967
23. Compernolle, R. van 'La clause territoriale du traité de 306/5 conclu entre Agathoclès et Carthage', *RBPhil.* 32 (1954) 395–421
24. Consolo Langher, S. 'Problemi di storia constituzionale siceliota', *Helikon* 9/10 (1969/70) 108–43
25. – 'La politica di Agatocle e i caratteri della tradizione del conflitto con Messana alla battaglia di Himera', *Archivio storico messinese* 1975/6, 29–89
26. – 'Agatocle: Il colpo di stato. "Quellenfrage" e ricostruzione storica', *Athenaeum* 54 (1976) 382–429
27. – 'La Sicilia e il pericolo punico', *Atti della Accademia Peloritana*, Classe di Lettere, Filosofia e Belle Arti 1977/8, 7–42
28. – 'La Sicilia della scomparsa di Timoleonte alle morte di Agatocle. La introduzione della "Basileia"', in *Storia della Sicilia*, ed. R. Romeo, 11.291–342 (with bibliography). Naples, 1979
29. – 'Lo stratagato di Agatocle e l'imperialismo siracusano sulla Sicilia greca nelle tradizioni diodorea e trogiana', *Kokalos* 25 (1979) 117–87
30. – 'I trattati tra Siracusa e Cartagine e la genesi e il significato della guerra del 312–306 A.C.', *Athenaeum* 58 (1980) 309–39
31. De Sanctis, G. 'Agatocle', in *Per la scienza dell' Antichità*, 141–206 (Turin, 1909) = *Scritti Minori* 1.205–48. Rome, 1966
32. Diesner, H.-J. 'Agathoklesprobleme: der Putsch vom Jahre 316', *Wissenschaftliche Zeitschrift der Martin-Luther-Universität Halle-Wittenberg* 7.4 .(1958) 931–8
33. Ehrenberg, V. 'Ophellas von Kyrene', in *Polis und Imperium*, ed. K. Stroheker and A. J. Graham, 539–47 (originally 'Ofella di Cirene', *Riv. Fil.* 66 (1938) 146–51). Stuttgart, 1965
34. Finley, M. I. *Ancient Sicily.* London, 1968
35. Freeman, E. A. and Evans, A. J. *History of Sicily* iv.356–491. Oxford, 1894
36. Giannelli, C. A. 'Gli interventi di Cleonimo e di Agatocle in Magna Grecia', *Critica storica* (Florence) 11 (1974) 353–80
37. Goldsberry, M. A. S. *Sicily and its Cities in Hellenistic and Roman Times* (diss. Univ. North Carolina, 1973)
38. Gsell, S. *Histoire de l'Afrique du Nord.* 4 vols. Paris, 1913–20 (especially iv.25ff.)
39. Holm, A. *Geschichte Siciliens im Alterthum.* 3 vols. Leipzig, 1870–98 (especially 11.219ff.)
40. Hüttl, W. *Verfassungsgeschichte von Syrakus.* Prague, 1929
41. Lévèque, P. 'De Timoléon à Pyrrhos', *Kokalos* 14/15 (1968/9) 135–56
42. Manni, E. 'Agatocle e la politica estera di Siracusa', *Kokalos* 12 (1966) 144–62
43. Meltzer, O. *Geschichte der Karthager.* 2 vols. Berlin, 1879–96 (especially 1.352ff.)
44. Mossé, C. *La tyrannie dans la Grèce antique.* Paris, 1969
45. Müller, M. *Der Feldzug des Agathokles in Afrika* (diss. Leipzig, 1928)

46. Niese, B. *PW* I (1893) 748–57 *s.v.* 'Agathokles (15)'
47. Pareti, L. *Sicilia antica*. Palermo, 1959
48. Rizzo, F. P. *La Sicilia e le potenze ellenistiche al tempo delle Guerre Puniche (Indagine storico-prosopografica)*. 1: *Rapporti con Cos, l'Egitto e l'Etolia* (Supplement to *Kokalos* 3). Palermo, 1973
49. Scaturro, I. 'Agatocle', *Archivio storico Siciliano* 9 (1943) 3–39
50. Schubert, R. *Geschichte des Agathokles*. Breslau, 1887
51. Tillyard, H. J. W. *Agathocles*. Cambridge, 1908
52. Waele, J. A. de *Acragas Graeca. Die historische Topographie des griechischen Akragas auf Sizilien* I: *Historischer Teil*. The Hague, 1971 (especially 137–42)
53. Wickert, L. *PW* IV.A (1932) cols. 1518–23 *s.v.* 'Syrakusai'

H. SOCIAL, CULTURAL AND ECONOMIC FEATURES

See also D 148, E68, J 173, 175 and 257
1. Adams, B. *Paramoné und verwandte Texte: Studien zum Dienstvertrag im Rechte der Papyri*, ed. E. Seidl. Berlin, 1964
2. Ashburner, W. *The Rhodian Sea-law*. Oxford, 1909
3. Asheri, D. 'Sulla legge di Epitadeo', *Athenaeum* 39 (1961) 45–68
4. – *Distribuzioni di terre nell'antica Grecia* (*Memorie dell'Accademia delle Scienze di Torino*, Class. sc. mor. stor. e fil.[4a] 10). Turin, 1966
5. – 'Leggi greche sul problema dei debiti', *Studi class. e orient.* 18 (1969) 1–122
6. Babakos, A. M. Σχέσεις οἰκογενειακοῦ δικαίου εἰς τὴν νῆσον Κάλυμνον τὸν Α΄. μ.Χ.αἰῶνα
7. – *Actes d'aliénation en commun et autres phénomènes apparentés d'après le droit de la Thessalie antique. Contribution à l'étude de la copropriété familiale chez les anciens Hellènes*. Thessalonica, 1966
8. Badian, E. 'A document of Artaxerxes IV?', in *Greece and the Eastern Mediterranean in Ancient History and Prehistory. Studies presented to F. Schachermeyr on the occasion of his 80th birthday*, ed. K. H. Kinzl, 40–50. Berlin-New York, 1977
9. Barth, B. *De Graecorum asylis* (diss. phil. Strasbourg, 1888)
10. Beloch, K. J. *Die Bevölkerung der griechisch-römischen Welt*. Leipzig, 1886
11. Bianchi Bandinelli, R. (ed.) *Storia e civiltà dei Greci*. VII: *La società ellenistica: quadro politico*; VIII: *La società ellenistica: economia, diritto, religione*. Milan, 1977
12. Bikerman, E. 'La cité grecque dans les monarchies hellénistiques', *Rev. Phil.* 65 (1939) 335–49
13. Blavatskaja, T. V., Golubcova, E. S. and Pavlovskaja, A. I. *Die Sklaverei in den hellenistischen Staaten in 3.–1. Jh. v. Chr.* Wiesbaden, 1972
14. Bloch, M. *Die Freilassungsbedingungen der delphischen Freilassungsurkunden* (diss. phil. Strasbourg, 1914)
15. Bogaert, R. 'Banquiers, courtiers et prêts maritimes à Athènes et à Alexandrie', *Chron. d'Égypte* 40 (1965) 140–56

16. – *Les origines antiques de la banque de depôt. Une mise au point accompagné d'une esquisse des opérations de banque en Mésopotamie.* Leiden, 1966
17. – *Banques et banquiers dans les cités grecques.* Leiden, 1968
18. – *Epigraphica* III: *Texts on Bankers, Banking, and Credit in the Greek World.* Leiden, 1976
19. – 'Il commercio internazionale e le banche', in Bianchi Bandinelli 1977, 375–99: (H 11)
20. Boll, F. *Sternglaube und Sterndeutung,* ed. W. Gundel. Ed. 4. Leipzig-Berlin, 1931
21. Bömer, Fr. *Untersuchungen über die Religion der Sklaven in Griechenland und Rom* II: *Die sogenannte sakrale Freilassung und die (δοῦλοι) ἱεροί (Abh. Akad. Mainz* 1960 no. 1). Wiesbaden, 1960
22. Boyancé, P. *Le culte des Muses chez les philosophes grecs. Études d'histoire et de psychologie religieuses.* Paris, 1972
23. Brady, T. A. *The Reception of the Egyptian Cults by the Greeks, 330–30* B.C. (U. of Missouri Studies x.1). Columbia, Mo., 1935
24. Braunert, H. 'Hegemoniale Bestrebungen der hellenistischen Gross-mächte in Politik und Wirtschaft', *Historia* 13 (1964) 80–104
25. – *Das Mittelmeer in Politik und Wirtschaft der hellenistischen Zeit.* Keil, 1967
26. Bravo, B. *Philologie, histoire, philosophie de l'histoire. Étude sur J. G. Droysen.* Warsaw, 1968
27. – 'Sulân: Représailles et justice privée contre les étrangers dans les cités grecques (Étude de vocabulaire et des constitutions)', *Annali di Pisa*[3] 10 (1980) 675–987
28. Briant, P. 'Des Achéménides aux rois hellénistiques: continuités et ruptures. (Bilan et propositions)', *Annali di Pisa*[3] 9.4 (1979) 1375–1414
29. Brulé, P. *La piraterie crétoise hellénistique* (Centre de recherches d'histoire ancienne 27: Annales littéraires de l'Université de Besançon 223). Paris, 1978
30. Bruneau, P. *Recherches sur les cultes de Délos.* Paris, 1970
31. Burford, A. M. 'Heavy transport in classical antiquity', *EHR* 13 (1960–1) 1–18
32. Cairns, F. *Generic Composition in Greek and Roman Poetry.* Edinburgh, 1972
33. Calderini, A. *La manomissione e la condizione dei liberti in Grecia.* Milan, 1908
34. Candiloro, E. 'Politica e cultura in Atene da Pidna alla guerra mitridatica', *Studi class. e orient.* 14 (1965) 134–76
35. Casson, L. 'The grain trade of the Hellenistic world', *TAPA* 85 (1954) 168–87
36. Cohn-Haft, L. *The Public Physicians of Ancient Greece.* Northampton, Mass., 1956
37. *Colloquium*: the papers of a colloquium on 'Die antike und die altoriental-ische Komponent im Hellenismus' are published in *Klio* 60 (1978) 1–219
38. Crawford, M. H. 'Rome and the Greek world: economic relationships', *EHR* 30 (1977) 42–52

39. – 'Trade and movement of coinage across the Adriatic in the Hellenistic period', in *Scripta Nummaria Romana: Essays presented to Humphrey Sutherland*, ed. R. A. G. Carson and C. M. Kraay, i–ii. London, 1978

40. Dandamayev, M. A. 'Politische und wirtschaftliche Geschichte', in *Beiträge zur Achämenidengeschichte*, ed. G. Walser, 15–58 (*Historia Einzelschr.* 18). Wiesbaden, 1972

41. Dareste, R. 'Du droit des représailles principalement chez les anciens Grecs', *Rev. Ét. Gr.* 2 (1889) 305–21

42. Davies, J. K. *Athenian Propertied Families 600–300 B.C.* Oxford, 1971

43. – 'Athenian citizenship: the descent group and the alternatives', *CJ* 73 (1977–8) 105–21

44. Debord, P. 'L'esclavage sacré: état de la question', *Actes Besançon 1971* (1972), 135–50

45. – 'Populations rurales de l'Anatolie gréco-romaine', *Studi vari di storia greca, ellenistica e romana, Atti del Centro ricerche e documentazione sull'antichità classica* (formerly *CSDIR*) 8, 43–69. Milan, 1976

46. Delorme, J. *Gymnasion. Étude sur les monuments consacrés à l'éducation en Grèce, des origines à la conquête romaine.* Paris, 1960

47. De Robertis, F. M. 'Lex Rhodia. Critica e anticritica su D. 14.2–9', in *Studi Arangio-Ruiz* III, 155–73. Naples, 1953

48. Dow, S. 'The Egyptian cults in Athens', *Harv. Theol. Rev.* 30 (1937) 183–232

49. – *Prytaneis: A Study of the Inscriptions Honouring the Athenian Councillors* (*Hesp.* Suppl. 1). Athens, 1937

50. Drijvers, H. J. W. *Cults and Beliefs at Edessa.* Leiden, 1980

51. Ducrey, P. *Le traitement des prisonniers de guerre dans la Grèce antique des origines à la conquête romaine.* Paris, 1968

52. Dunand, F. 'Sens et fonction de la fête dans la Grèce hellénistique', *DHA* 4 (1978) 201–18

53. Dunant, Chr. and Pouilloux, J. *Études thasiennes* V: *Recherches sur l'histoire et les cultes de Thasos* Pt 2: *De 196 avant J.-C. jusqu'à la fin de l'antiquité.* Paris, 1958 [1957 on title page]

54. Edelstein, E. and L. *Asclepius.* 2 vols. Baltimore, 1945

55. Engelmann, H. *The Delian Aretalogy of Sarapis.* Leiden, 1975

56. Engels, D. 'The problem of female infanticide in the Greco-Roman world', *CPhil.* 75 (1980) 112–20

57. Ferguson, W. S. 'The Attic orgeones', *Harv. Theol. Rev.* 37 (1944) 61–140

58. Festugière, A. J. *Études de religion grecque et hellénistique.* Paris, 1972

59. Finley, M. I. *Studies in Land and Credit in Ancient Athens, 500–200 B.C.* New Brunswick, N.J., 1952

60. – 'Land, debt, and the man of property in classical Athens', *Pol. Sci. Quart.* 68 (1953) 249–68

61. – 'The Black Sea and Danubian regions and the slave-trade in antiquity', *Klio* 40 (1962) 51–9

62. – 'Between slavery and freedom', *CSSH* 6 (1964) 233–49, reprinted in Finley 1981, 116–32; (H 65)

63. – 'Classical Greece', *Deuxième conférence internationale d'histoire économique, Aix en Provence 1962* I: *Trade and Politics in the Ancient World*, 11–36. Paris–The Hague, 1965

64. – *Ancient Slavery and Modern Ideology*. London, 1980

65. – *Economy and Society of Ancient Greece*, ed. R. P. Saller and B. D. Shaw. London, 1981

66. Forbes, C. A. *Neoi: A Contribution to the Study of Greek Associations*. Middletown, Conn., 1933

67. Fuchs, H. *Der geistige Widerstand gegen Rom*. Berlin, 1938

68. Fuks, A. 'Social revolution in Greece in the Hellenistic age', *PP* 21 (1966) 437–48

69. – 'Patterns and types of social-economic revolution in Greece from the fourth to the second century B.C.', *Anc. Soc.* 5 (1974) 51–81

70. Funck, B. 'Zu den Landschenkungen hellenistischer Könige', *Klio* 60 (1978) 45–55

71. Gardin, J. C. and Gentelle, P. 'L'exploitation du sol en Bactriane antique', *Bulletin de l'École Française de l'extrême orient* 66 (1979) 1–29

72. Garlan, Y. 'Signification historique de la piraterie grecque', *DHA* 4 (1978) 1–16

73. Garnsey, P. D. A. and Whittaker, C. R. (eds.) *Imperialism in the Ancient World*. Cambridge, 1978

74. Gauthier, Ph. *Symbola. Les étrangers et la justice dans les cités grecques*. Nancy, 1972

75. – ''Εξαγωγὴ σίτου: Samothrace, Hippomédon et les Lagides'' *Historia* 28 (1979) 76–89

76. Gawantka, W. *Isopolitie. Ein Beitrag zur Geschichte der zwischenstaatlichen Beziehungen in der griechischen Antike*. Munich, 1975

77. Geremek, H. *Karanis: communauté rurale de l'Égypte romaine au II-IVe siècle de n.è.* Wroclaw–Warsaw–Cracow, 1969

78. Gernet, L. *Recherches sur le développement de la pensée juridique et morale en Grèce*. Paris, 1917

79. Glotz, G. 'Le prix des denrées a Délos', *Journ, Sav.* 1913, 16–29

80. – 'L'histoire de Délos d'après les prix d'une denrée', *Rev.Ét.Gr.* 29 (1916) 281–325

81. Golden, M. 'The exposure of girls at Athens', *Phoenix* 35 (1981) 316–31

82. Gomme, A. W. *The Population of Athens in the Fifth and Fourth Centuries B.C.* Oxford, 1933 (repr. New York, 1967)

83. Grandjean, Y. *Une nouvelle arétalogie d'Isis à Maronée*. Leiden, 1975

84. Gschnitzer, F. 'Proxenos', *PW* Suppl. XIII (1974) cols. 629–730

85. Habicht, Chr. 'Die herrschende Gesellschaft in den hellenistischen Monarchien', *Vierteljahrschrift für Sozial- und Wirtschaftsgeschichte* 45 (1958) 1–16

86. Hands, A. R. *Charities and Social Aid in Greece and Rome*. London, 1968

87. Harmatta, J. and Komoroczy, G. (eds.) *Wirtschaft und Gesellschaft im alten Vorderasien (Act. ant. 22)*. Budapest, 1976

88. Hassall, M., Crawford, M. H. and Reynolds, J. 'Rome and the eastern

provinces at the end of the second century B.C.', *JRS* 64 (1974) 185–220

89. Hatzfeld, J. 'Esclaves italiens en Grèce', in *Mélanges Holleaux* (1913), 93–101

90. – *Les trafiquants italiens dans l'Orient hellénique.* Paris, 1919

91. Heichelheim, F. *Wirtschaftliche Schwankungen der Zeit von Alexander bis Augustus.* Jena, 1930

92. – 'Sitos', *PW* Suppl. VI (1935) cols. 819–92

93. Heinen, H. 'Zur Sklaverei in der hellenistischen Welt', *Anc. Soc.* 7 (1976) 127–49 (I); *Anc. Soc.* 8 (1977) 121–54 (II)

94. Henssler, O. *Formen des Asylie-Rechts und ihre Verbreitung bei den Germanen.* Frankfurt, 1954

95. Herrmann, J. 'Personenrechtliche Elemente der Paramone', *RIDA*[3] 10 (1963) 149–61

96. Herzog, R. '*ΚΡΗΤΙΚΟΣ ΠΟΛΕΜΟΣ*', *Klio* 2 (1902) 316–33

97. – *Die Wunderheilungen von Epidaurus (Philol.* Suppl. 22.3). Leipzig, 1931

98. Higgins, R. A. *Greek and Roman Jewellery.* London, 1961

99. – *Greek Terracottas.* London, 1967

100. Hiller von Gaertringen, F. 'Miletos (1): Geschichte", *PW* XV (1932) cols. 1586–622

101. Hintze, F. 'The kingdom of Kush: the Meroitic period', in *Africa in Antiquity: The Arts of Ancient Nubia and the Sudan* I: *The Essays*, pp. 63–7 and 75–88, and II: *The Catalogue*, pp. 65–101. New York, 1978

102. Hitzig, H. F. 'Altgriechische Staatsverträge über Rechtshilfe', in *Festgabe F. Regelsberger.* Zürich, 1907

103. – 'Der griechische Fremdenprozess', *ZSS* 28 (1907) 211–53

104. Holleaux, M. 'Antioche des Chrysaoriens', *Rev.Ét.Gr.* 12 (1899) 345–61 = *Études* III (1942) 141–57

105. – 'Remarques sur les décrets des villes de Crète relatifs a l'ἀσυλία des Téos', *Klio* 13 (1913) 137–57 = *Études* IV (1952) 178–203

106. – 'Sur la guerre crétoise (*Κρητικὸς πόλεμος*)', *Rev.Ét.Gr.* 30 (1917) 88–104 = *Études* IV (1952) 163–77

107. – 'L'expédition de Dikaiarchos dans les Cyclades et sur "Hellespont', *Rev.Ét.Gr* 23 (1920) 223 = 47 = *Études* IV (1952) 124–45

108. Hopkins, K. 'Taxes and trade in the Roman Empire (200 B.C.–A.D. 400)', *JRS* 70 (1980) 101–25

109. Huybrechs, F. 'Over de proxenie in Lakonië', *Belgisch Tijdschrift voor Philologie en Rechtsgeschiedenis* 37 (1959) 5–30

110. Jähne, A. 'Zwei Tendenzen gesellschaftlicher Entwicklung im Hellenismus', *Klio* 60 (1978) 137–50

111. Kagarow, E, *Griechische Fluchtafeln (Eos* Suppl. 4). Lemberg-Paris, 1929

112. Kamps, W, 'Les origines de la fondation cultuelle dans la Grèce ancienne', *AHDO* I (1937) 145–79

113. Klaffenbach, G. *Symbolae ad historiam collegiorum artificum Bacchiorum* (diss. phil. Berlin, 1914)

114. Knipovich, T. N. 'Naselenie Ol'bii v VI–I vv. do n.e. po dannym epigrafich eskich istochnikov' ('The population of Olbia from the vɪth to the 1st century B.C. from the data of epigraphic sources'). *Materialy i issledovaniya po arkheologii SSSR* 50: *Ol'biya nizhnee pobuzh'e v antichnuya epokhu*, 119–54. Moscow-Leningrad, 1956

115. Koschaker, P. *Über einige griechische Rechtsurkunden aus den östlichen Randgebieten des Hellenismus* (*Abh. Sächs. Akad.* 42). Leipzig, 1931

116. Köster, K. *Die Lebensmittelversorgung der altgriechischen Polis.* Berlin, 1939

117. Kreissig, H. 'Der Makkabäeraufstand. Zur Frage seiner sozialökonomi-schen Zusammenhänge und Wirkungen', *Studii Clasice* 4 (1962) 143–75

118. – 'Das Verhältnis der hellenistischen Stadt zur χώρα πολιτική und ihren Bewohnern', in *Die Krise der griechischen Polis*, edd. O. Jurewicz and H. Kuch, 57–62. Berlin, 1969

119. – 'Beobachtungen an hellenistischen Inschriften zur Frage des Tem-peleigentums an Land', *Klio* 52 (1970) 231–3

120. – *Die sozialen Zusammenhänge des judäischen Krieges.* Berlin, 1970

121. – 'Die Polis in Griechenland und im Orient in der hellenistischen Epoche', in Welskopf 1974, II.1074–84: (A 65)

122. Kreller, H. 'Lex Rhodia', *Zeitschrift für das gesamte Handelsrecht und Konkursrecht* 85 (1921) 257–367

123. Kroll, J. H. 'An archive of the Athenian cavalry', *Hesp.* 46 (1977) 83–140

124. Kuenzi, A, *Ἐπίδοσις.* Bern, 1923

125. Larsen, J. A. O. 'Representation and democracy in hellenistic federalism', *CPhil.* 40 (1945) 65–97

126. Latte, K. 'Συλᾶν', *PW* IV A.1 (1931) cols. 1035–8 = K, Latte, *Kleine Schriften* (Munich, 1968), 416–19

127. Laum, B. *Stiftungen in der griechischen und römischen Antike.* 2 vols. Leipzig-Berlin, 1914

128. Lejeune, M. *Observations sur la langue des actes d'affranchisement delphiques.* Paris, 1940

129. Lévêque, P. 'I regni del Medio Oriente'; 'I regni del Lontano Oriente', in Bianchi Bandinelli 1977, VII.192–227: (H 11)

130. Levi, M. A. *Né liberi né schiavi. Gruppi sociali e rapporti di lavoro nel mondo ellenistico-romano.* Milan, 1976

131. Lipinski, E. (ed.) *State and Temple Economy in the Ancient Near East* I–II (*Orientalia lovaniensia analecta* 6). Louvain, 1979

132. Long, A. A. *Hellenistic Philosophy: Stoics, Epicureans, Sceptics.* London, 1974

133. Lotze, D. *Μεταξὺ ἐλευθέρων καὶ δούλων.* Berlin, 1959

134. MacLean Harper Jr, G. 'A study in the commercial relations between Egypt and Syria in the 3rd century B.C.', *AJPhil.* 49 (1928) 1–35

135. MacMullen, R. *Enemies of the Roman Order.* Cambridge, Mass.-London, 1967

136. Marshall, A. J. 'The survival and development of international jurisdic-tion in the Greek world under Roman rule', *ANRW* II.13 (1980) 626–61

137. Masson, O. 'Recherches sur les Phéniciens dans le monde hellénistique', *BCH* 93 (1969) 679–700

138. McKendrick, P. L. *The Athenian Aristocracy 399 to 31 B.C.* Cambridge, Mass., 1969

139. Meincke, W. *Untersuchungen zu den enkomiastischen Gedichten Theokrits* (diss. phil. Kiel, 1965)

140. Mendelsohn, I. *Slavery in the Ancient Near East. A comparative study of slavery in Babylonia, Assyria, Syria, and Palestine from the middle of the third millenium to the end of the first millennium.* New York, 1949

141. Meyer, E. 'Demetrias', *PW* Suppl. IX (1962) cols. 24–6

142. Meyer, P. M. *Juristische Papyri. Erklärung von Urkunden zur Einführung in die juristische Papyruskunde.* Berlin, 1920

143. Michell, H. *The Economics of Ancient Greece.* Ed. 2. Cambridge, 1957

144. Mickwitz, G. 'Economic rationalism in Graeco-Roman agriculture', *EHR* 52 (1937) 577–89

145. Momigliano, A. D. 'Genesi storica e funzione attuale del concetto di Ellenismo', *Giornale critico della filosofia italiana.* 16 (1935) 10–35 = *Contributo* I (1955). 165–94: (A 35)

146. 'J. G. Droysen between Greeks and Jews', *History and Theory* 9 (1970) 139–53 = Momigliano 1977, 307–23 = *Contributo* V (1975), 109–26: (A 39)

147. Moretti, L. 'L'economia ellenistica', in Bianchi Bandinelli 1977, VIII.319–26, 333–74: (H 11)

148. – 'I regni ellenistici', in Bianchi Bandinelli 1977, VIII.326–33: (H 11)

149. Mouterde, R. 'Regards sur Beyrouth phénicienne, hellénistique et romaine', *Mél.USJ* 40 (1964) 156–61

150. Musti, D. 'Il regno ellenistico', in Bianchi Bandinelli 1977, VII.231–316: (H 11)

151. – 'Il commercio degli schiavi e del grano: il caso di Puteoli. Sui rapporti tra l'economia italiana della tarda repubblica e le economie ellenistiche', in *The Seaborne Commerce of Ancient Rome (MAAR 36)*, edd. J. H. D'Arms and E. C. Kopff, 197–215. Rome, 1980

152. Nilsson, M. P. *Die hellenistische Schule.* Munich, 1955

153. – *The Dionysiac Mysteries of the Hellenistic and Roman Age.* Lund, 1957

154. – *Geschichte der griechischen Religion* I: *Die Religion Griechenlands bis auf die griechische Weltherrschaft* II: *Die hellenistische und römische Zeit.* Ed. 3. Munich, 1967 and 1974

155. Oehler, J. 'Gymnasiarchos', *PW* VII (1912) 1969–2004

156. Oelsner, J. 'Zur Sklaverei in Babylonien in der chaldäischen, achämenidischen und hellenistischen Zeit', *Altorientalische Forschungen* 5 (1977) 71–80

157. Oertel, F. 'Katoikoi', *PW* XI (1921) cols. 1–26

158. Ormerod, H. A. *Piracy in the Ancient World: An Essay on Mediterranean History.* Liverpool, 1924

159. Parke, H. W. *The Oracles of Zeus: Dodona, Olympia, Ammon.* Oxford, 1967

160. Parke, H. W. and Wormell, D. E. W. *The Delphic Oracle* I: *The History* and II: *The Oracular Responses.* Oxford, 1956

161. Peek, W. *Der Isis-hymnos von Andros und verwandte Texte.* Berlin, 1930

162. Pélékidis, Chr. *Histoire de l'ephébie attique.* Paris, 1962

163. Pfister, F. 'Epiphanie', *PW* Suppl. IV (1924) cols. 277–323

164. Picard, Ch. 'Observations sur la société des Poseidoniastes de Bérytos et sur son histoire', *BCH* 44 (1920) 263–311
165. – *Délos* VI: *L'établissement des Poseidoniastes de Bérytus*. Paris, 1921
166. Pickard-Cambridge, A. W. *The Dramatic Festivals of Athens*. Ed. 2, revised by J. Gould and D. M. Lewis. Oxford, 1968
167. Pohl, R. *De Graecorum medicis publicis*. Berlin, 1905
168. Poland, F. *Geschichte des griechischen Vereinswesens*. Leipzig, 1909
169. – 'Technitai', *PW* V.A (1934) cols. 2473–558
170. Pomeroy, S. D. *Goddesses, Whores, Wives and Slaves: Women in Classical Antiquity*. London, 1976
171. – 'Τεχνικαὶ καὶ μουσικαί. The education of women in the fourth century and in the hellenistic period', *AJAH* 2 (1977) 51–68
172. Préaux, C. 'Les villes hellénistiques, principalement en Orient: leurs institutions administratives et judiciaires', in *Recueils de la société Jean Bodin* VI: *La ville* 1: *Institutions administratives et judiciaires*, 69–134. Brussels, 1954
173. – 'Institutions économiques et sociales des villes hellénistiques, principalement en Orient', in *Recueils de la société Jean Bodin* VI: *La ville* 2: *Institutions économiques et sociales*, 89–135. Brussels, 1955
174. – 'Le statut de la femme à l'époque hellénistique', in *Recueils de la société Jean Bodin* XI: *La Femme* 1, 127–75. Brussels, 1959
175. – 'Reflexions sur l'entité hellénistique', *Chron. d'Égypte* 40 (1965) 129–39
176. – 'Époque hellénistique', in *Troisième Conférence Internationale d'Histoire Économique, Munich 1965* III: *The Ancient Empires and the Economy*, 41–74. Paris-The Hague, 1969
177. Quandt, G. *De Baccho ab Alexandri aetate in Asia Minore culto* (diss. phil. Halle, 21.2). Halle, 1913
178. Rädle, H. *Untersuchungen zum griechischen Freilassungswesen* (diss. phil. Munich, 1969)
179. Raeder, A. *L'arbitrage international chez les Hellènes*. Christiania, 1912
180. Ranowitsch, A. B. *Der Hellenismus und seine geschichtliche Rolle*. Berlin, 1958
181. Rickman, G. E. *The Corn Supply of Ancient Rome*. Oxford, 1980
182. – 'The grain trade under the Roman Empire', in *Roman Seaborne Commerce* (*MAAR* 36), ed. J. H. D'Arms and E. C. Kopff, 261–76. Rome, 1980
183. Robert, L. 'Les juges étrangers dans la cité grecque', in Ξένιον. *Festschrift für Pan. J. Zepos* 1, 765–82. Athens/Freiburg-im-Breisgau/Cologne, 1973
184. Roehlig, J. *Der Handel von Milet* (diss. phil. Hamburg, 1933)
185. Rostovtzeff, M. I. *Studien zur Geschichte des römischen Kolonates* (*Arch. Pap.* I). Leipzig-Berlin, 1910
186. – 'Notes on the economic policy of the Pergamene kings', in *Anatolian Studies presented to Sir W. M. Ramsay*, ed. W. H. Buckler and W. M. Calder, 359–90. Manchester, 1923
187. – 'Foreign commerce of Ptolemaic Egypt', *Journ. Econ. Bus. Hist.* 4 (1932) 728–69

188. – 'The Hellenistic world and its economic development', *AHR* 41 (1936) 231–62

189. Roussel, P. *Délos, colonie athénienne.* Paris, 1916

190. – *Les cultes égyptiens à Délos.* Paris-Nancy, 1916

191. Sachs, A. 'Babylonian horoscopes', *JCS* 6 (1952) 49–75

192. Ste Croix, G. E. M. de 'Greek and Roman accounting', in *Studies in the History of Accounting*, ed. A. C. Littleton and B. S. Yamey, 14–74. London, 1956

193. – 'Ancient Greek and Roman maritime loans', in *Debts, Credits, Finance and Profits. Essays in honour of W. T. Baxter*, ed. H. Edey and B. S. Yamey, 41–59. London, 1974

194. – 'Political pay outside Athens', *CQ* 69/25 (1975) 48–52

195. – *The Class Struggle in the Ancient Greek World.* London, 1982

196. Samuel, A. E. 'The role of paramone clauses in ancient documents', *JJP* 15 (1965) 221–311

197. Saranidi, V. I. 'The treasure of the golden mound', *Archaeology* 33.3 (May–June 1980) 31–41

198. Sarkisian, G. Kh. 'Samoupravlyayushchiysaya gorod selevkidskoy Vavilonii ('The self-governing city in Seleucid Babylon')', *VDI* 1952 no. 1, 68–83

199. – 'O gorodskoy zemle v selevkidskoy Vavilonii', *VDI* 1953 no. 1, 59–73, reprinted as 'City land in Seleucid Babylonia', in Diakonov 1969, 312–31: (E 188)

200. 'Grecheskaya onomastika v Uruke i problema graeco-babyloniaca' ('Greek personal names in Uruk and the Graeco-Babylonian problem'). *Drevnij Vostok*² (Erevan, 1974), 181–217 (Eng. summary, *ibid.* 304–9). English version in Harmatta and Komdroczy 1976, 495–503: (H 87)

201. Schlesinger, E. *Die griechische Asylie* (diss. phil. Giessen, 1933)

202. Schlumberger, D. 'L'argent grec dans l'empire achéménide', in *Trésors monétaires d'Afghanistan*, edd. R. Curiel and D. Schlumberger, 1–63. Paris, 1953

203. – *L'Orient hellénisé.* Paris, 1970

204. Schönbauer, E. 'Rechtshistorische Urkundenstudien zum griechischen Recht im Zweiströmlande', *Arch. Pap.* 12 (1937) 194–217

205. Schweitzer, H. *Aberglaube und Zauberei bei Theokrit* (diss. phil. Basel, 1937)

206. Segre, M. 'L'asilia di Smirne e le Soterie di Delfi', *Historia* 5 (1931) 241–60

207. – 'L'institution des Nikephorie de Pergame', Appendix to Robert, *Hellenica* v (1948) 102–28

208. Seibert, J. *Die politischen Flüchtlinge und Verbannten in der griechischen Geschichte.* 2 vols. Darmstadt, 1979

209. Seyrig, H. 'Les rois Séleucides et la concession de l'asylie', *Syria* 20 (1939) 35–9

210. – 'Antiquités syriennes 47', *Syria* 28 (1951) 101–23

211. – 'Antiquités syriennes 48–51', *Syria* 28 (1951) 191–228

212. Shimron, B. 'Nabis of Sparta and the helots', *CPhil.* 61 (1966) 1–7

213. Shinnie, P. L. *Meroe: A Civilization of the Sudan*. London, 1967
214. Sifakis, G. M. *Studies in the History of Hellenistic Drama*. London, 1967
215. Sokolowski, F. 'The real meaning of sacral manumission', *Harv. Theol. Rev.* 47 (1954) 173–81
216. – *Lois sacrées d'Asie Mineure*. Paris, 1955
217. – *Lois sacrées des cités grecques. Supplément*. Paris, 1962
218. – *Lois sacrées des cités grecques*. Paris, 1969
219. Sonne, E. E. *De arbitris externis* (diss. phil. Göttingen, 1888)
220. Stefan, A. 'Die Getreidekrisen in den Städten an den westlichen und nördlichen Küsten des Pontos Euxeinos in der hellenistischen Zeit', in Welskopf 1974, II.648–63: (A 65)
221. Stewart, Z. 'La religione', in Bianchi Bandinelli 1977, 503–616: (H 11)
222. Stough, C. L. *Greek Scepticism*. Berkeley-Los Angeles, 1969
223. Svenciskaya, I. S. 'Raby'i vol'noot-pushchenniki v sel'skikh mestnoskyakh provintsii Azii' ('Slaves and freedmen in the rural areas of Asia Minor'). *VDI* 1963 no. 4, 127–30
224. Tchalenko, G. *Villages antiques de la Syrie du Nord. Le massif du Belus a l'époque romaine*. 3 vols. Paris, 1953–8
225. Timbal Duclaux de Martin, P. *Le droit d'asyle*. Paris, 1939
226. Tod, M. N. *International Arbitration among the Greeks*. Oxford, 1913
227. – *Sidelights on Greek History*. Oxford, 1932
228. Touloumakos, J. *Der Einfluss Roms auf die Staatsform der griechischen Stadtstaaten des Festlands und der Inseln im ersten und zweiten Jhdt.v. Chr.* Göttingen, 1967
229. Trofimova, M. K. 'Iz istorii ellinist-icheskogo piratstva' ('History of Hellenistic piracy'). *VDI* 1963 no. 4, 53–74
230. Vatin, C. *Recherches sur le mariage et la condition de la femme mariée à l'époque hellénistique*. Paris, 1970
231. Vidman, L. *Isis und Serapis bei den Griechen und Römern* (*RGVV* 29). Berlin, 1970
232. Warmington, B. H. *Carthage*. Ed. 2. Harmondsworth, 1964
233. Weinreich, O. *Antike Heilungs-wunder* (*RGVV* 3.1). Giesssen, 1909
234. Welles, C. B. 'The Greek city', in *Studi Calderini-Paribeni* (1936–7), 81–99
235. Welwei, K.-W. *Unfreie im antiken Kriegsdienst* I: *Athen und Sparta*; II: *Die kleineren und mittleren griechischen Staaten und die hellenistischen Reiche*. Wiesbaden, 1974 and 1977
236. Westermann, W. L. 'Athenaeus and the slaves of Athens', *HSCP* Suppl. 1 (1941) 451–70 = *Slavery in Classical Antiquity: Views and Controversies*, ed. M. I. Finley, 73–92. Cambridge, 1960
237. – 'Between slavery and freedom', *AHR* 50 (1945) 213–27
238. – 'The *Paramone* as a general service contract', *JJP* 2 (1948) 9–50
239. – 'Extinctions of claims in slave sales at Delphi', *JJP* 4 (1950) 49–61
240. – *The Slave Systems of Greek and Roman Antiquity*. Philadelphia, 1955
241. Wilhelm, A. 'Σιτομετρία', in *Mélanges Glotz* II, 899–909. Paris, 1932
242. Wirgin, W. 'On the right of asylum in Hellenistic Syria', in *Congrès international de numismatique, Paris, 6–11 Juillet 1953* II. *Actes*, edd. J. Babelon and J. Lafaurie. 137–48. Paris, 1957

243. Witt, R. E. *Isis in the Graeco-Roman World*. London, 1971
244. Woess, F. von *Das Asylwesen Aegyptens in der Ptolemäerzeit und die spätere Entwicklung*. Munich, 1923
245. – ''*Ασυλία*', *ZSS* 46 (1926) 32–67
246. Wolff, H. *Written and Unwritten Marriages in Hellenistic and Post-classical Roman Law*. Haverford, Pa., 1939
247. Woodhead, A. G. 'The state health service in ancient Greece', *Cambridge Historical Journal* 10 (1950–2) 235–53
248. Zawadski, T. 'Quelques remarques sur l'étendue et l'accroissement des domaines des grands temples d'Asie Mineure', *Eos* 46 (1952–3 [1954]) 83–96
249. Ziebarth, E. *Das griechische Vereinswesen*. Leipzig, 1896
250. – *Aus dem griechischen Schulwesen*. Ed. 2. Leipzig, 1914
251. – 'Hellenistische Banken', *Zeitschrift für Numismatik* 34 (1924) 36–50
252. – *Beiträge zur Geschichte des Seeraubs und Seehandels im alten Griechenland*. Hamburg, 1929
253. – 'Stiftungen', *PW* Suppl. VII (1940) cols. 1236–40
254. Ziegler, W. *Symbolai und Asylia* (diss. phil. Bonn, 1975)

I. MONARCHY

See also F 382

1. Aalders, G. J. D. *Die Theorie der gemischten Verfassung im Altertum*. Amsterdam, 1968
2. – '*ΝΟΜΟΣ 'ΕΜΨΥΧΟΣ*', in *Politeia und Respublica: Beiträge zum Verständnis von Politik, Recht und Staat in der Antike zum Andenken R. Starks gewidmet*, ed. P. Steinmetz, 315–29. Wiesbaden, 1969
3. – *Political Thought in Hellenistic Times*. Amsterdam, 1975
4. *Actes du colloque international sur l'idéologie monarchique dans l'antiquité. Cracovie-Mogilany du 23 au 26 octobre 1977.* Zeszyty Nauk Uniw. Jag. n. XXXVI, prace hist., z. 63. 1980
5. Adcock, F. E. 'Greek and Macedonian kingship', *Proc. Brit. Acad.* 39 (1953) 163–80
6. Aymard, A. 'L'usage du titre royal dans la Grèce classique et hellénistique', *Revue historique de droit français et étranger* 27 (1949) 579–90
7. – 'Tutelle et usurpation dans les monarchies hellénistiques. À propos d'un épisode de la sixième guerre de Syrie', in *Aegyptus*. [*Raccolta di scritti in onore di Girolamo Vitelli* II] 32 (1952) 85–96 = *Études d'histoire ancienne* (1967), 230–9: (A 2)
8. – *L'Orient et la Grèce*, esp. pp. 390–416, 'L'idéologie et le gouvernement monarchiques'. Paris, 1953
9. – *Études d'histoire ancienne* (=A 2), esp. 'Le protocole royal grec' (pp. 73–99), '*Βασιλεὺς Μακεδόνων*', (pp. 100–22), 'La monarchie hellénistique II: L'institution monarchique' (pp. 123–35), 'Sur l'assemblée macédonienne' (pp. 143–63), 'Tutelle et usurpation dans les monarchies hellénistiques' (pp. 230–9). Paris, 1967

10. Badian, E. 'The deification of Alexander the Great', in *Edson Studies* (1981), 27–71
11. Balsdon, J. P. V. D. 'The "divinity" of Alexander', *Historia* 1 (1950) 363–88
12. Bengtson, H. 'Einige Beziehungen swischen Sizilien und der hellenistischen Welt', *Kokalos* 10–11 (1964–5) 319–32
13. Bevan, E. R. 'The deification of kings in the Greek cities', *English Historical Review* 16 (1901) 625–39
14. Bikerman, E. 'Sur un passage d'Hypéride', *Athenaeum* 41 (1963) 70–85
15. Breccia, E. *Il diritto dinastico nelle monarchie dei Successori di Alessandro*. Rome, 1903
16. Burkert, W. 'Zur geistesgeschichtlichen Einordnung einiger Pseudo-pythagorica', *Pseudepigrapha* 1, ed. K. von Fritz (*Entretiens Hardt* 18), 25–55, 88–102 (discussion). Vandoeuvres-Geneva, 1972
17. Burstein, S. M. 'Arsinoe II Philadelphos: a revisionist view', in Adams and Borza 1982, 197–212: (C 1)
18. Cerfaux, L. and Tondriau, J. *Un concurrent du christianisme: le culte des souverains dans la civilisation gréco-romaine*. Paris-Tournai, 1957 (with excellent bibliography)
19. Charlesworth, M. P. 'Some observations on ruler-cult, especially in Rome', *Harv. Theol. Rev.* 28 (1935) 5–44
20. Delatte, L. *Les traités de la royauté d'Ecphante, Diotogène et Sthénidas*. Liège-Paris, 1942
21. Eddy, S. K. *The King is Dead*. Lincoln, Nebraska, 1961
22. Edson, C. F. 'Legitimus honor. A note on Hellenistic ruler-worship', *Harv. Theol. Rev.* 26 (1933) 324–5
23. Ehrenberg, V. *Alexander and the Greeks*. Oxford, 1938
24. Festugière, A. J. 'Les inscriptions d'Asoka et l'idéal du roi hellénistique', in his *Études de religion grecque hellénistiques*, 210–25. Paris, 1972
25. Fredericksmeyer, E. A. 'Three notes on Alexander's deification', *AJAH* 4 (1979) 1–9, esp. 3–5
26. – 'On the background of the ruler cult', in *Edson Studies* (1981), 145–56
27. Fritz, K. von 'Conservative reaction and One Man's rule in ancient Greece', *Pol. Sci. Quart.* 56 (1941) 51–83
28. Goodenough, E. 'The political philosophy of Hellenistic kingship', *YCS* 1 (1928) 53–102
29. Habicht, Chr. *Gottmenschentum und griechische Städte*. Ed. 2. (Zetemata 14). Munich, 1970
30. Hadot, P. 'Fürstenspiegel', in *Reallexikon für Antike und Christentum* VIII (1970) cols. 555–82
31. Hammond, N. G. L. '"Philip's tomb" in historical context', *GRBS* 19 (1978) 331–50
32. Herman, G. 'The "Friends" of the early Hellenistic rulers: servants or officials?', *Talanta* (1981) 103–49
33. Heuss, A. 'La monarchie hellénistique', in *Relazioni del X congresso internazionale di scienze storiche* II, 201–13. Florence, 1955
34. Hoïstad, R. *Cynic Hero and Cynic King*. Uppsala, 1948

35. Kaerst, J. 'Die Begründung des Alexander- und Ptolemäerkultes in Aegypten', *Rh. Mus.* 52 (1897) 42–68
36. – *Studien zur Entwicklung und theoretischen Begründung der Monarchie im Altertum.* Munich, 1898
37. – *Geschichte des Hellenismus.* Ed. 2. 2 vols. Leipzig, 1917–26. Esp. 11.376–404 ('Zum hellenistischen Herrscherkult')
38. Kornemann, E. 'Zur Geschichte der antiken Herrscherkulte', *Klio* 1 (1901) 51–146
39. Lenger, M.-Th. 'La notion de bienfait ("philanthropon") royal et les ordonnances des rois lagides', *Studi Arangio-Ruiz* 1 (1950). 483–99
40. MacEwan, C. W. *The Oriental Origin of Hellenistic Kingship.* Chicago, 1934
41. Macurdy, G. *Hellenistic Queens.* Baltimore, 1932
42. Meecham, H. G. *The Letter of Aristeas.* Manchester, 1935
42a. Mendels, D. '"On Kingship" in the "Temple Scroll" and the ideological *Vorlage* of the seven banquegs in the "Letter of Aristeas to Philocrates"', *Aegyptus* 59 (1979) 127–36
43. Meyer, E. 'Alexander der Grosse und die absolute Monarchie', in *Kleine Schriften* 1, 285–332. Halle, 1909
44. Momigliano, A. D. 'Per la data e la caratteristica della lettera di Aristea', in *Contributo* IV (1969). 213–24: (A 38)
45. – 'Re e popolo in Macedonia prima di Alessandro Magno', in *Contributo* V (1975). 1.445–64: (A 39)
46. Mossé, Cl. *La fin de la démocratie athénienne*, esp. pp. 375–99, 'Les tendances monarchiques dans la pensée politique grecque au IVe siècle'. Paris, 1962
47. – *Histoire des doctrines politiques en Grèce.* Paris, 1969
48. Murray, O. 'Aristeas and Ptolemaic kingship', *Journal of Theological Studies* 18 (1967) 337–71
49. – 'Hecataeus of Abdera and Pharaonic kingship', *JEA* 56 (1970) 141–71
50. – 'Herodotus and Hellenistic culture', *CQ* 22 (1972) 200–13
51. Musti, D. 'Morte e culto del sovrano in ambito ellenistico (in particolare sulle tombe-santuario dei sovrani della Commagene)', in *La mort, les morts dans les sociétés anciennes*, eds. G. Gnoli and J. P. Vernant, 188–201. Cambridge, 1982
52. Nenci, G. 'Il segno regale e la taumaturgia di Pirro', in *Miscellanea Rostagni* (1963), 152–61.
53. Nilsson, M. P. *Geschichte der griechischen Religion* II.132–85, 'Die Religion im Dienst des Königs'. Ed.2. Munich, 1961
54. Nock, A. D. *Essays on Religion and the Ancient World*, ed. Z. Stewart. 2 vols. Oxford, 1972. See especially 'Notes on ruler-cult' (1.134–59)
55. – '*Synnaos Theos*', *HSCP* 41 (1930) 1–62, = Nock 1972, 1.202–51: (I 54)
56. – '*Soter* and *Euergetes*', in *The Joy of Study (Papers on the New Testament and related subjects presented to honor Frederick Clifton Grant)*, ed. S. L. Johnson, 127–48 = Nock 1972, II.720–35: (I 54). New York, 1951
57. Passerini, A. 'La *tryphe* nella storiografia ellenistica', *Studi italiani di filologia classica* 2 (1934) 35–50
58. Pelletier, A. *Lettre d'Aristée à Philocrate (Sources chrétiennes* 89). Paris, 1962

59. Posener, G. *De la divinité du Pharaon*. Paris, 1960
60. Price, S. R. F. 'Between man and god: sacrifice in the Roman imperial cult', *JRS* 70 (1980) 28–43
61. Pugliese Caratelli, G. 'Asoka e i re ellenistici', *PP* 33 (1953) 449–54
62. Ritter, H. W. *Diadem und Königsherrschaft*. Munich, 1965
63. Robert, L. 'Sur un décret d'Ilion et sur un papyrus concernant des cultes royaux', in *Welles Essays* (1966), 175–211
64. Schmitthenner, W. 'Über eine Formveränderung der Monarchie seit Alexander dem Grossen', *Saeculum* 19 (1968) 31–46
65. Schubart, W. 'Das hellenistische Königsideal nach Inschriften und Papyri', *Arch. Pap.* 12 (1937) 1–26
66. – 'Das Königsbild des Hellenismus', *Die Antike* 13 (1937) 272–88
67. – *Die religiöse Haltung des frühen Hellenismus* (Der Alte Orient 35). Leipzig, 1937
68. Scott, K. 'The deification of Demetrius Poliorcetes', *AJPhil.* 49 (1928) 137–66, 217–39
69. Sinclair, T. A. *A History of Greek Political Thought*, esp. pp. 239–63, 'After Alexander'; 287–302, 'Hellenistic monarchy again'. London, 1951 [1952]
70. – 'Il pensiero politico dei primi due secoli dell'impero', *separatum* from *Il pensiero politico classico*. Bari, 1961
71. Sokolowski, F. 'Divine honors for Antiochos and Laodike at Teos and Iasos', *GRBS* 13 (1972) 171–6
72. Spoerri, W. *Späthellenistische Berichte über Welt Kultur und Götter*. Basel, 1959
73. Stroheker, K. F. 'Zu den Anfängen der monarchischen Theorie in der Sophistik', *Historia* 2 (1953/4) 381–412
74. Tcherikover, V. 'The ideology of the Letter to Aristeas', *Harv. Theol. Rev.* 31 (1958) 59–85
75. Taeger, F. 'Zum Kampf gegen den antiken Herrscherkult', *Archiv für Religionswissenschaft* 32 (1935) 282–92
76. – 'Isokrates und die Anfänge des hellenistischen Herrscherkultes', *Hermes* 72 (1937) 355–60
77. – 'Alexander der Grosse und die Anfänge des hellenistischen Herrscherkultes', *Historische Zeitschrift* 172 (1951) 225–44
78. – *Charisma: Studien zur Geschichte des antiken Herrscherkultes*. 2 vols. Stuttgart, 1957–60
79. Tarn, W. W. *The Greeks in Bactria and India*. Ed. 2. Esp. 414–36, 'Excursus: the Milindapañha and Pseudo-Aristeas'. Cambridge, 1951
80. Thesleff, H. *An Introduction to the Pythagorean Writings of the Hellenistic Period* (*Acta Academiae Aboensis, Humaniora* 24.3). Abo, 1961
81. – *The Pythagorean Texts of the Hellenistic Period* (*Acta Academiae Aboensis, Humaniora* 30). Abo, 1965
82. Tondriau, J. 'Les thiases dionysiaques royaux de la cour ptolémaïque', *Chron, d'Égypte* 41 (1946) 149–71
83. – 'La Tryphe, philosophie royale ptolémaïque', *Rev. Ét. Anc.* 50 (1948) 49–54

84. – 'Rois Lagides comparés ou identifiés à des divinités', *Chron. d'Égypte* 45–46 (1948) 127–46

85. – 'Souverains et souveraines séleucides en divinités', *Le Mouséon* 61 (1948) 171–82

86. – 'Heraclès, Héraclides et autres émules du héros', *Rend. Ist. Lomb.* 83 (1950) 397–406

87. – 'La dynastie ptolémaïque et la religion dionysiaque', *Chron. d'Égypte* 50 (1950) 283–316

88. – 'Dionysos, dieu royal. Du Bacchos tauromorphe primitif aux souverains hellénistiques Neoi Dionysoi', *Annuaire de l'Institut de philologie et d'histoire orientale de l'Université Libre de Bruxelles* 1953, 441–66

89. Treves, P. 'Les documents apocryphes du "Pro Corona"', *Les études classiques* 9 (1940) 138–74

90. Visser, E. *Götter und Kulte im Ptolemäischen Alexandrien.* Amsterdam, 1938

91. Volkmann, H. 'Der Herrscherkult der Ptolemäer in Phönikischen Inschriften und sein Beitrag zur Hellenisierung von Kypros', *Historia* 5 (1956) 448–55

92. – 'Die Basileia als *endoxos douleia.* Ein Beitrag zur Wortgeschichte der Duleia', *Historia* 16 (1967) 155–61

93. Weinreich, P. 'Antikes Gottmenschentum', *Neue Jahrbücher* 2 (1926) 633–5

94. Welwei, K. W. *Konige und Konigtum im Urteil des Polybios* (diss. Cologne). Herbede (Ruhr), 1963

95. Wilcken, U. 'Zur Entstehung des hellenistischen Königskultes', *Sitz. Berlin* 28 (1938) 298–321

96. Woodhead, A. G. 'Athens and Demetrios Poliorketes at the end of the fourth century B.C.', in *Edson Studies* (1981), 357–67

97. Zancan, P. *Il monarcato ellenistico nei suoi elementi federativi.* Padua, 1934

98. Zuntz, G. 'Aristeas Studies I: The Seven Banquets', *Journal of Semitic Studies* 4 (1959) 21–36

J. HELLENISTIC SCIENCE, WARFARE, AGRICULTURE, BUILDING

a. SCIENCE

(i) Ancient authors and works on these

1. The Lyceum after Aristotle

Theophrastus
1. *Theophrasti Eresii Opera quae Supersunt Omnia*, ed. F. Wimmer. 3 vols. Leipzig, 1854–62

2. *Theophrastus. Enquiry into Plants*, ed. Sir Arthur Hort (Loeb ed.). 2 vols. Cambridge, Mass., 1916

3. *Theophrastus. De Causis Plantarum*, edd. B. Einarson and G. K. K. Link (Loeb ed.). I: Books I and II. Cambridge, Mass., 1976

4. *Theophrastus. On Stones*, edd. E. R. Caley and J. F. C. Richards. Columbus, Ohio, 1956
5. *Theophrastus. De Lapidibus*, ed. D. E. Eichholz. Oxford, 1965
6. *Theophrastus. De Igne*, ed. V. Coutant. Assen, 1971

Strato and others
7. Wehrli, F. *Die Schule des Aristoteles.* 10 vols. Ed. 2. Basel, 1967–9
8. Gottschalk, H. B. 'Strato of Lampsacus: some texts', in *Proceedings of the Leeds Philosophical and Literary Society*, Literary and Historical Section, 11 (1964–6), Part 6 (1965)
9. Macran, H. S. *The Harmonics of Aristoxenus.* Oxford, 1902

2. Epicureans and Stoics

Epicureans
10. Usener, H. *Epicurea.* Leipzig, 1887
11. Bailey, C. *Epicurus.* Oxford, 1926
12. Arrighetti, G. *Epicuro. Opere.* Ed. 2. Turin, 1973
13. Bailey, C. *Lucretius.* 3 vols. Oxford, 1947

Stoics
14. Arnim, H. von *Stoicorum Veterum Fragmenta.* 4 vols. Leipzig, 1905–24
15. Edelstein, L. and Kidd, I. *Posidonius.* Vol. 1. Cambridge, 1972

3. Hellenistic mathematics, geography, astronomy and mechanics

Euclid
16. *Euclidis Opera Omnia*, edd. J. L. Heiberg and H. Menge. 8 vols. with supplement. Leipzig, 1883–1916 (for vols. i–v there is a 2nd ed., ed. E. S. Stamatis, Leipzig, 1969–77)
17. Heath, T. L. *The Thirteen Books of Euclid's Elements.* 3 vols. Ed. 2. Cambridge, 1926
18. Eecke, P. ver *Euclid: L'Optique et la catoptrique.* Paris-Bruges, 1938

Aristarchus
19. Heath, T. L. *Aristarchus of Samos.* Oxford, 1913

Archimedes
20. *Archimedis Opera Omnia cum Commentariis Eutocii*, ed. J. L. Heiberg. Ed. 2, E. S. Stamatis. 4 vols. Stuttgart, 1972–5
21. Heath, T. L. *The Works of Archimedes with the Method of Archimedes.* Cambridge, 1912 (repr. Dover, New York, no date)
22. Dijksterhuis, E. J. *Archimedes.* Copenhagen, 1956

Apollonius
23. *Apollonius Pergaeus quae Graece Exstant*, ed. J. L. Heiberg. 2 vols. Leipzig, 1891–3
24. Heath, T. L. *Apollonius of Perga.* Ed. 2. Cambridge, 1961
25. Eecke, P. ver *Les Coniques d'Apollonius de Perge.* Bruges, 1923

Philo
26. *Philo Byzantius. Mechanicae Syntaxis, Libri 4–5*, ed. R. Schöne. Berlin, 1893
27. *Exzerpte aus Philons Mechanik Buch* VII *und* VIII, ed. H. Diels and E. Schramm (*Abh. Akad. Berlin* 1919, 12). Berlin, 1920
    See also Marsden 1971, vol. II: (J 148), for *Belopoeica*

Hipparchus
28. *Hipparchus. In Arati et Eudoxi Phaenomena*, ed. C. Manitius. Leipzig, 1894
29. Dicks, D. R. *The Geographical Fragments of Hipparchus*. London, 1960

Geminus
30. *Gemini Elementa Astronomiae*, ed. C. Manitius. Leipzig, 1898
31. Aujac, G. *Géminos. Introduction aux Phénomènes*. Paris, 1975

Strabo
32. *Strabonis Geographica*, ed. G. Kramer. 3 vols. Berlin, 1844–52
33. Jones, H. L. *The Geography of Strabo*. 8 vols. (Loeb ed.) London-Cambridge, Mass., 1917–32

Hero
34. *Heronis Alexandrini Opera quae Supersunt Omnia*, edd. J. L. Heiberg, L. Nix, W. Schmidt, H. Schöne. 5 vols. Ed. 2. Stuttgart, 1976
35. *The Pneumatics of Hero of Alexandria*, trans. J. G. Greenwood, ed. M. B. Hall. London, 1971

The most important later sources are:
Ptolemy
36. *Claudii Ptolemaei Opera quae Exstant Omnia*
    I (2 parts): *Syntaxis Mathematica*, ed. J. L. Heiberg. Leipzig, 1898–1903
    II: *Opera Astronomica Minora*, ed. J. L. Heiberg. Leipzig, 1907
    III.1: *'ΑΠΟΤΕΛΕΣΜΑΤΙΚΑ*, edd. F. Boll and A. Boer. Ed. 2. Leipzig, 1954
    III.2: *ΠΕΡΙ ΚΡΙΤΗΡΙΟΥ ΚΑΙ 'ΗΓΕΜΟΝΙΚΟΥ, ΚΑΡΠΟΣ*, edd. F. Lammert, A. Boer. Ed. 2. Leipzig, 1961
37. *Claudii Ptolemaei Geographia*, ed. C. F. A. Nobbe. 3 vols. Ed. 2. 1898, 1966
38. Lejeune, A. *L'Optique de Claude Ptolémée*. Louvain, 1956
39. Düring, I. *Die Harmonielehre des Klaudios Ptolemaios* (Göteborgs Högskolas Årsskrift 36, 1). Göteborg, 1930
40. Manitius, C. *Ptolemäus, Handbuch der Astronomie*. 2 vols. Ed. 2. Leipzig, 1963
41. Taliaferro, R. C. *Ptolemy. The Almagest*. Chicago, 1952

Theon of Smyrna
42. *Theonis Smyrnaei Expositio Rerum Mathematicarum ad Legendum Platonem Utilium*, ed. E. Hiller. Leipzig, 1978

Cleomedes
43. *Cleomedis De Motu Circulari Corporum Caelestium*, ed. H. Ziegler. Leipzig, 1891

Pappus
44. *Pappi Alexandrini Collectionis quae Supersunt*, ed. F. Hultsch. 3 vols. Berlin,
    1876–8
45. Rome, A. *Pappus d'Alexandrie, Commentaire sur les livres 5 et 6 de l'Almageste*
    (Studi e Testi 54). Rome, 1931
46. *The Commentary of Pappus on Book x of Euclid's Elements*, edd. W. Thomson
    and G. Junge (Harvard Semitic Studies 8). Ed. 2. New York, 1968
47. Eecke, P. ver *Pappus d'Alexandrie. La Collection mathématique*. 2 vols. Paris-
    Bruges, 1933

Theon of Alexandria
48. Rome, A. *Théon d'Alexandrie. Commentaire sur les livres 1 et 2 de l'Almageste*
    (Studi e Testi 72). Rome, 1936
49. Rome, A. *Théon d'Alexandrie. Commentaire sur les livres 3 et 4 de l'Almageste*
    (Studi e Testi 106). Rome, 1943

Proclus
50. *Procli Diadochi In Primum Euclidis Elementorum Librum Commentarii*, ed. G.
    Friedlein. Ed. 2. Hildesheim, 1967
51. *Procli Diadochi Hypotyposis Astronomicarum Positionum*, ed. C. Manitius. Ed.
    2. Stuttgart, 1974
52. Morrow, G. R. *A Commentary on the First Book of Euclid's Elements*.
    Princeton, New Jersey, 1970

Simplicius and Philoponus
53. *Commentaria in Aristotelem Graeca*
    VII: *Simplicius. In Aristotelis De Caelo*, ed. J. L. Heiberg. Berlin, 1894
    IX and X: *Simplicius. In Aristotelis Physica*, ed. H. Diels. Berlin, 1882–95
    XVI and XVII: *Philoponus. In Aristotelis Physica*, ed. H. Vitelli. Berlin, 1887–8

4. Hellenistic medicine and the life sciences

Praxagoras
54. Steckerl, F. *The Fragments of Praxagoras of Cos and his School*. Leiden, 1958

Herophilus
55. Marx, K. F. H. *De Herophili Celeberrimi Medici Vita*. Göttingen, 1840
56. Staden, H. von *The Art of Medicine in Ptolemaic Alexandria: Herophilus and
    his School*. Cambridge, forthcoming
57. Dobson, J. F. 'Herophilus of Alexandria', *Proceedings of the Royal Society of
    Medicine* 18 (1925) 19–32

Erasistratus
58. Dobson, J. F. 'Erasistratus', *Proceedings of the Royal Society of Medicine* 20
    (1926–7) 825–32

Empiricists
59. Deichgräber, K. *Die griechische Empirikerschule: Sammlung und Darstellung.* Berlin, 1930

Pneumatists
60. Wellmann, M. *Die pneumatische Schule* (Philologische Untersuchungen 14). Berlin, 1895

Dioscorides
61. *Pedanii Dioscoridis Anazarbei De Materia Medica*, ed. M. Wellmann, 3 vols. Berlin, 1906–14

The most important ancient secondary sources are:
Celsus
62. *A Cornelii Celsi quae Supersunt*, ed. F. Marx (*Corpus Medicorum Latinorum* 1). Leipzig and Berlin, 1915
63. Spencer, W. G. *Celsus, De Medicina.* 3 vols. (Loeb ed.) Cambridge, Mass., 1935–8

Rufus
64. *Oeuvres de Rufus d'Éphèse*, edd. C. Daremberg and E. Ruelle. Paris, 1879

Soranus
65. *Sorani Gynaeciorum Libri* iv, ed. J. Ilberg (*Corpus Medicorum Graecorum* 4). Leipzig and Berlin, 1927
66. Temkin, O. *Soranus' Gynecology.* Baltimore, 1956

Galen
67. *Claudii Galeni Opera Omnia*, ed. C. G. Kühn. 20 vols. in 22. Leipzig, 1821–33
68. *Claudii Galeni Pergameni Scripta Minora*, edd. J. Marquardt, I. Müller, G. Helmreich. 3 vols. Leipzig, 1884–93
69. *Galeni De Usu Partium*, ed. G. Helmreich. 2 vols. Ed. 2. Stuttgart, 1968. Some works arc included in the *Corpus Medicorum Graecorum* edition, Berlin, in progress since 1914.

(*ii*) *Modern works*

A first orientation to the work of many Hellenistic scientists can be obtained either from the articles in *PW* or from those in the *Dictionary of Scientific Biography* (12 vols. plus supplement, ed. C. C. Gillispie, New York, 1970–8). See also H 167, J 148, and, on p. 602 (Addenda), J 93a, J 99a.
70. Bailey, C. *The Greek Atomists and Epicurus.* Oxford, 1928
71. Berthelot, M. and Ruelle, C. E. *Collection des anciens alchimistes grecs.* 3 vols. Ed. 2. Paris, 1967

72. Bouché-Leclercq, A. *L'astrologie grecque*. Paris, 1899
73. Clagett, M. *Greek Science in Antiquity*, London, 1957
74. Dicks, D. R. 'Ancient astronomical instruments', *Journal of the British Astronomical Association* 64 (1953–4) 77–85
75. Diels, H. *Antike Technik*. Ed. 3. Osnabrück. 1965
76. Drachmann, A. G. *Ktesibios Philon and Heron* (Acta Historica Scientiarum Naturalium et Medicinalium 4). Copenhagen, 1948
77. – *The Mechanical Technology of Greek and Roman Antiquity*. Copenhagen, 1963
78. Düring, I. *Ptolemaios und Porphyrios über die Musik* (Göteborgs Högskolas Årsskrift 40, 1). Göteborg, 1934
79. Edelstein, L. *Ancient Medicine*, edd. O. and C. L. Temkin. Baltimore, 1967
80. Farrington, B. *Greek Science*. Ed. 2. London, 1961
81. Festugière, A. J. *La Révélation d'Hermès Trismégiste*. 4 vols. Paris, 1944–54
82. Forbes, R. J. *Studies in Ancient Technology*. 9 vols. Ed. 2. Leiden, 1964–72
83. Fraser, P. M. 'The career of Erasistratus of Ceos', *Rend. Ist. Lomb.* (Classe di Lettere e Scienze Morali e Storiche) 103 (1969) 518–37
84. – *Ptolemaic Alexandria*. 3 vols, Oxford, 1972
85. Furley, D. J. *Two Studies in the Greek Atomists*. Princeton, 1967
86. Gatzemeier, M. *Die Naturphilosophie des Straton von Lampsakos*. Meisenheim, 1970
87. Gundel, R. G. *Weltbild und Astrologie in den griechischen Zauberpapyri*. Munich, 1968
88. Gundel, W. and Gundel, H. G. *Astrologumena: Die astrologische Literatur in der Antike und ihre Geschichte* (Sudhoffs Archiv, Beiheft 6). Wiesbaden, 1966
89. Harris, C. R. S. *The Heart and the Vascular System in Ancient Greek Medicine from Alcmaeon to Galen*. Oxford, 1973
90. Heath, T. L. *A History of Greek Mathematics*. 2 vols. Oxford, 1921
91. Heidel, W. A. *The Frame of the Ancient Greek Maps*. New York, 1937
92. Jones, W. H. S. *The Medical Writings of Anonymus Londinensis*. Cambridge, 1947
93. Kudlien, F. 'Herophilos und der Beginn der medizinischen Skepsis', *Gesnerus* 21 (1964) 1–13
94. Landels, J. G. *Engineering in the Ancient World*. London, 1978
95. Lejeune, A. *Euclide et Ptolémée: Deux stades de l'optique géometrique grecque*. Louvain, 1948
96. Lippmann, E. O. von *Entstehung und Ausbreitung der Alchemie*. Berlin, 1919
97. Lloyd, G. E. R. *Greek Science after Aristotle*. London, 1973
98. – 'A note on Erasistratus of Ceos', *JHS* 95 (1975) 172–5
99. – *Magic, Reason and Experience*. Cambridge, 1979
100. Lonie, I. M. 'Erasistratus, the Erasistrateans and Aristotle', *Bull. Hist. Med.* 38 (1964) 426–43
101. – 'The paradoxical text "On the Heart"', *Medical History* 17 (1973) 1–15 and 136–53
102. Michler, M. *Die hellenistische Chirurgie*. Vol. 1. Wiesbaden, 1968

103. Needham, J. *Science and Civilisation in China*. Vol. v.2: *Chemistry and Chemical Technology*. Cambridge, 1974

104. Neugebauer, O. *The Exact Sciences in Antiquity*. Ed. 2. Providence, R. I., 1957

105. – 'The equivalence of eccentric and epicyclic motion according to Apollonius', *Scripta Mathematica* 24 (1959) 5–21

106. – *A History of Ancient Mathematical Astronomy*. 3 vols. Berlin-New York. 1975

107. Neugebauer, O. and Hoesen, H. B. van *Greek Horoscopes* (American Philosophical Society Memoirs 48). Philadelphia, 1959

108. Nock, A. D. and Festugière, A. J. *Corpus Hermeticum*. 4 vols. Paris, 1945–54

109. Pedersen, O. *A Survey of the Almagest*. Odense, 1974

110. Phillips, E. D. *Greek Medicine*. London, 1973

111. Pohlenz, M. *Die Stoa*. Ed. 4. 2 vols. Göttingen, 1970–2

112. Potter, P. 'Herophilus of Chalcedon', *Bull. Hist. Med.* 50 (1976) 45–60

113. Préaux, C. 'Sur la stagnation de la pensée scientifique à l'époque hellénistique', in *Welles Essays* (1966), 235–50.

114. Preisendanz, K. *Papyri Graecae Magicae*, ed. A. Henrichs. Ed. 2. 2 vols. Stuttgart, 1973–4

115. Price, D. J. de S. 'Precision instruments: to 1500', in *A History of Technology* III, edd. C. Singer and others, 582 619. Oxford, 1957

116. – 'Gears from the Greeks. The Antikythera Mechanism', *Transactions of the American Philosophical Society* N.S. (1966) 64, 7 (1974)

117. Sambursky, S. *The Physical World of the Greeks*, trans. M. Dagut. London, 1956

118. – *Physics of the Stoics*. London, 1959

119. – 'Atomism versus continuum theory in ancient Greece', *Scientia* 96 (1961) 376–81

120. *The Physical World of Late Antiquity*. London, 1962

121. Sarton, G. *A History of Science*, 2 vols. London, 1953–9

122. Smith, W. D. *The Hippocratic Tradition*. Cornell, 1979

123. Solmsen, F. 'Greek philosophy and the discovery of the nerves', *Mus Helv.* 18 (1961) 150–67 169–97

124. Staden, H. von 'Experiment and Experience in Hellenistic medicine', *BICS* 22 (1975) 178–99

125. Steinmetz, P. *Die Physik des Theophrastos von Eresos*. Bad Homburg-Berlin-Zürich, 1964

126. Szabó, A. *The Beginnings of Greek Mathematics*, trans. A. M. Ungar. Budapest, 1978

127. Tannery, P. *Mémoires scientifiques*. 16 vols. Paris, 1912–43

128. Temkin, O. 'Celsus' "On Medicine" and the ancient medical sects', *Bulletin of the Institute of the History of Medicine* 3 (1935) 249–64

129. – 'Greek medicine as science and craft', *Isis* 44 (1953) 213–25

130. – 'Medicine and Graeco-Arabic alchemy', *Bull. Hist. Med.* 29 (1955) 134–53

131. Thomson, J. O. *History of Ancient Geography*. Cambridge, 1948
132. Thorndike, L. *A History of Magic and Experimental Science*. 8 vols. New York, 1923–58
133. Waerden, B. L. van der *Science Awakening*, trans. A. Dresden. Groningen, 1954
134. Wilson, L. G. 'Erasistratus, Galen and the Pneuma', *Bull. Hist. Med.* 33 (1959) 293–314

b. WARFARE

See also F(g) on Egypt, A 30, H 51 and 123, J 259
135. Adcock, F. E. *The Greek and Macedonian Art of War*. Berkeley-Los Angeles, 1957
136. Bar-Kochva, B. *The Seleucid Army. Organization and Tactics in the Great Campaigns*. Cambridge, 1976
137. Casson, L. *Ships and Seamanship in the Ancient World*. Princeton, 1971
138. Garlan, Y. 'Fortifications et histoire grecque', in Vernant 1968, 245–60: (J 154)
139. – *La guerre dans l'antiquité*. Paris, 1972 (= *War in the Ancient World: A Social History*. London, 1975.)
140. – *Recherches de poliorcétique grecque*. Paris, 1974
141. Griffith, G. T. *The Mercenaries of the Hellenistic World*. Cambridge, 1935
142. Kromayer, J. and Veith, G. *Heerwesen und Kriegführung der Griechen und Römer*. Munich, 1928
143. Launey, M. *Recherches sur les armées hellénistiques*. 2 vols. Paris, 1949–50
144. Lawrence, A. W. *Greek Aims in Fortification*. Oxford, 1979 [1980]
145. Lendle, O. *Texte und Untersuchungen zum technischen Bereich der antiken Poliorketik* (Palingenesia 19). Wiesbaden, 1983
146. Lévèque, P. 'La guerre à l'époque hellénistique', in Vernant 1968, 261–87: (J 154)
147. Markle, M. M. 'The Macedonian sarissa, spear and related armor', *AJArch.* 81 (1977) 323–39
148. Marsden, E. W. *Greek and Roman Artillery*
    I: *Historical Development*
    II: *Technical Treatises*. Oxford, 1969 and 1971
149. McCredie, J. R. *Fortified Military Camps in Attica* (*Hesp.* Suppl. 11). Princeton, 1966
150. Parke, H. W. *Greek Mercenary Soldiers*. Oxford, 1933
151. Pritchett, W. K. *The Greek State at War*. Berkeley, I (1971); II (1974); III (1979)
152. Snodgrass, A. M. *Arms and Armour of the Greeks*. London, 1967
153. Tarn, W. W. *Hellenistic Military and Naval Developments*. Cambridge, 1930
154. Vernant, J. P. (ed.) *Problèmes de la guerre en Grèce ancienne*. Paris, 1968
155. Volkmann, H. *Die Massenversklavungen der Einwohner eroberter Städte in der hellenistisch-römischen Zeit* (*Abh. Akad. Mainz* 3) 1961

c. AGRICULTURE

See also F 270, H 71 and 144

156. Butzer, K. W. *Early Hydraulic Civilisation in Egypt: A Study in Cultural Ecology.* Chicago-London, 1976

157. Cadell, H. 'La viticulture scientifique dans les archives de Zénon', *Aegyptus* 49 (1969) 105–20

158. Crawford, D. J. *Kerkeosiris: An Egyptian Village in the Ptolemaic Period.* Cambridge, 1971

159. – 'The opium poppy: a study in Ptolemaic agriculture', in *Problèmes de la terre en Grèce ancienne*, ed. M. I. Finley, 223–51. Paris-The Hague, 1973

160. Girard, M. P. S. 'Mémoire sur l'agriculture, l'industrie et le commerce de l'Égypte', *Description de l'Égypte. État moderne* II.491–714. Paris, 1813

161. Heichelheim, F. 'Roman Syria', in *ESAR* IV (1938) 123–257

162. Jardé, A. *Les céréales dans l'antiquité grecque.* Paris, 1925

163. Moritz, L. A. *Grain-mills and Flour in Classical Antiquity.* Oxford, 1958

164. Rostovtzeff, M. *A Large Estate in Egypt in the Third Century* B.C. *A study in economic history.* Madison, 1922

165. Schnebel, M. *Die Landwirtschaft im hellenistischen Ägypten (Münch. Beitr. Papyr.* 7). Munich, 1925

166. Thompson, H. A. 'Syrian wheat in Hellenistic Egypt', *Arch. Pap.* 9 (1930) 207–13

167. Vidal-Naquet, P. *Le bordereau d'ensemencement dans l'Égypte ptolémaïque.* Brussels, 1967

168. Wellmann, K. 'Die Georgika des Demokritos', *Abh. Akad. Berlin* 4 (1921)

d. BUILDING AND TOWNPLANNING

169. Adriani, A. 'Hellenistic architecture', in *Encyclopaedia of World Art* VIII.290–311. London, 1963

170. Akurgal, E. *Ancient Civilizations and Ruins of Turkey.* Ed. 4. Istanbul, 1978

171. Andronikos, M. *Vergina, the prehistoric necropolis and the Hellenistic palace* (Studies in Mediterranean Archaeology 13.) Lund 1964

172. Andronikos, M., Makaronas, Ch., Moutsopoulos, N. and Bakalabais, G. *Τὸ Ἀνάκτορο τῆς Βεργίνας.* Athens, 1961

173. Arnott, P. D. *The Ancient Greek and Roman Theatre.* New York, 1971

174. Audiat, J. *Délos* XXVIII: *Le gymnase.* Paris, 1970

175. Baldry, H. C. *The Greek Tragic Theatre.* London, 1971

176. Bammer, A. *Die Architektur des jüngeren Artemision von Ephesos.* Wiesbaden, 1972

177. – 'Der Altar des jüngeren Artemision von Ephesos', *Arch. Anz.* (1968) 400–23

178. Bean, G. E. *Aegean Turkey.* London, 1966

179. – *Turkey Beyond the Maeander.* London, 1971

180. – *Lycian Turkey.* London, 1978

181. Bernard, J. 'Chapiteaux corinthiens hellénistiques d'Asia centrale découverts à Ai-Khanoum', *Syria* 45 (1968) 111–51
182. Berve, H. and Gruben, G. *Tempel und Heiligtümer der Griechen*. Munich, 1978
183. Bieber, M. *History of the Greek and Roman Theater*. Ed. 2. Princeton, 1961
184. Boethius, A. *Etruscan and Roman Architecture* (with J. B. Ward-Perkins). Harmondsworth, 1970
185. Bohn, R. *Altertümer von Aegae*. Berlin, 1889
186. Borchhardt, J. 'Das Heroon von Limyra, Grabmal des lykischen Königs Perikles', *Arch. Anz.* 1970, 353–90
187. – *Die Bauskulptur des Heroons von Limyra* (*Istanb. Forsch.* 32). Berlin, 1976
188. Boyd, T. D. 'The arch and the vault in Greek architecture', *AJArch.* 82 (1978) 83–100
189. Bruneau, Ph. and Ducat, J. *Guide de Délos*. Paris, 1966
190. Bruneau, Ph. and others. *Délos* XXVII: *L'ilôt de la Maison des Comédiens*. Paris, 1970
191. Bulle, H. *Untersuchungen an griechischen Theatern* (*Abh. Bayer. Akad.* 33). Munich, 1928
192. Burford, A. *The Greek Temple Builders at Epidaurus*. Liverpool, 1969
193. Castagnoli, F. *Orthogonal Town Planning in Antiquity*. Cambridge, Mass., 1971
194. Clarke, J. T., Bacon, F. H. and Koldewey, R. *Investigations at Assos*. Cambridge, Mass., 1902–21
195. Coulton, J. J. 'The Stoa by the harbour at Perachora', *BSA* 59 (1964) 100–31
196. – *The Architectural Development of the Greek Stoa*. Oxford, 1976
197. – *Greek Architects at Work*. London, 1977
198. Delbrück, R. *Hellenistische Bauten in Latium*. 2 vols. Strasbourg, 1907–12
199. Delorme, J. 'La maison dite de l'Hermès à Délos', *BCH* 77 (1953) 444–96
200. – *Délos* XXV: *Les palèstres*. Paris, 1961
201. Demargne, P. and Coupel, P. *Fouilles de Xanthos* III: *Le monument des Néréides*. Paris, 1969
202. Dinsmoor, W. B. *The Architecture of Ancient Greece*. Ed. 3. London, 1950
203. Dyggve, E. *Lindos* III: *Le sanctuaire d'Athéna Lindia et l'architecture lindienne*. Berlin-Copenhagen, 1960
204. Fiechter, E. *Antike griechische Theaterbauten* V–VII and IX: *Das Dionysos-Theater in Athen*. Stuttgart, 1935–6 and 1950
205. Fyfe, T. *Hellenistic Architecture*. Cambridge, 1936
206. Gerkan, A. von *Das Theater von Priene*. Munich, 1921
207. – *Griechische Städteanlagen*. Berlin-Leipzig, 1924
208. – *Das Theater von Epidauros* (with W. Müller-Wiener). Stuttgart, 1961
209. Ginouvès, R. *L'établissement thermal de Gortys d'Arcadie*. Paris, 1959
210. – *Balaneutiké*. Paris, 1962
211. Gruben, G. 'Zum Artemis-Tempel von Sardis', *Ath. Mitt.* 76 (1961) 155–96
212. Hill, G. B. and Williams, C. K. *The Temple of Zeus at Nemea*. Princeton, 1966

213. Hörmann, H. *Die inneren Propyläen von Eleusis.* Berlin-Leipzig, 1932
214. Humann, C. *Magnesia am Maeander.* Berlin, 1904
215. Jantzen, U. (ed.) *Neue Forschungen in griechischen Heiligtümern. Internationales Symposion in Olympia vom 10. bis 12. Oktober 1974 anläss der Hundertjahrfeier der Abteilung Athen und der Deutschen Ausgrabungen in Olympia.* Tübingen, 1976
216. Jannoray, J. *Fouilles de Delphes* II.11: *Le gymnase de Delphes.* Paris, 1953
217. Jeppesen, K. 'Neue Ergebnisse zur Wiederherstellung des Mausolleions von Halikarnassos', *Istanb. Mitt.* 26 (1976) 47–99
218. Knackfuss, H. *Milet* I.2: *Das Rathaus von Milet.* Berlin, 1908
219. – *Didyma* I.1–3: *Die Baubeschreibung.* Berlin, 1941
220. Kontis, I. D. Αἱ ʽΕλληνιστικαὶ διαμορφώσεις τοῦ ʼΑσκληπείου τῆς Κῶ. Rhodes, 1956
221. – 'Zum antiken Stadtbauplan von Rhodos', *Ath. Mitt.* 73 (1958) 146–58
222. Krauss, F. and Herbig, R. *Der korinthisch-dorische Tempel am Forum von Paestum.* Berlin, 1939
223. Krischen, F. *Antike Rathäuser.* Berlin, 1941
224. Lawrence, A. W. *Greek Architecture.* Harmondsworth, 1957. Also Ed. 3, 1973
225. Lehmann, P. W. *Samothrace: Excavations conducted by the Institute of Fine Arts, New York University* III: *The Hieron.* New York, 1969
226. Maier, F.-G. *Griechische Mauerbauinschriften* I: *Texte und Kommentare* (*Vestigia* 1). Heidelberg, 1959
227. – *Griechische Mauerbauinschriften* II: *Untersuchungen* (*Vestigia* 2). Heidelberg, 1961
228. Martin, R. *Manuel d'architecture grecque* I: *Matériaux et techniques.* Paris, 1965
229. – 'Sculpture et peinture dans les façades monumentales au IV siècle av. J.-C.', *Revue Archéologique* (1968) 171–84
230. – Chapter on architecture in J. Charbonneaux, R. Martin and F. Villard, *Hellenistic Art.* London, 1973
231. – *L'urbanisme dans la Grèce antique.* Ed. 2. Paris, 1974
232. McDonald, W. A. *Political Meeting-Places of the Greeks.* Baltimore, 1943
233. Mussche, H. F. *Monumenta graeca et romana* IV: *Greek Architecture*, Pt 3: *Civil and military architecture.* Leiden, 1964
234. Napoli, Maria 'La ricerca archeologica di Velia', *PP* 21 (1966) 191–221
235. Neppi Modona, A. *Gli edifici teatrali greci e romani.* Florence, 1961
236. Onians, J. *Art and Thought in the Hellenistic Age.* London, 1979
237. Orlandos, A. *Les matériaux de construction et la technique architecturale des anciens grecs.* 2 vols. Paris, 1966–8
238. Petas, Ph. M. *Pella, Alexanser the Great's Capital.* Thessalonica, 1978
239. – ʽΟ τάφος τῶν Λευκαδίων. Athens, 1966
240. Pickard-Cambridge, A. W. *The Theatre of Dionysus in Athens.* Oxford, 1946
241. Robertson, D. S. *A Handbook of Greek and Roman Architecture.* Ed. 2. Cambridge, 1954
242. Ronczewski, K. 'Kapitelle aus Tarent', *Arch. Anz.* 1927, 263–96
243. – 'Tarentiner Kapitelle', *Arch. Anz.* 1934, 10–17
244. Roux, G. *L'architecture de l'Argolide aux IVe et IIIe siècles avant J.-C.* Paris, 1961

245. Salviat, F. *et al. Guide de Thasos.* Paris, 1968
246. Sauvaget, J. 'Le plan de Laodicée-sur-mer', *Bulletin d'études orientales* 4 (1934) 81–114
247. – *Alep.* Paris, 1941
248. – 'Le plan antique de Damas', *Syria* 26 (1949) 339–58
249. Schazmann, P. in R. Herzog (ed.), *Kos* I: *Asklepieion.* Berlin, 1932
250. Szalay, A. von and Boehringer, E. *Altertümer von Pergamon* X: *Die hellenistische Arsenale.* Berlin-Leipzig, 1937
251. Thompson, H. A. and Wycherley, R. E. *The Athenian Agora: The Results of Excavations Conducted by the American School of Classical Studies at Athens* XIV: *The Agora of Athens, the History, Shape and Uses of an Ancient City Center.* Princeton, 1972
252. Tölle-Kastenbein, R. *Samos* XIV: *Das Kastro Tigani.* Bonn, 1974
253. Travlos, J. *Pictorial Dictionary of Ancient Athens.* London, 1971
254. Vallois, R. and Poulsen, G. *Délos* II.2: *Nouvelles recherches sur la Salle Hypostyle.* Paris, 1914
255. Voigtländer, W. *Der jüngste Apollontempel von Didyma.* Tübingen, 1975
256. Ward-Perkins, J. B. *Cities of Ancient Greece and Italy.* London, 1974
257. Webster, T. B. L. *Greek Theatre Production.* Ed. 2. London, 1970
258. Williams, C. 'The Corinthian Temple of Zeus Olbios at Uzuncaburç: a reconsideration of the date', *AJArch.* 78 (1974) 405–14
259. Winter, F. E. *Greek Fortifications.* Toronto, 1971
260. Wycherley, R. E. *How the Greeks Built Cities.* Ed. 2. New York, 1962
261. – *The Stones of Athens.* Princeton, 1979

ADDENDA

D. *a.* MACEDONIA, EPIRUS AND ILLYRIA (p. 539)

17a. Errington, R. M. 'The historiographical origins of Macedonian *Staatsrecht*', *Ancient Macedonia* III (1983) 89–101
35a. Papazoglou, F. 'Sur l'organisation de la Macédoine des Antigonides', *Ancient Macedonia* III (1983) 195–210

E. *g.* IRAN, PARTHIA, THE PERSIAN GULF, BACTRIA (p. 553)

191a. Grenet, F. 'L'onomastique iranienne à Aï Khanoum', *BCH* 107 (1983) 373–81
197a. Rapin, Cl. 'Inscriptions économiques de la trésorerie hellénistique', *BCH* 107 (1983) 315–72

G. *b.* AGATHOCLES (p. 576)

38a. Hans, L.-M. *Karthago und Sizilien* (Historische Texte und Studien 7). Hildesheim-Zürich-New York, 1983

J. *a.* (ii) SCIENCE: *Modern works* (p. 596)

93a. Kudlien, F. *Der griechische Arzt im Zeitalter des Hellenismus* (*Abh. Akad. Mainz* 6) 1979
99a. Longrigg, J. 'Superlative achievement and comparative neglect: Alexandrian medical science and modern historical research', *History of Science* 19 (1981) 155–200

INDEX